H A C K E R S
READING

해커스 어학연구소

H
A
C
K
E
R
S
**R
E
A
D
I
N
G**

저자

David 조
언어학박사
前 UCLA교수
1998년 7월 Hackers TOEFL Program을 만듦

초판 1쇄 발행 2002년 4월 26일
초판 20쇄 발행 2013년 7월 22일
지은이 David Cho | 언어학 박사 前 UCLA 교수
펴낸곳 (주)해커스 어학연구소
펴낸이 해커스 어학연구소 출판팀
주소 서울시 서초구 서초동 1316-15 해커스 교육그룹
전화 02-566-0001 **FAX** 02-563-0622
홈페이지 www.goHackers.com
ISBN 978-89-951517-3-0 13740
값 16,900 원

Serial Number: 01-20-01

언어의 이해는 일상생활의 영위뿐만 아니라 학문의 발전에 있어서 기본적이며 필수적인 요소입니다. 언어의 이해란 언어가 내포하는 논리와 사고를 이해하는 것을 포함합니다. 이것은 모국어와 외국어에 공히 적용되는 것으로서 언어의 이해에는 풍부한 어휘력(vocabulary)과 문법(grammar)에 대한 기본 지식은 물론, 논리적 사고(logical thinking)가 바탕이 되어야 합니다.

그동안 논리적 사고를 발달시킬수 있는 독해의 고전을 꿈꾸어 왔습니다. 논리적 사고는 학문의 수단을 넘어서, 학문이라는 것 자체가 논리적 사고를 바탕으로 이루어져 있습니다. 학생들의 성공적 학문성취에 결정적 토대가 되는 논리력을 언어를 통해서 키워나갈 수 있도록 하는 것이 이책의 의도이자 목표입니다.

따라서 이책을 공부하면서 토론과 논의를 통하여 논리적으로 가장 적합한 해답을 찾아가는 과정이 필요합니다. 이러한 과정이 논리적 사고를 발달시키는데 중요한 역할을 할 뿐 아니라 독해의 마지막 벽을 넘는 초석이기도 합니다. 이책의 바탕을 이루는 Hackers의 독해수업은 해석보다는 토론과 논의로 이루어진 치열한 논쟁의 장이었습니다. 단순한 해답의 제시보다는 연결된 도전과 응전을 통해 가장 논리적인 해답을 찾아가는 과정을 밟아간 것입니다. 이러한 논쟁의 장을 통해 논리력과 독해력을 발달시키는 것이 이책이 추구하는 바입니다.

독해를 위한 준비과정으로 어휘습득이 기초를 이루어야함은 당연하고, 문법의 구조(structure)에 대한 지식을 갖추어야만 합니다. 기초 단어를 알지못하고 문장의 뜻을 파악할 수는 없으며 문장 구조의 도움없이 문장분석은 불가능합니다. 그 위에 논리적사고와 독해가 있는 것입니다. 독해와 더불어 이런 기초가 다져지도록 어휘와 문법의 충분한 선행학습을 권장합니다.

Hackers Reading이 태어나기까지 해커스 가족들의 헌신적인 도움이 있었습니다. 이책이 나오기 1년전 책표지를 준비하고 Carnegie Mellon으로 유학을 떠난 남희(5기)를 비롯하여, '민지엄마' 은혜(2기), 경원(9기)과 '진주반지팀', '어린왕자' 지원(16기), '16기 반장' 장만(16기), '대찬인생' 승돈(16기), 태영(4.5기), 수경(13기), 그리고 Heather, Elizabeth, John, 미승, 윤희기 선생님이 도움을 주었습니다. 또한 내 마음을 늘 편하게 해주던 Urbana-Champaign의 '애주가' 혜진(10기), 한결같은 성실함과 정확함으로 마음 든든하게 해주었던 '중문' 민혜(16기), 웃음을 선사해주던 '특수' 라경(14기), 만만찮은 책임감을 보여준 '마녀' 지연(11기), 그리고 '순수' 선경(16기)에게 고마움을 표합니다.

해커스 가족들의 또 하나의 아름다운 산물인 이책이 진정으로 공부를 하는 이들에게 작은 빛과 초석이 되기를 기원합니다.

| David 조 드림

Contents

HACKERS READING

TOEFL이란?

● TOEFL 이란 무엇인가?

TOEFL(Test of English as a Foreign Language)은 미국, 캐나다를 비롯한 영국, 호주, 뉴질랜드 등 영어권 국가에 유학을 가고자 하는 학생들을 대상으로 180 여개국에서 ETS (Education Testing Service)의 주관 하에 실시되는 국제적인 영어 시험이다. 미국 대학의 대부분은 입학허가 조건의 하나로 토플의 일정수준 이상 공식 점수를 요구하고 있는데 만점은 300점이다. 요구 점수는 각 대학과 학과에 따라 다르나 일반적으로 학부는 213점, 대학원은 230점 이상이며 요구 점수는 지원하려는 학교의 해당학과에 확인하는 것이 필요하다.

CBT TOEFL의 전체 구성

· Tutorials 컴퓨터 사용에 관한 교육	실시 시간	• 약 40분동안 CBT에서는 시험 시작하기 전 시험에 필요한 기초적인 컴퓨터 사용에 관한 교육을 실시한다.
· Section 1 Listening Comprehension (청취 능력 측정)	응시 시간	• 40~60 분 (문제 청취 시간 제외) 응시 시간이 일정하지 않은 것은 문제의 정 · 오답 여부에 따라 변별적으로 다음 문항이 변경되고, 경우에 따라 문항 수 자체도 가변적으로 주어질 수 있기 때문이다.
	Part A	• Short Conversations 11~17 문항
	Part B	• Longer Conversations / Discussions / Lectures 19~33 문항
· Section 2 Structure (문장 완성 및 오류 확인)	응시 시간 문항 수	• 15~20 분 • 20~25 문항
· Section 3 Reading Comprehension (독해 능력 측정)	응시 시간 문항 수	• 70~90 분 • 44~55 문항
· Section 4 Writing (주제에 따라 Essay 작성)	응시 시간 문항 수	• 30 분 • 1 문항

CBT TOEFL 신청안내

·등록안내	안내 전화	• (02) 3211-1233, 3275-4027
	등록 fax	• (02) 3275-4029
	등록 시간	• 오전 9시-오후5시(월-금요일)
	시험 장소	• 서울(고합빌딩, 한미교육위원단)과 대구
	등록비	• US $110
·시험 취소 및 변경	가능기한	• 등록된 시험일 3일 전(Business day) 오전 12시까지
	시험 일자 변경비	• US $40
	시험 취소	• US $65 환불 : Bulletin에 있는 양식을 이용하여, 시험 취소 후 60일 이내에 미국 ETS에 Refund를 요청하면 가능
·유의 사항	시험당일 신분 확인	• 본인의 서명이 들어있는 여권, 주민등록증, 운전면허증
	시험시간	• 4시간
	시험접수 준비	• 반드시 해당 시험의 Bulletin을 읽어 보기 : Fax나 우편등록시 International Test Scheduling Form을 다운받는다.
	시험 시간 30분 전에 시험장에 도착한다.	
·Fees for Testing	$110	• Computer-Based TOEFL Test
	$40	• Rescheduling Fee
	$12	• one Additional Score Report Request
	$50	• Essay rescore
	$10	• Reinstatement of canceled scores
	$25	• Fee for Returned Check and declined credit cards

CBT에서
Computer 사용방법

● CBT 화면 미리 보기

• Direction 화면

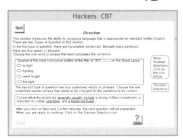

Directions

각 파트의 문제 시작 전에 출제 형식이나 정답 요령 등을 설명해 준다. 만일 바로 문제 풀이로 들어가고 싶은 경우에는 Dismiss Directions을 클릭한다.

• 문제 Tool

문제에 답을 표시한 후 새로운 문제로 넘어가기 위해서 Next를 클릭한다.

Next후 답을 Confirm함으로써 새로운 문제로 넘어갈 수 있다. CBT에서는 일단 풀고 Confirm한 문제는 다시 되돌아갈 수 없다.

바로 이전 문제나 화면으로 돌아가는 기능을 갖고 있다. 다만 Reading Section에서만 가능하다.

사용방법 등을 보여준다.

Time을 클릭하면 남은 시험시간 표시가 나타나며, 시험종료 5분전부터는 자동적으로 나타난다.

Writing Section에서 삭제하기 원하는 텍스트를 잘라낼 때 사용한다.

Writing Section에서 텍스트를 삽입하기 원할 때 사용한다. 붙여넣기를 원하는 텍스트를 잘라낸 후, 원하는 지점을 클릭한 뒤 Paste를 클릭한다.

바로 이전 행동을 취소하기 위해서 사용한다. 예컨대, 바로 이전에 텍스트를 잘라냈거나 붙여넣기 했다면 각각의 자료가 그 이전으로 복원된다.

Reading Comprehension Section

Computer-Based TOEFL Test

● 출제형식

• 소요시간 : 70~90분

• 문제수 : 44~55문제

  • 250~350단어 정도의 장문으로 4~5개 지문마다 각각 10~14문제가 출제 된다.

  • 새로운 문제의 유형 : 올바른 위치로의 문장 삽입과 지시어를 본문에서 직접 찾아 클릭하기

● 사용방법

• 지문을 읽은 후 proceed 버튼을 누르면 나누어진 화면에서 1문제씩 차례대로 풀게 된다.

• 질문에서 특정 단락을 언급한 경우 화면에서 찾기 쉽도록 그 단락의 첫 부분이 화살표로 표시되어 있다.

• one, it, those 등이 지칭하는 단어를 찾아내는 Reference 유형의 경우 지문 내에 대명사가 표시된다. 수험자는 4지 선다형 중 선택하는 것이 아니라 지칭되는 단어를 문장 내에서 클릭해야 한다.

● CBT 화면 보기

1

4개의 선택지 중에서 답을
고르는 문제

2

지시어를 본문에서 직접
찾아 클릭하는 문제

3

올바른 위치로 본문에 삽
입하는 문제

TOEFL READING 의 소개와 전략

1. TOEFL READING 이란?

● 토플에서 reading part는 수험자가 formal한 문어체 영어로 쓰인 글을 읽고 문제에 답하는 능력을 보는 시험이다. reading의 특이한 점은 다른 part와는 달리 CAT(computer adopted test)가 아니라는 점이다. 즉 다른 part에서는 앞의 문제에 대한 정답 여부에 따라 다음 문제가 결정되었지만 reading part에서는 모든 문제가 한 번에 주어진다. 수험자는 reading part의 시험이 시작되면 문제를 앞 뒤로 마음대로 오갈 수 있으며, 이런 특성 때문에 reading part의 strategy는 다른 part와 다르다.

● 일반적으로 실제 시험을 볼 때 보통 두 가지 set 중 한가지를 보게 되는데 LC 30문제, SW 25문제, RC 55문제인 set과 LC 50문제, SW 20문제, RC 44문제인 set 으로 나뉜다. 55문제인 경우는 지문이 5개, 44문제의 경우에는 지문이 4개 정도 나오며 한 지문에 나오는 문제는 대략 10-14문제 정도다.

● 지문은 보통 과학(물리학, 화학, 지학, 천문학, 생물학, 수학, 동물학, 식물학, 의학, 공학 등), 북미관련학(북미의 역사, 정부, 지리, 문화 등), 예술(음악, 문학, 회화, 조각, 건축, 춤, 드라마 등), 사회과학(인류학, 경제학, 심리학, 도시학, 사회학 등) 전기 등으로 이루어져 있다. 이러한 분야 중에서도 특히 천문학, 초기 인류, 미국역사, 재즈 등이 잘 나온다. 만일 국가적 특성을 띠는 지문이 나온다면, 이는 미국이나 캐나다에 대한 부분일 것이다. 즉 만일 역사에 관한 지문이 나온다면, 이는 미국이나 캐나다의 역사에 관한 지문일 것이다. 비록 지문이 다양한 토픽을 다루고 있긴 하지만, 쓰여진 스타일은 유사하며 보통 매우 간단한 구성 패턴을 따르고 있다.

● reading에 나오는 어휘는 약간 sophisticated 하지만 지나치게 복잡한 것은 나오지 않는다. 하지만 대부분의 경우에 수험자가 모르는 단어들이 나올 것이다. 때로는 문맥에 의거해 그 뜻을 추측해야 할 수도 있다. 문제에 답하기 위해 지문에 나오는 모든 단어를 이해해야 할 필요는 없다. 문제의 유형은 답하는 방식에 따라 나누면 4지선다형 문제, 문장과 문장 사이를 클릭하는 문제, 단어나 문장을 골라 클릭하는 문제 등으로 나눌 수 있고, 문제 내용에 따라 나누면 주제 찾기 문제, infer문제 등으로 나눌 수 있다.

● 토플 RC 파트 문제유형 분석표

문 제 유 형	사지선다형	클릭온패시지문제	문장 껴넣기 문제
Topic & Main Idea	○		
Tone & Attitude, Purpose	○		
Organization & Insertion	○	○	○
Restatement	○		
Negative (Exception)	○		
Scanning (Line)		○	
Inference	○		
Vocabulary	○	○	
Reference	○	○	

2. TOEFL READING STRATEGY

1) 전체 지문을 읽는 방법

reading section이 시작되면 먼저 instruction 이 나온다. 시험 전 미리 powerprep을 풀면서 읽어둔다. 실전에서는 dismiss 버튼을 눌러 넘기며 바로 시험을 시작하도록 한다. 시험이 시작되면 문제 없이 먼저 지문만 화면에 뜬다. 이때 지문을 끝까지 읽어야만 (혹은 가장 아래쪽까지 마우스를 내려 모든 지문이 화면에 나타나게 해야만) 다음으로 넘어갈 수 있다. 수험자는 다음 두 가지 중 한 가지 방법을 선택할 수 있다.

① 지문을 빠르게 한번 읽어보고 next버튼을 눌러 다음 화면이 나오면 첫 문제를 풀기 시작한다.

② 지문을 읽지 않고 마우스로 화면만을 내린 뒤 next를 눌러 문제가 나오면 먼저 문제를 읽고 지문을 읽기 시작한다.

2) 문제를 푸는 방법

reading test는 section 안에서 앞뒤 문제로 넘어갈 수 있다. 답하지 않고도 next를 누르거나, 세 번째 문제를 먼저 풀고 두 번째 문제로 돌아와 푸는 것이 가능하다. (단, reading section의 마지막 문제까지 도달하기 전에는 한 지문 내에서만 앞뒤로 움직일 수 있다. 즉 시험이 시작되어 수험자가 첫 지문을 풀고 두 번째 지문으로 넘어갔을 때 두 번째 지문 안에서는 마음대로 움직일 수 있지만 첫 지문을 지금 다시 볼 수는 없다. 마지막(네 번째 혹은 다섯 번째) 지문의 마지막 문제까지 다 본 후에는 다시 첫 지문으로 돌아갈 수 있다.) 따라서 이러한 점을 이용하여 수험자는 유리한 전략을 세워볼 수 있다.

① 문제를 푸는 도중에 시간이 부족할 때는 무작정 찍지 말고 가능한 빠른 속도로 지문을 대강 읽어보며 main idea를 집어낸 다음, 보통 전체 글의 목적이나 내용을 묻는 첫 문제를 먼저 답하고, next를 눌러서 문제 푸는 시간이 비교적 적게 드는 단어문제나 reference문제를 찾아내어 답한다. 그리고 남은 문제들에 대해 시간이 되는 만큼 빨리 읽고 답한다. 답이 잘 보이지 않을 때는 "내게 논리적이고 말이 되어 보이는" 것으로 보기를 고른다.

② reading test에서는 한 지문 안에서 첫 문제와 끝 문제를 제외한 대부분의 문제들이 글의 순서를 엄격하게 따른다. 따라서 문제를 풀다가 글에서 어디를 참조해야 할 지 잘 모를 경우 앞뒤 문제를 참고하여 그 문제를 풀어낼 수 있다.

Hackers Reading 특징

1. Pattern에 따른 문제 접근

토플(CBT)에 나오는 모든 문제 유형을 분석하여 Pattern별로 정리해서 학습자가 시험에 나오는 문제 유형을 정확히 익히고, 문제접근을 쉽게 할 수 있도록 구성했다.

2. 각 Pattern에 대한 자세한 전략 제시

각 Pattern에 대한 전략을 제시하고, 이러한 전략을 연습문제를 통하여 실전에 적용할 수 있도록 하였다.

3. 실제 토플(CBT) 독해와 가장 유사한 지문과 문제

Hackers TOEFL Reading에 나오는 모든 지문은 실제 TOEFL시험과 가장 유사한 지문을 사용하여 실제 TOEFL시험에 도움이 되도록 하였다.

4. 토플에 출제되는 전 분야에 해당하는 최대의 지문과 문제 수록

130 여개의 지문을 수록하여 기존의 유사 토플 문제집중 가장 많은 내용을 수록하고 있다.

5. 토플 시험에 출제되는 전 분야 수록

실제 토플 독해시험에 출제되는 실제지문과 같은 주제의 글을 전 분야를 수록하여 실제 토플 시험에 필요한 배경지식이 되도록 하였다. 그룹 스터디를 할 때 지문의 완전한 이해를 위한 정독과 토론은 Reading능력 향상에 큰 도움이 될 것이다.

6. Reading의 기본서

논리적인 추론 등을 포함한 독해를 하는데 중요한 훈련을 담고 있어서 TOEFL, TOEIC, TEPS, 고시영어 뿐만 아니라 모든 영어의 독해에 기본이 되는 책이다.

7. 스터디 자료로써의 완벽한 구성 (6 weeks / 4 weeks)

이 책의 학습 방법에서는 처음의 진단고사부터 마지막 Actual Test까지 매일 일정한 부분을 공부할 수 있도록 6 weeks program과 4 weeks program의 두 가지 방식으로 구성되어있고, 구체적인 schedule을 제시하고 있다.

8. TOEFL L/C의 Lecture part 공략에 도움

대부분의 지문이 L/C Lecture에 자주 나오는 지문과 같은 분야(지질, 해양, 생물, 인류, 정치, 예술, 문화, 역사 등)를 다루고 그 내용도 유사하기 때문에 L/C의 Lecture에서 그 내용을 잘 들을 수 없다고 하더라도 그에 대한 배경지식을 제공하며, 문제 푸는 데 도움을 줄 것이다.

9. 독해준비서와 실전문제집을 합쳐 놓은 책

Pattern별 연습을 위한 연습문제와 단원별 실전문제 외에도 일정한 양의 단원을 함께 test할 수 있는 Progressive Test와 모든 단원 공부가 끝난 뒤에 풀어볼 수 있는 실전문제 5회분을 포함하여 독해준비서와 실전문제집을 합쳐놓았다.

10. 해커스 Reading 게시판에서의 on-line 토론 가능

Hackers Grammar, Hackers Voca와 같이 Hackers Reading 역시 해커스 홈페이지에 Reading 게시판을 만들어 이책의 학습자들이 자유롭게 서로 묻고 답하며 토론을 할 수 있는 학습토론의 장을 마련했다.

www.goHackers.com

Hackers Reading 학습방법

Ⅰ. Schedule

1. Study Plan for 2 months (6 weeks, 42 days)

1st week	Day	1st	2nd	3rd	4th	5th	6th	7th
	Progress	진단고사	Ch1 전략과 HP	Ch1 HT	Ch2 전략과 HP	Ch2 HT	makeup	Review
	Homework	Ch1 전략과 HP	Ch1 HT	Ch2 전략과 HP	Ch2 HT	Ch3 전략과 HP		

2nd week	Day	8th	9th	10th	11th	12th	13th	14th
	Progress	Ch3 전략과 HP	Ch3 HT	Prog 1-1	Prog 1-2	Ch4 전략과 HP	makeup	Review
	Homework	Ch3 HT	Prog 1-1	Prog 1-2	Ch4 전략과 HP	Ch4 전략과 HP		

3rd week	Day	15th	16th	17th	18th	19th	20th	21st
	Progress	Ch4 전략과 HP	Ch5 HT(1)~(6)	Ch5 HT(7)~(10)	Ch6 전략과 HP	Ch6 HT	makeup	Review
	Homework	Ch5 HT(1)~(6)	Ch5 HT(7)~(13)	Ch6 전략과 HP	Ch6 HT	Prog 2-1		

4th week	Day	22nd	23rd	24th	25th	26th	27th	28th
	Progress	Prog 2-1	Prog 2-2	Ch7 전략과 HP	Ch7 HT	Ch8 전략과 HP	makeup	Review
	Homework	Prog 2-2	Ch7 전략과 HP	Ch7 HT	Ch8 전략과 HP	Ch8 HT		

5th week	Day	29th	30th	31st	32nd	33rd	34th	35th
	Progress	Ch8 HT	Ch9 전략과 HP	Ch9 HT	Prog 3-1	Prog 3-2	makeup	Review
	Homework	Ch9 전략과 HP	Ch9 HT	Prog 3-1	Prog 3-2			

6th week	Day	36th	37th	38th	39th	40th	41st	42nd
	Progress	AT1 시험	AT1 토론 AT2 시험	AT2 토론 AT3 시험	AT3 토론 AT4 시험	AT4 토론 AT5 시험	진단고사 진단고사 정독 AT5 토론	Review
	Homework	AT1 복습	AT2 복습	AT3 복습	AT4 복습	AT5 복습		

2.Study Plan for 1 months (4 weeks, 28 days)

1st week

	Day	1st	2nd	3rd	4th	5th	6th	7th
	Progress	진단고사	Ch1	Ch2	Ch3	Prog 1-1	Prog 1-2	makeup
	Homework	Ch1	Ch2	Ch3	Prog 1-1	Prog 1-2	Ch4	

2nd week

	Day	8th	9th	10th	11th	12th	13th	14th
	Progress	Ch4	Ch5-1	Ch5-2	Ch6	Prog 2-1	Review	makeup
	Homework	Ch5-1	Ch5-2	Ch6	Prog 2-1	Prog 2-2		

3rd week

	Day	15th	16th	17th	18th	19th	20th	21st
	Progress	Prog 2-2	Ch7	Ch8	Ch9	Prog 3-1	Prog 3-2	makeup
	Homework	Ch7	Ch8	Ch9	Prog 3-1	Prog 3-2	Review	

4th week

	Day	22nd	23rd	24th	25th	26th	27th	28th
	Progress	AT 1 시험 AT 2 시험	AT 1 토론 AT 3 시험	AT 2 토론 AT 3 시험	AT 3 토론 AT 4 시험	AT 4 토론 AT 5 시험	진단고사 진단고사 정독 AT 5 토론	makeup
	Homework	AT 1 복습	AT 2 복습	AT 3 복습	AT 4 복습	AT 5 복습		

- 전략 : 챕터 각 앞부분
- HT : Hackers Test
- HP : Hackers Practice
- AT : Actual Test
- Makeup : 당일 소화못한 분량을 보충하는날
- Review : 해당주의 학습내용을 복습하는날

II. How to Study

● 스터디 학습 – 해커스 리딩은 구성부분에 있어서 스터디 학습을 우선으로 한다.

● HOMEWORK : 숙제는 예습과 복습으로 이루어진다.

예습법

각 Chapter의 전략을 파악한 후, 그것을 적용하여 연습한다. 반드시 시간을 정해놓고 문제를 풀어야 하며, 문제를 풀고 난 후에 다시 처음으로 돌아가서 꼼꼼히 지문을 분석하고 선택지의 내용 중 정답이나 오답이 되는 이유를 모두 확인하여 스터디에서 토론을 할 수 있도록 한다. 이 때 자신이 정독을 맡은 지문에 관한한 구조파악 / 단어암기 / 배경지식 등을 완벽히 준비하여 스터디 팀원들에게 설명할 수 있어야 한다.

복습법

당일 스터디 시간에 학습한 부분을 다시 살펴보고, 그래도 이해되지 않는 경우 해커스 웹 사이트의 해커스 리딩 게시판을 이용하여(www.goHackers.com) 확인한다. 복습은 매일매일 해야 하지만 시간이 모자랄 경우, Review Day를 이용하여 보충한다.

● PROGRESS : 진도는 아래와 같은 3단계로 진행하며 정확한 시간배분을 해야 한다.

1st STEP 토론을 통한 답 수렴

전날 복습을 통해 풀어 온 문제에 대해 토론을 하면서 답을 수렴해 나간다. 이 때 정답과 해설은 보지 않고. 다만 서로의 답을 공개하고 왜 그 답을 선택하게 되었는지를 말한 후, 토론을 해야 한다. 결국 수렴되지 않는 문제의 경우, 너무 많은 시간을 소비하는 것은 좋지 않다. 문제를 해결하지 못하고 시간만 버리게 될 수도 있기 때문이다. 해결되지 않는 문제는 skip하고 나중에 정답과 해설을 확인한다.

2nd STEP 함께 정독

'함께 정독하기' 란 당일 분량의 지문 중 각 지문에 대한 담당자를 정하여 준비 해 온 지문을 강의하듯 정독하면서 스터디를 진행하는 것이다. 스터디 시간에는 각자 한 두 개의 지문을 직접 정독하지만 그 외의 다른 지문들도 스스로 정독해 와야 한다. 토론을 통해 잘못된 부분은 서로 지적하고, 의견을 조율하면서 지문을 정독해 나간다.

3rd STEP 최종적으로 해답을 맞추어본다.

이 과정은 점수확인보다는 스터디에 나온 결과와 비교하여 지문과 문제를 완전히 분석하고 이해하도록 하는 것이다.

● 개별 학습

● 개인 학습은 아래와 같은 3단계로 진행한다.

1st STEP 정해진 분량의 문제풀이

일정한 시간을 정해서 매일매일 문제를 풀어본다. 이때 챕터의 전략을 최대한 숙지하여 문제에 적용시키는 습관을 갖는다.

2nd STEP 정독과 선택지분석

문제를 다 풀었으면, 지문을 정독하면서 정답으로 고른 이유와 오답은 왜 정답이 될 수 없는 지를 기입한다.

3rd STEP 최종적으로 해답을 맞추어본다.

이 때 점수확인과 더불어, 꼼꼼하게 지문과 문제를 완전하게 분석하고 이해한다. 해결하지 못한 문제는 해커스 리딩 게시판을 이용하여 (www.goHackers.com) 반드시 확인해야 할 것이다.

1 1st Day를 월요일로 시작하는 것이 주말 makeup에 좋다. 특히 한 달 완성의 경우 하루 분량을 그날 못 마친 경우, 다음날로 미루지 말고, 진도는 그대로 나가되, makeup day를 이용하여, 반드시 그 주의 할 부분은 그 주에 끝내어 다음 주까지 미루지 않도록 한다.

2 첫 날 진단고사를 풀어본 다음 채점만하고, 답은 맞추지 않는다. 지문 당 틀린 개수와 총 틀린 개수를 적어 놓는다. 이는 Hackers Reading을 학습하기 전 스스로의 실력을 확인하기 위한 것이며, 이 책의 모든 문제를 다 풀어 본 후 마지막 날 다시 진단고사를 풀어 보고 자신의 실력을 가늠해 보도록 한다.

3 Review Day는 그 주에 학습한 부분을 복습하는 날이다. 특히 단어위주로 복습하면 매우 효과적이다.

4 문제를 풀 때는 반드시 시간을 정해놓고 풀어야 한다. CBT 방식으로 바뀌면서 PBT 때보다 비교적 시간여유가 있기는 하지만 시간제한 없이 문제를 푸는 것은 실전 시험에서의 시간 조절에 실패할 수도 있다.

5 Actual Test를 풀 때는 50분의 시간제한을 두고 실제 시험을 보는 것과 같이 한다.

6 정독을 맡은 사람은 '배경지식' 까지 함께 준비하면 지문을 이해하는 데 도움이 된다.

7 벌금제를 도입하는 것은 스터디의 효율을 높이는 데 효과적일 것이다. 특히 각자가 맡은 정독 지문을 준비하지 않은 경우 다른 팀원들에게도 피해를 줄 수 있으므로 더 많은 벌금을 부과한다. 이런 식으로 그 역할의 비중에 따른 유연한 벌금을 미리 정하고 꼭 지키도록 한다.

8 Chapter. 5의 Inference(2)는 특히 높은 논리력을 요구하는 부분인 만큼 스터디 날짜를 이틀로 했다. Inference 문제를 잘 풀기 위해서 심도있는 토론을 통해 지문에 제시된 정보뿐만 아니라 숨겨진 정보까지 정확히 찾아내는 능력을 길러야 한다.

9 1개월 동안 스터디를 할 경우 4 weeks program plan에 맞춰 스터디를 진행하면 되고, 2개월간의 스터디일 경우 6주 동안 이 책을 모두 학습한 뒤에 나머지 2 weeks는 powerprep과 같은 문제를 풀어보며 CBT시험 방식에 적응하는 훈련을 하는 것이 좋다. 또는 Hackers Reading의 chapter 부분은 모두 풀고 난 후 2주간 취약한 pattern을 보강하고 마지막에 최종 마무리로 Actual test를 풀어보는 것도 좋은 방법이다.

10 지문을 정독할 때 Hackers Grammar Pattern을 적용하면, 복잡한 장문의 문장도 정확한 해석이 가능하다.

11 스터디 학습이나 개별 학습 시 생기는, 스스로 해결할 수 없는 부분은 해커스 리딩 게시판(www.goHackers.com) 에서의 질문과 토론을 통해 해결한다.

12 문제를 다 푼 다음 단지 채점이나 주입식 암기에 그치는 것이 아니라 토론을 통해 논리력을 배양할 수 있도록 해커스식 토론 학습법을 적용하여 문제를 풀어야 한다. 이는 Reading 문제를 푸는 데 있어서 뿐만 아니라 단순 암기에 치우친 국내 학생들의 유학 생활에도 많은 도움이 될 수 있을 것이다.

Reading

HACKERS READING

진단고사

[1] Tropical rain forests are mainly the product of climatic interactions, particularly between temperature and rainfall. In general, tropical rain forests occur where a mean monthly temperature of between 20 and 28 degrees Celsius is combined with an annual rainfall of between 1.5 and 10 meters, evenly distributed throughout the year. This last proviso is very important because it is only to those tropical forests which experience little seasonal variation in terms of rainfall that the term rain forest can legitimately be applied.

It comes as no surprise to learn that among the plants which flourish in tropical rain forests, trees are the most abundant. The climate of the equatorial regions provides all the necessary ingredients for rapid plant growth, and it is not uncommon for trees to attain heights of up to, and sometimes over, 40 meters. Such immense plants require an extremely large leaf area in order to harness enough sunlight for photosynthesis, and the combined crowns of these enormous trees form an almost continuous canopy. Occasionally an exceptionally large tree pushes its way through the leaf cover, dominating the landscape. These trees are known as emergents, and form the uppermost layer of a rain forest's complex canopy structure.

■ Beneath the main canopy grow smaller trees that are either young or slow-growing, tending to have more elongated crowns than their taller counterparts. ■ Together with various large herbs and shrubs, these form a third canopy layer. ■ These three layers, or strata, together make up an almost impenetrable cover. Under normal conditions very little light—sometimes as little as 2 percent—is able to filter through to the forest floor. ■ It is because there are plenty of younger trees beneath just waiting for the opportunity to take advantage of the extra sunlight and join their fellows in the canopy.

All this makes for somewhat unfavorable growing conditions on the forest floor, and the result is that vegetation here is sparse. The exception to this rule occurs where rivers flow through the forests, and vegetation flourishes along their banks, making the forest thick and impenetrable. This is the typical image of the tropical rain forest, perhaps fuelled by the fact that many people's first impression is from a boat.

1   What does the passage mainly discuss?
   (a) The ecosystem of tropical rainforests
   (b) The deforestation of tropical rain forests
   (c) The canopy in tropical rainforests
   (d) The destruction of the rainforest canopy

2   The word legitimately in paragraph 1 is closest in meaning to
   (a) acceptably
   (b) splendidly
   (c) forcefully
   (d) illegally

3   According to the passage, why are trees the most abundant vegetation in tropical rain forests?
   (a) Trees are more resistant to diseases than other plants.
   (b) The roots of most plants, except trees, easily rot in rain forests' humidity.
   (c) Trees crowd out other plants by consuming most of the nourishment in the soil.
   (d) Trees are well-suited to the climate and environment of the rainforest.

4   According to the passage, the second canopy layer is composed of
    (a) regular trees found in tropical rain forests
    (b) trees with the smallest crowns of all the trees
    (c) rapid-growing young trees
    (d) big shrubs and lichens

5   The following sentence can be added to paragraph 3.

    Even when a large tree falls there is little respite.

    Where would it best fit in the passage?
    Clicke on the square [■] to add the sentence to the passage.

6   Inferring from the passage, a person walking in a tropical rain forest would be
    most likely to see which of the following?
    (a) A canopy of emergent trees that sits under the regular canopy
    (b) Sparse vegetation on riverbanks
    (c) Sunny areas where 40 meter high trees have collapsed
    (d) A third canopy of small trees and shrubs

7   It can be inferred from the passage that shrubs in tropical rain forests have
    features such as
    (a) dazzling colors
    (b) slippery outside roots
    (c) numerous fragranced flowers
    (d) wide leaves

8   According to the passage, which sentence is NOT true?
    (a) Tropical rain forests come about through a combination of temperature and
        rainfall factors.
    (b) Under the main canopy, trees grow slowly.
    (c) Under normal conditions, a large amount of light is able to filter down to the
        forest floor.
    (d) The climate of the equatorial regions supplies all the necessary ingredients
        for rapid plant growth.

9   Find the sentence in the passage that indicates why the canopy structure is related
    to vegetation density in the forest floor.

    Copy the sentence to the blank below.
    Such immense plants require an extremely large leaf area in order to

10 The word sparse in the passage is closest in meaning to
    (a) austere
    (b) meager
    (c) rash
    (d) quaint

11 The word their in the passage refers to
    (a) vegetation on the forest floor
    (b) younger trees
    (c) rivers
    (d) the forests

[2] Probably the most abundant frogs are the approximately 260 species of the genus Rana (GR. frog), found over all the temperate and tropical regions of the world except in New Zealand, the oceanic islands, and southern South America. They are usually found near water, although some, such as the wood frog R.sylvatica, spend most of their time on damp forest floors. The large bullfrogs, T. catesbeiana, and green frogs, R. clamitans, are nearly always found in or near permanent water or swampy regions. The leopard frogs, Rana pipiens and related species, are found in nearly every state and Canadian provinces and are the most widespread of all North American frogs. R. pipiens is the species most commonly used in biology laboratories and for classical electrophysiological research.

Within the range of any species, frogs are often restricted to certain localities—for instance, to specific streams or pools—and may be absent or scarce in similar habitats elsewhere. The pickerel frog (R. palustris) is especially noteworthy in this respect because it is known to be abundant only in certain localized regions. Recent studies have shown that many populations of frogs worldwide may be suffering declines in numbers and becoming even more patchy than usual in their distributions. The causes for decline in diminishing populations are unknown.

Most of the frogs are solitary in their habits except during the breeding season. During the breeding period most of them, especially the males, are very noisy. Each male usually takes possession of a particular perch near water, where he may remain for hours or even days, trying to attract a female to that spot.

When frogs are silent, their presence is not detected until they are disturbed. When they enter the water, they dart about swiftly and reach the bottom of the pool, where they kick up a cloud of muddy water. In swimming, they hold the forelimbs near the body and kick backward with their webbed hindlimbs, which propel them forward. When they come to the surface to breathe, only the head and foreparts are exposed and, since they usually take advantage of any protective vegetation, they are difficult to see.

1 What is the main topic of the passage?
(a) The adaptations of frogs
(b) The habitat and characteristics of frogs
(c) The distribution and reproductive behavior of frogs
(d) The life cycle of frogs

2 Why does the author mention New Zealand in the passage?
(a) To illustrate an area in which some frogs are not found
(b) To emphasize the influence of temperature in frog distribution
(c) To argue that frogs do not consider New Zealand a tropical area
(d) To compare frogs in different regions

3 The author organizes the discussion of frogs in paragraph 1 in terms of
(a) a description of biological characteristics
(b) a comparison of habitats
(c) an explanation of scientific names
(d) a ranking of various species of frogs

4 Which of the following statements about frogs and their habitats is NOT true?

(a) Bullfrogs and green frogs can be found in similar habitats.
(b) The leopard frog is found throughout North America.
(c) The R.sylvatica frog lives in the forest, not the swamp.
(d) There are leopard frogs in the oceanic islands.

5 The word scarce in the passage is OPPOSITE in meaning to

(a) abundant
(b) vacant
(c) substantial
(d) present

6 The author mentions the pickerel frog in the passage as a representative of frogs which are

(a) found in a few particular climate zones
(b) unevenly distributed
(c) rarely found in the same area as other frogs of the same species
(d) found only in specific areas

7 The word suffering in the passage is closest in meaning to

(a) tolerating
(b) reducing
(c) experiencing
(d) distressing

8 Find the sentence that talks about the recent decline in the frog population.

Copy the sentence to the blank below.

Recent studies have · · · _____

9 Which of the following statements about frogs during the breeding season is NOT true?

(a) The female frogs are noisy.
(b) Frogs prefer muddy water to clear water for breeding.
(c) Male and female frogs become more social.
(d) Male frogs choose particular spots to attract female frogs.

10 According to paragraph 4, which of the following statements about the swimming habits of frogs is true?

(a) Frogs avoid the bottom of the water because they hate mud.
(b) Frogs only swim if they are disturbed by an outside force.
(c) Even while swimming, frogs disguise and hide themselves.
(d) They get most of their swimming power from their powerful forelimbs.

11 The word detected in the passage is closest in meaning to

(a) dispersed
(b) discovered
(c) displayed
(d) abated

[3] Friendship quilts are the earliest of the private quilts. They have existed in the United States from at least the late 1830s to the present. Embroidering initials on textiles to indicate ownership and inventory was a housekeeping task, and inscribing sentimental messages, genealogies, verses, and alphabets was done on samplers, usually in counted cross stitch. But other than minutely worked names or initials, this sort of threadwork has not commonly been seen on quilts.

Friendship quilts or album quilts, given when one member of a group or family moved away or married, were frequently made from fabrics left from the dressmaking tasks of each named contributor—"cut from the same cloth," as it were—and served as a visual reminder of past associations. As the mobility of the population in the United States increased throughout the 19th century, with most people moving west, the very real possibility existed that those who migrated might never return to their family homes, and might not see friends and family again. And so the presentation of quilts with blocks contributed by those close to the recipient became common practice, investing the presentation with emotional and very personal feelings.

To a large extent the practice involved women making memories for other women, and sometimes for men. Signatures, affecting messages, bible verses, and sometimes addresses, all found their way onto quilts; usually each block was signed by its maker. As the recipient, and her descendants, migrated across the country, the quilts often ended up far from their point of origin. However far she, or occasionally he, might be from family and friends, the quilt owner could take comfort in the memories evoked by the quilt.

Sometimes the process of creation was reversed; a woman might write home to her family, begging signed blocks of family and friends in an attempt to alleviate loneliness and isolation. And as a further note, women did not only go west with their husbands and families; some went east as missionaries, or as missionary wives, dedicated to spreading Christianity to the "heathens" in Asia, Africa, India, Hawaii, and Polynesia. Many of these women not only carried friendship quilts with them, they also impressed quilt making skills upon their converts, whether quilts were practical in those locations or not.

1 What does the passage mainly discuss?
(a) The method of making of friendship quilts
(b) The function of friendship quilts
(c) Signatures on quilts
(d) The history of the quilt

2 The word evoked in paragraph 3 is closest in meaning to
(a) overlooked
(b) emitted
(c) considered
(d) aroused

3 The author organizes the discussion of friendship quilts in terms of
(a) their development from the 19th century to the present
(b) a comparison of their function to that of album quilts
(c) a description of their brief history and functions
(d) a presentation about their materials and methods

4 When did the practice of presenting friendship quilts to close people become popular?

(a) When many settlers began moving westward
(b) After the American folk culture revival
(c) When Christianity expanded to the east
(d) As migration to other countries increased

5 Find the sentence in paragraph 3 that tells what the quilt makers embroidered on fabric.

Copy the sentence to the blank below.

_____

6 It can be inferred from the passage that friendship quilts were given to men as well as women because

(a) men also enjoyed quilting as a hobby in the 19th century
(b) men thought quilts made from long lasting fabrics were very useful
(c) men who left home also found comfort in friendship quilts
(d) men often made quilts as a record of family history

7 According to the passage, which of the following statements about friendship quilts is true?

(a) They were the first quilts and thus the origin of quilting.
(b) They were usually sold at charity bazaars.
(c) They were always made from the clothing of the owner's friends and family.
(d) Friendship quilts were often sentimental and represented their makers' emotions.

8 According to the passage, friendship quilts were used for which of the following purposes?

(a) utilizing expensive pieces of cloth
(b) reminding family and friends
(c) converting heretics to Protestantism
(d) showing off one's sewing skills

9 The word some in paragraph 4 refers to

(a) friends
(b) women
(c) husbands
(d) families

10 According to the passage, which of the following statements about quilts is NOT true?

(a) Embroidered initials were commonly seen on quilts in the late 1830s.
(b) Women earned additional income in the 19th century from making quilts.
(c) Friendship quilts were given to family members who moved away.
(d) Usually each block of the quilt was signed by its maker.

11 The word heathens in paragraph 4 is closest in meaning to

(a) people who are barbarous
(b) people who are ignorant of quilt making skills
(c) people who are against foreign influx
(d) people who do not believe in God

[4] The skyscraper would not have been possible were it not for the invention of the elevator. Before the elevator, five or six stories was the maximum height of masonry buildings. Buildings could technically have been built taller, but fatigue and loss of time due to stairs reduced the commercial value of the higher stories. As soon as passenger elevators appeared, buildings were constructed twice as high. Steel skeleton construction, the introduction of the hydraulic elevator, and then the electric elevator, allowed buildings to rise taller and taller throughout the 19th and 20th centuries.

Hoists and primitive elevators operated by human and animal power or by water wheels were in use as early as the 3rd century B.C. ■ The pyramids of Egypt and the temples of Mexico and Guatemala were built using a rudimentary system powered by the muscular force of slaves. ■ The first modern elevator is said to have been built in 1743 in France for Louis XV at the Palace of Versailles. ■ The power elevator was developed in the 19th century. ■ Elevators use the same basic mechanical design today as they did when Elisha Otis invented his safety elevator in the 1850s. Cars ride up and down a vertical track, raised by a hydraulic system or a motor/counterweight combination. Clamping devices stop the cab from falling. If a cab over speeds, a safety brake slows and stops it.

Elisha Otis was a master mechanic at the Bedstead Manufacturing Company in Yonkers, New York. He invented the first safety elevator—a mechanism for a lifting platform—in 1852. He started the E.G. Otis Company and sold elevators which were used to carry freight. In 1857, Otis completed installation of the world's first commercial passenger elevator in the E.V. Haughwout & Company store in New York City.

1 What does the passage mainly discuss?
(a) The invention of the elevator and its effects
(b) The life and achievements of Elisha Otis
(c) Information on skyscraper manufacturing
(d) The ancient history of the elevator

2 Find the sentence in paragraph 1 that explains why buildings were not built more than 6 stories high in the past.

Copy the sentence to the blank below.

_____

3 Until the late 19th century, construction of higher buildings was obstructed by the problem of
(a) building structure
(b) availability of materials
(c) convenience
(d) aesthetics

4 The word rudimentary in the passage is closest in meaning to
(a) powerful
(b) incompatible
(c) beginning
(d) elementary

5 The word system in the paragraph 2 refers to

(a) water wheels
(b) elevators
(c) human power
(d) animal power

6 The following sentence can be added to paragraph 2

Some believe that he used the elevator to allow his mistress to arrive clandestinely.

Where would it best fit in the passage?
Click on the square[■] to add the sentence to the passage.

7 The word combination in the passage is closest in meaning to

(a) adhesion
(b) institution
(c) conjunction
(d) alliance

8 According to the passage, what was the importance of Elisha Otis' invention?

(a) His devices reduced the possibility of people having accidents in elevators.
(b) It was the first elevator powerful enough to carry humans.
(c) He improved elevator safety enough to enable the construction of skyscrapers.
(d) It successfully made use of a new energy source.

9 It can be inferred from the passage that the first skyscraper appeared

(a) around 1800
(b) before 1852
(c) after 1857
(d) in the 20th century

10 What can be inferred from the passage about the first passenger elevator in the E.V. Haughwout & Company store?

(a) The added gains of having it surpassed the cost of building it.
(b) It was powered by electricity.
(c) It had a safety system.
(d) Its mechanical design was too difficult for the Bedstead Manufacturing Company to make.

11 According to the passage, which of the following sentences about Elisha Otis is NOT true?

(a) He invented the first safety elevator in 1852.
(b) He sold elevators that were used to carry freight.
(c) He invented powerful electronic elevator.
(d) He completed the installation of the world's first commercial passenger elevator.

CHAPTER 1

Topic · Main Idea · Purpose

CHAPTER

1

Topic · Main Idea · Purpose

O v e r v i e w

독해에서 가장 기본이 되며, 또한 궁극적인 목표가 되는 것은 저자 (author)의 의도를 파악하고, 저자가 글에 담고 있는 내용이 무엇인지를 읽어내는 것이다. 바로 이러한 사항에 대한 문제 영역이 main idea, topic, title, purpose 찾기 등이다

Types of Questions

● Main topic은 해당지문에서 처음부터 끝까지 '무엇' 인가에 대해 일관되게 언급하고 있는 그 '무엇' 에 해당한다.
  - What is the main topic of this passage?
  - What does the passage mainly discuss?
  - The passage focuses on which of the following aspects of _____?
  - The best title of this whole passage is _____

● Main idea는 해당지문에서 전달하고 있는 내용 즉, 중심 생각을 의미한다. 글의 처음이나 마지막 부분 정도에 Topic sentence 안에서 직접적으로 나타나거나, key word나 key phrase를 통해 암시된다.
  - What is the main idea of this passage?

● Purpose는 왜 작가가 해당 단락 혹은 지문을 기술하였는지 혹은 특정부분에서 작가는 어떤 입장을 취하고 있는가를 말한다.
  - Why did the author write the passage?
  - What is the purpose of the third paragraph?
  - The author's purpose in writing is to _____

●Strategy

1 지문을 skimming 하되, 각 문단에서, 자주 반복되어 나오는 단어, 즉 key-words에 집중해서 읽는다.
- Key-words 중에 main topic 이 있다.

2 각 문단이나 지문에서 topic sentence (주제문장)를 찾는다.
- topic sentence는 주로 글의 맨 처음이나 마지막에 오지만, 반드시 그러한 것은 아니다.
- 예를 들거나, 부연설명 한 것은 주제문이 아니다.

3 전체 지문(passage)의 topic이나 main idea를 묻는 문제도 있지만, 각 문단 (paragraph)의 main idea를 묻는 문제도 출제되며 이에 대한 접근방법은 passage접근법과 동일하다.
Tip 위의 경우에는 글 전체의 내용에 너무 집착하지 말 것

4 보기의 내용이 아래와 같은 경우는 topic이나 main idea가 될 수 없으므로 이러한 것은 topic이나 main idea에서 제외된다.
- **Too Specific**: 해당지문의 일부분에 대해서만 언급하고 있을 때
- **Too General**: 해당지문에서 언급하는 것보다 더 폭 넓은 부분을 언급하고 있을 때
- **Incorrect**: 지문의 내용과 틀린 경우
- **Irrelevant**: 지문과 관련 없는 것

TOPIC류의 문제를 풀 때는, 언제나 위의 네 가지 함정에 빠지지 않도록 주의 해야 한다.

Ex 지문에서 '현재 미국의 경제가 불투명하다' 는 내용이 나올 때 선택지에서 다음과 같은 내용이 있을 경우를 보자.
TS 1. 현재 California 경제는 불투명하다
TG 2. 현재 세계 경제는 불투명하다
IC 3. 현재 미국 경제는 투명하다.
IR 4. 현재 미국인들의 대부분은 여가생활을 즐기고 있다.

여기서 1번은 미국의 일부에 국한되었기 때문에 too specific, 2번은 미국을 세계로 확대했기 때문에 too general, 3번은 미국경제가 불투명하다는 내용과 상반되므로 incorrect, 4번은 미국경제와 관련이 없기 때문에 irrelevant이므로 각각 틀리게 된다.
Tip 처음 문제를 푸는 단계에서는 반드시 오답의 유형을 확인하는 연습을 해야한다.(TS/TG/IC/IR로 체크)

Ex Read the following passage, then find the passage's topic sentence, and answer the question.

● The Conestoga wagon probably began as a farm wagon that was adapted for use on the rough, hilly ground in Lancaster County. A cover was added to protect the goods inside from the rain, the bottom was bowed in the middle to make it less likely that the material inside the wagon would slide as the wagon went up and down hill, and the wheels were large so the wagon could pass over streams without getting the products inside wet. Also, large wheels meant the wagon could pass over stumps in the roads or large rocks. In those days roads were not paved and the Conestoga wagon is a perfect example of how a farm wagon was modified to make it better able to move over the rolling hills, the many streams and the poor roads of Lancaster County.

· Topic sentence _____
· What does the paragraph mainly discuss?

    (a) The structure of a farm wagon

    (b) The influence of raindrops upon the Conestoga wagon

    (c) A wagon adapted for use on bumpy roads and hills

    (d) The inconvenience of the Conestoga wagon

> **Topic Sentence** The Conestoga Wagon probably began as a farm wagon that was adapted for use on the rough, hilly ground in Lancaster County.
>
> **Answer** (c)

Ex Read the passage and choose the one best answer to the question on the basis of what is stated in the passage. For each of the three distracters of the question, mark why they are incorrect using the following indications: TG (too general), TS (too specific), IC (incorrect), and IR (irrelevant).

● The major textile in Europe was wool until cotton from India became popular in the 1600s. The wool merchants felt threatened and so they lobbied to have the import of Indian cloth banned. They succeeded, but their action left a void; savvy entrepreneurs started importing raw cotton from the West Indies and Brazil and turning it into cloth. Wherever there was a fast flowing stream there was a source of power and water mills, cottages, shops, and support services soon developed. Inventors came up with better ways to spin and weave, canals were built, coal was harnessed as a fuel source, and factories were born. Blackburn's moist (most would say wet!) climate was ideal for cotton spinning and weaving. Cotton was big business and people moved to Blackburn in increasing numbers.

· What does the paragraph mainly discuss?

    _IC_ (a) Indian cloth took over the European market after the 1600s

    _C_ (b) Why was raw cotton imported and what did it bring about?

    _TS_ (c) What conditions contributed to the development of the cotton industry?

    _IR_ (d) The European textile industry was amazingly brisk before the 15th century

> **Answer** (a)-IC (b)-C (c)-TS (d)-IR

Hackers Practice

Read the passages and for each item, choose the one best answer based on what is stated in the passage. For each of the three distracters, mark why they are inaccurate using the following indications: TG(too general), TS(too specific), IC (incorrect), and IR(irrelevant).

1

The origins of traditional Chinese painting extend far back into China's history. Generally speaking, works dating from before the Tang dynasty (618-907 A.D.) are mainly line drawings of people engaged in various activities. This was the "golden age" of human figure drawing. By the mid-Tang dynasty, landscape and flower-and-bird paintings began their rise to prominence. Paintings of mountains, forests, fields, and gardens have the ability to transport one away from the vexations of the material world into a peaceful, carefree realm. For this reason, landscape paintings have always been highly regarded by China's literati and officials. The flowers, grass, trees, stones, birds, and other animals depicted in the lively and energetic flower-and-bird paintings are also widely admired. Thus, the landscape and flower-and-bird types of painting, together with the earlier human figure painting, comprise the three main categories of traditional Chinese painting.   주제문이지다.

● The passage is primarily concerned with

_IR_ (a) The famous works of traditional Chinese painting

_✓_ (b) The three main categories of traditional Chinese painting

_TS_ (c) The changes in painting of the Tang dynasty

_TG_ (d) The history of Chinese painting

2

Cave paintings in France leave no doubt that the horse was a prime food source for Stone-Age hunters. When the Stone Age ended and the Bronze Age began, human beings in Europe and Asia had had generations of experience working with animals, having mastered the skills of herding sheep, cattle and goats. They had also learned to herd horses, which they kept mainly for meat, and possibly also for milk (as nomads in Central Asia still do today). People also had learned to cultivate grain and had abandoned hunting in roving bands in favor of settling in permanent communities. By 3,000 BC, therefore, humans had established regular food supplies and thus had the time to appreciate the horse for qualities other than its ability to feed a family of four for a week or so.

- Which of the following is the passage mainly about?

_____ (a) As humans learned breeding and farming, the use of horses changed.

_____ (b) Cave paintings in France reveal the way humans could get enough food supplies in the Bronze Age.

_____ (c) Cave paintings show what life was like in ancient times.

_____ (d) The horse has been one of the most useful animals.

3

Piaget may be best known for his stages of cognitive development. Piaget discovered that children think and reason differently at different periods throughout their lives. He believed that everyone passes through an invariant sequence of four qualitatively distinct stages. Invariant means that a person cannot skip stages or reorder them. Although every normal child passes through the stages in exactly the same order, there is some variability in the ages at which children attain each stage. The four stages are: sensorimotor—birth to 2 years; preoperational—2 years to 7 years; concrete operational—7 years to 11 years; and formal operational (abstract thinking)—11 years and up. Each stage has major cognitive tasks which must be accomplished. In the sensorimotor stage, the mental structures are mainly concerned with the mastery of concrete objects. The mastery of symbols takes place in the preoperational stage. In the concrete stage, children learn mastery of classes, relations, and numbers, as well as how to reason. The last stage deals with the mastery of thought.

- Which of the following is the main point the author makes about Piaget's cognitive development theory?

_____ (a) Children develop cognitive capacity following 4 universal stages.

_____ (b) Every child experiences the same stages of development at the same age.

___(c) There are theories of cognitive development different from that of Piaget's.

___(d) Piaget theorized about the process of men's cognitive development.

4

Many centuries before European explorers found their way to the western hemisphere, the Pueblo Indians of what is now New Mexico developed a distinctive and complex civilization. These peace loving people created an urban life that harmonized with the environment and with each other. Their religion was pantheistic and deeply spiritual, constituting an important part of daily life. Within that life they created an equitable government, magnificent architecture, intensive agriculture with a sophisticated irrigation system and highly developed art in pottery, weaving, jewelry, leather work, and other crafts.

● What's the best title for this passage?

___(a) The Cultural History of the Pueblo Indians

___(b) The Civilization of the Pueblo Indians

___(c) The Discovery of European Explorers

___(d) Pantheistic Pueblo Indian Society

5

New York, host city of the United Nations, remains the country's most international city and is one of the world's primary magnets for foreign tourism. Because of its prominence, however, the city is also a natural target for terrorism, notably the bombing of the World Trade Center in 1993 that killed several people and caused extensive property damage. In the last decade of the 20th century, New York experienced sustained growth in both population and financial stability. Hundreds of thousands of immigrants were added to its population, while a sustained boom on Wall Street invigorated the economy of every borough. In addition, major renovations of its infrastructure were completed, such as the restoration of Grand Central Station. Thus, New York's position as the preeminent American city remained secure at the outset of the 21st century.

● Why did the author write the passage?

(a) To explain the importance and pre-eminence of New York as an international city

(b) To demonstrate New York's economic growth in the 20th century

(c) To prove the influence of world economic changes upon New York

(d) To show how New York became a prominent city through the years

6

Artistic nationalism was a prominent aspect of much of New Deal art. This interest in things American took many forms: muralists painted scenes depicting local history and color; folklorists recorded traditional stories; playwrights created plays about American heroes; photographers documented daily life; and writers produced state and regional histories. New Deal administrators encouraged this preoccupation with what one Writers' Project publication called "American Stuff." Celebrating the country's past and its character promoted a sense of national identity during difficult times and yielded art that people could easily understand and appreciate. But New Deal art could also move beyond mere celebration and probe deeper into issues of the American character and identity.

● What is the best title for this passage?

_____✓_ (a) American Themes in New Deal Art

__Tg_7ʊ_ (b) Nationalism and Paint

__Iᴧ_ (c) Early American Art Forms

__Iᶜ_ (d) Folk Art for the High Class

7

The sense of smell is important for almost all fishes. Certain eels with tiny eyes depend mostly on smell to locate food. The olfactory, or nasal, organ of fishes is located on the dorsal surface of the snout. The lining of the nasal organ has special sensory cells that perceive chemicals dissolved in water, such as substances from food material and send sensory information to the brain by way of the first cranial nerve. Odor also serves as an alarm system. Many fishes, especially various species of freshwater minnows, react with alarm to the body fluids produced by an injured member of their own species.

● What is this passage mainly concerned with?

ʊᴿIg___ (a) The effect of dorsal strength upon digestion in fish

__ɪᴧ__ (b) The predatory relationship between eels and minnows

__✓__ (c) The ways fish utilize their sense of smell for survival

__ɪ𝑠__ (d) Defense systems developed by fish using cranial nerves

8

There are four basic tastes: sweet, salty, sour, and bitter. Different parts of the tongue can detect all types of tastes. This has led to criticism of the simple tongue "taste map" that is found in many textbooks. The organ that actually detects taste is called the "taste bud". Each taste bud (and there about 10,000 taste buds in humans) is made up of many (between 50-150) receptor cells. Receptor cells live for only 1 to 2 weeks and then are replaced by new receptor cells. Each receptor in a taste bud responds best to one of the basic tastes. A receptor can respond to the other tastes, but it responds strongest to a particular taste.

● What is the main topic of this passage?

_UR_ (a) The discovery of four basic tastes

_TS_ (b) Criticism of the "taste map" explanation

_✓_ (c) The constitution and function of the taste bud

_TS_ (d) The role of receptor cells of taste buds

The word "laser" stands for "light amplification by stimulated emission of radiation." Lasers are possible because of the way light interacts with electrons. Electrons exist at specific energy levels or states characteristic of that particular atom or molecule. The energy levels can be imagined as rings or orbits around a nucleus. Electrons in outer rings are at higher energy levels than those in inner rings. Electrons can be bumped up to higher energy levels by the injection of energy—for example, by a flash of light. When an electron drops from an outer to an inner level, "excess" energy is given off as light. The wavelength or color of the emitted light is precisely related to the amount of energy released. Depending on the particular lasing material being used, specific wavelengths of light are absorbed (to energize or excite the electrons) and specific wavelengths are emitted (when the electrons fall back to their initial level).

● Which of the following is the main topic of the passage?

_TS_ (a) The characteristics of electrons

JR _TG_ (b) The invention of electricity from energy levels /

_✓_ (c) The interaction between light and electrons to produce lasers

TC _TR_ (d) The way in which lasers group together in orbits to form electrons

In the generation of hydroelectric power, water is collected or stored at a higher elevation and led downward through large pipes or tunnels (penstocks) to a lower elevation; the difference in these two elevations is known as the head. In the course of its passage down the steep pipes, the falling water rotates turbines. The turbines in turn drive generators, which convert the turbines' mechanical energy into electricity. Transformers change the alternating current produced by the generators into a very high-voltage current that is suitable for long-distance transmission. The structure that houses the turbines and generators, and into which the pipes or penstocks feed, is called the powerhouse.

● The passage is mainly concerned with

_UR_ (a) where hydroelectric power plants are usually located

v _TS_ (b) the production of electricity by water power ,

ZR _TG_ (c) the development of hydroelectric power in the 20th century

TS _✓_ (d) the structure of the powerhouse

Hackers Test

Read each passage then answer the questions that follow.

1　The beginning of the 20th century brought significant changes in the way and organization of life. Contemporary civilization, which was urged forward by technological progress, demanded appropriate forms of art. Traditional art forms were no longer able to express new feelings and experiences. The search for new art forms and for new methods of expression led to the destruction of existing systems of art and to the creation of new ones. The arts (painting, theater arts and literature) abandoned the mimetic character which had been canonized through tradition in western European art practice. Within the foundation of western European art tradition there was a concept of mimesis, imitating life through canonized art mediums. A work of art has its own meaning if it conveys some content, if it tells us a story (narration is the center of all art). In literature, narration (a story) is achieved through words, literary genres and styles; in ballet and theater it is achieved through stage effects, music, words and movements which express the flow of the plot and the emotions of the actor.

　The determined forms of presentation coded by tradition in the art of ballet led to the culmination of a formal aspect of dance in which, in addition to narrative aspects, the highest value was placed on the performing skill of the ballet dancer. The reformist stream of modern dance sharply opposed the classicist-formalist virtuosity of the dancer. The reformist spirit in art from the beginning of the century resisted the narrative nature of art as being essentially utilitarian (from the time of Horatio it was believed that the basic role of art was to entertain and educate). Reformers wanted to change the role of art in society, the role of the artist, as well as the illusionist or realistic (mimetic) nature of western European art. The emancipation of art demanded "pure" art, which relies on its own means and explores them, expressing nothing but itself. The discovery of new foundations of dance was linked to the realization that the art of dance is self-sufficient, that it is not necessary for dance to have music and scenography conjuring up an environment in which the plot takes place, nor is it necessary to tell a story of any kind. The reformers of new dance also abandoned the virtuous movements of ballet dancers and the entire system of training by which classical virtuosity was achieved. They believed that formalism should be rejected in favor of more natural movements which originate from the body itself, restricted only by its natural abilities and limitations.

1. What's the main topic of the first paragraph?

 (a) Big changes in the way of life in the early 20th century

 (b) Literary genres and styles

 (c) Characteristics of traditional art

 (d) Changes in traditional art

2. What's the best title for the second paragraph?

 (a) Reformist spirit in art

 (b) The role of art in society

 (c) Various changes in the art of ballet

 (d) The difference between reformist and classicist-formalist styles

3. What is the main purpose of the passage?

 (a) To point out significant changes in the art of ballet

 (b) To show the influence of 20th century civilization

 (c) To give a detailed explanation of significant changes in traditional art

 (d) To outline a brief history of the new style of art

---

2   Millions of children spend a part of the day in child care while their parents work. These settings—in centers and in homes—are places where children can learn and grow. In 1989, the President and the nation's governors developed a set of national education goals to improve the quality of education in America. Although the first goal focused on school readiness, child care has often been viewed as falling outside that picture. The tenth anniversary of the goals is an important opportunity to redefine education and recognize that quality child care is part of a system of learning that affects child development.

Children's language and cognitive skills thrive in quality child care programs, with responsive caregivers who are adequately trained and supported. In poor quality programs, opportunities to stimulate development are lost or squandered. In large groups with few trained staff, in centers and homes where children have few opportunities to be read to, to be listened to, or to be held, in programs where television or isolation replace human interaction and communication, children learn that they have little effect upon their environment—precisely the wrong message to promote readiness and school success.

Traditionally, three "places" have been seen to affect a child's education: family, school and community. Child care is part of all three. Child care is a family support. Not only is child care often provided by relatives and other family members, but from the perspective of the child as well as the family, child care is often an extension of the home. Child care provides many opportunities to help parents succeed as "first teachers."

1. What is the main topic of the second paragraph?
   (a) The importance of quality child care programs
   (b) Cognitive development in childhood
   (c) The quality of education in America
   (d) The direct link between environment and child development

2. What is the purpose of this passage?
   (a) To give responsibility to caregivers
   (b) To prevent child abuse in child care centers
   (c) To explain the roles of child care centers in the 20th century
   (d) To improve the quality of education in child care

3. What does the passage mainly discuss?
   (a) The tenth anniversary of setting national education goals
   (b) Factors that lead to school readiness and educational success
   (c) The four-way link between family, school, education and child care
   (d) The effect of child care upon learning and development

---

3　　The temperance crusade was perhaps the most widespread of all the reform movements. The census of 1810 reported some 14,000 distilleries producing 25 million gallons of spirits each year. With a hard-drinking population of just over 7 million, the "alcoholic republic" was producing well over three gallons per year for every man, woman, and child, not counting beer, wine, and cider. And the census takers no doubt missed a few stills. William Cobbett, an English reformer who traveled in the United States, noted in 1819 that "one could hardly go into any man's house without being asked to drink wine or spirits, even in the morning."

The temperance movement rested on a number of arguments. First and foremost was the religious demand that "soldiers of the cross" lead blameless lives. Others stressed the economic implications of sottish workers. The dynamic new economy, with factories and railroads moving on strict schedules, made tippling by the labor force a far greater problem than it had been in a simple agrarian economy. Humanitarians emphasized the relations between drinking and poverty. Much of the movement's propaganda focused on the suffering of innocent mothers and children. "Drink," said a pamphlet from the Sons of Temperance, "is the prolific source (directly or indirectly) of nearly all the ills that afflict the human family."

In 1833 a national convention was called in Philadelphia, where the American Temperance Union was formed. The convention, however, revealed internal tensions: was the goal moderation or total abstinence, and if the latter, abstinence merely from ardent spirits or also from wine, cider, and beer? Should the movement work by persuasion or by legislation? Like nearly every movement of the day, temperance had a wing of perfectionists who rejected all compromises, and they passed a resolution that the liquor traffic was morally wrong and ought to be prohibited by law. The union, at its spring convention in 1836, called for the abstinence from all alcoholic beverages—a costly victory that caused moderates to abstain from the movement instead. Still, between 1830 and 1860, the temperance agitation drastically reduced Americans' per-capita consumption of alcohol.

1. What is the main topic of this passage?

   (a) A brief history of the foundation of the American Temperance Union

   (b) American extremist fighting for abstinence from drinking

   (c) The reduction in America's consumption of alcohol

   (d) Summary of the American temperance movement of the 1800s

2. What is the main purpose of the second paragraph?

   (a) To illustrate the points of temperance supporters

   (b) To compare humanitarian and social views on drinking

   (c) To discuss the arguments against drinking

   (d) To support the temperance movement

3. The author's purpose in writing the 3rd paragraph is

   (a) to condemn moderates who did not support total abstinence

   (b) to examine the morality of the temperance movement

   (c) to show the problems the American Temperance Union had in coming to a
       consensus

   (d) to vindicate the victory of total abstinence by the wing of perfectionists

---

4   The Erie Canal is a historic waterway of the United States, connecting the Great Lakes
     with New York City via the Hudson River. By the beginning of the 19th century the
     desirability of a transportation link between the Atlantic coast and the trans-Allegheny
     region was evident. Governor DeWitt Clinton of New York saw the potential in the
     proposal for a canal from Buffalo, on the eastern shore of Lake Erie, to Albany, on the
     upper Hudson, passing through the gap in the mountains in the Mohawk Valley
     region. In 1817 he induced the state legislature to authorize the expenditure of $7
     million for construction of a canal 363 miles (584 km) long, 40 feet (12 meters) wide,
     and 4 feet (1.2 meters) deep. To cross the 500-foot (150-metre) rise in elevation
     west of Troy, the work required 83 locks. No roads existed for supply; horse and
     human power alone were available. Streams were crossed via aqueducts. In several
     places rock was blasted with black-powder charges. Despite all difficulties, the canal
     was opened on October 25, 1825, by the canal boat Seneca Chief.

     The effect of the canal on the growth of the upper Midwest was rivaled only by its
     effect on the growth of New York City. Settlers poured west (many using the canal)
     into Michigan, Ohio, Indiana, and Illinois, places from which they could ship farm
     produce via the Erie Canal to be marketed in the East; in return, barge loads of
     manufactured goods and supplies went west. Freight rates from Buffalo to New York
     City, which had been $100 a ton by land, were only $10 a ton by the canal. In nine
     years the tolls exceeded the cost of construction, and by 1882, when the tolls were
     abolished, the canal had paid for the cost of several feeder canals and contributed to
     the general revenue of the state.

     Enlarged to 70 feet (21 meters) in width and 7 feet (2.1 meters) in depth, the Erie
     Canal successfully resisted competition from the railroads and, despite suffering a
     period of neglect late in the 19th century, was the central artery in the 20th-century

development of New York canals that connected Lake Champlain, Lake Ontario, and the Finger Lakes. Completed in 1918, this waterway was called the New York State Barge Canal (later the New York State Canal System). The modern canal, though used largely for pleasure boating, is capable of accommodating barges of up to about 2,000 tons.

1. What is the main topic of paragraph 1?
   (a) The Erie Canal, one of the most international and important canals in the world
   (b) The political and economical importance of the Erie Canal
   (c) The construction of the Erie Canal
   (d) The difficulties of building the Erie Canal.

2. What is the main idea of paragraph 2?
   (a) The Erie Canal had important influence on the development of the upper Midwest.
   (b) Canals are the most important structure in the nation's economy.
   (c) It took several years to complete construction of the Erie Canal.
   (d) The building of the Erie Canal expanded the limitation in freight rates.

3. The best title of this whole passage is
   (a) the Economical Influence of the Erie Canal
   (b) why was the Erie Canal Built in America?
   (c) summary of the General History of the Erie Canal .
   (d) the Historical Structure, Erie Canal

5   Nevada began its transition to a modern economy during the Great Depression of the 1930s. After the legalization of gambling in 1931 and the reduction to six weeks of the residence requirement for divorce, Nevada became a marriage, divorce, and resort center. The principal resort areas are Las Vegas, Reno, Laughlin, and Lake Tahoe. Las Vegas attracts many tourists from southern California and foreign countries and also hosts business and professional conventions. Reno draws many pleasure seekers from the San Francisco Bay area and from the Pacific Northwest. Laughlin emerged as a tourist center in the 1980s, and Lake Tahoe continues to serve as a fashionable playground.

Construction of the Hoover Dam on the Colorado River substantially aided the economy of southern Nevada, and its cheap hydroelectric power opened the way for manufacturing. The importation of both hydroelectric power from the Bonneville Dam on the Columbia River and piped-in natural gas brought industrial development to the northwestern region.

In the 1950s the establishment of the Nevada Test Site by the federal government expanded employment opportunities and stimulated the development of technical industries within the state. Overshadowing the new industrialization, and fundamentally responsible for the current prosperity, is the diversification and expansion of the tourist trade to include not only the gaming and entertainment facilities of the Reno and Las Vegas areas but also the scenic and recreational opportunities statewide.

1. The first paragraph primarily describes
(a) Nevada's economy during the Great Depression
(b) Las Vegas, one of the most important centers in Nevada
(c) the way the change in marriage law in Nevada influenced the economy
(d) the booming tourist industry in Nevada since the Great Depression

2. Which of the following is the main topic of paragraph 2?
(a) The construction of the Hoover Dam
(b) Factors that contributed to the economic development of Nevada
(c) The Hoover Dam project in Nevada
(d) The significance of hydroelectric power

3. What is the best title for the whole passage?
(a) Nevada in the 20th century
(b) History of the tourist industry in Nevada
(c) The entertainment boom in Nevada in the 1950s
(d) The creation of a modern economy in Nevada

6 Like the California gold fields, the Oregon mines attracted single, unattached men almost exclusively. Heretofore, Oregon had been the destination of families, farmers, and settlers; the mines brought a distinctly unsavory element to the Territory. This might have had little impact on the character of white civilization in the area except that the Indians of southern Oregon were generally more hostile to whites than those in the north. The spring and summer of 1855 saw an escalating cycle of provocation, retribution, and retaliation that culminated in what was then described as the "most sanguinary war"—that is, the bloodiest—in Oregon's short history.

Tensions exploded in July, 1855, in the Humbug War, named for the creek along which the hostilities took place. More than two dozen Indians were cruelly and indiscriminately killed by shooting, hanging, or being thrown down abandoned prospect holes. On October 8, 23 noncombatant Indians (women, children, and old men) were killed in what was known as the Luptin Affair. The next day, 16 whites of all ages and both sexes were killed in the Rogue River Massacre. The fighting climaxed on October 17 at the Gallice Siege, wherein four whites and an undetermined number of Chinese were killed when Indians trapped a volunteer militia in buildings which they set ablaze with flaming arrows. The situation was eventually subdued by Indian Agent Joel Palmer, who spent 1855 imposing treaties on almost all the tribes of Oregon and sending them to reservations.

1. Which of the following best represents the topic of paragraph 1?
   (a) The beginning of conflicts in Oregon between southern Indians and the miners
   (b) Promotions the Oregon mines used to attract single, and unattached men
   (c) The prospering of the Oregon economy from the discovery of gold mines
   (d) The ferocity of southern Indians

2. The best topic for the second paragraph is
   (a) The outbreak of the Humbug war between southern Indians and miners
   (b) The escalation and resolution of the feud between southern Indians and miners
   (c) The conflicts' influence on the Oregon economy
   (d) The expansion of the conflicts between southern Indians and miners

3. This whole passage mainly describes
   (a) Economic damage in Oregon caused by the southern Indians
   (b) The difficulties of mining gold in California and Oregon
   (c) The cruelty of white Americans in Oregon during the 19th century
   (d) The history of conflicts between southern Indians and miners in Oregon

7   Bats are a fascinating group of animals. They are one of the few mammals that can use sound to navigate—a trick called echolocation. Of the some 900 species of bats, more than half rely on echolocation to detect obstacles in flight, find their way into roosts and forage for food.

Echolocation, the active use of sonar (Sound Navigation And Ranging) along with special morphological (physical features) and physiological adaptations, allows bats to "see" with sound. Most bats produce echolocation sounds by contracting their larynx (voice box). A few species, though, click their tongues. These sounds are generally emitted through the mouth, but Horseshoe bats (Rhinolophidae) and Old World leaf-nosed bats (Hipposideridae) emit their echolocation calls through their nostrils: there they have basal fleshy horseshoe or leaf-like structures that are well-adapted to function as megaphones.

Echolocation calls are usually ultrasonic—ranging in frequency from 20 to 200 kilohertz (kHz), whereas human hearing normally tops out at around 20 kHz. Even so, we can hear echolocation clicks from some bats, such as the Spotted bat (Euderma maculatum). These noises resemble the sounds made by hitting two round pebbles together. In general, echolocation calls are characterized by their frequency, their intensity in decibels (dB), and their duration in milliseconds. In terms of pitch, bats produce echolocation calls with both constant frequencies (CF calls) and varying frequencies that are frequently modulated (FM calls). Most bats produce a complicated sequence of calls, combining CF and FM components. Although low frequency sound travels further than high-frequency sound, calls at higher frequencies give the bats more detailed information—such as size, range, position, speed and direction of a prey's flight. Thus, these sounds are used more often.

---

1. What is the topic of the second paragraph?
   (a) Various sounds bats can make
   (b) The overdependence of bats on their sonar abilities
   (c) Ways in which bats produce echolocation
   (d) Physical adaptations bats have made to their environment

2. What does the third paragraph mainly discuss?
   (a) The characteristics of echolocation calls
   (b) The reason why bats rely on echolocation
   (c) The value of echolocation calls for getting information
   (d) The important role of CF calls and FM calls

3. What is the main idea of the whole passage?
   (a) Bats use echolocation to navigate.
   (b) Echolocation calls have various frequencies.
   (c) Humans cannot hear echolocation calls.
   (d) Most bats produce echolocation.

---

8   A plant is carnivorous if it attracts, captures, and kills animal life forms. It must also digest and absorb the nutrients from prey to qualify as a carnivorous plant. There are many noncarnivorous plants that do some (but not all) of these things. For example, flowers attract pollinators (insects, birds, and other creatures, even humans. Some plants (orchids, jack-in-the-pulpits, and waterlilies) temporarily trap insect pollinators to ensure pollen transfer. Plants such as members of the American genera Ibicella and Proboscidea trap and kill insects by their sticky leaves, but do not digest the prey. All plants absorb nutrients either through their roots or leaves. However, even though these plants do some of the things that carnivorous plants do, they do not fulfill all of the criteria necessary to qualify as a carnivorous plant. Only plants which attract, capture, kill, digest, and absorb prey are truly carnivorous.

In recent years people have been realizing that nature is not quite as black and white as we would like. Some plants are neither completely carnivorous, nor completely noncarnivorous. For example, there are sticky plants which harbor bugs on them. These bugs crawl freely on the plant and eat the insects trapped by the sticky leaves. The bugs excrete (i.e. poop) on the leaves, and the plant absorbs nutrients from the poop. Other plants rely on bacterial decomposition to break down their captured prey.

1.What is the purpose of the first paragraph?

    (a) To describe various types of plants

    (b) To compare the characteristics of noncarnivorous plants and carnivorous plants

    (c) To define which plants are true carnivorous plants

    (d) To inform about noncarnivorous plants

2. Why does the author mention sticky plants in paragraph 2?

    (a) To give detailed characteristics of noncarnivorous plants

    (b) To explain that carnivorous and noncarnivorous are not totally distinct from each other

    (c) To explain the relationship between sticky plants and harbor bugs

    (d) To illustrate that the plants must fulfill all of the criteria necessary to qualify as a carnivorous plant

3. What is the best title for the whole passage?

    (a) The classification of carnivorous and noncarnivorous plants ·

    (b) The criteria for distinguishing plants from animals

    (c) Why do some noncarnivorous plants have the features of carnivorous plants?

    (d) Carnivorous plants' strategy for seizing their prey

---

9   After scientists understood how the Sun produces its energy, they began developing theories to explain how the Sun's energy travels from the core to the Sun's atmosphere. For the first few decades after the discovery that fusion powers the Sun, scientists deduced the Sun's structure by comparing the theoretical output of the Sun's core to the energy actually released at the Sun's atmosphere. In the 1960s American physicist Robert Leighton developed a camera that could record Doppler shifts in light at the Sun's surface. A Doppler shift is a change in the wavelength of light caused by the movement of the object that is emitting the light. If the object is moving away from the observer, each wave will have to travel farther to reach the observer, making the distance between waves (the wavelength) longer. An object moving toward the observer will seem to emit light with a shorter wavelength. Leighton used this device to discover that the Sun seemed to pulsate in and out, making a complete cycle about every five minutes.

Leighton's discovery launched the field of helioseismology, or the study of the Sun's interior by observing the vibrations of the Sun and how sound waves move through it. In the 1970s scientists demonstrated that the entire Sun is vibrating with ponderous, organized rhythms that can extend to its very core. Scientists developed models of the interior of the Sun based on vibrations at its surface.

In 1995 six observatories around the world coordinated with each other to begin observing the oscillations of the Sun as a team. This project, a collaboration of 20 nations, is called the Global Oscillation Network Group (GONG). GONG can keep constant watch on the Sun because, at any given time, daytime is being experienced by at least one of the observatories. GONG has allowed scientists to get a better idea of the interior structure of the Sun through helioseismology.

1. With what topic is paragraph 1 mainly concerned?
   (a) The physics behind Doppler shifts
   (b) Robert Leighton's famous theory
   (c) The process of solar fusion and lunar Doppler shifts
   (d) Scientific advances in understanding the nature of the sun

2. What does the second paragraph mainly discuss?
   (a) The vibration of the sun's movement
   (b) The generation of energy by the sun
   (c) The study of how the sun's energy travels from the core
       to the Sun's atmosphere
   (d) The development of a field of study Leighton advanced

3. What is the main subject of this passage?
   (a) The development of the study of the sun
   (b) The influence of Robert Leighton's discovery of the camera
   (c) The history of the GONG project
   (d) Explanation of the Doppler shifts and oscillations of the Sun

10 Geologists classify rocks in three groups, according to the major Earth processes that formed them. The three rock groups are igneous, sedimentary, and metamorphic rocks. Anyone who wishes to collect rocks should become familiar with the characteristics of these three rock groups. Knowing how a geologist classifies rocks is important to transform a random group of rock specimens into a true collection.

Igneous rocks are formed from melted rock that has cooled and solidified. When rocks are buried deep within the Earth, they melt because of the high pressure and temperature; the molten rock (called magma) can then flow upward or even be erupted from a volcano onto the Earth's surface. When magma cools slowly, usually at depths of thousands of feet, crystals grow from the molten liquid, and a coarse-grained rock forms. When magma cools rapidly, usually at or near the Earth's surface, the crystals are extremely small, and a fine-grained rock results. A wide variety of rocks are formed by different cooling rates and different chemical compositions of the original magma. Obsidian (volcanic glass), granite, basalt, and andesite porphyry are four of the many types of igneous rock.

Sedimentary rocks are formed at the surface of the Earth, either in water or on land. They are layered accumulations of sediments-fragments of rocks, minerals, or animal or plant material. Temperatures and pressures are low at the Earth's surface, and sedimentary rocks show this fact by their appearance and the minerals they contain. Most sedimentary rocks become cemented together by minerals and chemicals or are held together by electrical attraction; some, however, remain loose and unconsolidated. The layers are normally parallel or nearly parallel to the Earth's surface; if they are at high angles to the surface or are twisted or broken, some kind of Earth movement has occurred since the rock was formed. Sedimentary rocks are forming around us all the time. Sand and gravel on beaches or in river bars look like the sandstone and conglomerate they will become. Compacted and dried mud flats harden into shale. Scuba divers who have seen mud and shells settling on the floors of lagoons find it easy to understand how sedimentary rocks form.

1. The purpose of the first paragraph is to
   (a) Demonstrate the importance of classifying rocks
   (b) Outline the classifications that geologists use with rocks
   (c) Present brief characteristics of three rock groups
   (d) Promote rock collecting as a hobby

2. What aspect of igneous rock does the second paragraph mainly discuss?
   (a) The process of forming
   (b) Various characters
   (c) The wide variety of rocks
   (d) Cooling and solidifying

3. The paragraph that follows this passage most likely deals with
   (a) The method of classifying rocks
   (b) Scuba divers' understanding of sedimentary rocks
   (c) The characteristics of metamorphic rocks
   (d) The process of forming metamorphic rocks

올림푸스(OlYmPUS) 의 12신

- **ZEOUS | JUPITER** | 하늘의 지배자 '찬란한 하늘'
  올림푸스(Olympus) 최고의 신으로 천상(天上)을 지배하는 천공(天空)·뇌정(雷霆)의 신인 동시에 인간사회의 정치·법률·도덕 등 모든 생활을 지배하였다.

- **HERA | JUNO** | 질투의 화신 '보호자'
  여성의 보호신이며 결혼과 출산을 관장했고, 질투의 여신이라는 이름이 잘 어울릴 정도로 질투가 심하여 제우스의 연인들은 물론이고 자식들까지 심하게 박해하였다

- **DEMETER | CERES** | 대지의 여신 '곡식의 어머니'
  데메테르는 대지의 생산력, 특히 곡식을 생육하는 곡식의 여신이다.

- **POSEIDON | NEPTUNE** | 바다의 지배자 '땅의 주(主)'
  '바다를 뒤흔드는 자'로 그의 무기인 삼지창 트라이아나(Triaina)를 휘둘러 암석을 분쇄하고, 폭풍우를 일으키고, 해안을 흔드는 지진의 신이다.

- **ATHENA | MINERVA** | 처녀의 수호신 '하늘의 여왕'
  제우스가 혼자 낳은 딸로서 제우스의 머리에서 무장한 채로 태어난 처녀 신으로 로마신화의 미네르바(Minerva)에 해당한다.

- **APOLLON | APOLLO** | 태양의 신 '미남 청년'
  태양의 신이자 궁술(弓術)과 예언·의료·음악 및 시의 신이기도 하다.

- **ARTEMIS | DIANA** | 순결의 여신
  수렵과 궁술을 맡아보고 또 야생동물, 어린이, 약한 자들을 수호하는 여신이다.

- **APHRODITE | VENUS** | 사랑과 미의 여신 '거품에서 태어났다'
  아프로디테는 여성의 생식력과 자연의 생식력을 표현하는 무서운 신이며 다산의 여신이기도 하다.

- **HEPHAESTUS | VULCAN** | 대장장이의 신 '낮을 빛내는 사람'
  화산(火山)의 신이자 대장장이 신으로 로마신화의 불칸(Vulcan)에 해당한다.

- **ARES | MARS** | 만물의 생성, 사랑의 신 '전사(戰士)'
  아레스는 행동과 결정을 주관하는 신이며 공포와 테러의 신이다.

- **HERMES | MERCURY** | 여행자의 수호신 '돌무더기'
  부와 행운의 신으로서 상업, 도박, 격투, 도둑질에 이르기까지 숙련과 기민성을 요하는 분야를 주관한다. 또 그는 통행인과 여행자의 수호신으로 길에 깔린 돌을 치워 도로를 정비한다고 일컬어진다

- **DIONYSOS | BACCHUS** | 술과 연극의 신 '불완전한 신'
  포도나무·포도주를 관장하며 술에 취하게 하는 힘을 상징할 뿐만 아니라 모든 속박으로부터의 해방의 신, 문명의 촉진자, 입법자, 그리고 평화의 애호자로 여겨지고 있다.

## CHAPTER 2

Organization & Insertion

2

Organization & Insertion

O v e r v i e w

작가는 개요(outline:작가의 의도를 포함하여 글의 전개방향을 제시한 것)를 가지고 글을 조직한다. 따라서 좋은 글은 단락마다, 일정한 구성방식(organization)을 지니게 되고, 또 이런 몇 개의 단락이 논리적 연관성을 가지고 엮어져서 전체 글을 구성하게 된다. Organization(구조파악)과 Insertion(삽입) 문제를 풀기 위해서는 글의 흐름을 파악하는 연습이 되어야 한다.

작가는 중심 단락에 자신이 말하고자 하는 바를 쓰고, 이 내용에 설득력을 주기 위해 뒷받침 단락에 중심 단락을 뒷받침 하는 결과에 대한 원인, 의견에 대한 사실, 주장에 대한 논리적 근거, 비교와 대조, 부연 설명 등을 쓰게 된다. 이러한 각 단락의 기능과 단락 간의 관계를 파악하고 글의 전개와 서술 방식을 이해함으로써 글의 정보를 정확히 파악하는 일이 가능해진다.

● Organization 문제는 detail한 내용보다는, 단락사이의 맥락(logical coherence)을 파악하고, 어떤 임의의 단락이 어떤 기능을 하고있는지 찾는 것이다. 유사하게, 단락을 구성하는 각각의 문장은 일정한 연관성을 가지고 나열되어서 결국 하나의 기능을 갖는 단락을 완성한다.

● Insertion 문제는 단락 전체를 구성하는 각각의 sentence(문장)이 글의 흐름을 유기적이고, 자연스럽게 연결될 수 있도록 문제에 제시된 문장을 삽입한다. (지문의 적절한 곳에 단락을 삽입하는 문제도 출제된다.)

● Following topic 문제는 마지막 단락과 자연스럽게 이어져 나올 내용이 무엇인지를 찾는 문제이다. 전체 글의 흐름을 파악하고 있어야 문제를 해결할 수 있다.

organization을 파악하는 것은 main idea, 작가의 purpose를 파악하는 초석이 된다. 이번 chapter에서는 organization과 insertion 문제에 접근하기 위한 연습문제와 실전문제를 풀어봄으로써, 글의 논리적 흐름을 읽는 연습을 하도록 하자.

●Strategy

Types of Questions

- The author organizes the passage of _____ in terms of _____.
- Which of the following best describes the organization of paragraph 1?
- Which of the following best describes the development of the passage?

1 문제에서 요구하는 단락 혹은 지문 전체를 Scanning

2 문단구성을 이해 시켜주는 단서가 되는 단어나 구를 확인

A. 시간 순서 전개(chronological order)/진행 순서 전개(process):
  · 년도별로 기술/ before~ then~ finally~등의 부사구가 순서대로 나타날 때 등

B. 두 가지 이상의 subject matter를 서로 비교(compare)/대조(contrast):
  · In comparison/ similarly /as well as / unlike/differently/in contrast/ on the other hand/whereas 등

C. subject matter에 대한 예를 들어서 설명(explain something with an example):
  · for example/ for instance/to illustrate/ a case in point 등

D. 사건의 원인(cause) 혹은 결과(effect, result):
  · because (of)/ since/ with theses reasons/ therefore/ after all/ consequently/ lastly 등

E. 전체에서 설명한 내용을 요약(summary) 할 때:
  · In short/ in brief/ in sum 등

F. subject matters의 성질이나 종류에 따른 분류(classification)를 할 때:
  · the first type/ the second category 등

G. subject matter에 대해 자세히 설명(definition, explanation)/묘사 (illustration, description):
  · in other words/ in addition 등
  * 이 경우는 단서를 찾기보다는 subject matter에 대한 접근 범위가 어떻게 발전하고 있는지에 주목하면 쉽게 파악할 수 있다.

3 보기 중에서 답을 고를 때, 문제의 초점을 다시 한번 상기하도록 하자.
즉, 문제에서 지문 전체에 대해서 묻고있는지, 특정 단락으로 한정하고 있는지를 분명히 인지 해야 한다. 특히 지문에서 여러 가지 개념을 동시에 다루고 있는 경우에는 함정에 빠지기 쉽다.

☑ Insertion

Types of Questions

- The following sentence can be added to the passage.
  SENTENCE: 삽입되어야 할 문장
  Where would it best fit in the passage?
  Click on the square [■] to add the sentence to the passage.
  ➤ 본문에 표시되어있는 네모 박스를 click하면 문장이 저절로 들어가게 된다.

---

1 문제에 나와있는 문장의 의미를 파악하고, 네모(■)가 나타난 단락을 정독하면서, 어디에 삽입되어야 단락의 논리적 흐름을 파괴하지 않는지 (Logical congruity)확인

---

2 삽입되는 문장은 아래의 7가지 패턴

A. 두괄식문장의 TOPIC 넣기

· 단락의 introduction이 빠져있는 경우로, 나머지 문장이 이 introduction에 대한 설명이나 예로 구성되어 있는 것이 특징이다. 대부분의 영어로된 글은 두괄식의 organization을 형성하기 때문에, missing된 부분인 introduction은 나머지 부분의 summary의 내용을 가지고 있다.

B. 구조에서 집합이 먼저 언급되고, 그의 부분이 나중에 언급되는 경우

Ex Two reasons for government regulation of industry stand out. First,......... Second, ...

C. 대명사로 확인하는 방법

· 대명사는 앞에 언급된 명사를 지칭하므로, 지문 내의 순서에 있어서 대명사가 있는 문장이 들어갈 부분은 그 대명사가 지칭하는 문장의 뒤에 온다.

Ex The brain of a computer is its central processing unit. In the case of a microcomputer, this is a chip called the microprocessor.

D. 연결어, 접속사로 확인하는 방법

· 연결어, 접속사는 글의 흐름을 원활히 해줄 뿐 아니라, 논의의 전환을 나타내기도 한다.

- ■ (Showing addition: and/ in addition/ furthermore/ not only... but also/ moreover
- ■ (Showing opposition: but/ although/ however/ in spite of
- ■ (Showing cause & effect: because/ since/ therefore/ as a result
- ■ (Showing condition: if/ unless/ otherwise

E. 정의 (definition) 뒤에 따라오는 예로 확인하는 방법

Ex Flexible plans allow for several contingencies. Contingencies are events that might affect what you plan to do, but are out of your control. For example, rain is a contingency that might affect the success of an outdoor event.

F. Additional Information으로 위치파악하기

추가정보는 유사정보의 뒤에 위치한다.

G. 동일단어 반복을 보고 위치 파악하기

동일한 단어가 반복될 경우 동일한 단어는 근접하여 있음에 주의한다.

3 Following topic

Types of Questions

- What would be mainly discussed in the following paragraph?
- What is the best topic following this passage?

 지문이 어떤 논리적 흐름을 따르고 있는지 파악하면 답은 쉽게 고를 수 있다.

 Following Topic 문제의 실마리

· 구조를 통해서 푸는 방법: 서론에서 제시된 글의 전개방향을 따라서, 다음 문단의 Topic을 예측

· 마지막 문단의 2문장 정도가 결정적인 힌트를 제공: 연관성을 지니고 글이 전개됨

Tip following topic문제는 전체 지문을 다시 한번 훑어 읽고(scanning) 문제를 푸는 것이 좋다.

Hackers Practice

Read the passages and for each item, choose the one best answer

Exercise I. Choose the one best description that identifies the relationship between sentences (A) and (B)

contrast	comparison	further definition
chronological order	cause and effect	process

1

(A) Rh is a family of proteins on the surface of red blood cells. (B) To clarify, when the most common form of these proteins is present, the blood type is Rh(+), and when it is absent, the blood type is Rh(-).

Answer _further definition_

2

The gross domestic product (GDP) is the amount of output of goods and services. Everyone knows the US has the strongest economy in the world. It has since the end of World War II, and will undoubtedly continue to hold that ranking for many years to come. In comparison to the second highest ranked country, China ($4.8 trillion), the US ($9.255 trillion) has almost 2 times the GDP. However, the statistic that really shows how well a country is doing is the GDP per capita. (A) In this category, the US ($33,900) is only second to the tiny (2,586 sq km & 437,389 pop.) land of Luxembourg ($34,200). (B) China, on the other hand, has a large GDP, but a small GDP per capita ($3,800), which basically means it is a very poor country.

Answer _contrast_

3

(A) As the rapid increase of power-driven machines produced yarn more cheaply, English merchants were able to capture a large proportion of the world market for cotton cloth. (B) More mills were established in England and Scotland to meet the demand, in turn creating greater demands for wood, iron, leather, bricks, timber, and so on needed to make the machines and mills, as well as the fuel to run them.

Answer *Cause & Effect*

4

(A) When a change in policy is being made, the government often first puts forward its proposals in a Green Paper, which is a discussion document on policy options. It originates in the department of the Ministry concerned and is then published for comment and ideas.

(B) This document forms the basis for a White Paper which is a broad statement of government policy. Comment may again be invited from interested parties. Once these inputs have been taken into account, the Minister and officials within the State department concerned may draft Legislative Proposals.

Answer *process*

Exercise II. Arrange the following sentences in the correct order.

5

(A) For example, a British encampment known as Salt Lick, located just southeast of New Stanton, was both a staging area and a battleground during the conquest of the western frontier in pre-revolutionary days.

(B) Not surprisingly, during the colonial period such locations became supply points for European soldiers.

(C) Indeed, so important were salt deposits that settlers used them to compose a series of names that today sound like the titles of dirty movies like *Two Lick Creek* or *the Indiana County Town of Black Lick.*

Answer *B* - *A* - *C*

C   B   A

6

(A) It was one of the great inventions of all time because of the contribution that the wheel, and its utilization in a vehicle, makes to applying supplemental sources of power to an individual's mobility.

(B) That is to say, horses and camels can travel faster than the humans riding on their backs, but to transport more than one person with a single animal—something most horses at one time had the strength to do—a vehicle was needed.

(C) After early efforts to domesticate animals for their burden-carrying abilities, the next significant development for human locomotion was the wheeled vehicle.

Answer _B_ - _C_ - _A_

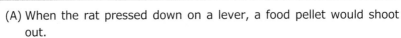

7

(A) When the rat pressed down on a lever, a food pellet would shoot out.
(B) A rat was placed in a cage with a pellet dispenser.
(C) Scientists outside of the cage could control when the pellet could come out, however, adjusting it so that the pellet would come out when the rat hit the bar two times, three times, etc.

Answer _B_ - _A_ - _C_

8

(A) Balloting in previous House elections for President (1801 and 1825) was secret, but many people today consider such a practice unthinkable.
(B) The fact that members of Congress might escape party discipline in secret balloting might have something to do with it too, one would think.
(C) For instance, on national television, Speaker Tom Foley claimed: "It would be impossible for the American people to be shut out from the actual undertaking and balloting of the House of Representatives. It'd be outrageous."

Answer _A_ - _C_ - _B_

Exercise III. Circle the square [■] to show where the following sentence would best fit in the paragraph.

9

The results of the present work indicated a different organization within the human brain with respect to the relation of testosterone to skilled movement compared to hand preference. ■ The serum testosterone was found to be associated mainly with right-hand skill in men and women. ■ Except for male right-handers with right-eye preference, the right hand skill was found to be directly related to serum testosterone in men, and inversely related to serum testosterone in women. ■ In other words, the right-hand skill increased with serum testosterone in men, which contrasts with the Geschwind-Behan hypothesis. ■ In women, the right-hand skill decreased with serum testosterone in accord with the Geschwind-Behan hypothesis

However, there were fundamental differences in the male and female patterns.

10

Early colored lithographs used one or two colors to tint the entire plate and create a watercolor-like tone to the image. ■ This atmospheric effect was primarily used for landscape or topographical illustrations. ■ Even for the well established tinted lithographs, it was only a small step to extend the range of color by the use of multiple tint blocks printed in succession. ■ Generally, these early chromolithographs were simple prints with flat areas of color, printed side-by-side. ■

For more detailed coloration, artists continued to rely on hand coloring over the lithograph.

Hackers Test

Read the following passages and the questions about them. Choose the one best answer for each question.

1 Gordon Strong and the New York Federal Reserve Bank were the main generators of inflation and cheap credit, but not the only ones. ■ The Treasury Department was another source: "As early as March 1927, Secretary Mellon assured everyone that 'an abundant supply of easy money' was available—and in January 1928, the Treasury announced that it would refund a 4 1/4 percent Liberty Bond issue, falling due in September, into 3 1/2 percent notes." ⟨■⟩ Bank credit rose accordingly, and other investors moved their bond funds into stock speculation. ■ With the federal government avidly pursuing inflationary policies, Rothbard concludes, the economy and the American people didn't stand a chance. ⟨■⟩

Hoover's overall rubric for his activism was "the coordination of business and governmental agencies in concerted action." How this translated into the real world was, among other things, Hoover's insistence that the "first shock of the depression must fall on profits and not on wages—precisely the reverse of sound policy," writes Rothbard, "since profits provide the motive power of business activity," an obvious statement that very few at the time seemed to wish to consider.

In short, Hoover persuaded industrialists and employers to keep wages at pre-crash levels. The result, as everyone knows, was the deepest and longest depression in U.S. history.

1. The following sentence can be added to the passage above.

   But his special condemnation falls on President Hoover, whose strongly activist programs exacerbated the already dire economic situation in the country.

   Circle the black square [■] that indicates the best position for the sentence.

2. Which of the following topics would best follow this passage?
   (a) The successful points of President Hoover's economic policies ✗
   (b) The way the economic crisis worsened because of government intervention
   (c) The structural problems of the American economy
   (d) International assistance received from Europe

2   Sewage treatment means removing impurities so that the remaining waste water can be safely returned to the river or sea and become part of the natural water cycle again.

Sewage treatment works by separating solids from liquids using physical processes and purifies the liquid through biological processes. Processes may vary but the following waste stream is typical.

In the preliminary treatment, solids like wood, paper, rags and plastic are removed by screens, washed, dried, and taken away for safe disposal at a licensed waste tip. Grit and sand, which would damage pumps, are also removed and disposed of in a similar way.

In the primary treatment, the remaining solids are separated from the liquid by passing the sewage through large settlement tanks, where most of the solid material sinks to the bottom. About 70% of solids settle out at this stage and are referred to as sludge. The sludge is used on farms after further treatment called sludge treatment.

Secondary treatment is a biological process which relies on naturally occurring micro-organisms acting to break down organic material and purify the liquid. In a simple sewage treatment process, micro-organisms are encouraged to grow on stones over which the sewage is trickled. The micro-organisms, which need oxygen to thrive, feed on the bacteria in the sewage and purify the water. These treatment units are called percolating filters. This process can be speeded up by blowing air into tanks of sewage where the micro-organisms float freely and feed on the bacteria. ■ These treatment units are called aeration tanks. ■ Following either form of secondary treatment, the waste water is settled in tanks to separate the biological sludge from the purified waste water.

■ This is known as tertiary treatment. Various methods may be used, including sand filters, reed beds or grass plots. ■ Disinfection, using ultra violet light to kill bacteria, is another method, and is being used at a number of coastal sewage treatment schemes.

---

1. The following sentence can be added to the passage above.

Sometimes, extra treatment is needed to give the waste water a final "polish".

Circle the black square [■] that indicates the best position for the sentence.

2. Which of the following best describes the organization of the passage?
(a) A discussion of the pros and cons concerning sewage treatment
(b) A random presentation about sewage systems
(c) A description of the necessity of micro-organisms
(d) An explanation of the sewage treatment process

3   Now, new evidence reveals that all or most of the West Antarctic ice sheet collapsed at least once during the past 1.3 million years—a period when global temperatures were probably not significantly higher than they are today and the ice sheet was assumed to have been stable. In geologic time, a million years is recent history.

The proof, which was published in *Science*, comes from a team of glaciologists from Uppsala University in Sweden and the California Institute of Technology in Pasadena, who drilled deep holes near the edge of the ice sheet. Within samples collected from sediments lying beneath the ice, they found fossils of microscopic marine plants called diatoms, which suggest that the region was not solid ice at the end of the Pleistocene Epoch, but rather an open ocean. As Hermann Engelhardt, a coauthor of the proof from Cal Tech, says, "the West Antarctic ice sheet has disappeared and can disappear again."

Of course, just because the ice sheet can disappear doesn't mean that it will. ■A host of unpredictable variables, such as global temperature changes or how the ice sheet responds to the breakdown of surrounding ice shelves, will help determine its fate. ■One major uncertainty involves the ice streams that drain the massive sheet.

■According to Engelhardt, one stream, called Ice Stream B, has been widening by 33 feet a year, a sign that the stream may be speeding up and the sheet breaking down. ■Other scientists, however, believe that the ice streams may be slowing.

---

1. Which of the following would best complete this passage?
    (a) A general question about the collapse of the West Antarctic ice sheet
    (b) Evidence to support the theory that the West Antarctic ice sheet is melting
    (c) A counterargument to the established theory of melting ice in West Antarctic
    (d) A proposal of solutions for reducing damage when the sea level rises

2. The following sentence can be added to the passage above.

    Like ocean currents, these streams, which can be 90 miles across, move up to 100 times faster than the sheet that houses them, providing a mechanism for rapid ice loss.

    Circle the black square [■] that indicates the best position for the sentence.

---

4   Private owners have strong incentives to raise their firm's profits, because they receive these profits as either direct income or as a capital gain when the value of their firm rises. In a competitive market, the profits that a firm earns can be increased by lowering production costs and by producing innovative, high-quality products that are popular with consumers. These activities are generally socially desirable allowing consumers to receive the best products at the cheapest possible prices.

But profit-maximizing activities need not be socially desirable. ■ The private saving received by the firm's owners is offset by the social loss created by the pollution. ■ This was the case in New Jersey in 1987 and Los Angeles in 1996. Private firms were employed to dispose of medical waste. ■ This usually involves high temperature incineration. ■ But to minimize costs, the private firms found that it was cheaper to simply dump the waste at sea. ■ The waste eventually washed up on local beaches leading to a public outcry. ■

In a market where competition is poor, private owners can also raise profits by raising the price that they charge consumers. Setting prices above the marginal cost of production increases firm profit but also creates a social loss as some buyers are squeezed out of the market.

□ Firms in every developed country face regulations that limit their ability to raise profits in socially undesirable ways such as by artificially reducing competition, creating excessive pollution or deliberately deceiving customers. □ In industries where there is a significant conflict between the private incentives to raise profit and public welfare, there often exists firm specific regulation. □ In the extreme, in industries such as water, electricity, public transport, and postal services, the firms have often been brought under direct government control. □

---

1. The following sentence can be added to the passage above.

   For example a firm might be able to reduce its own costs but at the same time increase pollution.

   Circle the black square [■] that indicates the best position for the sentence.

2. Which of the following best describes the relationship between paragraph 2 and paragraph 3?
   (A) Paragraph 3 summarizes paragraph 2.
   (B) Paragraph 3 develops the content about the New Jersey case presented in paragraph 2.
   (C) Paragraph 3 supports the topic sentence of paragraph 2.
   (D) Paragraph 3 objects to paragraph 2.

3. The following sentence can be added to the passage above.

   One way that governments have traditionally responded to these concerns about private ownership is through regulation.

   Circle the white square [□] that indicates the best position for the sentence.

4. Which of the following best describes the organization of the passage?
   (a) A summary of the limits of government regulation on private owners
   (b) An explanation of the causes and effects of profit maximizing
   (c) A comparison of the competitive market to the monopolized market
   (d) A survey on the amount of social loss created by profit maximizing activities

5   The ozone depletion process begins when CFCs and other ozone-depleting substances (ODS) leak from equipment. Winds efficiently mix the troposphere and evenly distribute the gases. CFCs are extremely stable, and they do not dissolve in rain. After a period of several years, ODS molecules reach the stratosphere, about 10 kilometers above the Earth's surface.

Strong UV light breaks apart ODS molecules. CFCs release chlorine atoms, and halons release bromine atoms. It is these atoms that actually destroy ozone, not the intact ODS molecules. It is estimated that one chlorine atom can destroy over 100,000 ozone molecules before finally being removed from the stratosphere. NASA provides a more detailed explanation of the ozone depletion reactions.

Ozone is constantly being produced and destroyed in a natural cycle. ■However, the overall amount of ozone is essentially stable. ■This balance can be thought of as a stream's depth at a particular location. ■Similarly, while ozone production and destruction are balanced, ozone levels remain stable. ■This was the situation until the past several decades.

■Large increases in stratospheric chlorine and bromine, however, have upset that balance. ■In effect, they have added a siphon downstream, removing ozone faster than natural ozone creation reactions can keep up. Therefore, ozone levels fall.

Since ozone filters out harmful UVB radiation, less ozone means higher UVB levels at the surface. □ The more depletion, the larger the increase in incoming UVB. □ UVB has been linked to skin cancer, cataracts, and damage to materials like plastics. □ Although some UVB reaches the surface even without ozone depletion, its harmful effects will increase as a result of this problem. □

---

1. Which of the following best describes the organization of paragraphs 1 and 2?
   - (a) A list of the effects of ozone depletion
   - (b) A description of the components of the ozone layer
   - (c) A comparison between general beliefs and NASA studies
   - (d) An explanation of the process by which ODS molecules exhaust the ozone

2. The following sentence can be added to the passage above.

   Although individual water molecules are moving past the observer, the total depth remains constant.

   Circle the black square [■] that indicates the best position for the sentence.

3. The following sentence can be added to the passage above.

   Furthermore, it harms certain crops and marine organisms.

   Circle the white square [□] that indicates the best position for the sentence.

6   Jane Addams, a member of a well-to-do, cultured family, was so distressed about the misery of the poor that she left home to spend her life in the slums of Chicago. ■ In 1889 she established a "settlement house" there, called Hull House, where she initiated many humanitarian projects. ■ Immigrants and other poor people came to Jane Addams's Hull House to get advice and help, as well as to learn and to have fun. ■ This remarkable woman also devoted herself to a number of other causes. ■ She was active in fighting against the use of child labor and against war; she worked for woman's suffrage and for improving the situation of the blacks; and she helped to establish playgrounds and public parks and initiated country vacation programs for poor city children.

Not everyone appreciated the work of Jane Addams. □ Indeed some disapproved of what they considered her meddling in other people's affairs. □ She promoted the idea of responsibility for the welfare of the underprivileged, and her programs were widely adopted. □ Settlement houses modeled on Hull House were founded in many poor neighborhoods to help children and adults to make their lives more meaningful. □

In recognition of her contributions to society, Jane Addams was awarded the Nobel Peace Prize in 1931.

1. The following sentence can be added to the passage above.

   Among these were hot-lunch service for factory workers, day-care centers for little children, free classes for young people and for adults, a gymnasium, and an art gallery.

   Circle the black square [■] that indicates the best position for the sentence.

2. The following sentence can be added to the passage.

   Nevertheless, she exerted great influence on the development of social work in the United States and also in other parts of the world.

   Circle the white square [□] that indicates the best position for the sentence.

3. The author organizes the story of Jane Addams in terms of
   (a) an evaluation of Addams' contributions and various opinions on her
   (b) a biography focusing on Addams' personality
   (c) an account of Hull House's propagation in the world
   (d) the author's description of Addams' work

7 The ocean responds simultaneously to inertia and to the gravitational force of both sun and moon. If the Earth, moon, and sun are all in a line, the lunar and solar tides will be additive, resulting in higher high tides and lower low tides. But if the moon, Earth and sun form a right angle, the solar tide will tend to diminish the lunar tide. Because the moon's contribution is more than twice that of the sun, the solar tide will not completely cancel the lunar tide.

■ The large tides caused by the linear alignment of sun, Earth, and moon are called spring tides. ■ During spring tides, high tides are very high and low tides are very low. ■ These tides occur at two-week intervals corresponding to the new and full moons. Neap tides occur when the moon, Earth, and sun form a right angle. ■ Neap tides also occur at two-week intervals, with the neap tide arriving a week after the spring tide. ■

Because their orbits are ellipses, not perfect circles, the moon and the sun are closer to the Earth at some times than at others. The difference between apogee (the moon's most distant point) and perigee (its closest) is 30,600 kilometers. Because the tidal force is inversely proportional to the cube of the distance between the bodies, the closer moon raises a noticeably higher tidal crest. □ The difference between perihelion (the Earth's closest approach to the sun) and aphelion (its greatest distance) is 3.7 million kilometers. □ If the moon and sun are over nearly the same latitude and if the Earth is also close to the sun, extreme spring tides will result. □ Interestingly, spring tides have greater ranges in Northern Hemisphere winter than in the Northern Hemisphere summer. □

---

1. Which of the following best describes the organization of paragraph 1?
   (a) A general explanation of tidal currents, supported by specific examples
   (b) A description of the roles of each earthly force
   (c) An explanation of the main forces that generate tides
   (d) A comparison between lunar energy and solar energy

2. The following sentence can be added to the passage above.

   During neap tides, high tides are not very high and low tides are not very low.

   Circle the black square [■] that indicates the best position for the sentence.

3. The following sentence can be added to the passage above.

   It is because Earth is closest to the sun during the northern winter.

   Circle the white square [□] that indicates the best position for the sentence.

8 A rapid means of long-distance transportation became a necessity for the United States as settlement spread ever farther westward. The early trains were impractical curiosities, and for a long time the railroad companies encountered troublesome mechanical problems. ■ The most serious ones were the construction of rails able to bear heavy loads, and the development of a safe, effective braking system. ■ Once these were solved, the railroad was established as the best means of land transportation. ■ By 1860 there were thousands of miles of track crossing the eastern mountain ranges and reaching westward to the Mississippi. ■

The high point in railroad building came with the construction of the first transcontinental system. In 1862 Congress authorized two western railroad companies to build lines from Nebraska westward and from California eastward to a meeting point, so as to complete a transcontinental crossing linking the Atlantic seaboard with the Pacific. ▢ The government helped the railroads generously with subsidies and grants of land. ▢ Actual work on this project began four years later. ▢ The Central Pacific Company, starting from California, used Chinese workers, while the Union Pacific Company employed crews of Irish immigrants. ▢ In 1869 they met at a place called Promontory in what is now the state of Utah. Many visitors came there for the great occasion. At the official ceremony a silver hammer was used to drive a golden spike, thus completing the union of the two railroads, while the newly developed telegraph broadcast the announcement to the whole United States. There were joyous celebrations all over the country, with parades and the ringing of church bells to honor the great achievement.

1. The following sentence can be added to the passage above.

   There were also regional southern and western lines.

   Circle the black square [■] that indicates the best position for the sentence.

2. The following sentence can be added to the passage above.

   The two groups worked at remarkable speeds, each trying to cover a greater distance than the other.

   Circle the white square [▢] that indicates the best position for the sentence.

3. Which of the following best describes the organization of the passage?
   (a) A description of the process of building railroads in the state of Utah
   (b) A comparison of the outcomes of the Ventral Pacific Company and the Union Pacific Company
   (c) A chronological discussion of the first transcontinental system
   (d) An analysis of difficulties faced by the railroad companies

9   It is generally believed that bat populations have declined worldwide in recent decades. ■ There is a developing concern about the conservation status of bats as many species of bats are increasingly affected by the actions of humans. ■ Bats face multiple threats of ignorance, suspicion, pesticide poisoning, roost destruction and closure, habitat loss, over-exploitation, and extermination as pests. ■ Among mammals, bats are the second most diverse order (after rodents) and occur on all continents except Antarctica. ■ Bats often range widely in their foraging activities, and habitat modifications such as urbanization, agriculture, and other land use practices may affect local plant and insect populations and thus the food resources of bats. At present, however, virtually nothing is known of the specific effects of global warming on bats although certain predictions can be made based on their biology. ■

Bats seem to have evolved as moderately long-lived (e.g., 5-30 years), intelligent creatures that are acutely in synchrony with global climates. □ Worldwide, bats are known to depend on a variety of natural resources. □ Not surprisingly, bats are frequent and important pollinators of plants, especially in tropical areas and on island ecosystems in the Pacific. □ Additionally, many bats rely on plants (especially trees) as roosting sites for varying periods of time. □ Disturbances to climate that interrupt or alter the phenology of plants, or greatly alter plant species occurrence or distribution, can be expected to affect bats.

There are several factors that bring about environmental change, and finally affect bats. However, it is believed that global warming is the gravest factor.

1. The following sentence can be added to the passage above.

   Because bats have low reproductive rates, populations are very susceptible to elevated mortality or depressed recruitment.

   Circle the black square [■] that indicates the best position for the sentence.

2. The following sentence can be added to the passage above.

   Many tropical species are dependent on nectar, pollen, and flowers and fruits of plants and are known to "track" the development of the plant resources upon which they depend.

   Circle the white square [□] that indicates the best position for the sentence.

3. Which of the following topics would be most likely to be discussed in the following paragraph?

   (a) The different weather conditions of Antarctica
   (b) Factors crucial for global warming
   (c) The role of bats as pollinators of plants
   (d) A description of the way global warming influences bats

10 Water has a simple molecular structure. ■ Water is composed of one oxygen atom and two hydrogen atoms. ■ Each hydrogen atom is covalently bonded to the oxygen via a shared pair of electrons. ■ Oxygen also has two unshared pairs of electrons. ■ That is to say, two pairs involved in covalent bonds with hydrogen, and two unshared pairs on the opposite side of the oxygen atom. Oxygen is an "electronegative" or electron "loving" atom, in comparison to hydrogen.

□ Water is a "polar" molecule, meaning that there is an uneven distribution of electron density. □ Water has a partial negative charge near the oxygen atom due to the unshared pairs of electrons, and partial positive charges near the hydrogen atoms. □ The ability of ions and other molecules to dissolve in water is also due to polarity. □

Many other unique properties of water are due to the hydrogen bonds. For example, ice floats because hydrogen bonds hold water molecules further apart in a solid than in a liquid, where there is one less hydrogen bond per molecule. The unique physical properties, including a high heat of vaporization, strong surface tension, high specific heat, and nearly universal solvent properties of water are also due to hydrogen bonding. The hydrophobic effect, or the exclusion of compounds containing carbon and hydrogen (non-polar compounds) is another unique property of water caused by the hydrogen bonds. The hydrophobic effect is particularly important in the formation of cell membranes. The best description is to say that water "squeezes" non-polar molecules together.

1. The following sentence can be added to the passage above.

   Thus, there are four pairs of electrons surrounding the oxygen atom.

   Circle the black square [■] that indicates the best position for the sentence.

2. The following sentence can be added to the passage above.

   An electrostatic attraction between the partial positive charge near the hydrogen atoms and the partial negative charge near the oxygen results in the formation of a hydrogen bond.

   Circle the white square [□] that indicates the best position for the sentence.

3. Which of the following best describes the organization of paragraph 3?
   (A) Definition of several unique properties of water
   (B) Summarization of many physical properties of water
   (C) Description of the role of hydrogen bonds in water
   (D) Explanation of the physical properties of the hydrophobic effect

FLUXUS

플럭서스는 흐름, 끊임없는 변화 움직임을 뜻하는 라틴어로 1960년대에서 1970년대에 걸쳐 주로 독일의 여러 도시들을 중심으로 일어난 국제적 전위 예술 운동이다.

1950년대 초 영국에서 그 전조를 보였으나 1950년대 중후반 미국에서 추상표현주의 주관적 엄숙성에 반대하고 매스 미디어와 광고 등 대중문화적 시각이미지를 미술의 영역 속에 적극적으로 수용하고자 했던 구상미술의 한 경향이라 할 수 있다.

60년대 전통적인 예술형식과 스타일을 벗어난 예술가들의 생각을 널리 알리기 위해 계획되었던 잡지의 제목으로 매키어너스라는 사람이 선택했던 것인데, 그 잡지는 발행되지 못했지만 플럭서스라는 명칭은 1962년 매키어너스가 비스바덴에서 조직한 최초의 콘서트 시리즈인 '새로운 음악'에서 처음 사용되어졌다.

플럭서스는 어떤 목표를 위해 협력하는 조직적인 화가의 그룹이라기 보다는 예술시장과는 거리가 있는 예술가 개개인과 아웃 사이더들의 자연스런 집단이라고 할 수 있다. 그러므로 플럭서스를 미술의 양식이라기 보다는 하나의 심리상태라고 보는 경향이 지배적이다.

플럭서스 미술가의 제작방식은 다양한 재료를 혼합하여 사용하는 것이었으며 여러 미술이 동시에 불협화음처럼 전개되는 플럭서스 이벤트는 유머러스하고 개방적인 경향을 특징으로 한다.

이러한 플럭서스 미술작품은 기상천외하며 부조리한 것 같지만 고정관념을 타파하려는 그 밑에 깔린 태도는 후대의 미술에 많을 영향을 끼쳤으며 개념 미술과 퍼포먼스 아트의 등장에 선도적인 역할을 했다.

CHAPTER **3**

Restatement Questions

3

Restatement Questions

O v e r v i e w

Restatement 문제는 지문에 명시적으로 주어진 정보를 묻는 문제로서, 지문의 내용을 정확하게 이해하고 있는 지에 대해 평가한다. 즉, 독해과 정의 최종점인 정보의 습득 여부를 확인하는 것이다. Restatement 문 제를 풀 때는 정확한 사실(fact)에 근거한 내용만을 고려해야 한다. 여기 서 사실이라고 하는 것은, 자신의 배경지식에 근거하는 것이 아니라, 지 문의 저자가 전달하는 사실을 말한다. 시험에 등장하는 지문은 대부분, 가장 근거 있는 학설이나, 사실이지만, 내용이 상식이나 이미 알고 있는 일반적인 이론에서 벗어나는 경우도 있을 수 있다.

Restatement 문제는 지문에서 언급한 세부사항에 대해서 여러 가지 각 도에서 물어 볼 수 있다.

처음 지문을 읽을 때는 전체적인 내용을 파악하는 scanning을 하지만, restatement 문제는 누가(who), 언제(when), 어디서(where), 왜 (why), 무엇을(what), 어떻게(how) 하였는지 꼼꼼히 확인해야 한다.

Types of Questions

● According to the passage/paragraph 1, what/when/where/ how _____ ?

● According to the passage/paragraph 2, which of the following statements about _____ is true?

● Which of the following is _____ that mentioned in the passage?

● For which of the following reasons, _____ (question) _____ ?

● It is significant that _____ because ....

● _____ (statement) _____ because ....

● Strategy

1 Restatement 문제를 풀때는 지문의 어느 부분에서 문제에서 확인하려고 하는 정보를 주고 있는지 빨리 찾아내야 한다.

A. 제일 먼저해야 할 일은, 문제에서 무엇을 물어보고 있는지 확인하는 것이다.
  · 의문사가 있으면, 의문사 확인(who /when /where /why /what /how 등)
  · 주어확인
  · as, about, for 등의 전치사와 다음에 나오는 명사 확인

B. 지문을 skimming하면서, 문제의 key-word 혹은 restatement(재진술: 동의어로 바꾸거나, paraphrase한 것)된 것이 걸리는 곳을 찾는다.
  · 물론, 지문전체에서 여러 번 나올 수 있다. 그러므로, 처음 scanning할 때, 글의 흐름을 파악하고 있어야 한다.

C. 문제 유형에 따라 다음의 것들을 함께 확인. 정확한 정보의 위치파악이 용이해진다.
  ■ when question: 접속사(since/after/while등), 연도(in 1779), 세기(in the late 18th century), 나이(the age of)
  ■ where question: 지명, 위치 전치사(at/under/beneath/above...), 방위 (southern part of /north등)
  ■ why question: 접속사(because/since/for), reason, due to, the need for, ~하기 위하여(to Verb)
  ■ who question에서는 직접적인 이름이 나올 수도 있지만 status(신분), organization(기관)등이 대상이 될 수도 있다는 점을 유념하자.

2 문제와 선택지는 지문에 나온 정보가 동의어 등으로 표현을 재구성하여 나오는 것임을 유의하여 읽어야 한다.

3 지문과 보기가 같은 뜻인지를 확인할 때는 중심어 뿐 아니라, 부사, 형용사, 접속사, 전치사 등도 세심히 검토해야 한다.

Ex Read the restated sentence below, then the passage underneath it. Underline any words or phrases in the passage that give clues for the restated sentence.

● Information from map rock shows us the importance of the rock in practical and ceremonial aspects.

> Map rock also depicts human figures and animals such as buffalo, deer, antelope, elk and mountain ship. These images suggest that the rock possessed pragmatic, ritualistic significance.

Answer depicts, suggest, pragmatic, ritualistic, significance

● The bad eating habits to eat nothing but one cornmeal resulted in the disease.

> The history of corn is still quite confusing. Grown by the Aztecs and Incas, adopted by the Spanish, widespread in Turkey, it also carried disease: pellagra, discovered in 1730. The disease was caused by an unbalanced diet based exclusively on polenta, made with cornmeal.

Answer was caused, unbalanced diet, exclusively

Ex **Read the sentence below and choose the answer that restates the sentence most accurately.**

● Children's moral reasoning follows the increasing cognitive complexity of their reasoning in general.

_____ The more cognitive complexity children's general reasoning gets, the higher moral reasoning becomes possible.

_____ Not until the reasoning ability on the whole has cognitive complexity can children do moral reasoning.

Answer 전자

Topic Sentence 주어진 문제 문장에서는, 아이들의 도덕적 reasoning은 general reasoning의 cognitive complexity가 늘어나는 것에 의해 (그 정도가) 결정된다고 말하고 있다.

보기의 첫번째 문장은 이와 같은 뜻이나, 두 번째 문장에서는 단지 cognitive complexity가 갖춰지면 아이들은 moral reasoning을 할 수 있다고 말하고 있다.

즉 degree의 기술이 빠져 있다.

● Other than young people leaving home in uniform and the news of letters and War Department telegrams, the most obvious signs of war on the Hoosier home front were the military installations and ordnance plants that sprang up overnight.

_____ The clearest token of war, the military installations and ordnance plants which were built up on the Hoosier home front overnight, had different meaning with that of conscripted young people and the news of letters and War Department telegrams.

_____ The scene, in front of the Hoosier home, of the military installations and ordnance plants which came into being in one night most evidently showed that they were at war, excluding conscripted youths, the news of letters and War Department telegrams.

Answer 후자

Topic Sentence 제복 입은 젊은이들이 집을 떠나는 모습과 편지, 육군성 전보 외에도, the Hoosier home front 에서 밤사이 생긴 군사시설과 무기공장은 가장 명백한 전쟁의 신호였다는 내용이며, 첫번째 문장에서는 전쟁의 상징인 군사시설과 무기공장은 또 다른 상징으로 뒤에 나온 것과는 다른 의미를 지닌다고 말하고 있으므로 답이 아니다.

Read the passages and choose the one best answer, based on how well it paraphrases the passage.

1

Based on a best-selling novel by Sinclair Lewis, *It Can't Happen Here* describes America under the control of a fascist dictatorship similar to the ones ruling Germany and Italy.

(a) Sinclair Lewis' best-selling novel, *It Can't Happen Here*, was written under the control of the dictators ruling Germany and Italy.

(b) Dealing with the topic of America under Fascism, *It Can't Happen Here* took the plot of its story from Sinclair Lewis's well-known novel.

(c) Sinclair Lewis wrote a best seller, *It can't Happen Here*, in which he compared the self-righteous American government to the German and Italian dictators.

(d) Antagonism to the fascism of the American government made the novel, *It Can't Happen Here*, by Sinclair Lewis, a best seller.

2

Water is one of the most powerful forces of nature, shaping the landscape, giving it character and providing contour and structure for the habitats of man, animal and plants.

(a) Water provides us with appropriate space to reside in alongside nature.

(b) Among nature's formidable forces, water is the only one that shapes the geographical features on the Earth.

(c) All the creatures of nature inhabit places that have been transformed by the marvelous power of water.

(d) Nature has various kinds of forces, one of which primarily organizes the structures of the Earth.

3   Printing has existed in some form since at least 1500 B.C., and Western civilization generally dates the beginning of modern printing from Johannes Gutenberg's invention of movable type in 1440.

(a) Printing commonly takes its origin from the movable type Johannes Gutenberg created in the 15th century.
(b) Johannes Gutenberg's modern type was prior to the advent of the first Western printing in some form.
(c) In Western civilization, the movable type Johannes Gutenberg designed encouraged the development of modern printing already initiated before 1500 B. C.
(d) The first modern type in Western civilization was made by Johannes Gutenberg about 3000 years after the birth of printing.

4   One of the New Deal's major achievements was bringing electrical power to rural parts of the country, and this success was most vividly demonstrated in the Tennessee River Valley.

(a) The power of electricity was finally demonstrated during the term of President Roosevelt in the Tennessee River Valley.
(b) Some New Deal policies achieved success in the vivid demonstration of extending urban electrical power to the rural parts of the country.
(c) Some countries, including the Tennessee River Valley, were first supplied with electric power during the New Deal movement.
(d) The New Deal's policy of distributing electricity to rural areas was a great success in the Tennessee River Valley.

5   Chief engineer Joseph Strauss and his colleagues intended to select a paint that would withstand the harsh winds and weather and the corrosive salt air—constant factors for a bridge across the Golden Gate.

(a) The Golden Gate was painted by Strauss and his colleagues with difficulty because of the harsh winds and weather and the corrosive salt air.
(b) Due to the hard natural conditions, Strauss and his colleagues painted the Golden Gate with caution.
(c) Strauss and his colleagues selected a paint that would be able to stand up to harsh weather conditions for the bridge across the Golden Gate.
(d) Strauss and his colleagues had to withstand the harsh environment to select a paint for a bridge across the Golden Gate.

6

During the 1870s, the federal government limited the role of silver in the monetary system, causing a decline in silver prices, the closing of many Nevada mines, and the decay of once thriving communities into ghost towns.

(a) In the 1870s, the decline in the mining industry in Nevada resulted in the reduction of silver in the monetary system and the decay of some communities.

(b) Controlled use of silver in producing money in the 1870s destroyed the mining industry of Nevada.

(c) During the 1870s, the price of silver was under the control of the federal government, which made the declining communities and mines in Nevada thrive again.

(d) The federal government limited the role of silver intending to damage the villages, once thriving in Nevada, step by step.

7

Baleen whales are usually solitary except during the breeding season, but odontocetes spend most of their lives in organized schools ranging in number from a few animals to 1,000 or more.

(a) Odontocetes organize schools only during the breeding season.

(b) During the breeding season, baleen whales try to organize groups to avoid the attacks of the grouped odontocetes.

(c) Odontocetes try to organize schools ranging in various numbers during the breeding season, while baleen whales usually try to be solitary during that period.

(d) In contrast to the odontocetes, which like grouping, baleen whales spend most of their lives in isolation.

8

For obvious reasons, human beings are poor subjects for experimental genetic studies; however, much that aids understanding heredity in humans has been learned from the "lower" forms of life.

(a) It is most difficult to understand heredity in humans because of the lack of experimental data.

(b) Experiments with animals make it possible to understand heredity in humans without experimenting with the human body.

(c) The "lower" forms of life are better subjects for experimental genetic studies because it is much easier to understand heredity in them than in humans.

(d) Experimental genetic studies are subject to the law of nature in that "lower" forms of life have inferior genes.

9

The surface currents of the ocean are characterized by large gyres, or currents that are kept in motion by prevailing winds, but the direction of which is altered by the rotation of the earth.

(a) The currents and gyres of the ocean are directed by the winds, which are kept in motion by the rotation of the earth.

(b) The gyres or currents comprising the surface currents are at the mercy of the winds and the rotation of the earth.

(c) The ocean is characterized by the prevailing winds, the strength degree of which comes from the rotation of the earth.

(d) The rotation of the earth influences the direction of winds, which is responsible for low and high tide.

10

The English scientists George Barger and Henry H. Dale first isolated histamine from the plant fungus ergot in 1910, and in 1911 they isolated the substance from animal tissues.

(a) Histamine was first separated from plant fungus by two English scientists in 1910, and then it was separated from animal tissues one year later.

(b) Barger and Dale extracted histamine from fungus ergot and animal tissues simultaneously.

(c) The English scientists George Barger and Henry H. Dale finally succeeded in planting fungus ergot into the isolated field for separating histamine.

(d) There is a keen difference between the histamine from plant fungus and that from animal tissues.

Hackers Test

Read the following passages and the questions about them.
Choose the one best answer for each question.

1 The Georgian style established itself in Ireland during the 18th century when English wealth was invested in Ireland, making Dublin the second most important city in Britain and Ireland, after London. Members of Parliament had seats in both London and Dublin, which created a need for respectable domestic housing and public buildings in Dublin. There was significant progress made in the building of churches, schools, bridges and town houses. Wealthy landlords took up the bulk of the building and footed the costs. Lord Gardiner was the main instigator of building on the north side of the city; while Lord Fitzwilliam, his rival, was responsible for most important building developments on the south side of the city.

Georgian architecture was initially dominated by a style known as 'Palladianism' — which aspired to recreate the effect of Ancient Roman architecture. This style remained influential from 1700 to 1760. The Parliament House in Dublin (now the Bank of Ireland, College Green) was designed by Sir Edward Lovett Pearce (1699-1733). It was the first large-scale Palladian building constructed in either Britain or Ireland. The Palladian style gave way to the Neo-Classical style in the late 18th century, a style that imitated the buildings of Ancient Greece. The greatest exponents of the Neo-Classical style are Sir William Chambers (1723-96), who designed what is now the Sir Hugh Lane Municipal Gallery; Thomas Ivory (1732-86), who designed King's Hospital in Blackhall Place, Dublin; and James Gandon (1743-1823) who designed Dublin's well-known Custom House and Four Courts.

Georgian houses were characterized above all by uniformity and practicality. Planning Acts decreed that red brick should be used to build houses, as a fire precaution. Architectural literature was published which encouraged townhouses that had standardized designs for doorways, chimneys, etc. Granite steps leading to the main door, above the servants' quarters, gave a grand look to the houses. Wrought iron railings that added to the effect were also a safety feature. Sash windows, decreasing in scale as they went up, lay flush with the brickwork. The familiar Georgian doorway, flanked by columns with Roman order capitals, was capped with a fanlight of intricate design. 'Street Furniture', such as wrought iron boot-scrapers and elegant lampposts, completed the Georgian look.

   1. For which of the following reasons did the construction of buildings in
      Dublin change remarkably?

(a) To equip the city with a look appropriate for its new position

(b) To develop its own architectural style

(c) To become the leading city in Britain and Ireland

(d) To satisfy wealthy landlords' desire to refresh themselves

2. According to paragraph 2, which of the following statements about architecture styles is true?

(a) The Georgian style was replaced by a reproduction of Ancient Greek style.

(b) Georgian architecture can be defined as a dominantly Palladian style.

(c) Thomas Ivory excellently represented the Neo-classical style.

(d) Palladianism was very popular throughout the 18th century.

3. What is the effect that the author discusses in paragraph 3?

(a) Practical effect

(b) Uniform effect

(c) Decorative effect

(d) Hygienic effect

4. Which of the following is mentioned as an example of an architectural detail that also served practical purpose?

(a) Wrought iron railings

(b) Granite steps

(c) Long doorways

(d) Marble columns

---

2   It can't be said that Fiorelli invented the concept of the big dig. Ernst Curtius, a German, had been attempting to amass funds for an extensive excavation since 1852, and by 1875 began excavating at Olympia. Like many sites in the classical world, Olympia had been the subject of much interest, primarily its statuary, which found its way into museums all over Europe. When Curtius came to Olympia, it was under the terms of a negotiated deal between the German and Greek governments. None of the artifacts would leave Greece except for "duplicates"; a small museum would be built on the grounds; and the German government could recoup the costs of the "big dig" by selling reproductions. The costs were indeed horrific, and Bismarck was forced to terminate the excavations in 1880, but the seeds of cooperative scientific investigations had been planted. So had the seeds of political influence in archaeology, which were to profoundly affect the young science during the early years of the 20th century.

The real increases toward the techniques and methodology of what we think of as modern archaeology were primarily the work of Schliemann, Pitt-Rivers, and Petrie. Although Heinrich Schliemann is often considered not much better than a treasure-hunter, by the latter years of his work at Hissarlik, he took on a German assistant, Wilhelm Dorpfeld, who had worked at Olympia with Curtius. Dorpfeld's influence on

Schliemann led to refinements in his technique and, by the end of his career, Schliemann carefully recorded his excavations, preserved the ordinary along with the extraordinary, and was prompt about publishing his reports.

A military man who spent a great deal of his early career studying the improvement of British fire-arms, Pitt-Rivers brought military precision and rigor to his archaeological excavations. In addition, he spent a not-inconsiderable inheritance building the first extensive comparative artifact collection, including contemporary ethnographic materials. His collection was decidedly not for beauty's sake; as he quoted T.H. Huxley: "The word 'importance' ought to be struck out of scientific dictionaries; that which is important is that which is persistent."

1. According to paragraph 1, which of the following statements about the "big dig" at Olympia is true?

   (a) The gain earned from selling duplicated statuary was excessive.
   (b) The Greek government agreed to the big dig under the condition that no artifacts would be sent abroad.
   (c) Ernst Curtius was not the first person to come up with the idea of a big dig.
   (d) All European museums acquired Olympian statuary in one way or another.

2. What was significant about Ernst Curtius attempt on the big dig?

   (a) His attempt paved the way for later excavations.
   (b) Germany's relationship with the Greek government would have been strained otherwise.
   (c) A world-class museum was built as a result.
   (d) Fiorelli had the same idea himself.

3. What was the result of Dorpfeld's influence on Schliemann?

   (a) The cultivation and development of his skills
   (b) The ability to record excavations in detail
   (c) An appreciation of real treasures
   (d) Attracting fame with his published reports

4. According to paragraph 3, which of the following statements about Pitt-Rivers is true?

   (a) He had no aesthetic sense.
   (b) He practiced archaeology with rigorous accuracy.
   (c) He thought that scientists didn't know what was 'important.'
   (d) His prior occupation was operating weaponry.

3   The power of the presidency makes it the most sought-after position in American politics. The keen competition for the post and the high cost of waging an effective campaign limit the pool of candidates to a select few. The Constitution originally provided for the election of the president and vice president by the Electoral College.

Members of the Electoral College, who are called electors, represented their states by casting votes for two candidates, with the person receiving the greatest number of votes becoming president and the second-place finisher, vice president. A tie vote in the 1800 election between Thomas Jefferson and Aaron Burr led to the enactment in 1804 of the 12th Amendment to the Constitution, which provided that the electoral college uses separate ballots, one for the president and one for the vice president.

By the mid-19th century the votes of the Electoral College had only symbolic importance. Electors from each state simply followed the will of the voting majority by giving their votes to the candidate receiving the most popular votes. However, in the Electoral College system, it is possible for candidates to win a majority of electoral votes, and therefore the presidency, without winning the nationwide popular vote. This scenario has occurred three times in United States history: in 1876, when Rutherford B. Hayes beat Samuel Tilden; in 1888, when Benjamin Harrison defeated Grover Cleveland; and in 2000, when George W. Bush prevailed over Al Gore. Another president who lost the popular vote was John Quincy Adams, who was elected in 1824 by the House of Representatives after no candidate received a majority in the Electoral College.

---

1. According to the passage, how was the vice president elected in the original Constitution?

   (a) All electors voted for the vice president from some candidates, and the one who got the most number of votes became the vice president.
   (b) The vice president was nominated by the president after the election.
   (c) The representative of each state voted for two candidates, and the one who received the second most votes became the vice president.
   (d) The Electoral College nominated the vice president with the agreement of the elected president after the election.

2. According to the passage, which of the following persons inspired an amendment for electing the president and the vice president?

   (a) Thomas Jefferson and Aaron Burr
   (b) Rutherford B. Hayes and Samuel Tilden
   (c) Benjamin Harrison and Grover Cleveland
   (d) The electoral college

3. According to the passage, to be elected president nowadays a candidate must

   (a) get the most numbers of votes from the nation-wide electors
   (b) win more than half of the votes from the electoral college
   (c) get the votes of the representatives from the major states
   (d) win more votes than the candidates for vice president

4. What do Rutherford B. Hayes, Benjamin Harrison, and George W. Bush have in common?

   (a) All of them amended the Constitution during their presidential term.
   (b) They didn't get the most popular support from the nation-wide voters.

(c) They were forced to accept the demands of the Electoral College to be elected as president.

(d) They had no matching rivals when they ran for presidential election.

---

4   Ancient Roman legend says that "soap" originally got its name from Mount Sapo where animals were sacrificed on altars with fire. Eventually the rains would wash the animal fats and wood ashes down the mountain into the Tiber River. The soap mixture was found useful for washing clothing, fur and skin. The first written formula for soap was discovered in 2200BC. By 312BC soaps were used in the Roman Baths and deemed good for cleansing and general health. When the Roman Empire fell in AD467, the popularity of soap and general bathing declined as well and the general lack of cleanliness contributed greatly to the plagues of the Middle Ages.

By about the 7th century, soap making guilds began to spring up with closely guarded trade secrets. Craftsmen were closely regulated and promoted within the trade.   By the 12th century, the English also began soap crafting. Soap was considered a luxury and highly valued. For many centuries after, soaps were heavily taxed as a luxury item and only available to the rich. In 1853, the soap tax was repealed causing a major shift in the cultural availability of soap. Social attitudes went hand in hand with cleanliness from then on.

In colonial times, women performed soap making. The soap was usually made once a year by using the collections of fat drippings and fireplace ashes from the previous year. Exact formulas were never really understood and the soaps tended to be quite caustic—but they cleaned well.

By the mid 1800's the chemistry of soap making was well understood, along with advanced methods of collecting soda ash from common salt (sodium hydroxide). Soap made for bathing, clothing and general cleaning became readily available on the market. Many of the low cost commercial soaps today are petrol-chemical based. These soaps have excellent cleaning capability, but they are also very drying for the skin. Other commercial soaps may be made with "tallow" (animal fat), but are often milled to remove the glycerin so it can be sold to the cosmetic or pharmaceutical industries. This soap without glycerin can also be hard on the skin, but still cleans well.

---

1. According to the passage, the epidemic in the Middle Ages resulted mostly from

  (a) Unbalanced diet

  (b) Unclean schools

  (c) Changes in bathing habits

  (d) The high price of medicine

2. Soap began to be used by ordinary people in the middle 19th century because

(a) its price was reduced ·
(b) fragrance was added to it
(c) soap making secrets were disclosed
(d) more awareness and concern for sanitation was spread

3. According to the passage, soap became widely accessible due to

(a) the shift in social attitudes
(b) the improvement in the methods of soap production
(c) the invention of better cleaning soaps
(d) the loosening of regulations on the soap making trade

4. A majority of inexpensive soaps are made from

(a) animal fat
(b) fireplace ashes
(e) petrol
(d) glycerin

---

5 The British Proclamation of 1763 ordered a halt to the westward movement at the Appalachians, but the decree was widely disregarded. Settlers scurried into Ohio, Tennessee, and Kentucky. After the American Revolution, a flood of people crossed the mountains into the fertile lands between the Appalachians and the Mississippi River. By 1810, Ohio, Tennessee, and Kentucky had been transformed from wilderness into a region of farms and towns.

Despite those decades of continuous westward pushing of the frontier line, it was not until the conclusion of the War of 1812 that the westward movement became a significant outpouring of people across the continent. By 1830 the Old Northwest and Old Southwest—areas scarcely populated before the war—were settled with enough people to warrant the admission of Illinois, Indiana, Missouri, Alabama, and Mississippi as states into the Union.

During the 1830s and '40s, the flood of pioneers poured unceasingly westward. Michigan, Arkansas, Wisconsin, and Iowa received most of them. A number of families even went as far as the Pacific coast, taking the Oregon Trail to areas in the Pacific Northwest. In 1849 fortune seekers rushed into California in search of gold. Meanwhile, the Mormons ended their long pilgrimage in Utah.

Between the gold rush and the Civil War, Americans in growing numbers filled the Mississippi River valley, Texas, the southwest territories, and the new states of Kansas and Nebraska. During the war, gold and silver discoveries drew prospectors—and later settlers—into Oregon, Colorado, Nevada, Idaho, and Montana.

By 1870 only portions of the Great Plains could truly be called unsettled. For most of the next two decades, that land functioned as the fabled open range, home to cowboys and their grazing cattle from ranches in Texas. But by the late 1880s, with the decline of the range-cattle industry, settlers moved in and fenced the Great Plains into family farms. That settlement—and the wild rush of pioneers into the Oklahoma Indian Territory—constituted the last chapter of the westward movement. By the early 1890s, a frontier had ceased to exist within the 48 continental states.

---

1. According to the passage, the British Proclamation of 1763
   (a) tried to halt the American Revolution
   (b) ordered people not to move westward .
   (c) influenced the increasing number of dwellers in West
   (d) was ignored by the people who had already left for the West

2. According to the passage, when did the number of westward settlers significantly increase?
   (a) Before the British Proclamation of 1763
   (b) When Ohio, Tennessee, and Kentucky changed from wild territory into towns
   (c) After the War of 1812
   (d) During the 1830s and 1840s

3. What was the main reason people moved into Oregon, Colorado, Nevada, Idaho, and Montana?
   (a) For their religious beliefs
   (b) To avoid and escape the war
   (c) Due to the discovery of gold and silver
   (d) Because of the discovery of the Great Plains

4. According to the passage, what happened in the late 19th century?
   (a) The British tried to halt the movement toward the West, but they couldn't stop it.
   (b) The Great Plains began to be changed into farmland.
   (c) The number of cowboys greatly increased.
   (d) The Gold Rush ended.

---

6   A vote-counting machine that Edison invented at the age of twenty was not accepted because it was not considered useful. After that disappointment, he decided not to work on any invention until he had made sure that it would fill a demand and be accepted.

Inventions that greatly improved the functioning of the telegraph earned him so much money that he was able to establish a laboratory for inventions. At the age of twenty-nine he set up such an "invention factory" at Menlo Park, a New Jersey village. His team of workers included toolmakers and a physicist, as well as practical designers of devices. There followed further telegraphic advances, then a number of solutions for problems in the operation of Alexander Graham Bell's invention, the telephone.

In 1878 Edison invented the phonograph. The incandescent bulb was patented in 1880, when a light bulb was produced that could burn for forty hours. Electric lighting had been invented early in the century, but the practical problems of lighting the streets electrically had never been worked out before. The great contribution of Edison was his applying of scientific discoveries and his modifying of older inventions so as to produce practical, usable devices. Together with his team he brought out a stream of inventions, accumulating over one thousand patents.

Edison's work in electricity lead to development in the electric power and light industries and eventually a new way of living for the people of the United States and much of the rest of the world. Many other inventions from the so-called invention factory proved to be of great importance, but the remarkable work in electricity had a truly revolutionary effect on modern life.

---

1. According to the passage, which of the following statements is true in regard to Edison's improvements of the telegraph?
   (a) It was not accepted by his contemporaries because it was considered useless.
   (b) He was only twenty-nine years old at the time, and a physicist.
   (c) It brought him the funds to start a laboratory for inventions.
   (d) He was able to solve some problems in the operation of Alexander Graham Bell's invention.

2. According to the passage, the vote-counting machine that Edison invented
   (a) earned him a lot of money
   (b) left him feeling like a failure
   (c) was similar to the machine used today
   (d) was in great demand

3. According to the passage, in his lifetime, Edison
   (a) donated money to many projects dealing with invention
   (b) acquired patents of more than one thousand kinds
   (c) did research without the help of any colleagues
   (d) was hostile to scientists who researched in the field of pure science

---

7 Macaques are highly adaptable generalists and are thus found in the widest range of habitats. In areas where they are considered sacred and therefore left unmolested, Rhesus macaques have even adapted to life in urbanized areas. These macaques are also found in environments ranging from semi-desert to dense forests, to mountains above the snowline. The genus includes the most northerly primate, the Japanese macaque. Similarly, the crab-eating macaque also manages to adapt to human settlements, although they prefer mangrove habitats. However, others are more specialized, e.g., the lion-tail macaque and pig-tailed macaque don't do well outside their forest homes. All macaques are found only in Asia, with the exception of the Barbary Ape, which is found in northern Africa.

Macaques eat mainly fruits. But they will also eat whatever is available: flowers, insects, eggs and perhaps some meat. Crab-eating macaques will hunt crabs and eat any other marine life they can catch.

To complement their varied diets, macaques have simple stomachs. They also have well-developed cheek pouches. Some are so large and extend down the neck that the pouches can contain the same amount of food as their stomachs. Macaques are stoutly built with strong limbs. They are dexterous with fully opposable thumbs. They move on all fours. Some such as the lion-tailed macaque and Barbary ape have virtually no tails, others have long tails.

Macaques are generally considered more terrestrial. But while most species come down to the ground to forage or move over long distances, a few are highly arboreal, e.g., the lion-tail macaque. But all prefer to sleep in trees or high above the ground. All macaques are more active during the day, but only the cooler portions, i.e., early morning or late afternoon to evening.

1. According to paragraph 1, which of the following statements about macaques is true?
   (a) Macaques are usually found in Africa.
   (b) All macaques are used to living with humans except for one species. ×
   (c) Some macaques don't mind humid climates when choosing their habitats.
   (d) All Asian people have considered macaques holy and do not touch them.

2. Which of the following animals does live in a different continent?
   (a) The Rhesus macaque
   (b) The lion-tail macaque
   (c) The Barbary Ape
   (d) The pig-tail macaque

3. According to the passage, lion-tail macaques tend to
   (a) live near human villages
   (b) be arboreal
   (c) move on two limbs
   (d) use both hands

4. Which of the following does the author mention as a feature all macaques have in common?
   (a) Sphere of habitats

(b) Limited diet due to simple stomachs

(c) Existence of tails

(d) Preference of being active when the sun is low to when the sun is high

---

8 The earliest known postcard is postmarked Dec. 1848. Further study of this area of postcard collecting will reveal many more postcards from the 1848 to 1893 time line. Most pre-1898 postcards share a few common traits: the postcard of this era is characterized by an undivided back (no line going down the center of the back of the postcard), and many contain printed lines on the back for the name of the addressee and his address only. Pioneer U.S. postcards are mostly from big Eastern cities. On May 19, 1898, by an act of Congress, private printers were granted permission to print and sell cards that bore the inscription "Private Mailing Card". During this period around 1900, Real Photo postcards began to filter into use. These early real photo images were mainly advertising pieces.

The use of the word "POST CARD/POSTCARD" (as one or two words) was granted by the government to private printers on Dec. 24, 1901. Writing was still not permitted on the address side. The publishing of printed postcards during this time frame doubled almost every six months. European publishers opened offices in the U.S. and imported millions of high quality postcards. By 1907, European publishers accounted for over 75% of all postcards sold in the U.S. The vogue of lithographed cards caught Eastman-Kodak's attention as well. They issued an affordable "Folding Pocket Kodak" camera around 1906. This allowed the mass public to take black & white photographs and have them printed directly onto paper with postcard backs.

Postcards with a divided back were finally permitted on March 1, 1907. The address had to be written on the right side of the back of the postcard while the left side was reserved for writing messages. At this time in American history the postcard hobby became a public addiction. Publishers printed millions of cards in this era. Most postcards were printed in Germany, the world leader in lithographic processes. At the height of the countrywide mania, World War I caused a crash in the hobby. The advent of World War I caused the supply of postcards from Germany to end. Poorer quality postcards came from English and U.S. publishers. The lowered quality of the printed postcard, recurrent influenza epidemics, and war shortages killed the American postcard hobby. During the war years the telephone replaced the postcard as a fast, reliable means to keep in touch.

---

1. Which of the following is mentioned as a characteristic of a postcard before 1898?

(a) It was a plain card with no line for messages.

(b) It needed no postage stamps.

(c) It was made by a private publisher.

(d) It had small decorative pictures on the back.

2. American postcards in the mid 19th century were made

   (a) mostly by private publishers

   (b) primarily by dilettantes

   (c) only by the government

   (d) by foreigners outside America

3. Why were European postcards popular in America in the early 1900s?

   (a) Their price was lower than in other countries.

   (b) They were superior in quality to others.

   (c) Their advertisements were very sensual.

   (d) Their size was convenient to use.

4. According to the passage, which of the following discouraged Americans from collecting postcards around World War I?

   (a) Mail sent abroad was strictly regulated.

   (b) The invention of the telephone made postcards less popular.

   (c) Most pictures on the back were government advertisements.

   (d) The quality of prints on postcards deteriorated.

---

9 A method of age-estimation, by counting growth-layers in teeth, was first developed in the southern elephant seal, Mirounga leonina. It has since been successfully applied to toothed whales and dolphins with some success. Layers can be seen in a length-wise thin-section of a tooth. Patterns of these layers, referred to as growth-layer groups, occur in cyclic fashion, somewhat like the growth rings in trees. The actual growth rates of deposition of layers are only known for a few species, but the method appears to work well in dolphins and pilot whales. The layered structure of cetacean teeth is essentially similar among species, varying only in detail, and it is recognized as a useful method of age-determination. Some researchers have determined the age of bottle-nose dolphins, Tursiops truncates, using this method. The cement of the tooth showed growth-layering which could be counted. This age-determination enabled researchers to state that females and males attain sexual maturity when 12 and 12-18 growth-layers, respectively, are laid down. The maximum number of layers was 50, but usually the average was 35. In the literature, the lengthwise thin-section examinations of the dolphin teeth have resulted in the observation that the growth layers are cyclic and appear in definite patterns, somewhat like growth rings in certain trees. Although most cetacean researchers agree that the growth layers are age equivalent, some investigators have questioned the actual rates of deposition and have questioned the relationship to age in some species of whale.

One method of preparation of the tooth for examination is by cutting the tooth into wafer-thin slices, as is performed on rocks. The tooth is first embedded in plastic in a vacuum, and then trimmed with a saw when cured. Then one side is ground down, using various sizes of grit, until highly polished. Finally the whole sample is affixed to a glass slide with epoxy. After curing for a couple of days, it is thinly sliced parallel to the glass slide with a special diamond saw and ground down, again using many grit sizes, until polished. After preparation the thin-section is examined under a polarizing microscope. The fine banding can be intensified with the use of crossed-polars and retardation plates.

1. Why does the author compare growth-layers in teeth to the growth rings in trees?
   (a) Layers and rings require similar amounts of time to grow.
   (b) Similar methods are used to prepare them for examination.
   (c) Similar information can be obtained from them. •
   (d) They are studied by researchers in the same field.

2. According to the passage, which of the following can be learned from the growth-layers in dolphin teeth?
   (a) The dolphin's species
   (b) The dolphin's maturity level
   (c) The dolphin's diet
   (d) The dolphin's health condition

3. According to the passage, researchers would agree that
   (a) the age of dolphins is related to their teeth growth-layers
   (b) a seal with 13 growth-layers is probably 13 years old
   (c) the actual rate of deposition in seals is confirmed to be reliable
   (d) some species of whales have different teeth layer structures from others

4. The last procedure to prepare the tooth for examination is
   (a) slicing it into very thin pieces
   (b) trimming it with a saw
   (c) grinding it with various sizes of grits .
   (d) attaching it to a glass slide

10 Despite the long periods of crisis, the abandoned fields, the famines and the drop in population during the Middle Ages, a true "technological revolution" occurred between the 13th and 14th centuries, along with the widespread spread of the figure of the miller.

The miller was not merely a technician: he collected on behalf of the feudal lord, he supervised the peasants so they could not elude the law and grind their own flour, and by law he kept only a third of the flour for himself. Although the millers lived outside of town and the bakers lived in the cities, both belonged to the most ancient of Corporations: the White Art.

Bakers were classified on the basis of the bread they produced: "white" bakers had the right to make soft white bread, while "black" bakers could bake only dark, compact bread.

After the traditional banquet of the Corporation, the newly admitted baker swore—in front of the authorities—to his honesty regarding the quantity and quality of his bread. At Hamburg, in the 14th century, the law decreed the immediate confiscation of bread that was too heavy or bad tasting and the baker was brought to court. In England, dishonest bakers were sent to the yoke, and dragged through the city by angry crowds. It was in the Middle Ages that the habit of delivering bread to homes began. Either the baker himself or a shop boy delivered the bread, bringing news and gossip along with it, much like the minstrels.

1. According to the passage, which of the following was the role of the miller?
   (a) The miller protected the landlord's profit as the landlord's proxy.
   (b) The miller helped the peasants overcome difficult situations.
   (c) The miller collected the peasants' words and relayed them to the landlord.
   (d) The miller supervised and controlled the activities of the White Art.

2. The White Art that the author mentions in paragraph 2 consisted of whom?
   (a) Millers and bakers
   (b) Bakers
   (c) White bakers
   (d) Black bakers

3. Which of the following is mentioned in the passage as a target for punishment by law?
   (a) A baker who buys flour directly from the peasants
   (b) A baker who is not in emotional harmony with his customers
   (c) A baker who refuses to bring bread to his customers' houses
   (d) A baker who makes bread with a strange flavor

4. Which of the following is mentioned in the passage as a similarity between the miller and the baker?
   (a) They were arranged according to their products.
   (b) They were subject to the same main body supervising them.
   (c) They both kept the skills of their trade secret from others.
   (d) They both were forced to follow laws based on vocational ethics.

Let It Be

When I find myself in times of trouble
Mother Mary comes to me speaking words of wisdom,
Let it be
And in my hour of darkness
She is standing right in front of me speaking words of wisdom,
Let it be.
And when the broken hearted people living in the world agree
There will be an answer,
Let it be
For though they may be parted There is still a chance that they will see,
There will be an answer, let it be
And when the night is cloudy, there is still a light that shines on me.
Shine until tomorrow, let it be.
I wake up to the sound of music,
Mother Mary comes to me, speaking words of wisdom,
Let it be.
# # #

내가 고통의 시간을 보내고 있을 때
성모마리아는 내게 다가와 현명한 말을 한다.
내버려 두어라.
그리고 내가 어둠 속에 빠져 있을 때,
그녀는 내 바로 앞에서, 현명한 말을 한다.
내버려 두어라.
그리고 이 세상의 상처 받은 사람들은
이것이 해답이 될 것으로 믿는다.
내버려 두어라.
만약 그들이 헤어지더라도 여전히 그들이 만날 기회는 있을 것이다.
이것이 해답이 될 것이다. 내버려 두어라.
그리고 구름 낀 밤에도, 여전히 희망은 남아있다.
희망은 계속될 것이다. 내버려 두어라.
난 음악의 소리에 깨어나고,
어머니 메어리는 내게 다가와, 현명한 말을 한다.
내버려 두어라.

Reading

HACKERS READING

Progressive Test 1-① / 1-②

Hackers Progressive Test 1-①

• Read through the passages and solve each question which covers the preceding 1st week's chapters;
  Ch. 1 Topic • Main Idea • Purpose, Ch.2 Organization & Insertion, Ch.3 Restatement Questions.

[1]   Modern dance began on the east and west coasts of the United States with Isadora
      Duncan, Loie Fuller, and Ruth St. Denis. The first modern dancers revolted against
      the classical ballet, which was considered European, and high culture-performance.

      Around the turn of the century Isadora Duncan was the first dancer and
      choreographer to try to change American dance. She looked to primitive dances and
      other cultures for inspiration. She thought these different styles of dance had
      something the European Ballet did not have. She also used more popular sorts of
      dance, like tap and jazz-dance. With all these different influences from various
      cultures Duncan wanted to create a new style. Although she was very successful,
      she only became popular in Europe and not in her native country. "Her career far
      remained oriented toward Europe and European taste."

      The Denishawn Company, the chief dance force in the U.S. during the 1920s, was
      developed by Ruth St. Denis and Ted Shawn. Denishawn schools were established
      across the country and the company toured in the United States and abroad. ■ The
      second wave of theatrical dance grew out of the Denishawn-school. Martha Graham,
      Doris Humphrey, and Charles Weidman all left Denishawn a few years after one
      another, and started making their own choreographs. ■ Their work reflected the
      influence of the Denishawn school. ■ Rebellion against the exotic romanticism of the
      Denishawn company was to be a major thrust of the modern dance movement, and
      Denishawn was formally disbanded by the end of 1931. ■

      1. What is the topic of the passage?
         (a) The greatest dancers of the early 20th century
         (b) European tradition found in modern dance
         (e) The early history of modern dance development
         (d) The Denishawn company's contribution to modern dance

2. What aspect of Isadora Duncun does the second paragraph mainly discuss?

  (a) Her new dance style led the European Ballet to decline in popularity.

  (b) She innovatively applied diverse cultures and styles to modern dance.

  (c) She admired European culture and spent much time in Europe.

  (d) One of her great achievements was popularizing primitive dances.

3. The following sentence can be added to the passage.

  Yet during the 1930s they developed their own direction in modern dance.

  Where would it best fit in the passage?
  Circle the correct square [■] to show where it would best fit in the passage.

4. Which of the following topics would best follow this passage?

  (a) The decline of modern dance after the 1930s

  (b) The importance of the Denishawn Company in modern dance history

  (c) The development of dance following the influence of the Denishawn Company

  (d) The removal of the European tradition from American modern dance in the 1930s

5. What did Isadora Duncan's dance and Ruth St. Denis' dance have in common?

  (a) The adoption of instinctive factors

  (b) Great popularity in their own homelands

  (c) Influence from other cultures

  (d) Rebellion against classical ballet

---

[2] The first Indian group to build mounds in what is now the United States is often called the Adenans. They began constructing earthen burial sites and fortifications around 600 B.C. Some mounds from that era are in the shape of birds or serpents, and probably served religious purposes not yet fully understood.

The Adenans appear to have been absorbed or displaced by various groups collectively known as the Hopewellians. One of the most important centers of their culture was found in southern Ohio, where the remains of several thousands of these mounds still lay. The Hopewellians, believed to be great traders, used and exchanged tools and materials across a region hundreds of kilometers wide.

By around 500 A.D., the Hopewellians disappeared, gradually giving way to a broad group of tribes generally known as the Mississippians or the Temple Mound culture. One city, Cahokia, just east of St. Louis, Missouri, is thought to have had a population of about 20,000 at its peak in the early 12th century. ■ At the center of the city stood a huge earthen mound, flattened at the top, which was 30 meters high and 37 hectares at the base. Eighty other mounds have been found nearby. ■

In what is now the southwest United States, the Anasazi, ancestors of the modern Hopi Indians, began building stone and adobe pueblos around the year 900. ■ These unique and amazing apartment-like structures were often built along cliff faces. The most famous, the "cliff palace" of Mesa Verde, Colorado, had over 200 rooms. ■

1. Which of the following would make the best title for this passage?
   (a) The origin of North American Indians
   (b) The mound builders of early America ·
   (c) The creation of a new building style by the Adenans
   (d) The history of Indian burial sites in America

2. Which of the following best describes the organization of the passage?
   (a) A comparison of Adenans and Hopewellians
   (b) A comparison of the structures of burial mounds
   (c) A chronological history of Indian mounds ·
   (d) An explanation of the various functions of Indian mounds

3. What aspect of the Adenans does paragraph 1 mainly discuss?
   (a) How they organized their society
   (b) Their technique of construction
   (c) Their culture of building mounds
   (d) The purpose of the mounds

4. According to the passage, which of the following is a true statement about mound building?
   (a) Mounds could be built in the shape of animals. ·
   (b) At its height, the Hopewellian mound city of Cahokia housed 20,000 people.
   (c) Even the largest mounds had only one room.
   (d) Mounds were built only for religious reasons.

5. The following sentence can be added to the passage.

   Another site, the Pueblo Bonito ruins along New Mexico's Chaco River, once contained more than 800 rooms.

   Where would it best fit in the passage?
   Circle the correct square [■] to show where it would best fit in the passage.

[3]   After the early periods of settlement, the first sharp increase in immigration took place in the 1830s and 1840s bringing North European craftspeople displaced by the Industrial Revolution, and then a great influx of Irish fleeing from the dreadful poverty of the Potato Famine. German political refugees arrived shortly after. Many

immigrants from northern and western Europe settled on farms in the Middle West. The Irish and others were eagerly absorbed as construction laborers on roads, bridges, and railroads, as well as in factories. Most of them remained in the northern cities.

In the 1880s a tremendous tide of immigration began this time largely from southern and eastern Europe. To most Americans, these newcomers seemed far stranger than their predecessors. ■ Their languages, customs, and ways of life were very different from those of established Americans. ■ The newcomers moved into the poorest neighborhoods of the large cities and tended to stay together in local ghettos, clinging to their old ways. ■ Being poor and accustomed to poverty, they were willing to work for very low wages. ■ Indeed, organized labor became one of the chief opponents of continued immigration. This opposition finally led to the immigration quota acts of the 1920s, which restricted further immigration, particularly from southern and eastern Europe. In 1965 these prejudicial laws were replaced by a new immigration act, which granted equal opportunity to foreigners, regardless of their place of origin. Asians, especially Koreans and Filipinos, then began to arrive, followed by Vietnamese at the end of the U.S.-Vietnam conflict. Many of these newcomers have worked very hard to establish themselves in their new land.

In the late 1970s and throughout the 1980s, immigration from Mexico and from Central America increased greatly. In ever-growing numbers, many of these immigrants simply walked across the very lone common border between the United States and Mexico. It was primarily to control this wave of immigration that the Immigration Reform Act was passed in 1986.

1. Which of the following is the main topic of the passage?

    (a) The beginning of immigration in America

    (b) The history of American immigration

    (c) The origins of the early immigrants

    (d) Settlement of the immigrants

2. What does paragraph 1 mainly discuss?

    (a) Economic crisis in the European countries in the early 19th century

    (b) The painful life of the early immigrants in America

    (c) The prerequisites of success for immigrants in America

    (d) The increase of immigration to America in the early 19th century

3. According to the passage, why did the government begin to restrict immigration?

    (a) Newcomers' culture shock was so great that their health deteriorated quickly.

    (b) Physical conflicts between established workers and new workers grew aggravated.

    (c) New immigrants disturbed the labor market. •

    (d) Asians' devotion to work comparatively lowered others' productivity.

4. According to the passage, which of the following statements about immigrants in the late 19th century is true?

    (a) They soon became adapted to the new culture.

    (b) They immigrated mostly for political reasons.

    (c) They eventually overcame their poverty.

    (d) They formed their own communities.

5. The following sentence can be added to the passage.

This made other workers, especially those in labor unions, afraid that the immigrants would thus lower wage levels and take jobs away from Americans.

Where would it best fit in the passage?

Circle the correct square [■] to show where it would best fit in the passage.

---

[4]   Hummingbirds have a fast breathing rate, a fast heartbeat, and a high body temperature. They must feed every 10 minutes or so all day, and they may consume 2/3 of their body weight in a single day. ■ A major part of a hummingbird's diet is sugar. ■ They get it from flower nectar and tree sap. ■ The tongue of a hummingbird has grooves on the side, which are used to catch insects in the air, as well as from leaves and spider webs. ■

Hummingbird bills are long and tapered, perfectly suited for probing into the center of tubular flowers for the nectar, which they take up at the rate of about 13 licks a second. Often one can see long translucent tongues spilling out of their long beaks, licking the air, as they approach bright colored flowers.

Hummingbirds have good memories; they can remember food sources from previous years. As they feed, hummingbirds accidentally collect pollen. By moving from flower to flower, they help the flowers to reproduce. Many flowers, like penstemons, seem specifically designed to accommodate hummingbirds.

Hummingbirds like to take baths on cupped leaves or in shallow pools. They flutter their wings or pull them straight back while lifting and spreading their tail. They dip their chins and bellies into the water. □ Sometimes a bathing hummer will throw its head back to toss droplets on its back. □ After bathing the bird will preen and dry its feathers. □ Hummingbirds also take shower baths while on the wing, and they sometimes sit in the rain on bare branches with their feathers ruffled up so they can soak their skin. □ One more thing hummingbirds like to do is to play in the fine mist of sprinklers. □

1. Which of the following would make the best title for this passage?
   (a) The uniqueness of the hummingbird
   (b) Nutrients in hummingbird food
   (c) The mental faculties of hummingbirds
   (d) General features of hummingbirds

2. According to the passage, for which of the following reasons does a hummingbird have a special bill?
   (a) To get nectar from specific kinds of flowers
   (b) To catch worms from deep holes underground
   (c) To bath and preen its feathers effectively
   (d) To collect pollen from tubular flowers

3. The following sentence can be added to the passage.

   Hummingbirds also need protein in order to build muscles, so they eat insects and pollen.

   Where would it best fit in the passage?
   Circle the correct square [■] to show where it would best fit in the passage.

4. Paragraph 2 focuses on which of the following aspects of Hummingbird bills?
   (a) The rate at which hummingbirds use them
   (b) How the hummingbirds utilize them in the hunt of insects
   (c) The relationship between their structure and function
   (d) The way they complement other physical traits of hummingbirds

5. The following sentence can be added to the passage.

   One woman, watering her flowers, had a Hummingbird dart several times through the mist of her garden hose, then finally land on her hand.

   Where would it best fit in the passage?
   Circle the correct square [□] to show where it would best fit in the passage.

Hackers Progressive Test 1-②

● Read through the passages and solve each question which covers the preceding 1st week's chapters; Ch. 1 Topic(Main Idea & Purpose), Ch.2 Organization & Insertion, Ch.3 Restatement.

[1]   Haunting photographs of starving African children in the news became commonplace during the 1980s and early 1990s, and many people became upset by the human suffering and misery that such pictures revealed. Positive news about hunger relief did occasionally appear, such as when medical treatment and balanced nutrition resulted in a reversal of nutritional deficiency diseases in certain populations. But it is clear that the specter of famine, which has been with humanity for thousands of years, has not disappeared. Despite advances made in many fields related to food production, numerous people—adults and children—still do not get enough food.

Producing enough food to feed the world's people is the largest single challenge in agriculture today, and the challenge grows more difficult each year as the human population expands. Currently, 1.4 billion metric tons (1.5 billion tons) of grains such as wheat, rice, corn, and barley are required to feed the world's population of 5.8 billion for 1 year. Each year, an additional 28 million metric tons of grain must be produced to account for that year's increase in population.

The food production challenge confronting agriculture is being met in a variety of ways, with genetic engineering being touted by some as the high-technology answer to agriculture's problems. Although it is true that genetic engineering has the potential to revolutionize agriculture, the changes will not occur overnight. A great deal of research must be done before most of "the envisioned benefits" from genetic engineering are realized.

Furthermore, genetic engineering is not the final solution to the challenge of producing enough food. The production of adequate food for the world's people will be an impossible goal until population growth is brought under control. Thus, the ultimate solution to world hunger is related to achieving a stable population in each nation at a level that it can support.

---

   1. What does paragraph 1 mainly discuss?

      (a) The news on hunger relief shed positive light on a solution to famine.
      (b) Many people are still suffering from hunger and starvation in the world.
      (c) Famine will soon disappear owing to medical treatment and balanced nutrition.
      (d) Photographs of starving children made famine a big issue.

2. Why does the author mention exact amounts of food when discussing the famine issue in paragraph 2?
   (a) To show the improvement of agricultural productivity
   (b) To bring out the seriousness of the famine issue
   (c) To illustrate the current world food deficit
   (d) To supply the accurate data for increasing the agricultural products

3. According to the passage, "the envisioned benefits" include
   (a) greater production of genetically engineered products
   (b) new kinds of products which can satisfy people of diverse tastes
   (c) invention of foods which have medical effects
   (d) flexible control of products in different quantities

4. Which of the following is mentioned as a prerequisite to resolving the food problem?
   (a) Agricultural revolution through gene manipulation
   (b) Careful long-term population planning
   (c) Medical breakthroughs
   (d) Worldwide advertisement of the miserable results of famine

5. Which of the following topics would best follow this passage?
   (a) Examples of how genetic engineering can improve the variety of food
   (b) Other suggestions for solving the global famine issue
   (c) Suggestions on how to control the world population growth
   (d) Problems caused by the unbalanced food supply in the world

[2]   In dry caves, preservation is often excellent, due to moistureless air and limited bacterial activity. Organic remains such as charred wood, nutshells, plant fibers, and bones are sometimes found intact. In wet caves, artifacts and other remains are often found encrusted with, or buried beneath, calcareous deposits of dripstone. The collected evidence of human habitation on the cave floor was often buried under rockfalls from the ceilings of caverns. Intentional burials have also been found in a number of cave sites.

Because of the unusual preservative nature of caves and the great age of many of the remains found in them, the fallacious belief has arisen that a race of cave people existed. Actually, most cave sites represent small, seasonal camps. Because prehistoric people spent much of the year in open-air camps, the caves contain the remains of only part of a group's total activities. Also, the cultural remains outside caves were subject to greater decay. Thus, the archaeological record of remote times is better seen in cave deposits.

Caves have been systematically excavated during the past one hundred years. ■ Since they often contain the remains of repeated occupations, caves can document changing cultures. ■ Some caves in the Old World continued to be inhabited even after the close of the Stone Age; relics from the Bronze and Iron ages have been found in cave deposits. ■ On occasion, material dating from the time of the Roman Empire has been recovered. ■ The famous Dead Sea Scrolls, discovered in 1947, were preserved in caves.

---

1. What does paragraph 1 mainly discuss?
   (a) Two types of caves
   (b) Preservation in caves
   (c) The way some caves can serve as historical sites
   (d) The damaged remains in caves

2. What is the main idea of paragraph 2?
   (a) Cave remains have proven that a race of cave people existed.
   (b) The remains found in caves are only parts of relics.
   (c) Relics in caves are clues for understanding the life of ancient people.
   (d) Prehistoric people used caves to record their activities.

3. Which of the following statements is a reason why some caves were believed to serve as fixed residences?
   (a) They contained remains of community life.
   (b) Formal burial sites were found nearby.
   (c) The ancient remains inside them were kept intact.
   (d) They contained some famous artifacts.

4. According to the passage, the best place to go and learn about ancient lifestyles is
   (a) famous Stone Age sites
   (b) dry caves used as periodic dwellings
   (c) accidental burials in mountains
   (d) caves in coastal areas

5. The following sentence can be added to the passage.

   For example, the economic transition from food collecting to agriculture is demonstrated by finds in highland Mexico and in Southeast Asia.

   Where would it best fit in the passage? Click the correct square [■] to show where it would best fit in the passage.

---

[3]   An important feature of energy flow is that most of it dissipates into the environment when going from one trophic level to another. The relative energy value at each trophic level is often graphically represented by an ecological pyramid. There are three main types of pyramids: pyramids of numbers, pyramids of biomass, and pyramids of energy.

A pyramid of numbers shows the number of organisms at each trophic level in a given ecosystem. In most pyramids of numbers, each successive trophic level is occupied by fewer organisms. Thus, in a typical African grassland, the number of products such as grasses is greater than the number of herbivores, such as zebras and wildebeests, which is greater than the number of carnivores, such as lions. Reverse pyramids of numbers, in which higher trophic levels have more organisms than lower trophic levels, are often observed among decomposers, parasites, tree-dwelling herbivorous insects, and similar organisms. For examaple, one tree can provide food for thousands of leaf-eating insects.

A pyramid of biomass illustrates the total biomass at each successive trophic level. Biomass is a quantitative estimate of the total mass, or amount, of living material. Its units of measure vary: biomass may be represented as total volume, as dry weight, or as live weight. ■ Typically, a pyramid of biomass illustrates a progressive reduction of biomass in succeeding trophic levels. ■ On the assumption that, on average, about a 90 percent reduction of biomass occurs for each trophic level, 10,000 kilograms of grass should be able to support 1,000 kilograms of frogs. ■ From this brief exercise one can see that although carnivores may eat no vegetation, a great deal of vegetation is still required to support them. ■

---

1. What does the first paragraph mainly discuss?
   (a) The method for putting ecosystems into categories
   (b) Ways of controlling energy flow
   (c) Different pyramid graphs for energy quantity ·
   (d) Using pyramid graphs for environmental problems

2. Paragraph 2 focuses on which of the following aspects of the pyramid of numbers?
   (a) The African grassland as a typical pyramid of numbers
   (b) The number of organisms at each tropic level ·
   (c) The flow of energy described by the numbers
   (d) Relations between two confronting ecosystems

3. Which of the following would make the best title for this passage?
   (a) The reversal of energy flow in each ecosystem
   (b) A Description of the flow of energy
   (c) Worsening environmental problems
   (d) Types of ecological pyramids ·

4. The following sentence can be added to the passage.

   By this logic, the biomass of frog eaters, such as herons, could weigh, at the most, only about 100 kg.

   Where would it best fit in the passage? Click the correct square [■] to show where it would best fit in the passage.

5. What topic could best continue this passage?

(a) The vegetation required to support carnivores
(b) Trophic levels of pyramids
(c) Pyramids of energy
(d) The relationship of carnivores to biomass

---

[4] When a wave reaches the boundary between one medium and another medium, a portion of the wave undergoes reflection and a portion of the wave undergoes transmission across the boundary. The reflected wave may or may not undergo a phase change depending on the relative densities of the two media. The amount of reflection is also dependent upon the dissimilarity of the two media. For this reason, acoustically minded builders of auditoriums and concert halls avoid the use of hard, smooth materials in the construction of their inside halls. A hard material such as concrete is as dissimilar as can be to the air through which the sound moves; subsequently, most of the sound wave is reflected by the walls and little is absorbed.

Reflection of sound waves off of surfaces can lead to one of two phenomenons—an echo or a reverberation. A reverberation often occurs in a small room with height, width, and length dimensions of approximately 17 meters or less. People observe reverberations when talking in an empty room, when honking the horn while driving through a highway tunnel or underpass, or when singing in the shower. In auditoriums and concert halls, reverberations occasionally occur and lead to the displeasing garbling of a sound.

But reflection of sound waves in auditoriums and concert halls do not always lead to displeasing results, especially if the reflections are designed right. Smooth walls have a tendency to direct sound waves in a specific direction. Subsequently, the use of smooth walls in an auditorium will cause spectators to receive a large amount of sound from one location along the wall; there would be only one possible path by which sound waves could travel from the speakers to the listeners. The auditorium would not seem to be as lively and full of sound. Rough walls tend to diffuse sound, reflecting it in a variety of directions. This allows a spectator to perceive sounds from every part of the room, making it seem lively and full. For this reason, auditorium and concert hall designers prefer construction materials which are rough rather than smooth.

---

1. What is the purpose of this passage?

(a) To explain why designers prefer rough construction materials in auditorium and concert halls
(b) To inform about the characteristics and effects of reflections of sound waves

(c) To list the advantages and disadvantages of sound waves

(d) To promote the use of the echo effect in concert halls

2. According to the author, listeners would feel sound most vividly in a concert hall where

   (a) all reverberation is removed

   (b) transmission occurs slowly

   (c) modified sound and echo distribution is produced

   (d) the height of the walls is over 20 meters

3. When a sound wave encounters an obstacle in its path, its direction is decided by

   (a) the frequency of the sound wave

   (b) the size of the room in which it is traveling

   (c) the speed of the wave at that point

   (d) the features of the obstacles' surface

4. Which of the following statements about sound wave reflections does the passage support?

   (a) Reflected sound waves can never be pleasant to the ear

   (b) Waves can be reverted based on echoes

   (c) Sound waves undergo reflection and transmission at boundaries

   (d) Architects prefer to use rough walls when building tunnels

5. Which of the following statements best describes the format of paragraph 2?

   (a) A general description and several examples of reverberations

   (b) A cause and effect of an echo and reverberation

   (c) A definition of a displeasing garbling sound

   (d) A summary of available reverberations

Inference Questions (I)

4

Inference Questions (Ⅰ)

O v e r v i e w

앞에서는 주로 지문에 제시된 정보의 확인과, 정확한 본문의 이해에 의의를 두는 사실적 사고 능력을 평가하는 문제를 다루었다. (direct description의 이해)

본 chapter에서는, 한단계 높은 차원의 능력인 "행간을 읽어야 하는" Inference 문제들을 만나게 된다. Inference 문제는 논리적 사고를 요하며, 추론은 반드시 근거가 뒷받침 되어야 한다. (indirect description의 이해)

Inference문제를 풀기 위해서는 지문에 제시된 사실적인 정보를 바탕으로 하여 지문 속에 숨겨진 내용이나, 주어진 정보 이상의 것을 미루어 추리해 내야 한다. 지문에 근거를 두지 않는 추리, 상상, 비약은 정답이 될 수 없다는 점을 명심하도록 한다.

● Inference는 RC part에서 가장 난이도가 높고, 또 출제비율이 높음을 감안하여 특별히 두개의 chapter로 나누어 충분한 연습을 하도록 배려하였다.

 - Chapter 4 에서는 inference에 대해 개괄하고 전략을 익힌 뒤 충분한 양의 연습문제를 풀어본다.

 - Chapter 5에서는 Chapter 4에서 연습한 전략을 토대로 다양한 실전문제를 풀어본다.

● 그러나 무엇보다도 inference 유형의 문제는 논리력이 가장 중요하기 때문에 여러 사람이 머리를 맞대고 토론하며 논리력을 기르는 시간을 갖기를 권장한다.

Types of Questions

● By stating ... , the author implies that

● From the first sentence in the passage, it can be inferred that _____

● It can be inferred from the passage that

● It can be inferred that which of the following was...

● The author implies/suggest that ...

 Tip Inference 문제 유형 분석

 1. 글에 제시된 내용을 바탕으로 숨겨진 사실을 미루어 알거나 생략된 정보를 추리

 2. 지문 내의 정보를 제시된 상황과 다른 상황에 적용

 3. 글쓴이가 글 속의 사건, 인물 등을 대하는 태도를 보고 글쓴이의 tone 혹은 attitude를 파악

●Strategy

1 지문내용의 정확한 이해

- 지문과 너무 동떨어져 있는 내용, 자신의 주장 혹은 선입견에 의한 판단을 삼가해야 하며, 글쓴이의 입장과 태도 또는 의도를 늘 생각하며 읽는다.
- 내용과 구조는 밀접한 관계를 갖기 때문에 내용의 흐름에 따라 구조를 예측할 수 있고, 구조를 통해 내용전개 또한 예측할 수 있다. 읽어내려가는 과정에서 내용을 요약하고 단락 간의 관계를 살펴보면, 글의 구조를 파악하는 동시에 생략된 구조 및 내용을 쉽게 추리할 수 있다.

2 오답을 유형화하여 자신의 답을 검토하거나, 맞는 답을 고르기 어려울 때 틀린 답을 제외시킴

- 오답의 유형
  - **IC : Incorrect** 보기가 지문의 내용과 상반되는 경우
  - **IR : Irrelevant** 보기가 지문의 내용과 전혀 상관없는 내용일 경우, 즉 언급 된 바 없음
  - **NS : Not Supported** 보기의 타당한 근거가 지문으로부터 추론되지 않는 경우, 혹은 비약이 심한 추론인 경우

Ex Read each of the follwing passages with 3 answer choices. Then, mark "C" in front of an answer choice if it can be inferred from the passage. For the wrong answer choices, mark why they are incorrect using the following indications: IC (Incorrect), NS (Not Supported) and IR (Irrelevant).

● When two people are talking to each other, they tend to stand a certain distance apart. Each person has an invisible boundary around their body which other people may not enter into. If someone pierces this boundary, they will feel uncomfortable and move away to increase the distance between them. (The major exception is family members and other loved ones.) This personal distance is not due to body odor or bad breath, but because closeness lends a sense of intimacy that is at odds with their relationship to the other individual.

IC The more closely strangers sit together, the more sense of intimacy they feel.

NS The average personal distance varies from culture to culture.

C The principle of personal distance is not applied to the relationship between a mother and her baby.

Answer IC, NS, C

● For instance, if an eight-year-old is shown eight yellow candies and four brown candies and asked, "Are there more yellow candies or more candies," he will say that there are more candies, whereas a five-year-old is likely to respond incorrectly that there are more yellow candies.

C The ability to reason about the whole and about part of the whole develops between five and eight-year-old.

IC Some eight-year-old children cannot differentiate yellow candies from brown candies.

__NS__ Most of the children became to learn logical thinking and mathematical analysis entirely after they reach the age of eight.

Answer C, IC, NS

---

3 **Tone이나 attitude를 파악하기 위해서, 지문에서 글쓴이가 사용하고 있는 표현, 특히 수사어구에 주의한다.**

· tone & attitude

A. 글쓴이가 글 속의 대상, 사건, 인물 등을 대하는 태도:

'긍정적(positive)', '부정적(negative)', '낙관적(optimistic)', '회의적(skeptic)', '존경하는(respectful)', '도전적/반항적(defiant)', '비판적(critical)' 태도

B. 글쓴이의 판단, 비판, 주장, 감정 등이 개입되어있는가에 따라:

'주관적'(subjective), '객관적'(objective/ impersonal/ neutral) 태도

More 부정적인 견해를 나타낼 때 비꼬면서 웃음 섞인 말투로 표현하면 '풍자적(sarcastic)'인 태도이며, 냉정한 지식인의 예리함으로 비판하면 '냉소적(cynical)' 태도로 나눌 수 있다.

Ex Underline any words or phrases that show the author's tone or attitude toward Van Gogh.

● When Van Gogh decided to become an artist, no one—not even himself—suspected that he had extraordinary artistic gifts. He evolved rapidly from an inept, but impassioned novice into a truly original master. He eventually proved to have an exceptional feel for bold, harmonious color effects and an infallible knack for choosing simple, but memorable compositions.

 허락되지않는 박자

Answer extraordinary, evolved rapidly, a truly original master, infallible knack

Ex Underline any words or phrases which show the author's tone or attitude toward the killer whale.

● The killer whale, one of the most intelligent of marine animals, hunts in packs and feeds on larger animals, such as fish, aquatic birds, seals, dolphins, and other whales. Despite its name, there have been no authenticated accounts of attacks on humans near Antarctica.

Answer the most intelligent

Ex **Read the following passages. If the statement can be inferred from the passage, mark O; otherwise mark X.**

A. 한 단어나 짧은 구, 절에서 함축된 의미를 찾아내기

From the outset, naval power was vital in determining the course of the war, lending to British strategy a flexibility that helped compensate for the comparatively small numbers of troops sent to America and ultimately enabling the French to help bring about the final British surrender at Yorktown, Va.

_____X____ America had a smaller number of troops than Britain.
_____O____ France and Britain fought a war in America.

Answer × ○

Topic Sentence 1번 질문은, 지문 중의 " British … the comparatively small numbers of troops" 라는 부분에서 영국군이 상대편보다 수적인 면에서 상대적으로 적었음을 알 수 있고, "enabling the French to help bring about the final British surrender" 라는 부분에서 영국군이 싸운 상대가 프랑스군이었음을 알 수 있다.

2번 질문에 대해서는, "troops sent to America" 라는 구에서 군대를 미국으로 보냈음을, 즉, 미국이 전쟁터였음을 알 수 있다.

Because the new immigration involved large numbers of sojourners, Mark Wyman's Round-trip to America is a necessary corrective to U.S.-centered views that assume all new arrivals are immigrants.

_____X____ Most early immigrants were Europeans who originally intended to visit America for only a short time.
_____O____ Before the sojourners began to settle in America, some other immigrant groups had settled down already.

Answer × ○

B. 두 개의 문장 내용을 조합하여 질문의 답 찾기

Compared with humans, the range of sound frequencies heard by fishes is greatly restricted. It is believed that many fishes actively communicate with each other by producing sounds in their swim bladders, throats, and various other body parts.

_____O____ Having a restricted sound frequency range doesn't mean that fish don't communicate with each other.
_____X____ Because humans have a wider range of sound frequencies than fish, they can hear the sound of fish.

Answer ○ ×

Topic Sentence 첫 문장에서 물고기가 들을 수 있는 sound frequency 범위가 인간의 것보다 훨씬 제한되어 있다고 하였고, 두번째 문장에서 많은 물고기들이 여러 방법을 써서 서로 communicate할 수 있다고 하였으므로 첫번째 보기를 유추해 낼 수 있다.

그러나 두번째 보기는 앞부분은 맞지만, 사람이 그러므로 물고기의 소리를 이해할 수 있다는 말은 나오지 않기 때문에 틀리다.

● In his failure to develop, Armstrong was typical of most jazz musicians, who generally have become reconciled to the style formulated at a comparatively early time of life.

_____ The reason for Armstrong's failure was that he couldn't develop his own creative style in jazz.

_____ Most jazz musicians come to compromise their style with the established form of jazz.

Answer × ○

C. 문단 구조를 통해 생략된 내용을 추리하거나, 직접 언급되어 있지 않은 새로운 정보를 추출해내기

● Children today find it hard to resist the urge to climb on a pony's back and it is not likely that human nature was much different in the Bronze Age.

_____ The children in the Bronze Age must have liked to ride ponies like children today.

_____ In the Bronze age, most ponies were smaller than they are now, so it was easier for children to ride them.

Answer ○ ×

Topic Sentence 지문의 내용을 정리하여 3단 논법을 적용해 보면,

1. 오늘날 아이들은 조랑말 타기에 충동을 느낀다
2. 청동기 시대에도 인간 본성은 비슷했을 것이다
3. 따라서 오늘날 아이들과 청동기 시대 아이들은 조랑말 타기에 비슷하게 충동을 느꼈을 것이다. 라는 결론이 나오게 된다. 그러므로 첫번째 보기는 지문에서 infer 가능한 지문이다. 그러나 두번째 보기는 지문에 전혀 암시되어 있지 않은 내용, 즉 청동기 시대 조랑말이 지금의 조랑말보다 작았다는 내용을 담고 있으므로 infer될 수 없다.

● The prevailing view among paleo-historians is that the first horses to be tamed were hitched to carts before being mounted. They base their conclusions on early depictions of horses that appear to be too small to carry an adult human. From studying skeletons, it does appear that Bronze Age horses were small, but so were Bronze Age people. And, size doesn't really count—even a pony can carry an adult a fair distance.

_____ Research conducted on skeletons did not agree with the prevalent view held by paleo-historians.

_____ People in the Bronze Age were smaller than they are today.

Answer ○ ○

Ex Read the following passages and choose the one best answer to each question, based on whether or not the statement can be inferred from the passage.

D. 지문의 내용을 새로운 상황에 적용해보기

There is another and less specific reason why caricature had to await the advent of printing and the wider dissemination of knowledge which resulted. The successful political cartoon presupposes a certain average degree of intelligence in a nation, an awakened civic conscience, a sense of responsibility for the nation's welfare. The cleverest cartoonist would waste his time appealing to a nation of feudal vassals; he could not expect to influence a people to whom the ballot box was closed. Caricature flourishes best in an atmosphere of democracy; there is an eternal incompatibility between its audacious irreverence and the doctrine of the divine right of kings.

· It can be inferred from the passage that a political cartoonist would most likely succeed in a society

(A) of people who can vote against their country's ruler

(B) that is heavily peopled and rich

(C) whose people love arts and literature.

Answer A

The cause of the cuckoo's demise is the same threat facing most endangered species—habitat loss. In the West, cuckoos are closely associated with broadleaf riparian (i.e. streamside) forests. Logging, cattle grazing, dams, water diversions, and water pumping have decimated the West's rivers and riparian forests, however, causing over a hundred birds, fish, amphibians, and mammals to be listed as federally endangered species. In most western states, 60-95% of the riparian forests have been destroyed. East of the Continental Divide, the cuckoo faces many of the same threats, but as the climate is generally more humid, it is able to tolerate greater levels of habitat destruction. Its decline in the East, therefore, was delayed, but is increasing rapidly.

· It can be inferred from the passage that, when considering the fact that riparian forests in the West and those in the East are being destroyed at the same rate, the cuckoo in the East

(A) lives on some kinds of insects which are found exclusively in riparian forests.

(B) also nests in a variety of nonriparian habitats.

(C) is less influenced by the construction of dams.

Answer B

Read the following passages and choose the one best answer to each question, based on whether or not the statement can be inferred from the passage.

Exercise I. Choose the statement that best describes what can be inferred from the passage.

1

Most New Deal artists were grateful to President Roosevelt for giving them work and enthusiastically supported the New Deal's liberal agenda. Not surprisingly, their art reflected this point of view.

(A) Portraits of President Roosevelt were the most popular painting genre among New Deal artists.

(B) President Roosevelt himself was an artistic man, so it is natural that he sponsored New Deal artists.

(C) Most of the works created by New Deal artists were not politically neutral.

2

The basilar membrane is not particularly well developed. It is short in comparison with that of most mammals, and its structural variation from basal to apical ends is only moderate in extent.

(A) The length of the basilar membrane is the shortest among all mammal membranes.

(B) Only more intelligent mammals have a basilar membrane.

(C) The structure of the basilar membrane is different between the basal and apical ends.

3

The only economically significant product derived from an orchid is the flavoring agent vanilla, which is obtained from the seedpod of several species of the genus Vanilla. However, many folk medicines, local beverages, and foods are prepared from various parts of orchid plants.

(A) Only the flavoring agent of orchids is useful to human beings.
(B) All orchids smell like vanilla.
(C) Orchid plants have many useful properties.

4

The Aurora consists of rapidly shifting patches and dancing columns of light of various hues. Extensive Auroral displays are accompanied by disturbances in the terrestrial magnetism and interference with radio, telephone and telegraph transmission. The period of maximum and minimum intensity of the Aurora follows almost exactly that of the sunspot cycle, which is an eleven-year cycle.

(A) Sunspots are associated with electrical interferences.
(B) Sunspot precedes a luminous meteoric phenomenon.
(C) Sunspots have phases of differing intensities.

5

In some areas where electric-power demand varies sharply at different times of the day, pumped-storage hydroelectric stations are used.

(A) In some areas where pumped-storage hydroelectric stations are used, the electric-power demand during the day is greater than during the night.
(B) Pumped-storage hydroelectric stations could be the solution to inconsistent electric-power demand.
(C) The areas that have pumped-storage hydroelectric stations use large amounts of electric power.

6

Contrary to the popular idea that sleep learning or integrated behavior patterns are the acting out of especially vivid dream experiences or a substitute for them, sleep talking occurs primarily in NREM sleep and sleepwalking exclusively during NREM sleep. Talking in one's sleep is a particular characteristic of lighter NREM sleep (stage 2), while sleepwalking is initiated from deeper NREM sleep (stage 4).

(A) Popular ideas or notions are commonly inconsistent with reality.
(B) Some acting can occur in other sleep as well as in NREM.
(C) Sleep talking and sleepwalking are a kind of substitute for vivid dream experiences.

7

Likewise, eastern Oregon was generally considered Indian country. Few others wanted to live there until the gold strikes in the Blue Mountains led to the forced relocation of the Nez Perce to make way for whites eager to exploit the newly-discovered gold fields. The search for gold became a dominant force not only in Oregon, but Idaho and Montana as well, altering the patterns of settlement that had until then been driven by emigrants looking for farmland.

(A) Before the gold strikes, Indians were superior in number to other groups of people in eastern Oregon.

(B) After the gold strikes, many farmers changed their careers to mining.

(C) American Indians didn't like gold as much as the whites did.

8

Elsewhere, canals could not compete with rail. They were limited both in the volume carried per unit and in speed; they were too small, too slow, and fragmented; and the railways, as they became integrated into national systems, provided a far more extensive service with greater flexibility. The canals were further handicapped because they were not, for the most part, common carriers themselves but were largely dependent on intermediate carrying companies. Although transport on the canals was initially cheaper than on rail, the railways gradually overcame this advantage.

(A) Most people still don't think canals are a good method of transportation.

(B) Sometimes price is not the most important factor in choosing a method of transportation.

(C) Canals were efficient in that they connected all the states with each other.

9

People believe that the first known terrestrial globe that has survived was made by Martin Behaim at Nurnberg in 1492. Many others were made during the 16th century. The principal centers of cartographic activity were Spain, Portugal, Italy, the Rhineland, the Netherlands, and Switzerland. England and France, with their growing maritime and colonial power, were soon to become primary map and chart centers. Capt. John Smith's maps of Virginia and New England, the first to come from the English colonies, were published in London in 1612.

(A) The rise in colonial power was a direct result of cartography.

(B) John Smith's map was the first to be introduced in London.

(C) Someone might have created the terrestrial globe before Behaim. •

10

Scientists still believe that the fastest part of the solar wind leaves the Sun through coronal holes, cool spots in the corona. The magnetic field of the Sun is relatively weak around coronal holes and thus allows particles in the solar wind to escape. Heavier particles seem to move more quickly than lighter particles in the same stream within coronal holes. The intermittent gusts from near the equator come from solar flares and coronal mass ejections.

(A) Spots in the corona were discovered only recently, so scientists have not yet determined their cause.

(B) The hypothesis on the function of coronal holes in the Sun has not changed much so far.

(C) The violent gust of the solar wind makes the earth rotate on its axis while revolving around the Sun.

Exercise II. Read the following passages and choose the one best answer to each question. If the statement can be inferred from the passage, mark ○, otherwise mark ×.

11

While such spelling reforms have been successful in other countries, and while Ben Franklin, Noah Webster, and others believed the benefits would clearly outweigh the temporary inconvenience, support for a major reform has never enjoyed widespread political support. It is as if tampering with the spelling system was tantamount to tampering with the Constitution.

Webster, due to the popularity of his dictionaries, was able to drop the silent [u] in color and implement a few other piece-meal reforms. However, Teddy Roosevelt's support for the replacement of "thru" for "through" was not enough to sway public opinion.

From a practical standpoint, resistance to change, even change for the better, is nearly insurmountable. Most scholars agree that having a spelling system similar to the one enjoyed by the Finns would increase literacy and speed the attainment of a 5th grade reading level by more than 25%. However, due to the lack of awareness and a variety of mostly invalid reasons, few people beyond those who have studied the topic are ready to advance or endorse any proposal for a spelling reform.

_X_ _O_ Finland was among the first countries to succeed in spelling reforms.

_O_ _X_ The American public considered the temporary inconvenience of spelling reforms to be greater than the benefits.

_V_ _O_ Americans have never succeeded in spelling reforms.

_X_ _O_ Americans objected to spelling reform because they thought it would be ineffective.

_X_ Teddy Roosevelt's support of "thru" for "through" failed because it was not reasonable.

12

The book is characterized by its use of writing or of some other system of visual symbols, such as pictures or musical notation, to convey meaning. As a sophisticated medium of communication, it requires mastery of the hard-won skills of reading and writing. Another distinguishing feature of the book is its publication for tangible circulation. A temple column with a message carved on it is not a book. Signs and placards that are easy enough to transport are made to attract the eyes of passers-by from a fixed location and thus are not usually considered books. Private documents not intended for circulation are also not considered to be books.

_X_ Only those people that acquire the skills of reading and writing can communicate with others.

_X_ Words are the most important factor in deciding whether something is a book or not.

_O_ Private diaries are considered books only if they get published.

_O_ According to the passage, the writer would classify the e-book—an electronic book that connects to the Internet, as a real book.

_X_ One of the characteristics of a good book is the usefulness of its contents.

13

In the years leading up to World War II, newspapers had reflected the socially gloomy atmosphere engendered by economic and political restrictions. In Britain, *The Times* supported government policy, and only *the Daily Mirror* was prepared to investigate in depth European political, diplomatic, and economic events. The continental press reflected all too faithfully the problematic state of affairs at the time. In Germany, Italy, Spain, and Portugal the press was subject to the rigid censorship associated with Fascism, while in the Soviet Union a different political system induced the same oppressive controls.

During the war, there was an expected clampdown on news coverage in most countries. However, in the United States and Britain a greater flow of information was allowed than had been the case during World War I. The British Ministry of Information and the U.S. Office of War Information issued vast amounts of official news and propaganda. In the United States, the Office of Censorship defined a "Code of Wartime Practices for the American Press," while in Britain newspapers voluntarily submitted any doubtful material for censorship, and a system of cooperative self-censorship prevailed. Nonetheless, as in any modern war, journalist heroes were created, the standards of photography reached great heights, and the horror and tragedy of the war frequently inspired excellence in writing and editing.

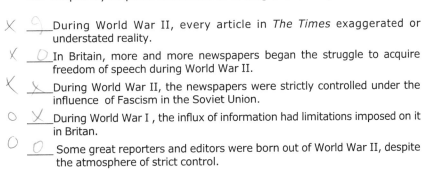

X _____ During World War II, every article in *The Times* exaggerated or understated reality.

X _____ In Britain, more and more newspapers began the struggle to acquire freedom of speech during World War II.

X _____ During World War II, the newspapers were strictly controlled under the influence of Fascism in the Soviet Union.

O _____ During World War I , the influx of information had limitations imposed on it in Britan.

O _____ Some great reporters and editors were born out of World War II, despite the atmosphere of strict control.

14　Changes in farming technique that increased productivity, introduced primarily in Great Britain and the Netherlands before the 1800s, made British farming the example to the world, even for the distant lands of America. However, the American continents, for both north and south, had indeed supplied Europe with very valuable plants. By the end of the 18th century, the production of North America was sufficient to supply some of the necessities of a warring Europe.

The New England settlements, like those of the Southern states, were expanding toward the west, as forest was claimed for farmland. Agriculture produced small surpluses for export. The Southern states had always exported staples like tobacco, cotton, and sugar, but the processes by which these plains were cultivated remained primitive.

Cattle raising expanded rapidly in the New World. The need for fresh and larger grazing areas drew cattle farming west into Ohio and Kentucky, where corn for fattening purposes could be raised at low cost. Consequently, cattle were being driven overland to seaboard markets by 1805.

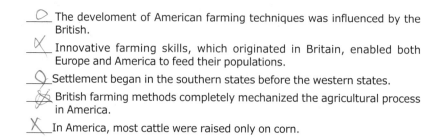

_____ The develoment of American farming techniques was influenced by the British.

_____ Innovative farming skills, which originated in Britain, enabled both Europe and America to feed their populations.

_____ Settlement began in the southern states before the western states.

_____ British farming methods completely mechanized the agricultural process in America.

_____ In America, most cattle were raised only on corn.

15

The most important aspect of post-medieval maps was their increasing accuracy, made possible by continuing exploration. Another significant characteristic was a trend toward artistic and colorful rendition, for the maps still had plenty of space where the artist could indulge his imagination. The cartouche, or title block, became more and more elaborate, amounting to a small work of art. Many of the map editions of this age have become collector's items.

The first map printings were made from woodcuts. Later they were engraved on copper, a process that made it possible to reproduce much finer lines. The finished plates were inked and wiped, leaving ink in the cut lines. Dampened paper was then pressed on the plate and into the engraved line work, resulting in extremely fine impressions. The process remained the basis of fine map reproduction until the comparatively recent advent of photolithography.

_____ Cartographical techniques were on the decline after the medieval ages.

_____ Post-medieval maps almost perfectly imitated the actual places they represented.

_____ The technique of engraving on copper made possible the inclusion of subtle and minute details on maps.   .

_____ Before the invention of photolithography, all maps were created in black and white.

_____ Water helped the paper effectively absorb ink in the cut lines.

16

In humans, sleep occurs in cyclical patterns. In each cycle of one and a half to two hours, a sleeper moves through four stages of sleep, from Stage 1 to Stage 4, and back again to Stage 1. In the first stage, low-frequency, low-amplitude theta waves characterize brain activity. The stage usually lasts only several minutes before the individual drifts into Stage 2, at which point the brain moves into low-frequency, high-amplitude waves. Stage 3 signals an increase of low-frequency, high-amplitude delta waves, and at Stage 4 these delta waves account for more than half of all brain waves.

Rapid-eye-movement (REM) sleep occurs during Stage 1, at the end of each cycle. People woken up at this time usually report that they have been dreaming. Dream deprivation or sleep deprivation results in detrimental changes in personality, perceptual processes, and intellectual functioning. There is some evidence that emotional and environmental deprivation disrupts the sleep patterns of young children, which in turn inhibits the secretion of growth hormones normally secreted maximally during sleep.

___√___About 20 minutes after a person falls asleep he/she usually starts dreaming.

___√___A person wakes up regularly after moving through Stage 4 of the sleep cycle.

___◯___Rapid-eye-movement is related to low-amplitude theta waves.

___✗___Every stage in the sleep cycle lasts the same amount of time.

___◯___A child who can't sleep well may have some growth problems.

Exercise III. Read the questions and choose the best answer for each.

17   Piaget's theory had a major impact on the views of intellectual development, but the theory no longer has the widespread acceptance it once did particularly from the 1950s through the 1970s. One reason for this is that the theory deals primarily with scientific and logical modes of thought and much less with aesthetic, intuitive, and other modes of thought. Another reason is that Piaget tended to overestimate the ages at which children could first perform certain cognitive tasks. Despite its diminished influence, however, Piaget's theory continues to serve as the basis for other theories.

1. What is the author's attitude toward Piaget's theory?
(a) sarcastic
(b) indifferent
(c) persuasive
(d) explanatory

18 Although urban-industrial life offers unprecedented opportunities for individual mobility and personal freedom, it can exact high social and psychological tolls. Such various observers as Karl Marx and Emile Durkheim cited the "alienation" and "anomie" of individual workers faced with seemingly meaningless tasks and rapidly altering goals. The fragmentation of the extended family and community tended to isolate individuals and to countervail traditional values. By the very mechanism of growth, industrialism appears to create a new strain of poverty, whose victims are unable to compete according to the rules of the industrial order. In the major industrialized nations of the late 20th century, such developments as automated technology, an expanding service sector, and increasing suburbanization signaled what some observers called the emergence of a post-industrial society.

1. What tone does the author take in this passage?
   (a) critical
   (b) angry
   (c) optimistic
   (d) defiant

2. What is the author's attitude toward industrialism?
   (a) positive
   (b) respectful
   (c) negative
   (d) neutral

19 In 1872 the inscrutable Rockefeller created the South Improvement Company, which he made the marketing agent for a large percentage of his oil shipments. By controlling this traffic he gained clout with the railroads, which in turn gave him large rebates on the standard freight rates in order to keep his high-volume business. In some cases, they even gave him information on competitors' shipments. Rockefeller then approached his Cleveland competitors and pressured them to sell out at his desired price. Most of them complied, and those who resisted were forced out. As one competitor recalled, they were told that "if we did not sell out, we should be crushed out." In less than six weeks, Rockefeller took over twenty-two of his twenty-six competitors. By 1879, Standard Oil controlled 90 to 95 percent of the oil refined throughout the country.

1. What does the author most likely think about Rockfeller?
   (a) He liked precision, order and tidiness.
   (b) He disliked competing with the competitors.
   (c) He was not a successful businessman.
   (d) He was a brutal businessman.

20 Architectural historians have praised Disney's development of Celebration, Florida, a new town south of Walt Disney World. Designed by New York architect Robert A.M. Stern, Celebration opened in 1996 as a traditional, pedestrian-friendly town. Cohesively arranged streets and squares, as well as homes with spacious porches and verandas in six different historical-revival styles, are intended to encourage old-fashioned neighborliness, according to the Celebration Company. Although not a gated community with its own security police, Celebration is an American theme town and an enclave for affluent citizens. Since the end of the Cold War, Disney's vision of "It's a Small World" seems to have been realized economically and technologically by the triumph of global capitalism and the computerized advent of the Internet. However, at the community level, the notion that the socially exclusive Celebration can serve as a model for new urbanism seems as naively optimistic as the town's corporately conceived name.

1. What is the author's attitude toward the town?

   (a) neutral
   (b) respectful
   (c) negative
   (d) positive

2. What tone does the author take in this passage?

   (a) approving
   (b) uncertain
   (c) indifferent
   (d) critical

Take a break

동팡이의 일기(1) : 종강파티

한국 대학에서의 종강..마지막 시험..칠판 오른쪽 한 귀퉁이에 꽈대가 모라고 써 놓습니다여..

'종강파티..아무개 주점..6시반..회비 만냥..빠지면 배짼다..'

이 동네만의 상황일지 모르겠지만..유학 바닥에서..술 마시는 사람..

소주 반 병이 치사량인 사람만 득시글득시글 합니다..

근데..기본 소주 2병..컨디션 좋다..3병..오늘 받는데..4병..그래 죽자.. 5병인..동팡이의 인기?..

거의 여고에서 강타 수준입니다..하늘을 찌릅니다..

(덕택에 동팡이 간은 멍들고 있습니다..T.T)

요즘처럼 종강 직후..학교가 문을 닫아 아무것도 못한다..

그럼..매니저를 둘까도 고민해야 한답니다..

어제는..수 차례의 호출과 독촉을 거듭하던 사람들과 술 자리를 가졌습니다..

역시 셋이서 750ml 짜리 소주 세 병을 나눠 마시고..그리고 간 노래방..

음주가무가 삶의 전부인 동팡이 앞에서..

음정무시 박자창조 가사창작은 아무리 술에 취한 상황이라도 참기 힘든 일입니다..

한국을 빛낸 100인의 위인들..아름다운 강산..모 이건 쏠렸지만..참을만 했습니다..

그러나 불후의 명곡 핑클의 내 남자친구에게를 망치는건 동팡이 인내력을 넘어서더군요..

신년 모임은 동팡이 집에서 전통의 강호들과 한자리를 가지려고 합니다..

뉴욕에 와 있는 동팡이 고등학교 모임 멤버들..망가져파..와 같이..

이들은 보드에 글 올릴 시간에 술 한잔을 더 마시자..라는 모토로..

술 먹는걸 일로 생각하기보다는 생활의 일부로 여기는 이들입니다..

이 날 모임을 위해 모후배는 서울서 오시는 어머님의 일정을 연기시켰고..(딸 맞아?..)

오하이오에서 개강했는데 비행기타고 날라오겠다는 후배 말리느라 죽을 줄 알았습니다..

이 모든 상황을 말로만 전해 듣다가 눈으로 확인하는 기쁨을 가지게 된 동팡이 동생..

아주 흥미진진한 눈초리로 안주거리 장만하느라 여념이 없답니다..

"오빠..정말 사람이 술 갖고 그리 잘 놀아?..(술이 사람 가지고 노는건 아닐까?..)"

이 글은 유학중인 이동행님이
www.goHackers.com에 올려주신 것입니다.

## CHAPTER 5

Inference Questions (Ⅱ)

Hackers Test

Read the following passages and the questions about them.
Choose the one best answer for each question.

1 Subterranean Termites, native to every state except Alaska, feed on wood and serve an important function in nature by converting dead trees into organic matter. Unfortunately, the wood in buildings is equally appetizing to termites and they cause serious damage to residential and commercial buildings. Eventually they can even threaten the structural integrity of a building. Their presence is not readily noticed and damage is often discovered before the termites are seen.

Subterranean Termites are social insects that live in nests or colonies in the soil. Termite colonies can range from hundreds of thousands to millions. Three termite forms or castes make up the colonies: reproductives, workers and soldiers. Reproductives can be winged (primary) or wingless (secondary). Each has the capability to produce new offspring. Primary reproductives, also called swarmers or alates, vary in body color from coal black to pale yellow-brown. Worker termites are small, creamy white insects. They are the most numerous and the cause of all termite damage. Soldiers resemble workers in color and general appearance. However, they have large, well-developed, brownish heads with strong mandibles or jaws. Soldiers defend the colony against invaders, primarily ants. When a colony is several years old and relatively large, it may produce another form of adult termite called a "swarmer." They are the colony's way of sending out new kings and queens to start colonies of their own. In the spring, great numbers of swarmers can fly from a single colony. Swarmers are the most visible form of termite. Usually a homeowner realizes termites are present in or around the home when a swarm is seen.

As their name indicates, Subterranean Termites usually live underground, excavating passageways to reach wood. Their passageways can be quite complex, extending 10 feet underground and over an acre in area. The soil provides a source of moisture that protects the termites from drying and shields them from predators. The soil also provides building materials for the protective shelter tubes the termites use to forage for wood above the ground. However, if water and wood is available from a source other than soil, subterranean termites can establish a colony with no ground contact. So, isolated, aboveground infestations may occur in buildings where termites have access to water from condensation, such as in leaking pipes, roofs, or other sources.

1. What can be inferred from the passage about soldier termites?
   (a) They produce young.
   (b) They rank lowest in the colony.
   (c) They usually live several years.
   (d) They can be mistaken for workers.

2. It can be inferred from paragraph 3 that Subterranean Termites can be prevented by
   (a) utilizing their natural enemies
   (b) eliminating contact points between the building and ground soil
   (c) replacing wood in the garden with shrubs
   (d) checking water leakages

3. It can be inferred from the passage that Subterranean Termites are usually found in
   (a) uninhabited areas
   (b) silent areas
   (c) arid areas
   (d) logging areas

4. It can be inferred that if a person sees flying yellow termites in his/her house, it means that
   (a) the termites will leave the house soon with all of their colony members
   (b) his house has already suffered a considerable sum of damage
   (c) there are no ants in his house
   (d) the yellow termites are the ones that have destroyed his house

2 Thomas Jefferson was never more typically a child of the Enlightenment than in his youthful conviction that reason and inquiry may lead man away from whatever is false, twisted, and capricious in human affairs toward the truths inherent in the nature of things. Man had been too long alienated from nature. For centuries he had been dominated by dogmatic authority and superstition, which was embodied, above all, in the alliance of kings and priests, Church and State. Now those false idols were crumbling, and man might take control of his destiny by discovering the laws of nature and using them in the service of the species. Newton had demonstrated the order of the physical universe; Locke had pointed the way to a science of mind as well as of government; Linnaeus and Buffon had begun to impose system on the chaos of living things; and Adam Smith, coincidentally in 1776, broached the idea of an autonomous economic order governed by immutable laws of nature. All such laws were permanent, universal, harmonious, intelligible, and beneficent, so man might feel at home in nature. The faith was aggressively secular, utilitarian, and progressive, its end being the increased freedom and happiness of humankind. In the great correspondence of their old age, his glum friend John Adams liked to twit Jefferson on the exploded hopes of the Enlightenment. But the sunny Virginian would have none of it. He went to his grave believing that the future would be better than the past and that the advance of freedom was irreversible. As he told Adams, he steered his bark "with hope in the head, leaving fear astern."

The optimistic faith of the Enlightenment informed all of Jefferson's work. We see it in Jefferson the scientist, Jefferson the educator, Jefferson the statesman – all facets of the multifaceted genius. His public policies often reflected the rationalism of the Enlightenment: thus the decimal system of coinage with the dollar unit; thus the rectilinear land-survey system for the Transappalachian West, the effects of which are still visible to anyone who flies over the prairies and plains today and views the linear patchwork of the fields below; thus, too, though it was not adopted, Jefferson's methodically developed plan for a uniform system of weights and measures based on a natural and universal standard.

1. It can be inferred from paragraph 1 that Thomas Jefferson believed that

   (a) man should return to nature and be freed from machinery
   (b) man should destroy false idols through violence as the first step to live in nature
   (c) man's reason and inquiry require full understanding of the laws of nature
   (d) man's destiny is to achieve supreme freedom and happiness in the end

2. According to the passage, it can be inferred that

   (a) Jefferson was the first to bring the Enlightenment to the United States
   (b) Thomas Jefferson's ideal world was fulfilled in his lifetime
   (c) immutable laws of nature were also false idols
   (d) John Adams didn't believe that reason and inquiry would bring a rosy and progressive future to humankind

3. It can be inferred from the passage that Thomas Jefferson's friend John Adams was a man who

   (a) wondered about the feasibility of his friend's ideal
   (b) was optimistic about the future of humanity when he was young
   (c) did not think highly of immutable laws of nature
   (d) usually liked to make fun of his friends

4. What is the author's attitude toward Thomas Jefferson?

   (a) critical
   (b) respectful
   (c) disregarding
   (d) neutral

3
The Navajo are part of the Athabaskan linguistic group and migrated from the North, apparently seeking a warmer climate. By 1400, they had settled north of the stone and adobe fortress villages of the Pueblo Indians of the Upper Rio Grande Valley in what is now New Mexico, and to the west in what is now Arizona. Trade appears to have been established between the Pueblo and the Navajo prior to the arrival of the Spanish in 1540.

Led by Coronado, the Spanish came up the Rio Grande Valley searching for the Seven Cities of Gold. In 1598, their conquest of the Pueblo Indians resulted in the establishment of settlements under a colonial government. The Navajo witnessed the plight of the Pueblo and kept their distance; historical records show that while they traded with the Spanish, they also raided their northern settlements. Over the next 250 years, despite the struggle for control of the Southwest between the Pueblo Indians, the Spanish, the Mexicans and United States troops, the Navajo developed and maintained an independent culture.

It was during this period, probably circa 1600-50, that the Navajo started turning cotton cloth-weaving on the primitive upright loom, learned from the Pueblo people, into a highly sophisticated textile art. They produced various types of finely woven textiles, including shirts, dresses and wearing blankets, using wool from stolen Spanish Churro sheep as their primary material. The primitive upright loom has continued to this day to be the only type of loom used by the Navajo weavers.

In 1795, the Spanish Governor of New Mexico, Fernando de Chacon, admitted that the rebel Navajo, 'work their wool with more delicacy and taste than the Spaniards'. Pedro Pino in his *Expedicion a Nuevo Mexico* (1812), described Navajo textiles as, 'woolen fabrics that are the most valuable goods in our province as well as Sonora and Chihuahua'. Even as far north as the Great Plains, traders recorded that during the 1840s, the Indians were willing to trade at least ten good buffalo robes for a single Navajo blanket. In 1849, Lieutenant James H. Simpson of the United States army commented on the Navajo, who 'seemed so poor', yet 'capable of making probably the best blankets in the world'.

1. It can be inferred from the passage that which of the following is true about the Pueblo Indians?
   (a) They had no awareness of the Navajo in the 15th century.
   (b) They continued to feud with the Spanish after colonization.
   (c) They also wove very refined textiles.
   (d) At first, they regarded the Navajo as invaders.

2. It can be inferred from the passage that the highly sophisticated Navajo textiles were
   (a) shared freely with their Pueblo neighbors
   (b) developed on a series of various looms
   (c) produced from their own wool
   (d) all made using a similar method

3. It can be inferred from the passage that the Spanish felt that the Navajo were
   (a) disobedient
   (b) concessive
   (c) respectful
   (d) arrogant

4. What can be inferred from the passage about the Navajo textiles?
   (a) They were primarily produced with techniques borrowed from the Spanish.
   (b) The Spanish prized their own textiles above those of the Navajo's.
   (c) Buffalo robes were more valuable than Navajo blankets.
   (d) They enjoyed a widespread reputation for quality.

---

4   Paper, whose manufacture was known only to the Chinese, followed the caravan routes of Central Asia to the markets at Samarkand. Here it was distributed as a commodity throughout the entire Arab world.

Papermaking manufacturing techniques seem to have followed the same caravan routes. Chinese prisoners taken at the Battle of Talas near Samarkand in 751 gave the secret to the Arabs. Paper mills proliferated from the end of the 8th century to the 13th century, from Baghdad and then on to Spain, then under Arab domination. Paper first penetrated Europe as a commodity in the 12th century through Italian ports that had active commercial relations with the Arab world and doubtless also by the overland route from Spain to France. Papermaking techniques may have been rediscovered by Europeans through an examination of the material from which the imported commodity was made. It is possible that the secret was brought back in the mid-13th century by returning crusaders or merchants in the Eastern trade. Papermaking centers evolved in Italy after 1275 and in France and Germany in the course of the 14th century.

But knowledge of the typographic process does not seem to have succeeded, as papermaking techniques had, in reaching Europe from China. It would seem that typography was assimilated by the Uighurs who lived on the borders of Mongolia and Turkistan, since a set of Uighur typefaces, carved on wooden cubes, has been found that date from the early 14th century. It would be surprising if the Uighurs, a nomadic people usually considered to have been the educators of other Turco-Mongolian peoples, had not spread the knowledge of typography as far as Egypt. There it may have encountered an obstacle to its progress toward Europe, namely, that, even though the Islamic religion had accepted paper in order to record the word of Allah, it may have refused to permit the word of Allah to be reproduced by artificial means.

1. It can be inferred from the passage that papermaking techniques were

   (a) first discovered by the Uighurs

   (b) probably taught to Europeans by the Arabs

   (c) not allowed to be distributed to foreigners in China

   (d) traded for a high price

2. By stating the Uighurs, a nomadic people usually considered to have been the educators of other Turco-Mongolian peoples, the author implies that

   (a) the Uighurs were the most intelligent of the Turco-Mongolians

   (b) the Uighurs were steadily employed by the Turco-Mongolians

   (c) the Uighurs had a reputation for spreading knowledge to others

   (d) neighboring peoples were forced to learn the Uighurs' culture and knowledge.

3. It can be inferred that if the Islamic religion had had no taboo about reproducing holy words by artificial means,

   (a) knowledge of typography would have reached Europe

   (b) the Uighurs would have been higher reputed in typography than the Chinese

   (c) the Uighurs would have made bronze typefaces

   (d) Islamic culture would have spread further

4. It can be inferred from the passage that Europeans did not learn typography from Muslims probably because

   (a) there was very little contact between Europe and Egypt at that time

   (b) Muslims considered it sacrilegious to reproduce the Koran through typography

   (c) typography was not regarded as essential to daily life

   (d) typography was kept secret by the Uighurs

---

5   The movement to defend American rights grew into the movement for independence in the meetings of the Continental Congress at Carpenters' Hall and the State House (Independence Hall) in Philadelphia. The spirit of independence ran high, as shown by spontaneous declarations of frontiersmen in the western areas and by the political events that displaced the old provincial government.

Pennsylvania troops took part in almost all the campaigns of the Revolution. A rifle battalion joined in the siege of Boston in August 1775. Others fought bravely in the ill-fated Canadian campaign of 1776 and in the New York and New Jersey campaigns. The British naturally considered Philadelphia of key importance and, in the summer of 1777, invaded the state and captured the capital. The battles of Brandywine, Germantown, and Whitemarsh were important engagements of this period. Following these battles, Washington went into winter quarters at Valley Forge from December 1777 to June 1778. News of the French alliance, which Benjamin Franklin had helped to negotiate, and the adoption of new strategy caused the British to leave Philadelphia in the spring of 1778. Frontier Pennsylvania suffered heavily from British and Indian raids until they were answered in 1779 by John

Sullivan's and Daniel Brodhead's expeditions against the Six Nations Indians. Pennsylvania soldiers formed a major portion of Washington's army, and such military leaders as Arthur St. Clair, Anthony Wayne, Thomas Mifflin, and Peter Muhlenberg gave valuable service. Pennsylvania also aided in the creation of the Continental navy, many ships being built or purchased in Philadelphia and manned by Pennsylvania sailors. The Irish-born John Barry became first in a long list of Pennsylvania's naval heroes.

The products of Pennsylvania farms, factories, and mines were essential to the success of the Revolutionary armies. At Carlisle a Continental ordnance arsenal turned out cannons, swords, pikes, and muskets. The state actively encouraged the manufacture of gunpowder. Pennsylvania's financial support, both from its government and from individuals, was of great importance. By 1780, the state had contributed more than $6 million to the Congress and, when the American states had reached financial exhaustion, ninety Philadelphians subscribed a loan of £300,000 to supply the army. Later, in 1782, the Bank of North America was chartered to support government fiscal needs. Robert Morris and Haym Salomon were important financial supporters of the Revolution.

1. What can be inferred from paragraph 2?
   (a) The Canadian campaign of 1776 ended in victory for the Americans.
   (b) The British sacked and burned Philadelphia in 1777.
   (c) The British defeated the Six Nations Indians in 1779.
   (d) Pennsylvania provided a number of naval heroes during the Revolution.

2. It can be inferred from the passage that the British considered Philadelphia to be crucial to their plans because
   (a) Pennsylvania produced the most war materials
   (b) Pennsylvania was located in a strategic place
   (c) Pennsylvanians aggressively participated in campaigns
   (d) Pennsylvania's naval force was a threat to Britain

3. It can be inferred from the passage that John Sullivan's and Daniel Brodhead's corps
   (a) helped Pennsylvania defend itself from British attacks
   (b) failed in expelling Indians from Pennsylvania
   (c) contributed greatly to enforcing Washington's army
   (d) were blamed for having a false strategy

4. It can be inferred from the passage that products from Pennsylvania were critical to the success of the Revolutionary armies because
   (a) Pennsylvania offered them to the Revolutionary army at no cost
   (b) Pennsylvania concentrated on producing what was needed during the war
   (c) they were produced only in Pennsylvania
   (d) those products were the highest quality in the nation

6   Postwar New York experienced an era in which alarming structural problems of urban society became ever more apparent. New York port lost its dominance, manufacturing began its long decline, massive city debt made it increasingly difficult to fund expensive services, and levels of municipal bureaucracy proliferated.

In the 1950s Robert Wagner granted collective bargaining rights to city unions but was often accused of ignoring long-term problems. Ultimately, he found it expedient to publicly break with Tammany Hall, which had twice gotten him elected. Wagner destroyed the power of the machine and its last boss, Carmine DeSapio. He was able to install his own Manhattan county leader and undermine Tammany's influence in the outer boroughs, but he did little to deal with the looming problems. Wagner prepared the electorate for another reform administration, as Republican-Liberal candidate John Lindsay unexpectedly won the election in 1965.

During Lindsay's two terms, New York's downward spiral accelerated as he attempted to impose administrative order. A massive transit strike coincided with his inauguration and was settled only with the first of several very generous union contracts. Lindsay's attempt to further undermine the power of the machine by merging departments and creating "super agencies" only added new levels of bureaucratic structure. His efforts to decentralize the school system and broaden minority participation in government led to greater ethnic animosity. Above all, he failed to gain control of a soaring municipal budget, even though he increased taxes. Denied renomination in 1969 by outraged Republicans, Lindsay won reelection as a Liberal-Independent candidate because the old Democratic machine had been gutted. His subsequent feud with a Republican governor led him to become a Democrat, but he had become a leader without followers. During his last years in office, the metropolis continued to deteriorate financially.

1. It can be inferred from paragraph 2 that Tammany Hall was a machine that
   (a) was financed by taxes
   (b) had strong political influence
   (c) was in favor of city unions
   (d) held elections

2. It can be inferred from paragraph 2 that the relationship between Wagner and DeSapio became
   (a) friendly since DeSapio helped Wagner win the election of New York mayor
   (b) hostile because DeSapio disagreed with Wagner's major housing policies
   (c) friendly because Wagner destroyed the power of the Tammany Hall machine
   (d) hostile because Wagner debilitated DeSapio's dominance after the election

3. Why does the author mention super agencies?
   (a) To give a concrete example of one of Lindsay's misleading policies
   (b) To emphasize the dominant power and authority Lindsay could possess
   (c) To explain how Lindsay could make his authority more firm
   (d) To show Lindsay's attempt at decentralizing the bureaucratic structure

4. What can be inferred about the policies Lindsay followed while in office?

    (a) His bad relationship with unions led to a transit strike.

    (b) By massively increasing taxes, he managed to balance the budget.

    (c) Their overall effect on the city's economy was negative.

    (d) They smoothed over previous problems in minority relations.

---

7   As trouble between the British government and the colonies grew with the approach of the American Revolution, Franklin's deep love for his native land and his devotion to individual freedom brought him back to America in 1775. There, while his illegitimate son, William Franklin, was becoming a leader of the Loyalists, Benjamin Franklin became one of the greatest statesmen of the American Revolution and of the newborn nation. He was a delegate to the Continental Congress, was appointed postmaster general, and was sent to Canada with Samuel Chase and Charles Carroll of Carrollton to persuade the people of Canada to join the patriot cause. He was appointed in 1776 to the committee that drafted the Declaration of Independence, which he signed.

Late in 1776 he sailed to France to join Arthur Lee and Silas Deane in their diplomatic efforts for the new republic. Franklin, with a high reputation in France well supported by his winning presence, did much to gain French recognition of the new republic in 1778. Franklin helped to direct U.S. naval operations and was a successful agent for the United States in Europe—the sole one after suspicions and quarrels caused Congress to annul the powers of the other American commissioners.

He was chosen in 1781 as one of the American diplomats to negotiate peace with Great Britain and laid the groundwork for the treaty before John Jay and John Adams arrived. British naval victory in the West Indies made the final treaty less advantageous to the United States than Franklin's original draft. The Treaty of Paris was, in contradiction of the orders of Congress, concluded in 1783 without the concurrence of France because Jay and Adams distrusted the French.

---

1. What can be inferred from the passage about Benjamin Franklin?

    (a) He returned to his country to participate in the independence movement.

    (b) He criticized Great Britain for suppressing personal freedom.

    (c) He was battled with his son, William Franklin.

    (d) He hesitated to draft the Declaration of Independence at first.

2. It can be inferred from paragraph 2 that when Benjamin Franklin visited France late in 1776

    (a) he had never been to France before

    (b) France already had an amicable relationship with colonial America

    (c) he was the first ambassador who was delegated to France

    (d) his personal repute played an important part in his mission

3. What can be inferred about the Treaty of Paris discussed in the 3rd paragraph?

   (a) Benjamin Franklin volunteered to negotiate peace with Great Britain.

   (b) Without Jon Jay, and John Adams' help, the treaty with Great Britain could not have been arranged

   (c) The West Indies were hostile to colonial America because America didn't help them when the war between the West Indies and Great Britain broke out.

   (d) At first, Congress intended to get France's support in negotiating with Great Britain

4. It can be inferred from the passage that the Treaty of Paris was

   (a) entirely negotiated secretly, without Congress' knowledge

   (b) originally intended to include France

   (c) signed by the French after a long delay

   (d) inspired by British victory in the West Indies

---

8 The Clean Water Act includes mandatory, enforceable requirements to control pollution from "point" sources such as factories and sewage treatment plants. Each source of pollution must have a permit through which requirements can be imposed, and a mechanism for enforcing these standards.

However, more than half of the remaining pollution of the Nation's surface waters is caused by polluted runoff ("non point source pollution"). Polluted runoff refers to pollution caused when precipitation washes toxic and other pollutants into surface waters from sources such as farms, streets, parking lots, and logging and mining operations. Other major sources of pollution, such as polluted municipal and industrial stormwater, combined sewer overflows, and irrigation return flows contaminated with pesticides and other pollutants, continue due to statutory or regulatory loopholes.

Attempts to deal with polluted runoff through vague planning programs and voluntary efforts have not worked, and this problem continues to wreak havoc on the Nation's water bodies. The time has come for Congress to prevent polluted runoff through strict, mandatory programs. Examples of ways to prevent polluted runoff include conversion to sustainable agriculture methods to reduce or eliminate pesticide use and to eliminate nutrient runoff from fertilizers; mandatory erosion controls and buffer strips to protect water bodies from overdevelopment; grading methods to divert runoff away from mining sites before it becomes contaminated; and the use of mandatory stormwater controls, such as retention basins, to treat urban runoff. Urban transportation patterns encourage overuse of automobiles and sprawl development—a primary cause of polluted runoff. These patterns must be changed through local land use planning integrated with stormwater controls. Increased federal funding of transportation alternatives is also needed.

1. It can be inferred from the passage that the control of polluted municipal stormwater
   (a) has been achieved by non-profit organizations
   (b) would benefit from more aid from the government
   (c) is publicly regulated by Congress
   (d) requires more voluntary point sources

2. It can be inferred from the third paragraph that prior attempts to deal with polluted runoff failed because
   (a) they had insufficient funds to perform programs
   (b) they lacked strong legal power
   (c) they were too strict for regular people to follow
   (d) they were performed against people's will

3. What is the author's attitude toward the attempts taken up until now to solve the polluted runoff problem?
   (a) indifferent
   (b) critical
   (c) favorable
   (d) vague

4. With which of the following statements would the author most probably agree?
   (a) Pesticides carried by rainstorms from an orchard can be regulated by The Clean Water Act.
   (b) The Clean Water Act can deal with most major sources of surface water pollution.
   (c) Major sources of water pollution require more strict and mandatory regulations.
   (d) Proper urban planning and stormwater controls can be an alternative to The Clean Water Act.

---

9   Henry Ford was a complex personality. Away from the shop floor he exhibited a variety of enthusiasms, prejudices, and from time to time, startling ignorance. His dictum that "history is more or less bunk" was widely publicized, as was his deficiency in that field, revealed during cross-examination in his million-dollar libel suit against the Chicago Tribune in 1919. A Tribune editorial had called him an "ignorant idealist" because of his opposition to U.S. involvement in World War I, and while the jury supported Ford, it awarded him only six cents. One of Ford's most publicized acts was his chartering of an ocean liner to conduct himself and a party of pacifists to Europe in November 1915 in an attempt to end the war by means of "continuous mediation." The so-called Peace Ship episode was widely ridiculed. In 1918, with the support of President Woodrow Wilson, Ford ran for a U.S. Senate seat from Michigan. He was narrowly defeated after a campaign of personal attacks by his opponent.

In 1918 Ford bought a newspaper, *The Dearborn Independent*, and in it published a series of scurrilous attacks on the "International Jew," a mythical figure he blamed for financing war; in 1927 he formally retracted his attacks and sold the paper. He gave old-fashioned dances at which capitalists, European royalty, and company executives were introduced to the polka, the Sir Roger de Coverley, the mazurka, the Virginia reel, and the quadrille. He established small village factories and he built one-room schools in which vocational training was emphasized. He experimented with soybeans for food and durable goods; he sponsored a weekly radio hour on which quaint essays were read to "plain folks"; he constructed Greenfield Village, a restored rural town. Finally, he built what later was named the Henry Ford Museum and filled it with American artifacts and antiques from the era of his youth when American society was almost wholly agrarian. In short, he was a man who baffled even those who had the opportunity to observe him closely. All, that is, except James Couzens, Ford's business manager from the founding of the company until his resignation in 1915. It was he who always said, "You cannot analyze genius and Ford is a genius."

1. By quoting Henry Ford's statement "history is more or less bunk", the author means that
   (a) Henry Ford was unconcerned about history
   (b) Henry Ford was remarkably straightforward
   (c) Henry Ford was very insightful
   (d) Henry Ford was a defiant man

2. It can be inferred from the passage that Henry Ford's candidacy in 1918 was
   (a) widely ridiculed by most people from the beginning
   (b) suspected to be corrupt
   (c) affected by his public reputation
   (d) welcomed by many pacifists

3. What is the author's attitude toward Henry Ford?
   (a) objective
   (b) negative
   (c) complimentary
   (d) worried

4. It can be inferred from the passage that James Couzens was a man who
   (a) could analyze genius
   (b) was very competent at his work
   (c) accepted all facets of Henry Ford
   (d) failed to realize Henry Ford's genius

10 Before Columbus discovered the New World, corn was grown only in the northern hemisphere. The Indians in North, Central and South America grew it for thousands of years. Corn has been found in places where Indians lived more than five thousand years ago. The cobs are so old they have petrified. The Indians called corn "MA-HIZ". Later it became known as maize.

Corn did not suffer the same indignities as did tomatoes and potatoes in being adopted by European cuisine. As soon as Columbus brought the grain back with him to Spain, it found its way into kitchens and farmlands, and was on its way to the rest of the world. By 1555, it was being written about in the Hunan province of China. Portugal soon exported it to Africa, where it became a key component of the diet.

Unable to supplement their diet, the European poor's reliance on corn led to a disease called pellagra. As a result, corn lost its favor with Europeans. In Africa and America, however, choices were fewer, and pellagra seemed a better option than starvation. Pellagra causes skin and mouth rashes, and can eventually lead to mental deterioration similar to that of syphilis. The disease was nearly unknown in Central and South America, due to inclusions of tomatoes, beans, and avocadoes in the diet. Only when the diet is primarily made up of the grain do problems occur.

The Indians showed the Pilgrims how best to grow this staple—a fish planted alongside the kernels in a mound, which provided a ready source of fertilizer. The Pilgrims quickly became dependent on the dish, adopting it into their own cultural dishes. Cornbread, also known as hoecake, ashcake, spidercake, or johnnycake was a staple of any traveler during this period, since cornbread didn't spoil as easily as other breads. Topped with molasses, it gave cooks the idea for Indian pudding, still a favorite in New England. Some dishes including hominy, grits, and succotash still mark Southern American cuisine.

1. It can be inferred from the first paragraph that about five thousand years ago, corn was
   (a) found only as wild plants
   (b) cultivated globally
   (c) regarded as sacred
   (d) raised as a crop

2. It can be inferred from the passage that after corn became a staple in Africa
   (a) the African public found a solution to the starvation crisis
   (b) the African diet was rich in animal protein
   (c) some of the African public suffered an illness
   (d) the African diet was lower in nutritional value

3. It can be inferred from paragraph 4 that
   (a) the land the Pilgrims settled in was too sterile to grow corn without any fertilizer
   (b) the Pilgrims found that when mixed with other foods, corn doesn't go bad easily
   (c) the Pilgrims used corn only as a supplement to their principle food
   (d) people made hominy with corn

4. It can be inferred from the passage that contrary to Europeans, Americans insisted on eating corn because
   (a) corn grew more rapidly than other plants
   (b) corn could be used for medical purposes
   (c) it was difficult to obtain other staples
   (d) various recipes could be applied to corn

동팡이의일기(2) : 토플 R/C ①

토플 중에서 유학가서 제일 쓸만한걸 들라면..당근 R/C져..

L/C가 제일 필요하다구요?..제 남자 애인(?)이었던 후배..미국에 나가 전화를 했답니다..

# # #

후 배 : 형..형은 햄버거 제대로 시켜먹어?..(당시 저도 미국에 있었구요..)

동 팡 : 그럼..당근빠다쥐..

후 배 : 우씨..그런데 왜 난 아직도 포테토 라지가 나오냐.. (이 후배 토플 600 넘겨가지고 나갔습니다..)

# # #

저도 솔직히 원하는거 먹을때까지 2주 걸렸답니다..

처음에 용감하게 주문대 앞으로 다가섰져..

그럼 까맣거나..하얗거나..어쨌든 우리와 좀 다르게 생긴 애가 보여요..

# # #

다르게 생긴애 : *%$#!@!#@%$

동 팡 : *.*?? (저게 몬소리야..)

다르게 생긴애 : (약간 갈구는 눈초리로) *%$#!@!#@%$

동 팡 : (눈치빨로 잽싸게 때린다..) 넘버투플리즈..

다르게 생긴애 : *#%$#^@!$@

동 팡 : - -! (이건 또 모래..)

다르게 생긴 애 : (이젠 거의 씹는다..) %$#^$&@$^^##%

동 팡 : (전혀 안 들린다..울고 싶다..) &.&

# # #

결국 내 앞에 놓여진건 햄버거+콜라+포테토 전부 라지..

먹고자한건 다이어트 콜라+포테토 미디엄..

보통 미국 도착하고 얼마가 흘러야 먹고 싶은 걸 먹습니다..

(2주동안 샌드위치에 오렌지 주스만 먹은 녀석도..세트메뉴라서..^^:)

이번에 만난 유학 온지 1년된 형..

그 형 : 동팡아..너 오렌지 쥬스 발음 제대로 되냐?.

난 아직까지 레스토랑에서 오렌지 쥬스 시켜 먹은적이 없다..

동 팡 : 형..그럼..메뉴판 보고..I`ll have this one..이럼 되잖아..꼭 말로 시켜야 돼?.

그 형 : 그럼 더 비참해..싫어..안해..   - 계속 -

## CHAPTER 6

Negative Questions

6

Negative Questions

Overview

Negative 문제 역시 본문의 세부적 사항에 대한 이해를 요구하는 문제이다. Restatement문제의 부분집합이라고 할 수 있다. 그렇기 때문에 Negative 문제에 접근 할 때도 정확히 기술된 내용만을 사실로 인정해야 한다. 다만, restatement와 negative 문제의 다른점은 마치 판화의 음양각과 같이 문제의 보기 중에서 옳게 기술된 것을 고르느냐, 아니면 옳게 기술된 것들 중에서 그르게 기술 된 하나를 골라내느냐의 차이라고 할 수 있다. 간혹 Negative 문제 유형으로 추론을 요하는 문제가 출제되기도 하는데, 역시 본문에서 기술된 사실로부터 추론 가능한지를 생각하도록 한다.

Types of Questions

A. 전체 지문에 대한 질문	B. 지문에서 다루었던 내용의 일부분에 관한 질문
■ According to the passage, all of the following are true EXCEPT ■ According to the passage, which sentence is NOT true?	■ According to the passage, which is NOT true about _____? ■ All of the followings are characteristics/statements of _____ EXCEPT ■ Which is NOT mentioned as _____?

●Strategy

 1 Negative 문제에 접근하는 단계에서는 본문에 대한 skimming이 되어 있어야 한다.

 2 질문하고 있는 내용의 scope(범위)를 확인해라.

A. 전체 지문에 대한 질문
· 이 경우에 정답지의 보기는 본문에 언급된 내용을 paraphrase한 문장으로 제시된다. 그러므로 각각의 보기가 지문의 어느 부분에서 언급되고 있는지 확인하면서 답을 골라내는 것이 가장 좋다.
· 문장의 key-word를 지문 내에서 match 시키는 과정이 필요하다.
· 이번 장에서는 문제 각각의 보기 옆에 지문의 몇째 줄에서 언급되었는지를 적으면서 푸는 연습을 해두자.

B. 지문에서 다루었던 내용의 일부분에 관한 질문
· 정답지의 보기를 paraphrase한 부분을 확인하는 것 만으로는 정답을 고를 수 없다. 왜냐하면 보기의 문장이 모두 옳게 진술 되었더라도, 문제에서 정한 scope에서 벗어나는 경우가 답으로 제시될 수 있기 때문이다.
· 이런 문제는 restatement문제와 같이 문제에서 key-word를 잡아내, 본문의 일부분을 scanning하면서 보기와 대조하는 쪽으로 접근한다.

3 Negative 문제의 정답유형

A. Unstated / Untruth
· 지문에서 전혀 언급된 바 없는 내용을 기술
· 지문과 다른 내용으로 기술된 것 (주어, 목적어, 동사 등이 엉뚱하게 기술)

B. Overstatement or Vice versa
· 진술을 과장 시킴
Ex 그 지역은 현재 물이 아주 부족하다 =〉 그 지역의 물이 고갈되었다. (overstated)

C. Out of Scope
· 지문에서 언급되었으나, 문제의 초점에서 벗어난
Ex 미국 현대 음악사에 관한 지문의 문제로 "1930년대 음악에 대한 설명이 아닌 것은?"
Answer 1940년대의 특징으로 언급된 내용

D. Tense Discord
· 문법적 불일치를 말하는 것이 아님
Ex 미국 사건의 흐름을 역행해서 진술한 경우/ 과거의 일을 현재처럼 기술한 경우

E. All Mixed Up
· Subject-Agent Inversion 주객이 전도된 경우
· Cause-Effect Inversion 원인과 결과가 뒤바뀐 경우

F. Illogically Inferred Idea
· 지문에서 근거를 찾을 수 없는 비논리적 추론

Ex Match the incorrect statements in the right column to the reasons they are incorrect in the left column.

● In all the nations engaged in World War I, the governments took on an increasing amount of control. Food production, raw materials, and manufacturing were put at the service of the war effort. For the first time in history, women played a major role as industrial workers, recruited in large numbers to work in factories.

Because of the British blockade, people in Germany faced major shortages. Germany and all the Central Powers lacked sufficient petroleum reserves, copper, and tropical products such as rubber and cotton. Even more serious was a food shortage. German farmers lost their horses to the army, and food production declined with both farm workers and draft animals in short supply. As a result, potatoes became the staple for everyone.

For the French and British, life was not so bleak. There was serious inflation and some shortages, but overall the civilian population remained comfortable. A series of governmental controls over wages, prices, labor, and profits appeared.

• According to the passage, which is NOT true about World War I?

A. Tense Discord   1 A shortage of rubber and cotton was the most severe problem.
                                    _____

B. Overstatement   2 The army gave out supplies to German farmers.
                                    _____

C. Untruth   3 Most of the people in France were victims of inflation.
                                    _____

D. Subject-Agent Inversion   4 Things were not easy for women employed as factory workers until the war broke out.
                                    _____

E. Illogically Inferred Idea   5 Everybody eats potatoes as the chief article of food after war.
                                    _____

Answer 1-C, 2-D, 3-B, 4-E, 5-A

Read the following passages and the questions about them.
Choose the one best answer for each question.

1

Most of the pottery were sandy-red, some red, some gray, and only a few were black and black-coated. The vessels were generally hand-made, with some refined by the wheel. During the late period, more gray pottery occurred and the potter's wheel came into being. The surfaces of the vessels were plain and polished, decorated with bowstring lines, rope lines, carving lines, embossed lines and engraved holes.

● According to the passage, all of the following are true EXCEPT that

(a) half the pottery was hand-made and half made on the wheel

(b) there were more gray pottery during the late period

(c) in the early period, reddish pottery was predominant

(d) bowstring lines were a way of decorating pottery

2

Ordinarily, only the hard parts of deceased organisms are preserved; for example, only the shells of invertebrates, and only the bones and teeth of vertebrates. In most instances we must make inferences about fossil organisms using only these hard parts. Despite this challenge, we must try to understand the soft-part anatomy of fossil organisms so that we can better appreciate them as organisms that were once alive; that consumed food, breathed oxygen, interacted with their physical and biological environments, etc. Taphonomy is the science that studies the information that is lost between the death of an individual and its eventual discovery.

● According to the passage, which sentence is NOT true?

(a) Fossil organisms were once alive.

(b) Often, only shells, bones and teeth remain after an animal dies.

(c) A fossil organism's soft-part anatomy gives information about how that animal lived.

(d) Taphonomy is the science of finding skeletons.

3

America's distinctive nominating process is an additional structural barrier to third parties. Among the world's democracies, the United States is unique in its reliance upon primary elections to nominate partisan candidates for state and congressional offices. It is also unique in its use of state-level presidential primaries in the selection of presidential nominees. In most nations, partisan nominations are controlled by the party organizations. But in the United States, it is the voters who make the ultimate determination of who the Republican and Democratic nominees will be. This system, of course, contributes to the fact that the United States has weaker formal party organizations than most other democracies.

● According to the passage, all of the following are true EXCEPT that

(a) Presidential nominees must first be elected in state-level primaries.

(b) There are few countries besides the United States that use this same system.

(c) The primary election system makes political party organizations strong.

(d) Both Republican and Democrat nominees are decided by the voters.

4

Atolls are ring-shaped islands of coral reefs and reef-derived sediment centered over submerged inactive volcanoes. The coral animals that build atolls can live only in the upper sunlight layer of seawater. How, then, did their skeletal remains end up at a depth of 1,280 meters within Eniwetok Atoll? This surprising discovery was made in 1954 when bore holes were being drilled in preparation for the first hydrogen bomb tests. Plate tectonics suggest an answer.

Coral animals can build atop the skeletons of their dead predecessors at a rate of about 1 centimeter each year. Coral animals living on a volcano's flanks can grow upward as the crust beneath the volcano slowly cools and contracts during its movement away from the warm spreading center where it formed. A deep column of coral skeletons can accumulate if the rate of sinking is less than about 1 centimeter per year. Thus, the coral record traces plate subsidence for millions of years into the past, supporting the plate tectonics theory.

● According to the passage, all of the following are true EXCEPT that

(a) coral animals can move upward by themselves

(b) coral animals can survive in a well lit saltwater environment

(c) coral animals reside on top of underwater dormant volcanoes

(d) dead coral amasses at a rate of about one centimeter per year

---

5

The Milwaukee Handcraft Project began in 1935 as an experiment aimed at employing workers who were considered unemployable because of age or disability. The project soon became a thriving business, employing up to 900 workers who made rugs, draperies, furniture, wall hangings, and toys that were purchased by public institutions such as hospitals and schools.

● All of the following are mentioned in the passage as explanations of the Milwaukee Handcraft Project EXCEPT that

(a) the Project grew and became successful quickly

(b) public institutions helped by managing and governing the Project

(c) as many as 900 workers were part of the Project at one time

(d) the Project gave the elderly and disabled jobs

6

A polygraph works based on the theory that when a person lies, it causes a certain amount of stress that can be picked up by changes in several involuntary physiological reactions. Using a series of different sensors attached to the body, a polygraph measures changes in an individual's breathing, blood pressure, pulse and perspiration while they are being questioned. During a test, the operator asks a series of control questions which are designed to set a pattern of definite true and false responses. Once the pattern is established, the actual questions are interspersed with filler questions. Over the course of a 2-hour exam, patterns in the questions develop which tell if the subject is lying.

● According to the passage, all of the following could explain the process of polygraph work EXCEPT that

(a) when people tell lies, their bodily reactions show that they are lying

(b) only the filler questions are used to decide whether the subject is lying

(c) the "exam" consists of answering questions for 2 hours

(d) the polygraph can sense whether the subject's pulse changes

7

Mars is by no means an easy object to study. It is a small world, only slightly more than half the diameter of the Earth, and even at its nearest, it never approaches closer than 140 times the distance of the Moon. Moreover, the features on its surface are of low contrast, thus are difficult to delineate accurately. To study Mars properly, perfect instruments and a steady atmosphere on Earth would be required.

● According to the passage, which is NOT mentioned as a difficulty in the study of Mars?

(a) Even the best instruments we have now are faulty.

(b) It is more than a hundred times as far from Earth as the Moon.

(c) It is difficult for us to see exactly what's on the surface of Mars.

(d) Good atmospheric conditions are necessary for such study.

8

Unlike mammals and birds, snakes cannot generate body heat through the digestion of food. They must depend on external sources of heat, such as sunlight, to maintain body temperature. Temperature control is particularly important when snakes are digesting a meal or, in the case of females, reproducing. Many snakes increase the amount of time spent basking in the sun after they have eaten a large meal in order to speed up the digestive process. To conserve their heat, snakes coil up tightly, so that only a small portion of their skin is exposed to cooler air.

● According to the passage, which of the following is NOT true about snakes?

(a) One reason snakes coil their bodies is to keep warm.

(b) A main way snakes get heat is by lying in sunlight.

(c) Maintaining body temperature is especially important for digestion.

(d) Snakes cannot digest large amounts of food.

9

Eagles lay from one to three eggs. Five to ten days after a successful copulation, the female lays a speckled off-white or buff colored egg about the size of a goose's. The second egg is laid a few days later, followed by a possible third. The 35 days of incubation duties are shared by both male and female, but it is the female who spends most of her time on the nest.

● According to the passage, which of the following is NOT true about eagles?

(a) They lay their eggs one by one.

(b) The female is mainly responsible for caring for the eggs.

(c) The color of the egg is usually dark brown.

(d) The egg can be laid as early as 5 days after fertilization.

10

Erosion is the removal of rock and soil material by natural processes, principally running water, glaciers, waves, and wind. Erosion transports rocky material after the process of weathering has broken bedrock down into smaller, moveable pieces.

● According to the passage, which of the following statements is NOT true?

(a) Weathering is the opposite of erosion.

(b) When rock erodes, it gets smaller.

(c) Erosion can be caused by the forces of water or wind.

(d) Erosion is a natural process.

Hackers Test

Read the following passages and the questions about them.
Choose the one best answer for each question.

1   What made the new dance 'modern' was its subject matter and, along with its revolutionary stance on stage, its progressive positions off the stage. The issues of the Spanish people's fight against fascist takeover during 1936-1939 and the worker's movement in the United States were linked by an overarching concern for the lower ranks of society. In this way it is comparable to other forms of art in the 1930s. Especially the theater plays in these years showed a concern for social and political issues. Dance, as a theater art, could do the same, but it was more in a symbolic, abstract way, since it was mostly non-verbal.

Martha Graham showed her concerns for social issues in her earliest works. Martha started creating her dances in 1929, with the dances 'Heretic' and 'Sketches for the People', which were studies for mass movement. Although they were apolitical, they had a clear social message. Some of her works were political. Between 1936 and 1939 she showed her support for the Spanish in the Franco war. Graham's dances 'Immediate Tragedy' and 'Deep Song' were about the Spanish war. The dances showed sympathy for Spain and commitment towards social relevance. It meant Martha Graham's movement toward social realism.

Some of Graham's works of the early thirties expressed a special interest in primitive culture. In that period she made a trip to New Mexico and became interested in the American Indian culture in that part of the country. She produced works like 'Primitive Canticles', 'Primitive Mysteries', 'Incantation' and 'Dolorosa' (all 1931), and 'Ceremonials' (1932), in which she distilled a pre-Christian religious sentiment into generally applicable terms. She later began to develop a line of choreography that dealt with the specifically American Mythic heritage. The first of these works was 'Frontier'.

1. According to the passage, which is NOT true about modern dance?
    (a) It was an art form performed on the stage.
    (b) It delivered its message in a mostly non-verbal way.
    (c) It was more symbolic and abstract than theater plays.
    (d) It did not demonstrate interest for social issues.

2. In the passage, which sentence about Martha Graham is NOT true?

   (a) From the beginning of her career, her work was socially aware.

   (b) In the 1930s, she supported Franco against the Spanish.

   (c) Her work 'Frontier' was part of her larger interest in primitive culture.

   (d) Most of her works about the primitive had religious themes.

2   In the 19th century North American archaeology was influenced both by cultural and Darwinian evolution, and, as an extension of this philosophy, the works of Lubbock. It was also influenced by the national idea of manifest destiny. Although a racist sentiment existed in North America prior to the 19th century, the works of Darwin and Lubbock justified and solidified this belief. Based on the Enlightenment concept of unilinear progress, Lubbock (1834-1913) maintained that European intervention in North America promoted the progress of man. Lubbock portrayed the "natural inferiority", and the general condition of Native Americans, as rooted in biological conditions. Therefore, his beliefs absolved the expansionist settlers from the responsibility of the native inhabitants' demise. The imposition of inferior roles on native groups was made to appear less a political act than a consequence of their limited natural abilities.

Due to the rise in "ethnic archaeology", based on the evolutionary approach, in the 1860's and 1870's archaeology and ethnology were allied. Ethnologists describing and recording the "primitiveness" of the native inhabitants could, in effect, supply all the information needed to know about an ancient culture. Between 1840 and 1914, explorers and scholars developed several models of cultural history to account for the numerous prehistoric ruins found in the American Southwest. In accordance with the Enlightenment concept of psychic unity, Morgan, in his *Ancient Society* (1877), presented a universal cultural evolution that placed Euro-American society at the forefront of human advancement. His sequence of evolution was based on a tripartite division of progress into lower/middle/upper, savagery, barbarism, and finally civilization. In Morgan's view, no indigenous New World society had progressed beyond Middle Barbarism. Although the cultural-historical approach still remained in use, in the early 20th century the functionalist approach also gained following. Functionalism was first concerned with how tools and artifacts were made and what use was made of them. Instead of an interest in the artifacts themselves, people were interested in their function, which later further extended to an interest in how the people who made the tools had lived.

1. North American archaeology in the 1800s was affected by all of the following EXCEPT
    (a) the national belief that settlers had the right to expand their territory
    (b) the pre-existing racist sentiment, combined with Darwin's evolution theory
    (c) Lubbock's theory that Native Americans could progress through biological conditions
    (d) the idea from the Enlightenment that progress took place in one line

2. According to the passage, all of the following are true EXCEPT that
    (a) Morgan considered Euro-American society to be at the beginning of his evolution sequence
    (b) Lubbok viewed European intervention in America as positive
    (c) Morgan's theory of evolution allied itself with the psychic unity concept of the Enlightenment
    (d) functionalism gained a following in the early 20th century

---

3 Although sound recording was independently invented in 1877 by Thomas Edison in the United States and by Charles Cros in France, the primary means of disseminating popular music until the 1920s was printed sheet music. By the late 19th century, the music-publishing business was centralized in New York City, particularly in an area of lower Manhattan called Tin Pan Alley. The first popular song to sell one million copies, "After the Ball" (1892) by Charles K. Harris, inspired rapid growth in the music-publishing industry.

Composers were hired to rapidly produce popular songs by the dozens, and the techniques of Foster and the pleasure-garden composers were further developed. Songs had to be simple, memorable, and emotionally appealing to sell to large audiences. Vaudeville had replaced minstrel shows as the dominant live-entertainment medium. Singers such as Al Jolson and Sophie Tucker promoted Tin Pan Alley songs on cross-country tours. Ragtime pieces written by professional composers such as Scott Joplin represented another stage in the influence of African American music on mainstream popular music.

The golden age of Tin Pan Alley occurred during the 1920s and 1930s. The best-known songs of this period were produced by a small group of composers and lyricists based in New York City. In most cases, composers and lyricists worked in pairs: George Gershwin and Ira Gershwin, Richard Rodgers and Lorenz Hart and, beginning in 1943, Richard Rodgers and Oscar Hammerstein II. Tin Pan Alley songs were popularized in Broadway musical comedies, the successor to vaudeville, and by popular singers accompanied by dance orchestras.

1. According to the passage, which of the following statements about the Tin Pan Alley songs is NOT true?

   (a) Ira Gershwin, Lorenz Hart, and Oscar Hammerstein II all wrote Tin Pan Alley songs.
   (b) Some songs gained attention when performed in Broadway musical comedies.
   (c) The songs were taken on national tours by vaudevile singers.
   (d) The first popular songs appealed to their audiences' emotions through their complexity.

2. According to the passage, which of the following historical figures is NOT mentioned as a musical artist?

   (a) Scott Joplin
   (b) Lorenz Hart
   (c) Charles K. Harris
   (d) Charles Cros

---

4 Only a few years after the Pilgrims set foot on American soil, Harvard College was established in 1634. Eight other colleges were already in existence before the Revolutionary War. The Land Ordinance of 1785, opening a large area between the Ohio and Mississippi Rivers for settlement, set aside one-sixteenth of the land to cover the expenses of public education. Later the Morrill Act of 1862 gave a large piece of land to each state so that the profit from that land would pay for establishing agricultural and technical colleges. Many of these state colleges have since grown into large universities.

Today there are a great variety of types of colleges and universities in the United States. Some are state-supported, others are privately endowed, and still others are supported by religious sects. Some of these institutions focus on a general liberal education, while others focus on technical and practical training, on specialized research, on the fine arts, or on preparation for the practice of a profession. Between 1900 and 1950 college enrollment multiplied tenfold, and it has grown much greater since then. The students represent all economic levels of society and all races.

State governments and other governmental agencies, special foundations, and the colleges themselves grant many scholarships to students with special abilities and to those with financial needs. And the federal government has also established a large-scale program offering long-term loans to students to help them meet their educational expenses. The goal is to make higher education available to everyone who is willing and capable, regardless of his or her financial situation.

---

1. All of the following are reasons why public education increased EXCEPT that
   (a) the Land Ordinance indirectly funded the costs of public education
   (b) the Morrill Act gave all states enough land on which to build their own college
   (c) the government came up with programs to help students pay their tuition bills
   (d) states were given resources to establish agricultural and technical college

2. In the passage, which is NOT mentioned as a scholarship source for students?
   (a) The federal government
   (b) State governments
   (c) Special foundations
   (d) Colleges and universities

---

5   Census is a term usually referring to an official count by a national government of its country's population. A population census determines the size of a country's population and the characteristics of its people, such as their age, sex, ethnic background, marital status, and income. National governments also conduct other types of censuses, particularly of economic activity. An economic census collects information on the number and characteristics of farms, factories, mines, or businesses.

Most countries of the world conduct population censuses at regular intervals. By comparing the results of successive censuses, analysts can see whether the population is growing, stable, or declining, both in the country as a whole and in particular geographic regions. They can also identify general trends in the characteristics of the population. Because censuses aim to count the entire population of a country, they are very expensive and have elaborate administrative operations, and thus are conducted relatively infrequently. The United States conducts a population census every ten years, a decennial census, and Canada conducts one every five years, a quinquennial census. Economic censuses are generally conducted on a different schedule from population census.

Censuses of population usually try to count everyone in the country as of a fixed date, often known as Census Day. Generally, governments collect the information by sending a questionnaire in the mail or a census taker to every household or residential address in the country. The recipients are instructed to complete the questionnaire and send it back to the government, which processes the answers. Trained interviewers visit households that do not respond to the questionnaire and individuals without mail service, such as the homeless or those living in remote areas.

1. A population census may be used to gather any of the following types of information EXCEPT

   (a) The number of minorities in a country
   (b) The number of illegal immigrants in a country
   (c) The number of married people in a country
   (d) The ratio of men to women in a country

2. According to the passage, which sentence about population censuses is NOT true?

   (a) The designated date for counting people for the Census is known as Census Day.
   (b) Most censuses are returned to the government through the mail.
   (c) Except in the US and Canada, censuses are inexpensive and regularly conducted.
   (d) Homeless and rural people are included in censuses.

---

6 A psychological test is any of a variety of testing procedures for measuring psychological traits and behavior, or for studying some specialized aspect of ability. Several forms of testing have arisen from the need to understand personality and its relationship to psychological disorders.

Projective tests attempt to measure personality based on the theory that individuals tend to project their own unconscious attitudes into ambiguous situations. Best known of the projective tests is that of the Swiss psychiatrist Hermann Rorschach (1884-1922), who used a group of standardized inkblots and asked the client to relate what the pictures brought to mind. The thematic apperception test (TAT), developed by the American psychologist Henry A. Murray, uses a standard series of provocative yet ambiguous pictures about which the client must tell a story. Each story is carefully analyzed to uncover underlying needs, attitudes, and patterns of reaction.

Other personality tests use questionnaires that limit the test-taker's responses to "true," "false," or "cannot say." These tests have a much higher level of standardization than projective tests, and hence are often called objective tests. One of the most widely used objective tests is the Minnesota Multiphasic Personality Inventory (MMPI), created in 1942 and updated in the early 1990s with the goal of defining a "normal" personality and detecting specific deviances. The test produces profiles that can predict class inclusion for such psychological disorders as schizophrenia, sociopathy depression, and hysteria. The MMPI has been useful in distinguishing individuals with mental illness from the normal population, but has been less helpful in diagnosing specific disorders.

1. Tests measuring psychological traits and behavior have all of the following characteristics EXCEPT that

    (a) they are used only for people with mental disorders

    (b) some ask true/false questions

    (c) they operate under the theory that personality and psychological disorders are connected

    (d) they analyze the answers the subject gives for personality clues

2. According to the passage, which of the following choices is NOT a true statement about the MMPI?

    (a) Its strength is its ability to distinguish exactly which mental disorder a subject has.

    (b) It does not consider sociopathy and hysteria to be "normal" personality types.

    (c) It is a popular test that has been used for over 50 years.

    (d) It has a more standardized format than the Rorschach and TAT tests.

---

7 Although generally associated with humid tropics, buffaloes have been reared for centuries in temperate countries such as Italy, Greece, Yugoslavia, Bulgaria, Hungary, Romania, and in the Azerbaijan and Georgian republics of the FSU (Former Soviet Union). In 1807 Napoleon brought Italian buffaloes to the Landes region of southwestern France and released them near Mont-de-Marsan. They became feral and multiplied prodigiously in the woods and dunes of the littoral, but unfortunately the local peasants found them easy targets. With the fall of Napoleon the whole herd was killed for meat. In the twelfth century Benedictine monks introduced buffaloes from their possessions in the Orient to work the lands of their abbey at Auge in northeastern France. In the thirteenth century a herd was introduced to England by the Earl of Cornwall, the brother of Henry III. Nothing is known about how well either herd survived. Buffaloes are also maintained on the high, snowy plateaus of Turkey as well as in Afghanistan and the northern mountains of Pakistan.

The buffalo has greater tolerance of cold weather than is commonly supposed. The current range of the buffalo extends as far north as 45 degrees latitude in Romania and the sizable herds in Italy and the FSU range over 40 degrees N latitude. Philadelphia and Peking are at comparable latitudes. In the Southern Hemisphere the 40-degree line of latitude easily encompasses Cape Town, Buenos Aries, Melbourne, and most of New Zealand's North Island. Cold winds and rapid drops in temperature, however, appear to have caused pneumonia and sometimes death. Most of the animals in Europe are the Mediterranean breed but other River type buffaloes, mainly Murrahs from India, have been introduced to Bulgaria and the FSU, which indicates that at least the River breeds have some cold tolerance.

1. According to the passage, which sentence about buffaloes is NOT true?

   (a) Napoleon introduced Italian buffaloes to France.

   (b) Buffalo breeds include Mediterranean, River and Murrah types.

   (c) In the 1900s, French peasants slaughtered buffaloes out of anger against Napoleon.

   (d) Monks used buffalo as farm animals to work their land.

2. The passage supports all of the following statements EXCEPT that

   (a) the buffalo is often misunderstood as being well tolerant to cold

   (b) buffaloes did not exist in Landes before Napoleon brought them

   (c) most of the buffaloes in Europe are the Mediterranean breed

   (d) buffaloes can live as wild animals or be domesticated for work

---

8   The tongue, a muscular organ located on the floor of the mouth, is an extremely mobile structure in humans and an important accessory organ in such motor functions as speech, chewing, and swallowing. In conjunction with the cheeks, it is able to guide and maintain food between the upper and lower teeth until mastication is completed. The tongue's mobility aids in creating a negative pressure within the oral cavity, thus enabling mammals to suckle.

The mucous membrane that covers the tongue varies greatly. Especially important as a peripheral sense organ, it contains groups of specialized epithelial cells, known as taste buds that carry stimuli from the oral cavity to the central nervous system. Furthermore, the tongue's glands produce some of the saliva necessary for swallowing.

The mammalian tongue consists of a mass of interwoven, striated muscles covered with mucous membrane and interspersed with glands and a variable amount of fat. By its extrinsic muscles, the tongue is attached to the lower jaw, the hyoid bone (a U-shaped bone between the lower jaw and the larynx), the skull, the soft palate, and the pharynx. It is bound to the floor of the mouth and to the epiglottis (a plate of cartilage that serves as a lid for the larynx) by folds of its mucous membrane.

---

1. The passage mentions all of the following as functions of the tongue EXCEPT

   (a) aidng in digestion by guiding food during chewing

   (b) helping to create a negative pressure in the mouth

   (c) making saliva using its mucous membrane

   (d) transmitting messages from the mouth to the central nervous system

2. According to the passage, all of the following describe the anatomy of the tongue EXCEPT that

(a) its interior makeup is muscle and its exterior membrane

(b) the fat layer of the tongue is located under the muscle

(c) the mucous membrane glues the tongue to the mouth with its layers

(d) muscles keep it connected to the jaw and skull

---

9 The solar interior is separated into four regions according to the different processes that occur in each. Energy is generated in the core. This energy diffuses outward by radiation—mostly gamma-rays and x-rays—through the radiative zone. Then by convective fluid it flows in a boiling motion through the outermost convection zone. The thin interface layer between the radiative zone and the convection zone is where the Sun's magnetic field is thought to be generated.

The Sun's core is the central region where nuclear reactions consume hydrogen to form helium. These reactions release the energy that ultimately leaves the surface as visible light. These reactions are highly sensitive to temperature and density. The individual hydrogen nuclei must collide with enough energy to give a reasonable probability of overcoming the repulsive electrical force between these two positively charged particles. The temperature at the very center of the Sun is about 15,000,000°C (27,000,000 °F) and the density is about 150 g/cm^3, about 10 times the density of gold or lead. Both the temperature and the density decrease as one moves away from the center of the Sun.

---

1. According to paragraph 1, all of the following are true EXCEPT that

(a) movement within the Sun happens through boiling motion and rays

(b) the regions of the Sun are differentiated from each other by their processes

(c) the Sun's magnetic field serves to block the radiation coming from the radiate zone

(d) next to the innermost zone of the Sun is the radiative zone

2. Which of the following is NOT true about the Sun's nuclear reactions?

(a) They are dependent upon proper conditions of temperature and density.

(b) They take place inside the Sun but their products eventually leave the Sun.

(c) During the reaction, hydrogen combines with helium to form positively charged particles.

(d) The chief product made by the Sun's reaction is energy.

10 One of the reasons that the water pollution problem is so severe is that it is not actually illegal to dump pollutants into water bodies. Sewage, sludge, garbage, and even toxic pollutants are all dumped into the water. Often, governments either do not care or simply look the other way. Across the world, about half of all sewage is dumped into water bodies in its original form. No efforts are made to disinfect the sewage or to remove especially harmful pollutants. Even if sewage is treated, problems still arise. Treated sewage forms sludge, which is sent out into the sea and dumped. Many cities and countries dump sewage out at sea. Often, they place it not far from their own coastline, killing all the sea wildlife in the dumping area.

In addition to sewage, chemicals dumped by industries and governments are another major source of water pollution. Oil, such as that spilled by transport ships, has been dumped into the water ever since the US Civil War. Every year, between 1 and 10 billion tons of oil are spilt, killing many species and destroying the ecosystem in the area. Cleanup efforts have been weak, as only about 10% of the oil is removed by the most successful efforts.

1. Which of the following is NOT mentioned in the passage as a cause of water pollution?
   (a) Dumping pollutants in their original form, without any treatment
   (b) Government disinterest in the problem
   (c) Failure to adequately warn people of the dangers of water pollution
   (d) Lack of appropriately stringent laws against dumping

2. Which of the following is NOT mentioned as a water pollutant?
   (a) oil
   (b) sludge
   (c) nuclear waste
   (d) garbage

동팡이의 일기 (2) : 토플 R/C ②

#

영어를 아주 잘해서 L/C가 나온다면 또 모를까..

학원에서 강의 하는 식으로 기계적으로 하면 나가서 망합니다..

토플 잘 나왔다고 영어 잘하는줄 아시면 곤란합니다..아닌경우도 꽤 있어여..

미국가서 here or to go..이거에 울지 않으신 분..손들어 봐요..그 보다 윗 버젼..tray or pack?..

#

R/C는 약이 없습니다..해석이 안되면..당합니다..

손싸매고 멍허니 본다고 해도 꼬부랑 글자가 읽혀질리도 없고..

GRE에 비한다면 비록 적지만..그래도..단어는 또 얼마나 많이 외워야 하는지..

결국 유학가서 전공서적 볼 때 가장 많이 도움이 된답니다..남들이..

(사실은 거기서 거기겠지만..다른 두 개보담야..)

또한 GRE 할때에도 다른 두 개 섹션은 없다고 보지만..

리딩은 죽어라고 꼬투리 잡습니다..미칩니다..환장합니다..돌아버립니다..

Reading

Progressive Test 2-① / 2-②

Hackers Progressive Test 2-①

● Read through the passages and solve each question which covers the preceding 2nd week's chapters; Ch.4&5 Inference Questions and Ch.6 Negative Questions.

[1] The two main theorists influencing the study of child development are Erikson and Piaget. Both believe that development occurs in stages and that in each stage the individual must grapple with certain universal developmental tasks before proceeding with the tasks of the following stages. Behaviorism is a different type of theory, but it is also influential and, at times, useful.

Erikson's *Eight Stages of Man* covers the psychosocial domain, relating to emotions and interactions, and transmutes Freudianism into something that ordinary people can understand. Erikson was the first to extend the theory of development into adulthood and was also interested in the way cultural differences in rearing may influence adult personality patterns. Erikson theorizes that there are eight stages of development and that in each, the individual faces a profound psychosocial conflict that must be resolved in either a healthy or an unhealthy way. For example, in infancy, the child's conflict relates to trust vs. mistrust, and on this resolution the rest of personality development depends. Erikson's ideas are extremely commonsensical and easy to grasp.

Piaget's Stages of Intellectual Development relate to how children think; particularly how they think about problems of logic, math, and spatial relations. He believed that throughout childhood and beyond, the individual constructs, through innumerable interactions with the environment, his or her version of the human knowledge that we all share. Piaget did a lot of observation of his own children, especially in infancy, and conducted interviews with older children to find out how they were thinking. While his ideas are rather difficult to grasp, they are fascinating when applied to that favorite parental pastime, child-watching.

Behaviorism is based on observations of animal behavior and tries to explain children's actions without reference to anything internal or introspective, seeing just sequences of behaviors and how they follow others. The concepts of reinforcement and punishment are valuable in understanding how to handle questions of discipline, something we all need help with at some time or another.

1. What does the passage mainly discuss?
   (a) Three psychological theories about child development
   (b) Intellectual development in childhood
   (c) The change in psychosocial conflicts from childhood to adulthood
   (d) Behaviorism and its relationship to Erikson's and Piaget's theory

2. According to the passage, which of the following can be explained using Behaviorism?

(a) A child who is suffering from psychological trauma because of his parents' death
(b) A child who hits his friend repeatedly
(c) A child who experiences emotional shock from a car accident
(d) A child who suffers from acrophobia

3. Why does the author give an example of trust vs. mistrust in infancy?

(a) To explain that Erickson's ideas are easy to grasp
(b) To discuss the significance of culture difference
(c) To give an example of an underlying psychosocial conflict
(d) To show that psychosocial conflict must be resolved

4. What does the author mainly discuss in paragraph 3?

(a) The main concepts of Piaget's theory are reinforcement and punishment.
(b) Piaget's stages are difficult but very important.
(c) Piaget's Stages of Intellectual Development are related to studies of children's way of thinking.
(d) Innumerable interactions with the environment are important to a child's development.

5. According to the passage, all of the following questions can be explained through child development theory EXCEPT

(a) What role does genetic inheritance play in personality?
(b) What is the most effective way to discipline a child?
(c) What role does the nurturing adult play in shaping the child?
(d) What are the different kinds of social influences that affect child development?

6. It can be inferred from the passage that when compared to Erikson, Piaget conducted his research

(a) in a completely objective manner using personal observation
(b) primarily focusing on personal experiences
(c) more biased on the aspects of social development
(d) concentrating more on the psychological domain

7. According to the passage, all of the following are true EXCEPT that

(a) psychosocial conflict could be resolved in an unhealthy way
(b) Erickson's eight stages of man are related to emotions and interaction
(c) Freud extended the theory of development into adulthood
(d) Piaget observed his own children to examine their thought process

8. Erikson's development theory included all of the following thoughts EXCEPT that

(a) children understand concepts differently at different stages
(b) personality characteristics appear to be heritable to some degree
(c) people are driven by many kinds of psychological and social forces
(d) development is an ongoing process

9. It can be inferred from paragraph 2 that Freudianism is

(a) a theory based on child development
(b) a theory that is not widely understood by the public
(c) a theory that contradicts Erikson's theory
(d) a scientifically well organized theory

10. According to Erikson's theory, that which influences personality development is

(a) accumulative
(b) commonsensical
(c) childlike
(d) cultural

---

[2] ■ At the dawn of the industrial age, whales were an important natural resource which humans had been exploiting for centuries. ■ Whales were especially valued for their oil, which was used primarily as fuel for lamps. ■ Regular whale oil, "train oil," was extracted from the blubber that encased the whale's body. ■ The best oil was spermaceti, found only in the nose of the sperm whale. If exposed to air it would congeal, and was used for smokeless candles, regarded as the finest quality candles ever made.

The sperm whale also sometimes produced ambergris, a sticky substance from the intestines used in the manufacture of perfume. Baleen, the bony, plankton-straining ribs in the mouths of most whales, excepting the sperm whale, was lightweight and had good tensile qualities. It was used for a variety of things, including corset stays, umbrella ribs, fishing rods, buggy whips, carriage springs, and skirt hoops. Bones from the body were generally used as fertilizer.

Whaling was a major industry in the 19th century, and the United States was the pre-eminent whaling nation. According to tradition, American commercial whaling began in 1712 in New England. Whaling expanded through the 18th century, but was disrupted by the American Revolution and the Napoleonic Wars. In 1815 came peace and rapid growth in the industry. By 1833 there were 392 American whaling vessels. By 1846 there were 735 whalers, comprising 80 percent of the whaling fleet of the entire world. Each year, whaling produced 4-5 million gallons of sperm oil, 6-10 million gallons of train oil, and 1.6-5.6 million pounds of bone. The price of train oil rose from 35 cents per gallon in 1825 to 95 cents in 1855.

---

1. What is the author's main point in paragraph 1?

(a) The whale is a very useful animal.
(b) Different whales produce different types of oil.
(c) Train oil contributed greatly to the development of world industry.
(d) Whale oil was considered a valuable industrial resource.

2. According to the passage, it can be inferred that spermaceti

(a) was considered a very precious material before electricity was invented
(b) was used for heating, for lubrication, soap, paint and varnish manufacturing
(c) became useless when it was exposed to air
(d) could be acquired from all kinds of whales

3. What topic is the passage primarily concerned with?

　　(a) Whaling to get natural resources
　　(b) The United States' role in the whaling industry
　　(c) The progress of civilization resulting from the whaling industry
　　(d) The whaling industry

4. The following sentence can be added to the passage.

**It was also used for heating, for lubrication, soap, paint and varnish
manufacturing, and the processing of textiles and rope.**

Where would it best fit in the passage? Click on the square[■] to add the
sentence to the passage.

5. According to the passage, baleen

　　(a) is a rib in the mouth found in all kinds of whales
　　(b) could be used for fishing rods
　　(c) was a very useful material in making perfume
　　(d) was sometimes used as fertilizer

6. It can be inferred from the passage that sperm whales were preferred
over other whales because

　　(a) it was easier to process them than others
　　(b) they had more profitable parts
　　(c) they had more blubber
　　(d) their meat was more savory

7. According to paragraph 2, which of the followings is true?

　　(a) Ambergis is used for manufacturing perfume.
　　(b) Ambergis is found in the mouth of sperm whales.
　　(c) Most whales' baleen are not valuable at all
　　(d) Sperm whale's baleen is not good enough in tensile quality to use for corset stays.

8. What can be inferred from the passage about the sperm whale?

　　(a) It doesn't eat plankton as a dietary substance.
　　(b) Its meat was widely popular all over the world.
　　(c) Some part of it was used to make carriage springs.
　　(d) People took advantage of it even before the industrial age.

9. According to the passage, in the mid 19th century, America

　　(a) owned 80 percent of whaling ships in the world
　　(b) produced more sperm oil than train oil
　　(c) was catching more and more whales, causing prices to decilne
　　(d) came to have 392 whaling vessels, with rapid growth in the industry

10. Which of the following best describes the organization of the passage?

　　(a) A biological analysis of the different whales in New England
　　(b) An explanation of the whaling industry and its expansion
　　(c) A chronological description of the whaling industry in the United States
　　(d) A contrast of the effects of the American Revolution to those of the Napoleonic Wars

[3]   Art Deco, a style popular in the·1920s and 1930s, was used primarily in the design of buildings, furniture, jewelry, and interior decor. ■ Art Deco is characterized by sleek, streamlined forms, geometric patterns, and experiments with industrial materials such as metals, plastics, and glass. ■ The term 'art deco' is a shortening of the title of a major Paris design exhibition held in 1925: Exposition Internationale des Arts Decoratifs et Industriels Modernes (International Exposition of Modern Industrial and Decorative Arts). ■ Art Deco quickly gained hold in the United States, where it reached the height of its achievement in architecture, especially in New York City's soaring skyscrapers of the late 1920s and early 1930s, such as the Chrysler, Daily News, and Empire State buildings. ■ Because many Art Deco buildings went up during a period of economic collapse known as the Great Depression, the style is sometimes referred to as "depression moderne". ■

Art Deco grew out of a conscious effort to simplify the elaborately curved shapes and plantlike motifs of Art Nouveau, the prevailing style in architecture and design at the beginning of the 20th century. Art Deco retained the tendency of art nouveau toward abstraction and repetition of forms but moved away from the shapes and motifs of the older style.

The clean lines, streamlining, and symmetry of Art Deco designs reflect the increasing importance of industrial products in everyday life, and a corresponding interest among modern artists and designers in the beauty of machinery. Art Deco objects were usually not mass-produced, yet many of them possess qualities belonging to mass production: simplicity, unvaried repetition, and geometric patterns. Designers began to look at industrial products less as utilitarian objects than as inspiration for art.

1. What does the passage mainly discuss?
    (a) The features of Art Deco
    (b) A popular painting style of the 1920s and 1930s.
    (c) Major differences between Art Deco and Art Nouveau.
    (d) Popular designs in the Great Depression.

2. The following sentence can be added to the passage.

    The style first became evident there.

    Where would it best fit in the passage? Click on the square[■] to add the sentence to the passage.

3. Why was art deco known as "depression moderne"?
    (a) Its simplicity reflected a shortage of materials.
    (b) The Great Depression destroyed most of the good Art Deco buildings
    (c) It was the newest modern style during the Great Depression.
    (d) Many Art Deco buildings were constructed during the Great Depression.

4. It can be inferred from the passage that Art Deco was popular in the 1920s and 1930s because

    (a) it correlated well with the manufacturing and industrial environment of the times

    (b) the economic situation greatly influenced architectural styles

    (c) it drew a clear line between art and manufacture

    (d) it was very cheap to produce, though not very beautiful

5. Which of the following is mentioned as a similarity between Art Deco and Art Nouveau?

    (a) Easily duplicable forms

    (b) Recurrence of patterns

    (c) Style of lines

    (d) Adorned details

6. Why does the author mention "simplicity, unvaried repetition and geometric patterns" in paragraph 3?

    (a) They were some characteristics of mass production exemplified by Art Deco.

    (b) They were unique qualities of Art Deco.

    (c) Because of these kinds of qualities, Art Deco designs influenced industrial products.

    (d) They are the main reasons art deco was popular in the 1920s and 1930s.

7. It can be inferred from the passage that when compared to Art Deco, Art Nouveau tends to

    (a) apply designs and configurations

    (b) use strong color contrasts

    (c) look more modern and concrete

    (d) give off a comfortable feeling

8. Which of the following is mentioned as an influence of industrial products on Art Deco?

    (a) Focus on functional aspects

    (b) Dynamic patterns

    (c) Sleek lines

    (d) Soft colors

9. According to the passage, which statement about Art Deco is NOT true?

    (a) It was applied to everyday life.

    (b) It was a retrospective style.

    (c) It had several similar forms.

    (d) It was popular in the early 20th century.

10. Which of the following best describes the organization of the passage?

    (a) A comparison of two mainstream art styles in the 1930s

    (b) A detailed description of the pragmatism of Art Deco

    (c) Highlights of the function of Art Deco in architecture

    (d) An explanation of the overall characteristics of Art Deco

[4] In the early 1800s, most newspapers were weeklies, though some dailies did exist in coastal cities. There were two types of newspapers: commercial and political. Both commercial and political newspapers were expensive, and sold for around six cents. People could not buy them on the street; instead, they had to pay for a full year's subscription. This meant that only the mercantile and political elites could afford to buy newspapers. Because of this, news focused mainly on politics, business and the comings and goings of ships in the port. Then, in the 1830s (closer to the 1870s and 1880s in Canada), the penny press revolutionized the way news was produced, distributed and consumed.

Instead of relying on subscriptions and political funding for revenue, the penny papers chose to rely on advertising. They were therefore able to offer their version of news to the public for merely a penny and sold their papers in the streets.

Since many more people could now afford to buy a paper, the penny press had to try to offer something for every type of reader. So it started hiring reporters to seek out up-to-date news about everyday life. As a result, the news emphasis shifted to local happenings, and papers began including illustrations, lifestyle tips and other things that would interest the working class. News also became less political, though no less colorful, because the penny papers refused to be affiliated with any political party. Much of this was because they needed mass audiences to attract advertisers, and could not afford to offend anyone with different political beliefs. Part of it was also because people really believed newspapers should be free from political influence. This period was the beginning of the modern press and journalism.

1. What does the passage mainly discuss?
   (a) The history of modern journalism
   (b) The two types of newspapers in the early 1800s
   (c) The origin and influence of the penny press
   (d) The difference and similarities between commercial and political newspapers

2. In 1810, the main consumers of commercial newspapers included
   (a) actors
   (b) inland traders
   (c) ranchers
   (d) statesmen

3. The author organizes the discussion of newspapers in the 19th century in terms of
   (a) a comparison of commercial and political newspapers
   (b) a description of the relationship between politics and advertising
   (c) an analysis of the spread of newspapers
   (d) a classification of dailies and weeklies

4. It can be inferred from the passage that the penny press was distinct from other papers because of its

   (a) lack of a subscription policy
   (b) biased but light political articles
   (c) way of arranging colors to draw attention
   (d) advertisements that appealed to the higher classes

5. How could the penny papers sell their newspapers for only a penny?

   (a) Merchants and political elites supported them.
   (b) The government wanted to publish a newspaper that was free from political influence.
   (c) They relied on advertising.
   (d) They relied on political funding for revenue.

6. How did the penny press revolutionize the way newspapers were produced?

   (a) It discovered a new revenue source for newspapers.
   (b) It maintained a firm political viewpoint.
   (c) It sold newspapers to the illiterate.
   (d) It published only enjoyable content.

7. It can be inferred from the passage that in the early 19th century, newspapers were not sold on the street because

   (a) publishers wanted to keep their dignity
   (b) they were too costly to print extra copies that might not be sold
   (c) the quality of ink and papers were too poor to endure sun and wind on the street
   (d) newspapers dealt with affairs too delicate to be read on the street

8. According to paragraph 3, which of the following statements is true?

   (a) The penny press sought out affiliations with political parties.
   (b) The penny press needed mass audiences to attract advertisers.
   (C) The penny press tried to offend anyone with different political beliefs.
   (d) People believed newspapers should have a political influence.

9. It can be inferred from paragraph 3 that

   (a) political news became more accessible than before after the rise of the penny papers
   (b) because many people bought newspapers, the price of newspapers went down
   (c) the penny press kept its focus on political matters while trying to attract the working class
   (d) reporters tended to write about current events that affected the majority of the population

10. What is the modern press and journalism that the author discusses in the last paragraph?

   (a) A politically neutral stance in regard to current affairs
   (b) A refusal to report about political affairs
   (c) Entertaining articles that appeal to most people
   (d) Newspapers that are affordable for everyone

Hackers Progressive Test 2-②

● Read through the passages and solve each question which covers the preceding 2nd week's chapters; Ch.4&5 Inference Questions and Ch.6 Negative Questions.

[1]   For better or for worse, the skyscraper is America's gift to architecture. ■ This kind of construction became possible when light but strong steel frames could be erected and after powerful elevators had been developed. ■

Louis Sullivan, the pioneer architect of skyscrapers, built the first one in Chicago in 1884. ■ Before long, New York began constructing them, and soon every large city—as well as every city that wished to be considered important—followed suit. ■ As the number of its skyscrapers increased, some of New York's central streets began to resemble canyons between high walls. Therefore a city law was passed, ruling that the upper stories of tall buildings must be set back so that some light and air could come through to the street. As a result, New York has a unique as well as a very interesting skyline. Although skyscrapers are built upward because of crowding in the city and the need for additional working and living space, they have actually worsened the congestion, since they draw large numbers of people into small areas.

Modern architecture in the United States has produced other creative styles. Perhaps the most famous is the work of Frank Lloyd Wright in the first half of the 20th century. Wright designed many original public buildings and homes, using interesting, unusual materials and trying to make each structure blend into its surroundings. His ideas have greatly influenced the architects of today.

1. What does the passage mainly discuss?
    (a) The life and work of Luis Sullivan as the pioneer architect of skyscrapers
    (b) Modern American architecture
    (c) The advantages and disadvantages of skyscrapers
    (d) The beginning of skyscrapers in New York

2. According to the passage, all of the following statements about the effect of skyscrapers are true EXCEPT that
    (a) they made possible the enlargement of working and living space in cities
    (b) they attracted a large number of people into small areas
    (c) they inspired the development of powerful elevators
    (d) they gave New York a unique and interesting skyline

3. The following sentence can be added to the passage.

    Concrete and plate glass also play an important part in building such tall structures.

    Where would it best fit in the passage? Click on the square [■] to add the sentence to the passage.

4. What is the main idea of paragraph 1?

   (a) Building skyscrapers required many precedent conditions.
   (b) Skyscrapers caused many unexpected health problems.
   (c) Concrete and plate glass are important materials in constructing buildings.
   (d) It was fashionable for cities to have skyscrapers.

5. What does the author mean by referring to the skyscraper as America's gift to architecture?

   (a) The skyscraper is America's greatest source of pride in architecture.
   (b) Americans never accomplished anything architecturally significant except make skyscrapers.
   (c) Americans patented the idea of skyscrapers first.
   (d) Americans are known for developing and improving methods of skyscraper building.

6. It can be inferred from paragraph 2 that most cities

   (a) regarded skyscrapers as a sort of status symbol
   (b) had no regulations related to designs of tall buildings
   (c) subsidized builders of skyscrapers
   (d) preferred skyscrapers over shorter buildings

7. According to the passage, which of the following statements is NOT true?

   (a) Skyscrapers are considered one of the greatest inventions in American history.
   (b) Chicago preceded New York in skyscraper construction.
   (c) Skyscrapers provided apartment space for cities experiencing high population density.
   (d) The government legally protected all buildings but skyscrapers in any area.

8. Which of the following does the author mention as the main cause of New York's famous skyline?

   (a) Buildings' heights
   (b) Seasonal winds
   (c) Over congestion
   (d) Canyons' location

9. What is the author's opinion of the existence of skyscrapers in the city?

   (a) influential
   (b) negligible
   (c) ironical
   (d) problematic

10. It can be inferred from paragraph 3 that Frank Lloyd Wright's architecture was similar to the pioneers' skyscrapers in that

    (a) their original ideas were not welcomed at first
    (b) they designed buildings focusing on saving space
    (c) they took into account the surroundings when planning their designs
    (d) their constructions were innovative and influential

[2] In 1610, shortly after viewing the sun with his new telescope, Galileo Galilei made the first European observations of sunspots. Daily observations were started at the Zurich Observatory in 1749 and with the addition of other observatories, continuous observations were obtained starting in 1849. The sunspot number is calculated by first counting the number of sunspot groups and then the number of individual sunspots. The "sunspot number" is then given by the sum of the number of individual sunspots and ten times the number of groups. Since most sunspot groups have, on average, about ten spots, this formula for counting sunspots gives reliable numbers even when the observing conditions are less than ideal and small spots are hard to see. Monthly averages, updated monthly, of the sunspot numbers show that the number of sunspots visible on the Sun waxes and wanes with an approximate 11-year cycle.

Early records of sunspots indicate that the Sun went through a period of inactivity in the late 17th century. Very few sunspots were seen on the Sun from about 1645 to 1715. Although the observations were not as extensive as in later years, the Sun was in fact well observed during this time and this lack of sunspots is well documented. This period of solar inactivity also corresponds to a climatic period called the "Little Ice Age" when rivers that were normally ice-free froze and snow fields remained year-round at lower altitudes. There is evidence that the Sun has had similar periods of inactivity in the more distant past: some Chinese observed sunspots with naked eyes. The connection between solar activity and terrestrial climate is an area of on-going research. ■

Detailed observations of sunspots have been obtained by the Royal Greenwich Observatory since 1874. ■ These data show that sunspots do not appear at random over the surface of the Sun, but rather are concentrated in two latitude bands on either side of the equator. ■ A butterfly diagram, updated monthly, showing the positions of the spots for each rotation of the sun since May 1874 shows that these bands first form at mid-latitudes, widen, and then move toward the equator as each cycle progresses. ■

1. What is the best title for this passage?
   (a) The development of equipment for observing sunspots
   (b) Causes of sunspots
   (c) Periodical change in the number of sunspots
   (d) The history of sunspot observation

2. What does paragraph 1 mainly discuss?
   (a) The importance of the Zurich Observatory in counting sunspots
   (b) The development of sunspot counting in the 17th century
   (c) The methodology of calculating the number of sunspots
   (d) Early 17th century mistakes in calculating sunspots

3. According to the passage, Galileo Galilei was

    (a) the first man to invent the telescope

    (b) the first scientist who tried to observe sunspots in Europe

    (c) a European astronomer who succeeded in seeing sunspots

    (d) a member of the famous Zurich Observatory

4. It can be inferred from the passage that observations of sunspots were performed

    (a) to show that sunspots wax and wane in number

    (b) to predict weather conditions on the earth

    (c) to diagram their location on the sun

    (d) to utilize solar energy

5. It can be inferred from paragraph 2 that in the late 17th century, the Sun

    (a) was observed by the Chinese without telescopes

    (b) did not affect territorial climate

    (c) was the principal cause of the "Little Ice Age"

    (d) had more sunspots than usual

6. The following sentence can be added to the passage.

    These observations include information on the sizes and positions of sunspots as well as their numbers.

    Where would it best fit in the passage? Click on the square[■] to add the sentence to the passage.

7. It can be inferred from the passage that when fields remain unseasonably covered with snow, it's possible that

    (a) the size of sunspots has become smaller

    (b) the direction of the solar wind has changed

    (c) the number of individual sunspots in a group has increased

    (d) the number of sunspot groups has decreased

8. According to the passage, a butterfly diagram

    (a) shows that sunspots form at random on the sun's surface

    (b) proves that the number of sunspot groups has decreased

    (c) is updated whenever new data are found

    (d) was first used by the Royal Greenwich Observatory in 1874

9. At the beginning of a solar rotation, sunspots are mostly found

    (a) all over the surface of the sun

    (b) at lower-latitudes

    (c) at mid-latitudes

    (d) on the equator

10. According to the passage, all of the following statements about sunspots are true EXCEPT that
   (a) observations on sunspots were taken at both the Zurich and the Royal Greenwich Observatories
   (b) when calculating the sunspot number, the number of sunspot groups multiplies by 10
   (c) Europeans were not the first people in the world to see sunspots
   (d) there is no regular pattern or cycle that applies to sunspots

[3] The study of archaeology goes back to ancient times. One of the first known archaeological expeditions was the excavation of the temple of Shamath at Sipper by Nabonidus, ruler of Babylon from 556 to 539 BC. The findings were displayed in a Babylonian museum after the project was over. Other classical peoples, such as the Greeks and Romans, excavated ancient burial grounds to learn about their own ancestors. After the fall of Rome, however, interest in archaeology waned as the Dark Ages cast a shadow over the past. During the Middle Ages, the study of archaeology came to a halt. History was almost completely based upon the Bible, and many people believed that artifacts that were found had been spontaneously generated by the earth, or placed there by the supernatural.

It was not until the 15th century that the study of the past was revitalized with the Renaissance. Intellectuals wished to regain the knowledge of Rome and Greece, and wealthy merchants and princes wanted to impress their peers and subjects with artifacts of the past. Some of the earliest major discoveries were the investigations of Pompeii and Herculaneum, which were destroyed by Mt. Vesuvius in 79 AD. Egypt had always been alluring, but until the discovery of the Rosetta Stone during the invasion of Napoleon's army, this ancient culture lay silent. During the 16th century in Europe, megalithic structures, such as Stonehenge, were being studied to determine their purpose. While the Renaissance marked the rebirth of archaeology, it was not until the 19th century that the field became the science that we now know it as.

A. H. Pitt-Rivers was one of the few people responsible for the establishment of archaeology as a scholarly field. Before Pitt-Rivers and others like him, archaeology was more of a treasure hunt than a science. During the mid and late 19th century, Pitt-Rivers and others demonstrated the importance of cataloging, detailed observation, and long-term preservation. He also focused more on small details and artifacts than beautiful or extraordinary findings, because he felt that ordinary things revealed more about the culture than rare items. While big finds are important, the true purpose of archaeology is to discover how ancient people lived. Everyday items, such as pots, tools, children's toys, and weapons, are the important aspects of the general population that archaeologists use to determine what life was like in ancient civilizations.

Pitt-Rivers's methods are still used today, and are the standard in the field of archaeology. An important part of archaeology is the order of the past—when a civilization lived in relation to others. To determine this, the "ages" system was used. This system was developed by the ancient Romans, and archaeologists and historians still use it today. The ages are divided up between three major ones— stone, bronze, and iron. When new civilizations are found, they can be fitted to one of these various ages. Up until this day, the boundaries of these divisions of time are changing with new findings and evidence.

1. What does the passage mainly discuss?
   (a) The important aspects of studying archeology
   (b) The dark ages of studying archeology
   (c) A brief history of archeology and archeological methods
   (d) The true purpose of studying archaeology

2. Which of the following statements about the study of the past can be inferred from the passage?
   (a) The knowledge of Romans and Greeks surpassed that of 15th century peoples.
   (b) Before the Middle Ages, digging the graves for archeological study was allowed for Greeks.
   (c) The spirit of the Renaissance partly included heretical ideas, when compared to the Middle Ages.
   (d) Though there remained no vestiges of lost cultures, stories about them were still handed down.

3. How does the author feel about the role of the Bible in archaeology?
   (a) It is absolutely right.
   (b) It is partly reliable.
   (c) It is not reasonable.
   (d) It is fairly logical.

4. According to the passage, which of the following statements is true?
   (a) There was decline of archeological study before the Middle Ages.
   (b) Ancient artifacts were not considered for royalties valuable in the 15th century.
   (c) Pitt-River asserted the importance of small details and artifacts in an aesthetic view.
   (d) "Age" system devised by Pitt-River is still influential for the today's archeologists.

5. There was great changeover of attitude toward archeology as a field of science
   (a) in the 16th century
   (b) during the Renaissance
   (c) when the megalithic culture was discovered
   (d) in the 19th century

6. What is the main topic of paragraph 3?

    (a) Pitt-Rivers' greatness as an archaeologist

    (b) The significance of everyday items in archaeology

    (c) Pitt-Rivers' method of studying archaeology

    (d) The history of the study of archaeology

7. According to the passage, Pitt-Rivers emphasized the importance of all of the following EXCEPT

    (a) finding rare items

    (b) itemizing lists

    (c) small details and tools

    (d) long-term preservation

8. According to the passage, the purpose of modern archaeology is

    (a) to revive ancient cultures in contemporary civilization

    (b) to identify new ages based on collected evidence

    (c) to determine what life was like in ancient cultures

    (d) to excavate ordinary things as well as precious ones

9. It can be inferred from paragraph 3 that most prior archaeologists before A.H. Pitt-Rivers tended to

    (a) apply aesthetic standards to findings

    (b) command their work from behind a desk with naive academic knowledge

    (c) focus more on classifying articles than on observing them accurately

    (d) collect adults' items rather than children's items

10. According to the passage, the "ages system" was used

    (a) to cross the boundaries of space and time

    (b) to document the time when the artifacts were discovered

    (c) to categorize findings into different periods

    (d) to determine the exact value of specific artifacts

[4]   The most obvious characteristics of the American crow are that it is big, black, and makes a lot of noise. The most obvious sound that crows make is the one written in English as 'caw'. Caws may be long or short, loud or relatively soft, given singly or in sequences, made by one bird alone or by two or more birds under a variety of circumstances. The caws of crows can sound different to human listeners. Within the same group of crows in a limited territory, there can be considerable variation in how the caws sound to a listener, and it has also often been noted that crows in different parts of the United States sound different from each other.

In addition to the distinctive caws, crows also make a variety of other sounds including, but not limited to, imitations of sounds of other species, including elements of human speech. ■ Of particular interest is a whole variety of other crow vocalizations that don't fit into the above categories, are fairly low volume and may be used by one crow alone or among a group of crows. ■

Observers over the centuries have noted that crows use specific sounds under specific circumstances. ■ One problem in interpreting these calls, however, has been the fact that different groups of crows, belonging to the same species but in different geographical areas, may not use or understand all of the same calls. ■

Hubert and Mable Frings (1959) noted, for example, that American eastern crows that breed in Pennsylvania and winter in the southern states among fish crows will respond to the distress call of the French jackdaw, a related bird not native to any portion of their range. Eastern crows that breed in Maine and apparently never mix with other crows, however, do not react to the jackdaw calls.

1. What is the main idea of paragraph 1?
   (a) Some unique characteristics of crows
   (b) The origin of the word, 'caw'
   (c) The characteristic sound of the crow
   (d) Differences and varieties in the sound 'caw'

2. What is the main purpose of the last paragraph?
   (a) To support that crows respond to certain sounds depending on their life experiences
   (b) To explain that crows migrate south
   (c) To illustrate the relationship between eastern crows
   (d) To describe the Frings's account with crows

3. It can be inferred from the passage that all the sounds American crows use are
   (a) genetically inherited
   (b) learned when young
   (c) learned and changed continuously throughout life
   (d) individually created

4. Which of the following factors can affect the sounds American crows make?
   (a) their diet
   (b) their habitat's climate
   (c) the size of their body
   (d) the situation they are in

5. What is the main topic of this passage?
   (a) The on-going research on crows
   (b) Some factors influencing the sounds of crows
   (c) Varieties of the sound that crows make
   (d) The characteristics of bird sounds

6. Which of the following could be a possible conclusion Hubert and Mable Frings could make based on their research?

   (a) Only American eastern crows recognize the sound of the French jackdaw because they are related.

   (b) Contact experiences with other animals make no difference between crows because they belong to the same species.

   (c) Fish crows and the French jackdaw are related, so their sounds are very similar to each other.

   (d) Crows have an ability to memorize and answer the sound of other crows.

7. The following sentence can be added to the passage.

   Alarm calls, assembly calls, distress calls, and many others have been noted.

   Where would it best fit in the passage? Click on the square[■] to add the sentence to the passage.

8. According to the passage, all of the following statements about crow caws are true EXCEPT that

   (a) crows can make caws singly or in a group

   (b) people ignored the sound of the crow until research was begun in the 20th century

   (c) while the caw is their signature sound, crows can make other sounds as well

   (d) much of the variance in crow caws is a result of habitat

9. Which of the following can be inferred from the passage?

   (a) Crows cannot live anywhere but America.

   (b) Only American eastern crows are big and black.

   (c) Eastern crows got their name from their habitat.

   (d) Crows from Pennsylvania can instinctively understand crows from Maine.

10. According to the passage, one reason crows caw is to

   (a) warn each other about danger

   (b) test if the other crow is a relative

   (c) safely exercise their voices at fairly low volume

   (d) humorously imitate the voices of humans

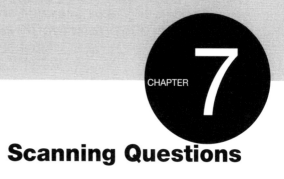

CHAPTER 7

Scanning Questions

7

Scanning Questions

O v e r v i e w

Scanning 문제는 역시 사실(fact)적 사고와 관련된 세부적 사항의 이해를 묻는 문제로, 앞서 학습했던 restatement문제의 파생형이라고 할 수 있다. 다만 4지 선다형 문제유형에서 탈피, 정답에 해당되는 부분에 직접 click 하도록 한 점이 다르다. Fact(사실) 접근 유형의 문제가 모두 그러하듯이, 문제에서 restate(재진술)되어있는 내용을 지문의 어느 부분에서 언급하고 있는지를 정확히 찾아내는 훈련이 요구된다.

Types of Questions

· Click on the paragraph in the passage that

· Click on the sentence in paragraph 1 that

| explains |
| describes |
| states |
| indicates |
| ⋮ |

....

● Strategy

 문제에서 요구하는 내용을 정확히 이해해야한다.

· 질문에서 요구하는 한 문장 만을 정확하게 찾아내야 하므로 동의어가 나타나는 부분을 찾는 것 만으로는 문제를 풀 수 없다.

· 정답은 단순히 동의어가 등장하는 문장이 아닌, 다른 문장, 즉 앞이나 뒤에 나오는 진술의 예시, 근거, 자세한 묘사 등을 물을 수 있다.

 Scanning 문제는 대부분 지문의 영역을 한정하므로, 그 부분 만큼은 정독한다.

Tip Restatement 단원의 전략을 다시 한번 상기하고 문제를 풀도록 한다.

Hackers Practice

For each item, find the sentence in the paragraph that the question asks about and underline them.

1   Though they moved into aboveground dwellings, Pueblo tribes continued to employ circular subterranean structures as kivas, or ritual spaces, where religious leaders descended into the earth to communicate with sacred clan animals or ancestral spirits. The cliff dwellings at Mesa Verde comprised the Pueblo living spaces above ground and the kivas. The kiva roofs, penetrated by ladders, served above ground as communal plazas. Here men, women, and children socialized, worked, and prepared food. But architectural historians have imagined these courtyards also as urban theaters, where the tribe's leading men would suddenly appear from below, climbing upward from the kiva's smoke hole to reenact the gods' act of creation.

● Find the sentence that describes the role kivas played in Pueblo family life.

2   Before the mid-nineteenth century, people in the United States ate most foods only in season. Drying, smoking, and salting could preserve meat for a short time, but the availability of fresh meat, like that of fresh milk, was very limited; there was no way to prevent spoilage. But in 1810 a French inventor named Nicolas Appert developed the

cooking-and-sealing process of canning. And in the 1850's an American named Gail Borden developed a means of condensing and preserving milk. Canned goods and condensed milk became more common during the 1860's, but supplies remained low because cans had to be made by hand. By 1880, however, inventors had fashioned stamping and soldering machines that mass-produced cans from tinplate.

● Find the sentence that explains why, at the start, the inventions of Nicolas and Gail couldn't be key solutions for the preservation of food.

3

During the latter half of the 1900s, the cinema industry entered into a profound crisis. With the rise of the nickelodeon, the number of theaters exhibiting films had grown so rapidly that producers were unable to meet demand. Forced to show the same film as the competitor down the block, theater owners looked to sound practices to differentiate their products. Where previous films had been only intermittently accompanied by a vaudeville orchestra, a lone untrained pianist, or not at all, exhibitors now sought to raise the tone of their establishments through sound. Eschewing popular music and ragtime, theaters instead increasingly featured light classical accompaniment performed by competent musicians.

● Find the sentence that describes why theatrical producers struggled to distinguish their films from others.

4

Christopher L. Sholes, a Milwaukee newspaperman, poet, and part-time inventor, was the main creator of the Sholes & Glidden (S&G). This machine typed only in capital letters, and it introduced the QWERTY keyboard, which is very much with us today. The keyboard was probably designed to separate frequently used pairs of typebars so that the typebars would not clash and get stuck at the printing point. The S&G was a decorative machine, boasting painted flowers and decals. The sewing machine department of the Remington arms company manufactured it. The Sholes & Glidden had limited success, but its successor, the Remington, soon became a dominant presence in the industry.

● Find the sentence that describes the success and legacy of the S&G.

5

Quilting originated in ancient times. The Chinese and Russians and the Native Americans of Mesoamerica wore quilted garments for warmth and protection. Crusaders from Western Europe encountered quilting when they met Saracens in the Holy Land. Saracen foot soldiers wore straw-filled, quilted canvas shirts in lieu of armor, and horsemen used quilted silk undershirts to keep their armor from chafing. The Crusaders took the idea back to Europe and adapted it for sleepwear and undergarments. Written records of quilts date from the 12th century. Being made of perishable materials, few early quilts have survived.

- Underline the sentence that describes the materials used in Saracens' quilts.

- Find the sentence that indicates whether the quilts made in ancient time still exist.

Hackers Test

For each item, locate the sentences in the paragraphs that the items ask about and underline them.

---

1 The size of the Earth—about 12,750 kilometers (km) in diameter—was known by the ancient Greeks, but it was not until the turn of the 20th century that scientists determined that our planet is made up of three main layers: crust, mantle, and core. This layered structure can be compared to that of a boiled egg. The crust, the outermost layer, is rigid and very thin compared with the other two. Beneath the oceans, the crust varies little in thickness, generally extending to only about 5 km. The thickness of the crust beneath continents is much more variable but averages about 30 km; under large mountain ranges, such as the Alps or the Sierra Nevada, however, the base of the crust can be as deep as 100 km. Like the shell of an egg, the Earth's crust is brittle and can break.

Below the crust is the mantle, a dense, hot layer of semi-solid rock approximately 2,900 km thick. The mantle, which contains more iron, magnesium, and calcium than the crust, is hotter and denser because temperature and pressure inside the Earth increase with depth. As a comparison, the mantle might be thought of as the white of a boiled egg. At the center of the Earth lies the core, which is nearly twice as dense as the mantle because its composition is metallic (iron-nickel alloy) rather than stony. Unlike the yolk of an egg, however, the Earth's core is actually made up of two distinct parts: a 2,200 km-thick liquid outer core and a 1,250 km-thick solid inner core. As the Earth rotates, the liquid outer core spins, creating the Earth's magnetic field.

---

1. Find the sentence in paragraph 1 that states the difference between the crust and the other layers.

_____

2. Find the sentence in paragraph 2 that states how temperature changes related to the deepness.

_____

3. Underline the sentence that explains the principle of magnetic field generation.

2   A U.S. citizen's right to seek a patent is designated by the U.S. Constitution. Actually, the Constitution doesn't explicitly grant people the right to get patents; it just says that Congress may provide inventors with rights to their inventions. However, even though it is only a suggestion, it is a suggestion made by the U.S. Constitution, therefore Congress generally felt obliged to set up some type of organization for granting patents. To this end, Congress set up the first patent board, which consisted of Thomas Jefferson, Henry Knox, and Edmund Randolph. That was about two hundred years ago, and the U.S. has been granting patents ever since.

The early patent boards were not too busy as the U.S. was primarily an agricultural society, and science and technology was a dominion shared by wealthy, over-educated Europeans, and as always, the military. But that all changed with the Industrial Revolution. Nineteenth-century businesses put a lot of stock in the power of patents to help them dominate markets and keep competitors at bay. In the "Great Telegraph Wars" of the 1870s, for example, financiers Cornelius Vanderbilt and Jay Gould hurled all manner of legal, financial and competitive assaults at each other as they ruthlessly schemed to control the most valuable assets in the industry: Thomas Edison's telegraph patents. Both these men knew, and rightly so, that huge fortunes depended on those patents.

Similarly, RCA purchased the patents of Marconi and other radio pioneers and made millions by controlling the patents of radio broadcasting. During the nineteen twenties RCA again waged a brutal battle for the patents on television, ultimately having to recognize Philo Farnsworth as the original inventor and true patent owner.

The sudden and enormous wealth of the U.S. manufacturing industry and the protections that patents provided to these industries, were not unnoticed by those wealthy, educated Europeans. These men saw that industry was the future and that a new class of European workers was being created who could capture this future. This new European class comprised engineers and technicians (and a few chemists) that were full of hope and bright ideas. The aristocracy immediately went to work calling their lawyers and representatives to make sure that laws would be put in place to accomplish two things; first to protect the valuable ideas and inventions of this new class of European workers; and second, and most importantly, to make sure that these patents were immediately to become the property of the companies that employed these engineers, lest this new class of worker actually own something of value. Japan, in turn, also adopted a U.S. style patent office to foster growth of technology and defense companies.

1. Find the sentence that indicates reason for Congress to institute the first patent board.

    _____

2. Find the sentence in paragraph 2 that explains what effects of patent were expected by businesses.

_____

3. Find the sentence that describes who were considered to be the new class of European.

_____

3   Samuel F.B. Morse led American artists in embracing the optical and chemical process that could "fit the image of the camera obscura". Ever since the Renaissance, artists had known of this "darkened chamber" or box, which could project exterior images onto a surface interior. But, until the nineteenth century, artists could preserve the naturalistic image only by tracing over it manually. Morse recalled that during his youth, while a student at Yale University, he had experimented with camera images. He had attempted to make them permanent through use of paper that had been made light sensitive by being "dipped into a solution of nitrate of silver". But he discovered to his frustration that the tonal areas were reversed in the final result: "light produced dark, and dark light." Morse had produced a negative image but did not yet know that negative film could be used to make positive photographic prints.

Later in his career, after he had become President of the National Academy of Design, Morse met the Parisian artist-inventor Louis Jacques Mande Daguerre, whose daguerreotype process employed polished, light-sensitized metal plates for producing positive images that did not invert light and dark areas. Using the vapors given off by heated mercury, Daguerre developed the film plate to "bring out" the latent image, fixed it by washing away the remaining photosensitive salts, and then toned the plate with gold chloride to heighten the light-dark contrast and the image's durability. Because of its fragility and the tendency of the silver plate to tarnish, the daguerreotype had to be further protected by a glass covering. Nevertheless, Daguerre had created clear, detailed pictures that amazed Morse.

1. Find the sentence in paragraph 1 that offers a description of why Morse was disappointed in his early experiments.

_____

2. Underline the sentence in paragraph 1 that shows Morse did not fully understand how to develop photograph prints.

3. Find the sentence in paragraph 2 that states the weak points of daguerreotype.

_____

4　　Though pollution can damage forests, much worse damage would occur from nuclear attack and fallout. Pine trees protect themselves against damage by exuding a resin which subsequently hardens and becomes amber. An explanation of the large amounts of amber found in some parts of the world could be that radiation or pollution severely damaged or stressed pine forests, leaving the trees to exude their natural defensive substance in large quantities.

After the disaster at Chernobyl, scientists studying the effects of fallout on coniferous forests found that the trees quickly absorbed dangerous radioactive cesium and incorporated it into their wood. But not by the root system—cesium sinks only slowly into the soil and it would take 25 years or more for it to begin to be taken up this way—pine needles directly absorbed the radioactive elements. Thus radioactive cesium is absorbed rapidly through pine needles and more slowly through roots subjecting the trees to severe stress for a long period without necessarily killing them. When the trees eventually did die, long lived isotopes would return to the soil to continue their damage in succeeding generations. Amber is variously dated. Baltic amber is usually dated in the Oligocene epoch of about 30 million years ago, but the Eocene epoch of 55 million years ago is also given. Valchovite, the amber from Czechoslovakia, is dated to the late Cretaceous period, the time of the extinction of the dinosaurs.

Radioactive emissions preserve. A dinosaur mummy hadrosaur discovered by Charles Sternberg died 65 million years ago, lying on its back apparently unharmed and with no signs of predators or scavengers having touched it. It is odd that it did not decay or get eaten. Supposedly it dried out in the sun, got swiftly washed downstream and got covered with fine mud so quickly that its dried skin had no time to rehydrate and decay. Dinosaur mummies are rare, but when found they are usually late Cretaceous hadrosaurs.

1. Find the sentence that explains what amber is composed of

_____

2. Find the sentence that indicates how radiation continues to affect trees long after exposure.

_____

3. Find the sentence that describes how scientists presume a dinosaur becomes a mummy.

_____

5   Seaweed, as a staple item of diet, has been used in Japan and China for a very long time. In 600 BC, Sze Teu wrote in China, "Some algae are a delicacy fit for the most honored guests, even for the King himself." Some 21 species are used in everyday cookery in Japan, six of them since the 8th century. In the west, seaweed is largely regarded as a health food and although there has been an upsurge of interest in seaweed as food in the last 20 years, it is unlikely that seaweed consumption in the west will ever be more than a fraction of that used by Japanese.

Regulations for the gathering of Palmaria palmata, a red seaweed, are mentioned in the Icelandic sagas of the 10th century. This edible seaweed has also been used in Ireland and Scotland for a very long time. Chondrus crispus (Irish Moss) was recommended as a health remedy in Ireland at the beginning of the 19th century, but its use appears to have been unknown before this. Various red algae have been used in the Mediterranean as sources of dying agents, as anthelmintics and, as other health remedies since pre-Christian times.

The use of kelps dates back to at least the 5th century in China. The main species used is Laminaria japonica, but 8-11 other species are used also, mainly in Japan. Plants are dried after harvesting and either cut into strips or powdered. In Japan, kombu—the other name for Kelp—is used in the preparation of fish, meat dishes, soups and also as a vegetable with rice. Powdered kombu is employed either in sauces and soups or is added to rice in the same way as curry. Some kinds are used in making an infusion similar to tea. In 1976, about 176,000 wet tons of Laminaria spp. were collected from wild sources in Japan and about 22,000 tons were cultivated. Laminaria is cultivated either by seeding blasted areas of rocky shores or by seeding ropes.

1. Find the sentence in paragraph 1 that offers a description of the variety of seaweed consumed in Japan.

   _____

2. Underline the sentence in paragraph 3 that tells how the kelps are prepared for consumption.

3. Find the sentence in paragraph 3 that states how Laminaria is grown.

   _____

버뮤다 삼각지대

마(魔)의 삼각지대'라고 불리는 버뮤다 삼각지대는 미국의 플로리다주 마이애미, 버뮤다, 푸에르토리코를 잇는 3각형 모양의 바다를 말하는 것이다. 이 지역에서 수많은 비행기와 선박 등이 실종되어 마의 삼각해역으로 불려 지고 있으며 그 원인으로서 UFO와 관련된 가설이 주장되기도 한다. 다른 가설로는 자연현상, 블랙홀, 4차원 공간지대 등 여러 가설들이 대두되고 있지만 완전한 해명을 못하고 있는 실정이다. 그러나 이 지역에서 심심치 않게 UFO가 바닷속에서 하늘로 치솟아 오르거나 하늘에서 바다로 들어가는 광경이 목격되기도 해 관심의 대상이 되고 있다.

이 괴현상을 설명하기 위해 많은 가설들이 나왔는데, 많은 지지를 받고 있는 이론으로는 지구 자기장의 변화를 들 수 있다. 지구의 자기장은 항상 일정한 것이 아니라 매 20~25만 년마다 자장이 바뀐다.

현재도 자장의 변화는 계속되고 있는데 그 때문에 자기적인 지진이 갑자기 발생할 수 있다는 것이며 버뮤다 삼각지대가 바로 대표적으로 자장이 불안정한 지역이라는 것이다.

더욱 심각한 것은 이런 공간이 일시적으로 형성되었다가 사라지므로 대비책을 세울 수 없다는 것이다.

버뮤다 삼각지대를 설명하기 위한 다른 이론들로는 아틀란티스의 침몰지점, 외계인의 지구인 납치설, 4차원의 세계로 통하는 문, 바닷속의 메탄 가스설(oceanic flatulence: 바닷속의 메탄 가스가 갑자기 위로 솟아나와 배가 침몰하게 되었다는 주장)등이 있다

CHAPTER **8**

Vocabulary in Context

8

Vocabulary in Context

Overview

어휘문제는 문맥상의 동의어, 반의어 등을 묻는 문제이다. 모든 단어는, meaning(의미)과 function(기능)을 동시에 가지고 있다. 가령 품사 (part of speech)가 동사인 run은 문장 내에서 주어 다음에 오는 동사 자리에 쓰일 수 있고, 의미는 "뛰다"이다. 또한 run은 뛰다 외에 "도망가 다", "인쇄되다", "경영하다" 등 여러 가지의 의미로 사용된다. 즉, 단순 히 단어 자체가 가지는 뜻만 파악하는 것으로는 문맥 안에서의 정확한 기능과 의미를 이해할 수 없다는 것이다. 단어는 문장, 문단을 구성하고, 그렇게 구성된 문맥 안에서 단어의 정확한 쓰임을 이해할 수 있게 된다. 언어능력이 어휘력과 직결된다고는 할 수 없지만, 어휘력을 탄탄히 쌓아 두어야만, 시험에서 좋은 성적을 거둘 수 있음은 의심의 여지가 없다. 단 어암기와 함께, 독해를 통해서 새로운 표현을 많이 접하는 과정을 병행 하면 어휘력 신장에 많은 도움이 된다.

Types of Questions

- According to the passage, what is "_____?"(사지선다형)
- Look at the word _____ in the passage. The word _____ is closest in meaning to ...... (사지선다형)
- Look at the word _____ in the passage. Click on the word or phrase in the bold text that has same meaning as ..... (지문에 클 릭하기)
- Look at the word _____ in the passage.
  Click on the word or phrase in the bold text that is OPPOSITE in meaning to _____

● Strategy

 동의어 혹은 반의어는 반드시 단어의 품사가 동일하게 제시된다.
- 의미가 비슷해도 품사가 다른 단어는 정답으로 고르지 말 것
- 동사는 타동사와 자동사를 구별할 것

 문맥을 통해서, 어휘문제의 정답에 접근한다.
- 단어의 사전적 의미를 외우지 못하더라도, 글의 문맥과 구조를 파악하여 문제를 해결할 수 있다.
- 지문으로부터 힌트가 될 수 있는 정보를 활용한다.

A. 관계절/부사절이 단어의 의미를 보충
- 종류:관계사 that, which, who, whom
  부사절 접속사: when, where

  Ex Doctors use jargons, which are special language used by a particular group, or profession, so that patients don't understand what they needn't know.
  : which가 이끄는 형용사절에서 jargons가 특별집단(전문집단)에서 쓰이는 언어임을 설명

B. 동격절/동격구

  Ex The shamrock, a small three-leafed clover-like plant, is the main symbol associated with the holiday Saint Patrick's Day.
  : shamrock의 의미를 컴마사이의 동격구에서 세잎식물의 일종임을 설명

C. 대명사 + 단서

  Ex Many people experience emotional problems in their adolescence. These people often wish their teenage years would fly by quickly.
  : these people, teenage years에서 adolescence가 사람의 십대시기를 말하는 것임을 확인

D. 대조되는 의미를 통한 파악
- 종류: but, however, in contrast, or, unlike, while, whereas

  Ex The fort appeared deserted, but inside it was full of government soldiers and officers.
  : but 이후의 내용과 desert가 상반됨을 이해

E. 예시를 통한 의미 파악
- 종류: as, like, for example, for instance, such as

  Ex Nutritionists say most of our diet should come from carbohydrates such as breads, cereals, rice and pasta.
  : 빵과, 곡물, 파스타 등의 예를 들어서 carbohydrates(탄수화물)의 의미를 설명

F. or 뒤에 나오는 동의어

Ex To become an astronaut, or an aviator that flies in outer space, one should complete a special 2 year training course.

: 같은 어휘의 중복을 피하면서 의미를 명확하게 해주는 or는 astronaut가 우주의 비행사임을 설명

G. 구두점의 이해

· 종류: , comma ( ) parentheses

— dash 〔 〕 bracket

" " ' '

Ex The Revolution of 1932 brought an end to monarchy—a state ruled or headed by a sole and absolute ruler—in its absolute form.

: 대쉬 사이의 구가 monarchy의 의미를 풀어서 설명

H. 접사(affixes)를 보고 의미 추측

· 접두사(prefixes): 단어의 의미에 영향을 미치는 요소

Ex maltreat hyperactive outstanding...

: mal-(이상) + treat(대우하다) = maltreat(함부로 대하다)

hyper-(과도) + active(활발한) = hyperactive(지나치게 활동적인)

out-(보다뛰어난) + standing(지위) = outstanding(저명한)

· 접미사(suffixes): 단어의 품사와 의미에 영향을 미치는 요소

Ex harm(v./n.) harmful(adj.) ⟨----⟩ harmless(adj.) harmlessly(adv.) harmlessness (n.)

: harm(해가 되다, 해) + -ful(~의 성질을 가진:형용사형 접미사) = harmful(해로운)

+ -less(~이 없는: 형용사형 접미사) = harmless(해가 없는)

harmless + - ly(양태:부사형 접미사) = harmlessly (해가 없게)

+ -ness(성질상태:추상명사 접미사) = harmlessness(해롭지 않음)

Tip 영어의 접두사와 접미사의 의미를 알아두면, 어휘력 신장에 도움이 된다.

Read the question and choose the one best answer that has a similar/opposite meaning to the shaded word in the sentence.

1

This article seeks to summarize the few similarities between these two psychology sub fields, in spite of the salient differences that distinguish them.

● The word salient is closest in meaning to

_____ (a) condign

_____ (b) conspicuous

_____ (c) coherent

_____ (c) unfamiliar

2

The biochemists, under standard biohazard code, began the tedious but necessary task of disinfecting their suits for possible contamination.

● The word tedious is closest in meaning to

_____ (a) wearisome

_____ (b) abnormal

_____ (c) sensible

_____ (d) degrading

3

During World War I, Germany had hoped that Britain would stay impartial, but German's breach of Belgian neutrality was enough for Britain to enter the war.

● The word impartial is closest in meaning to

_____ (a) unwary

_____ (b) distorted

_____ (c) honorable

_____ (d) unbiased

4

Artists from many different leftist points of view also embraced social causes, such as industrial unionism, civil rights for black Americans, and support for the anti-fascists in the Spanish Civil War.

● The word causes is closest in meaning to

_____ (a) tensions

_____ (b) goals

_____ (c) reprisals

_____ (d) results

5

Comedian Bob Hope's long career is documented in the Bob Hope Collection, which includes more than 100 scrapbooks—albums for pasting notes or pictures.

● The word scrapbooks is closest in meaning to

_____ (a) organizing envelopes

_____ (b) large-volume novels

_____ (c) high-quality inserts

_____ (d) books of collections

6

All the graduate scholarships are tenable for one year, while undergraduate scholarships can only be held for one academic semester.

● The word tenable is closest in meaning to

_____ (a) endurable

_____ (b) rational

_____ (c) maintained

_____ (d) defensible

---

7   Many dentists believe that grinding of teeth is caused by stress and advise their patients to stop moving together their teeth in such a manner, unless they want them to wear out quickly.

● The word grinding is closest in meaning to

_____ (a) rotating

_____ (b) rubbing

_____ (c) irritating

_____ (d) chewing

---

8   Insects become scarce in the winter in northern latitudes, so insectivorous birds, who are dependent upon insects for their diet, must move closer to the equator where insects are more abundant.

● The word insectivorous is closest in meaning to

_____ (a) insecticidal

_____ (b) insect-eating

_____ (c) insect-avoiding

_____ (d) intelligent

---

9   Animal skins and hides are treated to preserve them and make them suitable for use. The term "hide" is used to designate the skin of larger animals (e.g., cowhide or horsehide), whereas "skin" refers to that of smaller animals (e.g., calfskin or kidskin). The preservation process employed is a chemical treatment called tanning, which converts the otherwise perishable skin to a non-decaying material.

● Circle the word that is OPPOSITE in meaning to perishable

10   Some nocturnal mammals leave scent trails using special glands. This enables these night-active animals to move quickly and travel along familiar routes with ease.

● The word nocturnal is closest in meaning to

_____ (a) living in the forest

_____ (b) noxious to humans

_____ (c) keen of hearing

_____ (d) active mostly at night

Hackers Test

Read the following passages and choose the one best answer to each question.

1   The history of Chinese calligraphy is as long as that of China itself. Calligraphy is one of the highest forms of Chinese art. In studying Chinese calligraphy one must learn something of the origins of the Chinese language and of how they were originally written. However, except for people brought up in the artistic traditions of the country, its aesthetic significance seems to be very difficult to grasp.

Chinese calligraphy serves the purpose of conveying thought, but also emphasizes the 'abstract' beauty of the line. Rhythm, line, and structure are more perfectly embodied in calligraphy than in painting or sculpture.

One of the important factors contributing to the evolution of the distinctive style of traditional Chinese painting has been the close relationship between the materials used and their influence on artistic forms and techniques.

First, there is ink. Ink has been used in calligraphy and painting for over two thousand years. When ink cake is ground on a painter's stone slab with fresh water, ink of various consistencies can be prepared depending on the amount of water used. Thick ink is very deep and glossy when applied to paper or silk. Thin ink appears lively and translucent. As a result, in ink-and-wash paintings it is possible to use ink alone to create a rhythmic balance between brightness and darkness, and density and lightness, and to create an impression of the subject's texture, weight and coloring.

1. The phrase brought up in the passage is closest in meaning to
    _____ (a) mentioned
    _____ (b) raised
    _____ (c) living
    _____ (d) conveyed

2. The word grasp in the passage is closest in meaning to
    _____ (a) scrutinize
    _____ (b) apprehend
    _____ (c) clasp
    _____ (d) surpass

3. The word embodied in the passage is closest in meaning to
_____ (a) emanated
_____ (b) embedded
_____ (c) typified
_____ (d) immaterialized

4. The word consistencies in the passage is closest in meaning to
_____ (a) similarities
_____ (b) densities
_____ (c) equalities
_____ (d) harmonies

5. Which of the following is OPPOSITE meaning to the word translucent?
_____ (a) lucid
_____ (b) lubricious
_____ (c) opaque
_____ (d) judicious

2 In about 1 A.D., more than a thousand years before Christopher Columbus set foot on the New World, the Anasazi Basket Makers were excavating pit houses in the Southwest. The Anasazi ("the ancient ones") were the ancestors of the modern Pueblo Indians of New Mexico and Arizona. When Viking explorer Leif Ericson sailed for America around 1000 A.D., the Anasazi architects at Chaco Canyon in New Mexico had already built much of Pueblo Bonito, a spectacular multi-storied structure. Today, in modern Taos, Pueblo Indians dry chilies beside the same doors as their ancestors did long before the founding of the Jamestown Colony in 1607.

Early pit houses were saucer-shaped, made of sticks, smeared with mud, and built partially underground. Later pit houses had a framework of posts and cross-beams covered with brush to form the roof. A hole in the floor, the Sipapu, symbolized the place where the first Anasazi emerged into this world. Kivas, normally round stone structures used by later Pueblo Indians for religious ceremonies, are thought to be patterned after the early pit houses.

In time, the Anasazi built pit houses above ground with an entrance from a hole in the top. By around 750 A.D., the Anasazi began building different types of dwellings built of adobe (a mud/clay mixture) or terrones (square blocks cut from mud) used like bricks. When possible, a framework of slender upright poles plastered with mud (called jacal) was also used.

When sandstone was plentiful, dwellings were built of stone masonry, often around a central plaza. Vigas (wooden beams) formed the roof, small saplings (latillas) were laid between the vigas, followed by layers of twigs, reeds, mud, and finally topped with dry earth. Anasazi Cliff Dwellers built multi-storied stone structures, reached by ladders, near or under overhanging cliffs at Mesa Verde and other sites.

1. The word excavating in the passage is closest in meaning to
   _____ (a) quarrying
   _____ (b) hiding
   _____ (c) covering
   _____ (d) exhibiting

2. The word spectacular in the passage is closest in meaning to
   _____ (a) imminent
   _____ (b) impressive
   _____ (c) trivial
   _____ (d) lavish

3. Circle the word in the **bold** text that is similar in meaning to smeared

4. The word slender in the passage is closest in meaning to
   _____ (a) defamed
   _____ (b) slim
   _____ (c) slaughter
   _____ (d) slumber

5. The word plentiful in the passage is closest in meaning to
   _____ (a) splendid
   _____ (b) heedful
   _____ (c) stiff
   _____ (d) abundant

---

3   During the sensory-motor stage(birth to age 2), an infant learns through concrete actions: looking, touching, hearing, putting things in the mouth, sucking, and grasping. "Thinking" consists of coordinating sensory information with bodily movements. Soon these movements become more purposeful, as the child actively explores the environment and learns that specific movements will produce specific results. Unwrapping cloth will reveal a hidden toy; releasing one's grasp of a fuzzy duck will cause the duck to drop out of reach; banging on the table with a spoon will produce dinner (or Mom, taking the spoon away).

One of the baby's major accomplishments at this stage, said Piaget, is object permanence, the understanding that something continues to exist even if it can't be seen or touched. (In the first few months of life, he observed, infants seem to follow the motto "out of sight, out of mind.") They will look intently at a little toy, if the toy is hidden behind a piece of paper they will not look behind the paper or make an effort to get the toy. By about 6 months, infants begin to grasp the idea that a toy exists and the family cat exists, whether they can see the toy, or the cat, or not. If a baby of this age drops a toy from her playpen, she will look for it; she also will look under the cloth for a toy that is partially hidden. By 1 year of age, most babies have developed an awareness of the permanence of some objects. This is when they love to play peek-a-boo.

Object permanence, said Piaget, represents the beginning of representational thought, the capacity for using mental imagery and other symbolic systems. The child is able for the first time to hold a concept in mind, to learn that the word fly represents an annoying, buzzing creature, and that Daddy represents a friendly, playful one.

---

1. The word purposeful in the passage is closest in meaning to
    _____ (a) intentional
    _____ (b) pseudo
    _____ (c) careful
    _____ (d) perilous

2. Which of the following could best be substituted for the word Unwrapping in the passage ?
    _____ (a) denuding
    _____ (b) enfolding
    _____ (c) brandishing
    _____ (d) truncating

3. Which of the following is closest meaning to the word permanence?
    _____ (a) perception
    _____ (b) hindrance
    _____ (c) pursuit
    _____ (d) perpetuity

4. The word representational in the passage is OPPOSITE in meaning to
    _____ (a) abstract
    _____ (b) representative
    _____ (c) exceptional
    _____ (d) prudent

5. The word capacity in the passage is closest in meaning to
    _____ (a) magnitude
    _____ (b) impotence
    _____ (c) competence
    _____ (d) acceptance

4   Many politically active artists worked for the New Deal projects. United by a desire to use art to promote social change, these artists sympathized with the labor movement and exhibited an affinity for left-wing politics ranging from New Deal liberalism to socialism to communism. In the extreme, their art became a crude weapon aimed only at exposing capitalism's abuses and exalting the struggles of the working class. In other instances, their commitment to use art to create a better world resulted in "social realist" works that drew sensitively upon the lives of the poor or that captured the grim reality of Depression-era America. The Federal Art Project could usually accommodate moderate social realism. But in more controversial works, especially in public art such as murals and in Federal Theatre productions, it became ammunition for the projects' enemies to use against them.

1. The word affinity is closest in meaning to
   _____ (a) hostility
   _____ (b) connection
   _____ (c) unconcern
   _____ (d) dissension

2. The phrase In the extreme is closest in meaning to which of the following?
   _____ (a) In a radical point
   _____ (b) Most surprisingly
   _____ (c) To the greatest possible extent
   _____ (d) In a usual condition

3. Which of the following is closest in meaning to the word crude?
   _____ (a) frightening
   _____ (b) refined
   _____ (c) deathly
   _____ (d) coarse

4. The word accommodate is closest in meaning to
   _____ (a) commemorate
   _____ (b) alienate
   _____ (c) hold
   _____ (d) modify

5. Which of the following is closest in meaning to the word ammunition?
   _____ (a) defense
   _____ (b) missile
   _____ (c) fortification
   _____ (d) a means of attacking

5   The evolution of the Neolithic village into a city took at least 1,500 years-in the Old World from about 5000 to 3500 BC. The technological developments making it possible for man to live in urban places were, at first, mainly advances in agriculture. Neolithic man's domestication of plants and animals eventually led to improved methods of cultivation and stock breeding and the proliferation of crafts, which in turn produced a surplus and freed some of the population to work as artisans, craftsmen, and service workers.

As human settlements increased in size, by reason of the technological advances in irrigation and cultivation, the need for improving the circulation of goods and people became ever more acute. Pre-Neolithic man leading a nomadic existence in his never-ending search for food moved largely by foot and carried his essential goods with the help of his wife and children. Neolithic man achieved the domestication of animals and used them for transportation as well as for food and hides. Then came the use of draft animals in combination with a sledge equipped with runners for carrying heavier loads.

1. The word surplus is closest in meaning to
   _____ (a) oversupply
   _____ (b) disadvantage
   _____ (c) accumulation
   _____ (d) reap

2. Which of the following could best be substituted for the word freed in in the passage?
   _____ (a) changed
   _____ (b) fired
   _____ (c) released
   _____ (d) urged

3. The word circulation in the passage is closest in meaning to
   _____ (a) classification
   _____ (b) storage
   _____ (c) flow
   _____ (d) disposal

4. Which of the following is closest in meaning to the word nomadic in the passage?
   _____ (a) migratory
   _____ (b) constant
   _____ (c) bellicose
   _____ (d) tough

5. The phrase equipped with in the passage is closest in meaning to which of the following?

_____ (a) attached with

_____ (b) furnished with

_____ (c) carried with

_____ (d) saved with

---

6   The Egyptians possessed no lifting machinery to raise stones vertically. It is generally thought that the laying of successive courses of masonry was accomplished with earth or mud brick ramps, over which the stones were dragged to their places in the walls by animal and human muscle power. Later, as the ramps were removed, they served as platforms for the masons to apply the final touches to the stone surfaces. The remains of such ramps can still be seen at unfinished temples that were begun in the Ptolemaic period. The stones were usually laid with a bed of mortar made of gypsum, sand, and water, which perhaps acted more as a lubricant to push the stone into place than as a bonding agent. There was also limited use of metal dovetail anchors between blocks.

The great Pyramids of Giza, the tallest of which rose to a height of 147 meters (481 feet), are a marvelous technological achievement, and their visual impact is stunning even today; it was not until the 19th century that taller structures would be built. But they also represent a dead end in massive stone construction, which soon moved in the direction of lighter and more flexible stone frames and the creation of larger interior spaces. The free-standing stone column supporting stone beams appeared for the first time in the royal temples associated with the pyramids of about 2600 BC.

---

1. The word vertically in the passage is closest in meaning

_____ (a) uprightly

_____ (b) easily

_____ (c) outwardly

_____ (d) at one time

2. Which of the following is closest in meaning to the word remains ?

_____ (a) stay

_____ (b) residue

_____ (c) sequence

_____ (d) frame

3. The word limited in the passage is closest in meaning to

_____ (a) reserved

_____ (b) restricted

_____ (c) diverse

_____ (d) biased

4. Which of the following could best be substituted for the word marvelous in the passage?

_____ (a) ceaseless

_____ (b) strange

_____ (c) controversial

_____ (d) wonderful

5. The phrase associated with in the passage is closest in meaning to

_____ (a) simultaneous with

_____ (b) related with

_____ (c) in succession to

_____ (d) apart from

---

7   The localization of sounds from a stationary source in the horizontal plane is known to depend on the recognition of minute differences in the intensity and time of arrival of the sound at the two ears. A sound that arrives at the right ear a few microseconds sooner than it does at the left or that sounds a few decibels louder in that ear is recognized as coming from the right. In a real-life situation the head may also be turned to pinpoint the sound by facing it and thus canceling these differences. For low-frequency tones a difference in phase at the two ears is the criterion for localization, but for higher frequencies the difference in loudness caused by the sound shadow of the head becomes all-important. Such comparisons and discriminations appear to be carried out at brain stem and midbrain levels of the central auditory pathway. The spectral shapes of sounds have been shown to be most important for determining the elevation of a source that is not in the horizontal plane. Localization of sound that emanates from a moving source is a more complicated task for the nervous system, apparently involving the cerebral cortex and short-term memory. Experiments in animals have shown that injury to the auditory area of the cortex on one side of the brain interferes with the localization of a moving sound source on the opposite side of the body.

---

1. The word stationary in the passage is closest in meaning to

_____ (a) distant

_____ (b) vital

_____ (c) sizable

_____ (d) immobile

2. Which of the following is closest in meaning to the word pinpoint in the passage?

_____ (a) detect

_____ (b) ignore

_____ (c) reflect

_____ (d) transmit

3. The word criterion in the passage is closest in meaning to

_____ (a) cause

_____ (b) assistance

_____ (c) document

_____ (d) standard

4. Which of the following is closest in meaning to the word emanates in the passage?

_____ (a) emerges

_____ (b) results

_____ (c) echoes

_____ (d) emancipates

5. The phrase interferes with in the passage is closest in meaning to?

_____ (a) makes impossible

_____ (b) commutes

_____ (c) procreates

_____ (d) meddles

---

8 Rainforests are the most diverse ecosystems on earth because of the enormous numbers of animal species present. Most of this animal diversity is made up of insects, but many other invertebrate groups are also represented. A large rainforest region, such as the Amazon Basin, may have more than ten million animal species, although most of these have yet to be described scientifically. In contrast to temperate latitude forests, animal diversity in rainforests is heavily arboreal and always greater than that found living on the ground. Even some large vertebrates, such as the orangutan of North Sumatra and Borneo, have evolved to spend most of their lives in the trees. The great diversity of many animal groups, such as birds, can in large part be explained by the fact that various unique combinations of species tend to inhabit different layers of rain forest. In the riparian rain forests of the Amazon, vertebrate diversity is also greatly increased because of the large numbers of fish species that colonize these habitats during the annual floods to feed on fruits, seeds, insects, and other foods that fall out of the trees and into the water.

1. Which of the following could best be substituted for the word enormous in the passage?

_____ (a) numerous

_____ (b) ingenuous

_____ (c) ubiquitous

_____ (d) obvious

2. Which of the following is closest in meaning to the word represented

_____ (a) present

_____ (b) tampered

_____ (c) pretended

_____ (d) reprobated

3. The word diversity in the passage is closest in meaning to

_____ (a) contradictory

_____ (b) identity

_____ (c) manifoldness

_____ (d) pretense

4. Which of the following is closest in meaning to the word colonize?

_____ (a) subsidize

_____ (b) come-back

_____ (c) settle

_____ (d) reside

5. The word floods in the passage is closest in meaning to

_____ (a) brood

_____ (b) inundation

_____ (c) trickle

_____ (d) precipitation

9   Weather has a tremendous influence on human settlement patterns, food production, and personal comfort. Extremes of temperature and humidity cause discomfort and may lead to the transmission of disease; heavy rain can cause flooding, displacing people and interrupting economic activities; thunderstorms, tornadoes, hail, and sleet storms may damage or destroy crops, buildings, and transportation routes and vehicles. Storms may even kill or injure people and livestock. At sea and along adjacent coastal areas, tropical cyclones (hurricanes, typhoons, and willy-willies) can cause great damage through excessive rainfall and flooding, winds, and wave action to ships, buildings, trees, crops, roads, and railways, and they may interrupt air service and communications. Heavy snowfall and icy conditions can impede transportation and increase the frequency of accidents. The long absence of rainfall, by contrast, can cause droughts and severe

dust storms when winds blow over parched farmland, as with the "dustbowl" conditions of the U.S. plains states in the 1930s.

1. The word Extremes in the passage is closest in meaning to
_____ (a) Imbalances
_____ (b) Differences
_____ (c) Intensities
_____ (d) Whimsies

2. Which of the following could best be substituted for the word displacing in the passage?
_____ (a) removing
_____ (b) tormenting
_____ (c) arranging
_____ (d) confusing

3. The word adjacent in the passage is closest in meaning to
_____ (a) far-reaching
_____ (b) connected
_____ (c) nearby
_____ (d) similar

4. Click the word in the passage that is similar in meaning to impede.

5. The word parched in the passage is closest in meaning to
_____ (a) desolate
_____ (b) available
_____ (c) desiccated
_____ (d) contaminated

10   In prehistoric times, man found that his game would last longer if stored in the coolness of a cave or packed in snow. He realized the cold temperatures would keep game for times when food was not available. Later, ice was harvested in the winter to be used during the summer. As man became more industrialized and mechanized, ice was harvested from lakes and rivers or manufactured, stored, and transported to many countries. Even today, ice is manufactured for this use.

The intermediate stage in the history of cooling foods was to add chemicals like sodium nitrate or potassium nitrate to water causing the temperature to fall. Cooling wine via this method was recorded in 1550, as were the words "to refrigerate." The evolution to mechanical refrigeration, a compressor with refrigerant, was a long, slow process and was introduced in the last quarter of the 19th century.

The science of refrigeration continues to evolve. In 1996, there was a change made in the type of refrigerant used to comply with the Regulatory Clean Air Act, Title 6. The old refrigerant known to most people as "freon," a tradename, was replaced with HFC 134a, a new refrigerant less injurious to the ozone and still just as effective in keeping food cold. As consumers, we should notice no difference.

1. Which of the following could best be substituted for the word game?

_____ (a) jest

_____ (b) athletics

_____ (c) preys

_____ (d) implement

2. The word transported in the passage is closest in meaning to

_____ (a) exiled

_____ (b) deported

_____ (c) furnished

_____ (d) conveyed

3. The word intermediate in the passage is closest in meaning to

_____ (a) original

_____ (b) edge

_____ (c) middle

_____ (d) intimidate

4. The word via in the passage is closest in meaning to

_____ (a) by way of

_____ (b) according to

_____ (c) for account of

_____ (d) in the middle of

5. Which of the following is OPPOSITE in meaning to the word injurious?

_____ (a) deleterious

_____ (b) slanderous

_____ (c) pernicious

_____ (d) innoxious

Blues

16세기경에 "The Blue Devils"라는 용어가 처음 만들어져 우울하고 의기 소침한 정신적 상태를 글로 표현해 낼 수 있었다. 하지만 음악적 의미로서 미국 대중음악에 Blues란 말이 쓰이게 된 것은 남북전쟁 이후이며, 특히 흑인들의 우울한 정신 상태를 뜻하는 용어로서의 Blues는 1900년까지만 해도 기록상 거의 존재하지 않는다. Blues의 탄생에 있어서 Mississippi강 유역의 Delta지역은 아주 중요한 곳으로 등장한다. Delta 즉, 삼각주 지역은 천연의 비옥한 토지를 제공해주는 곳이기에 목화 재배지와 같은 많은 농장들이 있었으며, 당연히 그 힘든 노동력을 제공하는 것은 흑인 노예들의 몫이었다. 비인간적인 취급을 받으며 힘든 노동으로 어렵게 하루 하루를 살아가야 하는 이들에게 거의 유일한 안식은 음악이었다. 비록 음악이라고는 했지만 그들에게 있어선 한을 푸는 방법이었다고 하는 편이 더 가까울 것이다. 힘들 때 모두 어울려 부르는 Field Holler (누가 먼저 선창을 외치면 모두가 같이 따라 하는 형식의 외침)나 Work Song (노동가), Spiritual Song(흑인 영가)등이 바로 그것이다. 지금까지 말했던 상황에서 태어난 음악이기에 Blues엔 필연적으로 분노, 슬픔, 고뇌, 절망감과 같은 인간이 지닌 감정을 다루는 것이 많았으며, Melody 자체도 가슴이 아플 정도의 애수를 띤 것들이 즐겨 노래 되어 왔다. 그 후 시간이 흐르면서 차츰 기본적인 형식과 Style이 다져진 것이다. 연주자 대부분이 악보를 볼 줄 모르는 탓에 Blues는 입에서 입으로 구전됐으며, 어디를 가나 그렇듯 이들 중 음감이 뛰어난 사람의 Lead와 그들만의 독특한 정서, 그리고 해방후인 1920년대 초 영국, Scotland, Ireland계와 같은 백인과의 접촉 등으로 Blues라는 장르의 음악이 확실히 자기 고유의 지위를 확립하게 된다.

CHAPTER 9

Reference Questions

9

Reference Questions

Overview

작가는 글의 간결성을 위해서, 같은 단어의 반복적 사용을 피하고, 대명사 등의 지시어로 표현을 대신한다. 그러므로 지시어가 실제로 의미하고 있는 referent(지시물)가 무엇인지 찾아 내야만 문장의 의미를 정확히 이해할 수 있다. 문맥에 따라 의미가 유동적인 지시어가 지문의 무엇을 가리키고 있는지 고르는 문제가 바로 reference 문제이다.

Types of Questions

- Look at the word _____ in the passage. Click the word or phrase in the bold text that ____ refers to.
- The word ___ in paragraph 2 refers to (multiple-choice)

●Strategy

1 **Referent(지시물)는 지문의 지시어보다 앞서 언급된다.**

· 문제로 나온 지시어보다 앞의 문장, 문단을 검토하여 답을 고른다.
· 지시어가 Referent보다 먼저 나오는 단 하나의 예외는, 한 문장 내에서, 주절의 주어를 대명사로 취하여 부사(구)절 등이 (,)앞에 나오는 경우이다.

2 **지시어로 사용되는 단어**

		Single(단수)	Plural(복수)
A. 인칭대명사	Masculine(남성)	he/his/him	they/their/them
	Feminine(여성)	she/her/her	
	Neuter(중성)	it/its/it	
B. 지시대명사/지시형용사		this/that	these/those
		the former/the latter	
C. 부정대명사		one/(the)other/another/each/none	(the)others/all/both/several/either
		some/any	

– 문제에 등장한 지시어가
  A.단수인지 복수인지
  B.사물을 가리키는지 사람을 가리키는지
  C.사람인 경우, 남성인지 여성인지 확인하여 Referent의 범위를 좁힌다.

3 **Referent를 지시어 자리에 직접 대입하여 문장이 자연스러운지 확인한다.**

A. 지시어와 선택지의 답은 반드시 수 일치된다.
B. Referent(지시물)은 지문에 제시된 것 그대로 일 수도 있고, 문맥에 맞게 변형된 것으로 보기에 제시될 수 있다.

  Ex The human body produces a variety of hormones. Being deficient in any of it could cause serious disorders.

    : it의 referent는 hormones이지만 정답으로 hormone이 제시된다.

Tip Referent가 될 수 있는 요소는 대부분이 단어 혹은 구이지만, 경우에 따라서, 한 문장이나 혹은 여러 문장일 수도 있다.

Ex Decide which word or phrase in the passage is the correct referent for each of the highlighted words or phrases and underline them.

● Freshwater and saline lakes of Antarctica are found mainly in coastal regions, and in ice-free areas such as the Larsemann Hills, Schirmacher Oasis, Bunger Hills and Vestfold Hills. Such areas are rare in Antarctica and are often foci for human activities. These lakes are fed by glacier melt streams and many are particularly susceptible to contamination from human activities in the lake basins. In addition to those in ice-free areas, small lakes on ice are often associated with melt water from nunataks in inland Antarctica, and large lakes occur under the ice sheet in the central regions. Some, such as Lake Vostok, are very large.

Answer · Such areas: coastal regions, ice-free areas
· These lakes: Freshwater and saline lakes
· many: These lakes (Freshwater and saline lakes)
· Some: large lakes

● The human brain performs many operations simultaneously. It recognizes patterns all at once rather than as a sequence of information bits. It monitors bodily functions, perceives the environment, produces speech, and searches memory all at the same time. It can do this because millions of neurons are active at once, and each neuron communicates with thousands of others, which in turn communicate with millions more. Although no single neuron is terribly smart or terribly fast, millions of them working simultaneously produce the complexities of cognition.

Answer · It: brain
· this: It recognizes ~ all at the same time.
· others: neurons
· them: neurons

Hackers Practice

Read the passages. Decide which word or phrase in the passages is the correct referent for the highlighted word or phrase and mark the correct answer.

1   During the 17th century and up through the 19th century, quilting reached its height of popularity. It continues to be a popular form of artistic expression among today's arts and crafts community. Evidence of **its** use can be found all over the world from such locations as China, India, the Middle East and Africa.

_____ (a) quilting
_____ (b) artistic expression
_____ (c) the world
_____ (d) community

2   Woven fabrics are made of two sets of yarns—a lengthwise set called the warp and a crosswise set called the filling or weft. The warp yarns are threaded into a loom through a series of frames called harnesses. During the cloth-making process, the harnesses raise some warp yarns and lower **others**. This action creates a space, or shed, between the yarns.

_____ (a) fabrics
_____ (b) frames
_____ (c) harnesses
_____ (d) warp yarns

3

Jet lag is a disruption in sleep patterns following travel across time zones. It is a common problem for travelers, and more common in those over 50 than in those under 30. Incidence varies depending on how many time zones are crossed and the direction of travel.

_____ (a) sleep patterns
_____ (b) time zones
_____ (c) travelers
_____ (d) travel directions

4

The history of building is marked by a number of trends. One is the increasing durability of the materials used. Early building materials were perishable, such as leaves, branches, and animal hides. Later, more durable natural materials—such as clay, stone, and timber—and, finally, synthetic materials—such as brick, concrete, metals, and plastics-were used. Another is a quest for buildings of ever greater height and span; this was made possible by the development of stronger materials and by knowledge of how materials behave and how to exploit them to greater advantage.

_____ (a) history
_____ (b) trend
_____ (c) material
_____ (d) development

5

To a great extent, these students are not challenged or motivated by school, nor do they leave prepared for any particular career or occupation. The result is that some high school graduates end up unemployed, and many others find themselves jumping from one low-paying job to the next in search of skills and stability until the age of 23 or 24.

_____ (a) school
_____ (b) result
_____ (c) job
_____ (d) age

6
Einstein worked as a professor of physics at universities in Prague and Zurich before moving to Berlin in 1914 with his wife and two sons, Hans Albert and Eduard. He took a post at the Prussian Academy of Sciences, where he could continue his research and lecture. Unhappy with life there, his wife Mileva returned to Switzerland with their sons near the beginning of World War I.

_____ (a) Prague
_____ (b) Zurich
_____ (c) Berlin
_____ (d) Switzerland

7
Cybernetics is the analysis of the communication and control processes of biological organisms and their relationship to mechanical and electrical systems.

_____ (a) cybernetics
_____ (b) control processes
_____ (c) biological organisms
_____ (d) systems

8
The world of the crustaceans is a world of bizarre shapes and adaptations. This group of animals is probably best-known for their hard outer shell. As the animal grows, this shell must be removed and discarded. Once this takes place, the new shell takes time to harden. During this period, the animal is without its primary means of protection and vulnerable to attack from predators.

_____ (a) shapes
_____ (b) crustaceans
_____ (c) animals
_____ (d) predators

9

Prior to construction of the canal, New York City was the nation's fifth largest seaport, behind Boston, Baltimore, Philadelphia and New Orleans. Within 15 years of its opening, New York was the busiest port in America, moving tonnages greater than Boston, Baltimore and New Orleans combined.

_____ (a) canal
_____ (b) New York City
_____ (c) seaport
_____ (d) construction

10

Great Britain seems to be at least as economical as any of her neighbors. The military establishment, which she maintains for her own defense in time of peace, is more moderate than that of any European state which can pretend to rival her either in wealth or in power.

_____ (a) Great Britain
_____ (b) establishment
_____ (c) defense
_____ (d) wealth

Hackers Test

Read the passages. Decide which word or phrase in the passages is the correct referent for the highlighted word or phrase and underline it or(for Multiple-Choice items) mark the correct answer.

1   In a flute, the air jet from the player's lips travels across the embouchure-hole opening and strikes against the sharp further edge of the hole. If such a jet is disturbed, then a wave-like displacement travels along **it** and deflects it so that it may blow either into or out of the embouchure hole. The speed of this displacement wave on the jet is just about half the air-speed of the jet itself (which is typically in the range 20 to 60 meters per second, depending on the air pressure in the player's mouth). The origin of the disturbance of the jet is the sound vibration in the flute tube, which causes air to flow into and out of the embouchure hole. If the jet speed is carefully matched to the frequency of the note being played, then the jet will flow into and out of the embouchure hole at its further edge in just the right phase to reinforce the sound and cause the flute to produce a sustained note. To play a high note, the travel time of waves on the jet must be reduced to match the higher frequency, and **this** is done by increasing the blowing pressure (which increases the jet speed) and moving the lips forward to shorten the distance along the jet to the edge of the embouchure hole. These are the adjustments that people gradually learn to make automatically when playing the flute.

The flute is open at both ends. It's obvious that it's open at the far end. Anyone who looks closely at someone playing a flute, will see that, although the player's lower lip covers part of the embouchure hole, the player leaves a large part of the hole open to the atmosphere. For the purposes of this simple introduction to flute acoustics, we shall now make some serious approximations. First, we shall pretend that **it** is a simple cylindrical pipe—in other words we shall assume that all holes are closed (down to a certain point, at least), that the head is cylindrical, and we shall replace the side mounted embouchure hole with a hole at the end. It's a crude approximation, but it preserves much of the essential physics, and it's easier to discuss.

1. The word **it** in paragraph 1 refers to
_____ (a) embouchure-hole opening
_____ (b) a jet
_____ (c) edge of the hole
_____ (d) player's lip

2. The word this in paragraph 1 refers to

_____ (a) to reduce the travel time of wave

_____ (b) to play a high note

_____ (c) to match the higher frequency

_____ (d) to reinforce the sound

3. The word it in paragraph 2 refers to

_____ (A) flute

_____ (B) pipe

_____ (C) head

_____ (D) hole

---

2 The earliest cloth pieces were woven in narrow bands from a handful of warp threads of uniform length. One end of those threads could be tied into a single knot and held firmly by one person—or secured to a steady object such as a tree or pole —while the other end was held by the weaver, who would have the other hand free to move the weft thread over and under the narrow band of warp. In fact, the band could be woven in half the time if woven from each end by two different weavers. From this simplest of looming methods, there developed two weaving traditions that allowed the band to expand to broad cloth or broad loom—two terms in modern English that reveal the importance placed on this continuing development that began very far back in human history.

The ground loom first came into use in the Near East, Southern Asia and North Africa. It is the type still in use today in the North Arabian Desert. Two beams of timber hold the warp threads only a few inches off the desert sands while weavers crouch on either side of the warp and pass the shuttle which holds the weft threads back and forth, going over and under the warp threads. The warp-weighted loom, first in use from Hungary to Scandinavia, including Greece, was immortalized on a painted urn. With this type of loom, the warp beam hung on a wall or on two posts while the warp threads dangled from the beam, still with that ancient knotting technique for a certain measured amount of warp threads. The knot now acted as a weight to keep tension (along with ceramic loom weights) and the knot also acted as a counter for spacing warp threads when working patterns or "weaves" into the cloth. Both these two types of looms were used in Turkey at Catalhuyuk, a Neolithic settlement around 10,000 years ago.

---

1. The phrase this continuing development in paragraph 1 refers to

_____ (a) weaving traditions

_____ (b) modern English

_____ (c) securing the thread

_____ (d) looming methods

2. The word this in paragraph 2 refers to
_____ (a) the ground
_____ (b) the warp-weighted loom
_____ (c) a painted urn
_____ (d) the warp beam

3. The phrase Both these in paragraph 2 refers to
_____ (a) patterns and weaves
_____ (b) acting as a weight and a counter
_____ (c) ancient and today
_____ (d) the ground and warp-weighted

3   Infancy is the period between birth and the acquisition of language one to two years later. Besides a set of inherited reflexes that help them obtain nourishment and react to danger, newborns are equipped with a predilection for certain visual patterns, including that of the human face, and for certain sounds, including that of the human voice. Within a few months they are able to identify their mother by sight, and they show a striking sensitivity to the tones, rhythmic flow, and individual sounds that make up human speech. Even young infants are capable of complex perceptual judgments involving distance, shape, direction, and depth, and they are soon able to organize their experience by creating categories for objects and events (e.g., people, furniture, food, animals) in the same way older people do.

Infants make rapid advances in both recognition and recall memory, and this in turn increases their ability to understand and anticipate events in their environment. A fundamental advance at this time is the recognition of object permanence—i.e., the awareness that external objects exist independently of the infant's perception of them. The infant's physical interactions with his environment progress from simple uncoordinated reflex movements to more coordinated actions that are intentionally repeated because they are interesting or because they can be used to obtain an external goal. About 18 months of age, the child starts trying to solve physical problems by mentally imagining certain events and outcomes rather than through simple trial-and-error experimentation.

1. The word that in paragraph 1 refers to
_____ (a) an acquisition
_____ (b) a reflex
_____ (c) a predilection
_____ (d) a pattern

2. The word they in paragraph 1 refers to

_____(a) newborns

_____(b) human voices

_____(c) human faces

_____(d) young infants

3. The word they in paragraph 2 refers to

_____ (a) infants

_____ (b) reflex movements

_____ (c) perceptions

_____ (d) coordinated actions

4   The most famous governor of the Dutch period was Peter Stuyvesant, director general of New Netherland in 1647-64. Stuyvesant's military background enabled him to spruce up a disorderly town, and he soon granted it recognition as an independent city (1653). The religious orthodoxy he attempted to impose on his already multicultural domain, however, soon led him to clash with the Quaker population of Flushing (1657).

Ultimately, Stuyvesant was ordered by his superiors to "shut his eyes" to dissenters so long as they did not disrupt society or trade. The governor found such official blindness difficult, and his imperious nature continued to alienate town burghers. When a British fleet sent by James, Duke of York, the future James II, appeared off Gravesend in August 1664, Stuyvesant discovered that no one would fight for his colony.

"Old Peg Leg" was soon forced to surrender without even firing a shot. Interestingly, he chose to take an oath of allegiance to the English crown and lived out his life in the city. Despite a brief Dutch reoccupation in 1673-74, the destiny of the colony — which had been renamed in honor of James—had shifted to London. Within the conquered city, resident Dutch and incoming English merchants got along quite well, and representatives of both groups constituted a city elite into the 19th century.

1. Look at the phrase multicultural domain in the **bold** text below.

> **The most famous governor of the Dutch period was Peter Stuyvesant, director general of New Netherland in 1647-64. Stuyvesant's military background enabled him to spruce up a disorderly town, and he soon granted it recognition as an independent city (1653). The religious orthodoxy he attempted to impose on his already multicultural domain, however, soon led him to clash with the Quaker population of Flushing (1657).**

Underline the word or phrase in the **bold** text that multicultural domain refers to

2. The word they in the passage refers to

_____ (a) superiors

_____ (b) dissenters

_____ (c) town burghers

_____ (d) representatives

3. The name "Old Peg Leg" in passage refers to

_____ (a) Peter Stuyvesant

_____ (b) James, Duke of York

_____ (c) the Quaker governor

_____ (d) the British fleet

4. The word both groups in the passage refers to

_____ (a) the Dutch and the Quakers

_____ (b) the superiors and dissenters

_____ (c) the governor and town burghers

_____ (d) the Dutch and English merchants

---

5   American Indian horses are direct descendants of the horses that escaped from the Spanish Conquistadores. Captured by Native Americans and prized for their agility, stamina, and natural resistance to disease, horses became an integrated part of the Plains culture. The horse transformed the Plains Indians from pedestrians to nomadic hunters and warriors. Prior to the horse, hunting usually took the form of running a herd of game over a cliff. With the assistance of the horse, Indians were able to hunt within the herd of game and select only the most desirable targets. Horse stealing between tribes was considered an honored way for a young warrior to build his reputation.

Native Americans decorated their horses before important ceremonies or battles to convey their hopes, expectations, etc., just as modern automobile drivers place bumper stickers, signs and flags on their vehicles. Feathers, beads, natural stones such as amethyst and turquoise, and various types of paint including the blood of a defeated enemy were used to decorate the animals.

Horses were a sign of wealth and status, and were cared for as family members. Native Americans mourned the loss of their most favored war partner in similar manner as they did the loss of a fellow warrior. Mane hair and tail hair were often kept and woven into ceremonial objects. These pieces, treasured reminders of not only a great warhorse but also a noble friend, were thought to provide a strong protective spirit.

1. In paragraph 1, the word their refers to
   _____ (a) horses
   _____ (b) herds of game
   _____ (c) Spanish Conquistadores
   _____ (d) Plains Indians

2. Look at the word his in the **bold** text below.

   With the assistance of the horse, Indians were able to hunt within the herd of game and select only the most desirable targets. Horse stealing between tribes was considered an honored way for a young warrior to build his reputation.

   Underline the word or phrase in the **bold** text that his refers to

3. In paragraph 3, the phrase their most favored war partner refers to
   _____ (a) family members
   _____ (b) horses
   _____ (c) fellow warriors
   _____ (d) protective spirits

4. In paragraph 3, the phrase These pieces refers to
   _____ (a) Native Americans
   _____ (b) horses
   _____ (c) ceremonial objects
   _____ (d) mane hair and tail hair

6   Over the past 50 years, the government has endeavored to maintain a diversity of domestic mass transportation networks. In its efforts to maintain several alternatives for intercity travel, the government has focused on supporting railroads, and to ensure efficient travel within urban areas, the government has funded urban mass transit systems. Congress has responded to the increasing complexity of transportation policy with administrative reforms.

Following World War II, the increasing proportion of domestic travel accommodated by the automobile and then by the airplane made the private passenger rail industry substantially less profitable. The Transportation Act, passed in 1958, was an effort to revitalize the railroads. This law granted the Interstate Commerce Commission (ICC) $500 million for guaranteed loans to railroad companies as well as additional discretion in fixing price rates. Business remained slow, however, and in the 1960s many private railroads asked the ICC for permission to cancel their domestic rail services. Congress responded in 1970 by passing the Rail Passenger Service Act, a measure creating a semipublic for-profit corporation, the National Passenger Railroad Corporation (Amtrak), to operate intercity rail service previously conducted by private carriers. In exchange for their money, equipment, or labor, private companies received common stock in the corporation.

Amtrak's early losses coupled with concern that government monopolies would impede efficiency produced a trend toward deregulation beginning with the Amtrak Improvement Act of 1973. This law gave Amtrak more autonomy from the executive branch and its private stockholders. The Railroad Revitalization and Regulatory Reform ("4-R") Act, passed in 1976, diminished direct ICC control over the railroads. This bill also authorized subsidies and loans to the Consolidated Rail Corporation (Conrail), an agency that in 1975 took control of track owned by seven private freight carriers. In 1980, Congress further curtailed federal regulation of the rail industry and eliminated its antitrust exemption, effective January 1, 1984.

In contrast to the semipublic projects that characterize its intercity rail policy, the government role in promoting mass transit systems within urban areas has been directed at financial support of states and localities. In 1964, the Urban Mass Transportation Act authorized $375 million in matching funds for large scale public or private rail projects in urban areas, and a 1970 bill of the same name authorized an additional $12 billion.

1. Look at the word their in the **bold** text below

   This law granted the Interstate Commerce Commission (ICC) $500 million for guaranteed loans to railroad companies as well as additional discretion in fixing price rates. Business remained slow, however, and in the 1960s many private railroads asked the ICC for permission to cancel their domestic rail services

   Underline the word or phrase in the **bold** text that their refers to

2. In paragraph 3, the phrase This bill refers to

   _____ (a) the Amtrak Improvement Act of 1973
   _____ (b) ICC
   _____ (c) the Rail Passenger Service Act
   _____ (d) the Railroad Revitalization and Regulatory Reform ("4-R") Act,

3. The phrase the same name in paragraph 4 refers to

   _____ (a) the Urban Mass Transportation Act
   _____ (b) the Amtrak Improvement Act of 1973
   _____ (c) the Rail Passenger Service Act
   _____ (d) the Railroad Revitalization and Regulatory Reform ("4-R") Act,

7 Charles Darwin's *The Origin of Species* emphasized the hereditary nature of evolution, but at that time (1859), heredity was believed to be environmentally acquired. The next "pioneers" of medical genetics did not occur until the early 1900's, when Francis Galton and Archibald Garrod recognized the works of Mendel and postulated evolution occurs via "nature versus nurture" and that "inborn errors of metabolism" lead to biological abnormalities.

Little progress was made until 1953 when James Watson and Francis Crick described the molecular basis of DNA. They were awarded the Nobel Prize in 1962. In 1990 the "Human Genome Project" was started, with the goal of identifying every human gene by the year 2005. As of October 1999, it was 9% complete.

Classification of genetic disorders may be classified into one of three types: single gene disorders, chromosome disorders and multifactorial disorders. Although virtually all disease progresses as a combination of environment and genetics ("nature versus nurture"), the genetic contribution is now believed to play the most significant role.

Single gene defects are caused by mutant genes, usually a single critical error in the genetic code. Such disorders are usually phenotypically obvious, and include neurofibromatosis types I and II, osteogenesis imperfecta and cystic fibrosis. More than 4000 single gene disorders have been described.

Chromosome disorders are not due to a single genetic mistake but are due to an excess or deficiency in the number of genes contained within an entire chromosome. The most common example is Down Syndrome (Trisomy 21), which is an extra normal copy of chromosome 21. Other examples include Trisomy 13, Turner syndrome and Klinefelter syndrome. These disorders are usually fatal in utero, and are believed to account for more than half of all spontaneous abortions.

1. The word it in paragraph 2 refers to
_____ (a) DNA
_____ (b) Human Genome Project
_____ (c) the molecular basis
_____ (d) human gene

2. Look at the phrase Such disorders in the **bold** text below

Single gene defects are caused by mutant genes, usually a single critical error in the genetic code. Such disorders are usually phenotypically obvious, and include neurofibromatosis types I and II, osteogenesis imperfecta and cystic fibrosis. More than 4000 single gene disorders have been described.

Underline the word or phrase in the **bold** text that Such disorders refers to

3. The phrase Other examples in the passage refers to an example of
_____ (a) chromosome disorders
_____ (b) single gene defects
_____ (c) spontaneous abortions
_____ (d) fatal in utero disorders

8   During the 19th century it was widely held that there are four primary taste qualities (salt, sweet, sour, and bitter) and that all other gustatory experiences represent combinations of these. Some investigators have added to these an alkaline and a metallic taste, but others claim that they are not primary qualities. On the assumption that there are four primary taste qualities, chemicals supposedly exemplifying each of the classes (NaCl for salt, sugars for sweet, acids for sour, and alkaloids for bitter) have been applied to the tongues of man and laboratory animals in attempts to find regions of selective sensitivity or (by electrophysiological tests) to locate different types of taste receptors.

Unfortunately taste buds are compound structures, and their neural connections are complex. At any rate, impulses recorded from nerves, or even from single taste buds, fail to give direct evidence about what the individual receptor cells can do. While recordings can be made by inserting fine wires into individual taste buds, the exact cell sampled is not known. It is clear, however, that vertebrate taste receptor cells are not classifiable as sugar, cation, anion, or water receptors as they are among insects.

Some vertebrate cells respond to a fairly narrow range of chemicals, but most do not; those cells that respond to salts may also react to acids and sugars, or even water. Certain regions of the tongue tend to be selectively sensitive (e.g., the tip of the human tongue seems highly responsive to sweet chemicals, but not uniquely so). It is no longer expected that, by studying impulses in single gustatory nerves, specific salt, sweet, sour, and bitter receptor cells will be discovered. It seems that patterns of response (rather than specific receptor activation) set up among the sensory cells on the tongue mediate the different taste sensations in man.

1. The word these in paragraph 1 refers to
_____ (a) the four primary taste qualities
_____ (b) gustatory experiences
_____ (c) taste combinations
_____ (d) investigators

2. The word others in paragraph 1 refers to
_____ (a) investigators
_____ (b) taste receptors
_____ (c) laboratory animals
_____ (d) 19th century peoples

3. The word their in paragraph 2 refers to
_____ (a) taste buds
_____ (b) impulses
_____ (c) nerves
_____ (d) compound structures

9   The canal had an immediate and lasting impact on the Midwestern economy. First and foremost, it opened the region to development. Before the canal, northern Illinois had no paved roads or railroads. Farmers and others found it difficult to ship goods to market. Without reliable transportation, many farmers only grew enough to supply themselves or their local community with food. During rainy seasons the few trails turned into rivers of mud, and in the summer, clouds of dust choked horses and people alike. With the canal open, a journey that in 1818 took fur traders three weeks, and in the 1830s took farmers days on muddy roads, took only 24 hours on a canal boat. Suddenly people, corn, wheat, stone, and other products poured into Chicago, and finished goods from the East Coast streamed into the West.

The I&M Canal was the last great American waterway built during the canal era. In the 1850s and 1860s the nation increasingly shifted to rail transport and thousands of miles of railroad were built. Railroads had many advantages over canals: they could run all year long, while canals were closed during the winter when the water froze. They were faster and more flexible than canals, could be built anywhere and could build spurs to existing industries. Despite these advantages, the I&M Canal remained profitable until 1866, and shipped a record tonnage in 1882. The canal could best compete with the railroads by shipping heavy bulk items such as limestone, coal, and salt, and this competition kept railroad rates lower, giving Chicago an advantage over other Midwestern cities like St. Louis.

After 1900 use of the canal declined dramatically. There was a brief resurgence during World War I, but after this the canal fell into disrepair and was dubbed a "tadpole ditch." The opening of the Illinois Waterway in 1933 ended the shipping history of the canal, and saw the beginning of its transition to recreational use.

---

1. Look at the word they in the **bold** text below

   In the 1850s and 1860s the nation increasingly shifted to rail transport and thousands of miles of railroad were built. Railroads had many advantages over canals: they could run all year long, while canals were closed during the winter when the water froze.

   Underline the word or phrase in the **bold** text that they refers to

2. In paragraph 2, the phrase this competition refers to
   _____ (a) competition between Chicago and St. Louis
   _____ (b) competition between the Midwest and the East Coast
   _____ (c) competition between the I&M Canal and railroads
   _____ (d) competition between items to ship

3. In paragraph 3, the word this refers to

_____ (a) the dramatic decline

_____ (b) a brief resurgence

_____ (c) 1900

_____ (d) World War I

10 The output of industries, agriculture, and urban communities generally exceeds the biologic capacities of aquatic systems, causing waters to become choked with an excess of organic substances and organisms to be poisoned by toxic materials. When organic matter exceeds the capacity of those microorganisms in water that break it down and recycle it, the excess of nutrients in such matter encourages rapid growth, or blooms, of algae.

When they die, the remains of the dead algae add further to the organic wastes already in the water; eventually, the water becomes deficient in oxygen. Anaerobic organisms (those that do not require oxygen to live) then attack the organic wastes, releasing gases such as methane and hydrogen sulfide, which are harmful to the oxygen-requiring (aerobic) forms of life. The result is a foul-smelling, waste-filled body of water, a situation that has already occurred in such places as Lake Erie and the Baltic Sea and is a growing problem in freshwater lakes of Europe and North America.

The process by which a lake or any other body of water changes from a clean, clear condition—with a relatively low concentration of dissolved nutrients and a balanced aquatic community—to a nutrient-rich, algae-filled body and thence to an oxygen-deficient, waste-filled condition is known as accelerated eutrophication.

1. The word it in paragraph 1 refers to

_____ (a) the output

_____ (b) the excess

_____ (c) organic matter

_____ (d) toxic material

2. The word they in paragraph 2 refers to

_____ (a) nutrients

_____ (b) the remains

_____ (c) algae

_____ (d) the organic wastes

3. The word those in paragraph 2 refers to

_____ (a) the organic wastes

_____ (b) organisms

_____ (c) gases

_____ (d) the oxygen-requiring forms of life

별자리(Constellation)와 수호성

● **AQuarius** | **The Water Carrier** | 물병자리(1.21~2.18)
지성과 합리주의 그리고 생활의 아이디어를 주관하는 천황성(Uranus)

● **Pisces** | **The Fish** | 물고기자리(2.19~3.20)
포용력과 센스 ,영혼과 육체를 주관하는 해왕성(Neptune)

● **Aries** | **The Ram** | 양자리(3.21~4.19)
활동과 정렬을 주관하는 화성(Mars)

● **Taurus** | **The Bull** | 황소자리(4.20~5.20)
사랑과 평화를 주관하는 금성(Venus)

● **Gemini** | **The Twins** | 쌍둥이자리(5.21~6.21)
태양계의 9개 행성 중에 태양에 가장 가까운 수성(Mercury)

● **Cancer** | **The Crab** | 게자리(6.22~7.22)
방위와 여행을 맡아 다루는 달(Moon)

● **Leo** | **The Lion** | 사자자리(7.23~8.22)
젊음과 남성의 상징이며 생명과 질서의 보호자인 태양(Sun)

● **Virgo** | **The Virgin** | 처녀자리(8.23~9.22)
지혜와 기수를 관장하는 수성(Mercury)

● **Libra** | **The Balance Scales** | 천칭자리(9.23~10.23)
사랑과 아름다움 그리고 평화를 주관하는 금성(Venus)

● **Scorpius** | **The Scorpions** | 전갈자리(10.24~11.22)
탄생과 소멸 그리고 예리한 투시력을 상징하는 명왕성(Pluto)

● **Sagiffarius** | **The Archer** | 사수자리(11.23~12.21)
높은 이상과 우아한 품위를 주관하는 목성(Jupiter)

● **Capricornus** | **The Sea Goat** | 염소자리(12.22~1.20)
시간의 아버지이며 질서와 진실을 관장하는 토성(Saturn)

Reading

Progressive Test 3-① / 3-②

Hackers Progressive Test 3-①

● Read through the passages and solve each question which covers the preceding chapters; Ch.7 Scanning Questions, Ch.8 Vocabulary in Context and Ch.9 Reference Questions.

[1] Bald eagles' lifting power is about 4 pounds. They do not generally feed on chickens or other domestic livestock, but they will make use of available food sources. Bald eagles will take advantage of carrion, dead and decaying flesh. Because of its scavenger image, some people dislike the bald eagle. Other people do not care for powerful and aggressive birds. Still other people object merely on the grounds that it is a bird of prey, which kills other animals for food.

Once an eagle spots a fish swimming or floating near the surface of the water, it approaches its prey in a shallow glide and snatches the fish out of the water with a quick swipe of its talons. Eagles have a special locking mechanism for their talons. When the open talons hit the prey, they instantly close and cannot be opened again until the eagle pushes down on a solid surface.

Occasionally, bald eagles plunge into water while trying to catch a fish. The eagle cannot fly again until it's out of the water, so it uses its large wings to swim. The eagle is a strong swimmer, but if the water is very cold, it may be overcome by hypothermia.

An eagle can consume one pound of fish in about four minutes. The eagle holds its prey with one talon, holds onto its perch with the other, then tears off each bite with its bill. The bald eagle steals food from other bald eagles, as well as from other species. Chasing another raptor is usually enough to persuade it to drop its kill, but occasionally bald eagles will attack. Bald eagles do not have to eat every day. But if the bird goes too long without food, it may not be able to hunt effectively in order to survive. Eagles have an out pouching of the esophagus, called a crop, where they can store food. For a scavenger like the bald eagle, the carcass of a seal is an unexpectedly large food supply. Rich with fat and protein, the seal's body will feed a group of eagles for days. Though many calories will be obtained, they will be lost in fighting over the food.

1. Which of the following is the main topic of the passage?
   (a) Bald eagle's diets and feeding habits
   (b) Misleading images of bald eagles
   (c) The prey of Bald eagles
   (d) The hunting methods of bald eagles

2. The word available in the passage is closest in meaning to
   (a) obtainable
   (b) qualified
   (c) detected
   (d) reliable

3. It can be inferred from the passage that bald eagles prefer
   (a) preying on wild animals
   (b) hunting large prey
   (c) aggressively pursuing their prey
   (d) carrying prey back to their nest

4. The word plunge in the passage is closest in meaning to
   (a) fall
   (b) collapse
   (c) dive
   (d) creep

5. According to the passage, which of the following is NOT true about bald eagle's talons?
   (a) They are used to tear away pieces of prey.
   (b) They snap up the prey quickly and forcefully.
   (c) They help the eagle balance on a perch.
   (d) They have strong lifting power up to 4 pounds.

6. It can be inferred from the passage that relations between bald eagles are
   (a) hierarchic
   (b) competitive
   (c) indifferent
   (d) gregarious

7. The phrase the other in the passage refers to
   (a) the eagle
   (b) fish
   (c) perch
   (d) talon

8. Underline the sentence which states how bald eagles can do without everyday hunting.

9. The phrase Rich with in the passage is closest in meaning to
   (a) composed of
   (b) abundant in
   (c) requiring
   (d) storing

10. According to the passage, which of the following statements about bald eagles is true?
    (a) They don't damage human property.
    (b) They can be a threat to other raptors.
    (c) They prefer carcasses to live game for their rich nutrients.
    (d) They enjoy bathing in warm water.

[2] History shows that sustained economic development usually leads to smaller family size in the long run. Consider what happened in Europe, for example, where commercial, agricultural, and industrial revolutions in the seventeenth and eighteenth centuries triggered sustained population growth. Once launched, this growth spurred continuous economic, social, and political transformations over the next two centuries. Gradual declines in mortality occurred through improvements in hygiene and nutrition. But fertility fell also, as income, urbanization, education, and health reached certain thresholds.

Generalized as a "demographic transition," this European experience of better living standards leading to smaller family size has been found to apply to the more recent experiences of Latin America, Asia, and Africa, which did not have their own population explosions until after World War II. In these later cases the transition has taken place much more rapidly, with public health programs and family planning playing key roles in lowering mortality and fertility. Rapid increases in female education have also played a major role. While it took Europe nearly a century to complete its transition, many Asian and Latin countries have gone from sustained growth to fertility plunge in one to two generations.

Decisions about family size are part of what economists call the "utility maximization" process. Children contribute to parental well-being in many ways, but also compete for time, attention, and household resources. Economic development changes parental aspirations and values, increases the cost of children, and creates competing sources of parental utility. Fertility declines because couples, weighing all these factors, decide they want fewer children. Family planning programs work because they help couples reach goals that they set for themselves.

The widespread desire for smaller families does not mean that family planning programs are redundant. Some 40 percent of the decline in Third World fertility in recent decades is attributed to family planning, and the success of these programs may be responsible for the "ideational" demographic transition that we are also seeing today—the global shift toward the small-family norm even in countries that have not enjoyed sustained economic and social growth.

---

1. What does the passage mainly discuss?
   (a) The elements of deciding family size
   (b) Why economic development leads to small family size
   (c) The change in family size through history
   (d) Demographic transitions toward smaller family size

2. Why did demographic transitions happen rapidly in many Asian and Latin countries?
   (a) They didn't experience the second step in European transition.
   (b) More women took part in promoting economic growth.
   (c) The birthrate in Asian and Latin countries was lower than that in Europe.
   (d) Their governments actively improved public welfare.

3. The word triggered in the passage is closest in meaning to
   (a) accompanied
   (b) set off
   (c) assisted
   (d) transformed

4. The word sustained in the passage is closest in meaning to
   (a) prolonged
   (b) regressive
   (c) sensational
   (d) rapid

5. Which of the following best describes the organization of the passage?
   (a) a definition of the term "demographic transition"
   (b) a generalization of the impact of the Industrial Revolution in the 18th century
   (c) a presentation of the advantages and disadvantages of having a small family
   (d) a detailed description of the phenomenon and causes of smaller family size

6. The word themselves in the passage refers to
   (a) children
   (b) social workers
   (c) family planning programs
   (d) couples

7. By stating the "ideational" demographic transition, the author implies that
   (a) the recent decline in Third World fertility represents societal change through ideas
   (b) family planning programs were an "ideal" success
   (c) the Third World's transition to fertility decrease was more rapid than that of even many Asian and Latin countries
   (d) the Third World is experiencing transition in the reverse order from Europe

8. The word shift in the passage is closest in meaning to
   (a) favoritism
   (b) change
   (c) ideology
   (d) resolution

9. Which of the following statements does NOT describe the relationship between family size and economic growth as stated in the passage?
   (a) Demographic transition cannot occur without simultaneous economic revolution.
   (b) Better living standards often lead to smaller family size.
   (c) Continued economic development makes raising children expensive.
   (d) Initial economic development encourages population growth.

10. All of the following statements about the birthrate of a population are mentioned in the passage EXCEPT that

(a) lower birthrate was achieved through the government's control plan

(b) its rate of growth is not affected by improvements in nutrition

(c) it is related to economic development

(d) it declined after the 17th and 18th centuries in Europe

[3] Soil, which is composed of mineral particles, organic material, water, and air, is a valuable natural resource on which humans depend for food. Water, wind, ice, and other agents cause soil erosion, the wearing away or removal of soil from the land. Water and wind are particularly effective in removing soil: rainfall loosens soil particles that can then be transported away by moving water, while wind loosens soil and blows it away, particularly if the soil is exposed and dry.

Soil erosion is a national and international problem that does not make the headlines very often. To get a feeling for how serious the problem is, consider that approximately 2.7 billion metric tons (3.0 billion tons) of topsoil are lost from U.S. farmlands as a result of soil erosion each year. The U.S. Department of Agriculture estimates that approximately one fifth of U.S. cropland is vulnerable to soil erosion damage. Because erosion reduces the amount of soil in an area, it limits the growth of plants. Erosion also causes a loss in soil fertility, because essential minerals and organic matter that are part of the soil are removed. As a result of these losses, the productivity of eroded agricultural lands declines.

Humans often accelerate soil erosion through poor soil management practices. Agriculture is not the only culprit. The removal of natural plant communities during the construction of roads and buildings accelerates erosion. Unsound logging practices such as clear-cutting large forested areas for lumber and pulpwood cause severe erosion.

Soil erosion has a detrimental impact on other natural resources. Sediments that get into streams, rivers, and lakes, for example, affect water quality and fish habitats. If the sediments contain pesticide and fertilizer residues, as they often do, they further pollute the water.

Sufficient plant cover limits soil erosion: leaves and stems cushion the impact of rainfall, and roots help to hold the soil in place. Although soil erosion is a natural process, plant cover makes it negligible in many natural ecosystems.

1. What does the passage mainly discuss?

(a) Ways to prevent soil erosion

(b) The chemical composition of soil

(c) The causes and effects of soil erosion

(d) The consequences of soil erosion for agriculture

2. Which is NOT mentioned as a cause of soil erosion?

   (a) the destruction of forest

   (b) water and wind

   (c) inadequate soil management

   (d) the use of fertilizer

3. By stating Soil erosion is a national and international problem, the author means that

   (a) soil erosion is extensive everywhere

   (b) soil erosion deserves more attention and concern from people

   (c) soil erosion is a problem that requires wide cooperation

   (d) soil erosion is a problem that is impossible to solve

4. The word vulnerable in the passage is closest in meaning to

   (a) hazardous

   (b) tempted

   (c) injured

   (d) susceptible

5. The word removal in the passage is closest in meaning to

   (a) transfer

   (b) mutation

   (c) breakdown

   (d) elimination

6. The phrase get into in the passage is closest in meaning to

   (a) collide with

   (b) reach

   (c) accumulate in

   (d) slide down

7. In which of the following areas would soil erosion most likely occur?

   (a) a riverside

   (b) a wide prairie

   (c) a marsh

   (d) a bare mountain side

8. The word it in the passage refers to

   (a) the impact of rainfall

   (b) a natural process

   (c) soil erosion

   (d) plant cover

9. Find the sentence that states how erosion affects farming.

   _____

10. According to the passage, soil erosion can be lessened by

   (a) using organic fertilizer

(b) limiting the sprawling of cities

(c) constructing more dams

(d) placing stricter regulations on chemical plants

---

[4] During the depths of the Great Depression of the 1930s and into the early years of World War II, the Federal government supported the arts in unprecedented ways. For 11 years, between 1933 and 1943, federal tax dollars employed artists, musicians, actors, writers, photographers, and dancers. Never before or since has the government so extensively sponsored the arts.

The New Deal arts projects provided work for jobless artists, but they also had a larger mission: to promote American art and culture and to give more Americans access to what President Franklin Roosevelt described as "an abundant life." The projects saved thousands of artists from poverty and despair and enabled Americans all across the country to see an original painting for the first time, attend their first professional live theater, or take their first music or drawing class.

But the arts projects also sparked controversy. Some politicians believed them to be wasteful propaganda and wanted them ended; others wanted them expanded. Such controversy, along with the United States' entry into World War II, eventually killed the projects. But much of what they fashioned has survived through the efforts of museums, libraries, and archives, including the National Archives and Records Administration. One exhibition a few years ago described and displayed the work of the New Deal arts projects and discussed themes common to this government-sponsored art. The paintings, prints, books, playbills, posters, and music transcriptions displayed there were more than artifacts and documents of an emergency work program. They were examples of an extraordinary burst of American creativity that occurred during a time of tremendous change and trial.

---

1. What is the main topic of this passage?

    (a) Federal government funding of New Deal arts projects

    (b) Work for jobless artists

    (c) The American government's ideology in art

    (d) New Deal arts projects during the Great Depression

2. The author implies that the New Deal arts projects differed from most other emergency work programs because

    (a) they produced notably creative works in American art

    (b) they had a preparatory stage

    (c) they had unanimous national support

    (d) they influenced other countries' policies

3. The word unprecedented is closest in meaning to

    (a) novel

    (b) authorized

(c) predictable

(d) preposterous

4. The word their in the passage refers to

    (a) the arts projects

    (b) artists

    (c) Americans

    (d) politicians

5. According to the passage, what probably encouraged people to take their first art class?

    (a) An increasing number of American artists receiving international awards

    (b) The affluent economic situation

    (c) A government policy that made exposure to the arts easy

    (d) A spontaneous interest in American arts

6. The word sparked is closest in meaning to

    (a) twinkled

    (b) activated

    (c) amplified

    (d) extracted

7. It can be inferred from the passage that the artists' attitude toward the New Deal arts projects was

    (a) enthusiastic about the projects

    (b) capricious and changeable from project to project

    (c) damaging to their pride

    (d) indifferent to the projects

8. The word fashioned is closest in meaning to

    (a) created

    (b) admired

    (c) adapted

    (d) adjusted

9. According to the passage, some politicians objected to the New Deal arts projects, because they believed that the projects were

    (a) nominal and useless

    (b) unproductive but well-intentioned

    (c) helpful but low quality

    (d) abused commercially

10. According to the passage, which of the following is NOT characteristic of the New Deal art projects?

    (a) Their greater aim was to make America a more cultural nation.

    (b) They led to heated arguments between politicians.

    (c) They were funded by the President to be a national memorial of hard times.

    (d) They intended to relieve artists who were out of work.

Hackers Progressive Test 3-②

▷ Read through the passages and solve each question which covers the preceding chapters; Ch.7 Scannning Questions, Ch.8 Vacabulary in Context and Ch.9 Reference Questions.

[1]   During the 1920s, with five remarkable projects featured in an exhibition show, Frank Lloyd Wright developed architectural prototypes of far-reaching consequences. Exploring advanced building technologies and untried geometric patterns, he conceived rural and suburban building complexes that effectively restructured their sites in a manner calculated to heighten their natural grandeur. In earlier designs, Wright had approached settings more tentatively, with linkages achieved through such architectural extensions as loggias and terraces that left the sites themselves less changed. Now a new, more persuasive unity between building and site resulted, one in which roads and other movement systems were skillfully integrated on an unprecedented scale.

■ The complex geometries that Wright explored in the projects of the 1920s reflected far more than superficial pattern. ■ As his writings attest, he believed in the primacy of nature and in its underlying order, which he saw as essentially Euclidean. ■ Buildings were not meant to mimic their settings but to signal human presence through sympathetic alliance. ■ In his most evocative descriptions of landscape, it was this geometric order he perceived—cosmic in spirit, architectural in nature, often suggestive of ancient building and experienced while in motion across the land. It lay with the architect to extract and clarify these forms, shaping them, when necessary, to complete an order imperfectly revealed. These were means by which to represent the underlying order of the cosmos and to achieve a stronger connection to it.

In such ways, Wright sought universal meaning through attachment to place, varying his geometries not only to establish an indivisible bond with each specific location, but, more importantly, to complete that location's underlying structure. He remained sympathetic to his favorite nineteenth-century writers and to an earlier, more distant history by honoring a belief in the spirituality of nature, a belief which led him to reexamine issues of design that had been long unstudied. Yet he invigorated this approach by incorporating advances of his own era, so that mobility and a new awareness of natural, evolutionary change became part of his ideal landscape.

He thus effected connections with both place and time, envisioning a profound, richly layered architecture through which each place became more fully revealed as part of an ordered universe.

1. What is the best title for this passage?

    (a) The achievements and contributions of Frank Lloyd Wright

    (b) Frank Lloyd Wright's evocative description of landscape

    (c) Five remarkable projects in the 1920s

    (d) The meaning Frank Lloyd Wright pursued in his works in the 1920s

2. The word featured in the passage is closest in meaning to

    (a) appreciated

    (b) imagined

    (c) played down

    (d) displayed

3. The word extensions in the passage is closest in meaning to

    (a) elongations

    (b) additions

    (c) hallmarks

    (d) ranges

4. The word underlying in the passage is closest in meaning to

    (a) coordinated

    (b) elusive

    (c) basic

    (d) secretive

5. The word it in the passage refers to

    (a) the underlying order

    (b) ancient building

    (c) the architect

    (d) the form

6. How does the author feel about Frank Lloyd Wright?

    (a) He is an admirable architect .

    (b) He is an out-of-date architect.

    (c) He is a bigoted architect.

    (d) He is an important but not logical architect.

7. What is the purpose of paragraph 4?

    (a) To summarize Frank Lloyd Wright's contribution to architecture

    (b) To evaluate architectural trends in the 1920s

    (c) To describe how Frank Lloyd Wright's approach to architecture was different from that of others

    (d) To prove the significance of Frank Lloyd Wright's projects

8. It is clear that Frank Lloyd Wright had an attachment to

    (a) superficial unity with nature

    (b) fantastic and mysterious ideas

    (c) deriving hidden beauty through mimicry of nature

    (d) pursuing order through geometric rules

9. The following sentence can be added to the passage.

In Wright's approach they expressed special qualities of place.

Where would it best fit in the passage? Click on the square[■] to add the sentence to the passage.

10. According to paragraph 2, all of the following are true EXCEPT that
   (a) Wright's projects in the 1920s reflected far more than superficial pattern
   (b) Wright wanted to achieve a stronger connection to the geometric order
   (c) as Wright's writing attests, he believed in the primacy of nature
   (d) for Wright, buildings were meant to mimic their settings

---

[2] The belief that continents have not always been fixed in their present positions was suspected long before the 20th century; this notion was first suggested as early as 1596 by the Dutch map maker Abraham Ortelius in his work *Thesaurus Geographicus*. ■ Ortelius suggested that the Americas were "torn away from Europe and Africa . . . by earthquakes and floods" and went on to say: "The vestiges of the rupture reveal themselves, if someone brings forward a map of the world and considers carefully the coasts of the three continents." ■ However, it was not until 1912 that the idea of moving continents was seriously considered as a full-blown scientific theory—called Continental Drift—introduced in two articles published by a 32-year-old German meteorologist named Alfred Lothar Wegener. ■ He contended that, around 200 million years ago, the supercontinent Pangaea began to split apart. Alexander Du Toit, professor of Geology at Johannesburg University and one of Wegener's staunchest supporters, proposed that Pangaea first broke into two large continental landmasses, Laurasia in the northern hemisphere and Gondwanaland in the southern hemisphere. Laurasia and Gondwanaland then continued to break apart into the various smaller continents that exist today. ■

Wegener's theory was based in part on what appeared to him to be the remarkable fit of the South American and African continents, first noted by Abraham Ortelius three centuries earlier. Wegener was also intrigued by the occurrences of unusual geologic structures and of plant and animal fossils found on the matching coastlines of South America and Africa, which are now widely separated by the Atlantic Ocean. He reasoned that it was physically impossible for most of these organisms to have swum or have been transported across the vast oceans. To him, the presence of identical fossil species along the coastal parts of Africa and South America was the most compelling evidence that the two continents were once joined.

In Wegener's mind, the drifting of continents after the break-up of Pangaea explained not only the matching fossil occurrences but also the evidence of dramatic climate changes on some continents. For example, the discovery of fossils of tropical plants (in the form of coal deposits) in Antarctica led to the conclusion that this frozen land previously must have been situated closer to the equator, in a more temperate climate where lush, swampy vegetation could grow. Other mismatches of geology and climate included distinctive fossil ferns (Glossopteris) discovered in now-polar regions, and the occurrence of glacial deposits in present-day arid Africa, such as the Vaal River valley of South Africa.

1. What is the topic of this passage?
   (a) The influence of dramatic climate changes
   (b) The meaning of the discovery of identical fossil species.
   (c) Wegener's theory of continental drift
   (d) The change of belief in fixed continental idea

2. The phrase this notion in the passage means
   (a) the vestiges of the rupture
   (b) the idea of moving continents
   (c) Continental Drift
   (d) the supercontinent Pangaea

3. The following sentence can be added to the passage.

   Ortelius' idea surfaced again in the 19th century.

   Where would it best fit in the passage? Click on the square[■] to add the sentence to the passage.

4. When did the hypothesis about Laurasia become known to people?
   (a) the late 16th century
   (b) the early 18th century
   (c) the late 19th century
   (d) the early 20th century

5. The word full-blown in the passage is closest in meaning to
   (a) thorough
   (b) verified
   (c) astonishing
   (d) innovative

6. The phrase split apart in the passage is closest in meaning to
   (a) go away
   (b) revolve
   (c) disjoin
   (d) move

7. It can be inferred from the passage that Alfred Lothar Wegener's theory
   (a) was not widely welcomed
   (b) was first documented by archaeological evidence
   (c) supported the idea that Continental drift was caused by earthquakes and floods
   (d) was firmly supported by some intellectuals

8. The word intrigued in the passage is closest in meaning to

    (a) attracted

    (b) inquisitive

    (c) confused

    (d) reckless

9. The author mentions plant and animal fossils in paragraph 2 as evidence that

    (a) once there were mass migrations of ancient plants and animals

    (b) plant and animal fossils were transported by geological forces

    (c) there was little sea in the past earth

    (d) a larger landmass that existed in the past split in two parts

10. Alfred Lothar Wegener believed Continental Drift theory because of

    (a) the saw toothed coastline of South America

    (b) the resemblance of fish on the two different coasts

    (c) the identical botanical distribution between South America and Africa

    (d) the glacial deposits in Africa

---

[3]   Jefferson Davis became interested in politics, and in 1845, he won a seat in the U.S. House of Representatives. He did not stay in the House very long. In June of 1846 he resigned to become a colonel in the Mexican War serving under General Zachary Taylor, who later became president.

Davis was appointed by the governor of Mississippi in 1847 to fill out the term of a U.S. Senator who had died. The next year he was elected by the Mississippi state legislature to serve the rest of the term, and in 1850, he was elected to serve a full term. Davis, believing in strict interpretation of the Constitution, became involved in opposing the Compromise of 1850 in debates. Davis was a devoted supporter of Senator John C. Calhoun, a southern rights leader. Davis believed that Mississippi shouldn't accept the Compromise of 1850 and resigned from the senate to run for governor of Mississippi as a candidate for the States' Rights Democrats Party.

In 1857, Davis was re-elected to the U.S. Senate by the state of Mississippi. In the Senate, he defended the rights of the South and of slavery. He demanded that Congress protect the institution of slavery in the territories.

When Abraham Lincoln was elected President in 1860, Davis resigned from the Senate. Mississippi had passed the Ordinance of Secession and Davis hoped to be appointed head of the Confederate Army. ■ Instead, he was named provisional president of the Confederate States of America. He took the oath of office on February 18, 1861. ■

Davis was a good administrator for the Confederate States, but in the end, he was proven to be a poor planner. ■ His health was poor, but he managed his duties as President with devotion. ■

After the Civil War, Davis was captured and imprisoned at Fort Monroe. He was indicted for treason and was held in prison for two years to await his trial. Horace Greeley and a group of Northern men bailed Davis out of jail. He was never tried.

1. What does the passage mainly discuss?
   (a) Jefferson Davis's efforts to protect the institution of slavery
   (b) Jefferson Davis, Confederate President
   (c) The faith and desire of Jefferson Davis
   (d) The political career and life of Jefferson Davis

2. The word fill out in the passage is closest in meaning to
   (a) quit
   (b) complete
   (c) satisfy
   (d) supply

3. The word devoted in the passage is closest in meaning to
   (a) biased
   (b) fervid
   (c) addicted
   (d) demanding

4. Click the sentence in paragraph 2 which states the reason why Davis gave up his Senate position.

5. The word institution in the passage is closest in meaning to
   (a) establishment
   (b) deferment
   (c) propagation
   (d) creation

6. It can be inferred from the passage that when rigidly interpreted, the Constitution
   (a) didn't allow for states' rights
   (b) prescribed the equality of man except slaves
   (c) opposed the institution of slavery
   (d) applied different principles to each state

7. According to the passage, Jefferson Davis
   (a) was more a soldier than a politician
   (b) was better at carrying out plans than making them
   (c) betrayed his own beliefs before his trial
   (d) was too impatient to finish even a term

8. For which of the following reasons was Jefferson Davis accused of treason?

    (a) He was an enemy spy.

    (b) He enlisted in the Confederate Army.

    (c) He voted against Lincoln.

    (d) He didn't acknowledge the Federal government.

9. The word He in the passage refers to

    (a) Abraham Lincoln

    (b) Horace Greeley

    (c) Senator John C. Calhoun

    (d) Jefferson Davis

10. The following sentence can be added to the passage.

Davis was inaugurated one year later on February 22, 1862.

Where would it best fit in the passage? Click on the square[■] to add the sentence to the passage.

---

[4]   The Donner Party were among the wave of emigrants who would bring the US its "manifest destiny" to stretch from the Atlantic to the Pacific. Reports from California settlers, including John Sutter, a Swiss who had a "fort" at the confluence of the Sacramento and American Rivers (present Sacramento) and John Marsh, who had a ranch near Mt. Diablo, described the excellent climate, the ease of farming and the weakness of the Mexican government. These reports encouraged emigration from the economically depressed and malaria-ridden Mississippi Valley.

Several books published by 1845 described the trail to California. The books' glowing description of life in California, and the trail information, seemed to provide all one needed to know to make the crossing. Approximately 2,700 people set out on the trail in 1846. About 1,500 traveled to California, the rest to Oregon.

The trail to California had been established not by the government, but by members of the "Emigrant Societies" formed in the 1840's. The efforts of three parties had established a passable wagon road over the two main obstacles: the Great Salt Lake Desert in Utah, and the Sierra Nevada mountains in California. The result was a journey of 2,000 miles in a single summer and fall, by oxen or horses at 15 miles a day, which meant a voyage of about five months.

The first wagon road to California was the old Spanish trail through Santa Fe to Los Angeles. The first trail to Oregon was Lewis & Clark's route along the upper Missouri River to Oregon. But resistance from the tribes in the 1820's led fur trappers to use a trail along the North Platte River, crossing the Rockies at South Pass. From there the trappers reached the Hudson Bay Company's Fort Hall on the Snake River.

The trappers explored from the Great Salt Lake, over the Nevada desert all the way to California. In the Spring of 1828, Jedediah Smith returned from California by crossing the Sierra near the present Ebbetts Pass.

1. The passage is mainly concerned with
   (a) the two main obstacles of establishing a passable wagon trail
   (b) the emigration to California
   (c) the first wagon road to California
   (d) the route to California used by westward emigrants

2. The word manifest in the passage is closest in meaning to
   (a) obvious
   (b) authentic
   (c) intricate
   (d) prevalent

3. It can be inferred from paragraph 1 that emigrants to California
   (a) suffered troubles with natives
   (b) were mostly middle-class people
   (c) were attracted by precious minerals
   (d) were drawn by the living conditions

4. The word depressed in the passage is OPPOSITE in meaning to
   (a) exhilarated
   (b) dejected
   (c) prosperous
   (d) exulting

5. What is the author's purpose in paragraph 1?
   (a) to explain the economic depression in the Mississippi Valley
   (b) to present historical reasons for establishing the trail
   (c) to give an example of compelling reasons to emigrate to California
   (d) to point out the Donner Party's role in California emigration

6. The word Approximately in the passage is closest in meaning to
   (a) nearly
   (b) precisely
   (c) no more than
   (d) appropriately

7. The books mentioned in paragraph 2 were written
   (a) to discourage people from going to California
   (b) to warn people of the problems resulting from migration
   (c) to force people to use the wagon road
   (d) to encourage people to come to California

8. According to the passage, the early trails
   (a) could not be passed with oxen
   (b) were constructed by citizens
   (c) cut down traveling time to three seasons
   (d) were disregarded by some merchants

9. It can be inferred from the passage that the Donner Party made its way to California
   (a) traveling by train
   (b) because of the promise of a better life
   (c) trading with native tribes
   (d) in order to avoid war with Native Americans

10. A typical route to California would include which of the following?
   (a) Lewis & Clark's route along the upper Missouri River
   (b) crossing the Salt Lake Desert and Sierra Nevada mountain range
   (c) a trail from Los Angeles to Santa Fe
   (d) crossing the Snake River at South Pass

Reading

HACKERS READING

Actual Test

Beginning

[1] The growth of public education, spurred partly by the determination to "Americanize" immigrant children, helped quicken the emergence of a new America after the Civil War. By the 1870s, America's commitment to public education was nearly universal. In 1870 there were 7 million pupils in public schools; by 1920 the number had tripled. Despite such progress, educational leaders had to struggle against a pattern of political appointments, corruption, and incompetence in the public schools.

The spread of secondary schools accounted for much of the increased enrollment in public schools. In antebellum America, private academies had prepared those who intended to enter college. **At the beginning of the Civil War, there were only about 100 public high schools in the whole country, but their number grew rapidly to about 800 in 1880 and to 6,000 at the turn of the century.**

American colleges at this time sought to instill discipline, morality, and a curriculum heavy on mathematics and the classics; in church schools theology, along with ethnics and rhetoric. History, modern languages and literature, and some science courses were tolerated, although laboratory work was usually limited to a professor's demonstration in class. The college teacher was apt to be a young man seeking temporary refuge, or a broken-down preacher seeking safe harbor. In 1871 one writer called the typical professor "nondescript, a jack of all trades, equally ready to teach surveying and Latin eloquence, and thankful if his salary is not docked to whitewash the college fence."

➡Nevertheless, the demand for higher learning drove the college student population up from 52,000 in 1870 to 157,000 in 1890 and to 600,000 in 1920. During the same years, the number of institutions rose from 563 to about 1,000. To accommodate the diverse needs of these growing numbers, colleges moved away

---

1 What does the passage mainly discuss?
- (A) The growth of public education after the Civil War
- (B) The political incompetence between educational leaders
- (C) The history of American education
- (D) The new approach to Americanize immigrant children

2 The word universal in the passage is OPPOSITE in meaning to
- (A) compulsory
- (B) arbitrary
- (C) particular
- (D) far-reaching

3 It can be inferred from paragraph 1 that before the Civil War, most immigrant children
- (A) were educated according to their native customs
- (B) attained higher education
- (C) often got in trouble with non-immigrant children
- (D) were seen as non-American

4 The word spread in the passage is closest in meaning to
- (A) clustering
- (B) expansion
- (C) foundation
- (D) renewal

5 Look at the word their in the passage. Click on the word or phrase in the **bold** text that their refers to. *public high school*

6 The word tolerated in the passage is closest in meaning to
- (A) demanding
- (B) permitted
- (C) essential
- (D) neglected

7 The word docked in the passage is closest in meaning to
- (A) cut short
- (B) set aside
- (C) penalized
- (D) similar

End

from rigidly prescribed courses toward an elective system. **The new approach allowed students to favor their strong points and colleges to expand their scope. But as Henry Cabot Lodge complained, it also allowed students to "escape without learning anything at all by a judicious selection of unrelated subjects taken up only because they were easy or because the burden imposed by those who taught them was light."**

8 Look at the word it in the passage.

Click on the word or phrase in the **bold** text that it refers to.   *expand their scope*

9 It can be inferred from the passage that early American colleges were /

Ⓐ optimal for specialization in a certain field
Ⓑ good places to escape from harsh realities
Ⓒ ideal places through which to obtain a lifelong occupation
Ⓓ limited in their curriculum

10 In the late 19th century, American colleges suffered from the problem of

Ⓐ political infringement
Ⓑ financial crisis
Ⓒ discord between faculty members
Ⓓ incompetent faculty

11 Click on the sentence in paragraph 4 that explains why colleges changed their system.

Paragraph 4 is marked with an arrow (➡).

Beginning

[2] Soils found in arid and semiarid areas often contain high concentrations of inorganic mineral salts. In these areas, the amount of water that drains into lower soil layers is minimal because the little precipitation that falls quickly evaporates. **In contrast, humid climates have enough precipitation to leach salts out of the soils and into waterways and groundwater. Irrigation of agricultural fields often results in their becoming increasingly salty. Also, when irrigated soil becomes waterlogged, salts may move upward from groundwater to the soil surface, where they are deposited as a crystalized crust.**

Most plants cannot obtain all the water they need from salty soil, because such soil produces a water balance problem. **Under normal conditions, the dissolved materials in the watery cytoplasm of plant cells give them a concentration of water lower than that of soil. As a result, water moves by osmosis from the soil into plant roots.** When soil water contains a large quantity of dissolved salts, however, its concentration of water may be lower than that in plant cells; consequently, water moves out of plant roots and into the salty soil. Not surprisingly, most plants cannot survive under these conditions. Plant species that thrive in saline soils have special adaptations that enable them to tolerate the high amount of salt. Most crops, unless they have been genetically selected to tolerate high salt, are not productive in saline soil.

➡In principle, the way to remove excess salt from saline soils is to add enough water to leach it away. Although this sounds straightforward, it is extremely difficult and in many cases impossible. For one thing, saline soils usually occur in arid or semiarid lands where water is in short supply. Also, many soils don't have good drainage properties, so adding lots of water simply causes them to become waterlogged. Another factor that should not be overlooked

1   What is the main topic of the passage?
    Ⓐ Soil salinization
    Ⓑ The effect of saline on soil
    Ⓒ Minerals provided to plants by soil
    Ⓓ Necessary elements for plant growth

2   In which of the following areas can crystals of salt be found?
    Ⓐ A wheat field after a heavy rain
    Ⓑ A wild plain under hot sunrays
    Ⓒ A desert
    Ⓓ The shadows near a big lake

3   Look at the word their in the passage. Click on the word or phrase in the **bold** text that their refers to.   soils.

4   The word dissolved in the passage is closest in meaning to
    Ⓐ intensified
    Ⓑ solidified
    Ⓒ melted
    Ⓓ crushed

5   Look at the word that in the passage. Click on the word or phrase in the **bold** text that that refers to.
    concentration of water cytoplasm.

6   Click on the sentence in paragraph 2 that describes the kind of plants that could survive in saline soil.

7   The word flushed in the passage is closest in meaning to
    Ⓐ demolished
    Ⓑ emptied
    Ⓒ added to
    Ⓓ smoothed

8   Which of the following is NOT a disadvantage of the saline removal method known as 'leaching'?
    Ⓐ Saline soils usually occur in places where water is in short supply.
    Ⓑ Many soils have poor drainage properties.
    Ⓒ It is a very expensive method.
    Ⓓ Excess salt often pollutes groundwater or rivers.

End

is that even if the salt is flushed out of the soil, it has to go somewhere. The excess salt is usually carried to groundwater or to rivers and streams, where it becomes a water pollutant.

9 Look at the word it in paragraph 3. Click on the word or phrase in paragraph 3 that it refers to.

The excess salt,

Paragraph 3 is marked with an arrow (➡).

10 It can be inferred from paragraph 3 that adding enough water to remove redundant salt is

Ⓐ the best way without any side-effects
Ⓑ ineffective but harmless
Ⓒ not a good solution because it can increase the salt concentration
Ⓓ temporarily effective but can be harmful in the long run

11 Which of the following could be a good way to make soil less salty in semiarid areas?

Ⓐ Waterlogging
Ⓑ Light flushing
Ⓒ Crop rotation
Ⓓ Irrigation

Beginning

[3] **Performers of jazz improvise within the conventions of their chosen style. Typically, the improvisation is accompanied by the repeated chord progression of a popular song or an original composition.** Instrumentalists emulate black vocal styles, including the use of glissandi and slides, nuances of pitch—including blue notes, the microtonally flattened tones in the blues scale—and tonal effects such as growls and wails.

In striving to develop a personal sound or tone color—an idiosyncratic sense of rhythm and form and an individual style of execution—performers create rhythms characterized by constant syncopation, accents in unexpected places, and also by swing—a sensation of pull and momentum that arises as the melody is heard alternately together with, then slightly at variance with, the expected pulse. Written scores, if present, are used merely as guides, providing structure within which improvisation occurs. The typical instrumentation begins with a rhythm section consisting of piano, string bass, drums, and optional guitar, to which may be added any number of wind instruments. In big bands the winds are grouped into three sections—saxophones, trombones, and trumpets.

➡ Although exceptions occur in some styles, most jazz is based on the principle that an infinite number of melodies can fit the chord progressions of any song. The musician improvises new melodies that fit the chord progression, which is repeated again and again as each soloist is featured, for as many choruses as desired.

■ **Although pieces with many different formal patterns are used for jazz improvisation, two formal patterns in particular are frequently found in songs of the jazz genre.** ■ **One of them is the AABA form of popular-song choruses, which typically consist of 32 measures in meter, divided into four 8-**

1 What does the passage mainly discuss?
 Ⓐ Various historic jazz musicians and their unique styles
 Ⓑ Many different formal patterns for improvisation
 Ⓒ The main instruments used in jazz
 Ⓓ The characteristics of jazz

2 Look at the word their in the passage. Click on the word or phrase in the **bold** text that their refers to.
 performers (of jazz)

3 The word chosen in the passage is closest in meaning to
 Ⓐ ordinary
 Ⓑ destined
 Ⓒ picked
 Ⓓ unique

4 The phrase striving to in the passage is closest in meaning to
 Ⓐ attempting to
 Ⓑ building up to
 Ⓒ putting in to
 Ⓓ launching to

5 It can be inferred from the passage that scores of jazz music
 Ⓐ hardly exist
 Ⓑ record every chord rigidly
 Ⓒ were used mainly by black musicians
 Ⓓ were sold for high prices

6 The phrase at variance in the passage is closest in meaning to
 Ⓐ evenly
 Ⓑ by turns
 Ⓒ different
 Ⓓ without pause

7 Look at the word them in the passage. Click on the word or phrase in the **bold** text that them refers to.
 two formal patterns

8 Click on the sentence in paragraph 3 that states what jazz is mostly based on.

Paragraph 3 is marked with an arrow (➡).

End

measure sections: section A; repeat of section A; section B (the "bridge" or "release," often beginning in a new key); repeat of section A. ■ The other form, with roots deep in black American folk music, is the 12-bar blues form. ■

9　According to the passage, why do jazz performers make music with constant syncopation?

　Ⓐ To give music their own identifying marks

　Ⓑ To make the style of music free from rules

　Ⓒ To attract audiences' attention

　Ⓓ To give music a dramatic effect

10　The following sentence can be added to the passage.

　Unlike the 32-bar AABA form, blues songs have a fairly standardized chord progression.

　Where would it best fit in the passage? Click on the square [■] to add the sentence to the passage.

11　Which of the following is NOT mentioned as a feature of jazz music?

　Ⓐ Pulse variations

　Ⓑ Dynamic rhythms

　Ⓒ Gloomy melodies

　Ⓓ Strict format

Beginning

[4] Archaeological evidence indicates that condors have been revered by western Native Americans for thousands of years and played a major role in their legends and rituals. Condors were considered sacred and capable of providing communication with the supernatural world, as well as supernatural powers.

In more recent times, the California condor has become the subject of an intense and sometimes controversial effort to save the species from extinction. Faced with rapidly declining numbers, scientists began collecting wild-laid eggs and capturing free-flying birds to breed them in captivity with the goal of eventually restoring the condor to its rightful place in the California skies.

Condors were probably never very numerous in North America. The species once ranged along the entire Pacific Coast from British Columbia to Baja California. Fossils have been found as far east as Texas, Florida, and New York. More recently, however, they were confined to a horseshoe-shaped area of California that included portions of coastal mountain ranges, the Transverse range and the southern Sierra Nevada Mountains.

For years, no one knew precisely how many California condors existed, although they have been considered to be a declining species since the 1890s. **One estimate put their number at 100 in the early 1940s. Another indicated there were 50 to 60 in the early 1960s. By the late 1970s, the estimate had dropped to 25 to 30 birds.**

■ Some factors include illegal collection of condors and their eggs, poisoning from substances put out by ranchers to eradicate livestock predators, poisoning from ingesting lead fragments from bullets embedded in animal carcasses the condors feed on, and collisions with structures such as power lines. ■ In addition, the roads, cities, housing tracts, and weekend mountain retreats of modern

---

1 What is the main idea of the passage?

Ⓐ Western Native Americans have revered condors as supernatural birds.

Ⓑ Condors are declining mostly due to human carelessness.

Ⓒ Condors were never very numerous in North America.

Ⓓ Efforts to save the California condor from extinction are controversial.

2 The word sacred in the passage is closest in meaning to

Ⓐ potent

Ⓑ acute

Ⓒ admirable

Ⓓ holy

3 Click on the paragraph that explains what movement is taking place as condors become extinct.

4 Look at the word another in the passage. Click on the word or phrase in the **bold** text that another refers to. *number.*

5 The word embedded in the passage is closest in meaning to

Ⓐ included

Ⓑ buried

Ⓒ nurtured

Ⓓ encroached

6 The following sentence can be added to the passage.

Nor, despite years of study, can scientists pinpoint the reason for the bird's decline.

Where would it best fit in the passage? Click on the square [■] to add the sentence to the passage.

7 According to the passage, in ancient times condors lived

Ⓐ only in California

Ⓑ mostly along the mountain ranges

Ⓒ in many places in North America

Ⓓ all over the American continent

End

civilization have replaced much of the open country condors need to find food. ■ Their slow rate of reproduction and years spent reaching breeding maturity undoubtedly make the condor population as a whole more vulnerable to these threats. ■

8 It can be inferred from the passage that when its egg gets stolen, the condor
   Ⓐ abandons laying other eggs
   Ⓑ lays another egg the following year
   Ⓒ takes a while to lay another egg
   Ⓓ searches for the lost egg for a long period

9 For which of the following reasons did the number of condors decline?
   Ⓐ Extensive capturing by ranchers
   Ⓑ Diseases acquired through contact with humans
   Ⓒ Losing places where it could forage for food
   Ⓓ Low rate of mating

10 The effort to restore condors was
   Ⓐ made by government organizations
   Ⓑ somewhat disputatious
   Ⓒ taken all over North America
   Ⓓ proved to be ineffective at last

11 All of the following were reasons for the condors' decline EXCEPT
   Ⓐ death from poison intended to eradicate livestock predators
   Ⓑ collisions with structures
   Ⓒ regular overflowing of rivers
   Ⓓ the illegal collection of condors and their eggs

Beginning

[1] Historians use the word "revolution" in several different senses: for a violent uprising, for something strikingly innovative and influential, and for a process that works for deep and important changes. When discussing revolutions, it is easy to shift from one definition to another without realizing it. This is something to avoid, especially when discussing the Industrial Revolution. Although it is most popularly considered as a long process of great change, some writers prefer to emphasize the innovations and spend a good deal of time discussing the mining and use of coal and the principles and operation of the steam engine. However, neither of these was particularly new at the time.

In the year 1092, a monk of the Abbey of Saint James in Liege—in modern Belgium—wrote that a lot of "black rock" had been found under the soil in the vicinity and that it had great advantages, "giving warmth to the poor and fire to the artisan." In the nineteenth century, a significant steel industry was established at Liege using that coal deposit, but it had not really been developed until that time. The men and women of the Middle Ages found that their "black rock" "emitted noxious vapors" —we would call it "pollution"—and passed a law against using it. Back in Hellenistic times, Hiero, one of those bright chaps at the Museum of Alexandria, built an interesting gadget. He made a ball-shaped teapot with a tight-fitting lid and two spigots, one on each side and pointing in opposite directions. He put water in it and suspended it by a string above a small fire.

As the water started to boil, steam built up inside the vessel and began to escape through the spigots. The steam was shooting out in opposite directions, so the metal ball began to spin faster and faster. Hiero called his gadget an aeropile, and his friends thought it quite ingenious. It remained nothing more than a clever toy, however, much like the Mayan use of the

1   What is the best title for this passage?
    Ⓐ The meaning of the Industrial Revolution
    Ⓑ A different meaning of "revolution"
    Ⓒ The creative invention of Saint James
    Ⓓ The mechanical revolution in 1092

2   What is the purpose of paragraph 2 and 3?
    Ⓐ To clarify the Industrial Revolution
    Ⓑ To give an example of an invention
    Ⓒ To show the value of an aeropile
    Ⓓ To give insight on the early steam machine

3   According to the passage, when we mention the Industrial Revolution, the best definition of "revolution" is a process of
    Ⓐ remarkable creativity
    Ⓑ significant change
    Ⓒ rapid change
    Ⓓ epoch-making inventions

4   The author mentions black rock in order to demonstrate that
    Ⓐ some rediscovered inventions are regarded as new
    Ⓑ some archaeological findings wrongly indicate the time an invention was created
    Ⓒ some original thing caused the Industrial Revolution
    Ⓓ industrial success depends on the character of its source

5   It can be inferred from paragraph 2 that coal was first used
    Ⓐ in prehistoric times
    Ⓑ in the 11th century
    Ⓒ during the Middle Ages
    Ⓓ after the Industrial Revolution

6   The word it in the passage refers to
    Ⓐ the soil
    Ⓑ the vicinity
    Ⓒ the Abbey
    Ⓓ black rock

End

wheel only for pull-toys. The aeropile had a number of flaws, but if Hiero and his colleagues had had an important reason to do so, they could doubtless have developed it further into an effective steam turbine. There was no such reason, however, and so the principle of the aeropile was mostly forgotten.

7 Click on the sentence that describes the shape of the teapot Hiero invented.

8 The word suspended in the passage is closest in meaning to
Ⓐ dangled
Ⓑ erected
Ⓒ fabricated
Ⓓ barred

9 For which of the following reasons was the principle of the aeropile forgotten?
Ⓐ It had numerous defects.
Ⓑ There was no need for it.
Ⓒ It was interesting but too intricate.
Ⓓ It was too dangerous to use.

10 The word ingenious in the passage is closest in meaning to
Ⓐ curious
Ⓑ original
Ⓒ informative
Ⓓ witty

11 The author organizes the discussion of "revolution" in terms of
Ⓐ a summary of counter arguments about the Industrial Revolution
Ⓑ an introduction to the background of the Industrial Revolution
Ⓒ several definitions and additional explanations
Ⓓ a description of innovations of the Industrial Revolution

Beginning

[2] By about 5 billion years ago the solar nebula was a rotating disk-shaped mass of about 75% hydrogen 23% helium, and 2% other material, including heavier elements —gases,dust, and ice. Like a spinning skater bringing in his or her arms, the nebula spun faster as it condensed. Material that concentrated near its center became the protosun. Much of the outer material eventually became planets, the smaller bodies that orbit a star and do not shine by their own light.

The new planets formed in the disk of dust and debris surrounding the young sun through a process known as accretion—the dumping of small particles into large masses. Bigger clumps with stronger gravity pulled in most of the condensing matter. Near the protosun, where temperatures were highest, the first materials to solidify were substances with high boiling points—mainly metals and certain rocky minerals. The planet Mercury, closest to the sun, is mostly iron because iron is a solid at high temperatures. Somewhat farther out in the cooler regions, magnesium, silicon, water, and oxygen condensed. Methane and ammonia accumulated in the frigid outer zones. The Earth's array of water, silicon-oxygen compounds and metals results from its middle position within that accreting cloud. The planets of the outer solar system— Jupiter, Saturn, Uranus, and Neptune—are composed mostly of methane and ammonia ices because those gases can congeal only at cold temperatures.

➡The period of accretion lasted perhaps 50 to 70 million years. The protosun became a star when its internal temperature became high enough to fuse atoms of hydrogen into helium. The violence of these nuclear reactions sent radiation sweeping past the inner planets, clearing the area of excess particles and ending the period of rapid accretion. Gases like those we now see on the giant outer

1 What does the passage mainly discuss?
Ⓐ The origin of the earth
Ⓑ The lives of stars
Ⓒ The formation of new planets
Ⓓ The material makeup of stars

2 The word spun in the passage is closest in meaning to
Ⓐ expanded
Ⓑ ran
Ⓒ revolved
Ⓓ spread

3 It can be inferred from paragraph 1 that the materials that make up the protosun are
Ⓐ the heaviest materials
Ⓑ the lightest materials
Ⓒ the hardest materials
Ⓓ the softest materials

4 The word surrounding in the passage is closest in meaning to
Ⓐ accompanying
Ⓑ encircling
Ⓒ clinging to
Ⓓ bumping into

5 According to paragraph 2, the first material to solidify is
Ⓐ cadmium
Ⓑ iron
Ⓒ silicon
Ⓓ methane

6 The author mentions all of the following as features of the planet Mercury EXCEPT
Ⓐ uniform surface temperature
Ⓑ a position closest to the sun
Ⓒ mostly composed of iron
Ⓓ a solid body

7 The word lasted in the passage is OPPOSITE in meaning to
Ⓐ went over
Ⓑ revived
Ⓒ ceased
Ⓓ elongated

End

planets may once have surrounded the inner planets, but this rush of solar energy and particles stripped them away.

8 It can be inferred from paragraph 2 that solid ammonia

Ⓐ is found on stars

Ⓑ was swept from the center of a protosun to outer planets

Ⓒ is found on the farthest planets from the sun

Ⓓ is the lightest material in the process of forming the sun

9 Click on the sentence in paragraph 3 that tells the condition of the protosun being a star.

Paragraph 3 is marked with an arrow(➡).

10 The word them in the passage refers to

Ⓐ particles

Ⓑ the inner planets

Ⓒ the outer planets

Ⓓ gases

11 It can be inferred from the passage that a star is different from a planet in that

Ⓐ it's radiant by itself

Ⓑ it spins more quickly

Ⓒ it has more diverse components

Ⓓ it emits gases from its center

Beginning

[3] Many historians have characterized the period between the two world wars as the United States' traumatic "coming of age," despite the fact that U.S. direct involvement was relatively brief (1917-1918) and its casualties many fewer than those of its European allies and foes. **John Dos Passos expressed America's postwar disillusionment in the novel *Three Soldiers* (1921), when he noted that civilization was a "vast edifice of sham, and the war, instead of its crumbling, was its fullest and most ultimate expression."** ■ Shocked and permanently changed, Americans returned to their homeland but could never regain their innocence. ■

After experiencing the world, many now yearned for a modern, urban life. ■ New farm machines such as planters, harvesters, and binders had drastically reduced the demand for farm jobs; yet despite their increased productivity, farmers were poor. ■ Crop prices, like urban workers' wages, depended on unrestrained market forces heavily influenced by business interests. Government subsidies for farmers and effective workers' unions had not yet become established. "The chief business of the American people is business," President Calvin Coolidge proclaimed in 1925, and most agreed.

➡ In the postwar "Big Boom," business flourished and the successful prospered beyond their wildest dreams. For the first time, many Americans enrolled in higher education. In the 1920s college enrollment doubled. The middle-class prospered; Americans began to enjoy the world's highest national average income in that era. Many people purchased the ultimate status symbol—the automobile. The typical urban American home glowed with electric lights and boasted a radio that connected the house with the outside world, and perhaps a telephone, a camera, a typewriter, or a sewing machine. **Like the**

1 What is the main topic of this passage?
 Ⓐ The chracteristics of American life
 Ⓑ The postwar years in America
 Ⓒ The civilization illustrated in the novel *Three Soldiers*
 Ⓓ The modernization of America after the World Wars

2 The word edifice in the passage is closest in meaning to
 Ⓐ fragment
 Ⓑ condensation
 Ⓒ construction
 Ⓓ feature

3 By referring to the war as its fullest and most ultimate expression, the author implies that Americans realized that
 Ⓐ the essence of civilization is violent
 Ⓑ war comes from brutality inherent in human nature
 Ⓒ the war caused the destruction of civilization
 Ⓓ the war devastated the entire world

4 The word yearned in the passage is closest in meaning to
 Ⓐ defrosted
 Ⓑ craved
 Ⓒ denied
 Ⓓ executed

5 The following sentence can be added to the passage.
 Nor could soldiers from rural America easily return to their roots.

 Where would it best fit in the passage? Click on the square [■] to add the sentence to the passage.

6 The word proclaimed in the passage is closest in meaning to
 Ⓐ promulgated
 Ⓑ reckoned
 Ⓒ detained
 Ⓓ contrived

End

businessman protagonist of Sinclair Lewis's novel *Babbitt* in 1922, the average American approved of these machines because they were modern and because most were American inventions and American-made.

7   According to the passage, what is one reason that farmers left their farmland?

   Ⓐ The war deprived them of their inward peace.

   Ⓑ Agricultural demand increased just a little.

   Ⓒ New farm machines made the work too easy.

   Ⓓ The economic trend was against agricultural interests.

8   Click on the sentence in paragraph 3 that explains educational change in the "Big Boom" era.

   Paragraph 3 is marked with an arrow(➡).

9   It can be inferred from the passage that crop prices would have not fallen that much if there had been

   Ⓐ more productive farm machines

   Ⓑ active government aid

   Ⓒ a business center

   Ⓓ a completely competitive market

10 The author mentions a telephone, a camera, a typewriter, or a sewing machine as examples of items that

   Ⓐ most Americans bought as a symbol of wealth

   Ⓑ most Americans considered to be up-to-date

   Ⓒ allowed people to forget about the cruel war

   Ⓓ made American business most prosperous

11 Look at the word they in the passage.

   Click on the word or phrase in the **bold** text that they refers to.

Beginning

[4] Until the early 1950s, little was known about sleep. ■ Kleitman had assigned one of his graduate students, Eugene Aserinsky, the tedious task of finding out if the slow, rolling eye movements that characterize the onset of sleep continue throughout the night. ■ To both men's surprise, Aserinsky discovered that eye movements did indeed occur, but that they were rapid, not slow. ■ Using the electroencephalograph to measure the brain's electrical activity, these researchers, along with another of Kleitman's students, William Dement, were able to correlate the rapid eye movements of sleepers with changes in their brain-wave patterns. ■ **Adult volunteers were soon spending their nights sleeping in laboratories while scientists observed them and measured changes in their brain activity, muscle tension, breathing, and other physiological responses.**

➡As a result of this research, today we know that sleep is not an unbroken state of rest. In adults, periods of rapid eye movement (REM) alternate with periods of fewer eye movements, or non-REM (NREM), in an ultradian cycle that recurs, on the average, every 90 minutes. The REM periods last from a few minutes to as long as an hour, averaging about 20 minutes in length. Whenever they begin, the pattern of electrical activity of the sleeper's brain changes to resemble that of alert wakefulness. Non-REM periods are themselves divided into shorter, distinct stages, each associated with a particular brain-wave pattern.

When you first climb into bed, close your eyes, and relax, your brain emits bursts of alpha waves. On an EEG recording, alpha waves have a regular rhythm, high amplitude or height, and a low frequency of 8-12 cycles per second. Alpha activity is associated with relaxing or not concentrating on anything in particular. Gradually these waves slow down even further and you drift

1   What is the main topic of this passage?
Ⓐ The sequence of NREM and REM sleep
Ⓑ Success in studying the sleep patterns of Nathaniel Kleitman
Ⓒ Characteristics of REM sleep
Ⓓ Stages and characteristics of sleep

2   The word onset in the passage is closest in meaning to
Ⓐ resumption
Ⓑ beginning
Ⓒ pause
Ⓓ turning point

3   The following sentence can be added to the passage.

Then a breakthrough occurred in the laboratory of physiologist Nathaniel Kleitman, who at the time was the only person in the world who had spent an entire career studying sleep.

Where would it best fit in the passage?
Click on the square [■] to add the sentence to the passage.

4   By using the electroencephalograph, the researchers found
Ⓐ a relationship between REM and brain waves
Ⓑ changes in muscle tension during sleep
Ⓒ existence of eye movement during sleep
Ⓓ the effect of stimulation during sleep

5   The word them in the passage refers to
Ⓐ nights
Ⓑ Adult volunteers
Ⓒ laboratories
Ⓓ brain-wave patterns

6   It can be inferred from paragraph 1 that the discovery of rapid eye movements in sleep was
Ⓐ foreseen
Ⓑ unexpected
Ⓒ momentous
Ⓓ negligible

End

into the Land of Nod, passing through four stages, each deeper than the previous one.

REM and non-REM sleep continue to alternate throughout the night, with the REM periods tending to get longer and closer together as the hours pass. **An early REM period may last only a few minutes, whereas a later one may go on for 20 or 30 minutes and sometimes as long as an hour—which is why people are likely to be dreaming when the alarm goes off.**

7   Click on the sentence in paragraph 2 that indicates for how long REM periods last.

Paragraph 2 is marked with an arrow (➡)

8   The word recurs in the passage is closest in meaning to
   Ⓐ is consistent
   Ⓑ resorts
   Ⓒ happens again
   Ⓓ stands still

9   Which of the following statements about REM periods is true?
   Ⓐ At the start of REM sleep, there are changes in brain wave patterns.
   Ⓑ In REM sleep, breathing becomes shorter and lighter.
   Ⓒ When sleeping, REM occurs about 10 times a night.
   Ⓓ In REM sleep, people experience muscle tension.

10 The brain emits alpha waves when a person is
   Ⓐ studying
   Ⓑ in rapid eye movement
   Ⓒ dreaming
   Ⓓ resting

11 The word Gradually in the passage is closest in meaning to
   Ⓐ by chance
   Ⓑ by degrees
   Ⓒ on and on
   Ⓓ in leisure

Beginning

[5] There are approximately 20,000 species of lichens that typically possess one of the three different growth forms: crustose, foliose, and fruticose.

Although a lichen looks like a single organism, it is actually a symbiotic association between a photosynthetic organism and a fungus. The photosynthetic partner is usually a green algae or a cyanobacterium, and the fungus is most often an ascomycete. In some lichens in tropical regions, the fungal partner is a basidiomycete. The algae or cyanobacteria found in lichens are also found as free-living species in nature, but the fungal components of lichens are generally found only as part of lichens.

➡In a laboratory the fungal and photosynthetic partners of a lichen can be separated and grown individually in appropriate culture media. The algae or cyanobacterium grows more rapidly when separated, whereas the fungus grows slowly and requires a culture medium that provides many complex carbohydrates. ■ **Generally, the fungus does not produce fruiting bodies when separated from its photosynthetic partner. ■ As part of a lichen, however, the fungus does produce fruiting bodies, but only if they are placed together in a culture medium under conditions that cannot support either of them independently.**

➡■ In the past the lichen was considered a definitive example of mutualism, a symbiotic relationship equally beneficial to both species. ■ The photosynthetic partner carries on photosynthesis, producing carbohydrate molecules for itself and the fungus, and the fungus obtains water and minerals for the photosynthetic partner as well as protects it against desiccation. ■ Microscopic

1 What is the main topic of this passage?
   Ⓐ The characteristics of the partnership between fungi and lichen
   Ⓑ Fungi as a part of dual organisms called lichens
   Ⓒ The true nature of partnership in lichens
   Ⓓ The way fungi and photosynthetic partners react together

2 The word components in the passage is closest in meaning to
   Ⓐ parts
   Ⓑ methods
   Ⓒ junctions
   Ⓓ convocations

3 Look at the word its in the passage.
   Click on the word or phrase in the **bold** text that its refers to.

4 The passage supports all of the following statements about partnership of a lichen in the laboratory EXCEPT that
   Ⓐ fungus is generally sterile when separated from its photosynthetic partner
   Ⓑ the algae or cyanobacterium grows more rapidly if separated
   Ⓒ the fungal and photosynthetic partners of a lichen need appropriate culture media to be grown together
   Ⓓ when separated, the fungus grows slowly

5 The following sentence can be added to the passage.
   Some biologists, however, think that the lichen partnership is not a true case of mutualism but one of conrolled parasitism of the photosynthetic partner by the fungus.

   Where would it best fit in the passage?
   Click on the square [■] to add the sentence to paragraph 3 or 4. Paragraph 3 and 4 are marked with an arrow (➡).

6 The word desiccation in the passage is closest in meaning to
   Ⓐ vaporization
   Ⓑ dissemination
   Ⓒ dehydration
   Ⓓ conversion

End

examination reveals that some of the algae cells have been penetrated and destroyed by fungal hyphae. ■

7   What can be inferred from the theory of some biologists mentioned in paragraph 4?

Ⓐ Algae can live without water.

Ⓑ Photosynthesizing organisms don't need minerals.

Ⓒ Fungus is often harmful to its partner.

Ⓓ Fungi harm the algae cells to keep themselves adequately humid.

8   According to the passage, for its partner, the fungi offers

Ⓐ an energy source

Ⓑ shelter

Ⓒ moisture

Ⓓ inorganic matter

9   According to the passage, recent scientific studies oppose the theory that the lichen is

Ⓐ an independent species

Ⓑ a formation in which two partners are not supporting each other mutually

Ⓒ made up of two dependent organisms

Ⓓ composed of two different species mutually aiding each other

10 Which of the following statements about fungus is true?

Ⓐ The fungus produces fruiting bodies when separated from its photosynthetic partner.

Ⓑ The fungus produces carbohydrates for itself.

Ⓒ The fungus gives its partner indispensable help.

Ⓓ The fungus grows slower than the cyanobacterium.

11 The author mentions the example of fungal hyphae in paragraph 4 for which of the following reasons?

Ⓐ To introduce the species most closely related to the lichen

Ⓑ To refute the theory that lichen is a parasite

Ⓒ To clarify the process of fungal reproduction

Ⓓ To suggest that algae and fungus may not have a mutually beneficial relationship

Beginning

[1] **After the Civil War, agriculture began to decline while urban industry surged forward. Farmers knew they were being left behind. They suspected government indifference and hostility to their interests.** American farmers did not understand that they were caught up in an international crisis afflicting agriculture in many parts of the world.

The crisis for farmers of export staple crops—for example, wheat and cotton—resulted from the communication and transportation revolution that created an internationally accessible market for agricultural products. Ships first steamed through the Suez Canal in 1869, the year locomotives first steamed across the North American continent. In addition, vast new tracts of land were brought under cultivation in South America, Australia, and Canada, as well as in the trans-Mississippi West. Simultaneously, a new technology of mechanized cultivation exponentially increased productivity. The invention of the mechanical reaper in 1831 increased grain production six-fold.

Farmers were forced to compete in a world market without protection against their competitors or control over world output. Thus, prices of agricultural products declined as productivity mounted. In 1867, U.S. farmers produced 211 million bushels of wheat on 17 million acres of land and they received an average price per bushel of $2.01. In 1868, U.S. farmers produced 246 million bushels of wheat on 19 million acres of land and they received an average price per bushel of $1.46. In 1869, U.S. farmers produced 290 million bushels of wheat on 21 million acres of land and they received an average price of $.91 per bushel. From 1870 to 1873 cotton had averaged about 15.1 cents per pound. From 1894 to 1898 it dropped to an average of 5.8 cents per pound. In 1889 corn was selling for 10 cents a bushel in Kansas, and farmers were burning it for

1   What is the main topic of this passage?
    Ⓐ Agricultural development policy
    Ⓑ The state of agriculture in America at the end of the 19th century
    Ⓒ Government indifference toward the crisis of agriculture
    Ⓓ The decline of agriculture after the Civil War

2   The phrase surged forward in the passage is the best replaced by
    Ⓐ streamed
    Ⓑ precipitated
    Ⓒ diminished
    Ⓓ flourished

3   Look at the word their in the passage.
    Click on the word or phrase in the **bold** text that their refers to

4   By stating an international crisis in paragraph1, the author means
    Ⓐ a heavily regulated global market
    Ⓑ the collapse of a global market
    Ⓒ the disappearance of government subsidies
    Ⓓ a worldwide imbalance between demand and supply

5   The author mentions ships and locomotives in paragraph 2 to illustrate that
    Ⓐ the productivity of agriculture increased greatly
    Ⓑ advanced transportation accelerated the invention of new machines
    Ⓒ cities sprawled quickly due to them
    Ⓓ the global market was supported by transportation networks

6   The word simultaneously in the passage is closest in meaning to
    Ⓐ emphatically
    Ⓑ contemporarily
    Ⓒ intentionally
    Ⓓ collaboratively

End

fuel. Georgian farmers were getting 5 cents a pound for cotton when it cost about 7 cents per pound to produce it.

7   The passage supports all of the following statements about the agricultural situation EXCEPT that

Ⓐ in 1889 the price of corn was so cheap that farmers burned it for fuel in Kansas

Ⓑ Georgia farmers produced cotton at about 7 cents per pound but earned 5 cents per pound

Ⓒ prices of agricultural products declined as productivity went up

Ⓓ the number of acres used for agrarian residences increased between 1867 and 1868

8   All of the following are mentioned in the passage as reasons for the farming crisis EXCEPT that

Ⓐ the global food market was competitive

Ⓑ demand for wheat declined as tastes changed

Ⓒ the revolutionary increase in communication and transportaion

Ⓓ the government failed to protect farmers

9   How much was the average price of a bushel of wheat in 1869?

Ⓐ $2.01

Ⓑ $1.46

Ⓒ $0.91

Ⓓ $1.51

10   Why did farmers use corn as fuel?

Ⓐ Corn burns better than other crops.

Ⓑ Burning corn for fuel was more economical.

Ⓒ Production of corn was cheaper than of wood.

Ⓓ Corn's selling price dropped more than cotton's.

11   Why did American agriculture decline after the Civil War?

Ⓐ The government worked against farmers.

Ⓑ Farmers didn't utilize modern transportation well.

Ⓒ The supply increased rapidly due to new technology.

Ⓓ Productivity declined because of constant use of the farmland.

Beginning

[2] By the mid-1840s, America had become a two-ocean nation. As a result of the Treaty of Guadaloupe Hidalgo with Mexico and the earlier settlement of the Oregon question with Great Britain, the United States now had control over California, Oregon, and much of the interior of the continent. Recognizing the need to connect the vast area, in 1853 Congress charged Jefferson Davis, then Secretary of War, to conduct feasibility surveys for a transcontinental railroad. After years of debate on the best route, President Lincoln signed the Pacific Railroad Act on July 1, 1862, and one of the greatest adventures in American history began.

Two railroad companies, the Union Pacific and the Central Pacific, were authorized to construct a railroad and telegraph line that would span the continent. The Union Pacific was to build westward from the 100th meridian (near Omaha, Nebraska) across the Great Plains, and the Central Pacific was to build eastward from Sacramento through the Sierra Nevada.

➡In addition to the land grants, the government promised funds to each of the railroads according to how much track was laid, sparking a fierce competition between the two. Soon the silent lands that had been the province of nomadic Native Americans, fur traders, and explorers gave way to the bustle of surveyors, graders, trestle builders, tunnel blasters, and spikers. Thousands of workers, including Civil War veterans and immigrants, were enlisted to do the back-breaking work of laying track across the treeless deserts and through towering granite mountains. As the tracks from the Central Pacific and Union Pacific approached each other, the two railroads could not agree on a meeting point. As a solution, they surveyed and graded a parallel roadbed 320 kilometers long. Finally, they chose a meeting point—Promontory, Utah—and on May 10, 1869, a telegraph key clattered out a message indicating the line's completion.

1 What does paragraph 1 mainly discuss?
   Ⓐ The compromise of territorial conflicts between America and nearby countries
   Ⓑ The advent of the necessity of establishing transcontinental railroads
   Ⓒ The significance of American railroads
   Ⓓ One important event in American history

2 Which of the following can be inferred from paragraph 1?
   Ⓐ Americans often settled foreign lands illegally.
   Ⓑ The treaty with Mexico was against America.
   Ⓒ The surveys for a national railroad took about a quarter of a century.
   Ⓓ It was not simple to select the area for railroad.

3 The word feasibility in the passage is closest in meaning to
   Ⓐ stability
   Ⓑ practicability
   Ⓒ distrust
   Ⓓ compatibility

4 The phrase one of the greatest adventures in American history mentioned in paragraph 1 indicates
   Ⓐ the war with other countries
   Ⓑ a great change in Americans' life
   Ⓒ expanding the national border
   Ⓓ the installation of a new transportation system

5 The word nomadic in the passage is closest in meaning to
   Ⓐ aboriginal
   Ⓑ nominal
   Ⓒ peaceful
   Ⓓ itinerant

6 The phrase back-breaking in the passage is OPPOSITE in meaning to
   Ⓐ ethical
   Ⓑ effortless
   Ⓒ negligible
   Ⓓ outstanding

End

   During the next two decades, railroads experienced their greatest growth, adding 176,000 kilometers to the system and eventually constructing seven transcontinental rail routes. By the eve of the First World War, railroads had reached their peak in America, with over 400,000 kilometers of track.

7 The word they in the passage refers to
   Ⓐ thousands of workers
   Ⓑ governments
   Ⓒ the tracks
   Ⓓ the two railroads

8 According to paragraph 3, the American government prompted the railroad construction by
   Ⓐ igniting competition of companies
   Ⓑ subsidizing companies equally
   Ⓒ conducting it by itself
   Ⓓ using professional workers

9 Click on the sentence in paragraph 3 that indicates the changes of land caused by railroads.

   Paragraph 3 is marked with an arrow(➡).

10 When was construction of all the transcontinental railroads completed?
   Ⓐ 1853
   Ⓑ 1862
   Ⓒ 1869
   Ⓓ 1840

11 The paragraph that follows the passage most likely deals with
   Ⓐ reasons why America constructed railroads
   Ⓑ the effects of the war on railroad construction
   Ⓒ the government's role in establishing the railroads
   Ⓓ the benefits America experienced after the construction of railroads

Beginning

[3] The virtually infallible homing instinct of the Pacific salmon species is legendary. After migrating downstream as a smolt, a sockeye salmon ranges many hundreds of miles over the Pacific for nearly four years, grows to 2 to 5 kg in weight, and then returns almost unerringly to spawn in the headwaters of its parent stream. Some straying does occur and is an important means of increasing gene flow and populating new streams.

Experiments have shown that homing salmon are guided upstream by the characteristic odor of their parent stream. When the salmon finally reach the spawning beds of their parents, where they themselves were hatched, they spawn and die. The following spring, the newly hatched fry transform into smolts before and during the downstream migration. At this time they are imprinted with the distinctive odor of the stream, which is apparently a mosaic of compounds released by the characteristic vegetation and soil in the watershed of the parent stream. They also seem to imprint on the odors of other streams they pass while migrating downriver and use these odors in reverse sequence as a map during the upriver migration as returning adults.

➡ How do salmon find their way to the mouth of the coastal river from the trackless miles of the open ocean? Salmon move hundreds of miles away from the coast, much too far to be able to detect the odor of their parent stream. Experiments suggest that some migrating fish, like birds, can navigate by orienting to the position of the sun. However, migrant salmon can navigate on cloudy days and at night, indicating that solar navigation, if used at all, can not be the salmon's only navigational cue. Fish also, again like birds, appear able to detect the earth's magnetic field and to navigate by orientating to it. Finally, fishery biologists concede that salmon may not require precise navigational abilities at all, but instead may use ocean currents, temperature gradients, and food availability to reach the general

1   What is the main topic of this passage?
   Ⓐ The role of odor in a sockeye salmon's homing method
   Ⓑ Salmon's reroduction and growth
   Ⓒ The homing instinct and patterns of salmon
   Ⓓ The life cycle of fish

2   The word unerringly in the passage is closest in meaning to
   Ⓐ favorably
   Ⓑ easily
   Ⓒ without fail
   Ⓓ in time

3   According to paragraph 1, the salmon's ability to find its parent stream is
   Ⓐ nearly perfect
   Ⓑ powerless
   Ⓒ different depending on the subspecies
   Ⓓ determined by the surroundings in which the salmon hatched

4   The word they in the passage refers to
   Ⓐ fry
   Ⓑ smolts
   Ⓒ parents
   Ⓓ homing salmons

5   The word sequence in the passage is closest in meaning to
   Ⓐ deviation
   Ⓑ order
   Ⓒ rotation
   Ⓓ route

6   The experiments mentioned in paragraph 3 were done to find out
   Ⓐ how salmon locate their way from the open sea
   Ⓑ how salmon tell different odors
   Ⓒ how salmon find new streams
   Ⓓ how salmon remember odors

End

coastal area where "their" river is located. From this point, they would navigate by their imprinted odor map, making correct turns at each junction until they reach their natal stream.

7   Click on the word or phrase that indicates what salmon use as the main guidance for navigation near their breeding ground.

Paragraph 3 is marked with an arrow(➡).

8   It can be inferred from the passage that in the open ocean, salmons find routes by using
   Ⓐ vegetation odors
   Ⓑ the earth's magnetic field
   Ⓒ the location of stars
   Ⓓ the contour of the seabed

9   The word "their" in the passage refers to
   Ⓐ fishery biologists
   Ⓑ migrating fish
   Ⓒ salmon
   Ⓓ birds

10 The word imprinted in the passage is closest in meaning to
   Ⓐ infallible
   Ⓑ accurate
   Ⓒ fixed
   Ⓓ pictured

11 A salmon would probably NOT to be able to find its way to its parent stream if the stream were
   Ⓐ colored red by a red tide
   Ⓑ dominated by large noisy ships
   Ⓒ contaminated with stinky pollutants
   Ⓓ over populated with people

Beginning

[4] Today few scientists doubt that the atmosphere is warming. Most also agree that the rate of heating is accelerating and that the consequences of this temperature change could become increasingly disruptive. Even high school students can reel off some projected outcomes: the oceans will warm, and glaciers will melt, causing sea levels to rise and salt water to inundate settlements along many low-lying coasts. Meanwhile, the regions suitable for farming will shift. Weather patterns should also become more erratic and storms more severe.

Yet less familiar effects could be equally detrimental. Notably, computer models predict that global warming, and other climate alterations it induces, will expand the incidence and distribution of many serious medical disorders. Disturbingly, these forecasts seem to be coming true.

Heating of the atmosphere can influence health via several routes. Most directly, it can generate more, stronger and hotter heat waves, which will become especially treacherous if the evenings fail to bring cooling relief. Unfortunately, a lack of nighttime cooling seems probable. The atmosphere is heating unevenly and is showing the most significant rises at night, in winter and at latitudes higher than about 50 degrees. In some places, the number of deaths related to heat waves is projected to double by 2020. Prolonged heat can, moreover, enhance production of smog and the dispersal of allergens. Both effects have been linked to respiratory symptoms.

➡Global warming can also threaten human well-being profoundly, if somewhat less directly, by revising weather patterns— particularly by pumping up the frequency and intensity of floods and droughts and by causing rapid swings in the weather. As the atmosphere has warmed over the past century, droughts in arid areas have

1   What is the main idea of this passage?
Ⓐ Global warming threatens human life
Ⓑ Global warming relates to temperature change
Ⓒ Global warming is a big problem worldwide
Ⓓ Weather patterns will become more capricious.

2   Heating of the atmosphere would lead to all of the following phenomena EXCEPT that
Ⓐ some coastline would be altered
Ⓑ serious medical disorders would increase
Ⓒ the night temperature would rise
Ⓓ the density of salt in the ocean would be higher

3   The word Notably in the passage is closest in meaning to
Ⓐ especially
Ⓑ suspiciously
Ⓒ diversely
Ⓓ infamously

4   The word treacherous in the passage is closest in meaning to
Ⓐ hazardous
Ⓑ precarious
Ⓒ dependable
Ⓓ deceptive

5   The phrase Both effects in the passage refers to
Ⓐ heat waves and lack of nighttime cooling
Ⓑ allergens and heat waves
Ⓒ prolonged heat and smog
Ⓓ allergens and smog

6   According to the passage, heating of the atmosphere can bring about
Ⓐ reduced nighttime
Ⓑ ocean pollution
Ⓒ breathing problems
Ⓓ hypertension

End

persisted longer, and massive bursts of precipitation have become more common. Aside from causing death by drowning or starvation, these disasters promote, by various means, the emergence, resurgence and spread of infectious disease.

That prospect is deeply troubling, because infectious illness is a genie that can be very hard to put back into its bottle. It may kill fewer people in one fell swoop than a raging flood or an extended drought, but once it takes root in a community, it often defies eradication and can invade other areas.

7 Click on the sentence in paragraph 4 that explains what health problems the disasters caused by warming can bring about.

Paragraph 4 is marked with an arrow (➡).

8 The phrase Aside from in the passage is closest in meaning to
Ⓐ according to
Ⓑ except
Ⓒ in addition to
Ⓓ in spite of

9 By stating put back into its bottle, the author means to
Ⓐ prevent the emergence of disease
Ⓑ defeat contagious disease
Ⓒ ward off flood
Ⓓ eradicate supernatural beliefs

10 Which of the following is most likely to be a cause of an outbreak of infectious disease?
Ⓐ Inundation of the land by water
Ⓑ Changes in wind direction
Ⓒ Reduction of icebergs in the South Pole
Ⓓ Extinction of some crops

11 The author organizes the discussion of global warming in terms of
Ⓐ a description of its process and causes
Ⓑ different scientists' perspectives
Ⓒ a comparison of daytime and night
Ⓓ an explanation of likely phenomena and expected consequences

Beginning

[1] Sonar—sound navigation and ranging—is the projection and return through water of short pulses, pings, of high frequency sound. Crews aboard surface ships and submarines employ active sonar to search for objects in the ocean. Much progress has been made since Lieutenant Pryor's work in the 1930s. In a modern system, electrical current is passed through crystals, which respond by producing powerful sound pulses pitched above the limit of human hearing. Some of the sound from the transmitter bounces off objects larger than the wavelength of sound employed and returns to a microphone-like sensor. Signal processors then amplify the echo and reduce the frequency of the sound to within the range of human hearing. An experienced sonar operator can tell the direction of the contact, its size and heading, and even something about its composition— whale or submarine or school of fish—by analyzing the characteristics of the returned ping.

Side-scan sonar is a type of active sonar. Operating with as many as 60 transceivers turned to high sound frequencies, side-scan systems towed in the quiet water beneath a ship are sometimes capable of near-photographic resolution. Side-scan systems are used for geological investigations, archeological studies, and the locating of downed ships and airplanes.

Echo sounders also make use of sonar. An echo sounder transmits a pulse of sound toward the ocean floor, measures the time of its round trip from transducer to seabed and back, computes the depth from the time delay, and then displays the depth on a screen or strip chart. **This method can be used to depths of about 5,000 meters, but attenuation of sound and uncertainty about water conditions generally make it less accurate in deeper water.**

For deeper soundings, or to "see" into sediment layers below the surface, geologists use seismic reflection profilers

1. What is the main topic of this passage?
   Ⓐ Methods to investigate objects in the ocean
   Ⓑ The development of sound navigation and ranging
   Ⓒ The scientific contribution of active sonar in oceanography
   Ⓓ The types and uses of active sonar

2. Click on the sentence in paragraph 1 that tells how a modern transmitter generates sound pulses.

3. The phrase bounces off in the passage is closest in meaning to
   Ⓐ separates from
   Ⓑ is amplified by
   Ⓒ springs back from
   Ⓓ kicks out

4. Which of the following could be detected by using active sonar?
   Ⓐ The color of a whale
   Ⓑ The weight of a submarine
   Ⓒ The length of a wrecked ship
   Ⓓ The number of fish in a school

5. The word its in the passage refers to
   Ⓐ the sonar
   Ⓑ the contact
   Ⓒ sonar operator
   Ⓓ the ping

6. In the passage, all of the following are true EXCEPT that
   Ⓐ Lieutenant Pryor's work in the 1930s brought big advances to oceanography
   Ⓑ side-scan sonar used for geological investigations and archeological studies is a sort of active sonar
   Ⓒ even skilled sonar operators cannot catch the direction of the contact easily
   Ⓓ crews require active sonar, the projection and returned ping, when searching for objects in the ocean

End

employing powerful electrical sparks, explosives, or compressed air to generate a very energetic, low-frequency sound pulse. Again, the round-trip travel time of the sound waves is crucial. The low-frequency sound cannot resolve great detail, but the echo can usually provide an image of the sedimentary layers beneath the surface. Low-frequency sound also has the advantage of efficient travel with less absorption.

7 Which of the following statements about side-scan sounds can be inferred?

Ⓐ They take a long time to get information.

Ⓑ They can be used to locate pipelines on the seafloor.

Ⓒ They don't distort images at all.

Ⓓ They are not influenced by currents or the temperature of the sea.

8 The word downed in the passage is closest in meaning to

Ⓐ debased

Ⓑ archaic

Ⓒ lowered

Ⓓ sunken

9 Look at the word it in the passage.

Click on the word or phrase in the **bold** text that it refers to.

10 To get information about the earth under the ocean floor, what is necessary?

Ⓐ High frequency sounds

Ⓑ Low frequency sounds

Ⓒ Audible sounds

Ⓓ Ultrasounds

11 Why are low frequency sounds used in deeper water surveying?

Ⓐ They hardly weaken during sound travel.

Ⓑ They offer images true to life.

Ⓒ They are not affected by the earth's magnetism.

Ⓓ They provide information almost instantly.

Beginning

[2] Bats, the only group of flying mammals, are nocturnal and thus hold a niche unoccupied by most birds. Their achievement is attributed to two things: flight and the capacity to navigate by echolocation. Together these adaptations enable bats to fly and avoid obstacles in absolute darkness, to locate and catch insects with precision, and to find their way deep into caves—a habitat largely ignored by both mammals and birds—where they sleep away the daytime hours.

When in flight, bats emit short pulses 5 to 10 milliseconds in duration in a narrow directed beam from the mouth or nose. Each pulse is frequency modulated; that is, it is highest at the beginning, up to 100,000 hertz—Hz, cycles per second—and sweeps down to perhaps 30,000 Hz at the end. Sounds of this frequency are ultrasonic to the human ear, which has an upper limit of about 20,000 Hz. When a bat is searching for prey, it produces about 10 pulses per second. If a prey is detected, the rate increases rapidly up to 200 pulses per second in the final phase of approach and capture. The pulses are spaced so that the echo of each is received before the next pulse is emitted, an adaptation that prevents jamming. **Since the transmission-to-reception time decreases as the bat approaches an object, it can increase pulse frequency to obtain more information about the object. Pulse length is also shortened as the bat nears the object. It is interesting that some prey of bats, certain nocturnal moths for example, have evolved ultrasonic detectors used to detect and avoid approaching bats.**

The external ears of bats are large, like hearing trumpets, and shaped variously in different species. **Less is known about the inner ear of bats, but it obviously is capable of receiving the ultrasonic sounds emitted.** Biologists believe that bat navigations are so refined that a bat builds

---

1 What does this passage mainly discuss?
- (A) The flight and echolocation of bats
- (B) The communication methods of bats
- (C) The ecology of bats
- (D) Special ways bats search for prey

2 What does the author mean by stating that bats hold a niche unoccupied by most birds ?
- (A) Bats find and snatch insects with accuracy.
- (B) Bats' environment depends on birds.
- (C) Bats sleep in caves during the day.
- (D) Bats avoid competition with birds.

3 The word they in the passage refers to
- (A) adaptations
- (B) insects
- (C) mammals and birds
- (D) bats

4 Click on the sentence in paragraph 2 that indicates the range of sounds people can't sense.

5 Bats' ultrasonic sound pulses increase in frequency when they
- (A) recede from an object
- (B) are awake
- (C) near their prey
- (D) enter caves

6 It can be inferred from the passage that bats use sounds which are
- (A) unique to bats
- (B) more effective when not overlapped
- (C) not heard by other animals
- (D) reduced to the range of ultrasound

7 The word adaptation in the passage is closest in meaning to
- (A) organization
- (B) effect
- (C) regulation
- (D) modification

8 Look at the word nears in the passage. Click on the word in the **bold** text that is similar in meaning.

End

up a mental image of its surrounding from echo scanning that approaches the resolution of a visual image from eyes of diurnal animals.

9   Look at the word it in the passage.
    Click on the word or phrase in the **bold** text that it refers to.

10 The word diurnal in the passage is closest in meaning to
    Ⓐ omnivorous
    Ⓑ sound sensitive
    Ⓒ daytime active
    Ⓓ hibernating

11 According to the passage, which sentence is NOT true about bats?
    Ⓐ They are well adapted for their nocturnal environment.
    Ⓑ They regulate the frequency of their pulses to prevent jamming.
    Ⓒ They emit sound frequencies at a lower hertz than that of humans.
    Ⓓ They construct visual images with high resolution in their brains.

Beginning

[3] Fire is an essential component of many ecosystems. Over the millennia, plants and animals in these ecosystems have adapted to periodic fire, and indeed some have become dependant on burning. For example, certain chaparral species have a coating on their seeds that is quite hard; burning scars the seed and allows it to sprout. Lodgepole pine cones are held closed with a resin. Fire melts the resin and allows the cone to open and release seeds. A fungus that will eventually kill them often attacks year-old long-leaf pine seedlings. During the seedling's second year, it produces a clump of very long, grass-like needles but doesn't grow in height. A fire will kill the fungus, but the grassy tufts protect the seedling buds and allow it to start growing several feet a year. Suppressing the necessary fire element from fire-dependant ecosystems short-circuits their ecological processes as surely as removing water, oxygen or nitrogen would.

➡Fire in a natural regime generally burns quickly through underbrush or grass and shrubs. The fuel load is low because periodic fires clean house regularly and prevent fuel build up. ■ Established plants and soil are not usually adversely affected, and those species dependant upon fire retain their natural cycles. ■ On the other hand, fire suppression in ecosystems adapted to its frequent occurrence have high fuel densities. ■ Dead grass, brush, wood, twigs, barks, leaves and needles have accumulated, providing more fuel to feed larger wildfires than would otherwise be the case if the landscape was allowed to burn on a natural cycle. ■

➡Fires are caused by either lightening or people. Over the course of human history, people have learned to manupulated fire. ■ Native Americans deliberately set fires for various reasons, among them: to clear land for horticulture, to change the composition of the plant community so as to attract a diversity of game species, and to improve

1. What does the passage mainly discuss?
   Ⓐ Fire as a plant nutrient
   Ⓑ The necessity of natural fire for forest ecosystems
   Ⓒ Why people tried to control fire over the years
   Ⓓ The role of fire in human life

2. It can be inferred from the passage that chaparral species would not produce hard coated seeds if they grew in a forest that
   Ⓐ had a spreading fire
   Ⓑ didn't have a big fire
   Ⓒ didn't have a regular fire
   Ⓓ had only a man-made fire

3. The word Suppressing in the passage is closest in meaning to
   Ⓐ instigating
   Ⓑ conquering
   Ⓒ inhibiting
   Ⓓ fostering

4. According to the passage, why is natural fire necessary?
   Ⓐ It temporarily exterminates harmful insects .
   Ⓑ It helps some plants grow more easily.
   Ⓒ It disinfects the forest and revives it.
   Ⓓ It suppresses excessive growth of particular plants.

5. It can be inferred from the passage that ecologists would agree that for a healthier forest,
   Ⓐ wild fire is far more effectual than man-made fire
   Ⓑ fire suppression policy is essential
   Ⓒ removing fire fuel is essential
   Ⓓ periodic occurrences of wildfires are needed

6. The following sentence can be added to the passage.

   Thus the fires do not burn with great heat or intensity.

   Where would it best fit in the passage? Click on the square [■] to add the sentence to paragraph 2 or 3. Paragraph 2 and 3 are marked with an arrow (➡).

End

access. ■ Early settlers also set fires to ready land for agriculture and to eliminate the stubble of the previous year's crops. Today, land managers use fire as a tool for managing natural resources.

7 The word its in the passage refers to
   Ⓐ fire
   Ⓑ natural cycles
   Ⓒ ecosystems
   Ⓓ fire suppression

8 The word manipulated in the passage is closest in meaning to
   Ⓐ surged
   Ⓑ managed
   Ⓒ cherished
   Ⓓ halted

9 According to the passage, why did Native Americans set fires to forests?
   Ⓐ To manipulate the composition of the species of their environment
   Ⓑ To increase the amount of crops
   Ⓒ To control the size of forests
   Ⓓ To prevent contagious diseases

10 According to the passage,
   Ⓐ established plants are permanently affected by natural fire
   Ⓑ without fire, many ecosystems would be non-existent
   Ⓒ long-leaf pine seedlings usually don't survive fires
   Ⓓ fire suppression leads to low fuel density on forest floors

11 The word deliberately in the passage is closetest meaning to
   Ⓐ intermediately
   Ⓑ periodically
   Ⓒ thoughtfully
   Ⓓ intentionally

Beginning

[4] The pre-war decade from 1765 to 1775 witnessed a proliferation of visual media to propagandize against British tyranny. Printmakers published political cartoons in newspapers, magazines, and broadsides that were posted in shops, taverns, and coffeehouses. **The printer and almanac publisher Benjamin Franklin responded to Parliament's arbitrary taxation of the colonies by representing the British Empire as a dismembered woman. With her ships idle in the background, Britannia leans helplessly against a globe she once dominated.** A spear self-destructively points toward her breast. Severed arms and legs signifying the American colonies lie scattered upon the ground. Though critical of Britain's self-destructive imperial policies, Franklin's image suggested that most who initially denounced Parliament's imposition of taxes and trade duties did not envision political independence. For Franklin in 1765, the colonies were only separate limbs, entirely dependent upon the healthy body politic of the mother country.

However, as protests against trade duties and the monopolies enjoyed by London merchants intensified, political prints satirized the colonial model of dependency upon the mother country. On December 16, 1773, a group of Boston men, disguised as Mohawk Indians, secretly boarded ships of the East India Company, throwing into Boston harbor the duty-laden tea that symbolized Britain's monopolistic control of colonial trade. ■ Following the Boston Tea Party, Paul Revere, one of the participants, personified America as a violated Indian princess. ■ British government officials look up her dress and force tea down her throat. America's mother, Britannia, stands by helplessly while her daughter is sexually abused. ■ After independence, printmakers, painters, and sculptors transformed the personification of America into a Greek or Roman goddess, symbolizing Western

1 What is the purpose of this passage?
   Ⓐ To discuss Benjamin Franklin's role in American history
   Ⓑ To explain the causes of the Boston Tea Party
   Ⓒ To discuss the political propaganda used in the 18th century pre-war decade
   Ⓓ To criticize Britannia's unfair treatment of colonial America

2 The word dismembered in the passage is closest in meaning to
   Ⓐ disabled
   Ⓑ divided in pieces
   Ⓒ seceded
   Ⓓ inanimate

3 The word idle in the passage is closest in meaning to
   Ⓐ concealed
   Ⓑ harbored
   Ⓒ unused
   Ⓓ forsaken

4 Look at the word she in the passage. Click on the word in the **bold** text that she refers to.

5 In Benjamin Franklin's poster, what does A spear represent?
   Ⓐ English monopoly
   Ⓑ English taxation on the colonies
   Ⓒ English indifference to the colonies
   Ⓓ English political infringement

6 Click on the sentence in paragraph 2 that describes changes for woodworkers after independence.

7 Why did colonists partake in the Boston Tea Party?
   Ⓐ To expose the practice of illegal trade
   Ⓑ To object to the importation of English tea
   Ⓒ To show their discontent with unfair trade
   Ⓓ To steal precious tea

End

civilization and the ideals of Liberty and Wisdom. ■ American wood carvers who normally crafted the figureheads of ships were now called upon to decorate courthouses and other public buildings with personifications of Liberty and Wisdom. ■

After the Seven Years' War, which forced Catholic France to abandon Canada, Americans dreamed of territorial expansion far beyond the eastern seaboard, proclaiming that the course of civilization was moving westward with the sun. Magazines and newspapers quoted "Verses on the Prospect of Planting Arts and Learning in America," by George Berkeley, contrasting a decaying Europe with America's "virgin earth," fertile for a millennial "golden age."

8 Through the image of a violated Indian princess, Paul Revere intended to portray America as

Ⓐ regal
Ⓑ separate from England
Ⓒ deserving money
Ⓓ unfairly exploited

9 The following sentence can be added to the passage.
With white pine and paint, they imicked the pristine marble of classical sculpture.

Where would it best fit in the passage? Click on the square [■] to add the sentence to the passage.

10 It can be inferred from paragraph 3 that Americans' attitude toward their future was

Ⓐ excited
Ⓑ anxious
Ⓒ composed
Ⓓ pessimistic

11 The word abandon in the passage is OPPOSITE in meaning to

Ⓐ advance into
Ⓑ reconcile with
Ⓒ retain
Ⓓ occupy

Beginning

[5] The era of the talking film began in late 1927 with the enormous success of Warner Brothers' *The Jazz Singer*. The first totally sound film, *Lights of New York*, followed in 1928. Although experimentation with synchronizing sound and picture was as old as the cinema itself (Dickson, for example, made a rough synchronization of the two for Edison in 1894), the feasibility of sound film was widely publicized only after Warner Brothers purchased the Vitaphone from Western Electric in 1926. The original Vitaphone system synchronized the picture with a separate phonographic disk, rather than using the more accurate method of recording (based on the principle of the oscilloscope) a sound track on the film itself. Warners originally used the Vitaphone to make short musical films featuring both classical and popular performers and to record musical sound tracks for otherwise silent films. For *The Jazz Singer*, Warners added four synchronized musical sequences to the silent film. When Al Jolson sang and then delivered several lines of dialogue, audiences were electrified. The silent film was dead within a year.

The conversion to synchronized sound caused serious problems for the film industry. **Sound recording was difficult. Cameras had to shoot from inside glass booths and studios had to build special soundproof stages. Theaters required expensive new equipment, writers had to be hired, who had an ear for dialogue, and actors had to be found whose voices could deliver it.** Many of the earliest talkies were ugly and static, the visual images serving merely as an accompaniment to endless dialogue, sound effects, and musical numbers. Serious film critics mourned the passing of the motion picture, which no longer seemed to contain either motion or picture.

The most effective early sound films were those that played most adventurously with the union of picture and sound track.

1 What does the author mainly discuss?
   Ⓐ The problem of conversion to synchronized sound
   Ⓑ Reasons for the success of Warner Brothers
   Ⓒ The history of American film
   Ⓓ The development of synchronized sound and picture in American film

2 Which of the following statements about the movie, *The Jazz Singer*, is true?
   Ⓐ It contained several musical sequences, which made it a sound film.
   Ⓑ Its sound was recorded by a method that is still widely used to make talking films.
   Ⓒ It was Al Jolson's last film, as he died within a year after the film was made.
   Ⓓ Its recording method was kept secret for a long time.

3 The word synchronized in the passage is closest in meaning to
   Ⓐ disjoined
   Ⓑ harmonized
   Ⓒ resounded
   Ⓓ recorded

4 The word electrified in paragraph 1 could be best replaced by
   Ⓐ charged
   Ⓑ amplified
   Ⓒ irritated
   Ⓓ thrilled

5 Look at the word it in the passage.
   Click on the word or phrase in the **bold** text that it refers to.

6 By stating the passing of the motion picture, the author implies that
   Ⓐ the introduction of sound made the silent film disappear
   Ⓑ film makers' neglect of visual effects resulted in ruining the quality of the film itself
   Ⓒ disgusted with the excessive use of sounds, people no longer watched movies
   Ⓓ the motion picture industry collapsed and gave way to the recording industry

Test Quit   ? Help   ← Prev   → Next

End

In his cartoons Walt Disney combined surprising sights with inventive sounds, carefully orchestrating animated motion and musical rhythm. Ernst Lubitsch also played very cleverly with sound, contrasting the action depicted visually with the information on the sound track in dazzlingly funny or revealing ways. By 1930 the U.S. film industry had conquered both the technical and the artistic problems involved in using sight and sound harmoniously, and the European industry was quick to follow.

7 It can be inferred from the passage that, after the appearance of the talking film, the silent movie

Ⓐ was not made at all
Ⓑ was soon conquered by the talking film
Ⓒ continued to be preferred to the talking film
Ⓓ transformed itself into cartoons

8 The word animated in the passage is OPPOSITE in meaning to

Ⓐ spirited
Ⓑ emboldened
Ⓒ inert
Ⓓ vivacious

9 It can be inferred form paragraph 3 that Ernst Lubitsch made

Ⓐ humorous films
Ⓑ gloomy films
Ⓒ boring films
Ⓓ soft films

10 Which topic could best continue this passage?

Ⓐ Why silent film lost popularity
Ⓑ An introduction to the new vitaphone used in Disney cartoons
Ⓒ Ways in which Disney and Warners differed
Ⓓ The development of sound in the European film industry

11 According to the passage, conversion to synchronized sound caused serious problems in all of the following ways EXCEPT

Ⓐ studios had to build special soundproof stages
Ⓑ movie theaters needed expensive new equipment
Ⓒ actors had to sing songs by themselves
Ⓓ cameras had to film from inside glass booths

Beginning

[1] **As the original settlers of an unpopulated and untamed wilderness, North American Indians preceded Europeans as the mapmakers and architects of a New World in the Western Hemisphere. By naming and mapping their environment, they created webs of meaningful relationships with the natural world. Their maps established regional networks of trade and communication.** Few Native American maps survive today because they were part of an oral tradition that described the landscape in experiential terms, associating different sites with specific spiritual forces and gods as well as animal, vegetable, and mineral resources. When necessary, maps were sketched from memory in the dirt or sand or, more permanently, on other natural materials such as animal skins, tree bark, and rocks.

At a site on the Snake River near Givens Hot Springs, Idaho, pre-Columbian Shoshone Indians covered a large basalt boulder with pictographic signs. Known as Map Rock, this petroglyph, or example of rock art with deeply etched markings, apparently represents the Shoshone's tribal territory centered on the Snake and Salmon Rivers. Situated within a field of other petroglyphs and near the architectural remains of Indian lodges that date from 4,000 years ago, Map Rock also depicts human figures and animals such as buffalo, deer, antelope, elk, and mountain sheep. These images suggest that the rock possessed pragmatic ritualistic significance, guaranteeing successful hunts, while demonstrating spiritual harmony between the territory's human and animal realms.

Rather than attempting to conquer or set themselves above nature, Native Americans sought to find their place within the natural processes of earth, water, and sky. They did not regard land as a commodity that could be sold or traded for the exclusive use of an individual owner.

1   What is the main topic of this passage?
    (A) The relationship between Native American culture and nature
    (B) Native American map-making
    (C) Primitive map-making
    (D) Native American lifestyle and characteristics

2   According to the passage, all of the following were styles of how Native Americans documented maps EXCEPT
    (A) tattoos on the body
    (B) marking on wood
    (C) drawings on animal skins
    (D) engravings on rocks

3   Look at the word Their in the passage.
    Click on the word or phrase in the **bold** text that Their refers to.

4   Click on the sentence in paragraph 1 that describes what North American Indians used to draw maps on.

5   The word Situated in the passage is closest in meaning to
    (A) merged
    (B) located
    (C) scattered
    (D) clustered

6   According to paragraph 2, Map Rock was made to pray for
    (A) the discovery of new routes
    (B) safe hunting
    (C) spiritual triumph over animals
    (D) expansion of territory

7   The word sedentary in the passage is the most opposite in meaning to
    (A) meditative
    (B) bellicose
    (C) settled
    (D) migratory

End

Land was communally owned by members of a tribe, although its resources and use might be shared with other tribes through mutual agreement. No Indian group was entirely sedentary. Depending on the source of food, tribes generally occupied more than one home, village, or town and moved with the change of seasons between summer and winter living sites.

8 According to the passage, images carved on Map Rock represented all of the following EXCEPT
Ⓐ a ceremonial act
Ⓑ a prayer for food
Ⓒ artistic inheritance
Ⓓ spiritual accord with animals

9 According to the passage, what was the Native American culture's perspective on nature?
Ⓐ They controlled the power of nature
Ⓑ They sought to take advantage of its resources by transforming it
Ⓒ They considered themselves to be part of their surroundings
Ⓓ Nature could be sold or traded for the use of an individual owner

10 Which of the following statements about American Indians is true?
Ⓐ They recognized animals as co-owners of the land.
Ⓑ They tabooed leaving permanent records of religious things.
Ⓒ They guided Europeans in mapmaking.
Ⓓ They made maps in oral forms for entertaining purposes.

11 If a tribe found a new place that it wanted to use for a summer camp, but that was owned by another tribe, which of the following could it do?
Ⓐ Buy it for an agreed-upon price
Ⓑ Lend it for an agreed-upon price
Ⓒ Use it together under agreement
Ⓓ Not use it

Beginning

[2] One of the most sophisticated and complex of all nonhuman communication systems is the symbolic language of bees. Honeybees are able to communicate by dances, which are mainly of two forms. The form having the most communicative richness is the waggle dance. Bees most commonly execute this dance when a forager has returned from a rich source, carrying either nectar in her stomach or pollen grains packed in basketlike spaces formed by hairs on her legs. The waggle dance is roughly in the pattern of a figure-eight made against the vertical surface on the comb inside the hive. One cycle of the dance consists of three components: (1) a circle with a diameter about three times the length of the bee, (2) a straight run while waggling the abdomen from side to side and emitting a pulsed, low-frequency sound, and (3) another circle, turning in the opposite direction from the first. This dance is repeated many times with the circling alternating clockwise and counterclockwise.

➡The straight waggle run is the important informational component of the dance. ■ Waggle dances are almost always performed in clear position of the sun. ■ **If the forager has located food directly toward the sun, she will make her waggle run straight upward over the vertical surface of the comb.** ■ If food is located 60 degrees to the right of the sun, her waggle run is 60 degrees to the right of vertical. ■ The waggle run points at the same angle relative to the vertical as the food is located relative to the sun.

➡ ■ If the food is close to the hive, the forager employs a simpler dance called the round dance. ■The forager simply turns a complete clockwise circle, then turns, and completes a counterclockwise circle, a performance that is repeated many times. ■Other workers cluster around the scout and become stimulated by the dance as well as by the odor of nectar and pollen grains gathered from the flowers she has visited. ■

1 What is the purpose of the passage?
ⓐ To establish unequivocally the accuracy of a nonhuman way of exchanging information
ⓑ To describe what was previously unknown about honeybees' communication
ⓒ To present dancing in relation to the communication of honeybees
ⓓ To compare two kinds of symbolic language used by honeybees

2 It can be inferred from the first paragraph that
ⓐ bees are the most inteligent animals next to human
ⓑ bees' language is highly organized and refined
ⓒ bees' language varies depending on the individual
ⓓ bees' language can express abstract and arbitrary meanings

3 According to the passage, all of the following are descriptive of honeybees' communication EXCEPT that
ⓐ it is complicated
ⓑ it is indelicate
ⓒ it is active
ⓓ it is nonverbal

4 The word waggling in the passage is closest in meaning to
ⓐ upsetting
ⓑ vibrating
ⓒ shaking
ⓓ pushing forward

5 Click on the sentence in paragraph 1 that indicates where bees store nectar to take home.

6 The following sentence can be added to the passage.

Distance of the food source is also coded into bee dances.

Where would it best fit in the passage? Click on the square [■] to add the sentence to paragraph 2 or 3. Paragraph 2 and 3 are marked with an arrow (➡).

End

The recruits then fly out and search in all directions but do not stray far. The round dance carries the message that food is to be found in the vicinity of the hive.

7   Look at the word she in the passage. Click on the word in the **bold** text that she refers to.

8   Which of the following information can be acquired from the round dance of the honeybee?
Ⓐ The direction of the food's location
Ⓑ The amount of available food
Ⓒ The distance between the hive and the food
Ⓓ The existence of enemies.

9   The word stimulated in the passage is closest meaning to
Ⓐ accompanied
Ⓑ benumbed
Ⓒ incriminated
Ⓓ aroused

10 It can be inferred that the waggle dance and the round dance are similar in
Ⓐ the sound that accompanies the dances
Ⓑ the time it takes to complete the dance
Ⓒ the dance pattern
Ⓓ the directions of rotation

11 The word vicinity in the passage is closest in meaning to
Ⓐ exterior
Ⓑ neighborhood
Ⓒ shade
Ⓓ degree

Beginning

[3] Life in the American West was reshaped by a series of patents for a simple tool that helped ranchers tame the land: barbed wire. Nine patents for improvements to wire fencing were granted by the U.S. Patent Office to American inventors, beginning with Michael Kelly in November 1868 and ending with Joseph Glidden in November 1874. Barbed wire not only simplified the work of the rancher and farmer, but it significantly affected political, social, and economic practices throughout the region. The swift emergence of this highly effective tool as the favored fencing method influenced life in the region as dramatically as the rifle, six-shooter, telegraph, windmill, and locomotive.

Barbed wire was extensively adopted because it proved ideal for western conditions. Vast and undefined prairies and plains yielded to range management, farming, and, ultimately, widespread settlement. As the use of barbed wire increased, wide open spaces became less wide, less open, and less spacious. The days of the free roaming cowboy were numbered. Today, cowboy ballads remain as nostalgic reminders of life before barbed wire became an accepted symbol of control, transforming space to place and giving new meaning to private property.

Before the invention of barbed wire, the lack of effective fencing limited the range of farming and ranching practices, and with it, the number of people who could settle in an area. ■ Wooden fences were costly and difficult to acquire on the prairie, and plains, where few trees grew. ■ Lumber was in such short supply in the region that farmers were forced to build houses of sod. ■ Shrubs and hedges, early substitutes for wood and rock fencing materials, took too long to grow to

---

1 With what topic is the passage mainly concerned?
- Ⓐ The effects of the invention of barbed wire on the American West
- Ⓑ Life in the American West in the late 19th century
- Ⓒ Inventions of the American West
- Ⓓ American patent procedures

2 The word patents is closest in meaning to
- Ⓐ instruments
- Ⓑ ranches
- Ⓒ licenses
- Ⓓ laws

3 Click on the sentence in paragraph 1 that indicates that wire was redeveloped several times after its invention.

4 Which of the following words is the closest in meaning to tame?
- Ⓐ reduce
- Ⓑ humiliate
- Ⓒ control
- Ⓓ repress

5 Which of the following is NOT mentioned as an effect of barbed wire?
- Ⓐ It made work eaiser for ranchers and farmers.
- Ⓑ It proved not ideal for eastern conditions.
- Ⓒ It was fit for conditions in the West.
- Ⓓ It could be used to limit open spaces.

6 The author mentions the rifle, six-shooter, telegraph, windmill, and locomotive as examples of
- Ⓐ classics in modern technology
- Ⓑ tools that emerged at the same time as barbed wire
- Ⓒ tools that revolutionized human life
- Ⓓ economically important inventions

End

become of much use in the rapidly expanding West. ■ Barbed wire was cheaper, easier, and quicker to use than any of these other alternatives.

7   By stating Today, cowboy ballads remain as nostalgic reminders of life before barbed wire became an accepted symbol of control, the author means that after the advent of barbed wire,

Ⓐ cowboy songs lost their popularity
Ⓑ cowboys guarded cattle in wild areas
Ⓒ cowboys no longer controlled cattle
Ⓓ the need for cattle watchers decreased

8   The following sentence can be added to the passage.

Likewise, rocks for stone walls— commonly found in New England— were scarce on the plains.

Where would it best fit in the passage? Click on the square [■] to add the sentence to the passage.

9   Which of the following words could be best substituted for alternatives?

Ⓐ reciprocals
Ⓑ intervals
Ⓒ variances
Ⓓ options

10 It can be inferred from paragraph 3 that shrubs and hedges as early fencing materials were

Ⓐ very costly to produce
Ⓑ preferred in the view of aesthetic sense
Ⓒ not strong enough to confine cattle
Ⓓ very time consuming to prepare for use

11 It can be inferred from the passage that barbed wire would be critical to people living

Ⓐ in forests
Ⓑ on the savannah
Ⓒ in a coastal area
Ⓓ on a bare mountain

Beginning

[4] Deserts in the Southwestern United States are areas of extreme heat and dryness, just as most of us envision them. More scientifically, deserts, also called arid regions, characteristically receive less than 10 inches of precipitation a year. In some deserts, the amount of evaporation is greater than the amount of rainfall. Semiarid regions average 10 to 20 inches of annual precipitation. Typically, desert moisture occurs in brief intervals and is unpredictable from year to year. About one-third of the earth's land mass is arid to semiarid—either desert or semi-desert.

Evaporation is also an important factor contributing to aridity. In some deserts, the amount of water evaporating exceeds the amount of rainfall. Rising air cools and can hold less moisture, producing clouds and precipitation; falling air warms, absorbing moisture. Areas with few clouds, bodies of water and little vegetation absorb most of the sun's radiation, thus heating the air at the soil surface. More humid areas deflect heat in clouds, water and vegetation, consequently remaining cooler. High winds in open country also contribute to evaporation.

➡ Locations of deserts have changed throughout geologic time as the result of continental drift and the uplifting of mountain ranges. **Modern desert regions are centered in the "horse latitudes", typically straddling the Tropic of Cancer and the Tropic of Capricorn, between 15 and 30 degrees north and south of the equator. Some, such as the Kalahari in central Africa, are geologically ancient. The Sahara Desert in northern Africa is 65 million years old, while the Sonoran Desert of North America reached its northern limits only within the last 10,000 years.**

Because they are poised in such harsh extremes of heat and aridity, deserts are among the most fragile ecosystems on the planet. Three of the four major deserts of North America are contained within a

1 What is the purpose of paragraph 1?
Ⓐ To give a general description of deserts
Ⓑ To compare the characteristics of desert and semi-desert weather
Ⓒ To give an example of deserts in the Southwestern United States
Ⓓ To summarize a scientific survey on deserts

2 It can be inferred from the passage that in a typical desert
Ⓐ the existing animal species never change
Ⓑ temperatures do not fall even at night
Ⓒ gusty winds increase the aridity
Ⓓ there are many mountain ranges

3 The word envision is closest in meaning to
Ⓐ endure
Ⓑ constrain
Ⓒ conceive
Ⓓ reiterate

4 According to the passage, which of the following is NOT mentioned as a possible characteristic of arid regions?
Ⓐ The amount of evaporation is greater than that of rainfall.
Ⓑ The ecosystems of arid regions are extremely fragile.
Ⓒ There is little water, but much vegetation.
Ⓓ The air at ground level is heated.

5 According to the passage, in what way does vegetation influence climate?
Ⓐ It absorbs the sun's heat.
Ⓑ It contrubutes to aridity.
Ⓒ It cools the soil surface.
Ⓓ It facilitates evaporation.

6 Look at the word aridity in paragraph 2. Click the word in paragraph 1 whose meaning is OPPOSITE.

7 Look at the word its in the passage. Click on the word or phrase in the **bold** text that its refers to.

End

geological region called the Basin and Range Province, lying between the Rocky Mountains to the east and the Sierra Nevadas to the west. While the distinctiveness of each desert is based on the types of plant life found there, determined both by evolutionary history and climates, the geological structures of these three deserts are rather similar.

8   Click on the sentence in paragraph 3 that tells the location of deserts today.

Paragraph 3 is marked with an arrow (➡).

9   What does the author mean by stating Some, such as the Kalahari in central Africa, are geologically ancient ?

Ⓐ Some deserts are older than other deserts.
Ⓑ The deserts' locations have not changed for a long time.
Ⓒ Some deserts were unknown to humans for ages.
Ⓓ Some deserts have recently moved to new sites but the deserts themselves are ancient.

10 Individual deserts are characterized by which of the following factors?

Ⓐ Their site
Ⓑ The degree of heat
Ⓒ Their flora
Ⓓ The amount of precipitation

11 The word fragile in the passage is closest in meaning to

Ⓐ weak
Ⓑ divisive
Ⓒ incredible
Ⓓ sparse

www.goHackers.com

Reading

HACKERS READING

Answer Key

[1] **1** c⟨ch1⟩ **2** a⟨ch8⟩ **3** d⟨ch3⟩ **4** a⟨ch3⟩ **5** 4th ■ ⟨ch2⟩ **6** d⟨ch4/5⟩
7 d⟨ch4/5⟩ **8** c⟨ch6⟩ **9** All this makes~.⟨ch7⟩
10 b⟨ch8⟩ **11** c⟨ch9⟩

[2] **1** b⟨ch1⟩ **2** a⟨ch1⟩ **3** b⟨ch2⟩ **4** d⟨ch6⟩ **5** a⟨ch8⟩ **6** d⟨ch3⟩
7 c⟨ch8⟩ **8** Recent studies have~.⟨ch7⟩
9 b⟨ch6⟩ **10** c⟨ch3⟩ **11** b⟨ch8⟩

[3] **1** b⟨ch1⟩ **2** d⟨ch8⟩ **3** c⟨ch2⟩ **4** a⟨ch3⟩
5 Signatures, affecting messages~.⟨ch7⟩
6 c⟨ch4/5⟩ **7** d⟨ch3⟩ **8** b⟨ch4/5⟩ **9** b⟨ch9⟩ **10** b⟨ch6⟩ **11** d⟨ch8⟩

[4] **1** a⟨ch1⟩ **2** Buildings could have~.⟨ch7⟩ **3** c⟨ch3⟩
4 d⟨ch8⟩ **5** b⟨ch9⟩ **6** 3rd ■ ⟨ch2⟩ **7** c⟨ch8⟩ **8** a⟨ch4/5⟩
9 c⟨ch3⟩ **10** c⟨ch4/5⟩ **11** c⟨ch6⟩

Chapter 1 Topic • Main Idea • Purpose

Hackers Practice

[1] 정답 b 해설 (a)-IR (b)-C (c)-TS (d)-TG

[2] 정답 a 해설 (a)-C (b)-IC (c)-IR (d)-TG

[3] 정답 a 해설 (a)-C (b)-IC (c)-IR (d)-TG

[4] 정답 b 해설 (a)-IR (b)-C (c)-IR (d)-TS

[5] 정답 a

[6] 정답 a 해설 (a)-C (b)-TG (c)-IR (d)-IC

[7] 정답 c 해설 (a)-IR (b)-IR (c)-C (d)-TS

[8] 정답 c 해설 (a)-IR (b)-TS (c)-C (d)-TS

[9] 정답 c 해설 (a)-TS (b)-IR (c)-C (d)-IC

[10]정답 b 해설 (a)-IR (b)-C (c)-IR (d)-TS

Hackers Test

[1] **1** d **2** c **3** c

[2] **1** a **2** d **3** d

[3] **1** d **2** a **3** c

[4] **1** c **2** a **3** c

[5] **1** d **2** b **3** d

[6] **1** a **2** b **3** d

[7] **1** c **2** a **3** a

[8] **1** c **2** b **3** a

[9] **1** d **2** d **3** a

[10]1 b **2** a **3** d

Chapter 2 Organization & Insertion

Hackers Practice

[1] 정답 Further definition

[2] 정답 Contrast

[3] 정답 Cause & Effect

[4] 정답 Process

[5] 정답 (c)-(b)-(a)

[6] 정답 (c)-(a)-(b)

[7] 정답 (b)-(a)-(c)

[8] 정답 (a)-(c)-(b)

[9] 정답 2nd ■

[10] 정답 2nd ■

Hackers Test

[1] **1** 4th ■ **2** b

[2] **1** 3rd ■ **2** d

[3] **1** c **2** 3rd ■

[4] **1** 1st ■ **2** c **3** 1st □ **4** b

[5] **1** d **2** 3rd ■ **3** 3rd □

[6] **1** 2nd ■ **2** 2nd □ **3** d

[7] **1** c **2** 4th ■ **3** 4th □

[8] **1** 4th ■ **2** 4th □ **3** c

[9] **1** 1st ■ **2** 2nd □ **3** d

[10] **1** 4th ■ **2** 3rd □ **3** c

Chapter 3 Restatement Questions

Hackers Practice

[1] 정답 b   **[2]** 정답 c   **[3]** 정답 d   **[4]** 정답 d
[5] 정답 c   **[6]** 정답 b   **[7]** 정답 d   **[8]** 정답 b
[9] 정답 b   **[10]** 정답 a

Hackers Test

[1] **1** a **2** c **3** c **4** a

[2] **1** b **2** a **3** a **4** b

[3] **1** c **2** a **3** b **4** b

[4] **1** c **2** a **3** b **4** c

[5] **1** b **2** c **3** c **4** b

[6] **1** c **2** b **3** b

[7] **1** c **2** c **3** b **4** d

[8] **1** a **2** c **3** b **4** d

[9] **1** c **2** b **3** a **4** c

[10] **1** a **2** a **3** d **4** d

Progressive Test 1-1

[1] 1 c **2** b **3** 3rd ■
   4 c **5** d

[2] 1 b **2** c **3** c
   4 a **5** 4th ■

[3] 1 b **2** d **3** c
   4 d **5** 4th ■

[4] 1 d **2** a **3** 3rd ■
   4 c **5** 5th ■

Progressive Test 1-2

[1] 1 b **2** c **3** a
   4 b **5** c

[2] 1 b **2** c **3** a
   4 b **5** 2nd ■

[3] 1 c **2** b **3** d
   4 3rd ■ **5** c

[4] 1 b **2** c **3** d
   4 c **5** a

Chapter 4 Inference Questions(I)

Hackers Practice

[1] 정답 c
[2] 정답 c
[3] 정답 c
[4] 정답 c
[5] 정답 b
[6] 정답 b
[7] 정답 a
[8] 정답 b
[9] 정답 c
[10] 정답 b
[11] 정답 × ○ × × ×
[12] 정답 × × ○ ○ ×
[13] 정답 × × × ○ ○
[14] 정답 ○ × ○ × ×
[15] 정답 × × ○ × ○
[16] 정답 × × ○ × ○
[17] 정답 d
[18] 정답 **1** a **2** c
[19] 정답 d
[20] 정답 **1** c **2** d

Chapter 5 Inference Questions(II)

Hackers Test

[1] 1 d **2** d **3** d **4** b
[2] 1 c **2** d **3** a **4** b
[3] 1 b **2** d **3** a **4** d
[4] 1 b **2** c **3** a **4** b
[5] 1 d **2** c **3** a **4** b

[6] 1 b **2** d **3** a **4** c
[7] 1 a **2** d **3** d **4** b
[8] 1 b **2** b **3** b **4** c
[9] 1 a **2** c **3** a **4** c
[10] 1 d **2** c **3** d **4** c

Chapter 6 Negative Questions

Hackers Practice

[1] 정답 a
[2] 정답 d
[3] 정답 c
[4] 정답 a
[5] 정답 b
[6] 정답 b
[7] 정답 a
[8] 정답 d
[9] 정답 c
[10] 정답 a

Hackers Test

[1] 1 d **2** b
[2] 1 c **2** a
[3] 1 d **2** d
[4] 1 b **2** a
[5] 1 b **2** c
[6] 1 a **2** a
[7] 1 c **2** a
[8] 1 c **2** b
[9] 1 c **2** c
[10] 1 c **2** c

Progressive Test 2-1

[1] 1 a 2 b 3 c
4 c 5 a 6 b
7 c 8 b 9 b 10 d

[2] 1 d 2 a 3 d
4 3rd ■ 5 b 6 b
7 a 8 d 9 a 10 b

[3] 1 a 2 3rd ■ 3 d
4 a 5 b 6 a
7 a 8 c 9 b 10 d

[4] 1 c 2 d 3 c
4 a 5 c 6 a
7 b 8 b 9 d 10 a

Progressive Test 2-2

[1] 1 b 2 c 3 2nd ■
4 a 5 d 6 a
7 d 8 a 9 a 10 d

[2] 1 d 2 c 3 c
4 b 5 c 6 2nd ■
7 d 8 d 9 c 10 d

[3] 1 c 2 b 3 c 4 a
5 d 6 c 7 a 8 c
9 a 10 c

[4] 1 c 2 a 3 c 4 d 5 c
6 d 7 3rd ■ 8 b 9 c 10 a

Chapter 7 Scanning Questions

Hackers Practice

[1] 정답 Here men, women, and children socialized, worked, and prepared food.

[2] 정답 Canned goods and condensed milk became more common during the 1860's, but supplies remained low because cans had to be made by hand.

[3] 정답 Forced to show the same film as the competitor down the block, theater owners looked to sound practices to differentiate their products.

[4] 정답 The Sholes & Glidden had limited success, but its successor, the Remington, soon became a dominant presence in the industry.

[5] 정답 1. Saracen foot soldiers wore straw-filled, quilted canvas shirts in lieu of armor, and horsemen used quilted silk undershirts to keep their armor from chafing.
2. Being made of perishable materials, few early quilts have survived.

Hackers Test

[1] 1 The crust, the outermost layer, is rigid and very thin compared with the other two.
2 The mantle, which contains more iron, magesium, and calcium than the crust, is hotter and denser because temperature and pressure inside the Earth increase with depth.
3 As the Earth rotates, the liquid outer core spins, creating the Earth's magnetic field.

[2] 1 However, even though it is only a suggestion, it is a suggestion made by the U.S. Constitution, therefore Congress generally felt obliged to set up some type of organization for granting patents.
2 Nineteenth-century businesses put a lot of stock in the power of patents to help them dominate markets and keep competitors at bay.
3 This new European class comprised engineers and technicians (and a few chemists) that were full of hope and bright ideas.

[3] 1 But he discovered to his frustration that the tonal areas were reversed in the final result: "light produced dark, and dark light".
2 Morse had produced a negative image but did not yet know that negative film could be used to make positive photographic prints.
3 Because of its fragility and the tendency of the silver plate to tarnish, the daguerrotype had to be protected further by a glass covering.

[4] 1 Pine trees protect themselves against damage by exuding a resin which subsequently hardens and becomes amber.
2 When the trees eventually did die, long lived isotopes would return to the soil to continue their damage in succeeding generations.
3 Supposedly it dried out in the sun, got swiftly washed downstream and got covered with fine mud so quickly that its dried skin had no time to rehydrate and decay.

[5] 1 Some 21 species are used in everday cookery in Japan, six of them since the 8th century.
2 Plants are dried after harvesting and either cut into strips or powdered.
3 Laminaria is cultivated either by seeding blasted areas of rocky shores or by seeding ropes.

Chapter 8 Vocabulary in Context

Hackers Practice

[1] 정답 b
[2] 정답 a
[3] 정답 d
[4] 정답 b
[5] 정답 d
[6] 정답 c
[7] 정답 b
[8] 정답 b
[9] 정답 non-decaying
[10]정답 d

Hackers Test

[1] 1 b **2** b **3** c **4** b **5** c
[2] 1 a **2** b **3** plastered **4** b **5** d
[3] 1 a **2** a **3** d **4** a **5** c
[4] 1 b **2** a **3** d **4** c **5** d
[5] 1 a **2** c **3** c **4** a **5** b
[6] 1 a **2** b **3** b **4** d **5** b
[7] 1 d **2** a **3** d **4** a **5** d
[8] 1 a **2** a **3** c **4** c **5** b
[9] 1 c **2** a **3** c **4** interrupt **5** c
[10] 1 c **2** d **3** c **4** a **5** d

Chapter 9 Reference Questions

Hackers Practice

[1] 정답 a
[2] 정답 d
[3] 정답 c
[4] 정답 b
[5] 정답 c
[6] 정답 c
[7] 정답 c
[8] 정답 b
[9] 정답 a
[10] 정답 b

Hackers Test

[1] 1 b **2** a **3** a
[2] 1 d **2** b **3** d
[3] 1 d **2** a **3** d
[4] 1 New Netherland **2** b **3** a **4** d
[5] 1 a **2** A Young Warrior **3** b **4** c
[6] 1 Private railroads **2** d **3** a
[7] 1 b **2** Single gene defects **3** a
[8] 1 a **2** a **3** a
[9] 1 Railroads **2** c **3** b
[10] 1 c **2** c **3** b

Progressive Test

Progressive Test 3-1

[1] 1 a **2** a **3** a
4 c **5** a **6** b
7 d **8** Eagles have an~ **9** b **10** b
[2] 1 d **2** d **3** b
4 a **5** d **6** d
7 a **8** b **9** a **10** b
[3] 1 c **2** d **3** b
4 d **5** d **6** b
7 d **8** c **9** As a result~ **10** b
[4] 1 d **2** a **3** a
4 c **5** c **6** b
7 a **8** a **9** a **10** c

Progressive Test 3-2

[1] 1 d **2** d **3** b
4 c **5** a **6** a
7 a **8** d **9** 2nd ■ **10** d
[2] 1 c **2** b **3** 2nd ■
4 d **5** a **6** c
7 d **8** a **9** d **10** d
[3] 1 d **2** b **3** b
4 Davis believed that~ **5** a **6** b
7 b **8** d **9** d **10** 2nd ■
[4] 1 d **2** a **3** d
4 c **5** c **6** a
7 d **8** b **9** b **10** b

Actual Test 1

[1] **1** a **2** c **3** a **4** b
5 public high schools **6** b
7 a **8** The new approach **9** d **10** d
11 To accommodate the diverse needs
of these growing numbers, colleges
moved away from rigidly prescribed
courses toward an elective system.

[2] **1** a **2** a **3** agricultural fields
4 c **5** concentration of water
6 Plant species that thrive in saline soils
have special adaptations that enable
them to tolerate the high amount of
salt.
7 b **8** c **9** The excess salt **10** d **11** b

[3] **1** d **2** Performers **3** c **4** a **5** a **6** c
7 two formal patterns
8 Although exceptions occur in some
styles, most jazz is based on the
principle that an infinite number of
melodies can fit the chord progressions
of any song.
9 a **10** 4th ■ **11** d

[4] **1** b **2** d
3 2nd paragraph
4 estimate **5** b **6** 1st ■
7 c **8** c **9** c **10** b **11** c

Actual Test 2

[1] **1** a **2** b **3** b **4** a **5** b **6** d
7 He made a ball-shaped teapot (of
course, they didn't have tea at the time)
with a tight-fitting lid and two spigots,
one on each side and pointing in
opposite directions.
8 a **9** b **10** b **11** c

[2] **1** c **2** c **3** a **4** b **5** b **6** a
7 c **8** c **9** The protosun became a star
when its internal temperature became
high enough to fuse atoms of hydrogen
into helium.
10 d **11** a

[3] **1** d **2** c **3** a **4** b
5 2nd ■ **6** a **7** d
8 For the first time, many Americans
enrolled in higher education -- in the
1920s college enrollment doubled.
9 b **10** b **11** These machines

[4] **1** d **2** b **3** 1st ■ **4** a **5** b **6** b
7 The REM periods last from a few
minutes to as long as an hour,
averaging about 20 minutes in length.
8 c **9** a **10** d **11** b

[5] **1** c **2** a **3** the fungus
4 c **5** 5th ■ **6** c
7 c **8** c **9** d **10** d **11** d

Actual Test 3

[1] **1** d **2** d **3** Farmers
4 d **5** d **6** b **7** d
8 b **9** c **10** b **11** c

[2] **1** b **2** d **3** b **4** d **5** d **6** b
7 d **8** a
9 Soon the silent lands that had been
the province of nomadic Native
Americans, fur traders, and explorers
gave way to the bustle of surveyors,
graders, treastle builders, tunnel
blasters, and spikers.
10 c **11** b

[3] **1** c **2** c **3** a **4** b
5 b **6** a **7** Odor map
8 b **9** c **10** c **11** c

[4] **1** a **2** d **3** a **4** a **5** d **6** c
7 Aside from causing death by
drowning or starvation, these disasters
promote by various means the
emergence, resurgence and spread of
infectious disease.
8 c **9** b **10** a **11** d

Actual Test 4

[1] **1** d
2 In a modern system, electrical current
is passed through crystals, which
respond by producing powerful sound
pulses pitched above the limit of human
hearing.
3 c **4** c **5** b **6** c **7** b
8 d **9** This method **10** b **11** a

[2] **1** a **2** d **3** d
4 Sounds of this frequency are
ultrasonic to the human ear, which has
an upper limit of about 20,000Hz.
5 c **6** b **7** d **8** approaches
9 The inner ear **10** c **11** c

[3] **1** b **2** c **3** c **4** b
5 d **6** 1st ■ **7** a **8** b
9 a **10** b **11** d

[4] **1** c **2** b **3** c **4** Britannia **5** b
6 American wood carvers who normally
crafted the figureheads of ships were
now called upon to decorate
courthouses and other public buildings
with personifications of Liberty and
Wisdom.
7 c **8** d **9** 5th ■ **10** a **11** c

[5] **1** d **2** a **3** b **4** d
5 dialogue **6** b **7** b
8 c **9** a **10** d **11** c

Actual Test 5

[1] 1 b **2** a **3** North American Indians
4 When necessary, maps were sketched from memory in the dirt or sand or, more permanently, on other natural materials such as animal skins, tree bark, and rocks.
5 b **6** b **7** d **8** c
9 c **10** a **11** c

[2] 1 c **2** b **3** b **4** c
5 Bees most commonly execute these dances when a forager has returned from the rich source, carrying either nectar in her stomach or pollen grains packed in basketlike spaces formed by hairs on her legs.
6 5th ■ **7** forager **8** c
9 d **10** d **11** b

[3] 1 a **2** c
3 Nine patents for improvements to wire fencing were granted by the U.S. Patent Office to American inventors, beginning with Michael Kelly in November 1868 and ending with Joseph Glidden in November 1874.
4 c **5** b **6** c **7** d
8 3rd ■ **9** d **10** d **11** b

[4] 1 a **2** c **3** c **4** c
5 c **6** moisture **7** the Sonoran Desert
8 Modern desert regions are centered in the "horse latitudes", typically straddling the Tropic of Cancer and the Tropic of Capricorn, between 15 and 30 degrees north and south of the equator.
9 b **10** c **11** a

Reading

해석

1 열대 우림은 주로 기후, 특히 기온과 강수량의 상호작용에 의한 산물이다. 일반적으로 열대 우림은 월평균 섭씨 20도와 28도 사이의 기온이 1.5에서 10 미터 사이의 연간 강수량 – 연중 고르게 분포된 – 과 조합되는 곳에서 발생한다. 이 마지막 단서 – 연중 고르게 분포된이라는 – 가 매우 중요한데 그 이유는 강우에 있어서 거의 어떤 계절적 차이를 보이지 않는 열대 숲에만 우림이라는 용어가 적절하게 적용될 수 있기 때문이다.

열대 우림에서 번성하는 식물들 중에 나무가 가장 풍부하다는 것을 알게 되는 것은 그다지 놀라운 것이 아니다. 그 적도 지역의 기후는 급속한 식물의 성장을 위한 모든 필수 요소를 제공하며 나무의 높이가 40미터나 때로는 그 이상의 높이까지 도달하는 것은 흔히 있는 일이다. 그러한 거대한 식물들은 광합성에 필요한 충분한 햇빛을 이용하기 위해 굉장히 큰 잎 부분을 필요로 하고 이러한 거대한 나무들의 crown(잎으로 이루어진 꼭대기층)들은 서로 결합되어 거의 뚫린 곳이 없는 하나의 덮개(차양)를 형성하게 된다. 때때로, 예외적으로 큰 나무가 그 나뭇잎 층을 뚫고 위로 솟아나 그곳의 경관을 지배한다. 이러한 나무들은 emergents(우뚝이들)라고 알려져 있으며 그 열대 우림의 복잡한 덮개 구조의 최상위층을 형성하고 있다.

주 덮개 아래에 더 작은 나무들 – 어리거나 성장이 느린 – 이 자라고 이들은 큰 나무들보다 더 가늘고 긴 crown을 갖고 있는 편이다. 다양한 종류의 큰 풀, 관목과 함께 이러한 작은 나무들이 제 3의 덮개 층을 형성한다. 이러한 3개의 층은 뚫린 곳이 거의 없는 하나의 덮개를 형성하여 정상적인 상황에서는 거의 어떠한 빛 – 간혹 약 2% 정도 만큼 적은 – 도 그 숲의 바닥까지 투과할 수 없다. **큰 나무 하나가 쓰러질 때 조차도 여지가 거의 없다.** 이것은 여분의 햇빛을 이용하여 그 덮개층에 있는 동료들에 합류할 기회를 잡기 위해 바로 밑에서 대기하고 있는 어린 나무들이 많이 있기 때문이다.

이러한 상황들이 숲 바닥에 다소 좋지 않은 성장 조건을 만들게 되고 그 결과 이 곳의 식물은 희박하다. 이러한 규칙에 대한 예외는 강이 숲을 통과해 흘러 강 둑을 따라 관목들이 번성하여 그 숲을 울창하고 빽빽하게 만드는 곳에서 발생한다. 이것이 열대 우림의 전형적인 이미지이다 – 아마도 많은 사람들이 (열대 우림에 대해 갖는) 첫인상이 보트에서 보는 것이라는 사실에 기초해 본다면.

2 가장 숫자가 많은 개구리는 아마도 뉴질랜드, 해양섬들, 남아메리카 남부지역을 제외한 전 세계의 온난지역과 열대 지역에 걸쳐 발견되는 Rana 속(屬)에 속하는 개구리 약 260종이다. 그 개구리들은 주로 물가에서 발견되지만 나무 개구리 R.Sylvatica와 같은 몇몇 종은 주로 습한 숲 바닥에서 지낸다. 큰 황소개구리 T. catesbeiana와 청개구리 R. clamitans는 물이나 습지 지역에서 또는 그 근처에서 거의 항상 발견된다. 표범 개구리인 Rana pipiens와 그 동종들은 거의 모든 (미국의)주와 캐나다 주들에서 발견되며 북아메리카 개구리 중 가장 넓게 분포되어 있다. R.pipiens는 생물 실험실과 전통적인 전기생리학 연구에 가장 흔히 사용되는 종이다.

어떤 종들의 범위 내에서 보면(註: 어떤 종들에 한정된 설명이라는 의미), 개구리들은 종종 특정 지역(예를 들면, 특정 개울이나 연못 등)에만 있고 그 밖의 다른 그와 유사한 서식지에는 거의 살지 않거나 아주 드물 것이다. 피커럴(창꼬치) 개구리(R. palustris)는 이런 점에서 특히 주목할 만한데 그 이유는 그 개구리들이 특정한 국부 지역에서만 그 수가 많이 있다고 알려져 있기 때문이다. 최근 연구에서는 전세계 개구리 개체군들이 그 수에 있어서 감소를 겪고 있으며 분포에 있어서도 평상시에 비해 더 국지적으로 분포하고 있음을 보여준다. 감소를 겪고 있는 개체군 대부분에 있어서 그 원인들은 알려져 있지 않다.

그 개구리들 대부분은 번식기 동안을 제외하고는 그들의 서식지에서 고립된 생활을 한다. 번식기 동안에 그 개구리들 대부분, 특히 수컷들은 매우 시끄럽다. 각 수컷은 주로 물 근처에 특정 지점을 차지하고는 거기에서 몇 시간씩 또는 심지어 며칠씩 머물러 있으면서 그 지점으로 암컷을 유인하려고 한다.

개구리들이 조용할 때는 그들이 방해를 받게 되기 전까지는 거의 그들의 존재를 알아채지 못할 정도이다. 그들이 물 속으로 들어갈 때 그들은 재빠르게 돌진하여 연못 바닥에 도달하여 그곳에서 뿌연 흙탕물을 쳐낸다. 헤엄을 칠 때 그들은 앞 발은 몸 근처에 붙이고 물갈퀴가 달린 뒷다리로 뒤쪽 방향으로 차서 앞으로 돌진해나간다. 그들이 호흡하기 위해 물 표면에 나올 때는 단지 머리와 몸의 앞 부분만 노출되며 그들은 대개 식물을 보호용으로 이용하기 때문에 그들을 보기는 쉽지 않다.

3 친선 퀼트는 사적 퀼트 중에 가장 초기의 것이다. 그것들은 적어도 1830년대 후반부터 현재까지 미국에서 찾아볼 수 있다. 소유권과 재산 목록을 표시하기 위해 천 위에 이니셜(머리글자)을 수놓는 것이 가사일의 한 부분이었고 감상적인 메시지, 가계도, 시구, 알파벳을 십자 수로 새기는 것들이 견본집에 행해졌다. 그러나 정교하게 작업되는 이름이나 이니셜 이외에는 이런 종류의 바느질은 퀼트에서는 흔하게 볼 수 있는 것은 아니다.

그룹이나 가족의 일원이 멀리 이사를 가거나 결혼을 하게 될 때 받게 되는 친선 퀼트나 앨범 퀼트는 이름을 쓴 각 제공자들의 옷을 만들고 남은 천으로 - 말하자면 " (자신의 옷 천과) 같은 천에서 자른"- 종종 만들어졌으며 (그 퀼트는) 과거의 친선관계를 (떠올릴 수 있는) 시각적인 기념품으로 기능하였다. 미국의 인구 이동 - 대부분은 서부로 이동 - 이 19세기 전반에 걸쳐 증가했기 때문에 이사 가는 사람들이 그들의 고향으로 돌아오지 못할지도 모르며 다시는 친구들이나 가족을 보지 못할지도 모른다는 현실적 가능성이 생기게 되었다. 그래서 (그것을) 받는 사람과 가까운 사람들이 제공한 천 조각들을 가지고 만든 퀼트를 주는 것은 흔히 있는 한 관행이 되었고 그러한 증정을 통해 감정적이고 아주 개인적인 감정을 나타낼 수 있었다.

대부분의 경우에 그런 관행은 여성들이 다른 여성을 기억하기 위해, 그리고 가끔은 남성들을 기억하기 위해 행해졌다. 서명, 감동적인 메시지, 성서 문구, 때때로 주소 이 모든 것들이 퀼트 위에 새겨졌으며 대부분의 경우 각 조각에는 그것을 만든 사람의 서명이 있었다.

그것을 받는 사람과 그녀의 자녀들이 그 나라를 가로질러 이주하였기 때문에 그 퀼트들은 종종 그것이 만들어진 곳으로부터 아주 먼 곳에서 끝을 보았다. 그녀가 (때때로 그가) 가족과 친구들로부터 아무리 멀리 떨어져 있다 하더라도 그 퀼트를 가지고 있는 사람은 그 퀼트에 의해 유발된 기억들로부터 안정감을 얻을 수 있었다.

때때로 그것이 만들어지는 과정이 뒤바뀌기도 했다 - 한 여성이 고향에 있는 그녀의 가족에게 글을 써서 외로움과 고독을 달랠 요량으로 가족과 친구들의 서명이 새겨진 천 조각을 요청했을 수도 있다. 게다가 덧붙여 말하면, 여성들이 그들의 남편, 가족과 함께 서부로만 간 것은 아니었다. 어떤 여성들은 선교사로 또는 선교사의 아내로 동쪽으로 가서 아시아, 아프리카, 인도, 하와이, 폴리네시아의 이교도들에게 기독교를 전파하는 일에 헌신했다. 이런 여성들 중 많은 사람들이 친선 퀼트를 가지고 갔을 뿐 아니라 그들의 개종자들에게 - 퀼트가 그 지역에서 실용적이건 그렇지 않건 간에 - 퀼트 만드는 기술을 배우도록 하였다.

4 엘리베이터가 발명되지 않았다면 고층 건물은 가능하지 않았을 것이다. 엘리베이터가 생기 전에는 5~6층이 석조 건물의 최대 높이였다. 건물들은 기술적인 면에서는 더 높아질 수도 있었겠지만 계단을 오르는데 드는 시간 손실과 노동이 더 높은 빌딩이 갖게 될 상업적인 가치를 감소시켰다. 승객용 엘리베이터가 등장 하자마자 빌딩은 2배로 높아졌다. 철근 골격의 구조물과 유압식 엘리베이터의 등장 그리고 전기 엘리베이터는 19세기와 20세기동안 빌딩이 점점 높아지는데 기여했다.

인간과 동물의 노동력 또는 물레방아에 의해 작동되는, 감아 올리는 기계장치와 원시적 형태의 엘리베이터는 B.C 3세기 초에 이미 사용되었다. 이집트의 피라미드와 멕시코와 과테말라의 사원은 노예의 강인한 노동력으로 작동되는 원시적 시스템의 사용으로 건설되었다. 첫번째 현대식 엘리베이터는 1743년 프랑스에서 베르사유 궁전의 루이 15세를 위해 지어졌다고 한다. **어떤 사람들은 그가 자신의 애인을 비밀리에 들어오게 하는 데 그 엘리베이터를 사용했다고 믿기도 한다.** 동력 엘리베이터는 19세기에 개발되었다. 오늘날 엘리베이터는 1850년대에 Elisha Otis가 안전 엘리베이터를 발명했을 때 사용했던 것과 똑같은 기본적 기계 장치 패턴을 사용한다. (엘리베이터의)

타는 칸은 유압 시스템 혹은 모터/평형추의 공동작용에 의해 들어올려져 수직 트랙을 위 아래로 이동한다. 거밀못 역할을 하는 장치는 차체의 추락을 막는다. 만약 그 차체가 너무 빠르게 움직이면 안전 브레이크가 속도를 낮추거나 멈추게 한다.

Elisha Otis는 뉴욕의 Yonkers에 있는 Bedstead 제조 회사의 수석 정비사였다. 그는 1852년에 최초의 안전 엘리베이터 - 승강대 장치 - 를 발명했다. 그는 E.G. Otis 회사를 열었고 화물을 운송하는데 사용되는 엘리베이터를 판매했다. 1857년, Otis는 뉴욕에 있는 E.V. Haughwout & Company에 세계 최초의 상업용 승객운반 엘리베이터의 설치를 완성했다.

## Chapter 1

Hackers Practice

1 전통적인 중국 회화의 기원은 중국의 역사로 한참 거슬러 올라간다. 일반적으로 말하자면, Tang 왕조 이전부터 비롯된 작품들은 대부분 다양한 활동에 종사하는 사람들을 그린 선화(線畵)이다. 이 시대는 인물 그림의 황금기였다. Tang 왕조 중반까지는, 풍경화와 화조도가 두드러지게 나타나기 시작했다. 산, 숲, 들판, 그리고 정원을 그린 그림들은 물질 세계의 번뇌로부터 평화롭고 근심 없는 영역으로 사람을 데려가는 능력을 가지고 있다. 이 때문에, 풍경화는 중국의 문인과 관료들에 의해 항상 상당히 중시되었다. 생생하고 활기찬 화조도에 묘사된 꽃, 풀, 나무, 바위, 새 그리고 다른 동물들도 또한 널리 사랑을 받는다. 그래서 풍경화와 화조도는 초기의 인물 그림과 더불어 전통적인 중국 회화의 3대 주요 범주를 이룬다.

2 프랑스의 동굴 벽화는 말이 석기시대의 사냥꾼들에게 주요 음식 공급원이었다는 사실을 명백히 드러낸다. 석기시대가 끝나고 청동시대가 시작되었을 때, 유럽과 아시아의 사람들은 수 세대에 걸쳐 동물과 일하는 경험을 갖고 있었고 양, 소 그리고 염소를 사육하는 법을 잘 알게 되었다. 또한 그들은 말 - 주로 고기를 위해 그리고 또한 우유를 얻기 위해 (오늘날 중앙 아시아의 nomads가 여전히 그러듯이) - 을 사육하는 법도 알게 되었다. 사람들은 또한 곡식을 경작하는 것을 배우게 되자, 집단으로 떠돌아다니며 사냥하는 것을 포기하고 영구적인 거주지에 정착하는 것을 택했다. 그래서, 기원전 3,000년 까지 인간은 정기적인 식량 공급이 확보되자 말을 단지 네 식구를 일주일 가량 먹여 살릴 수 있는 능력 그 이상의 어떤 자질을 가지고 있는 것으로 평가하게 되었다.

3 Piaget는 그의 인지 발달 단계론으로 가장 잘 알려져 있을지도 모른다. Piaget는 아이들이 그들 생의 각 다른 시기에 다르게 생각하고 추론한다는 것을 알아냈다. 그는 모든 사람이 일정한 일련의 네 가지 질적으로 다른 단계를 거치게 된다고 하였다. 일정하다(invariant)는 것은 단계를 건너뛰거나 순서가 바뀔 수 없다는 것을 의미한다. 모든 정상적인 아이가 정확히 똑같은 순서로 그 단계들을 거치게 된다고 하여도, 아이들이 각 단계에 도달하는 나이에는 차이가 있다. 네 단계는 다음과 같다: 지각 운동 단계 - 태어나서 2세까지; 전조작기 - 2세에서 7세까지; 구체적 조작기 - 7세에서 11세까지; 그리고 형식적 조작기 (추상적 사고) - 11세에서 그 이상. 각 단계에는 성취되어야만 하는 주요한 인지 과업들이 있다. 지각운동단계에서는 정신 구조가 주로 구체적 사물에 숙달되는 것과 관련되어 있다. 상징적인 것들에 익숙해 지는 것은 전조작기 단계에서 일어난다. 구체적 조작기에서는, 아이들은 부류, 관계, 숫자, 그리고 추론하는 법을 알게 된다. 마지막 단계는 사고에 숙달되는 것과 관련되어 있다.

4 유럽 탐험가들이 서반구에 도착하기 수 세기 이전에, 현재 뉴 멕시코 지역의 Pueblo 인디언들은 하나의 독특하고 복잡한 문명을 이루고 있었다. 이 평화를 사랑하는 사람들은 환경과 그리고 서로간에 조화를 이루는 도시 생활을 영위하였다. 그들의 종교는 범신론이었고 상당히 영적이었으며 일상 생활의 중요한 부분을 차지하였다. 그 안에서 그들은 공평한 정부, 훌륭한 건축, 정교한 관개 시스템

을 가진 집약적 농업, 그리고 도기류, 직조법, 보석, 가죽을 다루는 일, 그리고 다른 수공예에서 고도로 발달된 기술을 이룩해냈다.

5 유엔이 위치해 있는 뉴욕은 미국의 가장 국제적인 도시이고, 외국 관광객을 끌어들이는 세계의 주요한 곳들 중 하나이다. 그러나, 두드러지기 때문에, 자연스럽게 테러의 목표가 된다 - 특히 대 여섯 명이 사망하고 엄청난 재산상의 피해를 입힌 1993년의 세계무역센터 폭격은 (주목할 만하다.) 20세기의 마지막 십년 간, 뉴욕은 인구와 경제적 안정성 둘 다에 있어서 지속적인 성장을 경험했다. 수십만의 이민자들이 그 인구에 편입되는 한편, 월 스트리트의 지속적인 붐은 모든 독립(자치)구의 경제를 활성화시켰다. 게다가, 기간 산업의 주요 혁신 - Grand Central Station의 재건과 같은 - 이 완성되었다. 그래서, 빼어난 미국 도시로서의 뉴욕의 위치는 21세기 초에도 여전히 안정적인 위치를 구축하고 있다.

6 예술 민족주의는 많은 New Deal 예술의 두드러진 일면이다. 미국적인 것에 대한 이러한 관심은 많은 형태를 취했는데, 벽 화가는 지방의 역사와 개성을 묘사하는 그림을 그렸고 민속학자들은 전통적인 이야기들을 기록했고 극작가들은 미국 영웅에 대한 희곡을 썼고 사진사들은 일상생활을 사진으로 찍어 남겼고 그리고 작가들은 나라와 지방의 역사를 썼다. New Deal 집행자들은 한 작가 프로젝트 출판물이 "American Stuff"라고 부른 것에 이렇게 몰두하는 것을 격려했다. 그 나라의 과거와 그 인물들을 찬양하는 것은 어려운 시대에 국가 정체성 의식을 장려했고 사람들이 쉽게 이해하고 감상할 수 있는 예술을 만들어냈다. 그러나 New Deal 예술은 단순한 찬양을 넘어 미국의 특성과 정체성의 문제로 더 깊이 파고들 수 있었다.

7 후각은 거의 모든 물고기에게 중요하다. 매우 작은 눈을 가진 특정한 뱀장어들은 먹이의 위치를 찾아내는데 주로 냄새에 의존한다. 물고기의 후각기관은 주둥이의 등쪽 표면에 위치해 있다. 후각기관의 내층에는 특수 감각 세포들이 있어 음식물에서 나온 물질과 같은 물에 용해된 화학물질을 감지하여 제1 뇌신경을 거쳐 두뇌로 감각 정보를 전달한다. 냄새는 또한 경보체계로서의 역할을 한다. 많은 물고기, 특히 다양한 종의 민물 잉어들은 자신과 같은 종의 상처 입은 동료에게서 분비되는 체액에 놀라서 반응한다.

8 네 가지의 기본적인 미각이 있다: 단맛, 짠맛, 신맛, 그리고 쓴맛. 혀의 서로 다른 부분들이 모든 종류의 미각을 탐지할 수 있다. 이것이 많은 교과서에서 찾아볼 수 있는 간단한 혀 "미각 지도"에 대한 비판을 야기시켰다. 실제로 미각을 감지하는 기관은 "미각돌기"라고 불린다. 각각의 미각 돌기(인간에게는 대략 10,000 개의 미각 돌기가 있다)는 많은(50에서 150개 정도의) 수용 세포들로 구성된다. 수용 세포들은 겨우 1~2주 정도 살고 새로운 수용 세포에 의해 대체된다. 미각 돌기에 있는 각각의 수용기는 그 기본 미각들 중의 하나에 가장 잘 반응한다. 하나의 수용기는 그 외의 다른 미각들에도 반응할 수 있지만, 특정한 미각에 가장 강하게 반응한다.

9 laser라는 단어는 "복사의 자극 방출에 의한 빛의 증폭"을 나타낸다. laser가 가능한 것은 빛이 전자와 상호 작용하는 방식 때문이다. 전자는 그 특정한 원자나 분자를 특징짓는 특정 에너지 준위나 상태에서 존재한다. 에너지 준위는 핵 주위의 고리나 궤도로 상상되어 질 수 있다. 바깥 고리의 전자들은 안쪽 고리의 전자들보다 더 높은 에너지 준위에 있다. 전자들은 예를 들어, 번쩍하는 빛과 같은 에너지의 주입에 의해 더 높은 에너지 수준으로 튀어 오를 수 있다. 전자가 바깥에서 안쪽 준위로 떨어질 때, "잉여" 에너지는 빛으로서 방출된다. 방출된 빛의 파장 또는 색은 방출된 에너지의 양과 정확하게 관련되어 있다. 사용되는 (laser광선을 발하는) 특정 물질에 따라, 빛의 특정 파장이 흡수되어 (전자를 활성화시키거나 자극하고) (전자들이 최초의 수준으로 다시 떨어질 때) 특정 파장이 방출된다.

10 수력 발전에서, 물은 보다 높은 높이에 모아지거나 저장되어, 큰 파이프나 터널(수로)을 통해 보다

낮은 높이로 내려가게 된다; 이러한 두 높이의 차가 낙차로 알려져 있다. 가파른 파이프를 따라 내려가는 과정에서, 떨어지는 물이 터빈들을 회전시킨다. 터빈들이 이번에는 발전기를 작동시키게 되고 발전기는 터빈의 기계적 에너지를 전기로 변환시킨다. 변압기들은 발전기에 의해 생산되는 교류를 장거리 전송에 적합한 매우 높은 전압의 전류로 변화시킨다. 터빈과 발전기가 들어있고 파이프나 수로가 연결되어 있는 그 구조를 발전소라고 부른다.

Hackers Test

1　20세기의 시작은 삶의 방식과 구성에 있어서 중요한 변화를 가져왔다. 기술적인 진보에 의해 앞으로 나아가게 된 당시의 문명은 적절한 형태의 예술을 요구했다. 전통적인 예술 방식은 새로운 느낌과 경험을 더 이상 표현할 수 없었다. 새로운 예술 형태와 새로운 표현 방식의 탐색은 기존 예술 체계의 붕괴와 새로운 예술 체계의 창조로 이끌었다. 예술(회화, 극장 예술, 그리고 문학)은 서유럽의 예술 관행에서 전통적으로 규범화 되어온 모방의 특성을 버렸다. 서유럽 예술 전통의 토대 속에는 하나의 모방 – 규범화 된 예술 매체를 통해 삶을 흉내내는 – 철학이 있었다. 하나의 예술 작품은 그것이 어떤 내용을 포함하고 있고 우리에게 어떤 이야기(서술은 모든 예술의 중심이다)를 해주면 그 자체의 의미를 갖게 된다. 문학에 있어서, 서술(이야기)은 어휘, 문학 장르, 문체에 의해 이루어지고 발레와 연극에서는, 무대 효과, 음악, 대사와 동작 – 줄거리의 흐름과 연기자의 감정을 표현하는 –에 의해 이루어진다.

　발레예술에서 전통적으로 규범화 되어온 제한된 표현 형식들은 형식적인 측면에 있어서 는 춤 – 서술적인 측면에 덧붙여, 거기에서는 최고의 가치가 발레 무용가의 연기 기술에 두어졌다 – 을 정점으로 이끌었다. 현대 춤의 혁신주의적 경향은 무용가의 고전주의자-형식주의자 기교에 아주 심하게 반대했다. 20세기 초부터 예술의 혁신주의 정신은 예술의 서술적인 특성이 본질적으로 실용주의적(Horatio시대부터 예술의 기본적인 역할은 사람을 즐겁게 하고 교육시키는 것이라고 믿어졌다)일 수 밖에 없다고 반대했다. 개혁자들은 사회에서 예술의 역할, 예술가 – 환상가 뿐 아니라 – 의 역할, 서유럽 예술의 현실적인(모방적인) 본질을 바꾸기를 원했다. 예술의 해방은 "순수" 예술 – 그 자체의 방식에 의존하고 그것을 탐구하여 그 자체만을 표현하는 – 을 요구했다. 춤의 새로운 토대의 발견은 '춤의 예술은 자급자족할 수 있어 이야기가 전개될 배경을 만들어내기 위해 음악과 배경화법이 필요하지 않으며 어떤 종류의 이야기를 하는 것이 불필요하다' 는 깨달음으로 이어졌다. 새로운 춤의 개혁자들은 또한 발레 무용수들의 정돈된 동작과 전반적인 훈련 시스템 – 그 시스템에 의해 고전적인 기교를 달성하게 하였던 – 을 버렸다. 그들은 형식주의가 몸 자체에서 일어나는 보다 자연스런 동작 – 몸의 자연스런 능력과 한계에 의해 제한을 받는 – 을 위하여 없어져야 한다고 생각했다.

> **mimetic** 모방의　**canonize** (정전)으로 인정하다; 찬미하다; (특히 종교적으로)신성시하다
> **mimesis** 모의, 모방　**virtuosity** 묘기, 탁월한 기량　**Horatio** (고유명사) 남자이름
> **emancipation** 해방, 이탈　**nothing but** 단지... 일 따름(only)
> **scenography** 배경도법, 원근 도법

2　수백만의 아이들이 부모들이 일하는 동안 탁아되어 낮 시간의 일부를 보낸다. 이러한 환경들 – 센터와 가정에서의 – 은 아이들이 배우고 성장할 수 있는 장소이다. 1989년에, 대통령과 주지사들은 미국 교육의 질을 향상시키기 위한 일련의 국가 교육 목표를 설정했다. 첫번째 목표가 학교 준비에 초점을 두고 있었음에도 불구하고 탁아가 자주 그 그림(목표)에서 벗어나는 것으로 보여졌다. 그 목표(설정) 10주년 기념일이 교육을 재정의하고 질적인 탁아소가 아동 발달에 영향을 끼치는 학습 시스템의 일부분이라는 것을 인식하는 중요한 기회라고 할 수 있다.

　아이들의 언어와 인지적 기술들은 질적인 탁아 프로그램 – 적절히 훈련되고 지지 받는　호의적인 보모가 있는 – 에서 성장한다. 질적으로 낮은 프로그램에서는, 발달을 자극하는 기회가 없어지거나

잘못 쓰여진다. 훈련 받은 직원이 거의 없는 큰 집단, 아이들이 책 읽는 것을 듣거나, 이야기를 듣게 되거나, 껴안아질 기회가 거의 없는 센터나 집, 그리고 인간의 상호작용과 의사소통 대신 텔레비전이나 고립이 있는 프로그램에서 아이들은 그들이 그들의 환경에 거의 영향력을 갖지 못한다는 것 - 정확하게는 (이것은) 학교 준비와 성공적인 학교 생활을 조장하는데 전혀 맞지 않는 메시지 - 을 알게 된다.

전통적으로, 세 개의 "장소"들이 아이의 교육에 영향을 끼치는 것으로 알려져 있다 - 가족, 학교, 그리고 지역사회. 탁아는 이 세가지 모두의 일부이다. 탁아는 가족을 지지해준다. 탁아는 종종 친척이나 다른 가족 구성원에 의해 제공되어질 뿐만 아니라, (가족뿐만 아니라 아이의 관점에서 보면), 탁아는 종종 가정의 연장이다. 탁아는 부모들이 "첫 교사"로서 성공하도록 도와줄 많은 기회를 제공한다.

readiness 준비(성), 자진해서 함, 신속   **cognitive** 인식의, 인식력 있는
squander (시간 ,돈을)낭비하다, (기회를)놓치다, 흩어지다

3   금주운동은 아마도 모든 개혁 운동 중에서 가장 널리 퍼진 것이었을 것이다. 1810년 조사는 대략 14,000개의 증류소가 매년 2500만 갤론의 알코올을 생산한다고 보고했다. 700만 명이 넘는 과도한 음주가들이 있는 "음주 공화국"은 모든 남성과 여성, 아이들 일인당 - 맥주, 와인, 사과술을 포함시키지 않고도 - 년간 3갤론 이상의 술을 생산해냈다. 그리고 이 조사자들은 틀림없이 몇 개의 증류소를 빠뜨렸을 것이다. 미국을 여행했던 영국 개혁가 William Cobbett는 1819년에 사람들은 "와인이나 알코올을 마실 것을 요구 받지 않고서는 좀처럼 누군가의 집에 들어가기 어렵다, 심지어 아침에도."라고 말했다.

금주운동은 수많은 주장에 기초하고 있다. 맨 먼저 "열성적인 그리스도교 전도자"가 비난 받지 않는 삶에 앞장서야 한다는 종교적인 요구가 있었다. 다른 사람들은 술에 취한 노동자들이 경제에 미치는 영향을 강조했다. 역동적인 새로운 경제 - 공장과 철도가 꽉 짜여진 스케줄로 가동되는 - 에서는 술에 취해 있는 것이 단순 농업 경제에서 그랬던 것 보다 훨씬 더 큰 문제가 되었다. 인도주의자들은 음주와 가난 사이의 관계를 강조했다. 그 운동에서 주장하는 것들 중 많은 부분이 무고한 엄마와 아이들이 겪게 되는 고통에 그 초점을 맞추었다. Sons of Temperance에서 나온 소책자에서는 "음주는 가족을 괴롭히는 거의 모든 악의 (직접 또는 간접적인) 원인이다" 라고 언급하기도 했다.

1833년에 그 연합 단체는 American Temperance Union이 형성되었던 필라델피아에서 국가 회의를 소집했다. 그러나 그 회의는 내부적인 긴장들을 드러내었다 : 목표가 완화인지 혹은 절대 금주인지, 그리고 만일 후자의 경우라면 단지 독한 술로부터의 금주인지 아니면 와인이나 사과술, 맥주 까지도 포함되는가? 그 운동이 설득(권고)선에서 진행되어야 하는가? 혹은 법에 의해서 진행되어야 하는가? 그 시대의 대부분의 운동처럼 금주 운동에도 모든 타협을 거부하는 일단의 완벽주의자들이 있었고 그들은 알코올 음료의 거래는 도덕적으로 잘못된 것이고 법에 의해 금지되어야 한다는 결의안을 통과시켰다. 1836년 봄 정기 회의에서 그 연합 단체는 모든 알코올 음료의 금주 - 대신에 온건주의자들로 하여금 그 운동을 그만두게 만든 값비싼 승리 - 를 요구했다. 그러나 1830년과 1860년 사이에 그 금주 운동은 미국의 일인당 알코올 소비량을 급격하게 감소시켰다.

crusade 개혁운동   **distillery** 증류소   **sottish** 술고래의, 주정뱅이의
tipple (독한 술을) 조금씩 습관적으로 마시다, 알코올 음료   **abstinence** 절제, 금욕, 금주

4   Erie 운하는 5대호를 Hudson 강을 거쳐 뉴욕시에 연결하는 미국의 역사적인 수로이다. 19세기 초반까지 대서양 연안과 Allegheny를 통과하는 지역 사이를 연결하는 운송수단이 (갖는) 가치는 명백했다. 뉴욕 주지사 DeWitt Clinton은 Erie호 동쪽 해안의 Buffalo부터 Hudson강 - Mohawk 계곡 지역 산맥의 협곡을 통해 흘러가는 - 위쪽의 Albany를 잇는 운하를 (제안한) 계획서에서 잠재적 가

능성을 보았다. 1817년에 그는 주의회에 길이 363마일(584킬로미터), 넓이 40피트(12미터), 깊이 4피트(1.2미터)인 운하의 건설을 위해 7백만 달러의 지출을 승인해주도록 설득했다. Troy 서쪽으로 500피트 융기되어 있는 지역을 가로지르기 위해서는 83개의 수문이 필요했다. 물자 운반을 위한 어떤 도로도 없었고 말과 사람의 힘만을 이용할 수 있었다. 개울이 수관을 통해 가로지르고 있었다. 몇몇 지역에서는 바위가 검은 화약으로 폭파되었다. 모든 어려움에도 불구하고, 그 운하는 운하 보트(길고 좁은 운하에서 사용되는) Seneca Chief에 의해 1825년 10월 25일에 개통되었다.

북쪽 중서부의 성장에 끼친 운하의 영향은 뉴욕시의 성장에 끼친 영향에 견주어질 수 있는 유일한 것이었다. 정착민들은 (많은 사람들이 운하를 이용하여) 서쪽 Michigan, Ohio, Indiana, Illinois - 그들이 Erie 운하를 통해 동부에 내다팔 농산물을 선적할 수 있는 지역인 -으로 몰려갔다; 그 대가로 짐배 가득한 공산품과 일용품이 서쪽으로 운반되었다. 버팔로부터 뉴욕 시가지의 화물 운송비 - 육로로 톤당 100달러였던 - 는 운하로는 톤당 단 10달러 밖에 되지 않았다. 9년 만에 통행료는 건설비를 넘어섰고, 1882년 통행료가 폐지되었을 때까지 운하는 몇몇 지류 운하의 비용을 지불했고 주의 총 세입에 기여했다.

넓이는 70피트(21미터), 깊이는 7피트(2.1미터)로 확장된 Erie 운하는 성공적으로 철도와의 경쟁에서 버텼고, 19세기 후반에 방치되는(거의 이용되지 않는) 시기를 겪었음에도 불구하고 20세기 뉴욕 운하들 - Champlain호, Ontario호, 그리고 the Finger Lakes를 잇는-의 개발에 있어서 주요 동맥이었다. 1918년에 완성된 이 수로는 the New York State Barge Canal이라고 불렸다 (후에 the New York State Canal System이라고 불림). 현대의 운하는 대체로 유람용으로 사용되지만, 대략 2,000톤까지의 짐배들을 수용할 수 있다.

lock (운하의) 수문, 자물쇠, (자동차의) 제륜 장치,   **blast** 폭파하다
barge 바닥이 편편한 짐배   **revenue** 세입, 수입(항목)
artery 동맥, 주요 도로, 중추   **accommodate** 수용하다, 숙박시키다, 적응시키다, 화해하다

5   Nevada는 1930년대의 대공황 기간동안 현대 경제체계로의 전환을 시작했다. 1931년 도박의 적법화와 (결혼한 부부가) 이혼을 하기 위한 동거 의무 기간을 6주로 줄인 후에, Nevada는 결혼, 이혼, 유흥의 중심지가 되었다. 주요 유흥 지역은 Las Vegas, Reno, Laughlin, 그리고 Lake Tahoe이다. Las Vegas는 남부 캘리포니아와 외국 나라들로부터 많은 여행객들을 끌어들이고 또한 비즈니스와 전문 집회를 주최한다. Reno는 샌프란시스코 만 지역과 태평양 북서쪽으로부터 많은 행락객들을 끌어들인다. Laughlin은 1980년대에 여행 중심지로 떠올랐고, Lake Tahoe는 계속해서 현대풍의 행락지로 역할을 한다.

Colorado강에 Hoover댐의 건설은 남부 Nevada 경제를 실질적으로 도왔고, 그것의 값싼 수력은 생산의 길을 열어주었다. Columbia강 Bonneville댐으로부터 수력과 파이프를 통해 보내지는 천연가스의 수입이 또한 북서지역에서의 산업발달을 가져왔다.

1950년대에 연방정부에 의한 Nevada Test Site의 설립은 고용기회를 확대했고 그 주 내부의 기술산업의 발달을 자극했다. 그 새로운 산업화를 무색하게 하고 본질적으로 현재의 번영을 가져다 준 것은 관광산업의 다양화와 확대 - Reno와 Las Vegas 지역의 도박과 오락 시설 뿐만 아니라 주 전역에서 경치와 휴양을 즐길 기회까지 포함시키게 된 - 라고 할 수 있다.

reduction 축소, 저하, 적응, 항복   **overshadow** 무색하게 하다, 가리다, 빛을 잃게 하다
diversification 다양화, 변형, (투자 대상의)분산   **gaming** 도박, 내기(gambling)

6   캘리포니아 금광지대처럼, Oregon광산은 거의 배타적으로 독신의 부양식구가 없는 남자들을 끌어들였다. 이전에는, Oregon은 가족, 농부, 그리고 정착민들의 행선지였는데 그 광산들이 그 지역에 명백히 불쾌한 요소를 일으키게 되었다. 이것은 그 지역의 백인 문명의 특성에 거의 영향을 끼치지 않았을지도 모른다. 남부 Oregon의 인디언들이 북부의 인디언들보다 일반적으로 백인들에게 더 적

대적이라는 것을 제외하고는 말이다. 1855년의 봄과 여름에는 분노에서 징벌, 징벌에서 보복으로 이어지는 점점 더 강도가 세지는 일련의 과정이 있었고 그것은 결국 Oregon의 짧은 역사에서 가장 "살벌한 전쟁" - 가장 피비린내 나는 - 으로 묘사되었던 것을 유발시키게 되었다.

1855년 7월에 그 교전이 일어난 곳을 따라 흐르던 시내의 이름을 따서 지어진 Humbug War에서 긴장상태가 폭발했다. 스무 명이 넘는 인디언들이 잔인하게 무차별적으로 총에 맞거나, 교수형에 처해지거나, 시굴용 광산 구멍에 내던져짐으로써 살해되었다. 10월 8일에 23명의 비전투원인 인디언들 (여자들, 아이들, 그리고 나이든 남자들)이 Luptin Affair로 알려진 사건에서 살해되었다. 그 다음 날, 다양한 연령의 남녀 16명의 백인들이 Rogue강 학살에서 살해되었다. 그 싸움은 10월 17일 Gallice Siege에서 정점에 달했는데, 그곳에서 인디언들이 불화살로 불 타오르게 한 건물에 자원 시민군을 가두게 되면서 네 명의 백인과 미확인 숫자의 중국인들이 죽었다. 그 상황은 결국에는 인디언 감독관 Joel Palmer - 1855년 동안 Oregon에 있는 거의 모든 부족들에게 조약을 강요하고 그들을 인디언 보호구역으로 보냈던 - 에 의해 진정되었다.

unattached 부속되지 않은, 약혼(결혼)하지 않은, 중립의　heretofore 지금까지, 이전에는
unsavory (맛, 냄새 등)불쾌한, (도덕적으로)불미스러운　escalate 단계적으로 확대되다, 차츰 오르다
provocation 성나게 함, 자극　retribution (나쁜 행동에 대한)보복, 징벌
retaliation (같은 수단으로의)보복, 앙갚음　sanguinary 피비린내 나는, 살벌한
creek 시내, 샛강　noncombatant (비)전투원의
siege 포위공격, 공성(攻城)　militia (집합적)시민군, (미)국민군
ablaze 밝게 빛나는, 흥분한, 격한, set~불타오르게 하다

7 박쥐들은 하나의 흥미로운 동물군이다. 그들은 이동하는데 음파를 사용할 수 있는 - echolocation(자신이 보낸 초음파의 반사를 잡아 물체의 존재를 확인하는 능력)라고 불리는 능력 - 몇 안 되는 포유동물중의 하나이다. 약 900종에 이르는 박쥐들 중에서, 반 이상이 echolocation에 의존하여 비행 중에 장애물을 감지하고, 보금자리로 가는 길을 찾고, 먹을 것을 찾아다닌다.

echolocation - 특별한 형태학(신체적 특징)적, 생리학적 적응과 더불어 sonar의 적극적인 사용 - 은 박쥐들이 소리를 통해 "보는 것"을 가능하게 한다. 대부분의 박쥐들은 그들의 후두(소리 상자)를 수축시킴으로써 echolocation 소리를 만들어낸다. 그러나 몇몇 종은 그들의 혀를 딸각 소리나게 한다. 이 소리들은 일반적으로 입을 통해 나오지만, Horseshoe(편자) 박쥐(Rhinolophidae)와 Old World leaf-nosed 박쥐(Hipposideridae)는 echolocation 소리를 그들의 콧구멍을 통해 낸다: 거기에 (콧구멍에) 그들은 확성기로서 역할을 하도록 잘 개조된 편자(살로 이뤄진)나 나뭇잎 같은 구조들을 가지고 있다.

Echolocation 소리는 초음파로 보통 주파수가 20에서 200kilohertz(kHz)에 이른다. 반면 인간의 청력은 정상적으로 20kHz 정도가 최고이다. 그렇다 하더라도, 우리는 Spotted(얼룩이 있는) 박쥐(Euderma maculatum)와 같은 몇몇 박쥐들이 내는 echolocation 딸각 소리를 들을 수 있다. 이러한 소리들은 두개의 둥근 조약돌을 부딪힘으로써 만들어지는 소리와 닮았다. 일반적으로, echolocation 소리는 주파수, 데시벨(dB)의 강도, 그리고 1000분의 1초 단위의 지속 시간에 의해 특징 지워진다. 음의 고저의 관점에서 보면, 박쥐는 일정한 주파수(CF)와 주파수 변조(FM)된 변화하는 주파수를 가지고 echolocation 소리를 만들어낸다. 대부분의 박쥐들은 CF와 FM 요소로 구성된 복잡한 일련의 소리를 만들어낸다. 비록 저주파의 소리가 고주파의 소리보다 더 멀리 가기는 하지만, 고주파 소리가 박쥐에게 크기, 거리, 위치, 속력, 먹이의 비행 방향 등의 더 자세한 정보를 준다. 그래서, 이 소리들은 더 자주 사용된다.

forage (식량을) 찾아 다니다, 약탈하다　morphological 형태학상의
larynx 후두　modulate 조정하다, 변화시키다

8 식물이 동물을 유인하고, 포획해서, 죽인다면 그것은 식충 식물이다. 또한 그것이 식충식물로서의 자격을 갖기 위해서는 먹이로부터 영양분을 소화하고 흡수해야만 한다. 이러한 것들 중 일부분만 (전부가 아닌)을 하는 많은 비 식충식물이 있다. 예를 들어, 꽃은 수분자(곤충, 새, 그리고 다른 생물, 심지어는 인간)를 유인하고, 어떤 식물(난초, 천남성류, 그리고 물백합)들은 꽃가루를 확실히 옮기기 위해 잠시 곤충 수분자를 가둬두고, 미국의 Ibicella와 Proboscidea 속의 구성원인 식물들은 끈적끈적한 잎으로 곤충들을 가두고 죽인다 (그러나 먹이를 소화시키지는 않는다). 모든 식물들은 뿌리나 잎을 통해 영양분을 흡수한다. 그러나, 이 식물들이 식충식물이 하는 일들 중 일부를 할지라도, 그들은 식충식물로서의 자격을 얻기에 필요한 모든 기준을 충족시키지 않는다. 먹이를 유인하고, 포획하고, 죽이고, 소화하고, 흡수하는 식물만이 진정한 의미의 식충식물 이다.

최근에 사람들은 자연이 우리들이 바라는 것처럼 흑과 백이 뚜렷하지 않다는 것을 깨닫고 있다. 몇몇 식물들은 완전하게 육식성도 아니고 완전하게 비 육식성도 아니다. 예를 들어, 자신들 위에 벌레들을 숨겨주는 끈끈이 식물이 있다. 이 벌레들은 식물 위를 자유롭게 기어 다니고 끈적끈적한 잎에 잡힌 곤충을 먹는다. 벌레들은 잎사귀 위에 배설하고, 식물은 그 배설물로부터 영양분을 흡수한다. 다른 식물들은 잡힌 먹이를 분해하기 박테리아의 부패 작용에 의존한다.

> **carnivorous** 육식성의 **pollinate** 수분(가루받이)시키다
> **orchid** 난초, 연보라 빛의 **jack in the pulpit** 천남성류 (북미산)
> **genera** genus의 복수, (생물의)속, 부류
> **harbor** 피난 시키다, (벌레, 곤충의)집이 되다, (감정, 사상)품다
> **crawl** 기어가다, 포복하다 **excrete** 배설하다, 방출하다
> **poop** 선미루, 엉덩이

9 과학자들이 어떻게 태양이 에너지를 만들어내는 지를 이해한 후에, 그들은 어떻게 태양의 에너지가 중심으로부터 태양의 대기권으로 이동하는 지 설명해 줄 이론을 만들기 시작했다. 핵융합이 태양에 동력을 공급한다는 발견이 있은 후 처음 수 십년 간, 과학자들은 태양 중심부의 이론적인 산출량과 태양의 대기권에서 실제로 방출되는 에너지를 비교함으로써 태양의 구조를 추론했다. 1960년대에 미국의 물리학자인 Robert Leighton은 태양 표면에서 빛의 도플러 변동을 기록할 수 있는 카메라를 개발했다. 도플러 변동은 빛을 방출하는 물체의 움직임에 의해 생기는 빛의 파장의 변화이다. 그 물체가 관찰자로부터 멀어지고 있다면, 각 파장은 관찰자에게 도달하기 위해 더 멀리 이동해야만 할 것이다 – 그것이 파간의 거리(파장)를 더 길게 한다. 관찰자쪽으로 움직이는 물체는 더 짧은 파장을 가진 빛을 방출하는 것으로 보일 것이다. Leighton은 이 장치를 사용하여 태양이 안팎으로 고동치는 것 – 약 5분 단위로 하나의 완전한 주기를 이루면서 – 처럼 보이는 것을 발견하였다.

Leighton의 발견은 태양 지진학 – 태양의 진동과 어떻게 음파가 태양을 통과해 이동하는지를 관찰함으로써 태양의 내부를 연구하는 것 – 분야를 출범시켰다. 1970년대에 과학자들은 태양 전체가 대단히 무겁고 조직적인 리듬 – 그것의 중심부까지 미칠 수 있는 – 으로 진동하고 있다는 것을 증명했다. 과학자들은 표면에서의 진동에 근거하여 태양 내부의 모형을 개발했다.

1995년에 전 세계 여섯 개 관측소가 팀으로 태양의 진동 관찰을 시작하기 위하여 서로 협동작업을 하였다. 20개 국가 공동 연구인 이 프로젝트는 the Global Oscillation Network Group (GONG)으로 불린다. GONG은 태양을 계속해서 관찰할 수 있다, 어떤 시간이건 적어도 그 관측소들 중의 하나는 낮을 경험하고 있기 때문에. GONG은 과학자들이 태양 지진학을 통해 태양의 내부 구조에 대해 더 잘 알 수 있도록 해주고 있다.

> **pulsate** (심장, 맥박이)뛰다, 진동하다
> **heliosesismology** 태양 지진학
> **oscillation** 진동, 진폭, 주저

10 지질학자들은 세 개의 그룹으로 암석을 구분한다. 암석을 형성한 주요 지구 작용에 따라. 그 세 개의 암석 그룹은 화성암, 퇴적암, 변성암이다. 암석을 수집하기를 원하는 사람이면 누구나 이 세 개의 암석 그룹의 특징에 친숙해져야만 한다. 일단의 무작위적인 암석 견본을 정확한 수집물로 바꾸기 위해서는 지질학자가 암석을 어떻게 분류하는 지를 아는 것이 중요하다.

화성암은 차가워져서 굳은 용해 암석으로부터 형성된다. 암석이 지구 내부에 깊이 묻혀 있을 때, 그것들은 높은 압력과 온도 때문에 녹는다. magma 라고 불리는 용해된 암석은 위로 흐르거나 심지어 화산으로부터 지구표면으로 분출할 수도 있다. 보통 수 천 피트의 깊이에서 magma가 서서히 냉각할 때, 결정들이 녹은 액체로부터 생겨나고, 거친 입자의 암석이 형성된다. 지구의 표면이나 근처에서 magma가 빠르게 냉각할 때 그 결정은 매우 작아 결과적으로 입자가 고운 암석이 생긴다. 다양한 종류의 암석이 다양한 냉각 속도와 원 magma의 다양한 화학적 구성에 의해 형성된다. 흑요석(화산 유리), 화강암, 현무암, 그리고 안산암 반암은 화성암의 많은 유형들 중 네 가지이다.

퇴적암은 지구의 표면- 물속이나 땅 위- 에서 형성된다. 그것들은 암석, 광물, 동,식물 물질의 침전물, 파편물 들이 층으로 축적된 것이다. 온도와 압력은 지구의 표면에서 낮은데, 퇴적암은 그것의 모양과 그것이 포함하는 광물을 통해 이 사실을 보여준다. 대부분의 퇴적암은 광물과 화학물질에 의해 접합되기도 하고 전기력에 의해 뭉쳐진다. 그러나, 몇몇은 느슨하고 굳어지지 않은 채로 남는다. 층들은 보통은 지구의 표면에 평행이거나 거의 평행이다; 그것이 표면과 높은 각도를 이루거나 꼬여있거나 깨져있다면, 암석이 형성된 이후에 어떤 종류의 지구 움직임이 있었다는 것이다. 퇴적암은 우리 주위에서 항상 형성되고 있다. 해변가나 강가의 모래와 자갈은 그것들이 변하게 될 사암과 역암처럼 보인다. 단단하게 결속된 마른 진흙판들은 이판암으로 굳어진다. 진흙과 조가비가 얕은 바다의 밑바닥에 가라앉는 것을 본 적이 있는 스쿠버 다이빙 선수는 어떻게 퇴적암이 형성되는 지 이해하기가 쉽다는 것을 안다.

> **igneous** 불의, 불같은, 화성의 **sedimentary** 침전물의, 침전작용에 의한, 침적의
> **metamorphic** 변형의, 변성의 **grained** 나뭇결(돌결)이 있는, 거죽이 도돌도돌한
> **obsidian** 〔광물〕흑요석 **granite** 화강암 **basalt** 현무암 **andesite** 안산암
> **porphyry** 반암 **gravel** 자갈, 요사, 요결석 **conglomerate** 둥글게 뭉친 것, 역암
> **shale** 혈암 **lagoon** 석호, (강. 호수로 통하는) 늪, 못

## Chapter 2

Hackers Practice

1 Rh는 적혈구 표면상에 있는 하나의 단백질군이다. 명확히 설명하자면 이러한 단백질의 가장 일반적인 형태가 존재하면 혈액형이 Rh(+)가 되고 그것이 없으면 혈액형이 Rh(-)가 된다.

2 국내 총생산은 재화와 용역의 생산량을 말한다. 미국이 세계에서 가장 강력한 경제를 갖고 있다는 사실은 누구나 알고 있다. 미국은 세계 2차 대전이 끝난 이후부터 그래왔으며 또한 앞으로 다가올 수년 동안 의심할 여지 없이 그 순위를 계속 유지할 것이다. 두 번째 순위 국가인 중국($4.8조)과 비교하여 미국($9.255조)은 거의 GDP가 2배 가량 된다. 그러나 정말 한 국가가 얼마나 만족스러운 부를 가지는가 하는 것을 보여주는 통계치는 일인당 GDP이다. 이 기준(일인당 GDP)에서 미국(33,900)은 아주 작은 국가(2,586 평방 킬로미터 & 437,389 인구)인 룩셈부르크($34,200) 다음 순위가 된다. 그러나 중국은 GDP는 많지만 일인당 GDP($3,800)는 아주 적다 – 이것은 기본적으로 중국이 가난한 나라라는 것을 의미한다.

3 동력엔진 기계의 급속한 증가로 실을 더욱 싸게 생산할 수 있었기 때문에 영국 상인들은 전 세계 면직물 시장에서 아주 큰 비중을 차지할 수 있었다. 그 수요를 충족시키기 위해 더 많은 공장들이 영국과 스코틀랜드에 세워졌고, 그것은 이번에는 그 기계와 공장을 세우는데 필요한 나무, 철, 가죽, 벽돌, 목재 등과 그것들을 가동시키는데 필요한 연료에 대한 보다 많은 수요를 창출하게 되었다.

4 정책에 어떤 변경이 행해질 때, 종종 정부는 먼저 그것의 계획안을 Green Paper - 정책 대안들에 대한 검토 문서 - 에 제안하게 된다. 그것은 관련 부서에서 처음으로 만들어지고 비평과 아이디어를 구하기 위해 출판되어진다. 이 문서는 White Paper - 정부 정책에 대한 대략적인 기술 - 의 초안이 된다. 관련된 정당으로부터의 비평에 대한 문이 열려있다. 일단 이러한 입력 사항들을 참작하여 관련된 정부 부처의 장관과 공무원들은 입법 제안서의 초안을 작성하게 된다.

5 (A) 예를 들면, Salt Lick - New Stanton 바로 남동쪽에 위치한 - 으로 알려진 한 영국 야영지는 독립전쟁 이전 시대 서부 국경 정복과정에서 하나의 작전지이면서 동시에 전투지였다.
(B) 식민지 기간동안 그러한 지역들이 유럽 군사들을 위한 보급소가 되었다는 것은 별로 놀랄만한 일이 아니다.
(C) 실제로 소금 퇴적층들은 아주 중요했기 대문에 정착민들은 그것들을 일련의 이름 - Two Lick Creek 또는 Indiana County town인 Black Lick 등과 같은 오늘날 음란 영화 제목처럼 들리는 -을 짓는데 사용하였다.

    lick - 핥기, 함염지

6 (A) 그것은 유례없는 위대한 발명 중의 하나로 볼 수 있는데 그 이유는 바퀴와, 탈것에 그 바퀴를 이용한 것이 개인의 기동성에 부가적 동력원을 제공한 공헌을 했기 때문이다.
(B) 말하자면 말과 낙타는 그들의 등에 탄 인간들보다 더 빠르게 이동할 수 있지만, 한 마리의 동물에 한 사람 이상을 실고 가기 위해서는 - 대부분의 말들이 할 수 있는 힘을 가지고 있었던 것- 탈것이 필요했다.
(C) 짐 운반용으로 동물을 길들인 초기의 노력 이후 인간의 이동에 있어 그 다음 중요한 단계(추가)는 바퀴가 달린 탈것이었다.

7 (A) 그 쥐가 지레 위를 내려 누르면 그 먹이 덩이가 튀어나온다.
(B) 한 마리의 쥐가 먹이(둥글게 뭉친 것) 분배기가 있는 우리에 놓여졌다.
(C) 그러나 그 우리 밖에 있는 과학자들은 그 먹이가 나올 수 있는 때를 조절할 수 있다. 쥐가 그 막대를 두 번 칠 때, 또는 세 번 등등으로 칠 때 먹이가 나올 수 있도록 조정하면서.

8 (A) 이전의 하원 의장 선출을 위한 선거(1801과 1825년)는 비밀 투표였으나, 오늘날 많은 사람들은 그러한 관행을 있을 수 없는 일이라고 생각한다.
(B) 국회 의원들이 비밀투표에서 당의 징계를 피할 수 있었을 지도 모른다는 사실이 또한 그것과 어떤 관련이 있었을 것이라고 생각할 수 도 있다.
(C) 한 예로, 국영 TV에서 하원 의장 Tom Foley는 "미국 국민들이 하원의 실질적인 업무와 투표로부터 차단되는 것은 불가능할 것이다. 그것은 정말 있을 수도 없는 일이다" 라고 주장했다.

9 현재 연구의 결과들은 테스토스테론과 숙련을 요하는 움직임 - 손 선호에 비유되는 - 과의 관계에 관하여 인간 두뇌의 내부에 어떤 다른 체제가 있음을 보여주었다. 혈청 테스토스테론이 주로 남자와 여자에서 주로 오른손 기술과 관계가 있는 것으로 알려졌다. **그러나 남자와 여자의 패턴에는 근본적으로 다른 점이 있다.** 오른쪽 눈을 선호하는 오른손잡이 남자를 제외하고는 오른손 기술은 남자에게 있어서는 혈청 테스토스테론과 직접적으로 관련되어 있지만 여성에게는 반대로 관련되어 있는 것으로 밝혀졌다. 다시 말하자면, 오른손 기술을 남성에게 있어서 혈청 테스토스테론과 함께 증가했는데, 이것은 Geschwind-Behan 가설과는 반대이다. 여성에게 있어서 오른손 기술은, Geschwind Behan 가설에 일치하여, 혈청 테스토스테론에 따라 감소했다.

10 초기 색깔이 있는 석판화는 한 두 가지 색을 사용하여 전체 판에 엷게 색을 칠하여 그 이미지에 수채화 같은 색조를 만들어냈다. 이런 분위기 효과는 주로 풍경이나 지형학적 삽화를 그리는데 사용되어졌다. **더욱 정교한 채색을 위해 화가들은 석판화의 채색을 손으로 하는 것에 계속 의존해 왔다.** 심지어 잘 만들어진 채색 석판화의 경우에도 연달아 인쇄된 다수의 색 판들을 사용하여 색의 범위를 확장시킨 것은 단지 작은 진척에 불과했다. 일반적으로 이러한 초기 다색 석판 그림들은 평평한 색 면들 - 나란히 인쇄된- 을 갖고 있는 단순한 판화였다.

Hackers Test

1 Gordon Strong과 미 연방 준비은행은 인플레이션과 저리의 신용대부를 유발시킨 주요 원인이기는 하지만 전적인 원인은 아니었다. 재무부가 또 다른 원인이었다. 1927년 3월 초 Mellon 장관은 저금리 자금에 대한 충분한 공급이 가능할 것이라고 단언했고, 1928년에 재무부는 만기가 9월인 4 1/4% 자유공채 발행분을 3 1/2% 어음으로 차환할 것이라고 발표했다. 따라서 은행 신용 대부가 증가하였고, 다른 투자자들은 그들의 채권 자금을 주식 투기로 이동시켰다. Rothbard는 연방정부가 인플레이션 정책을 열렬히 추구했지만 "(미국) 경제와 미국 국민들은 성공을 거두지 못했다" 라고 결론내린다. **그러나 그의 이례적인 비난은 Hoover 대통령 - 그의 강력한 행동주의 정책이 이미 비참해진 그 국가의 경제상황을 더 악화시켰다고 - 에게 쏟아졌다.**

Hoover가 자신의 행동주의를 위해 (제시한) 전반적인 기조는 "기업과 정부 기관이 일치된 행위로 협동하는 것" 이었다. 그 중에서도 어떻게 이것이 현실 세계에 적용되었는가 하는 것은 "불황의 첫 번째 충격이 임금에 부과되는 것이 아니라 이윤에 부과되어야 한다 -라는 Hoover의 주장이었다. 이 것은 건전한 정책과 정반대 되는 것이다, 왜냐하면 이윤이 경제 활동의 원동력을 제공해주기 때문에" (그 당시 사람들은 거의 염두에 두고 싶어하지 않았던 하나의 명백한 진술) 라고 Rothbard는 썼다.

요컨대, Hoover는 기업들과 고용주들에게 충격(불황) 이전 수준으로 임금을 유지하도록 설득했다. 그 결과는 모든 사람이 알고 있는 것처럼 미국의 역사상 가장 심하고 긴 불황이었다.

> **treasure** 금고,자금 (the T~) 재무부 **bond** 채권, 보증(금) **stock** 주식, 재고품, 축적
> **speculation** 투기, 심사숙고, 사색, 견해 **avidly** 탐욕스럽게, 열심히, 갈망하여
> **rubric** 항목, 전례법규, 붉게 인쇄한 것

2 하수처리는 불순물을 제거하여 그 남은 폐수가 안전하게 강이나 바다로 돌아가, 다시 자연적인 물 순환 사이클의 일부가 될 수 있도록 하는 것을 의미한다.

하수처리는 물리적인 처리 과정들을 이용하여 액체로부터 고체를 분리시키고 생물학적 처리 과정들을 통해 그 액체를 정화시킨다. 처리 과정들은 다양하지만, 다음에 나오는 waste stream(폐수를 흐르게 하면서 처리하는 것)이 전형적인 방법이다.

예비 처리 단계에서는 나무, 종이, 넝마조각, 플라스틱과 같은 고체들이 칸막이들에 의해 걸러져, 씻겨지고, 건조되어, 안전한 처리를 위해 허가된 쓰레기 처리장에 버려진다. 양수기를 손상시킬 수 있는 자갈과 모래 또한 유사한 방법으로 제거되어 처리되어진다.

1차 처리에서, (예비처리 후에도) 남아 있는 고체들은 하수를 큰 침전 탱크 - 그곳에서 고체 물질 대부분이 바닥으로 가라앉는다 - 에 통과시키는 과정에서 액체로부터 분리된다. 고체의 약 70%가 이 단계에서 가라 앉게 되며 침전물로 불리게 된다. 그 침전물은 침전물 처리라고 불리는 추후 처리를 거친 후 농장에 사용된다.

2차 처리는 생물학적 처리과정 - 유기물질을 분해하여 액체를 정화시키는 역할을 하는 자연 발생 미생물들에 의존하는 - 생물학적 과정이다. 간단한 하수 처리 과정에서는 미생물들이 하수가 스치고 지나가는 돌 위에서 자라게 조장되어진다. 변성하기 위해서는 산소를 필요로 하는 미생물은 그

하수에 있는 박테리아를 먹어 물을 정화시킨다. 이러한 처리 장치를 여과 필터라고 부른다. 이 과정은 하수탱크 – 미생물이 자유롭게 떠다니며 박테리아를 먹는 장소인 – 안으로 공기를 주입함으로써 가속화 될 수 있다. 이러한 처리 장치는 통기 탱크라고 불린다. 2차 처리 과정의 어떤 한 방식(여과 필터나 통기 탱크)을 거치면 그 폐수는 탱크에 가라앉아 생물학적 침전물과 정화된 폐수로 분리된다.

가끔은 그 폐수에 마지막 "광택(정화)"을 위해 추가 처리가 필요하기도 한다. 이것은 3차 처리로 알려져 있다. 다양한 방법 – 모래필터, 갈대짚단, 잔디 구획들 등을 포함한 – 들이 사용될 수 있다. 박테리아를 죽이기 위해 자외선을 사용하는 살균작용은 또 다른 방법이며 많은 해안의 하수처리 계획에 사용되어 지고 있다.

> **sewage** 하수, 오물 **rag** 넝마 누더기 **disposal** 처분 (권), 처리
> **grit** (기계등에 끼이는) 잔 모래, 거친 가루 **sludge** 진창, 진흙, 찌꺼기
> **trickle** (액체가) 똑똑 떨어지다, 졸졸 흐르다 **percolate** (액체가) 여과되다, 스며 나오다
> **aeration** 통기, 탄산가스포화, **tertiary** 제 3차의, 제 3급의 **reed** 갈대

3   지금, 새로운 증거는 서 남극 빙상(氷床)의 전부 또는 대부분이 지난 130만년 동안 – 지구 온도가 아마도 현재보다 그리 많이 높지 않고 그 빙상도 안정되어 있었던 것으로 추정되었던 시기 – 적어도 한 번은 무너졌다는 것을 보여준다. 지질학적 시간에서 백 만년은 최근 역사이다.

사이언스지에 실린 그 증거는 스웨덴의 Uppsala 대학과 Pasadena에 있는 캘리포니아 기술 연구소의 한 팀의 빙하학자들 – 그 빙상의 가장자리 근처에 깊은 구멍들을 뚫은 –로부터 나왔다. 그 얼음 아래 있는 퇴적물로부터 수집된 표본 내에서 그들은 규조라는 극히 미세한 해양 식물의 화석을 발견했는데 그것은 그 지역이 홍적세 말기에 딱딱한 얼음이 아니라 열린 해양이었다는 사실을 시사한다. 칼 텍의 공저자 Hermann Engelhardt가 말한 것처럼 "서 남극 빙상은 사라진 적이 있고 다시 사라질 수도 있다"

물론 빙상이 사라질 수도 있다고 해서 그것이 그렇게 된다는 것을 의미하지는 않는다. 여러 가지 예측할 수 없는 변수들 – 세계 기온의 변화나 그 빙상이 주변 얼음판의 붕괴에 어떤 식으로 반응하는지 등 – 이 그것의 운명을 결정하는데 일조를 하게 될 것이다. 하나의 주요 변수는 그 거대한 판을 갉아먹는 빙류와 관련되어 있다.

해류와 마찬가지로 이러한 빙류들 – 폭이 90마일이 되기도 하는 – 은 그것들을 담고 있는 빙상보다 100까지 더 빠르게 이동하여 빠른 빙하손실 메커니즘을 만들어 낸다. Engelhardt에 의하면 빙류 B라고 불리는 하나의 빙류가 1년에 33피트씩 넓히고 있으며 그것은 그 빙류가 가속화되어 판이 붕괴될 지도 모른다는 하나의 징후이다. 그러나 다른 과학자들은 빙류(의 속도가) 늦어질 수도 있다고 믿는다.

> **diatom** 규조, 돌말 **Pleistocene** 홍적세
> **coauthor** 공저자, 공동 집필하다 **a host of** 많은

4   사적 기업가들은 그들 기업의 이윤을 증가시키기 위한 강한 동기를 가지고 있는데, 그 이유는 그들이 이러한 이윤들을 직접적인 수입이나 (그들 기업의 가치가 성장하게 될 때 쓸) 자본금 확득이라는 형태로 받기 때문이다. 경쟁시장에서, 한 회사가 창출하게 되는 이윤은 생산비용을 낮춤으로써 그리고 혁신적인 고품질 상품 – 소비자들에게 인기있는 – 을 생산함으로써 증가될 수 있다. 이러한 활동들은 소비자들로 하여금 가능한 가장 싼 가격에 최상의 상품을 구입할 수 있도록 해주므로 대개 사회적으로 바람직하다.

그러나 수익을 극대화시키는 활동들이 사회적으로 바람직할 필요는 없다. **예를 들어 한 기업은 그 자체의 비용을 감소시킬 수 있지만 동시에 오염을 증가시킬 수도 있는 것이다.** 그 회사

주인이 얻게 된 개인적 절약은 오염으로 생긴 사회적 손실에 의해 상쇄된다. 이것은 1987년 뉴저지, 1996년 로스엔젤레스에서 있었던 사례였다. 사기업들이 의학 폐기물을 처리하도록 고용되었다. 이것은 일반적으로 고온의 소각과정을 필요로 한다. 그러나 비용을 최소화 하기 위해 그 사기업들은 그 폐기물을 단순히 바다에 던지기만 한다면 더 쌀 것이라는 것을 깨달았다. 결국 쓰레기는 지역 해변으로 떠오르게 되었고 그것은 대중의 항의를 불러 일으키게 되었다.

경쟁이 심하지 않은 시장에서는 사기업 경영자들은 그들이 소비자들에게 부담시키는 가격을 올림으로써 수익을 높일 수 있다. 생산에 드는 한계 비용보다 높이 가격을 책정하는 것은 기업 이윤을 증가시키긴 하지만 또한 몇몇 구매자들이 그 시장으로부터 밀려나게 되므로 사회적 손실을 야기시킨다.

정부가 사적 기업들에 대한 이러한 문제에 전통적으로 대응해온 방법은 규제를 통한 것이다. 모든 선진 국가의 기업들은 규제들- 인위적으로 경쟁을 줄이거나 과도한 오염을 일으키거나 고의로 소비자들을 속이는 것과 같은 사회적으로 바람직하지 않은 방식으로 이윤을 증대 시키려는 능력을 제한하려는 - 에 맞닥뜨린다. 이익을 증대 시키려는 사적 의욕과 공공복지 사이에 현저한 갈등이 있는 산업에서는 종종 기업 세부 규제 조항이 있다. 극단적인 경우에는 물, 전기, 대중교통, 그리고 우체국 서비스와 같은 산업에서 그 기업들은 종종 직접적인 정부 통제 아래 있어왔다.

> offset 상쇄되다, 파생하다 dispose of 처분, 처리하다, 결말을 짓다.
> incineration 소각, 화장 wash up 물가에 밀어올리다, 세수하다, 설거지하다
> outcry 비명, (대중의)강력한 항의, 경매
> squeeze 짜내다; 밀어내다; 계략을 써서 파산(폐업)시키다

5 오존 고갈 과정은 CFC와 다른 오존고갈 물질(ODS)이 기기로부터 누수되어 나오면서 시작된다. 바람이 대류권을 효과적으로 섞어 그 가스들을 고르게 분포시킨다. CFC는 극도로 안정적이어서 그들은 비에도 용해되지 않는다. 몇 년의 기간이 지난 후 ODS 분자들이 성층권 - 지구 표면 위 약 10km 되는 - 도달한다.

강한 UV광선은 ODS분자를 분리시킨다. CFC는 염소 원자를 방출하고 halon은 브롬 원자를 방출한다. 이런 원자들이 실제로 오존을 파괴하는 것이지 분리되지 않은 ODS 분자들이 (파괴하는 것은) 아니다. 하나의 염소 원자가 마침내 성층권으로부터 제거되어지기 전까지, 십만 개 이상의 오존 분자를 파괴할 수 있는 것으로 추정된다. NASA는 오존 고갈 반응에 대한 더 세부적인 설명을 제공하고 있다.

오존은 자연적인 싸이클에서 계속 생산되고 파괴된다. 그러나 오존의 전체 양은 본질적으로 변동이 없다. 이러한 균형은 특정한 지역에 (흐르고) 있는 시내의 깊이로 생각되어질 수 있다. **개별 물 분자들은 그 관측자를 지나 이동하고 있지만, 전체 깊이는 일정하게 유지된다.** 그와 유사하게, 오존의 생산과 파괴가 균형을 이루고 있는 동안에 오존의 수치는 일정하게 유지된다. 이것은 과거 몇 십년까지의 상황이었다.

그러나 성층권에 있는 염소와 브롬의 엄청난 증가가 그 균형을 깨트리고 있다. 사실상, 그것들은 자연적인 오존 생성이 따라갈 수 있는 것보다 더 빨리 오존을 파괴하여 하나의 사이펀(관)을 아래쪽으로 증가시키고 있다. 그러므로 오존의 수치는 떨어진다.

오존은 해로운 UVB 방사선을 여과해 내기 때문에 더 적은 오존은 지표에서 더 높은 UVB 수치를 의미한다. (오존이) 더욱 많이 고갈될수록 흡수되는 UVB는 더욱 많아진다. UVB는 피부암, 백내장과 플라스틱 같은 물질들의 손상과 관계가 있다. **게다가 그것은 몇몇 농작물과 해양 유기체에도 해를 끼친다.** 비록 일부 UVB는 오존 파괴가 없어도 표면에 도달하긴 하지만 그것의 해는 결국 이러한 문제의 결과로서 증가하게 될 것이다.

> troposphere 대류권 stratosphere 성층권 chlorine 염소 bromine 브롬
> intact 손상되지 않은, 변하지 않은 siphon 사이펀(한쪽이 짧고 다른 한쪽이 긴 구부러진 관)
> cataract 백내장

6 유복하고 교양있는 가문의 구성원인 Jane Addams는 가난한 사람들의 고통에 대해 너무 괴로워하여 결국 집을 떠나 시카고 슬램가에서 그녀의 생을 보냈다. 1889년에 그녀는 그곳에 Hull House 라는 사회 복지관을 세워 그 곳에서 많은 인도주의적인 사업을 시작했다. **이것들 중에는 공장 노동자들을 위한 점심식사 제공과 어린 아이들을 위한 어린이집, 젊은이들과 성인들을 위한 무료 강좌, 체육관과 미술화랑 등이 있었다.** 이민자와 다른 가난한 사람들은 배움과 즐거움을 얻는 것 뿐만 아니라 조언과 도움을 받기 위해 Jane Addams의 Hull House로 왔다. 이 훌륭한 여성은 또한 많은 다른 대의에 자신을 헌신하였다. 그녀는 어린이 노동력의 사용과 전쟁에 대항해 싸우는데 적극적이었다. 게다가 그녀는 여성의 참정권과 흑인들의 지위 개선을 위해 일했다. 그리고 그녀는 운동장과 공원을 만드는 것을 도왔고 가난한 도시 아이들을 위한 지역 휴가 프로그램을 시작했다.

모든 사람들이 Jane Addams의 행동을 높이 평가한 것은 아니었다. 실제로 어떤 사람들은 다른 사람의 개인적인 문제에 있어서 그녀가 간섭한다고 불만을 표시했다. **그럼에도 불구하고 그녀는 미국과 또한 세계의 다른 지역에서 있어서의 사회사업 발전에 막대한 영향을 미쳤다.** 그녀는 혜택 받지 못한 사람들의 복지에 대한 책임감을 조장하였고, 그녀의 프로그램은 널리 채택되었다. Hull House를 모델로 삼은 사회 복지관이 많은 가난한 지역에 설립되어 어린이들과 어른들이 그들의 삶을 더욱 의미있게 영위하도록 도왔다.

그녀의 사회에 대한 공헌이 인정되어 Jane Addams 는 1931년 노벨 평화상을 수상했다.

> **humanitarian** 인도주의적인
> **underprivileged** 권리가 적은, 혜택 받지 못한

7 해양은 관성과 (태양과 달의) 중력에 대해 동시에 반응한다. 만일 지구, 달, 태양이 모두 일직선 상에 있다면 달과 태양의 조수가 부가작용을 하여 높은 조수는 더 높아 지고 낮은 조수는 더 낮아지는 결과가 생긴다. 그러나 만일 달, 지구, 태양이 90도를 이루면 태양의 조수는 달의 조수를 감소시키게 될 것이다. 달의 영향이 태양의 두 배 이상이기 때문에 태양의 조수는 달의 조수를 완전히 없애지는 못할 것이다.

태양, 지구 그리고 달의 일직선 배치에 의해 야기되는 큰 조수는 spring tide(한사리)이라고 부른다. 그 조수 동안 만조는 매우 높고, 간조는 매우 낮다. 이러한 조수는 초승과 보름에 해당하는 2주 간격으로 발생한다. 최저조는 달, 지구, 태양이 90도를 이룰 때 발생한다. **최저조 동안에 만조는 매우 높지 않고 간조도 그다지 낮지 않다.** 최저조도 2주 간격으로 발생하며 그 최저조는 한사리 1주 후에 나타난다.

그것들의 궤도는 완벽한 원이 아니고 타원이기 때문에 달과 태양이 지구에 더 가까워 지는 때(다른 때보다)가 있다. 원지점(달이 가장 먼 지점)과 근지점(가장 가까운 지점) 사이의 차이는 30,600km이다. 조수의 힘은 그 천체들 사이 거리의 세제곱에 반비례하므로 더 가까운 달이 현저하게 더 높은 조수(의 최고치)를 야기시킨다. 근일점(지구가 태양에 가장 근접하는 것)과 원일점(가장 먼 거리) 사이의 차이는 370만km이다. 만일 달과 태양이 거의 같은 위도에 있고 지구가 또한 태양에 가까이 있다면 최고의 한사리가 야기될 것이다. 흥미롭게도 한사리는 북반구의 여름보다 북반구 겨울에 더 큰 (변동) 범위를 보인다. **그것은 지구가 북부지방의 겨울 동안 태양과 가장 가깝게 있기 때문이다.**

> **inertia** 〔물리〕 관성, 타성, 〔의학〕 무력(증) **gravitational** 중력의, 인력작용의
> **neap** 소조(의), 최저조((~tides) (상현, 하현시의)
> **apogee** 원지점 **perigee** 근지점 **inversely** 거꾸로, 반대로
> **proportional** 비례하는(to) **crest** 최상,꼭대기
> **perihelion** 〔천문〕 근일점, 태양계의 천체가 태양과 가장 가까워지는 위치
> **aphelion** 원일점

8 빠른 장거리 교통 수단은 거주지가 서부로 더 멀리 확장됨에 따라 미국의 필수품이 되었다. 초기 기차는 비실용적인 신기한 것일 뿐이었고 오랫동안 철도회사는 성가신 기계적 문제에 봉착했다. 가장 심각한 것은 무거운 짐을 운반할 수 있는 철도(레일)의 건설과 안전하고 효과적인 제동 시스템의 개발이었다. 일단 이러한 문제들이 해결되자, 철도는 최고의 육로 교통 수단이 되었다. 1860년까지 동부 산맥을 가로질러 서쪽으로 미시시피 강 까지 도달하는 수 천 마일의 선로가 있었다. **또한 남부와 서부의 지역 선로도 있었다.**

철도 건설에 있어서 가장 중요한 시점은 첫번째 대륙횡단 시스템의 건설로 시작했다. 1862년 의회는 두개의 서부 철도 회사로 하여금 서쪽으로는 네브라스카로부터 그리고 동쪽으로는 캘리포니아로부터 (시작하여) 하나의 만나는 지점까지 연결하는 철도선을 -대서양을 태평양에 연결하는 대륙횡단선을 완성하기 위해 - 만들도록 승인했다. 정부는 보조금과 토지의 허가를 통해 관대하게 철도회사에 도움을 주었다. 이러한 계획의 실질적인 작업은 4년 후에나 시작하게 되었다. Union Pacifc Company가 아일랜드 이주민을 고용했던 반면 캘리포니아에 세워진 Central Pacific Company는 중국의 노동자를 고용했다. **그 두 그룹은 각각 다른 쪽보다 더 많은 거리를 커버하기 위해 놀랄 정도로 빠른 속도로 일했다.** 1869년에 그들은 Promontory라는 곳에서 만났는데 그곳은 지금 유타주이다. 많은 방문객들이 그 큰 행사를 위해 그 곳으로 왔다. 그 공식행사에서 은으로 된 방망이가 금으로 된 대못을 박는데 사용되어졌고 - 이로써 두 철도의 결합이 완성되었고 - 새로 개발된 전보가 미국 전역으로 그 소식을 알렸다. 미국 전역에 그 위대한 업적을 기리기 위한 축하 행렬과 교회 벨 소리를 동반한 즐거운 축제가 있었다.

> **bear** (짐을)싣다 **ranges** 열, 줄, 산맥. 범위
> **seaboard** 해안선, 해안지대(의) **subsidy** 보조금, 기부금

9 일반적으로 최근 몇 십년 간 세계 전역의 박쥐 수가 감소하고 있다고 믿어진다. **박쥐는 번식력이 낮기 때문에 개체수는 증가된 사망률과 낮아진 출생률에 민감하다.** 많은 종의 박쥐가 인간활동에 의해 점차 많은 영향을 주었기 때문에 박쥐의 보존 상태에 대한 관심이 높아지고 있다. 박쥐는 많은 위험 - 무지와 의심, 살충제 중독, 보금자리의 파괴와 폐쇄, 서식지 상실, 과잉 개발 그리고 해충(으로 간주되어) 박멸되는 것과 같은 - 에 직면해 있다. 포유 동물 중에서 박쥐는 (설치목 다음의) 두 번째로 가장 다양한 목(目)이며, 남극 대륙을 제외한 모든 대륙에서 발견된다. 박쥐들은 종종 먹이를 찾는 방식이 아주 다양하며 서식지의 변형 - 도시화, 농업, 기타 다른 땅 사용 행위들과 같은 - 이 지역 식물과 곤충 개체수 그리고 그에 따른 박쥐의 먹이원에 영향을 끼칠 수 있다. 그러나 현재 실제로 박쥐에 대한 지구 온난화의 구체적인 효과에 대해 알려진 것은 아무것도 없다. 비록 그들의 생태에 기초하여 어떤 예측들이 만들어질 수 있다 하더라도.

박쥐는 지구의 기후에 그 때 그 때 잘 적응하여 적절하게 긴 수명(5-30년)을 가진 지적 동물로 진화해 온 것 같다. 전 세계적으로 박쥐들은 다양한 많은 천연자원에 의존하는 것으로 알려져 있다. **많은 열대 종들은 화밀, 꽃가루, 그리고 식물의 꽃과 열매에 의존하며, 그들이 의존하는 그 식물 자원의 발달과정을 "따라가는 것"으로 알려져 있다.** 당연히, 박쥐는 식물 - 특히 열대지역과 태평양에 있는 생태계에서 - 의 잦은 그리고 중요한 수분자이다. 게다가, 박쥐들은 다양한 기간동안 보금자리로 식물(특히 나무)에 의존한다. 기후 변동들 - 식물들의 생물 계절학을 교란시키거나 바꾸거나 또는 식물 종의 발생과 분포를 크게 바꾸게 되는 - 이 박쥐에게 영향을 미칠 것이라고 예상할 수 있다.

환경의 변화를 가져와 궁극적으로 박쥐에게 영향을 미치는 몇 가지 요소가 있지만 지구 온난화가 가장 큰(영향을 미치는) 요소라고 믿어진다.

> **roost** (가금 특히 닭의) 홰, 새들의 보금자리, 숙소
> **exploitation** (산림, 광산, 시장의) 개척, 개발, (노동력의)착취
> **forage** 먹이를 찾아다니다 **modification** 조절, 완화, 변형

10 물은 단순한 분자 구조를 가진다. 물은 한 개의 산소원자와 두 개의 수소 원자로 구성되어 있다. 각각의 수소 원자는 공유된 전자 쌍에 의해 공유결합으로 묶여 있다. 또한 산소는 두 개의 비공유 전자 쌍을 갖고 있다. **그러므로 산소 원자 둘레에는 4쌍의 전자가 있는 것이다.** 말하자면, 두 쌍은 수소와 공유 결합되어 있는 두 쌍과 산소 원자 반대 편에 있는 두개의 비공유 전자쌍. 산소는 수소와 비교해 볼 때 음전기성 즉 전자를 "좋아하는" 원자이다.

물은 "극성" – 전자 밀도에 있어서 불균형 배치를 의미하는 – 분자 이다. 물은 비공유 전자쌍 때문에 산소 근처에서는 부분적 음전하를 띠고, 수소 원자 근처에서는 부분적 양전하를 띤다. **수소 근처의 부분적 양전하와 산소 근처의 부분적 음전하 사이의 정전기적 인력으로 인해 수소 결합이 생성되게 되는 것이다.** 이온과 다른 분자들이 물에 용해될 수 있는 것 또한 극성 때문이다.

물이 갖는 많은 다른 독특한 특성들은 수소 결합 때문이다. 예를 들어 얼음이 뜨는 이유는 수소 결합이 액체 – 분자 당 한 개 미만의 수소 결합이 이루어지는 곳 – 에서 보다 고체에서 물 분자들을 더 멀리 떨어져 있는 상태로 붙잡고 있기 때문이다. 독특한 물리적 특성들 – 높은 기화열, 강한 표면장력, 높은 비열, 그리고 거의 보편적이라고 할 수 있는 용해성 – 또한 수소결합 때문이다. 소수성 효과, 즉 탄소와 수소를 함유하는 화합물(비극성 화합물)의 배제는 수소 결합에 의해 야기되는 또 다른 물의 특징이다. 소수성 효과는 특히 세포막 형성에 있어서 중요하다. 가장 최고의 설명은 물은 비극성 분자들을 모두 "짜낸다"라고 말하는 것이다.

> **molecular** 분자의, 분자로 된   **covalent** 분자 쌍을 공유하는 (~bond 공유결합)
> **electronegative** 음성의, 음전기의 (물질), 비금속성의
> **polarity** 양극이 있음, 인력, 정반대   **vaporization** 증발작용, 기화

Chapter 3

Hackers Practice

1 Sinclair Lewis의 베스트셀러 소설에 기초한 "It Can't Happen Here"은 독일과 이태리를 지배했던 것과 유사한 파시스트 독재 통치 하에 있던 미국을 묘사하고 있다.

2 물은 가장 강력한 자연의 힘 중 하나로, 풍경을 만들고, 그 풍경에 특징을 주며 인간과 동식물의 거주지에 윤곽과 구조를 제공해 준다.

3 인쇄술은 어떤 형태로든 적어도 B.C. 1500 년 이후부터 존재해 왔고, 서구 문명은 일반적으로 근대 인쇄술의 시작을 1440년의 Johannes Gutenberg의 활자의 발명으로 본다.

4 뉴 딜 정책의 큰 성과중의 하나는 전력을 시골까지 끌어온 것이었으며 이 성공은 테네시 강 유역에서 매우 생생하게 드러났다.

5 수석 엔지니어 Joseph Strauss와 그의 동료들은 거친 바람과 날씨 그리고 부식성의 소금 낀 공기 – 금문을 가로지르는 다리에 항상 있는 요소- 에도 견딜 수 있는 페인트를 고를 작정이었다.

6 1870년대에 연방정부는 통화 체계에서 은의 역할을 제한하였고 이것은 은의 가격 하락, 많은 네바다 광산의 폐광, 한때 번성했던 마을들을 유령마을로 쇠퇴하게 만들었다.

7 수염고래는 번식기를 제외하고는 거의 혼자 다니지만 odontocetes는 대부분의 생애를 몇 마리에서 천마리 이상씩 되는 무리로 지낸다.

8 명백한 이유들로 인해 인간들은 실험적 유전학 연구의 피실험자로 부족하다. 그러나, 인간의 유전에 대한 이해를 돕는 많은 것들은 "하등한" 생명체로부터 알아왔다.

9 대양의 표면해류는 큰 소용돌이 - 즉 우세한 바람에 의해 움직이지만 그것의 방향은 지구회전에 의해 바뀌는 해류 - 에 의해 특징 지워진다.

10 영국과학자인 George Barger와 Henry H. Dale은 처음으로 1910년에 식물 맥각균에서 히스타민을 분리했고, 1911년에는 동물 조직에서 그 물질을 분리했다.

Hackers Test

1 조지 왕조시대 양식은 18세기 동안 - 영국의 부가 아일랜드에 투자되어 더블린을 영국과 아일랜드에서 런던 다음으로 두 번째로 중요한 도시로 만들었던 시기인 - 아일랜드에서 확고한 그 위치를 굳혔다. 국회의원들은 런던과 더블린에 모두 의석이 있었고 그것이 더블린에 괜찮은 주택과 공공건물에 대한 필요를 창출하게 되었다. 교회, 학교, 다리, 저택의 건축에 획기적인 발전이 있었다. 부유한 토지 소유주들이 그 건축의 대부분을 차지하고 값을 치렀다. Gardiner경은 도시 북쪽에서 건축을 부추긴 장본인이었고, 반면 그의 경쟁자인 Fitzwilliam 경은 남쪽에서 중요한 건축 단지를 맡았다. 조지 왕조시대 건축은 처음에는 '팔라디오풍' - 고대 로마시대 건축의 영향을 재생하려고 열망했던 - 으로 알려진 스타일의 지배를 받았다. 이 양식은 1700년에서 1760년까지 영향력이 남아 있었다. 더블린에 있는 국회의사당(현재 아일랜드 은행, 칼리지 그린)은 Edward Lovett Pearce (1699-1733)에 의해 디자인되었다. 그것은 영국과 아일랜드에 처음 대규모로 지어진 팔라디오식 건축이었다. 18세기 말에 팔라디오식 양식에서 고대 그리스 건축을 모방한 신고전주의 양식으로 넘어갔다. 신 고전주의 양식의 대표자들은 현재 Sir Hugh Lane 시 박물관을 디자인한 William Chambers (1723-96), 더블린의 Blackhall Place에 있는 King's 병원을 디자인한 Thomas Ivory(1732-86), 더블린의 유명한 Custom House와 Four Courts를 디자인한 James Gandon (1743-1823)이다.

조지왕조시대의 집들은 무엇보다도 통일성과 실용성이 특징이다. 계획법령들은 집을 지을 때 화재 예방조치로서 빨간 벽돌이 반드시 사용되어야 한다고 공포했다. 출입구, 굴뚝 등의 디자인을 표준화한 저택들을 장려했던 건축문학이 출판되었다. 하인들 숙소 위쪽에 있는 현관으로 가는 화강암 계단은 주택에 웅장한 광경을 제공했다. 그 외양에 더해졌던 연철로 된 난간들은 또한 안전의 특징이기도 했다. 위로 갈수록 크기가 작아지는 새시 창은 벽돌구조에 맞닿아 있었다. 그 친숙한 조지 왕조양식의 출입구 - 측면에 로마기둥양식의 머리받침을 가진 기둥들이 있었고 - 는 섬세하게 디자인된 부채꼴의 채광창으로 덮여있었다. '거리 가구' - 연철로 된 흙떨이와 우아한 가등주 같은 - 가 그 조지 왕조양식을 완성시켰다.

> **Palladianism** 팔라디오풍의 **exponent** 대표자 **granite** 화강암
> **quarters** 막사, 숙소 **wrought** 세공한, (철물 등)두들겨 만든
> flush 불그스레한, 평평하게, 같은 높이로 **flank** 옆구리(살), ~측면에 서다, 위치하다
> **cap** 덮다, 붙이다, 끝손질하다 **fanlight** 부채꼴, 채광창
> **scraper** 흙떨개 **lamppost** 가로등의 기둥

2 Fiorelli가 대형 발굴의 개념을 발명했다고 할 수 없다. 독일인 Ernst Curtius가 1852년부터 광범위한 발굴을 위해 기금을 모으려 하고 있었고 1875년 까지는 올림피아에서 발굴을 시작했다. 고전시대의 많은 유적지처럼 올림피아는, 주로 그곳의 조각상들이 - 유럽전역의 박물관으로 보내졌던 - 많은 흥미의 대상이었다. Curtius가 올림피아에 갔을 때는 Olympia는 독일과 그리스 정부 사이에 협상된 거래의 협정 하에 있었다. 복제품을 제외하고는 어떤 문화유물도 그리스를 떠나지 못한다.

작은 박물관이 그 발굴지에 세워지고 독일정부는 복제품을 팔아서 '대형 발굴' 의 비용을 메울 수 있다. 비용은 실제 엄청나게 많이 들었고 비스마르크는 1880년에 발굴을 중지하도록 압력을 받았지만, 공동 과학 조사의 씨앗은 뿌려 졌다. 고고학에 대한 정치적 영향이라는 씨앗 또한 뿌려졌고, 이는 20세기 초반에 초기 과학에 깊은 영향을 미쳤다.

우리가 현대 고고학이라고 간주하는 것의 기술과 방법론을 향한 실질적인 증진은 주로 Schliemann, Pitt-Rivers 그리고 Petrie 의 작업이다. 비록 Heinrich Schliemann이 Hissarlik에서의 후기 작업 때문에 보물 사냥꾼 이상으로 종종 간주되지 않았지만 그는 독일인 조수 Wilhelm Dorpfeld - 올림피아에서 Curtius와 함께 일했던 - 를 고용했다. Schliemann에 대한 Dorpfeld의 영향은 그의 기술을 세련되게 했고, 그의 경력을 마칠 때 까지 Schliemann은 발굴에 대해 꼼꼼히 기록했고, 일상적인 것들을 비일상적인 것들과 함께 보존했고, 그의 보고서를 기꺼이 출판하였다.

경력의 초반기에 영국 무기 발전을 연구하는데 많은 시간을 투자했던 군인, Pitt-Rivers는 군대식의 정확성과 엄격함을 그의 고고학적 발굴에 도입했다. 또한, 적지 않은 상속재산을 첫 광범위한 비교 문화 유물 컬렉션 - 동시대의 민족지 물건들을 포함하여 - 을 이룩하는데 썼다. 그의 컬렉션은 단연코 미를 위한 것이 아니었다. 그는 T.H. Huxley의 말을 인용했다. '중요성이란 단어는 과학 사전에서 삭제되어야 한다. 중요한 것은 지속되는 것이다.'

> **statuary** 조각(상), 조소술(의) **recoup** 공제하다, 보상(변상)하다
> **rigor** 엄밀, 엄정, 엄격 **inconsiderable** 중요치 않은, 사소한
> **ethnographic** 민족지학상의, 민족지(誌)적인 **sake** (~을)위함, 목적, 이유

3 대통령의 권력은 그것을 미국정치에서 가장 추구되는 지위로 만들었다. 그 직책에 대한 치열한 경쟁과 효과적인 선거전을 위한 높은 비용은 후보자들의 수를 선발된 몇 명으로 줄였다. 헌법에는 원래 선거인단에 의해 대통령과 부통령을 뽑도록 했다. 선거인단의 구성원, 즉 선거인은 두 후보에게 투표를 함으로써 주를 대표하였는데 가장 많은 표를 얻으면 대통령, 두 번째는 부통령이 되었다. Thomas Jefferson과 Aaron Burr의 1800년 선거에서의 동점은 1804년 12번째 개헌 - 선거인단이 한 표는 대통령에 한 표는 부통령에 각각 투표하도록 규정한 - 을 시행케 했다.

19세기 중엽까지만 해도 선거인단의 투표는 상징적인 중요성만 가지고 있었다. 각 주에서 온 투표인은 가장 많은 일반투표를 받은 후보에게 투표하므로 써 대다수의 의지를 따랐다. 그러나, 선거인단 투표체계에서는 후보자들이 전국적인 일반투표에서 승리하지 않고도 선거인단 투표에서 다수를 차지하면 대통령이 될 수 있다. 이런 시나리오는 미국 역사에서 3번 일어났다. 1876년 Rutherford B. Hayes가 Samuel Tilden, 1888년 Benjamin Harrison이 Grover Cleveland를, 2000년 George W. Bush가 over Al Gore를 이겼을 때이다. 일반투표에서 진 또 다른 대통령은 John Quincy Adams인데 그는 어떤 후보도 선거인단 투표에서 과반수를 확보하지 못한 후 하원에서 1824년에 선출되었다.

> **presidency** 대통령의 지위, 임기, 통솔, 통할 **electoral** 선거(인)의,
> **ballot** (무기명) 투표용지, 추첨, 후보자 명부

4 고대 로마 전설에서는 "비누" 라는 이름은 원래 Mount Sapo - 그곳에서 동물들은 제단에서 불로 태워졌다 - 로부터 왔다고 한다. 종국에는 비가 내려 동물의 지방과 나무재를 그 산 아래 Tiber 강으로 썻어 내리곤 했다. 비누 혼합물은 옷감, 모피, 피부 등을 씻는데 유용하다는 것을 알아냈다. 비누에 대한 첫번째 기록된 제조법은 B.C 2200년에 발견되었다. B.C 312년까지 세척과 전반적인 건강에 좋다고 하여 비누는 로마 목욕탕에서 사용되었다. A.D 467년 로마제국의 붕괴와 함께 비누와 일반적인 목욕도 인기가 시들해졌고 전반적인 청결의 부재가 중세 흑사병에 큰 역할을 했다.

약 7세기까지는 비누제작 길드가 엄밀하게 보호되는 장사 비법을 가지고 생겨나기 시작했다. 숙련

공들은 그 장사에서 규제되고 활성화되었다. 12세기 까지는 영국도 또한 비누제작을 시작했다. 비누는 고가품으로 여겨지고 매우 가치 있게 여겨졌다. 여러 세기동안 비누가 고가품으로 높은 세금이 메겨지고 부자들만 이용할 수 있었다. 1853년에 비누세가 폐지 되자 문화적인 비누사용에 큰 변이가 있었다. 그 때부터 사회적 태도는 청결과 함께 가게 됐다.

식민지시대에는 여성들이 비누를 제작하였다. 비누는 주로 일년에 한번 씩 전년도의 기름 방울 모인 것과 벽난로 재를 수집한 것으로 만들어 졌다. 정확한 제작공식은 결코 실제적으로 알려지지 않아 비누는 꽤 부식성이 있었지만 잘 씻어냈다.

1800년대 중반까지는 비누제작은 화학적으로 잘 이해되었는데 일반소금(가성소다)으로부터 소다 재를 모으는 발전된 방법과 더불어 였다. 목욕, 세탁, 일반 세척을 위한 비누제작은 시장에서 즉시 이용 가능해 졌다. 오늘날 많은 저 원가 상업용 비누는 석유화학에 근간했다. 이 비누들은 뛰어난 세척능력을 가졌지만 또한 피부를 매우 건조 시켰다. 다른 상업용 비누는 "짐승기름"을 가지고 만들어졌지만, 종종 글리세린을 제거하여 그것(글리세린)을 화장품이나 의약품 산업에 팔았다. 글리세린을 제거한 비누도 피부에는 좋지 않지만 역시 여전히 잘 세척한다.

> **deem** 생각하다, 간주하다(consider)   **formula** 제조법, (일정한)법규, 공식규격
> **guild** (중세의)상인 단체, 동업 조합   **repeal** 무효가 되다, 폐지,철회하다
> **dripping** 물방울, 뚝뚝 떨어짐, [~s]떨어지는 기름방울
> **sodium** 나트륨,소듐   **hydroxide** 수산화물   **petrol** 휘발유, 가솔린
> **tallow** 짐승기름, 수지   **mill** 맷돌로 갈다, 제분하다   **glycerin** 글리세린
> **pharmaceutical** 조제의, 약학의, 약제(사)의

5   1763년의 영국포고령은 애팔래치아 산맥에서 서쪽으로 이동을 금지하였지만, 그 법령은 주로 무시되었다. 정착민들은 오하이오, 테네시, 켄터키로 총총 이주했다. 미국독립전쟁이후 많은 사람들이 산맥을 넘어 애팔래치아 산맥과 미시시피 강 사이에 있는 비옥한 땅으로 갔다. 1810년까지는 오하이오, 테네시, 켄터키는 황량한 곳에서 농장과 마을이 있는 지역으로 변모해 갔다.

서쪽으로 계속해서 서부 변경선을 밀어붙인 그 수 십 년에도 불구하고, 1812년의 전쟁이 끝나고 나서야 서부이동이 대륙을 가로지른 엄청난 사람들의 이동이 되었다. 1830년 까지는 구 북서지역과 구 남서지역 (전쟁 전에는 거주인구가 거의 없었던)은 일리노이, 인디애나, 미주리, 알라바마, 미시시피를 주로써 연방에 가입할 수 있을 정도로 충분한 인구가 거주했다.

1830년대와 1840년대 동안에는 개척자들의 행렬이 끊임없이 서부로 이어졌다. 미시간, 알칸사, 위스콘신, 아이오와는 그들의 대부분을 받아들였다. 많은 가족들은 심지어 태평양 해안까지 가서 Oregon Trail을 타고 태평양 북서부 지역까지 갔다. 1849년에는 일확천금을 노리는 사람들이 금을 찾아 캘리포니아로 몰려갔다. 한편, 몰몬교 사람들은 그들의 긴 순례를 유타에서 멈췄다.

Gold rush 와 남북전쟁사이에 늘어나는 미국인들은 미시시피강 유역, 텍사스, 남서국경지역, 그리고 새로운 주(로 편입된) 켄사스, 네브래스카를 채웠다. 전쟁동안 금,은의 발견은 채굴자들 (나중의 거주민) 을 오레곤, 콜로라도, 네바다, 아이다오, 몬타나로 끌어들였다.

1870년 까지는 오직 대평원의 일부만이 진정 비정착지로 불렸다. 그 후 20년 대부분 동안 그 땅은 전설적인 방목구역으로서 기능하며 카우보이와 (텍사스의 목장으로부터 온) 풀 뜯는 소들의 고향이었다. 그러나 1880년대 말까지는 방목 소 산업의 쇠퇴와 함께 정착민들이 대평원으로 들어와 펜스를 쳐서 가족 농장을 만들었다. 그 정착(과 오클라호마 인디안 정착지로의 개척자들의 열광적인 쇄도)는 서부 이동의 마지막 장을 장식했다. 1890년대 초까지는 국경은 멈춰 48개 대륙 주내에 존재하였다.

> **halt** 정지, 휴식, 정거장   **scurry** 허둥지둥 달리다, 잰 걸음으로 서두르다.
> **outpouring** 유출(물), 분출   **pilgrimage** 성지순례, 긴 여행
> **ranch** 목장, 농장

6   Edison이 20세에 발명한 투표용지를 세는 기계는 유용하다고 생각되지 않아서 받아들여 지지 않았다. 그러한 낙담 이후에 그는 그것이(발명품) 수요를 충족시키고 받아들여 진다는 확신이 서기 전까지는 어떠한 발명도 하지 않기로 결심했다.

전보의 기능을 크게 향상시킨 발명품들은 그가 많은 돈을 벌 수 있도록 했고 그 결과 그는 발명을 위한 실험실을 설립할 수 있었다. 29세에 그는 한 뉴저지 마을인 Menlo Park에 그런 "발명 공장"을 세웠다. 그의 연구팀은 고안품의 실질적인 디자이너 뿐만 아니라 연장 제작공과 물리학자들도 포함되어 있었다. 더 많은 전신기의 진보가 뒤를 이었고 그 후 Alexander Graham Bell의 발명품인 전화기의 작동상의 문제들에 대한 많은 해결책이 있었다.

1878년에 Edison은 축음기를 발명했다. 백열구는 1880년 –40시간 동안 탈 수 있는 백열 전구가 나왔을 때인– 에 특허를 받았다. 전기불은 그 세기 초에 발명되었으나 거리를 전기적으로 밝게 하는 실질적인 문제들은 결코 전에 해결된 적이 없었다. 에디슨의 가장 위대한 공헌은 실질적이고 유용한 장치를 생산하기 위해 그의 과학적인 발견들을 적용하는 것과 예전 발명품에 수정을 하는 것이었다. 그의 팀과 함께 그는 많은 발명품을 만들었으며 천 개 이상의 특허를 취득하였다.

전기(부분)에서의 Edison이 이룩한 업적으로부터 전력과 조명 산업, 궁극적으로는 미국과 나머지 다른 세계의 많은 사람들의 삶의 새로운 방식에 발전이 있었다. 소위 "발명 제작소"로부터의 많은 다른 발명품들도 매우 중요한 것으로 인정되었지만 전기에 있어서의 정말 주목할 만한 업적이 현대 삶에 혁명적인 결과를 가져왔다.

> **phonograph** 축음기, 레코드 플레이어 **incandescent** 백열의, 빛나는, 열렬한
> **work out** 점점 나오다, 풀리다, 잘 되어가다

7   짧은 꼬리 원숭이는 매우 순응력 높은 만능 선수이므로 넓은 범위의 서식지에서 발견된다. 그들이 신성시되어 방해 받지 않은 채 남아있을 수 있는 지역에서, Rhesus 원숭이들은 도시화된 지역에서의 삶에 적응해왔다. 이러한 짧은 꼬리 원숭이는 또한 반사막에서부터 조밀한 숲, 설선 위의 산맥에 이르는 환경에서 발견된다. 이러한 속(屬)에는 가장 북쪽의 영장류인 Japanese 원숭이가 포함된다. 이와 유사하게, 게를 먹는 원숭이는 또한 비록 그들이 홍수림의 서식지를 더 좋아할지라도 인간의 정착지에서 그럭저럭 잘 적응한다. 그러나 다른 원숭이들은 훨씬 더 분화되어 있다. 예를 들어 lion-tale 원숭이와 pig tailed 원숭이는 그들의 숲 속 서식지 밖에서는 잘 지내지 못한다. 모든 짧은 꼬리 원숭이들은 (북부 아프리카에서 발견되는 꼬리 없는 원숭이만을 제외하고) 아시아에서만 발견된다. 짧은 꼬리 원숭이는 주로 과일을 먹는다. 그러나 손에 넣을 수 있는 것은 무엇이든 – 꽃, 곤충, 알 그리고 아마도 몇몇 고기 – 먹을 수 있다. 게를 먹는 원숭이는 게를 사냥하며, 그들이 잡을 수 있는 또 다른 해양 생물을 먹을 것이다.

그들의 다양한 식단을 보완하기 위해 짧은 꼬리 원숭이는 단순한 위를 가지고 있다. 그들은 또한 잘 발달된 볼 주머니를 가지고 있는데 어떤 것들은 매우 크고 목 아래까지 늘어져 있기 때문에 그들의 위에 담을 수 있는 만큼의 음식을 가질 수 있다. 짧은 꼬리 원숭이는 강한 팔다리를 가지고 있으며 단단한 체격을 이루고 있다. 그들은 완전히 마주보게 할 수 있는 엄지손가락이 있어 능숙하다. 그들은 4개 손가락 모두로 짚고 움직인다. 어떤 것들 – lion-tailed macaque, Barbary ape – 은 사실상 꼬리가 없고 다른 것들은 긴 꼬리를 가지고 있다.

짧은 꼬리 원숭이는 일반적으로 육지(지상) 생물로 여겨진다. 그러나 대부분의 종이 음식을 구하거나 장거리 이동 시에 땅으로 내려오는 반면, lion-tailed 원숭이와 같은 몇몇 종은 주로 나무생활을 한다. 그렇지만 모든 종이 나무나 땅 위의 높은 곳에서 잠자는 것을 더 좋아한다. 모든 짧은 꼬리 원숭이들은 낮 시간 – 그러나 시원한 때(아침 일찍이나 늦은 오후부터 저녁까지) – 에 더 활동적이다.

> **macaque** 짧은 꼬리 원숭이 **unmolested** 곤란을 받지 않은, 평온한
> **genus** 종류, 속 **primate** 영장류 **pouch** 유대류 **limb** 팔, 다리, 큰 가지
> **dexterous** 솜씨 좋은, 교묘한, 민첩한 **arboreal** 나무의, 교목성의 (동물이)나무에서 사는

8　가장 최초로 알려진 엽서는 1848년 12월 소인이 찍혀 있다. 엽서 수집 분야에 대한 더 많은 연구는 1848년부터 1893년까지 더욱 많은 엽서를 보여줄 것이다. 대부분 1898년 이전의 엽서들은 몇 가지 공통점을 가지고 있다. 이 시대의 엽서는 분할되지 않은 뒷면(엽서 뒤 중앙에 그려진 선이 없음)으로 특징지어 지고 많은 것들이 단지 수취인의 이름과 주소를 위해 뒷면에 인쇄된 선만을 가지고 있다. 미국 우편 엽서의 개척자는 대부분 큰 동부도시로부터 왔다. 1898년 5월 19일에 의회의 법령에 의하여 개인 인쇄 업자들은 카드 – "사적 우편 엽서"라는 제명이 기재되어 있는 – 의 인쇄와 판매에 대한 허가를 받았고 대략 1900년의 기간 동안 사진 우편 엽서가 사용되기 시작했다. 이러한 초기의 실제 사진 그림들은 주로 광고용 작품들이었다.

"POST CARD / POSTCARD"(1개 또는 2개의 단어로 된)라는 용어의 사용은 1901년 12월 24일에 정부에 의해 개인 인쇄업자들에게 양도되었다. 주소면에 글쓰기는 여전히 허용되지 않았다. 이러한 시대의 틀 동안에 인쇄된 우편엽서의 출판은 거의 매 6개월 동안 2배가 되었다. 유럽의 출판사들은 미국에 사무실을 열고 무수한 양질의 우편 엽서를 수입했다. 1907년까지 유럽의 출판들은 미국에서 팔린 모든 엽서 중 75% 이상을 차지했다. 석판으로 인쇄된 카드의 유행은 또한 Eastman-Kodak의 관심을 끌었다. 그들은 1906년쯤 적정한 가격의 "접이식 주머니용 코닥(Folding Pocket Kodak)"을 내놓았다. 이것은 일반 대중이 흑백사진을 찍어서 우편 엽서 뒷면이 있는 종이 위에 직접 그것들을 인쇄하는 것을 가능하게 해주었다.

마침내 뒷면이 분할된 우편엽서가 1907년 3월 1일에 허용되었다. 주소는 엽서 뒷면 오른 쪽에 쓰여지게 되었고 반면 왼쪽은 메시지를 쓰기 위해 남겨졌다. 미국 역사상 이 시기에 postcard 취미가 대중적 열광이 되었다. 출판업자들은 이 시기에 수백만 장의 카드를 인쇄했다. 대부분의 우편 엽서는 석판 인쇄 과정에 있어서 세계 제일인 독일에서 인쇄되었다. 그 국가의 폭 넓은 몰두의 정점에서 세계 1차 대전은 그러한 취미의 붕괴를 야기 시켰다. 세계 1차 대전의 도래는 독일에서의 엽서 공급이 끝나도록 만들었다. 질이 좋지 않은 우편 엽서가 영국과 미국 출판업자들로부터 만들어졌다. 낮은 질의 인쇄된 우편엽서와 재발하는 유행성 감기 그리고 전쟁에 따른 결핍은 미국의 postcard 취미를 사양화 시켰다. 전쟁동안 서로 연락하기 위한 빠르고 믿을 만한 수단으로서 전화가 엽서를 대신 하게 되었다.

> postmark 소인을 찍다　inscription 비문, 명각
> lithograph 석판으로 인쇄하다　account for ~의 계정으로 팔다
> recurrent 재발하는, 순환하는

9　치아에 있는 성장 층의 수를 세서 나이를 추정하는 방법이 남부 해마, Mirounga leonine에게서 처음 개발되었다. 그것은 이후 치아가 있는 고래와 돌고래에게 성공적으로 적용되어 어느 정도 성공을 거두고 있다. 층들은 치아를 길게 자른 단면에서 보여질 수 있다. 성장 층 그룹으로 불리는 이러한 층의 패턴은 나무의 나이테와 같이 주기적인 양상으로 발생한다. 층 침착의 실제 성장률은 오직 몇몇의 종류에게만 (해당된다고) 알려져 있지만, 그 방법이 돌고래와 pilot whales의 경우에 잘 들어맞는다. 고래류의 이빨에 있는 층 구조는 본질적으로는 종들 사이에서 유사하며 – 세부적으로만 차이를 보이며, 그것이 나이를 측정하는 유용한 방법으로 인식되어진다. 몇몇 조사자들은 이러한 방법을 사용하여 bottle-nose 돌고래, Tursiops truncates 의 나이를 결정한다. 치아의 시멘트질이 셀 수 있는 성장층을 드러내 보였다. 이러한 나이 측정법은 조사자들로 하여금 암컷과 수컷이 각각 12개와 12-18개의 성장 층이 있을 때 성적 성숙에 도달한다는 진술을 할 수 있도록 했다. 층의 최대 수는 50개 정도 되지만 보통 평균은 35개 이다. 그 보고서에서 돌고래 치아의 세로 단면 부분에 대한 조사에 의해 성장 층이 주기적이며 특정 패턴 – 나무의 나이테처럼 – 으로 나타난다는 관찰을 가능하게 하였다. 비록 대부분의 고래류 조사자들이 나이테가 나이의 수와 같다는데 동의할지라도 몇몇 조사자들은 실제 침착률에 대해 의문을 가지기도 하고 (고래의 몇몇 종에 있어서는) 그것과 나이와의 관계에 대해서도 의문을 가진다.

실험에 쓸 치아를 준비하는 한 가지 방법은 치아를 박편으로 자르는 것이다. 암석(박편) 작업에서

하는 것처럼. 치아는 먼저 진공 상태로 플라스틱에 끼워넣은 후 건조되었을 때 톱으로 다듬어진다. 그리고 나서 다양한 크기의 숫돌을 사용하여 한쪽을 광택이 날 때까지 갈아낸다. 마지막으로. 그 전체 표본은 에폭시로 유리 슬라이드에 부착된다. 이틀 정도 지난 후에 특수 다이아몬드 톱으로 슬라이드에 평행이 되게 얇게 잘라, 광택이 날 때까지 다시 다양한 크기의 숫돌로 간다. 준비 완료 후, 그 얇은 박편은 편광 현미경으로 조사된다. 세밀한 띠(나이테)는 교차 극선과 감속판의 사용으로 더 강화된다.

> **seal** 바다표범, 물개(의 가죽) **cetacean** 고래류의 동물
> **truncate** (나무, 원추 등의) 꼭대기를 자르다, (인용구를)생략하여 줄이다
> **lengthwise** 세로의(로) 긴(길게) **wafer-thin** 매우 얇은, 근소한 차이의
> **embed** 파묻다, 깊이 간직하다 **grit** 잔모래, 거친 가루
> **affix** 첨부하다, (우표를)붙이다, (서명을)써넣다 **retardation** 지연, 저지, 방해(물)
> **plate** (파충류, 물고기 등의) 등딱지, 판금갑옷, 금속판, 판유리

10 오랜 기간의 위기, 버려진 들판, 기근 그리고 중세 동안의 인구 감소 등에도 불구하고 진짜 "기술적 혁명"은 제분업자의 수가 널리 퍼짐에 따라 13,14세기 사이에 발생했다.
제분업자는 단지 기술자가 아니었다. : 그는 봉건 영주를 대신하여 수금을 하기도 했고 농부들이 법을 피하여 그들의 밀가루를 빻을 수 없도록 그들을 감독했으며, 법에 의해 밀가루의 3분의 1만 자기 몫으로 가질 수 있었다. 비록 제분업자들은 마을 외곽에 살았고 제빵업자들은 도시 내에 살았지만, 둘 다 가장 오래된 조합인 White Art에 속해 있었다.
제빵업자는 그들이 생산했던 빵을 기준으로 분류되어졌다. "white(흰빵)" 제빵업자는 부드러운 white bread를 만들기 위한 권리를 가졌던 반면 "black(흑빵)" 제빵업자들은 단지 검정색 고밀도의 빵만 구울 수 있었다. 조합의 전통 연회 이후에 새로 입회한 제빵 업자는 -당국 앞에서- 그의 빵의 질과 양에 관한 그의 정직을 맹세했다. 14세기에 Hamburg에서 너무 설 구워지거나(덜 부풀거나) 맛이 좋지 않은 빵에 대한 즉각적인 압수를 법으로 공포하였고 그 제빵업자는 법정으로 끌려갔다. 영국에서는 부정한 제빵업자들은 멍에가 씌워져 성난 군중들에 의해 도시 전역으로 끌려다녔다. 빵을 집으로 배달하는 관습이 시작된 것은 중세 때 였다. 제빵업자 본인이 또는 가게의 소년이 빵을 배달하면서 (마치 음유시인처럼) 뉴스와 가십거리를 알려주었다.

> **flour** 밀가루, 소백분 **banquet** 연회 **confiscation** 몰수, 압수
> **minstrel** (중세의) 음유시인, 가수

Progressive Test 1-1

1 현대 무용은 미국의 동부와 서부의 해안 지방에서 Isodora Duncan, Loie Fuller, and Ruth St. Denis 와 함께 시작되었다. 최초의 현대 무용가들은 유럽식의 교양있는 행위예술로 간주되는 고전 발레에 대항해서 혁신을 일으켰다.
세기의 전환기 즈음 Isodora Duncan은 미국 무용을 변화시키고자 노력한 첫번째 무용수이자 안무가였다. 그녀는 영감을 얻기 위해, 원시적인 무용과 다른 문화를 살펴 보았다. 그녀는 춤을 추는데 있어서 이러한 다른 스타일은 유럽의 발레에서는 볼 수 없는 무언가를 지니고 있다고 생각했다. 그녀는 텝 댄스와 재즈 댄스 같은 좀 더 대중적인 종류의 춤을 또한 다루었다. 다른 문화들로부터 모든 이러한 서로 다른 영향을 받아, 던컨은 새로운 스타일을 창조하기를 원했다. 비록 그녀는 큰 성공을 이루었지만, 단지 유럽에서만 인기가 있었고 그녀의 조국에서는 그렇지 못했다. "그녀의 춤은 유럽과 유럽인의 취향에 오랜 기간 맞춰진 채로 있었다."
1920년대 동안 미국 최고의 무용 단체였던 Denishawn 극단은 Ruth St. Denis and Ted Shawn 에 의해 발전되었다. Denishawn 학교가 국가 전역에 설립되었고, 그 극단은 미국과 해외로 순회공

연을 다녔다. 연극 무용의 두 번째 밀려오는 집단(물결)은 Denishawn 학교로부터 성장했다. Martha Graham, Doris Humphrey, and Charles Weidman은 몇 년의 간격을 두고 차례로 Denishawn을 떠났고, 그들 자신만의 안무를 만들기 시작했다. 그들의 작품은 Denishawn 학교에서 받은 영향을 반영했다. **그러나 1930년대에 그들은 현대무용에서의 그들 각자의 진로를 발전시켰다.** Denishawn 극단의 이국적인 낭만주의에 대항한 반란은 현대무용운동의 주요 추진력이 되었으며, Denishawn은 공식적으로 1931년 말까지 해산되었다.

2   지금은 미국인 곳에 토루를 지은 최초 인디언 무리는 종종 Adenans로 불린다. 그들은 B.C 600년 경에 흙으로 된 매장장소와 요새를 짓기 시작했다. 그 시기의 몇몇 토루는 새나 뱀의 모양이었으며, 아직까지 명확하게 알 수 없는 종교적인 목적들을 위해 아마도 쓰여졌을 것이다.

Adenans는 집합적으로 Hopewellians로 알려진 다양한 그룹에 의해 흡수되고 교체되어 온 것으로 나타난다. 그들 문화의 가장 중요한 중심지 중의 하나가 남부 오하이오에서 발견되었는데, 그 곳에는 아직도 이러한 고분들 수천개의 유물이 그대로 남아있다. 뛰어난 상인들로 알려진 Hopewellians는 수백킬로미터의 넓은 지역에 걸쳐 도구와 물품을 사용하고 교환했다.

A.D 500년 경까지 미시시피족 혹은 사원 토루(Temple Mound) 문화로 일반적으로 알려진 부족 무리들에게 점차 굴복하면서, Hopewellians 또한 사라졌다. 미주리주 세인트 루이스의 정동쪽에 Cahokia라는 한 도시는 12세기 초 한창때 대략 2만 명의 인구가 살았을 것으로 생각된다. 그 도시의 중앙에는 거대한 토루가 서있었는데, 30미터 높이에, 기반은 37헥타르였고, 정상은 평평하게 되어 있었다. 80개의 다른 토루들이 근처에서 발견되었다.

지금은 미국의 남서부인 곳에서, 현대 Hopi 인디언의 조상인 Anasazi가 900년 경에 돌과 벽돌 푸에블로를 짓기 시작했다. 이 독특하고 놀라운 아파트 같은 구조물들은 자주 절벽(경사) 면을 따라 세워졌고, 콜로라도 Mesa Verde의 가장 유명한 "절벽 궁전"은 200개 개가 넘는 방을 갖고 있었다. **또 다른 곳, 뉴 멕시코의 Chaco 강가의 푸에블로 보니토 유적은 한 때 800개 이상의 방을 가지고 있었다.**

3   초기 정착기간 이후, 이민의 첫번째 급속한 증가는 산업혁명에 의해 면직된 북유럽의 수공업자들과 감자 기근의 혹독한 가난으로부터 도망쳐 나온 아일랜드인들의 거대한 유입이 있었던 1830년대와 1840년대에 발생했다. 곧이어 독일의 정치적 피난민들이 도착했다. 북부와 서부 유럽에서 온 많은 이민자들이 중서부의 농장에 정착했다. 아일랜드인과 다른 사람들은 공장에서 뿐만 아니라 길, 다리, 철도의 건설 노동자로 열심히 일했다. 그들 대부분은 북부의 도시에 남았다.

1880년대에 주로 남부와 동부 유럽으로부터의 대규모의 이민이 시작되었다. 대부분의 미국인들에게 이러한 새로운 이민자들은 그들의 조상(먼저 온 이민자들)보다 훨씬 이상해 보였다. 그들의 언어와 관습 그리고 생활 양식은 미국인들이 만들어 왔던 것과 매우 달랐다. 그 새로운 이주자들은 큰 도시들의 가장 가난한 동네로 이주했고, 지역 빈민가에 함께 머무르면서, 그들의 옛날 방식을 고수하는 경향이 있었다. 가난하고 가난에 익숙한 그들은 매우 낮은 임금을 위해 기꺼이 일했다. **이것은 다른 노동자들 특히 노동조합의 사람들이 이민자들이 급료수준을 낮추고 미국인들로부터 일을 빼앗을 것이라고 두려워하도록 만들었다.** 실제로, 노동조합에 가입된 노동자는 계속되는 이민의 주요 반대자들 중 하나가 되었다. 이러한 반대는 마침내 1920년대에 이민 제한 법을 만들게 되었는데, 그것은 특히 남부와 동부 유럽으로부터의 더 많은 이민을 제한하는 것이었다. 1965년 이러한 편협한 법은 새로운 이민법으로 교체되었는데, 그것은 그들의 원래 국적과 상관없이 외국인들을 위한 동등한 기회를 인정하는 것이었다. 아시아인들, 특히 한국인과 필리핀인들은 미국과 베트남의 전쟁 끝 무렵에 베트남 사람들의 뒤를 이어 도착하기 시작했다. 이러한 새로운 이주자들의 상당수가 그들의 새로운 땅에서 자립하기 위해 매우 열심히 일했다.

1970년대 후반과 1980년대에 멕시코와 중앙 아메리카로부터 이민자들이 크게 증가했다. 점점 더 많이, 이러한 이민자들의 상당수가 간단히 미국과 멕시코 사이의 매우 인적이 드문 공동경계를 넘어서 걸어왔다. 1986년 이민개혁법이 통과된 것은 주로 이러한 이민자들의 물결을 통제하기 위한 것이었다.

4 벌새는 빠른 호흡속도, 빠른 심장박동, 높은 체온을 가지고 있다. 그들은 하루종일 10분마다 먹이를 먹어야만 하고, 하루에 그들 체중의 3분의 2정도를 소비한다. 벌새 식단의 중요한 부분은 설탕이다. 그들은 꽃의 즙액과 나무의 수액으로부터 그것을 얻는다. **벌새는 또한 근육을 만들기 위해 단백질이 필요하므로, 곤충과 화분을 먹는다.** 벌새의 혀는 옆면에 홈이 파여 있는데, 그것은 공중에서 - 또한 잎과 거미줄에 있는 곤충을 잡기 위해 사용된다.

벌새의 부리는 길고 끝으로 갈수록 좁아서, 화밀을 찾아 꽃관의 중앙으로 들어가기에 매우 적합한데, 그들은 초당 대략 13번 핥기의 속도로 빨아들인다. 종종 우리는 그들이 밝은 색의 꽃에 다가가면서, 공기를 핥는 그들의 긴 부리 밖에 나온 긴 반 투명한 혀를 볼 수 있다.

벌새는 좋은 기억력을 갖고 있다. 즉, 그들은 지난 해의 식량의 출처를 기억할 수 있다. 그들은 먹이를 먹으며 우연히 화분을 모은다. 꽃에서 꽃으로 이동하면서 그들은 꽃들이 번식할 수 있도록 도와준다. Penstemon 같은 많은 꽃들은 특히 벌새들을 고려해 디자인 되어진 것처럼 보인다.

벌새는 컵 모양의 잎이나 얕은 웅덩이에서 목욕하는 것을 좋아한다. 그들은 날개를 펄럭거리고 그들의 꼬리를 올렸다 펼쳤다 하면서 날개를 뒤로 쭉 펼치고, 그들의 턱과 배를 물속에 살짝 담근다. 가끔 목욕하고 있는 벌새는 등에 있는 물방울을 떨어뜨리기 위해 머리를 뒤로 젖힐 것이다. 목욕 후 그 새는 깃털을 다듬고 말릴 것이다. 벌새는 또한 날고 있는 동안 목욕을 하며, 때로는 몸을 젖게 하기 위해 깃털을 곤두세운 채 비 속에서 잎이 다 떨어진 나뭇가지 위에 앉아 있기도 한다. 벌새가 하기 좋아하는 또 한가지는 스프링클러(살수장치)가 뿜어낸 가는 물 안개 속에서 노는 것이다. **꽃들에 물을 주면서, 한 여성은 그녀의 정원용 호스가 뿜어낸 물 안개를 통과해 몇 번을 휙 지나치다가 마침내 그녀의 손에 앉는 벌새를 경험했다.**

Progressive Test 1-2

1 뉴스에 나오는 굶주리는 아프리카 아이들의 잊혀지지 않는 사진들은 1980년대와 1990년대 초기에 일상적인 것이 되었고, 대부분의 사람들은 그러한 사진이 보여주는 인간의 고통과 비참함에 괴로워했다. 기아 구제에 대한 긍정적인 뉴스들이 때때로 등장했는데, 의학적 치료와 균형 잡힌 영양물 섭취가 특정한 사람들에게 있어 영양 결핍으로 인한 병들이 퇴치되는 결과를 가져올 때 같은 경우였다. 그러나 수 천년동안 인류와 함께 한 기근이라는 망령이 사라지지 않았다는 사실은 명백하다. 식량 생산과 관련된 많은 영역에서 진보가 이루어 졌음에도 불구하고, 수많은 사람들이(어른과 아이들) 여전히 충분한 음식을 공급 받지 못한다.

전 세계 인구를 먹여 살리기에 충분한 음식을 생산하는 것은 오늘날 농업에 있어서 가장 큰 하나의 도전이며, 그 도전은 인구가 팽창함에 따라 매년 점점 더 어려워진다. 현재, 밀, 쌀, 옥수수, 보리와 같은 곡물의 14억 메트릭 톤(15억 톤)이 1년 동안 58억의 세계 인구를 먹여 살리는데 요구된다. 매년 추가로 곡물 2천 8백만 매트릭 톤이 그 해 인구 증가분을 책임지기 위해 생산 되어야만 한다.

농업이 직면하고 있는 식량생산의 도전은 몇몇에 의해 농업 문제들에 대한 첨단기술 해결책으로 극찬 되고 있는 유전공학과 더불어, 다양한 방법으로 맞닥뜨려지고 있다. 비록 유전공학이 농업에 혁명을 일으킬 잠재력을 갖고 있는 것이 사실일지라도, 그 변화가 하룻밤 사이에 일어나지는 않을 것이다. 많은 연구조사가 유전공학으로부터 기대되는 혜택의 대부분이 실현되기 전에 행해져야만 한다.

게다가 유전공학은 충분한 음식을 생산하는 도전에 대한 궁극적인 해결책이 아니다. 전 세계 인구를 위한 충분한 음식 생산은 인구성장이 통제될 때까지 불가능한 목표가 될 것이다. 그러므로, 세계 기근에 대한 궁극적 해결책은 각 나라에서 부양할 수 있는 수준의 안정된 인구를 달성하는 것과 관계가 있다.

2 건조한 동굴들에서는 습기가 적은 공기와 제한된 박테리아의 활동 때문에 종종 보전상태가 훌륭하다. 까맣게 탄 나무, 견과의 껍질, 식물의 섬유조직 그리고 뼈와 같은 유기체의 잔재가 때때로 손상되지 않은 채 발견된다. 축축한 동굴에서는 인공물과 다른 잔재들이 종종 (종유석ㆍ석순 모양의) 점적석 이라는 석회석의 퇴적물로 덮이거나 아래에 묻힌 채 발견된다. 동굴바닥의 인간거주에 대해 수집되는 증거는 종종 동굴의 천장으로부터 떨어진 돌 조각 아래에 매장되었다. 의도적으로 매장한 것이 수많은 동굴 터에서 또한 발견되었다.

동굴의 보기 드문 보존성과 그 안에서 발견되는 많은 잔재들의 오랜 나이 때문에, 한 일족의 동굴 인이 존재했다는 그릇된 믿음을 가져왔다. 실제로, 대부분의 동굴 터는 작은, 계절적인 막사를 나타낸다. 선사시대 사람들이 개방된 막사에서 일년의 대부분을 보냈기 때문에, 동굴은 한 집단의 총체적인 활동 중 일부분만의 유물을 포함하고 있다. 또한 동굴 밖의 문화 유물들은 더 많이 부패되기 쉬웠다. 그러므로 먼 시대의 고고학적 기록은 동굴의 퇴적물에서 더 잘 보여진다.

동굴은 과거 백년동안 체계적으로 발굴되어 왔다. 종종 그것들은 반복 활동과 관련된 유물을 포함하고 있기 때문에, 변천하는 문화에 대한 증거를 보여줄 수 있다. **예를 들어, 채집 경제에서 농경경제로의 이행은 고지의 멕시코와 동남아시아에서의 유물에 의해 증명된다.** 구 세계의 몇몇 동굴들은 석기시대가 끝난 이후에도 계속해서 거주 되었고, 청동기, 철기 시대의 유물들이 동굴 퇴적물들에서 발견되었다. 때때로, 로마 제국 시대로부터 기원하는 자료가 재발견되었다. 1947년에 발견된 유명한 사해 두루마리 책(Dead Sea Scrolls)도 동굴 안에서 보존되었다.

3 에너지 흐름의 중요한 특징은 하나의 영양단계에서 다른 영양단계로 갈 때 그것의 대부분이 환경 속으로 흩어져 없어진다는 것이다. 각각의 영양단계의 상대적 에너지 가치는 종종 생태학적 피라미드에 의해 여실히 나타난다. 피라미드의 3가지 주요 형태들이 있는데, 숫자 피라미드, 생물량 피라미드, 에너지 피라미드이다.

숫자로 된 피라미드는 주어진 생태계에 각각의 영양단계에서 유기체의 수를 보여준다. 대부분의 숫자 피라미드에서, 각각의 연속적인 영양단계는 더 적은 유기체에 의해 차지된다. 그러므로, 전형적인 아프리카 초원에서 풀과 같은 생산자의 수는 얼룩말과 영양과 같은 초식동물의 수 보다 더 많고, 이것은 사자와 같은 육식동물의 수보다 더 많다. 높은 영양단계가 낮은 영양단계보다 더 많은 유기체를 가지는 숫자 피라미드의 역전은 종종 분해자와 기생충, 나무에 사는 초식 곤충과 그와 유사한 유기체 사이에서 관찰된다. 예를 들어, 한 그루의 나무는 수천 개의 잎을 먹는 곤충들에게 먹을 것을 제공할 수 있다.

생물량 피라미드는 각각의 연속하는 영양 단계에서 전체 생물량을 보여준다. 생물량은 살아있는 물질의 전체 크기와 양에 대한 양적인 평가이다. 그것의 측정 단위들은 다양하다: 생물량은 전체 부피, 말린 무게 또는 산 그대로의 무게로 나타내어질 지 모른다. 전형적으로, 생물량 피라미드는 연속되는 영양단계에서 점진적인 생물량의 감소를 보여준다. 평균적으로, 생물량의 약 90%의 감소가 각 영양 단계에서 일어난다는 가정 하에, 풀 1만 킬로 그램이 개구리 1천 킬로 그램을 부양할 수 있어야 한다. **이러한 논리에 의해, 왜가리와 같은 개구리를 먹는 동물의 생물량은 기껏해야 단지 약 100 킬로 그램의 무게가 나갈 수 있다.** 이러한 간단한 연습으로부터, 우리는 비록 육식동물이 식물을 먹지 않을 지라도, 많은 양의 식물이 여전히 그것들을 부양하기 위해 요구되어진다는 것을 알 수 있다.

4 파동이 한 매체에서 다른 매체 사이의 경계에 도달할 때, 그 파동의 일부는 반사되고 일부는 그 경계를 거쳐 전달된다. 반사된 파동은 두 매개체의 상대적 밀도에 따라 위상 변화를 겪거나 겪지 않을 지도 모르며, 반사량 또한 두 매개체의 차이점에 의존한다. 이러한 이유로, 공연장과 콘서트 홀에 대해 음향학적으로 신경을 쓰는 건축업자들은 내부 홀의 건축에 있어서 단단하거나 부드러운 물질의 사용을 피한다. 콘크리트 같은 단단한 물질은 소리가 통과하는 공기와 상당히 다르고, 그 결과 대부분의 소리 파동은 벽에 의해 반사되어지고, 거의 흡수되지 않는다.

표면을 떠난 소리 파동의 반사는 메아리와 반향음의 두 현상중 하나를 가져올 수 있다. 반향음은 대략 17미터나 그 보다 작은 높이, 가로, 세로 치수들을 가진 작은 방에서 종종 발생한다. 사람들은 빈 방에서 대화할 때, 고속도로의 터널이나 지하도를 통과하여 운전하는 동안 경적을 울릴 때, 또는 샤워하면서 노래를 부를 때 반향음을 깨닫게 된다. 공연장과 콘서트 홀에서, 반향음이 때때로 발생하고 소리의 불쾌한 왜곡을 이끈다.

그러나, 공연장과 콘서트 홀에서 소리 파동의 반사가 특히 만일 그 반사가 정확히 계획된 것이라면 항상 불쾌한 결과를 이끌지는 않는다. 부드러운 벽은 소리 파동을 특정한 방향으로 향하게 하는 경향이 있다. 결과적으로 공연장에서 부드러운 벽을 사용하는 것은 관객이 벽을 따라 한 위치에서 많은 양의 소리를 받도록 할 것이고, 소리 파동이 스피커들에서 청중에게 로 이동할 수 있는 단 하나의 가능한 경로가 있을 것이다. 그 공연장은 생생하고 소리로 가득찬 것처럼 보이지 않을 것이다. 거친 벽은 소리를 다양한 방향으로 반사 시키면서 퍼트리는 경향이 있다. 이것은 공간을 생생하고 가득찬 것으로 보이게 만들면서, 관객이 공간의 모든 부분으로부터 소리를 인식하도록 한다. 이러한 이유로, 공연장과 콘서트 홀 설계자들은 부드러운 것보다 오히려 거친 건축 재료들을 선호한다.

## Chapter 4

Hackers Practice

1   대부분의 뉴딜시대의 예술가들은 그들에게 일자리를 준 루즈벨트 대통령에게 감사했고 뉴딜정책의 자유주의적 협의사항을 열정적으로 지지했다. 당연히, 그들의 작품은 이러한 관점을 반영했다.

2   기초 세포막은 특별히 잘 발달되어 있지 않다; 그것은 대부분의 포유류의 그것과 비교하여 짧은 편이고, 아래부분부터 꼭대기까지 그 구조적 변화는 정도에 있어서 보통일 뿐 이다.

3   난초로부터 추출되는 경제적으로 중요한 유일한 생산품은 맛을 내는 작용제인 바닐라인데, 이것은 바닐라에 속하는 여러 종의 깍지로부터 얻어진다. 많은 전통 의약품, 토속 음료와 음식들이 난초의 다양한 부분으로부터 마련된다.

4   오로라는 빠르게 바뀌는 얼룩들과 다양한 빛깔의 출렁이는 빛 줄기들로 구성된다. 넓은 범위에 걸친 오로라의 출현은 지구자기력의 동요와 라디오, 전화망 그리고 전신 전달의 간섭을 동반한다. 오로라의 최대최소 강도의 주기는 11년을 주기로 하는 흑점주기의 최대최소 강도의 주기를 거의 정확히 따른다.

5   하루 중 전력의 수요가 시간대별로 아주 급변하는 지역에서는 양수 수력발전소가 사용된다.

6   수면 학습이나 통합된 행동양식은 생생한 꿈의 경험에서 나온 행동이거나 그것들의 대체물이라는 일반적인 생각과 대조적으로, 잠꼬대는 NREM 수면 동안에 주로 발생하고 몽유병은 오로지 NREM 수면에서만 발생한다. 잠꼬대는 가벼운 NREM 수면 단계인 stage 2의 독특한 특성인 반면, 몽유병은 깊은 NREM수면 단계인 stage 4에서 시작된다.

7   마찬가지로, 동부 오레건은 인디언 지역으로 여겨졌다. Blue Mountain 산맥에서의 금광 발견이 새롭게 발견된 금광의 탐사를 열망하는 백인들을 위한 길을 만들기 위해 강압적으로 Nez Perce을 이주하도록 이끌기 전까지는 그곳에 살고 싶어하는 다른 사람들은 거의 없었다. 금 찾기는 오레건 뿐만 아니라 아이다호와 몬타나에서도 지배적인 영향력이 되었고, 그 당시까지 농장을 찾는 이주민에 의해 이끌려 온 정착의 양식들을 바꾸어 놓았다.

8 다른 곳에서 운하는 철도와 경쟁이 될 수 없었다. 운하는 단위 당 실어 나를 수 있는 양과 속도 둘 다에서 한계가 있었다; 그것들은 너무 작고 느리고 지엽적이었다. 그리고, 철도는, 국가적 체계로 통합되면서, 매우 유동적인 훨씬 더 광범위한 서비스를 제공했다. 운하는 보통 자체적으로 운반하는 것이 아니라, 중개 운송 회사들에게 많이 의존했기 때문에 더욱 더 불리한 위치에 서게 되었다. 운하를 통한 수송이 초기에는 철도에 비해 가격이 저렴했지만 철도는 이런 (운하의) 강점을 점차 극복했다.

9 사람들은 현존하는 처음으로 알려진 지구의는 Martin Behaim에 의해 1492년 뉘른베르그에서 만들어졌다고 믿고 있다. 많은 다른 것들은 16세기 동안 만들어졌다. 지도 제작 활동의 주요 중심지들은 스페인, 포르투칼, 이탈리아, 라인 지방, 네덜란드, 스위스였다. 영국과 프랑스는 증대하는 해상과 식민지의 세력과 더불어 곧 중요한 지도와 해도의 중심지가 될 예정이었다. 존 스미스 선장의 버지니아와 뉴 잉글랜드 지도, 영국식민지로부터 온 것 중 첫번째, 는 1612년 런던에서 출판되었다.

10 과학자들은 여전히 태양풍의 가장 빠른 부분은 코로나에서 차가운 부분인 코로나 구멍을 통해 태양을 빠져 나간다고 생각한다. 태양의 자기장은 상대적으로 코로나의 구멍들 주위에서 약하고 그래서 태양풍의 입자들이 빠져나갈 수 있다. 코로나 구멍내의 같은 흐름에서 무거운 입자들이 가벼운 입자들보다 더 빨리 움직이는 것처럼 보인다. 태양적도 부근으로부터의 간헐적인 돌풍은 태양 섬광과 코로나의 대규모 분출로부터 온다.

11 그러한 철자 개정이 다른 나라들에서 성공적이었고 Ben Franklin, Noah Webster, 그리고 다른 사람들이 그 이익이 일시적인 불편함을 분명히 능가할 거라고 믿었던 반면에, 주요 개정에 대한 지지는 폭 넓은 정치적 지지를 결코 누리지 못했다. 마치 철자 체계에 간섭하는 것이 헌법에 간섭하는 것과 동등한 것처럼 말이다.
Webster 사전이 대중적인 덕택에, Webster는 color에서 묵음〔u〕를 탈락시키고 몇몇 다른 단편적인 개정을 이행할 수 있었다. 그러나 'through'를 'thru'로 교체하는 데 대한 Teddy Roosevelt의 지지는 여론을 움직이는 데는 충분하지 못했다.
실제적인 관점에서 보자면, 더 좋은 것을 위한 변화일지라도 변화에 대한 저항은 거의 이겨내기 어려운 것이다. 대부분의 학자들은 핀란드 인이 사용하는 것과 유사한 철자체계를 갖는 것이 읽고 쓸 줄 아는 능력을 증가시키고 5학년 독해 수준의 습득을 25%이상 빠르게 할 것이라는 데 동의한다. 인식의 부족과 다양한 대개가 가치 없는 이유들 때문에, 그 주제를 연구해온 사람들 이외에는 철자개정을 위한 어떤 제안도 진척시키거나 뒷받침할 준비가 되어 있는 사람은 거의 없다.

12 책은 의미를 전달하기 위해 글 또는 (그림이나 음악 표시법 같은) 몇몇 다른 시각적 상징들의 체계를 사용하는 것에 의해 특징 지워진다. 의사소통의 정교한 매개체로서, 책은 독해와 작문이라는 힘들게 얻어지는 기술들의 숙달을 필요로 한다. 책의 또다른 두드러진 특징은 유형의 유통을 위한 출판이다. 메시지가 그 위에 새겨진 사원의 기둥은 책이 아니다. 운송하기 쉬운 간판과 벽보는 통행자의 눈을 고정된 위치로부터 유인하기 위해 만들어지고, 따라서 보통 책으로 간주되지 않는다. 유포를 위해 의도된 것이 아닌 사적인 서류들도 또한 책으로 간주되지 않는다.

13 세계 2차 대전으로 이어지는 시기에, 신문은 경제적 정치적인 규제에서 발생되는 사회적으로 우울한 분위기를 반영했다. 영국에서, Times지는 정부의 정책을 지지했고, Daily Mirror지만이 유럽의 정치, 외교, 경제 사건을 철저히 조사할 준비가 되어 있었다. 유럽대륙의 언론은 불행한 사태를 너무나 성실하게 반영했다. 독일, 이태리, 스페인과 포르투갈에서, 언론은 그 당시의 파시즘과 관련된 엄격한 검열을 받아야 했던 반면에, 소련에서는 다른 정치적인 체계가 그와 같은 억압적인 통제를 야기했다.

전쟁(2차 대전)중에 대부분의 국가에서는 뉴스 취재범위에 대한 예측된 탄압이 있었다. 그러나 미국과 영국에서는 세계 1차 대전 때의 경우보다는 더 많은 정보의 흐름이 허락되었다. 영국의 정보부와 미국의 전쟁 정보국은 방대한 양의 공식 뉴스와 선전을 유포했다. 미국에서 검열국이 '미 언론의 전시 실천 규약' 을 규정지은 반면에, 영국에서는 신문사들이 자발적으로 검열을 위해 모든 의심이 가는 자료를 제출했고, 협조적인 자체 검열 제도가 보편화되었다. 그럼에도 불구하고, 모든 현대전에서처럼, 언론인 영웅들이 탄생했고, 사진술의 기준이 절정에 도달했으며, 전쟁의 공포와 비극은 종종 글쓰기와 편집에 우수함을 불어넣었다.

14 1800년대 전에 영국과 네덜란드에 주로 소개된 생산성을 증가시키는 농업 기술의 변화들이 영국 농업을 멀리 떨어진 아메리카에 알릴 만큼 전세계에 농업의 전형으로 만들었다. 그러나 미국의 대륙들, 북부와 남부는 정말로 유럽에 매우 귀중한 식물들을 공급했다. 18세기 말까지, 북아메리카의 생산량은 전쟁중인 유럽의 필수품들 중 일부를 공급하기에 충분했다.
남부 주들의 개척지들처럼, 뉴잉글랜드의 개척지들은 토지가 숲에서 개간 되어 짐에 따라 서쪽으로 확장되어 가고 있었다. 농업은 수출을 위해 약간의 잉여농산물들을 생산했다. 남부 주들은 담배, 목화, 설탕과 같은 기본적인 농산물들을 항상 수출해왔다; 그러나, 이러한 대초원들을 경작하는 과정은 원시 상태로 남아있었다.
가축 사육은 신세계에서 빠르게 발전했다. 신선하고 더 넓은 목초 지역에 대한 필요성이 서쪽 오하이오와 켄터키로 가축농장을 이끌었는데, 그 곳에서는 살찌우는 목적으로 이용되는 옥수수가 낮은 비용으로 재배될 수 있었다. 그 결과, 가축은 1805년까지 육로를 통해 해안의 시장들로 몰아졌다.

15 후기 중세 시대 지도들의 가장 중요한 측면은 지도의 증가하는 정확도였는데, 그것은 계속되는 탐험에 의해 가능하게 되었다. 또 다른 중요한 특징은 예술적이고 색채가 풍부한 연출을 하려는 경향이었는데, 왜냐하면 지도는 여전히 예술가가 그의 상상력을 몰입할 수 있는 많은 공간을 가지고 있었기 때문이다. 카르투시 즉 제목의 장식테두리는 점점 더 정교하게 되어, 작은 예술작품과 같게 되었다. 이 시대의 지도 판들의 상당수가 수집가의 품목들이 되었다. 최초의 지도 인쇄물들은 목판을 재료로 만들어졌다. 나중에, 그것들은 구리 위에 새겨졌는데, 그것은 훨씬 더 가는 선들을 복사하는 것을 가능하게 하는 방법이었다. 그 완성된 금속판들은 잉크가 칠해지고 닦여서, 그 새긴 선들에 잉크를 남겼다. 축축한 종이가 그 후에 금속판 위에 눌러 붙여져서 그 새긴 선 작품으로 되어 매우 정교한 느낌을 주게 되었다. 그 방법은 비교적 최근에 사진 평판술이 출현할 때까지 정교한 지도 복사의 기본으로 남았다.

16 인간에게 있어서, 수면은 주기적인 양식으로 발생한다. 1시간 30분에서 2시간의 각 주기에서, 수면자는 1단계부터 4단계까지 수면의 네 가지 단계를 거치고, 다시 1단계로 돌아온다. 첫번째 단계에서, 저주파 저진폭의 세타파들이 두뇌 활동을 특징 짓는다. 그 단계는 사람이 2단계 수면-이 지점에서 두뇌는 저주파 고진폭의 파로 이동한다-으로 이동하기 전에 보통 몇 분간만 지속된다. 3단계는 저주파 고진폭의 델타파들의 증가를 나타내고, 4단계 수면에서 이 델타파들은 모든 뇌파의 반 이상의 비율을 차지한다.
빠른 눈 운동(REM)수면은 각 주기의 마지막의 1단계 수면동안 발생하고, 이 시간에 깨어난 사람들은 보통 그들이 꿈을 꾸고 있었다고 보고한다. 꿈의 부족상태나 수면의 부족상태는 성격, 지각 방법들 그리고 지적인 기능에 해로운 변화들을 결과로 가져온다. 정서적, 환경적 궁핍은 어린 아이들의 수면 패턴을 혼란 시켜서, 정상적으로는 수면 중에 최대로 분비되는 성장호르몬의 분비를 억제한다는 몇몇 증거가 있다.

17 Piaget의 이론이 지적인 발달을 보는 견해들에 중요한 영향을 끼쳤지만 그 이론은 더 이상 한때, 특히 1950년대부터 1970년대까지 그것이 누렸던 그 폭 넓은 지지를 받고 있지 않다. 이에 대한 한가지 이유는 그 이론이 사고의 과학적, 논리적인 방법들을 주로 다루고, 사고의 미적, 직관적 그리고

다른 방법들을 훨씬 덜 다룬다는 것이다. 또 다른 이유는 Piaget가 아이들이 처음으로 특정한 인지적 과제들을 수행할 수 있는 나이들을 과대평가하는 경향이 있었다는 것이다. 그러나, 그 이론의 영향력이 줄어들었음에도 불구하고, Piaget의 이론은 계속해서 다른 이론들의 기초로서 역할을 한다.

18 비록 도시의 산업적인 생활이 개인의 기동성이나 개인적 자유에 유례없는 기회들을 제공하기는 하지만, 그것은 높은 사회적 심리적 대가를 가져올 수 있다. Karl Marx와 Emile Durkheim과 같은 다양한 관찰자들은 표면적으로 무의미해 보이는 일들과 빠르게 바뀌는 목표에 직면한 개개 노동자의 "소외감"과 "사회적 무질서"를 언급했다. 대가족과 공동체의 분열은 개인들을 고립시키고 전통적 가치들을 상쇄하는 경향이 있었다. 성장의 바로 그 정해진 절차에 의해, 산업주의는 가난이라는 새로운 부담을 만들어내는 것처럼 보이는 데, 가난의 희생자들은 그 산업적 질서의 규정들에 따라 경쟁할 수 없다. 20세기 후반의 주요 산업 국가들에서, 자동화된 기술, 팽창하는 서비스 부문과 증가하는 교외화와 같은 발전들이 일부 관찰자들이 탈 공업화 사회의 출현이라고 부르는 것의 신호였다.

19 1872년에 이해하기 어려운 Rockefeller는 the South Improvement Company를 설립했는데, 그는 그것을 그의 석유 선적의 큰 비율을 담당할 매매 대행자로 만들었다. 이 무역을 통제함으로써, 그는 철도에 대한 영향력을 얻었는데, 그것은 그에게 그의 큰 부피의 사업을 유지하기 위한 그 표준 화물 운송 요금에 있어 많은 환불을 가져다 주었다. 몇몇 경우에, 그들은 심지어 경쟁사들의 선적량에 대한 정보를 그에게 주었다. Rockefeller는 그 다음에 그의 Cleveland 경쟁자들에게 접근해서 그들에게 그가 제시한 가격에 팔도록 압력을 가했다. 그들 대부분이 순응했다. 저항한 자들은 강제로 밀려났다. 한 경쟁자는 우리는 "만약 우리가 팔지 않으면 끝장날 것이다."라고 들었다고 회상했다. 육 주도 채 안되어, Rockefeller는 그의 스물 여섯 개의 경쟁 상대들 중에 스물 두개를 접수했다. 1879년까지, Standard Oil사는 나라전체를 통틀어 정제된 석유의 90%에서 95%를 통제하게 되었다.

20 건축 역사가들은 디즈니의 Walt Disney World 남쪽 새로운 마을인 Celebration, Florida 개발을 칭찬했다. New York 건축가 Robert A.M. Stern에 의해 설계된, Celebration은 1996년에 전통적인, 보행자를 배려한 마을로서 문을 열었다. 여섯 개의 서로 다른 복고풍의 널찍한 현관과 베란다가 있는 집들뿐만 아니라 밀착하여 정돈된 거리들과 구획들은 the Celebration Company에 따라 구시대의 친절함을 촉진하도록 의도되어진다. 비록 그 자신의 치안 경찰이 있는 문이 있는 공동체는 아니지만, Celebration은 미국의 주제 도시이고 부유한 시민들을 위한 영토이다. 냉전이 끝난 이후로, "하나의 작은 세계"를 꿈꾸는 디즈니의 상상력은 세계 자본주의의 승리와 인터넷의 컴퓨터화된 출현에 의해 경제적으로, 기술적으로 실현된 것으로 보인다. 그러나, 공동 사회 수준에서, 사회적으로 배타적인 Celebration, Florida가 새로운 도시화를 위한 하나의 모형으로서 역할을 할 수 있다는 개념은 그 마을의 공동으로 착상된 이름만큼이나 순진하게 낙천적인 것으로 보인다.

Chapter 5

Hackers Test

1 알라스카 주를 제외하고 미국 전역에 서식하는 지하 흰개미들은 나무를 먹고 살면서 죽은 나무를 유기물로 바꾸어 줌으로써 생태계에 중요한 역할을 하고 있다. 불행한 일은 건물의 자재로 사용되는 나무 역시 이 흰개미의 식욕을 자극시키는 대상이 된다는 것이며, 따라서 이 흰개미들이 주택이나 상가 건물에 큰 피해를 입힐 수도 있다는 것이다. 결국 심한 경우 건축물 구조 자체에 위험을 주기도 한다. 이 흰개미들은 쉽게 눈에 띄지 않는데, 어떤 경우 건물의 파손을 발견하고 나서야 비로소 흰개미들이 있다는 것을 알게 되기도 한다.

지하 흰개미들은 땅속에 둥지나 군락을 이루어 사는 사회성 곤충이다. 흰개미 군락들은 수십만 개에서 수백만 개에 달한다. 세가지 흰개미 형태 즉 세 계급이 그 군락을 구성한다: 생식 개미 (reproductives), 일개미(workers), 병정개미(soldiers). 생식 개미는 날개가 있기도 하고 없기도 하다. 각각은 자손을 생산해 낼 수 있는 능력을 갖추고 있다. 날개 달린 생식 개미 - 또한 'swarmers'나 'alates'라고도 불리는 - 의 몸 색깔은 석탄처럼 까만 색부터 연한 황토 빛을 띄는 색까지 매우 다양하다. 일개미들은 크기가 작고 크림색을 띠는 곤충이다. 그들은 가장 수가 많으며, 모든 흰개미 피해의 원인이다. 병정개미들은 그 색깔이나 외관상 일개미와 유사하다. 그러나 그들은 크고 잘 발달된 갈색 머리 - 강한 하악골 즉 턱이 붙어 있는 - 를 가지고 있다. 병정개미들은 침입자들 - 대개의 경우 일반 개미들 - 로부터 자신들의 군락을 방어한다. 한 군락이 생긴지 수년이 흘렀거나 그 크기가 상대적으로 커지면 그 군락은 일명 'swarmer'라고 불리는 어른 흰개미들로 하나의 다른 군락을 형성하게 된다. 이것이 새 왕과 여왕을 파견하여 그들 자신의 군락을 이루는 방식이다. 봄이 되면 각 군락에서 생겨난 수많은 swarmer들이 날아다닌다. 흰개미 종류 중 가장 눈에 잘 띄는 것이 바로 이 swarmer들이다. 보통 집주인이 흰개미가 자기 집에 또는 집 근처에 서식하고 있다는 것을 알게 되는 경우는 이 swarmer를 보게 되면서부터 이다.

그들의 이름이 나타내는 것처럼, 지하 흰개미들은 지하에 서식하며, 나무에 다다를 수 있도록 통로를 뚫는다. 그들의 지하 통로는 상당히 복잡하여 지하 10피트가 넘고 면적이 1 에이커 이상에 달하기도 한다. 흙은 흰개미들이 건조해지는 것을 막아주는 수분의 원천이며 외부 침입자들로부터 그들을 방어해준다. 흙은 그 흰개미들이 땅 위의 나무 먹이를 찾는데 사용하게 되는 보호 통로 터널을 만들기 위한 재료가 되기도 한다. 하지만, 만약 물과 나무를 흙이 아닌 다른 것으로부터 얻을 수만 있다면 이 지하 흰개미들은 땅과 전혀 접촉 없이도 군락을 형성할 수 있다. 그래서 물이 새는 수도관이나 지붕 등과 같이 액화 현상을 통해 수분을 공급 받을 수 있는 건물에 꼭 땅과 연결되어 있지 않더라도 흰개미가 들끓게 되는 곳이 존재할 수 있는 것이다.

subterranean 지하의, 지하에 사는, 숨은 **termite** 흰개미
integrity 고결, 성실, 보전, 완전 **caste** 계급
swarmer 우글우글 떼짓는 것(사람) **alate** 날개가 있는 것들의, 날개 모양의
mandible 하악골, (새의)아랫부리 **infestation** 침략, 만연

2 전형적인 계몽주의 정신의 계승자로서의 Thomas Jefferson의 면모는 그의 청년기의 신념 - 즉 호기심을 가진 탐구와 이성이 인간으로 하여금 인간사 내부에 존재하는 모든 그릇되고, 왜곡되고, 변덕스러운 것들로부터 벗어나 사물 자체에 본질적으로 내재된 진리로 이끌어 줄 수 있다고 믿었던 - 에서 가장 잘 드러난다. 인간은 그 동안 자연적 본질로부터 너무나 멀리 떨어져 지내왔었다. 수세기 동안 인간은 교회의 권위와 맹목적 신앙 - 그것도 왕과 성직자들, 그러니까 곧 교회와 국가의 유대 하에서 구체화된 - 에 의해 지배되어 왔다. 이제 그러한 잘못된 우상들은 무너지려 하고 있었고, 인간은 자연의 법칙을 발견해 내고 그것을 자신들을 위해 사용함으로써 자기 자신들의 운명을 결정할 수 있을 것이다. Newton은 물리적 우주의 법칙을 증명해 내었고, Locke는 통치 과학뿐만 아니라 정신 과학 측면까지 다루었으며, Linnaeus와 Buffon은 혼돈 속에 존재하던 생명체들에게 질서 있는 체계를 부여했다. 그리고 1776년 우연하게도 Adam Smith는 불변의 자연 법칙에 의해 지배되는 자율적 경제 질서에 대한 생각을 내어놓았다. 이러한 모든 법칙들은 영구적이고 보편적인 것이며 또한 조화롭고 지적이고 인간들에게 유익한 것들이었으므로 사람들은 본질적으로 안락함을 느낄 수 있을 것 같아 보였다. 이러한 신념은 그 목표가 인간의 자유와 행복을 증진시키는 것으로 당시 교회와 종교사상에 반대한 상당히 공격적인 것이었으며 실용적이고 급진적인 것이었다. 나이가 들었을 때 주고 받았던 훌륭한 서신에서, Jefferson의 무뚝뚝한 친구 John Adams는 Jefferson이 계몽주의에 대해 지나친 희망을 가지고 있다고 비웃기도 했다. 하지만 그 쾌활한 버지니아인은 그것에 대해 전혀 개의치 않았다. 그는 무덤에 갈 때까지도 미래가 과거보다 더 나을 것이며, 자유의 증진은 되돌릴 수 없는 것이라고 믿었다. Adams에게 그가 예전에 말한 것처럼, 그는 "두려움은 고물(배의 뒤편)에 두고 이물(배의 앞머리)에는 희망을 싣고" 자신의 배를 조종하였다.

이러한 낙관적 계몽주의 신념이 Jefferson의 모든 업적에 들어 있다. 우리는 과학자 Jefferson, 교육자 Jefferson, 정치인 Jefferson의 모습 – 다재 다능한 천재의 모든 면모 – 에서 그것을 볼 수 있다. 그의 공공 정책들은 종종 계몽주의적 이성주의를 반영한 것이었다: 달러 단위로 십진법 화폐 주조 시스템, Transappalachian West에 대한 직선적 측량 시스템(오늘날 프레어리 대초원 위를 날아본 경험이 있는 사람이라면 그 아래로 놓여진 바둑판 모양으로 짜여진 평야의 모습을 통해 그 결과를 한 눈에 알아 볼 수가 있을 것이다) 그리고 (비록 채택되지는 않았지만) 자연적이고 보편적인 기준에 근거하여 그가 체계적으로 고안했던 무게와 측량 시스템에 대한 단일화 계획안.

superstition 미신(적 습관, 행위) **crumble** 가루로 만들다, 무너지다
broach (이야기를)끄집어 내다, 발의하다 **glum** 무뚝뚝한, 시무룩한, 음울한
twit 조롱하다, 비웃다 **steer** 돌리다 **bark** 범선 **multifaceted** 다면적인
rectilinear 직선의, 직선으로 둘러싸인 **patchwork** 쪽모이 세공, 잡동사니

3   나바호(Navajo) 원주민들의 언어는 Athabaskan어족에 해당하며, 그들은 북쪽 지방으로부터 이주해 왔는데 분명 그 이유는 온화한 기후를 찾아서 였을 것이다. 1400년까지는 그들은 Upper Rio Grande Valley – 지금의 New Mexico 와 서쪽으로는 지금의 Arizona지방에 해당하는 – 의 푸에블로(Pueblo) 원주민들이 돌과 어도비(adobe) 벽돌을 사용하여 세운 성곽 마을 북쪽에 정착했었다. 1540년 스페인 사람들이 이곳으로 오기 이전에 이미 푸에블로족과 나바호족 사이에 무역이 이루어 졌던 것으로 보인다.
Coronado의 지휘아래 그 스페인 사람들은 7개의 금광도시(Seven Cities of Gold)를 찾아 Rio Grande Valley에 왔다. 1598년에는 푸에블로 원주민들을 정복한 그들은 자신들의 식민 통치 하에 있는 거주지를 설립하기에 이르렀다. 나바호족은 푸에블로 족의 곤경을 목격했으며, 그들과 거리를 유지하게 되었다: 역사적 자료는 나바호족이 스페인 사람들과 무역을 해 오면서도 그들의 북쪽 주거지역을 습격했음을 보여준다. 그 후 250년이 넘는 시간 동안 푸에블로 원주민들과 스페인, 그리고 멕시코와 미연방 군대 사이에서 서남부 지역을 차지하기 위한 싸움이 계속되었음에도 불구하고 나바호족은 자신들의 고유한 문화를 발전 계승시켜 왔다.
나바호 원주민들이 푸에블로 원주민들로부터 배웠던 원시적 형태의 수직형 베틀을 이용한 면직물 짜기 기법을 아주 정교한 형태의 직물 공예로까지 발전 시켰던 시점이 1600-50년경으로 추정되는 바로 이 기간 이었다. 그들은 훔친 스페인산 Churro sheep에서 빼낸 양모를 주 재료로 사용하여 셔츠에서부터 원피스 종류 그리고 담요에 이르기까지 아주 다양한 종류의 정교한 직물을 짜 냈다. 원시적 형태의 수직형 베틀은 나바호 원주민에 의해 사용된 단일 형태의 베틀로 오늘날까지 계속 사용되고 있다.
1795년에는 New Mexico 스페인 사령관 Fernando de Chacon은 반란자 나바호 원주민들에 대해 '스페인 양모를 스페인 사람들보다 더 정교하고 예쁘게 직조해 내고 있다'고 인정하게 되었다. Pedro Pino는 그의 저서, "Expedicion a Nuevo Mexico"(1812)에서 나바호 원주민들의 직물에 대해 'Sonora와 Chihuahua와 더불어 이 지방에서 가장 중요한 모직물 특산품'이라고 표현한 바 있다. 교역자들의 기록에 의하면 심지어는 1840년대쯤 저 멀리 대평원 북쪽에 사는 원주민들이 나바호족 담요 한 벌과 최소 10벌 정도의 버팔로로 만든 가죽옷과 기꺼이 맞바꾸었다고 전해진다. 1849년에는 미합중국 육군 대령 James H. Simpson이 나바호 원주민들에 대해 평하기를, '아주 가난해 보이는 사람들이지만, 아마도 세상에서 최고의 담요를 만들어 낼 수 있는 능력을 가진 사람들'이라고 했었다.

raid 침입, 급습하다(빼앗다) **loom** 배틀, 직기기술
Spaniard 스페인 사람
robe 길고 헐거운 옷, 무릎덮개, 의복

4 제조법이 유일하게 중국인에게만 알려져 있었던 종이는 중앙 아시아의 무역 대상로를 따라 Samarkand에 있는 시장까지 오게 되었다. 이로부터 종이는 아랍 국가 전역에 일용품으로 보급되었다.

종이 제조 기법 역시 이와 똑같은 대상로를 따라 전해 진 것으로 보인다. 751년 Samarkand근처에서 발생했던 Talas 전쟁에서 체포된 중국 포로들이 아랍인들에게 그 비법을 전수해 주었다. 종이 제조 공장은 8세기 말엽부터 13세기까지 바그다드에서부터 당시 아랍 영토였던 스페인에 이르기까지 번성했다. 종이는 12세기 경에 당시 아랍권 세계와 활발한 상업 교역이 이루어지던 이탈리아 항구와 또한 의심의 여지 없이 스페인에서 프랑스에 이르는 육상로를 통해 처음 소개되어 유럽 전 대륙에 일용품으로 침투하게 되었다. 유럽인들은 당시 수입되던 종이를 무엇으로 만들어 내는지 연구 조사하기 시작하였고, 아마도 그런 과정을 통해서 종이 제조 기법을 발견해 내었을 것이다. 물론 그 비법이 13세기 중엽 동방 무역에 종사하던 상인이나 고향으로 돌아온 십자군들에 의해서 유럽으로 전달되었을 가능성도 있다. 종이제조 공장은 1275년 이후에 이탈리아에서 14세기 동안 프랑스와 독일에서 성장했다.

하지만 종이 제조 기법이 중국에서 유럽으로 성공적으로 전달되었던 것과는 달리 인쇄술은 유럽 대륙에 전파되는데 성공을 거두지 못했다. 인쇄술은 Mongolia와 Turkistan 접경지대에 살았던 위구르족에게 마지막으로 전해 진 것으로 보이는데, 그렇게 보는 이유는 14세기 초엽의 것으로 보이는 (목판에 새겨진) 한 세트의 위구르족 활자들이 발견되었기 때문이다. 위구르족 – 보통 다른 터키–몽골 족들에게 문화를 보급하는 교육자로서의 역할을 해온 것으로 인식된 유목민족 – 이 인쇄술을 저 멀리 이집트까지 전파시키지 못했다면 놀라운 일일 것이다. 어쩌면, 유럽으로 전달하는 과정 중에 뜻하지 않은 장애물에 부닥뜨렸을 수도 있는 일이다. 즉, 당시 이슬람 종교가 알라신의 말을 기록하기 위해 종이를 받아들였지만, 알라신의 말씀이 인위적인 방법에 의해 재생되는 것을 허용하지 않으려 했을 수도 있었을 것이다.

> **caravan** (순례자) 여행자단 **onward** 전방으로(의), 전진하는
> **crusader** 십자군 전사, 개혁 운동가 **typographic** 인쇄상의
> **typeface** 활자면, (활자)서체

5 미국의 권리 수호를 위한 움직임은 필라델피아 Carpenter Hall과 주의회 의사당(State House(Independence Hall))에서 열린 대륙회의를 통해 그 성질이 점차 독립운동으로 바뀌어 갔다. 서부 지역 개척의 자발적인 선언이나 낡은 지방 정부를 와해시켰던 일련의 정치적 사건들이 보여주는 것처럼 독립 정신은 고양되어 있었다.

펜실베니아주 군대는 거의 모든 독립 혁명 전투에 참여하였다. 한 소총대대가 1775년 보스턴을 점령하는데 참여했다. 다른 부대들 역시 불운의 1776년 캐나다 전투에서 그리고 뉴욕과 뉴 져지 전투에서 용감하게 싸웠다. 당연히 영국은 필라델피아를 주요 거점 지역으로 생각했고 1777년 여름 펜실베니아 주를 침략하여 수도를 점령했다. 이 시기 Brandywine전투와 Germantown전투, 그리고 Whitemarsh전투는 아주 중요한 교전들이었다. 이 일련의 전투에 출전하였던 Washington은 1777년 12월부터 1778년 6월까지 Valley Forge에 있는 겨울 진영으로 옮겨갔다. Benjamin Franklin의 협상 성공으로 인한 프랑스 연합군의 출전 소식과 미국의 새로운 전술의 채택은 1778년 봄 영국을 필라델피아에서 떠나도록 만들었다. 펜실베니아주 접경 지대는 영국과 원주민들의 습격으로 골머리를 앓고 있었다. 6개 부족 원주민에 대한 John Sullivan과 Daniel Brodhead의 원정 공격이 이루어진 1779년까지. 펜실베니아주 군인들은 워싱톤이 지휘하는 군대의 중요한 부분을 차지하였고 Arthur St. Clair나 Anthony Wayne, Thomas Mifflin, 그리고 Peter Muhlenberg와 같은 훌륭한 장교들이 훌륭하게 군대를 이끌어 갔다. 또한 수많은 전함들이 필라델피아에서 구입되거나 만들어졌고 펜실베니아 지역 선원들이 그 전함에 군인으로 참전함으로써 펜실베니아주는 미 대륙의 해군을 창설하는 데 일조했다. 아일랜드 태생 John Berry는 펜실베니아주의 해군 영웅 리스트에 그 첫 이름을 장식하는 인물이 되었다.

펜실베니아주의 농장과 공장, 그리고 광산에서 나오는 생산물들은 독립군의 승리에 있어서 본질적인 것이었다. Carlisle에 있던 미 대륙 군수품 병기창고에서는 대포와 검, 창, 소총들을 만들어 내었다. 펜실베니아주는 화약 제조를 아주 적극적으로 권장하기도 했다. 펜실베니아주에서 제공한 재정 지원은 그것이 주 정부에서 나온 것과 민간인에게서 나온 것 둘 다 매우 중요한 것이었다. 1780년까지 이 주에서 6백만 달러가 넘는 돈을 국회에 기부했으며, 미국의 많은 주들이 재정적으로 궁핍한 상태에 있었을 때 90명의 필라델피아 시민들이 군대를 지원하기 위해 30만 파운드를 빌려주었다. 후에 1782년에는 Bank of North America가 정부의 재정적 요구를 지원하기 위한 특허를 받았다. Robert Morris와 Haym Salomon은 미국 독립 전쟁에 있어서 중요한 재정 지원자였다.

> **battalion** 대대, 많은 사람들　**man** 인력을 배치하다, 배에 태우다
> **ordnance** 무기, 병기　**arsenal** 병기고, 군수공장, 군수물자
> **fiscal** 국고의, 국가세입의

6　전후 뉴욕에서는 심각한 도심지역의 구조적 문제점들이 그 어느 때보다도 더 극명하게 나타나고 있었다. 뉴욕 항은 이미 그 우위를 상실했고 제조업이 오랫동안 하락세를 보였고 엄청난 양의 뉴욕 시 채무로 인해 돈이 많이 드는 공공사업에 지원을 하는 것이 어려워 졌고 시 관료조직의 규모가 급격히 늘어났다.
1950년대 Robert Wagner는 도시 노동조합에게 단체 교섭권을 허용했지만, 장기적 문제점들을 묵과한다는 비난을 받았다. 결국에 그는 자신을 두 번이나 시장으로 당선되도록 도와주었던 Tammany Hall과 공식적으로 결별하는 것이 문제 해결의 지름길이라고 판단하게 되었다. Wagner는 그 조직(Tammany Hall)의 힘과 그것의 마지막 의장이었던 Carmine DeSapio를 와해시켰다. 그는 자신의 측근으로 맨하튼 카운티의 지도자를 세우고 외부 자치구에서의 Tammany의 영향력을 감소시키는 데는 성공했으나 급박한 문제들에 대해서는 거의 대처하지 못했다. Wagner는 새로운 개혁 행정부를 위해 유권자를 준비시켰다. 1965년 선거에서 공화자유당 후보였던 John Lindsay가 뜻하지 않게 승리를 하게 되었기 때문에.
Lindsay의 두 번의 재임기간 동안 뉴욕의 이러한 하락 추세는 그가 행정 질서의 강요를 시도하면서 더욱 가속화되어 갔다. 대규모 운송기관 파업이 그의 취임식 날에 겹쳐 일어났는데, 몇 개의 매우 관대한 노동조합 계약 중 단지 첫 번째만으로 해결되었다. 각 부서들을 통합하여 "super agency"들을 만들어 그 조직의 힘을 좀 더 감소시키려 했던 Lindsay의 시도는 오히려 새로운 관료 조직을 더 추가 시키는 결과만 낳았다. 집단 시스템을 분산화 시키고 정부 기구에 소수 인종의 참여를 확대시키려 했던 그의 노력은 인종 적대감을 심화 시켰다. 무엇보다 세금을 올렸음에도 불구하고 그는 솟아오르는 시 예산을 조절하는 데 실패했다. 1969년 분노한 공화당원들에 의해 재지명이 거부되었던 Lindsay는 그 낡아빠진 민주당 조직은 속이 텅 비어있었기(권력이 없었기) 때문에 선거에 자유 무소속(Liberal-Independent) 후보로 나와 재당선 되었다. 그의 계속되는 공화당 주지사와의 불화는 그를 민주당원이 되도록 했고, 그는 결국 추종자 없는 지도자가 되어 버렸다. 그의 마지막 재임 기간 동안에도 그 도시의 재정 상태는 계속해서 악화되어 갔다.

> **bargaining** 거래, 교섭, 단체 교섭의　**break with** 절교하다, 탈퇴하다, (낡은 상고방식)버리다
> **borough** 자치도시　**loom** 베틀, 어렴풋이 나타나다
> **electorate** 선거민(전체)　**transit** 통과, 변화
> **animosity** 악의, 증오　**gut** 깡그리 약탈하다, 파괴하다

7　영국 정부와 식민지 국가들 사이에서 마찰이 고조되어 미국 독립전쟁 발발로 이어지게 되자 Franklin은 고향에 대한 깊은 애정과 개인의 자유에 대한 깊은 신념으로 인해 1775년 다시 미국으로 되돌아 왔다. 당시 그의 서자 William Franklin은 미국 독립을 반대하는 왕당파의 지도자가 되어 가고 있었던 반면, Benjamin Franklin은 미국 독립 전쟁과 신생 국가를 지지하는 위대한 정치

인들 중의 한 명이 되었다. 그는 대륙회의에 대표위원이었고, 우정 장관으로 임명되었으며, 캐나다 사람들을 그 애국 운동에 동참하는데 설득하도록 Samuel chase와 Carrollton의 Charles Carroll과 함께 캐나다로 보내지기도 했다. 1776년에 그는 독립 선언문의 초안을 작성한 위원회에 임명되었고, (나중에) 그가 서명했다.

1776년 후반 Arthur Lee와 Silas Deane을 새 공화국 건설을 위한 외교적 시도에 동참시키기 위해 배를 타고 프랑스에 갔다. 자신의 매력적인 풍채(당당한 이미지)에 힘입어 프랑스에서 높은 명성을 쌓은 Franklin은 1778년에는 새 공화국에 대한 프랑스의 승인을 얻어내는데 많은 기여를 했다. Franklin은 또 미국 해군 작전을 지휘하는 데에도 많은 도움을 주었을 뿐 아니라 유럽에서 미국을 대변한 성공한 외교 위원 – 국회가 불신과 반목으로 다른 미국 위원들의 권한을 무효화시키고 난 후에는 유일한 외교 위원 – 이었다.

1781년 그는 대영 제국과의 평화협상을 체결하기 위한 미국 외교관중 한 명으로 선택되었고 John Jay와 John Adams가 도착하기 이전 조약 체결을 위한 기초 작업을 했다. 서인도 제도에서 영국 해군의 승리는 그 최종 조약을 Franklin이 작성한 원안보다는 미국에 덜 유리하게 만들어 버렸다. 파리 조약은, 국회법에 반하여, 1783년 프랑스와의 동의 없이 체결되었다. Jay와 Adams가 프랑스 사람들을 신뢰하지 않았기 때문에.

illegitimate 불법의, 부조리한 **postmaster** 우체국장
presence 존재, 출석, 풍채, 당당한 사람 **groundwork** 기초(작업), 기본원리

---

8 수질환경보전법령(Clean Water Act)에는, 일반 공장이나 하수처리 공장 등과 같은 일명 "점" 오염 원(point source)으로부터의 오염을 통제하기 위한, 강제적이고 실행 가능한 의무 조항들이 포함되어 있다. 각 오염원들은 먼저 – 그것을 통해 의무 조항들이 부과될 수 있는 – 를 가지고 있어야 하며, 이런 기준들을 집행할 수 있는 장치를 갖추고 있어야 한다.

하지만 나머지 국가 지표수 오염의 절반 이상이 오염된 빗물(runoff) ("非점오염원")로 인해 야기되고 있다. 오염된 runoff는 땅에 떨어진 빗물이 독성물질이나 오염물질을 오염원 – 농장이나 길거리, 주차장, 또는 벌목현장이나 광산현장 – 으로부터 지표수로 흘러보내게 될 때 생기는 오염을 말한다. 다른 주요 오염원들 – 시나 기업에서 나오는 오염된stormwater, (연결된) 하수구의 범람, 살충제와 기타 오염물질로 오염된 관개수가 다시 흘러 돌아오는 것과 같은 – 은 바로 법적, 제도적 허점 때문에 계속되고 있다.

막연하게 계획된 프로그램과 자발적인 노력을 통해 오염된 runoff를 해결하려던 시도는 유효하지 못했고, 이러한 문제는 국가 전체의 수질 상태를 계속해서 황폐화했다. 지금은 강력하고 의무적인 프로그램을 통해서 runoff 오염을 방지할 수 있도록 국회가 나서야 할 때이다. runoff 오염 방지를 위한 법 규제 대책을 몇 가지 예로 들자면, 살충제 사용을 최소화하고 화학 비료에서 나오는 양분 유출을 없애기 위한 친 환경 농사법으로의 전환, water body가 지나치게 커지는 것을 막기위한 침식 방지사업과 완충지대의 의무적 설치, 광산현장에서 애초부터 runoff를 오염시키지 못하도록 runoff를 그 광산현장으로부터 멀리 보내기 위한 경사 조절 방법, 또는 도심지의 runoff를 처리하기 위해 저장 수반을 설치하게 하는 것과 같은 의무적인 stormwater 조절. 도심지 교통수단 이용 형태는 자동차의 과잉 사용과 스프롤 현상(무분별한 팽창, 발달) – 지표수 오염의 가장 큰 원인이 되고 있는 – 을 부추겼다. 이러한 패턴은 지역토지 사용계획을 통해 – stormwater 조절과 통합되어 – 바뀌어져야 한다. 또한 대체 교통 수단 촉진을 위한 연방 정부의 지원금을 늘리는 것도 필요할 것이다.

enforceable 시행할 수 있는 **runoff** 땅 위를 흐르는 빗물
sewer 하수(도) **statutory** 법정의, 법령에 의한
loophole 공기 빼는 구멍, 틈새기 **wreak** (해,벌 등을)가하다, (분노를)터뜨리다
buffer 완충기, 완충장치, 완화하다 **retention** 보류, 유지, 감금
basin 웅덩이, (하천의)유역, 대야, 수반
sprawl 팔,다리를 펴다, (불규칙하게)뻗어나다

9   Henry Ford는 복잡한 성격의 소유자였다. 자신의 가게에서 벗어나 있을 때면, 그는 아주 다양한 열정과 편견, 가끔은 깜짝 놀랄 정도로 무식한 모습을 드러내기도 했다. "역사는 다소 터무니없는 것"이라고 했던 그의 말은 1919년 Chicago Tribune을 상대로 한 백만 달러 명예훼손 소송의 반대심문 과정 중 드러났던 그 방면에 있어서 그의 무식함 만큼이나 잘 알려져 있다; Tribune의 한 사설은 그를 세계 1차 대전에 미국의 참전을 반대했다는 이유로 "무식한 이상주의자"라고 칭했으며 배심원이 비록 Ford의 편을 들어주기는 했으나, 그는 손해배상 재정액으로 단 6센트 밖에 받지 못했다. 세인의 이목을 가장 집중시켰던 Ford의 몇몇 행동 중 그 한가지는 "지속적인 중재"라는 수단을 통해 그 전쟁을 종식시키려던 시도로, 1915년 11월 자신을 비롯한 일단의 평화주의자들을 유럽으로 안내할 원양 여객선을 전세낸 것이다. 소위 "평화의 배(Peace Ship)" 에피소드는 널리 세인의 웃음거리가 되었다. 1918년에 그는 Woodrow Wilson 대통령의 지지에 힘입어 미시간주 상원 의원에 출마했었다. 상대편 출마자가 Ford에 대해 인신 공격을 가하는 선거전을 벌인 후 그는 근소한 차이로 선거에서 패했다.

1918년 Ford는 Dearborn Independent지를 사서 거기에 "국제적인 유태인" – 그가 전쟁에 자금 지원을 했다고 비난한 한 가공의 인물 – 에 대한 심한 악평을 연재했다가 1927년 공식적으로 그 발언을 철회하고 신문을 팔아 버리기도 했다. 그는 또 구식사교춤 파티를 열어 자본가들과 유럽의 귀족들, 그리고 회사 임원진들에게 Polka춤과 Sir Roger de Coverley, Mazurka, Virgini reel, quadrille과 같은 춤을 소개하기도 하였고, 소규모 공장 단지를 조성하기도 하였으며, 직업교육이 강조되는 one-room 학교를 세우기도 했다. 음식과 내구재를 만들어 내기 위해 콩으로 실험을 하기도 했었고, 주말 라디오 방송 시간 – "평범한 사람들"에게 희한한 이야기들을 들려주는 – 에 스폰서를 하기도 하였으며, 복원된 시골 마을인 Greenfield Village를 세우기도 했다. 그는 또한 후에 Henry Ford 박물관으로 명명된 건물을 세워 자신의 청년기 시대 – 미국 사회 거의 대부분이 농업 사회였을 때 – 의 미국 물품과 골동품들로 그곳을 채웠다. 간단히 말해서, 그는 그를 가까이서 관찰할 수 있는 기회를 가졌던 사람들조차도 당황하게 만들었던 그런 사람이었다. 단 한 사람 예외는 James Couzen이라는 사람 – 그 회사 설립 때부터 1915년 사임할 때 까지 Ford의 사업 매니저였던 – 으로 그는 항상 "여러분이 천재를 분석할 수 없으며 Ford가 바로 그런 천재다"라고 말했었다.

> **bunk** 속임수, 허풍   **libel** 중상하는 글, 모욕   **cross-examination** 반대 심문
> **charter** (비행기, 선박 따위를) 전세내다   **scurrilous** (사람,말씨 등이) 야비한, 상스러운
> **mazurka** 폴란드의 3박자의 경쾌한 무용   **reel** 스코틀랜드 고지 사람의 경쾌한 춤곡
> **quadrille** 방향끼리 2,4 사람씩 짝지어 추는 구식 춤

10   Columbus가 신세계를 발견하기 이전, 옥수수는 오직 북반구에서만 재배되고 있었다. 아메리카 대륙의 북부, 중부, 남부 지역의 인디안들이 수천 년이 넘도록 그것을 재배해 왔다. 옥수수는 인디언 원주민들이 오천 년 이상 살았던 곳에서 살았던 지역에서 발견된다. 발견된 옥수수 속대는 너무 오래되어서 이미 화석화 되었다. 원주민들은 옥수수를 "MA-HIZ"라고 불렀다. 후에 이것은 "maize"로 알려지게 되었다.

옥수수는 토마토나 감자가 처음 유럽 요리법으로 적용되었을 때와 같은 냉대를 받지 않았다. Columbus가 이 곡식을 스페인으로 가져가자마자 그곳의 부엌과 농장을 통해서 쉽게 보급되었고 세계의 다른 지역으로까지 퍼졌다. 1555년까지는 옥수수가 중국 Hunan 지방에 기록되고 있었다. 포르투갈은 곧바로 옥수수를 아프리카로 수출했고, 거기서 옥수수는 중요한 주식의 종류로 자리잡았다.

대체할 다른 음식물이 없었기에, 유럽의 빈민들이 옥수수에만 의존하여 "pellagra"란 병이 생겨나게 되었다. 그 결과, 유럽인들은 옥수수를 좋아하지 않게 되었다. 그러나 아프리카나 미국에서는 선택의 여지가 거의 없었으므로 굶어 죽는 것보다는 Pellagra를 앓는 것이 더 나은 선택이었다. (Pellagra는 피부와 입에 붉은 반점을 일으키며, 궁극적으로는 매독의 증세와 유사한 정신적 혼란을

야기한다.) 이 병은 중앙 아메리카와 남아메리카에서는 거의 발견되지 않았는데, 그 이유는 그들은 식단에 토마토와 콩, 그리고 아보카도가 포함되어 있었기 때문이다. 식단이 주로 그 곡물(옥수수)로 구성되어 있을 때만 문제가 발생한 것이다.

인디안들은 청교도들에게 이 기본 식품을 가장 잘 재배할 수 있는 방법 - 비결은 씨앗들을 따라 흙더미 안에 물고기를 심어두어 비료로 쓰일 수 있도록 하는 것 - 을 그들에게 알려 주었다. 청교도들은 빠르게 그 요리에 의존하게 되었고 그것을 그들 자신의 요리로 채택하게 되었다. 옥수수빵 - hoecake ashcake, spidercake, 또는 johnnycake 라고 알려진 -은 다른 빵처럼 쉽게 썩지 않았기 때문에 이 시기 여행자들의 주식이 되었다. molasses를 얹어 먹게 되는 그 빵은 요리사들에게 인디언 푸딩 - 여전히 New England 지방에서 인기 있는 음식 - 에 대한 아이디어를 제공해 주었다. hominy나 grits, 그리고 succotash와 같은 일부 요리들은 여전히 미국 남부지방의 대표 요리로 꼽힌다.

> **petrify** 석질화하다, (깜짝 놀라서)돌처럼 굳다 **maize** 옥수수 열매
> **pellagra** 니코틴산 결핍 증후군 **rash** 발진, 뾰루지
> **syphilis** 매독 (신을 모독한 벌로 이병에 걸린 양치기의 이름에서 유래)
> **kernel** (밀 등의)낟알 **mound** 흙무더기, 제방, 작은 언덕
> **staple** 주요 산물, 기본 식료품, 재료 **molasses** 당밀
> **hominy** 굵게 간 옥수수(로 쑨 죽) **grit** 거칠게 찧은 곡식(특히 밀)
> **succotash** 강낭콩과 옥수수(귀리와 보리)를 끓인 콩요리

Chapter 6

Hackers Practice

1 도기류의 대부분이 모래 빛이 감도는 적색이고, 어떤 것들은 붉은 색이거나 회색이며, 극소수만이 검은색이나 검은 색으로 코팅 되어있었다. 그 그릇들은 대개 수제품으로 일부는 녹로로 정교하게 다듬어졌다. 후기에 들어 회색 도기류가 더 많이 나타났고, 도공용 녹로도 나타나게 되었다. 그 그릇들의 표면들은 무늬 없이 밋밋하고 윤이 나게 닦아지고 활시위 선, 밧줄 선, 조각한 선, 양각으로 새긴 선들 그리고 새겨진 구멍들로 장식되었다.

2 보통 죽은 물체들의 단단한 부분들만이 보존 된다(예를 들면, 무척추동물의 단단한 껍질이나 척추동물의 뼈와 이빨 등). 대개의 경우 우리는 이런 단단한 부분들만을 이용하여 화석 생물체에 관해 추론해야만 한다. 이런 어려움에도 불구하고, 한때 살아있었고, 먹이를 소비하고 산소를 흡혹하며 물리적, 생물학적 환경 등과 서로 영향을 주고받았던 생물체들로서 그들을 보다 잘 인식할 수 있도록 하기 위하여, 우리는 화석 생물체의 부드러운 부분의 해부적 구조를 이해하도록 노력해야만 하는 것이다. 화석학(Taphonomy)은 한 개체의 사망과 그 개체의 최종 발견 사이에 상실된 정보를 연구하는 과학 분야이다.

3 미국의 독특한 후보자 추천 과정은 제 3정당들에게는 부가적인 구조적 장애이다. 세계의 민주국가 중에서, 미국은 주정부 직이나 의회 직에 입후보하는 각 정당 후보들을 지명하기 위해 예비 선거에 의존하는 점, 그리고 (이러한 예비선거는) 대통령 후보 선출에 있어 주 단위로 행해지는 대통령 예비선거에도 또한 사용된다는 점에 있어, 독특하다. 대부분의 국가들에서는 당의 후보 지명이 그 당 임원회에 의해 통제된다. 그러나 미국에서는 누가 공화당과 민주당의 지명자가 될지를 최종적으로 결정하는 것은 유권자이다. 당연히 이 제도는 미국이 대부분의 다른 민주국가들 보다 더 약한 형식적인 정당의 임원회들을 가진다는 사실에 공헌한다.

4 Atoll(환상산호섬)은 수중의 휴화산 위를 중심으로 산호초와 산호초로부터 나온 침전물로 된 고리 모양의 섬이다. 환상산호섬을 짓는 산호충은 해수의 위쪽 햇볕이 드는 층에서만 살 수 있다. 그렇다면, 어떻게 그들의 골격의 잔해가 Eniwetok 환상산호섬 내에 1,280미터 깊이에서 끝났을까? 이 놀

라운 발견은 첫번째 수소 폭탄 시험 준비를 위해 천공기 구멍이 뚫리고 있던 1954년에 이루어졌다. 암판 구조 학이 해답을 제시한다.

산호충들은 그들의 죽은 조상의 해골 꼭대기에 일년에 대략 1센티미터의 속도로 축적될 수 있다. 화산의 측면에 사는 산호충들은 화산 아래의 지각이 천천히 냉각하고 수축함에 따라 위쪽으로 자라나게 되며, 그 동안 그것이 형성된 따뜻하며 확장되어가는 중심지로부터 멀리 움직여 나가게 된다. 산호 해골의 깊은 기둥은 가라앉는 속도가 일년에 대략 1센티미터 이하이면 축적될 수 있다. 그래서, 산호 기록은 과거 수백만년 동안의 암판 함몰을 추적하도록 해 주며, 암판 구조학 이론을 뒷받침한다.

5 밀워키 수공예 프로젝트는 연령이나 신체 장애로 취직이 용이하지 않은 노동자들을 채용하고자 하는 목적으로 1935년에 실험적으로 실시되기 시작했다. 그 프로젝트는 곧 번창하는 사업이 되어, 병원이나 학교와 같은 공공 단체에서 구입했던 양탄자, 휘장, 가구, 벽걸이 장식, 장난감 등을 만들도록 900여명에 이르는 노동자들을 채용하게 되었다.

6 거짓말 탐지기는 사람이 거짓말을 할 때면 일정한 양의 스트레스가 발생하는데, 그 스트레스를 몇 가지 무의식적인 생리적인 반응에 나타나는 변화를 보고 알아낼 수 있다는 이론에 바탕을 둔 것이다. 사람 몸에 부착된 여러 가지 센서를 사용하여 거짓말 탐지기는 사람들이 심문을 받는 동안 그들의 호흡, 혈압, 맥박과 땀 등에 나타나는 변화를 측정한다. 심문을 하는 동안 거짓말 탐지기 집행자는 명확한 진실 반응과 거짓 반응의 패턴을 세우기 위해 고안된 일련의 대조표준질문을 던진다. 그래서 일단 패턴이 파악되면 간간이 단편적인 보충 질문이 섞인 실제 질문이 이어지게 된다. 2시간에 걸친 심문 과정에서 그 조사 대상자가 거짓말을 하고 있는지 아닌지를 판별하게 해줄 질문의 패턴이 만들어지게 된다.

7 화성은 결코 쉬운 연구대상이 아니다. 화성은 그 직경이 지구 직경의 반이 조금 넘는 작은 세계이고, (지구와) 가장 가까울 때라도 달과의 거리의 140배 이상으로 더 가까워지지는 않는다. 더욱이, 화성 표면의 모습은 윤곽이 뚜렷하지 않아 정확하게 그 모습을 그려내기가 어렵다. 화성을 좀 더 정확히 연구하려면 완벽한 장비가 필요하고 지구 대기가 일정해야 한다.

8 포유동물이나 조류와는 달리 뱀은 음식물 소화를 통해 몸의 열을 발생시킬 수가 없다. 그러므로 뱀은 체온을 유지하기 위해 햇빛과 같은 외부의 열에 의존한다. 뱀이 먹이를 소화시킬 때나 암컷의 경우 알을 낳을 때 체온 조절이 특히 중요하다. 따라서 많은 뱀들이 먹이를 잔뜩 먹은 뒤에는 소화의 과정을 촉진시키기 위해 햇볕을 쬐는 시간을 늘린다. 그리고 몸의 열을 보존하기 위해 자신의 몸을 잔뜩 또아리 틀어 아주 작은 부분의 피부만이 찬 공기에 노출되도록 하는 것이다.

9 독수리는 한 개에서 세 개까지 알을 낳는다. 교미가 성공하고 5일에서 10일이 지나고 나면 암컷은 거위 알 크기의, 반점이 있고 누런 빛이 도는 흰색 또는 황갈색의 알을 하나 낳는다. 두 번째 알은 며칠 뒤에 낳고, 그 다음에 세 번째 알이 이어지기도 한다. 35일 간의 알 품는 역할은 암컷과 수컷이 공동으로 나누어 하게 되지만, 실제로 둥지에서 대부분의 시간을 보내게 되는 것은 암컷이다.

10 침식은 주로 흐르는 물이나 빙하, 파도, 바람 등과 같은 자연 현상에 의해 암석이나 토양이 제거되는 것을 말한다. 풍화작용에 의해 단단한 암반이 작고 움직일만한 조각으로 깨지고 나면 침식작용이 그 조각들을 쓸어 가는 것이다.

Hackers Test

1 새로운 무용을 '모던' 한 것으로 만든 것은 무용의 주제, 그리고 그 무용이 무대 위에서 내보이는 혁명적 자세와 무대 밖에서의 진보적 위치이다. 파시스트 정권(1936-1939)의 집정에 대항하는 스페인 사람들의 투쟁에 관한 이슈와 미국에서의 노동운동에 관련된 이슈는 사회의 하층계급 사람들에

관련된 전반적 관심사라는 점에 있어서 서로 연계되어 있다. 이런 점에서 새로운 무용은 1930년대의 다른 예술 양식과 비교될 수 있다. 특히 그 당시의 연극은 사회적 정치적 문제에 많은 관심을 보였다. 무대 예술의 하나인 무용도 연극과 비슷한 역할을 하였지만 그 방식은 좀 더 상징적이고 추상적인 방식이 될 수밖에 없었는데, 그것은 무용이 대개 비언어적 예술이었기 때문이었다.

마샤 그라함은 초기 작품에서 사회 문제에 대한 자신의 관심을 표출했다. 마샤는 1929년 대중 운동을 주제로 다룬 '이단자', '국민들을 위한 스케치'란 제목의 무용으로 자신만의 무용을 창조하기 시작했다. 비록 처음의 그 무용들이 비정치적이긴 했지만 분명한 사회적 메시지는 담고 있었다. 그녀 작품의 일부는 정치적이었다. 1936년에서 1939년 사이에 그녀는 프랑코 전쟁에서 스페인 국민들에 대한 지지를 표명하였다. 그라함의 '목전의 비극', '나지막한 노래'는 모두 스페인 내란에 관련된 무용으로, 스페인에 대한 공감과 사회 문제에 대한 책임을 보여주고 있다. 또한 그것은 그라함이 사회주의적 리얼리즘으로 나아가고 있다는 것을 의미했다.

30년대 초 그라함의 작품 가운데는 원시 문화에 대해 각별한 관심을 보인 작품들이 있다. 그 시기에 그녀는 뉴멕시코를 여행하는 가운데 그 지역의 미국 인디언 문화에 관심을 보였다. 그 시기에 그녀가 만들어낸 작품들이 '원시 성가(聖歌)', '원시 신비들', '주술', '돌로로사'(이상 1931), 그리고 '제식'(1932) 등으로, 이 작품들에서 그녀는 기독교 이전의 종교적 감성을 일반적으로 통용되는 양식으로 순화시켰던 것이다. 후에 그녀는 특수하게 미국의 신화적 유산을 다룬 독특한 발레 무용의 계보를 발전시키게 된다. 그 첫 작품이 '변경'이었다.

stance 발의 위치,자세,발판, 태도   fascist 국수주의자, 파시즘 신봉자
overarch ~의 위에 아치를 만들다, 아치형이 되다
heretic 이교도, 이단자   commitment 위탁, 투옥, 약속, 범행
relevance 적절, 타당(성), 관련   incantation 주문, 마법, 요술
choreography 무도법, 안무   canticle 성가, 찬송가

2 19세기 북미 고고학은 문화적, 다원주의적 진화론 그리고 이 철학의 연장선상에서 러보크의 저술의 영향을 받게 되었다. 그것은 또한 운명은 이미 결정되었다는 당시의 국가적 사고의 영향도 받았다. 19세기 이전에도 북미에 인종차별적 정서가 존재하긴 했지만, 다윈과 러보크의 저서가 그런 믿음을 정당화하고 더욱 공고화한 셈이었다. 단선적 진보라는 계몽주의 개념을 바탕으로 러보크(1834-1913)는 북미에 대한 유럽의 개입이 인간의 진보를 촉진하였다고 주장하였다. 러보크는 북미 원주민들의 "타고난 열등성"과 기타 그들의 전반적 상황을 생물학적 조건 속에 뿌리 박혀 있는 것으로 묘사하였다. 결과적으로 그러한 그의 신념들이 그곳에 정착한 팽창주의자들을 원주민 말살에 대한 책임으로부터 해방시켜 주었다. 원주민들에게 열등한 역할을 부과하는 것은 사실은 어떤 정치적 행위에서 이루어진 것이라기보다는 원주민들이 타고난 제한된 능력의 결과였던 것으로 보이게 했다.

진화론적 접근방법에 기초한 "소수민족 고고학"이 발생함에 따라 1860년대와 1870년대에 고고학과 인종학(민족학)이 한데 결합되었다. 원주민들의 "원시성"을 묘사하고 기록하는 인종학자들은 실제로 고대문화에 관해 필요한 모든 정보를 제공해 줄 수 있다. 1840년과 1914년 사이에 탐험가들과 학자들은 미국 남서부에서 발견된 많은 선사시대 유적들을 설명할 수 있는 몇 가지 문화 역사의 모델을 개발하였다. 한편 영혼 일체성이라는 계몽주의 개념에 따라 모간은 그의 저서 "고대사회" (1877)에서 전 세계의 문화 진화도를 제시하면서 유럽-미국 사회를 인류 발전의 최선두에 위치시켰다. 그가 제시한 진화의 순서는 하부/중간/상부, 즉 야만, 미개상태, 그리고 문명이라는 3단계로 구분된 발전항목을 바탕으로 한다. 모간의 견해에 따르면, 모든 신세계의 토착(원주민) 사회는 중간 단계인 미개상태를 벗어나지 못했다는 것이다. 문화 역사적 접근방법이 아직 통용되고는 있었지만 20세기 초에는 기능주의적 접근방법도 점점 추종자들이 생겨나기 시작했다. 처음에 기능주의는 도구나 공예품들이 어떻게 만들어졌는지, 무슨 용도로 만들어진 것인지에 관심을 가졌다. 말하자면, 공예품 그 자체에 대한 관심보다는 그것의 기능에 관심을 가졌다 (기능주의는 나중에 그 도구를 만든 사람들의 생활 방식에까지도 그 관심을 확대하나가게 되었다.)

racist 인종차별 주의자 inferiority 열등 unilinear 단선적인
imposition (의무, 짐, 세금 등을) 지움, 부과(물) archaeology 고고학
ethnology 민족학, 인종학 psychic 영혼의, 심령의, 정신적인
tripartite 셋으로 나누어진 savagery 야만상태, 잔인 barbarism 미개
indigenous 토착의, 그 지역고유의

3 축음기가 1877년 미국에서는 토마스 에디슨에 의해, 프랑스에서는 샤를르 크로에 의해 독자적으로
발명되긴 했지만 1920년대까지 대중음악을 확산시키는 주요 수단은 여전히 인쇄된 악보였다. 19세
기 후반 경에 음악 출판 사업은 뉴욕 시, 특히 틴 팬 엘리라 불리는 맨하탄 의 한 지역에 집중되었다.
백만 장이 팔린 최초의 대중가요는 찰스 K. 해리스의 "무도회가 끝난 뒤"(1892)였는데, 이것은 음
악 출판 사업의 급속한 성장을 촉진시켰다.
신속하게 대중 가요를 생산하도록 수 십명 단위로 작곡가들이 고용되었고, 포스터와 유원지 작곡가들
의 기법도 더욱 발전되었다. 노래가 많은 대중들에게 팔리기 위해선 단순하면서도 쉽게 기억할 수 있
고, 또 정서적으로 호소력이 있어야 했다. 보드빌(노래, 춤, 연극 등이 한데 곁들인 쇼)은 흑인 분장쇼
를 대신하여 가장 대중적인 라이브 쇼가 되었고, 알 졸슨과 소피 터커와 같은 가수들이 틴 팬 엘리에서
만들어진 노래들을 전국적으로 흥행되도록 촉진시켰다. 한편 스콧 조플린과 같은 전문 작곡가들이 쓴
랙타임 노래들은 주류 대중가요에 미친 흑인 음악의 영향의 또 다른 단계를 반영하는 것이었다.
틴 팬 엘리의 황금기는 1920년대와 30년대였다. 이 시기 가장 잘 알려진 노래들은 뉴욕 시에 기반
을 둔 소수의 작곡가들과 작사자들에 의해 창작되었다. 대부분의 경우 작곡가와 작사자는 짝을 이
뤄 함께 일했다. 조지 거쉰과 이라 거쉰, 리차드 로저스와 로렌즈 하트, 그리고 1943부터 함께 일하
기 시작한 리차드 로저스와 오스카 햄머스타인 2세가 대표적인 경우다. 틴 팬 엘리의 노래는 보드빌
의 뒤를 이은 브로드웨이 뮤지컬 코메디에서, 그리고 댄스 오케스트라와 함께 공연하는 대중가수들
에 의해 더욱 인기를 끌게 되었다.

sheet 낱장 악보 pleasure-garden 유원지, 공원 vaudeville 가벼운 회가극
minstrel show 얼굴을 거멓게 칠하여 흑인으로 분장하고 흑인 가곡 등을 부르는 쇼
lyricist 서정 시인, 작사가

4 영국 청교도단들이 미국 땅에 발을 내디디고 난 뒤 불과 몇 년이 지나지 않은 1634년에 하버드 대
학이 설립되었다. 미국 독립전쟁 이전에 부터도 이미 8개 이상의 대학들이 존재했다. 1785년 오하
이오 강과 미시시피 강 사이의 대규모 토지를 개척한 국유지 사용 규정에서는 그 토지의 16분의 1
을 공공교육 비용을 충당하기 위해 따로 떼어놓았다. 그 후, 1862년의 모릴 법령은 대규모 토지를
각 주에 기부하여 그 토지에서 발생하는 수익금으로 각 주의 농업과 기술 단과 대학의 설립 비용을
충당하게 했다. 그런 주립 단과 대학들이 그 이후 지금의 종합 대학으로 성장하게 되었다.
오늘날 미국에서 대단히 다양한 형태의 단과대학과 종합대학이 있다. 그 중에는 주 정부의 지원을
받는 대학도 있고 사립 대학도 있으며, 종교단체에서 지원 받는 대학도 있다. 이런 대학들 가운데는
일반 교양 교육에 치중하는 대학도 있고, 기술교육이나 실용교육, 전문적인 연구, 미술, 혹은 전문직
개업을 위한 준비교육 등에 초점을 맞춘 대학들도 있었다. 1900년에서 1950년 사이에 대학에 등록
한 학생 수가 10배로 증가하였으며, 그 이후 그 수는 더욱 늘어나게 되었다. 학생들은 경제적으로
사회의 다양한 계층 출신이었으며, 모든 인종을 다 망라하였다.
주 정부나 기타 정부 기관들, 특수 재단, 그리고 대학 자체에서 특수한 재능을 지닌 학생들이나 재정
적 도움이 필요한 학생들에게 많은 장학금을 수여한다. 그리고 연방정부에서는 학생들에게 교육비
용을 감당하는데 도움이 되도록 장기 대출을 제공하는 대규모 프로그램을 설립하였다. 그 목적은
그들이 처한 경제적인 상황에 상관없이 교육을 받을 의사가 있고 능력이 있는 모든 사람들에게 고
등교육을 받게 하자는 것이다.

ordinance 법령, 포고, 성찬식 tenfold 10배(겹)의, 으로

5 인구조사 (센서스)는 보통 한 국가의 인구수를 대상으로 그 정부에 의해 시행되는 공식적 통계를 지칭하는 용어이다. 인구조사는 한 국가의 총 인구수, 그리고 연령, 성, 인종 배경, 결혼여부, 소득 등 그 국민의 특성을 조사한다. 정부에서는 그 밖의 다른 형태의 센서스, 특히 경제활동과 관련된 조사를 실시한다. 경제활동 센서스의 경우는 농장, 공장, 광산, 각종 사업체 등의 수와 특징에 관한 정보를 수집한다.

세계 대부분의 국가는 정기적인 간격으로 인구조사를 실시한다. 연속되는 인구조사 결과를 비교함으로써 분석가들은 국가 전체 단위에서나 특정 지역에서 인구가 증가하는지, 안정적인지, 감소하고 있는지를 알아낼 수 있다. 또한 분석가들은 주민의 특성에서 보이는 보편적인 성향도 확인할 수 있다. 인구조사가 한 국가의 전체 인구를 조사를 목적으로 하기 때문에 실시 비용이 많이 들고 복잡한 행정 정책이며, 따라서 비교적 드물게 실시된다. 미국은 10년에 한 번 인구조사를 실시하며(10년 주기 인구조사), 캐나다는 5년에 한 번 실시한다(5년 주기 인구조사). 경제활동 조사는 보통 인구조사와는 다른 일정에 의해 실시된다.

인구조사는 보통 인구조사일(센서스 데이)라고 하는 어느 특정한 날 현재 그 국가에 살고 있는 모든 사람들의 수를 세는 것이다. 일반적으로 정부에서는 설문지를 우편이나 인구조사 요원을 통해 그 나라의 모든 가구 혹은 주거지로 보내 정보를 수집한다. 설문지를 받은 주민들은 설문지를 다 채워 다시 해당 정부기관에 보내도록 요구되며, 정부에서 그 대답을 처리하게 된다. 설문지에 응답을 하지 않은 가구들, 우편 서비스를 받지 못하는 개인들, 가령 노숙자나 먼 곳에 살고 있는 사람들의 경우는 잘 교육 받은 설문 요원들이 직접 방문한다.

martial 부부의, 결혼의 **successive** 계속적인, 연속하는 **recipient** 수령인

6 심리 테스트란 심리적인 특성이나 행동을 측정하거나 사람 능력의 특수한 측면을 연구하는 다양한 테스트 절차 모두를 말한다. 사람의 개성을 이해하고, 그 개성과 정신 이상과의 관계를 이해하려는 필요에 의해 여러 가지 테스트 형태가 나타났다.

주관 투사 테스트는 사람들이 자신의 무의식적인 태도를 어떤 애매모호한 상황에 투사하는 경향이 있다는 이론에 근거해서 개인의 특성(개성)을 측정하려고 시도한다. 이 주관 투사 테스트 가운데 가장 잘 알려진 것이 스위스의 정신병리학자인 헤르만 로르샤하(1884-1922)의 테스트로, 로르샤하는 표준화된 잉크 얼룩 그림을 이용하여 테스트 대상자들에게 그 그림을 보면 무엇이 떠오르는지 말하도록 물었던 것이다. 미국의 심리학자인 헨리 A. 머레이가 개발한 주제별 유화(類化) 테스트(TAT)는 자극적이면서도 애매모호한 일련의 표준화된 그림들을 이용하여 대상자가 그 그림에 대해 이야기를 하도록 시키는 테스트다. 각각의 이야기들은 면밀히 분석되어 마음 깊숙한 곳에 있는 욕구나 태도, 그리고 반응의 양상을 드러내게 된다.

그 밖의 다른 성격 테스트들은 테스트 대상자들의 반응을 "맞다", "틀리다", 혹은 "말할 수 없다"로 제한하는 질문지를 이용한다. 이런 테스트들은 주관 투사 테스트들 보다 훨씬 높은 수준의 표준화 정도를 지니며, 따라서 보통 〈객관〉 테스트라고도 부른다. 가장 널리 사용되는 객관 테스트의 하나는 "정상적"인 성격이 어떤 것인가를 규정하고 (그에 따라) 특정한 이상 성격을 탐지해 내기 위한 목적으로 1942년에 만들어진 (그리고 1990년대 초에 개정된) 미네소타 다면 성격 목록표(MMPI)이다. 이 테스트는 그 대상자가 정신분열증, 반사회적 성격, 우울증, 신경증 등과 같은 정신이상의 범주에 포함되는지 아닌지를 예측할 수 있도록 해주는 대략적 범주표를 만들어낸다. 이 MMPI는 정신병에 걸린 사람과 정상인을 구별하는 데는 매우 유용했으나 특정의 정신이상을 진단하는 데는 크게 도움이 되지 못했다.

projective test 투영 검사법 (도형에 대한 성격 테스트의 일종) **psychiatrist** 정신병의사(학자)
inkblot (심리테스트용의) 잉크얼룩 **thematic** 주제(논제)의, 어간의
deviance (성욕, 사회적응에서) 이상(의 행동), 일탈
schizophrenia 정신 분열증, 조발성 치매

7　보통 습한 열대지방과 관련이 있는 것으로 알려져 있지만 실제로 들소는 수세기 동안 이탈리아, 그리스, 유고슬라비아, 불가리아, 헝가리, 루마니아, 그리고 구 소비에트 연방의 아제르바이잔 공화국과 그루지아 공화국과 같은 온대지역 국가에서 사육되어 왔다. 1807년에 나폴레옹이 이탈리아산 들소를 프랑스 서남부의 랑데 지방으로 가져온 후, 몽 드 마르상 근처에 방면하였다. 그러자 이 들소들은 이내 야성을 되찾아 그 해안 지방의 숲과 모래언덕에서 엄청나게 그 수가 불어나기 시작했지만 불행하게도 그 지역 시골 농부들의 손쉬운 표적이 되고 말았으며, 급기야 나폴레옹의 몰락과 더불어 모두 식용으로 도살되고 말았다. 12세기에는 베네딕트 수도승들이 프랑스 동북부 오그에 있는 그들 수도원에서 땅을 갈도록 하기 위해, 동방에 있는 그들의 영지에서 들소를 도입하였다. 13세기에는 헨리 3세의 형제인 콘월 백작이 들소 무리를 영국에 도입하기도 했다. 프랑스나 영국에서 들소들이 얼마나 잘 견뎠는지는 알려진 바가 없다. 아무튼 들소들은 아프가니스탄이나 파키스탄 북부 산악지대에서 뿐 아니라 터키의 눈 덮인 고원에서도 잘 지내는 것으로 알려져 있다.

　들소는 일반적으로 사람들이 생각하는 것 이상으로 추위를 잘 견딘다. 오늘날 들소의 분포도를 보면 북위 45도의 루마니아까지 퍼져 있으며, 북위 40도 이상의 이탈리아와 구 소련 연방에도 상당한 수의 들소가 서식하고 있다. 필라델피아나 베이징도 비슷한 위도에 있다. 남반구에서는 케이프 타운, 부에노스아이레스, 멜버른, 그리고 뉴질랜드 북부 섬의 대부분이 위도 40도 상에 걸쳐 있다. 그러나 추운 바람과 급속한 온도 하강 등이 폐렴과 같은 병을 발생하게 하고 때로는 죽음으로도 몰아갈 수 있다. 유럽에 서식하는 들소들 대부분은 지중해 품종이지만, 다른 강 유역의 들소들(대개가 인도산 무라 종이다)이 불가리아와 구 소련연방에 유입되었는데, 이것은 강 유역의 들소들이 적어도 어느 정도 추위에 대한 내성을 가짐을 보여주는 것이다.

> **rear** 재배, 사육하다　**Azerbaijan** 아제르 바이잔(옛 소련의 한 공화국)
> **feral** 야생의, 야생적인, 흉포한　**prodigiously** 경이적으로, 엄청나게
> **littoral** 해안의, 물가에 사는, 연해지방　**plateau** 고원, 높고 편편한 땅
> **Peking** 북경　**pneumonia** 폐렴　**Mediterranean** 지중해의, (the~)지중해

8　입안 바닥에 위치한 근육 기관인 혀는 사람의 신체 가운데 지극히 많이 움직이는 구조이며, 말을 하거나 음식물을 씹고 삼키는 등의 근육 운동 기능에 있어서 아주 중요한 보조 기관이다. 뺨과 함께 혀는 음식물을 씹는 운동이 완료될 때까지 음식물을 윗니와 아랫니 사이로 몰아넣고 그 사이에 머물도록 할 수 있다. 혀의 이동성은 구강 내에 네거티브 압력(흡입력)을 생기게 하는 데에도 도움을 주어 포유동물이 젖을 빨 수 있게 한다.

　혀를 덮고 있는 점막은 매우 다양하다. 점막은 특히 말초 감각 기관으로도 중요하지만 그 안에 구강 내의 자극을 중앙 신경조직으로 전달해주는 미뢰(맛봉오리)라고 알려진 일단의 특수한 상피 세포를 포함하고 있다. 더 나아가 혀의 분비선은 음식물을 삼키는 데 필요한 타액을 생산한다.

　포유동물의 혀는 복잡하게 얽힌 줄무늬 근육 덩어리로 구성되어 있는데, (이 근육 덩어리는) 점막으로 덮여 있으며 분비선과 다양한 양의 지방이 산재해 있다. 외부로 연결된 근육에 의해 혀는 아래 턱, 설골(舌骨: 아래턱과 후두 사이의 U자 모양의 뼈), 두개골, 연구개, 그리고 인두와 연결되어 있다. 혀는 겹겹의 점막에 의해 입안 바닥과 후두개(후두의 덮개 기능을 하는 연골 판)에 부착되어 있다.

> **mastication** 씹음　**suckle** 젖을 빨다　**mucous** 점액
> **epithelial** 상피의, 피망조직의　**gland** 선, 분비 기관
> **mammalian** 포유류의 (동물)　**hyoid** 설골 (의)
> **pharynx** 인두　**epiglottis** 후두개, 회염연골
> **cartilage** 연골(조직)　**larynx** 후두　**anatomy** 해부(학), 조직

9　태양의 내부는 그 내부에서 일어나는 상이한 과정에 따라 4개의 지역으로 나뉜다. 에너지는 핵에서 발생된다. 이 에너지는 방사선(대개가 감마선과 X선)에 의해 방사권을 통과한다. 그리고 대류 이동

에 의해 가장 바깥쪽에 있는 대류권을 통과하여 외부로 확산된다. 방사권과 대류권 사이에 있는 얇은 중간층에서는 태양의 자기장이 발생하는 것으로 알려져 있다.

태양의 핵은 핵반응을 통해 수소를 연소시켜 헬륨을 만들어내는 중추 지역이다. 이런 핵반응은 마지막에는 눈에 감지되는 빛의 형태로 태양의 표면으로부터 이탈하는 에너지를 방출한다. 태양의 핵반응은 온도와 밀도에 지극히 민감하다. 개개의 수소 원자단은 두 양극 분자 사이의 반발 전기력을 극복할 수 있는 가능성을 확보할 수 있을 만큼의 충분한 에너지를 가지고 충돌해야 한다. 태양 중심의 온도는 섭씨 약 15,000,000도(화씨 27,000,000도)이며, 밀도는 약 150 g/cm3 (금이나 납의 밀도의 약 10배)이다. 태양의 중심에서 멀어질수록 온도와 밀도 모두 감소한다.

radiate 복사상의, 발산하는   convective 대류적인, 전달성의
nuclei nucleus의 복수, 핵심, 핵

10   수질 오염의 문제가 그렇게 심각한 이유 중의 하나는 물에 오염물질을 쏟아 붓는 일이 실제로는 불법이 아니라는 사실에 있다. 생활하수, 슬러지(진흙 모양의 각종 공업 폐기물), 쓰레기, 심지어 독성 오염물질까지 모두가 하천이나 강에 버려진다. 대부분 정부에서는 상관하지 않거나, 간단히 무시한다. 전 세계에 걸쳐 하수의 반 정도가 원래의 형태로 그대로 하천이나 강에 버려지고 있다. 하수를 살균하거나 특히 유해한 오염물질을 제거하는 어떤 노력도 이루어지고 있지 않는 것이다. 혹 하수를 처리한다 해도 여전히 문제가 발생한다. 처리된 하수가 슬러지로 만들어져 바다로 방출돼 버려지기 때문이다. 많은 도시나 국가에서 하수를 바다에 버리고 있다. 종종 이들은(도시나 국가들) 슬러지를 해안선에서 별로 멀지 않은 곳에 버리기 때문에, 그 쓰레기 처리 지역의 모든 해양 생물들을 죽이게 되기도 한다.

하수 이외에도 공장이나 정부에서 버리는 화학물질이 수질오염의 또 다른 주범이다. 미국 남북전쟁 이후, 수송선에서 새어 나오는 것과 같은 기름이 강이나 바다에 버려졌다. 매년 10억 톤에서 100억 톤에 이르는 기름이 선박에서 새어 나와 많은 생물들을 죽이고 그 지역의 생태계를 파괴하고 있다. 기름 제거 노력은 아직 미미하여 가장 성공적인 작업에 의해서도 버려진 기름의 약 10%만이 제거되고 있는 실정이다.

sludge 진흙, 진창 (하수 등의)찌끼   spill 흘리다, 엎지르다
amphibious 수륙 양생의

Progressive Test 2-1

1   어린이 성장발달 연구에 영향을 미치는 두 명의 주요한 이론가는 Erikson과 Piaget이다. 두 사람 다 발달은 단계적으로 발생하고 각 단계에서 개인이 다음 단계들의 과업으로 나아가기 전에 특정한 공통된 발달 과업들과 씨름을 해야 한다고 믿는다. 행동주의는 또 다른 형태의 이론이지만, 그것은 또한 영향력 있고, 때로는 유용하다.

Erikson의 인간의 8단계는 사회 심리학 영역(감정과 상호작용과 관련 있는)을 포함하고, 프로이드 설(정신분석학)을 보통 사람들이 이해할 수 있는 것으로 변화시킨다. Erikson은 발달이론을 성인기까지 확대시킨 첫번째 사람이고, 또한 양육에서의 문화적 차이들이 성인의 성격 패턴에 영향을 미칠지 모르는 방식에 관심을 가졌다. Erikson은 성장발달의 8단계가 있고, 각각의 단계에서 개인은 유익한 방법과 유익하지 않은 방법 중 한가지로 해결해야만 하는 심각한 사회 심리적 갈등에 직면한다는 것을 이론화한다. 예를 들어, 유아기에, 아이의 갈등은 신뢰와 불신과 관계 있고, 이것의 해결에 인격 발달의 나머지 부분이 의존한다. Erikson의 생각은 지극히 상식적이고 이해하기 쉽다.

Piaget의 지적발달의 단계들은 아이들이 어떻게 생각하는가 특히, 논리, 수학, 공간 관계의 문제들에 대해서 어떻게 생각하는가와 관련이 있다. 그는 어린시절(그리고 그 이후에) 내내, 개인은 환경

과의 수많은 상호작용을 통해, 우리 모두가 공유하는 인간 지식의 나름대로의 변형을 형성한다고 믿었다. Piaget는 자신의 아이들을 특히 유아기 때 많이 관찰했고, 좀 더 나이든 아이들과 인터뷰를 하여 그들이 어떻게 생각하고 있는지를 알아냈다. Piaget의 견해를 이해하기란 다소 어렵지만, 부모가 가장 좋아하는 활동인 아이들 관찰에 적용될 때 그 견해는 상당히 흥미롭다.

행동주의는 동물행동을 관찰한 것들에 기초해 있고, 연속적인 행동들과 그것들이 어떻게 다음으로 이어지는가 만을 보면서, 내적인 것에 개의치 않고 아이들의 행동들을 설명하려고 시도한다. 강화와 처벌의 개념들은 우리 모두가 때때로 도움을 필요로 하는 것인 단련의 문제들을 어떻게 다룰 것인지를 이해하는데 있어서 중요하다.

2 산업시대가 막 시작되려는 시점에서, 고래는 인간이 수 세기 동안 이용해 온 중요한 천연 자원이었다. 고래는 특히 그 기름이 가치가 있었는데 주로 램프의 연료로 사용되었다. **그것은 또한 난방과 윤활제, 비누, 페인트, 광택제 제조와 직물과 밧줄의 가공에 또한 사용되었다.** 표준 고래 기름인 "train oil(경유)"은 고래 몸체를 싸고있는 지방으로부터 추출되었다. 그러나 최고의 기름은 향유고래의 코에서만 발견되는 경랍이었다. 그것은 공기에 노출되면 응고되고, 지금까지 만들어진 가장 좋은 질의 양초라고 간주되는 그을음 없는 양초에 사용되었다.

또한, 향유고래는 때때로 용연향(고래의 내장으로부터 나오는, 향수를 제조하는데 쓰이는 끈적끈적한 물질)을 만들어냈다. 고래수염과 대부분의 고래(향유고래를 제외한)의 입안의 뼈 같은 플랑크톤을 분리하는 갈빗대는 무게가 가벼웠고 신축성이 좋았다. 그것은 코르셋 지지물, 우산 대, 낚싯대, 4륜 마차의 채찍, 운반차량 용수철, 스커트 버팀대를 포함한 다양한 물건들을 위해 사용되었다. 몸에서 나온 뼈는 일반적으로 비료로 사용되었다.

고래잡이는 19세기 주요 산업이었으며, 미국은 최고의 포경 국가였다. 구전에 의하면, 미국의 상업적 고래잡이는 뉴 잉글랜드에서 1712년에 시작했다. 고래잡이는 18세기 내내 팽창했으나, 미국혁명과 나폴레옹 전쟁으로 인해 중단되었다. 1815년에 평화가 찾아왔고 산업의 급속한 성장이 이루어졌다. 1833년까지 392척의 미국 포경선이 있었다. 1846년까지 전 세계 포경선의 80%를 차지하는 735척의 포경선이 있었다. 해마다 포경업은 향유고래 기름 4백만에서 5백만 갤론, 경유 6백만에서 천만 갤론, 그리고 뼈 1백 60만에서 5백 60만 파운드를 생산했다. 경유의 가격은 1825년 1갤론당 35센트에서 1855년 95센트로 상승했다.

3 1920년대와 1930년대의 유행하는 스타일이었던 Art Deco는 빌딩, 가구, 보석 그리고 인테리어 장식의 디자인에 주로 사용되었다. Art Deco는 매끄러운 유선의 형태, 기하학적 패턴, 금속, 플라스틱, 유리와 같은 산업 재료를 이용한 실험으로 특징지어 진다. Art Deco라는 용어는 1925년에 열린 중요한 파리 디자인 전시회의 명칭인 "현대 산업 장식 예술 국제 박람회"를 줄인 것이다. **거기서 처음으로 그 스타일이 명확하게 드러났다.** Art Deco는 빠르게 미국에서 지지를 얻었고, 건축 특히, Chrysler, Daily News, Empire State 빌딩과 같은 1920년대 후반과 1930년대 초반의 뉴욕의 높게 치솟은 마천루들에 있어 그것의 성취의 절정에 도달했다. 많은 Art Deco 빌딩들은 대공황으로 알려진 경제적 붕괴 기간동안 세워졌기 때문에, 그 스타일은 때때로 "depression moderne"으로 알려져 있다.

Art Deco는 정교하게 굽은 모양과 20세기 초 건축과 디자인 분야에서 만연했던 스타일인 Art Nouveau의 식물 같은 주제를 단순화하려는 의식적인 노력으로부터 성장했다. Art Deco는 추상과 형태의 반복을 향한 art nouveau 경향을 유지했지만, 예전 스타일의 형태와 주제로부터 멀어졌다. Art Deco 디자인의 명확한 선, 유선, 균형은 일상생활에서 산업상품의 중요성의 증가와 기계류의 미에 있어서 현대 예술가들과 디자이너들 사이에 일치하는 관심을 반영한다. Art Deco 대상물들은 보통 대량생산 되지 않았지만, 그것들 중 상당수가 대량생산에 속하는 단순성, 단조로운 반복, 기하학적인 패턴과 같은 특징을 가진다. 디자이너들은 실용적인 물건보다는 예술을 위한 영감으로서 산업상품을 보기 시작했다.

4　1800년대 초기, 몇몇 일간지가 해안가 도시에 있긴 했지만, 대부분의 신문들은 주간지였다. 신문에는 상업적인 것과 정치적인 것, 이렇게 두 가지 유형이 있었다. 상업신문과 정치신문 둘 다 값이 비쌌고 대략 6센트 정도로 팔렸다. 사람들은 그것을 길거리에서 살 수 없었고, 대신 1년 구독료를 지불해야 했다. 이것은 상인과 정치 엘리트만이 신문을 살 수 있었다는 것을 의미했다. 이 때문에, 뉴스는 정치, 사업 그리고 항구에 있는 배의 입출항에 초점을 두었다. 그리고 나서, 1830년대(캐나다는 1870 ~1880년대에 가까워서)쯤에 penny 신문은 뉴스가 생산, 분배, 소비되는 방식을 개혁했다.

Penny 신문은 수입을 정기구독과 정치기금에 의존하는 대신에 광고에 의존하는 쪽을 선택했다. 그래서, 그들은 단지 1 페니로 대중에게 그들의 신문 판을 제공할 수 있었고, 길거리에서 그들의 신문을 팔았다.

보다 많은 사람들이 이제는 신문을 살 수 있었기 때문에, penny 신문사는 모든 유형의 독자에게 무언가를 제공하기 위해 노력해야만 했다. 그래서 일상 생활에 대한 최신 뉴스를 찾아 내기 위해 리포터를 고용하기 시작했다. 이 때문에, 뉴스의 중점은 지방의 사건들로 그 방향이 바뀌었고, 신문은 노동계층의 흥미를 불러일으킬 삽화, 생활양식 조언, 그리고 다른 것들을 포함하기 시작했다. 뉴스들은 또한 비록 덜 다채롭지는 않았지만 덜 정치적이 되었는데, 이것은 Penny 신문이 어떠한 정당과 특별 관계를 맺는 것을 거절했기 때문이다. 이러한 결과의 상당부분이 그들이 광고주들을 끌어들이기 위해서는 대규모의 독자들을 필요로 하고, 다른 정치적 신념을 가진 누군가를 성나게 하는 것을 감당할 수 없었기 때문이었다. 또한 부분적으로는 사람들이 신문은 정치적인 영향력으로부터 자유로워야 한다고 믿었기 때문이었다. 이 시기는 현대 언론계와 저널리즘의 시초였다.

Progressive Test 2-2

1　좋든 나쁘든, 마천루는 건축에 있어서 미국의 선물이다. 이러한 종류의 건축은 가볍지만 튼튼한 철강 구조물을 세울 수 있게 되고, 강력한 엘리베이터가 발전된 후에 가능하게 되었다. **또한 콘크리트와 판유리도 그러한 높은 구조물들의 건축에 있어서 중요한 역할을 한다.**

마천루의 개척자적인 건축가, Louis Sullivan은 1884년 시카고에 첫번째 빌딩을 건설했다. 곧 뉴욕에서 그것들을 건축하기 시작했고, 중요하게 생각되기를 희망하는 모든 도시뿐만 아니라 모든 큰 도시가 곧 뒤를 따라 똑같이 했다. 마천루의 수가 증가함에 따라, 몇몇 뉴욕 중심가는 높은 벽들 사이의 깊은 협곡을 닮기 시작했다. 그래서 도시 법이 통과 되었는데, 그것은 고층 건물들의 상층들은 얼마간의 빛과 공기가 길까지 올 수 있도록 떨어져 있어야만 한다고 규정한다. 그 결과, 뉴욕은 매우 흥미로울 뿐만 아니라 독특한 윤곽을 가지고있다. 비록 마천루들이 도시의 혼잡과 추가적인 직장과 생활 공간을 위한 필요성 때문에 높이 지어졌지만, 그것들은 작은 영역들로 많은 수의 사람들을 끌어 들이기 때문에 실제로는 혼잡을 더 악화시켰다.

미국의 현대 건축은 다른 창조적인 스타일을 생산해왔다. 아마도 가장 유명한 것은 20세기 초반의 Frank Lloyd Wright의 작품일 것이다. Wright는 흥미롭고 특이한 재료를 사용하고 각각의 구조물이 주변 환경과 조화되도록 만들려고 노력하면서, 많은 독창적인 공공 건물과 집을 디자인했다. 그의 아이디어는 오늘날의 건축에 크게 영향을 미쳤다.

2　1610년, 그의 새로운 망원경을 가지고 태양을 본 이후 얼마 지나지 않아, Galileo Galilei는 유럽에서 최초로 태양흑점을 관찰했다. 매일매일의 관측이 1749년 Zurich 관측소에서 시작되었고, 다른 관측소들이 더해져서, 1849년 이래로 계속적인 관측이 이루어졌다. 태양흑점 수는 처음 태양흑점 집단들의 수를 세고 나서 개개의 태양 흑점 수를 셈으로써 계산되어진다. "태양흑점 수"는 개개의 태양 흑점 수와 집단들 수의 10배의 총계로 결정된다. 대부분의 태양흑점 집단들은 평균적으로 10개 정도의 점을 가지고 있기 때문에, 태양흑점을 세는 데 있어 이러한 공식은 관찰 조건이 덜 이상적이고 작은 흑점은 보기가 어려울 때 조차도 믿을 만한 수치들을 제공한다. 태양 흑점 수의 월 평균들

(매달 갱신되는)은 태양 표면에 보이는 태양 흑점의 수가 대략 11년 주기로 증가하고 감소함을 보여준다.

태양 흑점의 초기 기록은 태양이 17세기 후반에 비활동성의 기간을 거쳤다는 것을 알려준다. 대략 1645년부터 1715년까지 매우 적은 흑점들이 관찰되었다. 비록 그 관측들이 나중에 행해진 것 만큼 광범하지 않았지만, 태양은 사실상 이 시기동안 잘 관찰되었고 이러한 태양 흑점의 부족은 문서로 잘 증명된다. 이러한 태양의 비활동 기간은 또한 평상시 얼음이 없는 강이 얼고 눈 쌓인 들판이 낮은 고도에서 1년 내내 그대로였던 때인 "Little Ice Age"라고 불리는 기후상의 기간과 일치한다. 태양이 더 먼 과거에 유사한 비활동성 기간들을 가졌다는 증거가 있다: 몇몇 중국인들은 맨눈으로 태양 흑점들을 관찰했다. 태양활동과 지구상의 기후 사이의 연관성이 계속 진행 중인 연구 분야이다.

태양흑점의 세부적인 관찰들이 1874년 이래로 Royal Greenwich 관측소에 의해 이루어졌다. **이러한 관찰들은 그들의 숫자 뿐만 아니라 태양 흑점의 위치와 크기에 관한 정보도 포함한다.** 이러한 자료는 태양흑점은 태양 표면 위에 무작위로 나타나는 것이 아니라 적도 양쪽 부분에 두 위도의 띠에 집중된다는 것을 보여준다. 1874년 5월 이래로 태양이 자전하는 동안 흑점의 위치를 보여주는 나비 꼴의 도표(매달 갱신되는)는 이러한 띠가 중간 위도에서 처음 형성되고, 확장되며, 각 주기가 진행되면서 적도 쪽으로 이동함을 보여준다.

3 고고학의 연구는 고대로 거슬러 올라간다. 최초로 알려진 고고학적 탐험 중 하나는 B.C 556년부터 539년까지 바빌론의 통치자 Nabonidus에 의한 Shipper에 있는 Shamath 사원의 발굴이었다. 그 유적은 작업이 끝난 후 바빌론의 박물관에 진열되었다. 그리스인과 로마인 같은 다른 고대 민족들은 그들 자신의 조상에 대해 알기 위해 고대의 매장 터들을 발굴했다. 그러나 로마의 몰락 후, 고고학에 대한 흥미는 암흑시대가 과거에 그림자를 던지면서 줄어들었다. 중세 동안, 고고학 연구는 중단되었다. 역사는 거의 완전히 성경에 기초하게 되었고, 많은 사람들이 발견된 유물들이 대지에 의해 자연스럽게 생겨나고 초자연적 현상에 의해 거기에 놓이게 되었다라고 믿었다.

15세기가 되어서야 르네상스와 더불어 과거에 대한 연구가 부활되었다. 지식인들은 로마와 그리스에 대한 지식을 다시 얻기를 희망했고, 부유한 상인들과 왕자들은 과거의 유물들을 가지고 그들의 동료와 신하들을 감동시키기를 원했다. 최초의 주요 발견들 중에 몇몇은 A.D 79년에 Mt. Vesuvius에 의해 파괴된 Pompeii 와 Herculaneum의 연구조사 였다. 이집트는 항상 매혹적이었지만, 나폴레옹 군대의 침입기간에 Rosetta 석이 발견될 때까지 이러한 고대문화는 조용히 묻혀 있었다. 16세기의 유럽에서, Stonehenge와 같은 거석으로 된 구조물들이 그것들의 쓰임을 결정하기 위해 연구되었다. 르네상스가 고고학의 부활을 나타냈지만, 19세기가 되어서야 그 분야는 우리가 지금 알고 있는 것과 같은 과학이 되었다.

A.H Pitt-Rivers는 학문 분야로써 고고학의 정립에 책임이 있는 몇 사람들 중의 하나이다. Pitt-Rivers 그와 같은 사람들 이전에, 고고학은 과학이라기보다 보물사냥에 더 가까웠다. 19세기 중반, 후반 동안, Pitt-Rivers와 다른 사람들은 (발견물의)분류 목록과 자세한 관찰 그리고 오랜 기간의 보존에 대한 중요성을 증명했다. 그는 또한 드문 물건들보다 일상적인 것들이 문화에 대해 더 많이 보여준다고 느꼈기 때문에, 아름답고 특이한 유물보다 작은 세부 사항들과 인공 유물들에 더 초점을 맞추었다. 큰 유물들이 중요하지만, 고고학의 진정한 목적은 고대인들이 어떻게 살았나를 발견하는 것이다. 항아리, 공구, 아이들의 장난감 그리고 무기와 같은 모든 물품들은 고고학자들이 고대 문명의 삶은 어떠했는가를 결정하는 데 이용하는 일반 대중의 중요한 외관들이다.

Pitt-Rivers의 방식은 오늘날 여전히 이용되고 있으며 고고학 분야의 표준이다. 고고학의 중요한 부분은 한 문명이 다른 문명과 연계되어 살았을 때인 과거의 순서이다. 이것을 결정하기 위해, "시대"의 체계가 사용되었다. 이 시스템은 고대 로마인들에 의해 발전되었고, 오늘날 고고학자와 역사가들은 여전히 그것을 사용한다. 그 다양한 시대들은 세 개의 주요 시대, 석기, 청동기, 철기로 나누어진다. 새로운 문명들이 발견될 때, 그것들은 이러한 다양한 시대 중 하나에 맞춰질 수 있다. 오늘날까지, 시간에 대한 이러한 분할의 경계는 새로운 유물과 증거로 인해 변화하고 있다.

4   미국 까마귀의 가장 명확한 특징들은 크기가 크고, 검정 색이며, 많은 소음을 낸다는 것이다. 까마귀들이 내는 가장 분명한 소리는 영어에서 "까악까악(caw)"으로 쓰여지는 것이다. 까악까악 소리는 다양한 환경에 따라 길거나 짧을 수도 있고, 크거나 비교적 부드러울 수도 있으며, 한번 또는 연속해서 울 수도 있고, 한 마리가 혼자 울거나 두 마리나 그 이상의 새들이 울 수도 있다. 까마귀의 까악까악 소리는 듣는 사람에 따라 다르게 들릴 수도 있다. 제한된 영역 안에 있는 까마귀의 같은 무리 내에서도 까악까악 소리가 듣는 사람에게 어떻게 들리느냐에 상당한 다양함이 있을 수 있고, 또한 미국의 서로 다른 지역의 까마귀들은 서로 다른 소리를 낸다는 것도 자주 언급되었다.

그 특징적인 까악까악 소리와 더불어, 까마귀는 또한 사람 말의 요소들을 포함하여 다른 종들의 소리를 모방하는 (그러나 그것에만 제한되어 있지는 않은) 것 등의 다양한 다른 소리들을 만들어 낸다. 특히 흥미를 끄는 것은 위의 범주들에 들어맞지 않는 다양한 다른 까마귀 발성법은 꽤 낮은 음량이고, 혼자 또는 까마귀 무리에 의해 사용될 지 모른다는 것이다.

수세기에 걸쳐 관찰자들은 까마귀들이 특정한 환경 하에서 특정한 소리를 사용한다는 것에 주목해 왔다. **경보 소리, 집합호출 소리, 조난 소리, 그리고 많은 다른 것들이 관찰되어졌다.** 그러나, 이러한 울음소리들을 해석하는데 한가지 문제는 같은 종에 속하지만 다른 지리적 영역에 분포하는 까마귀의 서로 다른 집단들이 같은 울음소리 모두를 사용하거나 이해하지 못할지 모른다는 사실이었다.

예를 들어, Hubert와 Mable Frings (1959)는 펜실베니아에서 자라고, 남부의 물고기 까마귀 사이에서 겨울을 보내는 미국의 동부 까마귀들이 그들 영역의 어느 부분도 원산지로 하지 않는 동족의 새인 프랑스 갈가마귀의 조난 소리에 반응할 것이라는 사실을 주목했다. 하지만, 메인 주에서 자라고 분명히 다른 까마귀들과 결코 섞이지 않는 동부 까마귀들은 갈가마귀의 울음 소리에 반응하지 않는다.

Chapter 7

Hackers Practice

1   비록 그들이 땅 위의 주거지로 이동했지만 Pueblo 부족들은 원형 지하 구조를 kiva 즉 종교의식의 장소 – 종교 지도자들이 그 땅으로 내려와 신성시되는 동물 종이나 조상의 영혼과 교통을 하는 곳 – 로써 계속 사용했다. Mesa Verde에 있는 절벽 주거지들은 땅 위의 Pueblo의 생활 장소와 kiva로 이루어 졌다. 사다리를 통해서 들어갈 수 있는 kiva의 지붕은 지상에서 공공 광장으로 이용되어졌다. 여기서 남성과 여성, 아이들은 서로 교제하고 노동을 하며 음식을 준비하기도 했다. 그러나 건축 역사가들은 이러한 안마당 또한 도시의 공연장 – 그 부족을 이끄는 남성들이 갑자기 땅 아래로부터 나타나 kiva의 연기구멍으로부터 위로 올라 신의 창조행위를 재연하는 곳인 – 으로 생각했다.

2   19세기 중반 이전에 미국에 있는 사람들은 제철 음식만을 먹었다. 건조, 훈제, 염장으로 단기간동안 육류를 보존할 수 있었지만 신선한 고기를 얻기가, 신선한 우유를 얻는 것과 마찬가지로, 매우 제한적이어서 부패를 막을 방법이 없었다. 그러나 1810년에 Nicolas Appert라는 이름의 한 프랑스 발명가가 통조림의 조리-밀폐 제조 과정을 개발하였다. 그리고 1850년대에 Gail Borden이라는 이름의 한 미국인이 우유를 응축시켜 보존하는 방법을 개발하였다. 통조림 제품과 응축 우유는 1860년대 동안 보급되긴 했지만 공급량이 낮았다. 왜냐하면 캔이 손으로 만들어져야만 했기 때문이다. 그러나 1880년 까지는 발명가들이 양철판으로 캔을 대량 생산하는 압형 납땜기를 개발하였다.

3   1900년대 후기에 영화 산업은 심각한 위기를 맞게 되었다. 5센트 짜리 극장의 성장으로 영화를 상영하는 극장들의 수가 급속도로 많아져 그 결과 제작자들이 그 수요를 충족시킬 수 없게 되었다. 바로 아래 구역의 경쟁자와 같은 영화를 상영할 수 밖에 없게 되자 극장 소유자들은 그들의 상품을 차별화하기 위해 음향 실행으로 관심을 돌렸다. 예전의 영화들이 보더빌(가벼운 희극) 오케스트라나 미숙한 피아니스트 혼자 간헐적으로만 나오거나 혹은 음악이 전혀 없기도 했던 곳에

서 이제 영화관의 경영자는 음악을 통해 그들 시설물의 격조를 높이려고 애를 썼다. 대중음악과 래그타임은 피하고 대신 극장들은 점차 재능있는 음악가에 의해 공연되는 가벼운 클래식 반주에 주안점을 둔다.

4 Milwankee의 신문기자이자 시인, 발명가이기도 한 Christopher L. Sholes는 S&G의 주요 고안자였다. 이 기계는 오직 대문자로만 타이프되었고 QWERTY 키보드를 도입했었는데 그것은 오늘날 우리에게 매우 일반적인 것이다. 그 키보드는 자주 쓰여지는 타이프바 짝들을 서로 떼어 놓기 위해서 고안되어진 것 같다, 그 타이프바들이 프린팅 지점에서 서로 부딪쳐 엉키지 않도록. 그 결과 S&G는 채색된 꽃들과 도안의 전사 인쇄를 자랑으로 삼는 장식적인 기계였다. Remington 병기 회사의 재봉틀 부서에서 그것을 제조했다. Sholes & Glidden은 얼마 안 되는 성공을 거두었지만 그것의 계승자 Remington은 곧 그 산업에서 주요한 존재로 자리 잡았다.

5 퀼트는 고대로부터 기원한다. 중국인과 러시아인, 그리고 중앙 아메리카의 원주민 보온과 방어를 위해 누빈 의복을 입었다. 서 유럽으로부터 온 십자군들은 그들이 팔레스타인 성지에서 사라센 사람을 만났을 때 우연히 누빈 천을 보게 되었다. 사라센 보병들은 갑옷 대신에 짚으로 채워진 누빈 캔버스 셔츠를 입었고 기수는 그들의 갑옷이 쓸려서 아프게 하는 것을 막기 위해 누빈 실크 속옷을 사용했다. 십자군은 그 아이디어를 얻어 유럽으로 돌아갔고, 그것을 잠옷이나 속옷에 적용시켰다. 퀼트에 대한 기록은 12세기부터 나타났다. 썩기 쉬운 물질로 만들어졌기 때문에 초기의 퀼트는 거의 남아 있지 않다.

Hackers Test

1 지구의 크기 - 대략 직경 12,750km - 는 고대 그리스인에 의해서 알려졌다. 하지만 20세기의 전환기가 되어서야 우리의 행성이 크게 지각, 맨틀, 핵 3가지 주요 층으로 구성되어 있다는 것을 과학자들은 확신하게 되었다. 이렇게 층으로 이루어진 구조는 마치 삶은 계란의 구조에 비유될 수 있다. 가장 바깥 층인 지각은 딱딱하고 다른 두개와 비교해서 상당히 얇다. 해양 아래의 지각은 두께가 거의 변화하지 않는데, 일반적으로 대략 5km 정도까지 이른다. 대륙 아래의 지각의 두께는 좀 더 변화가 심한데 평균 30km정도 된다. 그러나 Alps나 Sierra Nevada와 같은 큰 산맥 아래에 있는 지각의 기저부분은 100km 까지 달한다. 계란의 껍질처럼 지구의 지각도 취성(깨지기 쉬운 성질)이며, 부서지기 쉽다.
지각 밑에는 맨틀 - 대략 2900km 정도 두께의 높은 밀도의 뜨거운 준고체 암석층 - 이 있다. 지각보다 더 많은 철, 마그네슘, 칼슘을 함유하고 있는 맨틀은 더 뜨겁고 더 밀도가 높은데 이유는 지구 내부의 온도와 압력은 깊이에 따라 증가하기 때문이다. 비유적으로 보면, 맨틀은 삶은 계란의 흰자로 생각될 수 있다. 지구의 중앙부분에는 맨틀보다 두 배 정도로 밀도가 높은 - 그 구성이 암석성이기 보다는 금속성 (철-니켈 합금)이기 때문에 - 핵이 위치해 있다. 하지만 계란의 노른자와는 달리 지구의 핵은 실제로 두 개의 다른 부분 - 2200km 두께의 액체로 된 외핵과 1250km 두께의 고체로 된 내핵 - 으로 구성되어 있다. 지구가 자전 할 때, 액체로 된 외핵은 회전하여 지구의 자기장을 형성하게 된다.

yolk 노른자위, 양털기름

2 미국시민이 특허권을 추구할 권리는 미국의 헌법으로 부터 나온다. 실제로 헌법은 사람들에게 특허권을 얻을 권리를 명시적으로 부여하고 있지는 않고 다만 국회가 발명자들에게 그들의 발명품에 대한 권리를 줄 것이라고만 말하고 있다. 그러나 그것이 단지 제안에 불과하였더라도 헌법에 의해 정해진 제안이므로 국회는 특허를 주기 위해서 어떠한 유형의 조직을 세워야 한다는 의무감을 느꼈다. 이것 때문에, 국회는 Thomas Jefferson, Henry Knox, Edmund Randolph로 구성된 최초의

특허청을 설립했다. 그것이 약 200년 전이었고, 그 이후로 미국은 계속해서 특허권을 주고 있다.

초기의 특허청은 미국이 근본적으로 농업 사회였으므로 그렇게 분주하지는 않았고, 과학과 기술은 부유하고, 잘 교육 받은 유럽인들과 항상 그렇듯이 군인들에게 할당된 영역이었다. 그러나 그 모든 것이 산업혁명과 함께 변했다. 19세기 기업들은 그들이 시장을 지배하고 경쟁자들을 견제하는 데 도움이 되는 특허권에 많은 비중을 두었다. 예를 들어 1870년대의 Great Telegraph Wars에서 자본가 Cornelius Vanderbilt와 Jay Gould는 그 산업에서 가장 가치 있는 자산 - Thomas Edison의 전보 특허권 - 을 장악하기 위해 무자비한 계획을 세움으로써 모든 법적, 재정적, 경쟁적인 공격을 서로에게 퍼부었다. 이들 둘 다 막대한 부가 이러한 특허권에 좌우된다는 것을 알고 있었고, 당연히 그러했다.

이와 유사하게, RCA(Radio Corporation of America)는 Marconi와 다른 라디오 개척자의 특허권을 구매했고 라디오 방송의 특허를 장악함으로써 수백만 달러를 벌었다. 1920년대 동안 RCA는 텔레비전의 특허권을 따내기 위해 무자비한 전쟁을 치뤘지만 궁극적으로는 Philo Farnsworth를 원발명자이며 진정한 특허권의 소유자로 인정해야만 했다.

미국 제조업의 갑작스럽고 거대한 부와 그 보호 조치들 - 특허권이 이런 산업들에게 제공한 - 이 부유하고 교육 받은 유럽인들의 눈에 띄지 않을 수 없었다. 이들은 산업이 미래라는 것 그리고 이 미래를 손에 넣을 수 있는 새로운 유럽 노동자 계층이 형성되고 있다고 보았다. 이런 새로운 유럽인 계층은 희망과 총명한 아이디어로 가득 차 있는 공학자와 기술자(소수의 화학자 포함)로 구성되었다. 그 일류들은 즉시 업무에 착수하여 그들의 변호사와 대리인들에게 법이 두 가지 - 첫째는 이 새로운 유럽인 노동자 계층의 가치 있는 아이디어와 발명품들을 보호하는 것이고 더 중요시 되었던 두 번째는 새로운 노동자 계층이 실제로 어떠한 가치를 소유하지 않도록 이러한 특허권이 즉시 기술자를 고용한 회사의 재산이 되도록 하는 것 - 를 수행하기 위해 적용될 수 있는 지를 확인하라고 요청하였다. 이번에는 일본 또한 기술의 성장과 방위산업체의 성장을 육성하기 위해 미국 방식의 특허청을 채택했다.

dominion 지배(통치)권, 주권   **scheme** 계획하다, 음모를 꾸미다.
aristocracy 귀족, (각 분야의) 일류의 사람들

3 Samuel F. B. Morse는 미국 예술가들을 "카메라의 상을 맞출 수 있는" 그 광학적, 화학적 과정을 받아들이도록 이끌었다. 르네상스 이래로 예술가들은 이 "어두운 작은 방" 또는 상자에 대해서 알고 있었는데, 그것은 외부의 상을 내부의 표면으로 투사할 수 있는 것이었다. 그러나 19세기까지 예술가들은 그것을 손으로 그림으로써만 그 자연적인 상을 보존할 수 있었다. Morse는 젊은 시절, 예일대 학생이었을 때 그가 그 카메라 상을 실험했던 것을 회상한다. 그는 "질산은 용액에 담금"으로써 빛에 대해 고감도로 만들어진 종이의 사용을 통해 카메라 상들을 영구적으로 만들기를 시도하였다. 그러나 그는 절망스럽게도 명암 부분이 마지막 결과물에서 뒤바뀐 것을 알게 되었다. 즉, 빛 부분은 어두웠고 어두운 부분은 밝았다. Morse는 음화 상을 만들어냈지만 음화필름이 양화 사진 인화지를 만드는데 사용될 수 있다는 것을 알지 못했다.

그의 인생 후반기에, 그는 국립 디자인 학술원의 대표가 된 이후 Morse는 파리의 예술가이자 발명가인 Louis Jacques Mande Daguerre - 그의 은판 사진 과정에 광택이 나고 감광성인 금속판을 사용하여 빛과 어두운 부분이 바뀌지 않는 양화를 만들어 냈던 - 를 만났다. 가열된 수은에서 발산된 증기를 사용하여 Daguerre는 표면에 드러나지 않은 (숨어있는) 상을 "드러나게 한" 필름 판을 발명하여 남아있는 감광염을 씻어냄으로서 그것을 고정했으며 그리고 나서 그 판을 빛과 어둠의 대비와 그 상의 내구성을 높이기 위해 금 염화물로 조색했다. 그러한 은판의 깨지기 쉬운 성질과 변색되는 경향 때문에 은판은 유리 덮개로 더욱 보호되어야 했다. 그럼에도 불구하고 Daguerre는 Morse를 놀라게 했던 깨끗하고 세밀한 사진을 고안해 냈다.

daguerreotype 은판사진(으로 찍다)   **chloride** 염화물

4　오염이 산림에 피해를 주긴 하지만 핵 공격과 낙진은 훨씬 더 많은 손상을 준다. 소나무는 후에 딱딱하게 굳어 호박이 될 송진을 배출시킴으로써 손상으로부터 스스로를 지킨다. 세계 몇몇 지역에서 발견되는 많은 양의 호박은 방사능이나 오염이 소나무 숲에 손상을 가해 그 나무들로 하여금 엄청난 양의 자연적 방어 물질을 배출하게 했다는 것을 설명해준다.

체르노빌원전 참사 이후, 침엽수림에 가해지는 낙진의 영향을 연구하는 과학자들은 그 나무들이 위험한 방사성 세슘을 빠르게 흡수하여 그것을 그들의 나무 내부로 통합시킨다는 것을 알아냈다. 뿌리 시스템 - 세슘이 천천히 땅으로 가라앉아 그것이 이런 식으로 흡수되기 시작하는데 25년 이상 걸린 - 에 의해서가 아니라 소나무 잎이 직접 방사능 물질을 흡수한다. 그래서 방사능 세슘은 소나무 잎을 통해 급속히 흡수되고 훨씬 천천히 뿌리를 통해 흡수되어 그 나무에 장기간 심각한 스트레스를 입히게 된다. 반드시 나무를 죽이는 것은 아닐 지라도. 결국 나무가 죽게 되었을 때, 수명이 긴 동위체는 흙으로 돌아가 다음 세대에도 계속해서 손상을 주게 된다. 호박은 다양한 연대에서 기원하고 있다. Baltic 호박은 대략 삼천만년 전인 점신세(Oligocene: 지질학에서 규정되는 시대)로 거슬러 올라가지만 5500만년 전인 시신제(Eocene) 시기라고도 알려졌다. 체코슬로바키아의 호박 Valchovite는 공룡이 멸종한 시기인 후기 백악기시대로 거슬러 올라간다.

방사성 방출물은 보존된다. Charles Sternberg에 의해 발견된 공룡 미라 hadrosaur는 6천 5백만년 전에 죽었고, 손상되지 않은 채 등을 대고 누워있으며 포식자나 청소 동물들이 그것을 손댔다는 어떤 증거도 보이지 않았다. 그것이 썩지도 않고 먹히지도 않은 것은 이상한 일이다. 추측컨대 태양에 의해 건조되어 재빨리 하류로 씻겨 내려가 고운 진흙으로 신속하게 덮여서 그것의 건조한 표피에 물이 다시 들어오거나 썩을 시간이 없었던 것이다. 공룡 미라는 드물지만, 발견된 것들은 보통 후기 백악기 시대의 공룡이다.

> **fallout** 낙진, 결과　**exude** 스며 나오다, 발산하다　**resin** 송진, 합성수지
> **amber** 호박(색)의　**coniferous** 구과를 맺는, 구과 식물의, a ~ tree 침엽수의
> **cesium** 세슘　**isotope** 동위 원소　**Baltic** 발트해(의), 발트해 연안 제국의
> **Oligocene** 점신세(의)　**Eocene** 제 3기의, 시신세의　**Cretaceous** 백악기(층,계)(의)
> **scavenger** 썩은 고기를 먹는 청소 동물(독수리, 게, 개미 등), 폐품 수집자, 살균 소독제
> **rehydrate** 수화하다, (건조식품을) 원상으로 돌아가게 하다

5　해초는 식단의 주요 품목으로 오랫동안 일본과 중국에서 사용되어왔다. 기원전 600년경, Sze Teu는 중국에서 "몇몇 해조는 최고의 손님을 대접하는데 심지어 왕에게도 아주 좋은 진미다"라고 언급했다. 일본에서는 약 21종류가 일상 요리에 사용되어지고 그것들 중 6종은 8세기 때부터 사용되었다. 서구에서도 해조류가 크게 건강식품으로 인식되어 있고, 지난 20년 동안에 음식으로서의 해조류에 대한 관심이 급증했지만 해조류 소비가 일본의 일부 보다 더 많을 것 같지는 않다.

적색 해조류인 Palmaria palmata의 채집에 대한 규정이 10세기경의 아이슬랜드인의 무용담에 나와있다. 이 식용 가능한 해조는 아일랜드와 스코틀랜드에서 아주 오랫동안 사용되었다. Chondrus crispus(아일랜드 이끼)는 19세기 초에 아일랜드에서 건강 보조제로 추천되어졌지만 이전에는 그것의 사용이 알려지지 않은 것 같다. 다양한 적색 해조가 기원 이전부터 지중해 연안에서 염료의 원료로 그리고 구충제나 다른 건강 보조제로 사용되어왔다.

다시마의 사용은 중국에서 최소한 5세기 경까지 거슬러 올라간다. 사용된 주된 종류는 Laminaria japonica이지만 8~11개의 다른 종류가 주로 일본에서 사용되었다. 식물은 수확 이후에 건조되어지고 가늘게 잘려지거나 분말로 으깨진다. 일본에서 Kombu는 - 다시마의 다른 이름 - 생선이나 고기 요리, 야채스프를 만드는데 사용되고, 밥과 함께 먹는 야채로써 사용되기도 한다. 분말 kombu는 소스나 스프에 사용되거나 카레와 같은 방식으로 밥에 첨가되어진다. 어떤 종류는 차와 유사한 우려낸 물을 만드는 데에도 사용된다. 1976년에 대략 176000톤의 Laminaria spp가 일본에서 야생에서 채집되었으며 22000톤이 양식으로 재배되었다. Laminaria는 암석 해안의 폭파된 지역이나 밧줄에 씨를 뿌려서 경작되어진다.

staple 요소, 주성분, 주요한, 주요산물   upsurge 급증, 쇄도, 돌발
saga 중세북유럽 전설, 모험담   anthelmintic 구충제, 구충의
kelp 켈프(다시마 등의 대형 갈조)   japonica 동백나무, 모과나무
rope 줄, 로프 (복수)새끼줄은 친 곳

Chapter 8

Hackers Practice

1   이 기사는 이 두 심리학의 하위 분야 사이에 존재하는 몇몇 유사성 – 그들을 구별해주는 현저한 차이에도 불구하고 – 을 간략히 정리하는 것을 목적으로 한다.

2   생화학자들은 표준 생물학적 위험 코드 하에서 일어날 수 있는 오염에 대해 그들의 옷을 소독하는 지루하지만 필수적인 임무를 시작했다.

3   1차 세계 대전 동안 독일은 영국이 공정한 입장에 머물기를 원했으나, 벨기에의 중립에 대한 독일의 조약 위반은 영국이 전쟁에 돌입하도록 하는데 충분한 이유가 되었다.

4   다양한 좌파적 견해를 수용함으로써 예술가들은 또한 산업 노동 조합주의, 미국 흑인들의 공민권, 스페인 내전에서 반 파시스트에 대한 지지와 같은 사회적 주장들을 포용하게 되었다.

5   코미디언 Bob Hope의 오랜 경력은 Bob Hope 콜렉션에 상세히 자료화되어 있는데, 이 콜렉션은 100개 이상의 스크랩북–메모나 사진들을 붙이기 위한 앨범–을 포함하고 있다.

6   모든 대학원 장학금은 일년간 지속되는 반면에, 대학 장학금들은 한 학기동안만 유지될 수 있다.

7   많은 치과 의사들이 이를 가는 것은 스트레스에 의해 발생한다고 믿고, 환자들에게 치아를 빨리 닳게 하고 싶지 않다면 치아를 그런 식으로 한꺼번에 움직이는 것을 멈추라고 충고한다.

8   북반구에서는 겨울에 곤충들이 적어지므로, 먹이를 위해 곤충들에 의존하는 식충성의 새들은 곤충들이 더 풍부한 적도쪽으로 더 가까이 이동해야 한다.

9   동물의 표피와 가죽은 이들을 보존하여 사용에 적합하도록 하기 위해 화학처리 된다. Hide라는 용어는 더 큰 동물들의 표피를 지칭하기 위해 사용되는 반면에 (예를 들어, 소가죽 또는 말가죽) , "Skin"은 더 작은 동물들의 가죽을 가리킨다 (송아지 가죽 또는 새끼 염소가죽). (대부분) 사용되는 보존 과정은 제혁법(tanning)이라고 불리는 화학적 처리이고, 이러한 처리를 하지 않을 경우 쉽게 부패하게 되는 표피를 잘 썩지 않는 물질로 변화시킨다.

10   몇몇 야행성 포유 동물들은 특별한 분비기관을 사용하여 냄새 흔적들을 남긴다. 이것은 이 야행성의 동물들이 빨리 움직이고 쉽게 익숙한 길들을 따라 이동하도록 해 준다.

Hackers Test

1 중국 서예(書藝)의 역사는 중국 자체의 역사만큼이나 오래된다. 서예는 중국 예술의 최고의 형태 중의 하나이다. 중국 서예를 공부하기 위해서는 한자의 기원들과 어떻게 그것들이 처음에 쓰여졌는지에 대해 배워야만 한다. 그러나 중국의 예술적 전통들 속에서 길러진 사람들을 제외하고는 서예의 미학적 가치를 파악하기란 매우 어려워보인다.

중국의 서예는 사상을 전달하고자 하는 목적에도 기여하지만 선(線)이 지니고 있는 '추상적' 아름다움도 강조한다. 리듬, 선, 구조가 그림이나 조각에서 보다 서예에서 더 완벽하게 구현되어진다. 전통적인 중국화의 그 독특한 스타일의 발전에 기여한 중요한 요소들 중의 하나가 사용된 재료들과 그것들이 예술적 형식과 기법들에 미친 영향 사이의 밀접한 관계였다.

첫째는, 먹물이다. 먹물은 서예나 그림에서 이 천년 넘게 사용되어 왔다. 먹이 화가의 벼루 위에 깨끗한 물과 함께 갈아질 때 사용한 물의 양에 따라 다양한 농도의 먹물이 만들어질 수 있다. 진한 먹물이 종이나 실크 위에 사용되면 매우 깊고 광택이 난다. 엷은 먹물은 선명하고 투명하게 나타난다. 결과적으로, 먹을 사용한 묵화에서는 먹물만을 사용하여 명과 암, 농도의 진함과 엷음 사이의 율동적인 균형을 만들어내고, 주제의 감촉과 중량과 채색의 인상을 만들어내는 것이 가능하다.

  calligraphy 서예, 달필
  slab 석판, 널빤지

2 Christopher Columbus가 신세계에 발을 내딛기 천년도 훨씬 전인 약 1세기경에 Anasazi 바구니 제작자들은 서남부에 구덩이 집을 파고 있었다. Anasazi("고대 사람들")들은 New Mexico와 Arizona에 살고 있는 현재 Pueblo 인디언들의 조상들이었다. 바이킹 족의 탐험가인 Leif Ericson이 기원 후 1000년쯤에 미국으로 항해했을 때, New Mexico의 Chaco 협곡에 있던 Anasazi 건축가들은 Pueblo Bonito라는 여러 층으로 된 웅장한 건축구조물을 이미 상당 부분 건설해둔 상태였다. 오늘날, 현대의 Taos에 거주하는 Pueblo 인디언들은 1607년Jamestown 식민도시가 건설되기 오래 전에 그들의 조상들이 했던 것처럼, 그때와 똑같은 문들 옆에서 고추를 건조 시키고있다.

초기의 구덩이 집들은 나무 막대기에 진흙을 발라 만든 접시 모양으로, 부분적으로 지하에 숨어 지어졌다. 나중에 구덩이 집들은 지붕을 구성하는 풀로 뒤덮인 기둥과 십자 이음새의 구조를 가지게 된다. 바닥에 있는 구멍, Sipapu는 최초의 Anasazi인이 세상에 출현했던 그 장소를 상징하였다. 후에 Pueblo 인디언들에 의해 종교적 의식들에 사용된 보통 둥근 석조 구조물인 Kivas는, 초기의 구덩이 집들을 본떠서 만들어진 것으로 여겨진다.

시간이 흐르면서, Anasazi인들은 꼭대기에 구멍을 내어 입구를 만든 땅 위에 구덩이 집을 지었다. 서기 750년 경까지, Anasazi인들은 벽돌처럼 사용되는 adobe나 terrone로 만들어진 다양한 유형의 거주지들을 짓기 시작했다. 가능한 경우에는, 진흙을 더덕더덕 바른 가느다란 수직의 기둥들의 구조(jacal이라 불림)가 또한 사용되었다.

사암이 풍부한 경우라면, 거주지들은 대개 중앙 광장 주변에 석조 건축으로 지어졌다. Vigas(목재 들보)가 지붕을 형성했고, 그 vigas 사이에 작은 어린 나무들(latillas)을 놓고 그 위에 잔가지, 갈대, 진흙의 층들, 그리고 마지막으로 마른 흙으로 덮었다. Anasazi 절벽 거주자들은 Mesa Verde와 다른 터들의 돌출한 절벽들 근처나 아래에 사다리들로 닿는 여러 층의 석조 구조물들을 쌓았다.

  saucer 받침 접시(모양의), 밑받침   **adobe** 어도비 벽돌(제조용 점토)-햇볕에 말려서 만듦
  plaster 회반죽(바르다) 장식하다   **jacal** 토벽 초가집   **sapling** 어린나무, 풋내기
  reed 갈대(밭), 마른 갈대

3 감각 운동 단계(생후 2살까지)동안, 갓난아기들은 보고, 만지고, 듣고, 입안에 물건을 넣고, 빨고, 손으로 잡는 등의 구체적인 행동을 통해 학습을 한다. "사고"는 감각을 통해 얻은 정보를 신체의 움직임과 통합시키는 것으로 구성된다. 아이가 주변 환경을 적극적으로 탐구하게 되고, 또한 특정한 행동들이 특정한 결과들을 낳는다는 것을 학습하게 됨에 따라, 곧 이런 움직임들은 좀 더 목적 지향

적이 되어간다. 천 조각을 풀면 숨겨진 장난감이 드러나고, 푹신푹신한 오리를 잡았다 놓으면 오리가 떨어지고, 숟가락으로 식탁을 탕탕 두드리면 저녁이 나타날 것이다(또는 엄마가 숟가락을 빼앗아 가든지).

Piaget의 말에 의하면, 이 단계에서 아이의 중요한 성취들 중의 하나는 대상의 영속성, 즉, 사물을 볼 수도 없고 만질 수도 없지만 계속해서 존재한다는 것을 이해하는 것이다. 그는 생후 첫 몇 개월 동안 갓난아기들이 "보이지 않으면, 마음에서도 멀어진다"는 격언을 따르는 것처럼 보이는 것을 관찰하였다. 갓난아기가 어떤 작은 장난감을 뚫어지게 바라보다가도 만일 당신이 그 장난감을 종이 뒤에 감춰버리면 구태여 종이 뒤를 찾아 본다든지 혹은 장난감을 다시 얻어내려는 노력 등을 하지는 않을 것이다. (대략 6개월까지, 아기들은 그들이 장난감이나 집안의 고양이를 볼 수 있든 아니든 간에 그 장난감, 혹은 그 집안 고양이가 존재한다는 생각을 이해하기 시작한다. 이 나이의 아기는 자기의 놀이터에서 장난감을 떨어뜨리면, 그것을 찾으려고 할 것이다. 또한 부분적으로 가려져 있는 장난감을 찾아내려고 헝겊 아래도 살펴볼 것이다. 1살 까지, 대부분의 아기들은 몇몇 사물들의 영속성에 대한 인식을 발전시켜 왔다. 이 때가 아기들이 아웅, 까꿍 놀이를 좋아할 때이다.)

Piaget는 사물의 영속성이 구상적인 사고, 즉 정신적 이미지와 다른 상징 체계들을 이용할 수 있는 능력의 시초를 알린다고 말했다. 아이는 처음으로 마음속에 어떤 개념을 포착할 수 있게 되고, 파리라는 단어가 윙윙거리며 성가시게 구는 생물을 나타내고 아빠가 다정스럽고 장난치기 좋아하는 사람을 나타낸다는 것을 배울 수 있다.

> **sucking** 빨아들이는, 미숙한 **fuzzy** 잔털 모양의, 보풀이 선, 흐트러진
> **drop out of** ~에서 손을 떼다, 그만두다, 뒤떨어지다
> **bang** 탕치다, 쾅 부딪치다 **peek-a-boo** '까꿍' (숨어 있다가 아이를 놀리는)
> **buzz** 윙윙(와글와글)거리는

4 정치적으로 활발히 활동해온 많은 예술가들이 뉴딜 프로젝트들을 위해 일했다. 예술을 이용하여 사회변화를 촉진시키고자 하는 욕망으로 한데 뭉친 이 예술가들은 노동 운동에 동감을 표하고, 뉴딜 자유주의에서 사회주의, 그리고 공산주의에 이르는 좌익 정치에 친근감을 보였다. 극단적인 경우, 그들의 예술은 오로지 자본주의의 폐단만을 들춰내고 노동자 계급의 투쟁들을 찬양하는 데에만 목표를 둔 조잡한 무기가 되었다. 다른 경우들에서는, 더 나은 세계를 창조하기 위해 예술을 이용하고자 하는 그들의 현실참여 의지는 가난한 사람들의 삶을 섬세하게 그려내거나 단지 대공황 시기 미국의 암울한 현실을 포착한 "사회주의 현실주의자" 작품들로 끝났다. 연방 예술 사업은 보통 온건한 사회적 현실주의를 수용할 수 있었다. 그러나 좀 더 논의의 여지가 있는 작품들, 특히 벽화와 같은 대중 예술과 연방 극장 공연물 등에 있어서, 온건한 사회적 현실주의는 그 프로젝트들의 적들이 그들에게 대항해 사용할 수 있는 공격수단이 되었다.

> **grim** 엄격한, 완강한, 불길한, 잔인한 **ammunition** 탄약, 공격(방어)수단

5 신석기 시대의 부락이 하나의 도시로 발전하기까지는 적어도 1,500년의 세월 - 기원전 약 5,000년에서 3,500년 까지의 구세계에서는 - 이 걸렸다. 인류를 도시 지역에서 살 수 있도록 만들어준 기술 발달은 처음에는 주로 농업 분야에서의 일어났다. 신석기 사람들의 농작물 경작과 가축 사육은 결국에는 경작과 목축, 그리고 각종 기술의 확산을 이끌었고, 이러한 기술의 확산은 그 결과 사실상 여분량을 생산하도록 함으로써 인구의 일부를 기능공이나 기술자, 혹은 서비스업에 종사하는 사람들로 일하도록 자유롭게 해주었다.

관개와 경작에서의 기술적 발달들에 의해 인간 거주지들의 규모가 커져 감에 따라, 상품과 사람들의 유통을 향상시킬 필요성이 어느 때 보다도 더 강했다. 먹을 것을 끊임없이 찾아야 하는 유목생활을 영위하는 신석기 이전의 사람은 대체로 걸어서 이동했고, 중요한 소유물들은 그의 아내와 아이들의 도움을 받아 운반했다. 신석기 시대 사람은 동물을 사육하였고, 그 동물들을 식량과 가죽을 위

해서 뿐 아니라 운반수단으로도 활용하였다. 그 다음에는 더 무거운 짐을 나르기 위해 활주부들을 갖춘 썰매와 결합한 짐수레용 동물들이 이용되기 시작했다.

domestication 교화, 길들임 **sledge** (화물용) 썰매

6 이집트인들은 돌들을 수직으로 들어올리기 위한 어떤 기중기 기계류도 보유하지 않았다. 층층이 벽돌을 쌓아올리는 연속적인 과정은 흙, 혹은 진흙 벽돌로 된 경사로를 사용했는데, 그 경사로들 위로 동물과 사람의 근력에 의해 돌은 벽에서 필요한 자신의 위치로 끌어올려졌다고 일반적으로 여겨진다. 나중에 그 경사로들이 제거된 후, 그것들 석공들이 돌의 표면에 마지막 손질을 하기 위한 지지대로서 역할을 하게 되었다. 그런 경사로들의 잔해는 이집트 톨레미 왕조 때 시작되어 미완성인 채로 남아 있는 신전들에서 여전히 발견되어 진다. 돌들은 보통 석고, 모래와 물로 만들어진 회 반죽 판을 이용해 쌓였고, 물은 아마도 접착제로서 보다는 돌을 제자리에 밀어 넣기 위한 윤활제로서 더 많은 역할을 했을 것이다. 또한 벽돌 사이에는 금속으로 된 서로 꼭 들어맞는 고정쇠들이 제한적으로 사용되었다.
기자의 거대 피라미드들 - 그 중 가장 높은 것은 높이가 147미터(481피트)에 이른다 - 은 놀랄만한 기술적 업적이고, 그것들의 시각적 효과는 심지어 오늘날에 조차도 매우 놀랍다. 사실 19세기가 되어서야 그 보다(피라미드 보다) 더 높은 건축물들이 세워질 수 있었다. 그러나 이러한 피라미드들은 또한 거대 석조 건축의 종말을 상징하기도 하는데, 사실 피라미드 이후로 곧 거대 석조 건축은 곧 보다 가볍고 유연한 석조 구조들과 더 넓은 실내 공간을 창조하는 방향으로 변화해갔다. 석조 가로대를 떠받치는 버팀 없이 서 있는 돌기둥은 기원전 2600년경의 피라미드들과 연관이 있는 왕조의 사원들에서 처음으로 나타났다.

ramp 경사로, 진입로, 이동식 계단 **masonry** 석공(직,술), 벽돌공, 석조 공사
Ptolemaic 프톨레마이오스의, 천동설의 **gypsum** 석고, 깁스

7 수평면의 어느 고정된 지점에서 들리는 소리의 위치 측정은, 사람의 양쪽 귀에 그 소리가 도달하는 강도, 그리고 그 시간차에 있어서의 그 미세한 차이도 인지에 의해 결정된다고 알려져 있다. 왼쪽 귀보다 오른쪽 귀에 약 백만 분의 2, 3초 정도 빨리 도달하거나 혹은 오른쪽 귀에 몇 데시벨 정도 더 크게 들리는 소리는 오른쪽에서 나는 것으로 인식된다. 실제 상황에서는 (무의식적으로) 고개를 돌려 그 소리를 정확히 감지해낼 수 있게 되는데 그것은 그 소리쪽을 향하게 되어 결과적으로 이러한 소리 크기의 차이를 없애게 됨으로써 (가능한 것이다.) 저주파 음조인 경우 두 귀에 도달하는 소리 전달 과정에서의 차이가 소리 위치 측정의 기준이나, 고주파의 경우에는 두뇌의 소리 공명에 의해 야기되는 소리 강도 차이가 가장 중요하다. 이러한 비교와 구별작업은 중앙 청각 통로의 뇌간과 중뇌 단계에서 실행되는 것으로 보여진다. 각각의 소리가 가진 다양한 형태들은, 수평면에 위치하지 않은 소리의 근원지 높이를 측정하는 데 가장 중요한 요소로서 생각되어져 왔다. 움직이는 근원지로부터 발생하는 소리의 위치를 확인하는 작업은 신경체계에는 좀 더 복잡한 일이며, 분명 명백히 뇌 피질, 그리고 단기 기억과 연관이 있다. 동물들에게 실시된 실험에서는 어느 한쪽 뇌피질의 청각 영역 손상이, 그 반대편쪽의 신체방향에 있는 움직이는 소리 근원지 위치 측정을 어렵게 한다는 것을 보여주었다.

microsecond 마이크로 초 (100만분의 1초) **auditory** 귀의, 청각의
cerebral 대뇌의, 지적인, 사색적인 **cortex** 피질, 외피

8 열대 우림들은 굉장히 많은 수의 동물 종들이 있기 때문에 지상에서 가장 다양한 생태계들이다. 이런 동물 다양성의 대부분이 곤충들로 구성되어 있지만, 많은 다른 무척추동물 집단들 또한 (이 생태계를) 대표하기도 한다. 비록 이들 대다수의 종이 아직 과학적으로 설명되지 않고 있을지라 하더라

도, 아마존 유역과 같은 대규모 열대 우림 지역은 대략 천만 종 이상의 동물들을 보유하고 있을 것이다. 온대 지역의 산림과는 대조적으로, 열대 우림에서는 많은 수의 다양한 동물들이 주로 나무에 살고있고, 그 수는 땅 위에 사는 것으로 알려진 동물의 수 보다 항상 훨씬 더 많다. 수마트라 북부와 보르네오에 사는 오랑우탄과 같은 몸집이 큰 척추 동물들까지도 나무 위에서 그들 삶의 대부분을 보내도록 진화해 왔다. 조류의 예에서와 같이, 많은 동물 집단들의 엄청난 다양성은, 가지각색의 독특한 종들이 서로 조화를 이루어 각각 열대 우림의 서로 다른 층들에 거주하는 경향이 있다는 사실로써 대부분 설명되어 진다. 아마존의 강기슭 열대 우림 들에서, 척추 동물의 다양성이 또한 크게 증가되는데, 그것은 매년 홍수기에 나무들에서 물로 떨어진 과일들, 씨앗들, 곤충들 및 다른 먹이들을 먹고 살기 위해 이 서식지들을 개척한 많은 수의 어종들 때문이다.

arboreal 나무의, 교목성의 (동물이)나무에 사는　**vertebrate** 척추동물, 척추가 있는, 튼튼한
riparian 강기슭의(소유자), 호수가의, 강가에 사는

9 날씨는 인간 거주지 형태, 식량 생산, 그리고 개인의 안위에 엄청난 영향을 미친다. 극단적인 온도와 습도는 불편함의 원인이 되고 질병의 확산을 야기시킬지도 모른다. 폭우는 홍수를 일으켜 사람들을 강제로 옮기게 하고 경제 활동들을 방해할 수 있다. 뇌우, 토네이도, 우박, 그리고 진눈깨비 폭풍우는 농작물, 건물, 그리고 도로 및 차에 피해를 입히거나 파괴할 지도 모른다. 폭풍우는 사람과 가축을 다치게 하거나 심지어는 죽일지도 모른다. 바다와 인접한 연안 지역들을 따라, 열대성 폭풍들(허리케인, 태풍, 그리고 윌리-윌리)은 집중 폭우와 홍수, 바람, 파도를 발생시켜 선박, 건물, 나무, 농작물, 도로 및 철도에 막대한 피해를 끼칠 수 있고, 항공 운송이나 통신을 방해할 지 모른다. 폭설과 얼음으로 덮인 상황은 교통을 방해하고, 사고들의 빈도를 늘릴 수 있다. 이와는 대조적으로 오랫동안 비가 내리지 않는 것은 1930년대 미국의 대초원 주들에서의 "먼지그릇" 현상에서와 같이 바람이 바짝 마른 농지 위로 불 때 가뭄들과 심각한 먼지 폭풍들을 야기할 수 있다.

sleet 진눈깨비(가 오다)
dustbowl 먼지바람이 부는 지역, 황진 지대(미시시피 서부의 평원지대)

10 선사시대에 사람은 서늘한 동굴에 저장하거나 눈 속에 보관하면 사냥한 고기가 더 오래간다는 것을 알게 되었다. 그들은 차가운 온도가 먹을 것을 구할 수 없는 때를 대비해 사냥한 고기들을 보존해 줄 수 있다는 것을 깨달았다. 나중에는, 여름에 사용할 목적으로 겨울에 얼음이 거두어들여졌다. 인간이 좀 더 산업화되고 기계화 됨에 따라, 얼음이 호수나 강에서 수확되거나 만들어져서 저장되고 많은 나라들로 운반되었다. 심지어 오늘날에도 얼음이 이런 용도로 여전히 만들어지고 있다.
식량 냉동 보관의 역사의 중간단계 즈음에서는, 질산나트륨이나 질산칼륨과 같은 화학물질을 물에 첨가하여 온도가 떨어지도록 했다. "냉동하다"라는 단어가 그랬듯(1550년대에 기록되었듯), 이러한 방식으로 포도주를 차갑게 만드는 것 역시 1550년에 들어서야 기록되었다. 냉각제를 사용하는 압축기와 같은 기계적인 냉동으로의 발전은 길고 느린 과정이었고 19세기 말엽이 되어서야 소개되었다.
냉동의 과학은 계속해서 발전한다. 1996년, 대기오염 방지 규제법 제6조에 따르기 위해 사용되는 냉각제의 유형에 변화가 있었다. 대부분의 사람들에게 상품명, "프레온"으로 알려져 있는 구 냉각제가 오존층에 덜 해로우면서도 여전히 음식을 차게 보관하는데 구 냉각제만큼 효과적인 새로운 냉매, 즉 HFC 134a로 대체되었다. 소비자인 우리가 차이를 알아차리지 못하는 것이 당연하다.

sodium nitrate 질산나트륨　**potassium nitrate** 질산칼륨
refrigerant 식히는, 얼게하는, 냉각제, 완화제
tradename 상품명, 상표명

## Chapter 9

Hackers Practice

1   17세기에서 19세기 동안 퀼트 기술은 상당한 인기를 얻게 되고, 계속하여 오늘날 예술과 공예 영역 사이에서의 예술적 표현의 대중적인 형태가 되었다. 그것의 사용 흔적은 중국, 인도, 중동 그리고 아프리카와 같이 전세계에 걸쳐 발견된다.

2   직조 직물은 두 부분의 실로 만들어진다. - 세로 쪽은 날실이라고 하고 가로 쪽은 씨실 이라고 한다. 날실 가닥들이 harness(날실의 오르 내리 장치)라고 불리는 일련의 틀을 통해 베틀에 엮어진다. 옷을 만드는 과정 동안 그 harness는 날실 몇 가닥을 집어 올리고 다른 것들을 아래쪽으로 내린다. 이러한 동작은 실 가닥 사이에 하나의 공간, 즉 shed를 만들어준다.

3   jet lag는 시간대를 통과하는 여행을 한 후에 발생하는 수면 패턴의 혼란을 지칭한다. 그것은 여행자들에게 흔한 일이며, 30살 이하 보다는 50세 이상의 사람들에게 더욱 많이 일어난다. 그 발생률은 여행할 때 얼마나 많은 시간대를 통과해야 하는지, 그리고 어떤 방향으로 움직이는지에 따라 다양하다.

4   빌딩의 역사는 다양한 유행들로 특징 지워진다. 한 예로 사용된 자재의 내구성이 증가되었다. 초기의 건축 자재들은 나뭇잎, 나뭇가지, 동물 가죽과 같이 썩거나 부서지기 쉬운 것들이었다. 나중에는 진흙, 돌, 그리고 목재 등 보다 내구성이 강한 천연 재료들이 이용되었고, 마침내는 벽돌, 콘크리트, 철제, 그리고 플라스틱 등의 합성 재료들이 사용되었다. 또 다른 예로 보다 높고 넓은 건물을 추구하는 경향이다. 이것은 보다 튼튼한 건축 재료의 개발과 그 재료들의 특성과 이들을 어떻게 더욱 유리하게 활용할 수 있는지에 대한 이해로부터 가능하게 되었다.

5   대부분, 요즘 학생들은 학교에 의해 자극되거나 어떠한 동기를 부여 받지 못한다. 그것들은 더 이상 어떤 특정한 경력이나 직업을 준비시키지 않는다. 그 결과 일부 고등학교 졸업생은 일자리를 찾지 못한 채 고등학교를 마치게 되거나, 일자리를 찾은 다른 학생들의 경우에도 많은 수가 대부분 23세나 24세까지는 기술과 안정성을 얻기 위해서 저임금 직업에서 또 다른 저임금 직업으로 옮겨가는 일을 계속하게 된다.

6   아인슈타인은 1914년 그의 아내, 그리고 두 아들 Hans Albert와 Eduard와 함께 베를린으로 이사하기 전에는 프라하와 취리히에 있는 대학들에서 물리학 교수로 재직했었다. 이사 후 그는 Prussian 과학 아카데미에서 근무하게 되어 거기에서 그의 연구와 강의를 계속해나갔다. (하지만) 그곳에서의 삶이 불행했던 그의 부인 Mileva는 1차 세계대전의 시작쯤에 두 명의 아들과 함께 다시 스위스로 돌아갔다.

7   인공 두뇌학이란 생물 유기체의 의사 소통과 조절과정에 대한, 그리고 그 유기체들이 기계적이고 전기적인 시스템과 어떻게 연관되었는지를 분석하는 학문이다.

8   갑각류 동물의 세계는 기이한 모양과 구조의 세계이다. 아마도 이 동물군은 딱딱한 겉껍질을 지니고 있는 것으로 가장 잘 알려져 있을 것이다. 그들이 성장함에 따라 그 껍질은 점점 벗겨지고 제거된다. 일단 이렇게 껍질이 벗겨지게 되면, 새로 생긴 껍질이 단단해지기까지는 많은 시간이 필요하다. 따라서 이 기간동안 이 갑각류 동물들은 자신을 보호할 주요 수단이 없는 상태에 놓이게 되고, 자연히 약탈자의 공격에 취약하게 된다.

9 운하가 건설되기 이전에 뉴욕 시는 보스턴, 볼티모어, 필라델피아, 그리고 뉴 올리온즈 다음으로 미국에서 다섯 번째로 큰 항구였다. 그러나 운하가 개통되고 15년이 채 지나지 않아 뉴욕은 보스턴과 볼티모어, 그리고 뉴 올리온즈를 한데 합한 것보다 더 많은 화물을 수송하는, 미국에서 가장 분주한 항구가 되었다.

10 영국은 적어도 최소한 여느 이웃 국가 만큼은 경제적인 것 같아 보인다. 영국이 평화의 시대에 스스로의 국방을 위해 유지하고 있는 군대는 부 혹은 권력에 있어서 영국과 맞먹는다고 생각하는 여느 유럽 국가의 그것보다 더욱 온건하다.

Hackers Test

1 플루트를 불 때, 연주자의 입술에서 분출되는 공기는 플루트의 주둥이 구멍을 거쳐서 그 구멍의 날카로운 더 먼 가장자리에 부딪치게 된다. 만일 이 공기 흐름이 방해를 받게 되면, 물결모양의 공기 파장이 그 공기 기류를 따라 움직여 기류를 빗나가게 함으로써, 그 공기가 플루트의 주둥이 안으로 들어가거나 혹은 바깥으로 나오도록 하게 된다. 연주자 입에서 나온 기류에 가해지는 공기 파장의 속도는 기류 자체 속도(기류의 속도는 연주자 입에서 가해지는 공기 압력에 따라 약 초당 20 미터에서 60 미터 정도이다)의 약 절반 정도의 속도이다. 이러한 기류 방해의 원인은 플루트 관(통)에서 발생하는 소리의 진동으로, 이 소리의 진동이 공기를 플루트의 주둥이 안쪽과 바깥쪽으로 흘러가도록 만드는 것이다. 만일 기류의 속도가 연주되는 가락의 주파수와 일치하게 되면, 그 기류는 플루트의 주둥이 구멍으로부터 가장 먼 부분에서 적절한 속도로 플루트의 안쪽 혹은 바깥쪽으로 흘러 들어가 플루트의 소리를 강화하고 플루트가 고른 가락을 내도록 할 수 있게 해준다. 고음을 연주하기 위해서 기류에 가해지는 파장의 이동 시간이 고주파와 일치하게끔 감소되어야 하며, 공기를 불어넣는 압력(이 압력이 기류의 속도를 증가시킨다)을 증가시키고, 기류가 입을 대는 구멍의 가장자리에 닿는 거리를 짧게 하기위해 입술을 앞으로 이동시킴으로서 그 파장의 이동시간 감소가 가능해진다. 이런 것들이 바로 플루트를 연주할 때 플룻 연주자 들이 저절로 학습하여 점진적으로 발전시키는 연주 조절 방법들이다.

플루트는 양쪽 끝이 열려 있다. 플루트의 양 면 끝이 열려있는 것은 명백하다. 플루트 연주하는 사람을 세밀하게 관찰하는 사람은 연주자의 아랫입술이 플루트의 주둥이 구멍 부분을 덮고 있는 것으로 보겠지만, 사실 연주자는 그 구멍의 상당 부분을 대기에 노출시킨다. 플루트 음향학에 대해 간단한 소개를 하기 위해, 우선 그와 비슷한 것을 예로 들어보자. 먼저, 플루트를 단순한 원통형의 파이프로 생각해보자 – 달리 말해, 모든 구멍이 (적어도 아래 일정 지점까지는) 다 막혀 있고 머리부분이 원통이고, 맨 끝의 구멍을 측면에 붙어있는 입을 대는 구멍으로 생각하자. 이것이 아마 조잡하긴 해도 플루트의 기본 물리적인 구조는 갖추고 있고, 그러면 훨씬 논의하기가 쉬워진다.

> **jet** 분출구, 분출물 **embouchure** 강어귀, 하구, (관악기의)주둥이, 입술 대는 법
> **acoustics** 음향학, 음향상태, 효과(강당, 극장 등의) **approximation** 접근, 근사치
> **cylindrical** 원통(모양)의

2 초기의 옷감 조각들은 동일한 길이의 날실 타래를 움켜잡은 손을 이용하여 좁은 띠 모양의 끈들로 짜여졌다. 이 날실 타래의 한쪽 끝을 하나의 매듭으로 묶어 다른 사람에게 그 매듭을 단단히 잡도록 한다.– 또는 나무나 기둥 같은 고정된 물체에 단단히 묶을 수도 있다.– 다른 한쪽 끝은 직조자가 잡고 있도록 하는데, 이 경우 그의 나머지 한 손은 날실의 (매듭이 지어진) 좁은 띠 아래 위로 자유롭게 씨실을 움직일 수 있게 된다. 사실상, 그 띠를 양쪽 끝에서부터 두 명의 직조자가 함께 짠다면, 그 띠는 삼 십분 안에 짜여질 수 있었다. 이처럼 가장 간단한 직조방식으로부터 그 가는 띠조각을 좀더 넓은 천으로, 혹은 넓은 베틀 – 인류 역사 오래 전부터 시작된 연속적인 직조기술 발달의 중요성을 말해주는 현대 영어의 두 용어인 – 로 넓혀가는 두 가지 직조 전통들이 발달했다.

지면 베틀은 근동지역, 남아시아 및 북아프리카에서 처음으로 사용되었다. 그것은 북 아라비아 사막에서 오늘날 여전히 사용중인 형태이다. 사막 모래사장에서 불과 몇 인치 안 떨어진 곳에 세워진 나무 가로대 두 개가 날실 타래를 고정시키고 날실 양쪽 끝에 천을 짜는 사람들이 웅크리고 앉아 씨실 타래를 감은 북을 앞 뒤로 통과시키며 날실 타래 위, 아래로 움직이는 것이다. 헝가리부터 스칸디나비아 및 그리스에서 처음 사용된 날실이 걸린 베틀 모양은 채색된 항아리 위에 새겨져 오래도록 남아있다. 이 유형의 베틀의 경우, 날실 가로대를 벽이나 두 기둥에 걸어 놓고는, 동시에 정해진 양만큼의 날실 타래를 그 오래된 매듭 기술로 묶어 가로대에 매달아 놓는다. 그 매듭은 (사기로 된 베틀 추와 함께) 장력을 유지하기 위한 추로서 역할을 했고 또한 천에 무늬를 넣거나 짜 나갈 때 날실 타래들이 일정한 간격을 두도록 하기 위한 계산지표로의 역할을 하기도 했다. 이 두 가지 유형의 베틀 모두가 약 10,000년 전 신석기 시대 거주지였던 터키의 Catalhuyuk에서 사용되었다.

> warp 휘다, 왜곡하다, 날(실)을 베틀에 걸다　loom 직기(베틀로) 짜다, 흐릿하게 보이다
> crouch (비굴하게)굽실거리다. 위축되다　shuttle (베틀, 재봉틀의) 밀실 넣는 곳
> urn 항아리　dangle 매달(리)다

3　요람기는 출생부터 약 1, 2년 뒤의 언어 습득 사이의 기간이다. 갓난아기는 영양분을 섭취하고 위험에 대응하는 데 도움을 주는 일련의 타고난 반사 작용들 이외에도, 사람의 얼굴을 포함한 특정한 시각적인 모양들과 사람의 목소리를 포함한 특정한 소리들에 대해 애착감을 갖게 된다. 그래서 몇 개월이 지나지 않아 갓난아기는 시각으로 어머니의 모습을 확인할 수 있으며, 사람의 목소리를 구성하는 어조와 억양의 흐름, 그리고 개별 소리들에 놀랍도록 민감한 반응을 보인다. 심지어 어린 아기들도 거리, 모양, 방향, 그리고 깊이를 포함하는 복잡한 지각 판단을 할 수 있고, 곧 나이가 많은 사람들이 하는 것과 같은 방식으로 물체나 사건(예를 들어, 사람, 가구, 음식, 동물)과 관련된 범주들을 만들어가며 그들의 경험을 체계화할 수 있게 된다.

아기들은 지각과 회상 기억 능력 둘 다에서 급속도의 진전을 보이게 되고, 이것은 차례로 환경에서 사건들을 이해하고 예측하는 그들의 능력을 증진시킨다. 이 시기의 하나의 중요한 발달은 사물의 영속성에 대한 인식, 즉 외부의 사물들이 유아의 지각과는 독립적으로 존재한다는 인식의 발달이다. 아기의 주변 환경과의 신체적인 상호작용은 단순하고 개별적인 반사 운동들에서 좀 더 통합적인 행동들로 발전하는데, 이러한 통합적인 행동들은 재미있기 때문에, 혹은 외부의 목적을 달성하는데 사용될 수 있기 때문에 의도적으로 반복된다. 약 18개월쯤 되면 아이는 단순한 시행착오의 실험을 통해서 보다는 어떤 사건과 결과들을 머리 속에서 상상함으로써 신체적인 문제들을 해결하려고 애쓰기 시작한다.

> reflex 반사작용, 반사신경
> predilection 선입적 애호, 편애

4　네덜란드 점령기의 가장 유명한 총독은 1647년에서 64년까지 새로운 네덜란드의 총독이었던 Peter Stuyvesant였다. 그의 군사적인 배경은 그가 무질서한 도시를 말끔히 정리하는 하는 것을 가능하게 했고, 그는 곧 그것을 하나의 독립된 도시로 인정해 주었다(1653). 그러나 그는 이미 여러 문화가 뒤섞여있는 지역에 자신의 종교적 교리를 강요하려고 시도함으로써 Flushing 시에 거주하는 퀘이커 교도들과의 충돌을 낳게 된다. (1657).

마침내 Stuyvesant는 상부로부터 사회질서나 무역거래를 어지럽히지 않는 한 국교 반대자들을 "눈 감아 주라"고 명령을 받았다. 하지만 총독은 그러한 공식적 승인은 할 수 없다고 생각하였고, 이러한 그의 오만한 태도는 도시 주민들과의 계속적인 불화를 낳게 된다. (alienate: 불화하게 하다)1664년 8월쯤 Gravesend 앞 바다에 영국 요크의 공작인 제임스(미래의 제임스 2세)가 파견한 영국 함대가 나타났을 때 그는 어느 누구도 자신의 식민지를 위해 싸우지 않을 것이라는 것을 깨닫게 되었다.

"나이든 의족을 한 사람"은 곧 총 한 번 쏴보지 못하고 항복할 수밖에 없었다. 흥미롭게도, 그는 영국 왕실에 충성을 맹세하고 평생을 그 도시에서 살았다. 1673년에서 74년까지 잠시 네덜란드가 그 도시를 재 점령하기도 했지만, 그 식민지(제임스 왕을 기념하여 다시 이름 지어진)의 운명은 런던으로 방향을 바꾸었다. 그 정복된 도시 안에서, 네덜란드 출신 주민과 흘러 들어온 영국 상인들이 서로 잘 지냈고, 두 집단의 대표자들이 도시 엘리트 집단이 되어 19세기에 이르렀다.

spruce 모양내다, 말쑥하게 꾸미다　　clash (의견 등이) 충돌(하다), 전투
Quaker 퀘이커 교도가 창시한 개신교의 일파인 프렌드회의 회원 : 절대평화 주의자
dissenter 반대자 [D~](영)국교 반대자　　burgher 공민, 시민(중산층)
fleet 함대, 해군력, 비행대　　reoccupation 미리 점령함(점거), 거주, 점유(권)

5 미국 인디언의 말들은 스페인 사람들에게서 도망쳐 나온 말들의 직계 후손들이다. 미국 인디언들에게 붙잡혀 그 민첩성과 지구력, 그리고 질병에 대한 타고난 저항력 등 때문에 귀중한 대접을 받으면서, 말들은 미국 대초원 문화의 하나의 완전한 일부가 되었다. 이 말들은 The Plains Indians(대초원의 인디언들)을 보행자로부터 유목 사냥꾼과 전사들로 변화시켰다. 말이 도입되기 이전에는, 사냥은 보통 사냥감 한 떼를 절벽 아래로 몰아 떨어뜨리는 형태를 취했다. 말의 도움을 이용하여, 인디언들은 사냥감 무리 가운데 가장 바람직한 목표물만을 골라 사냥할 수 있게 되었다. 각 부족들 사이에서는 말을 훔쳐오는 일이 젊은 전사가 명성을 쌓을 수 있는 명예로운 방법으로 여겨졌다.
미국 원주민들은, 오늘날의 자동차 운전자들이 그들 자동차에 범퍼 스티커, 각종 표시, 깃발 등을 장식하는 것과 마찬가지로, 중요한 의식이나 전투를 벌이기 전에 자신들의 희망과 기대를 전달한다는 뜻에서 말에 온갖 장식을 달았다. 깃털, 구슬, 자수정이나 터키 옥과 같은 천연석, 그리고 물리친 적의 혈흔을 포함한 각종 물감이 그 동물들을 장식하는데 사용되었다.
말은 부와 지위의 상징이었으며, 가족의 구성원으로 소중히 다루어졌다. 미국 인디언들은 동료 전사를 죽음에 대해 애도하는 것과 비슷한 방식으로 그들이 가장 아끼는 전쟁 파트너의 죽음을 슬퍼했다. 종종 말의 갈기와 꼬리털은 보존된 후 짜여져 의식에 쓰이는 물건들이 되었다. 이러한 물건들은, 위대한 전투마일 뿐만 아니라 고귀한 친구(이기도 한 말을)를 기억하게 하는 소중한 것으로서 강한 수호자의 정령이 깃들여 있다고 여겨지기도 했다.

Conquistador 신대륙 정복자(16c 멕시코, 페루를 정복한 스페인 사람)
amethyst 자수정, 자주색
mane (말, 사자의)갈기, 긴 머리

6 지난 50년에 걸쳐, 정부는 국내의 대중 교통망들의 다양성을 유지하려고 노력해 왔다. 도시간 여행을 위한 여러 대체 교통 수단들을 확보하려는 노력에 있어서, 정부는 철도를 지원하는데 초점을 맞추어 왔고, 도시 지역들 내의 효율적인 이동을 보장하기 위해, 정부는 도시 대중 운송 조직에 자금을 투자해 왔다. 의회는 행정상의 개혁들과 더불어 날로 복잡해지는 교통 정책에 대응해 왔다.
2차 세계 대전 이후, 자동차와 항공기가 수용하는 국내 이동의 비율이 증가하여 민영 여객 철도 산업을 상당히 수익이 낮게 만들었다. 1958년에 통과된 교통 법안은 철도 사업을 소생시키기 위한 하나의 노력이었다. 이 법안은 고정된 운임 가격에 자유 재량을 추가해 주었을 뿐 아니라, 철도 회사들을 위한 대출금을 보장하도록 주간(州間) 통상 위원회(ICC)에 5억 달러를 주었다. 그러나 철도 사업은 여전히 부진했고, 1960년대에 많은 민영 철도 회사는 ICC에 그들의 국내 철도 사업 취소를 허락해 줄 것을 요청했다. 의회는 1970년에 예전에 민영 회사들에 의해 운영되던 도시간 철도 서비스를 운영할 수 있도록, 이윤 목적의 반국립 회사인 철도 여객 공사(Amtrak)를 설립하는 방안으로써 철도 여객 서비스 법안을 통과 시켜 이에 대처했다. 민영 회사들은 회사 설립 자금과 장비 및 노동을 교환하는 대가로, 그 주식회사의 보통주를 받았다.
Amtrak의 초기 손실은 정부 독점이 효율성을 저해할 것이라는 우려와 결부되어, 1973년의

Amtrak 개선 법안을 시작으로 규제를 완화하려는 경향을 가져오게 되었다. 이 법안은 Amtrak에 행정부와 개인 주주들의 규제로부터 보다 많은 자치권을 부여해 주었다. 1976년 통과된 철도 활성화 및 규제 개혁 법안("4-R")은 철도에 대한 ICC의 직접적인 통제력을 축소시켰다. 이 법안은 또한 일곱 개의 민영 화물 수송업자들이 소유했던 철로 경영권을 1975년 떠맡은 기관인 통합 철도 회사(Conrail)에 보조금과 대출금을 보장해주었다. 1980년에 의회는 철도 사업에 대한 연방 정부의 규제를 더 줄이고, 반트러스트 면제권을 삭제하여 1984년 1월 1일부터 효력을 발생했다.

도시간 철도 정책의 특성을 나타내는 반국립 프로젝트들과는 대조적으로, 도시 지역들 내의 대중 통행 체계들을 향상시키는 데 있어서의 정부의 역할은 주 정부와 시 당국을 재정적 지원하는 쪽으로 실시되었다. 1964년, 도시 대중 교통 법안은 도시 지역들에서의 대단위 공영 혹은 민영 철도 프로젝트들을 위한 보조금들로 3억 7천 5백만 달러를 승인했고, 같은 이름의 1970년 법안은 추가로 120억 달러를 승인했다.

> **endeavor** 노력, 시도하다 **discretion** 행동(판단, 선택)의 자유 분별, 신중
> **deregulation** 규칙 폐지 **stockholder** 주주
> **subsidy** 보조금, 장려금 **freight** 화문(운송), 운임(료), 뱃짐

7 찰스 다윈의 〈종의 기원〉은 진화의 유전적 본질을 강조했지만, 그 당시에(1859년), 유전은 환경적으로 습득되는 것으로 여겨졌다. 의학 유전학의 그 다음 "선구자들"은 Francis Galton과 Archibald Garrod가 멘델의 연구를 인정하고, 진화가 "자연 대 양육"의 구도를 통해 일어날 뿐 아니라 "타고날 때부터의 신진대사의 결함"은 생물학적으로 비정상인 상태로 이끈다고 가정한 1900년대 초에야 비로서 나타났다.

진전이 거의 이루어지지 않다가 1953년 James Watson과 Francis Crick이 DNA의 분자 원리를 설명해내게 되었다. 그들은 1962년 노벨상을 수상하였다. 1990년 2005년까지 모든 인간의 유전자를 판독한다는 목표를 가지고 "인간 게놈 프로젝트"가 시작되었다. 1999년 10월 현재 그 프로젝트는 9%를 완료했다.

유전자 결함의 분류는 3가지 중 하나로 분류될 지 모른다: 단일 유전자 결함, 염색체 결함, 그리고 다른 원인에서 유래된 결함이다. 사실상 모든 질병이 환경과 유전학의 결합으로("자연 대 양육") 진행되지만, 현재에는 유전적인 기여가 가장 중요한 역할을 하는 것으로 믿어진다.

단일 유전자 결함들은 돌연변이 유전자들, 보통 유전자 코드에서 발생하는 하나의 치명적인 오류에 의해 야기된다. 그러한 결함들은 보통 겉으로는 금방 눈에 띄며, neurofibromatosis I과 II 유형들, 골 유전자 결함, 포낭 섬유조직 증식들이 이에 포함된다. 4000개 이상의 단일 유전자 결함들이 밝혀져 왔다.

염색체 결함들은 단일 유전자 결함에서 기인하는 것이 아니라 하나의 온전한 염색체 내에 포함된 유전자들의 수가 넘쳐 나거나 부족한 것에서 기인한다. 가장 흔한 예가 다운 증후군인데(Trisomy 21), 그것은 21번 염색체가 추가적으로 하나 더 있는 것이다. 다른 예들로는 Trisomy 13, Turner 증후군, 그리고 Klinefelter 증후군이 있다. 이러한 결함들은 보통 태내에서 치명적이라, 모든 자연 유산들의 반 이상의 원인으로 믿어진다.

> **hereditary** 유전적인, 세습의 **postulate** 가정하다, 요구하다
> **metabolism** (물질)대사, 신진대사 **chromosome** 염색체
> **multifactorial** 다른 원인(영향)에서 유래된
> **versus** (소송, 경기 등에서) ~에 대한, 와 비교하여
> **nurture** 양육하다 **mutant** 돌연변이(체), 변종(에 의한)
> **phenotypically** 표현형(육안으로 볼 수 있는 생물의 형질)으로,
> **osteogenesis** 골 유전자 **imperfecta** 결함
> **cystic** 포낭이 있는 방광의 **fibrosis** 섬유증, 섬유형성
> **trisomy** 3염색체성: 2배체의 체세포의 염색체 수가 2n+1이 되는 현상
> **abortion** 유산(아), 낙태, 실패

8 19세기에는 네 가지 주요 미각 특성들(짠맛, 단맛, 신맛, 쓴맛)이 존재하고, 모든 다른 미각 경험들은 이 네 가지의 결합들을 나타낸다고 널리 여겨졌다. 어떤 연구가들은 이것들에 알칼리성과 금속의 맛을 덧붙였지만, 다른 이들은 그것들이 주요 (미각) 특성들에는 포함되지 않는다고 주장한다. 네 가지 중요한 미각 특성들이 있다는 그 가정 하에, 각각의(selective) 맛에 민감한 영역들과 (전기생리학 검사들에 의해) 각 상이한 모습의 미각 세포들의 분포위치를 알아내려고 시도하는 과정에서, 각 각의 분야(맛의 분야)를 나타낸다고 여겨졌던 화학 물질들(짠맛은 염화나트륨, 단맛은 당분, 신맛은 산, 쓴맛은 알칼로이드)을 사람과 표본 동물들의 혀에 발랐다.

불행하게도, 미뢰(맛봉오리)들은 복합 구조체들이고, 그 신경 연결 관계들은 복잡하다. 어쨌든, 신경조직이나 또는 단일 미뢰들로부터 기록된 자극들은 개개의 수용 세포들이 무엇을 할 수 있는 지에 대한 직접적인 증거를 제공하지 못한다. 가느다란 와이어들을 개개의 미뢰에 넣음으로써 (자극들을) 기록할 수 있지만, 정확하게 반응한 세포를 알아내지 못한다. 그러나 분명한 것은, 척추동물의 미각 수용 세포들은 곤충들에게 있어서 처럼 당분, 양이온, 음이온, 또는 수분 수용기들로 분류될 수 없다는 것이다.

일부 척추동물 세포들이 상당히 좁은 범위의 화학 물질들에 반응하지만 대부분은 그렇지 않다; 소금에 반응하는 그러한 세포들은 또한 산과 설탕 또는 심지어 물에도 반응할 지 모른다. 혀의 특정 부분들이 선택적으로 민감한 경향이 있다(예를 들어, 사람 혀의 끝은 단맛의 화학물질에 상당히 민감해 보이지만, 유일하게 그런 것은 아니다). 단일한 미각 신경들에 가해지는 자극들을 연구함으로써, 특정한 짠맛, 단맛, 신맛, 쓴맛 수용 세포들이 발견될 것이라고 더 이상 기대하지 않게 되었다. 혀 위의 감각 세포들 사이에 만들어진 어떤 반응 양식들(특정한 수용기의 활성화 라기보다는)이 사람의 서로 다른 미각적 지각을 조정하는 것으로 보인다.

> **gustatory** 미각의 **alkaline** 알칼리성의 **metallic** 금속(제)의, 금속을 함유하는
> **bud** 싹, 돌기 **cation** 카티온, 양이온 **anion** 음이온

9 운하는 중서부 지역 경제에 직접적이면서 지속적인 영향을 미쳤다. 무엇보다 먼저, 그것은 그 지역 개발의 문을 열어주었다. 운하가 생기기 전에 일리노이 북부에는 포장된 도로나 철로가 없었다. 농부나 그 밖의 다른 사람들은 상품을 시장까지 운송하기 어려웠다. 확실한 운송 수단이 없었으므로 많은 농부들이 자신들, 혹은 그들의 지역사회에다 충분히 공급할 수 있는 정도로만 농사를 지었다. 우기 동안은 그나마 있던 길도 진흙강이 되었고, 여름에는 구름처럼 피어오르는 흙먼지가 말과 사람들 모두의 숨을 막히게 했다. 운하가 개통되면서 1818년 당시 3주가 걸리던 모피상인들의 여정과 1830년대 농부들이 진흙탕 길을 걸어 며칠씩 걸렸던 길이 운하의 배를 통해 단 하루에 해결되었다. 갑자기 사람과 옥수수와 밀과 석재, 그리고 그 밖의 생산품들이 시카고로 쏟아져 들어왔으며, 동부 해안에서 서부로 완제품이 유입되기 시작했다.

I&M 운하는 운하 시대에 건설된 미국의 대규모 수로 가운데 마지막 수로였다. 1850년대와 60년대 미국은 점차적으로 철도운송으로 눈을 돌리기 시작했으며, 수천 마일의 철도들이 건설되었다. 철도는 운하보다 많은 장점을 지니고 있었다. 철도는 일년 내내 운행할 수 있었고 반면에, 운하는 물이 얼어붙는 겨울에는 문을 닫아야 했다. 그리고 철도는 운하보다 더 빠르고 더 유용성이 있어 어느 곳에든 철로를 놓을 수 있고, 따라서 기존의 산업에도 더욱 힘을 불어넣을 수가 있다. 철도가 이런 장점들을 지니고 있었지만 I&M 운하는 1866년까지는 수익을 남겼으며, 1882년에는 기록적인 수송량을 나타내기도 했다. 이 운하는 석회석, 석탄, 소금 같은 대규모 화물을 실어 나르는 일에 철도와 경쟁을 했으며, 이러한 경쟁은 철도의 수송량을 낮추어, 세인트 루이스와 같은 중서부의 다른 도시보다 시카고에 여러 이점을 제공하기도 하였다.

1900년 이후 운하의 사용은 급격히 줄어들기 시작했다. 제1차 세계 대전 동안 잠시 운하의 통행이 늘어나기도 했지만 그 이후 운하가 손상되면서부터 "올챙이 도랑"이란 명칭이 붙기도 했다. 1933년 일리노이 수로가 개통되면서 그 운하의 수송 역사는 종말을 고하게 되었고, 이후 그 운하는 유원지화 되었다.

choke 질식시키다, 억제하다   tonnage (선박, 적하의) 톤세, 용적톤수
limestone 석회암   resurgence 재기, 부활
dub 기사작위를 주다, (명칭, 별명을)붙이다, ~라고 부르다
tadpole 올챙이

10 산업과 농업, 그리고 도시 지역의 폐기물들은 수생 시스템의 생물학적 능력치를 초과하여, 하천을 유기 물질과 독성 물질에 오염된 유기체로 넘쳐 나도록 만들었다. 유기 물질이 그것을 분해해서 재활용하게 만드는 물 속의 미생물의 능력을 초과하는 경우 그 유기 물질 속에 있는 과도한 영양분은 해조류의 성장을 급속도로 촉진시키게 된다.

이 해조류들이 죽을 때 그 찌꺼기가 이미 물 속에 있는 유기체 쓰레기에 더해지게 되고, 궁극적으로는 그 물은 산소량이 부족하게 된다. 무기성 생물(생존에 산소를 필요로 하지 않는 생물)은 메탄이나 황화 수소와 같은 가스를 배출하여 유기체 잔해를 공격하게 되는데, 이것은 산소를 필요로 하는 생명체에 해로운 것이다. 그 결과로 물은 역겨운 냄새를 풍기며, 온갖 오물로 가득 차게 되는 상태가 되는데, 이는 이미 에리 호수나 발트 해에서 발생하고 있는 현상이며, 점차 유럽과 북미의 깨끗했던 호수에서도 심각한 문제로 대두되고 있다.

이러한 과정을 통해, 호수나 강과 같은 하천은 깨끗하고 맑은 상태 – 용해된 영양분의 농도가 비교적 낮고, 따라서 수생계의 균형이 이루어지고 있는 상태 – 에서 영양분이 넘쳐 나고 해조류가 가득한 상태로 나아가게 되며, 그래서 결국엔 산소가 부족하며 오염물질이 넘쳐나게 되는데 이러한 과정은 가속 부영양화 과정(영양 오염화 과정)으로써 알려져 있다.

bloom (꽃의)개화   algae 조류, (민물, 바닷물의)말   methane 메탄
sulfide 황화물   foul 불결한, 더러운   anaerobic 무기성 생물의, 미생물의
aerobic 호기성 생물의   eutrophication (호수의)부영양화, 영양오염

Progressive Test 3-1

1 대머리 독수리의 들어올리는 힘은 약 4파운드 정도 된다. 그들은 일반적으로 닭이나 다른 기르는 가축들을 먹지 않지만, 입수할 수 있는 식량 자원들을 이용할 것이다. 대머리 독수리는 썩은 고기(죽거나 부패한 식육)를 이용할 것이다. 그 청소동물의 이미지 때문에, 몇몇 사람들은 대머리 독수리를 싫어한다. 다른 사람들은 강하고 공격적인 새들을 좋아하지 않는다. 또 다른 사람들은 단지 그들이 식량으로 다른 동물을 죽여서 먹이로 삼는 새라는 이유로 반감을 가진다.

일단 독수리가 수면 가까이 떠다니거나 헤엄치는 물고기를 발견하면, 그것은 얕은 활공으로 먹이에 접근하여 갈고리 발톱으로 재빠르게 쳐서 물 밖으로 고기를 낚아챈다. 독수리는 그들의 발톱에 특별한 잠금 장치를 가지고 있다. 벌어진 발톱이 먹이를 칠 때, 그것들은 즉각적으로 닫히고 독수리가 단단한 표면에 밀어 내릴 때까지 다시 벌어지지 않는다.

이따금, 대머리 독수리는 물고기를 잡으려고 하면서 물속으로 뛰어든다. 독수리는 물밖으로 나올 때까지 다시 날 수 없으므로, 그것은 큰 날개를 헤엄치기 위해 사용한다. 독수리는 힘이 센 헤엄을 치는 짐승이지만, 물이 너무 차가우면, 저 체온 증에 압도될 지 모른다.

독수리는 약 4분 이내에 1파운드의 물고기를 소비할 수 있다. 독수리는 하나의 발톱으로 그것이 먹이를 잡고, 다른 하나로 그것의 횟대를 잡고 나서, 부리를 이용해 한 입씩 찢어 먹는다. 대머리 독수리는 다른 종들 뿐만 아니라 다른 대머리 독수리들에게서도 먹이를 훔친다. 다른 맹수를 뒤쫓는 것이 보통 그것이 잡은 사냥감을 떨어뜨리도록 설득하기에 충분하지만, 때때로 대머리 독수리들은 공격할 것이다. 대머리 독수리는 매일 음식을 먹을 필요가 없다. 그러나, 만일 독수리가 먹을 것 없이 너무 오래 지낸다면, 그것은 살아 남기 위해 효과적으로 사냥할 수 없을 지 모른다. 독수리는 먹이를 저장할 수 있는 소낭 이라 불리는 식도의 바깥 주머니를 가지고 있다. 대머리 독수리와 같은 청소 동물에게, 바다 표범의 시체는 예기치 않은 큰 먹이 공급원이다. 지방과 단백질이 풍부한, 바다 표범의

시체는 며칠 동안 독수리 떼에게 먹이를 줄 것이다. 비록 많은 칼로리를 얻을 지라도, 음식을 가지고 싸우면서 그것들을 잃을 것이다.

2   역사는 보통 지속적인 경제 발전이 더 작은 가족 규모를 결국에 초래한다는 사실을 보여준다. 예를 들어, 17, 18세기의 상업, 농업, 산업 혁명들이 지속적인 인구성장을 시작케한 유럽에서 무슨 일이 일어났는지를 생각해 보자. 일단 시작되어, 이러한 성장은 다음 두 세기에 걸쳐 계속적인 경제적, 사회적, 정치적 변형들을 자극했다. 사망률의 점차적인 감소가 위생학과 영양학의 진보를 통해 일어났다. 그러나, 소득, 도시화, 교육 그리고 건강상태가 특정한 문턱에 다다르면서 출생률 또한 하락했다.
"인구 통계학적 변화"로 일반화 되어지는, 이러한 유럽에서의 소규모의 가족으로 이끄는 더 나은 생활 수준의 경험은 2차 세계대전 후에야 인구 폭발을 겪은 라틴 아메리카, 아시아, 아프리카의 보다 최근의 경험들에 적용되는 것으로 알려졌다. 이러한 나중의 경우들에서는, 공중 위생 프로그램과 가족계획이 사망률과 출생률을 낮추는 중요한 역할을 하면서, 그러한 변화가 훨씬 더 빨리 일어났다. 여성교육의 빠른 성장 또한 중요한 역할을 했다. 유럽이 변화를 끝마치는데 거의 한 세기가 걸린 반면에, 많은 아시아와 라틴 국가들은 한 두 세대 안에 지속된 인구 성장에서 출생률의 하락으로 넘어갔다.
가족의 규모에 대한 결정은 경제학자들이 "효용 극대화" 과정이라고 부르는 것의 일부분이다. 아이들은 많은 방법으로 부모의 행복에 기여하지만, 또한 시간, 관심, 가족의 물자들을 얻으려고 겨룬다. 경제적 성장은 부모의 소망의 대상들과 가치관을 바꾸고, 아이들에게 드는 비용을 증가시키며, 부모의 효용에 대한 경쟁적인 원천들을 만들어 낸다. 이러한 모든 요소들을 비교 검토하여, 부부가 더 적은 수의 아이들을 원한다고 결심하기 때문에, 출생률은 하락하게 된다. 가족 계획 프로그램들은 부부가 그들 스스로 정해 놓은 목표들을 달성하도록 돕기 때문에 효과가 있다.
더 작은 가정을 향한 광범위한 욕구가 가족 계획 프로그램들이 과다하다는 사실을 의미하지는 않는다. 최근 수 십 년간 제 3세계 출생률의 약 40% 감소는 가족계획에 그 원인이 있고, 이러한 프로그램들의 성공은 우리가 또한 오늘날 마주치고 있는 "관념화 된" 인구통계학적 변화 –지속된 경제적 사회적 성장을 누려 본 적이 없는 나라들에서 조차 작은 가족이라는 표준을 향한 세계적인 변화– 에 책임이 있을지도 모른다.

3   광물 입자들, 유기 물질, 물 그리고 공기로 구성되어 있는 토양은 인간이 식량을 위해 의존하는 소중한 천연 자원이다. 물, 바람, 얼음과 다른 자연력은 땅으로부터 흙을 닳아 없애거나 없애는 토양 침식을 야기시킨다. 물과 바람은 특히 흙을 제거하는데 효과적이다: 강우가 흙 입자들을 느슨하게 하여 그것이 이동하는 물에 의해 운반되게 하는 반면, 바람은 특히 흙이 노출되고 건조한 상태라면 흙 입자를 느슨하게 해서 그것을 날려 보낸다.
토양 침식은 매우 자주 신문의 큰 표제가 되지는 않는 국가적이고 세계적인 문제이다. 그 문제가 얼마나 심각한지 느낌을 알기 위해, 해마다 토양 침식의 결과로서, 약 27억 미터톤(30억 톤)의 표토가 미국 농장으로부터 유실된다는 것을 생각해 보자. 미국 농림부는 미국 농경지의 약 5분의 1이 토양 침식으로 인한 피해에 취약하다고 추정한다. 침식은 한 지역에 있는 토양의 양을 감소시키기 때문에, 그것은 식물의 성장을 제한한다. 침식은 또한 흙의 일부분인 필수 광물들과 유기물을 제거하기 때문에, 토지의 산출력에 손실을 가져온다. 이러한 손실들의 결과로, 침식된 농경지의 생산성은 감소한다.
인간은 자주 서투른 토양 관리 습속으로 토양 침식을 촉진한다. 농업만이 피해를 주는 것은 아니다. 도로와 건물들을 건축하는 동안, 자연 식물계의 제거는 침식을 가속화한다. 재목과 펄프용 재를 얻기 위하여 큰 숲이 우거진 지역들을 깨끗이 베어버리는 것과 같은 불합리한 벌목 습속은 심각한 침식을 일으킨다.
토양 침식은 다른 천연 자원들에 해로운 영향력을 가지고 있다. 예를 들어, 개울, 강, 그리고 호수로 흘러 들어가는 침전물은 수질과 물고기 서식지들에 영향을 미친다. 만일 침전물들이 자주 그렇듯이, 살충제와 화학 비료의 잔류물을 포함하고 있다면, 그것은 훨씬 더 많이 물을 오염시킨다.

충분한 식물 덮개는 토양 침식을 제한한다: 잎이나 줄기는 강우의 충격을 완화하고, 뿌리는 흙이 제 자리에 있도록 돕는다. 비록 토양 침식이 자연적인 과정이라고 할 지라도, 식물 덮개는 많은 자연 생태계에서 그것(침식)을 무시해도 좋을 정도로 만들어 준다.

4   1930년대의 대공황의 절정 동안, 그리고 2차 세계대전 초기까지, 연방정부는 유례없는 방식으로 예술을 후원했다. 1933년과 1943년 사이의 11년 동안, 연방정부의 세금은 화가, 음악가, 배우, 작가, 사진사 그리고 무용수들을 고용했다. 정부가 그렇게 광범하게 예술을 후원한 적은 과거에도 없었고 그 이후에도 없었다.

뉴딜 예술 프로젝트는 일자리가 없는 예술가들에게 일을 주었지만, 그들은 또한 미국 예술과 문화를 장려하고, Franklin Roosevelt 대통령이 "풍부한 삶"으로 묘사한 것에 더 많은 미국인들이 접근할 수 있도록 하는 더 큰 임무를 가지고 있었다. 그 프로젝트는 가난과 절망으로부터 수 천명의 예술가들을 구했고, 나라 전역의 미국인이 처음으로 진품의 그림을 보고, 처음으로 전문 라이브 극장에 참석하거나, 처음으로 음악이나 그림 수업을 받는 것을 가능하게 했다.

그러나, 이러한 예술 프로젝트는 또한 논쟁을 유발했다. 몇몇 정치인들은 그것이 낭비적인 선전이라고 생각하고, 그것이 끝나기를 원했다; 다른 정치인들은 그것이 확대되기를 원했다. 그러한 논쟁은, 미국이 2차 세계 대전에 참전함에 따라, 결국 그 (예술)프로젝트를 소멸시켰다. 그러나, 그들이 만든 것의 상당수가 박물관, 도서관, 국가 공문서와 공적기록부를 포함하는 기록 보관소들의 노력을 통해 살아 남았다. 몇 년 전에 한 전시회가 뉴딜 예술프로젝트의 작품을 설명하고 전시했으며, 이러한 정부 후원 예술에 공통된 주제들을 토론했다. 거기에 전시된 그림, 인쇄물, 책, 연극 광고표, 포스터와 편곡들은 비상용의 작업 프로그램의 예술품과 문헌들 이상이었다. 그것들은 중대한 변화와 시련의 시간에 발생한 미국적 창조성을 보기 드물게 분출한 예들이었다.

Progressive Test 3-2

1   1920년대, 한 전시회에서 보여진 다섯 개의 놀랄 만한 프로젝트들과 관련하여, Frank Lloyd Wright는 영향이 크고 중요한 건축적 원형들을 발전시켰다. 진보된 건축기술과 시도되지 않은 기하학적인 패턴을 탐구하던 그는 자연적 위대함을 강조하기 위해 계산된 방식으로 그들의 대지들을 효과적으로 재구성한 시골과 교외의 건물 복합체를 착상해 냈다. 초기 디자인에서, Wright는 대지 자체를 덜 변화된 채로 두는 로지아(한 쪽이 트인 주랑)와 테라스 같은 건축학적 확장을 통해 이루어지는 연계를 이용해 좀 더 시험적으로 주위 환경에 접근했다. 이제야 건물과 대지 사이의 새롭고, 좀 더 설득력 있는 통일체가 생겼는데, 그것은 도로와 다른 이동 체계들이 유례없는 규모로 교묘하게 통합되어 있는 것이었다.

1920년대의 프로젝트들에서 Wright가 탐구했던 복잡한 기하학적 구조들은 피상적인 패턴보다 훨씬 더 많은 것을 나타냈다. **Wright의 접근법에서 그것들은 공간의 특별한 질을 표현했다.** 그의 글들이 증명하듯이, Wright는 자연의 탁월함과 거기에 내재하는 질서를 믿었는데, 그는 그것을 본질적으로 유클리드 기하학과 관련된 것으로 보았다. 건축물은 그들의 주위 환경을 흉내내도록 의도되는 것이 아니라, 교감적인 연합을 통해 인간의 존재를 알리도록 의도되었다. 풍경을 가장 많이 환기시키는 그의 묘사들에 있어서, 그가 이해한 것은 바로 이러한 기하학적인 질서였다 -정신적으로 질서정연하고, 본질적으로 건축적이며, 고대 건축물을 종종 연상시키고, 대지를 가로질러 움직이는 동안 자주 경험되는 것. 불완전하게 드러난 질서를 완성하기 위해 이러한 형태들을 필요할 때 구체화하면서, 그것들을 뽑아내고 명백하게 하는 것은 건축가의 몫이었다. 이것들은 우주의 내재하는 질서를 나타내고, 질서와 더 확고한 관계를 성취하기 위한 수단이었다.

그런 식으로, Wright는 각각의 특정한 위치와 끈끈한 결속을 수립할 뿐만 아니라 더욱 중요하게는 그 장소의 내재하는 구조를 완성하기 위해 그의 기하학적 구조들을 다양화 하면서, 장소와의 연결을 통해 보편적인 의미를 추구했다. 그는 오랫동안 연구되지 않아온 디자인의 문제점을 재조사하도록 이끈 믿음인, 자연의 숭고함에 대한 믿음을 경배함으로써, 그가 가장 좋아하는 19세기의 작가들과 초기의 더 먼 역사와 여전히 교감했다. 그러나, 그는 그 시대의 진보들을 통합시킴으로써 이러한 접근을 고무했고, 그 결과 기동성과 자연적, 진화적 변화의 새로운 인식이 그의 이상적인 조경의 일부가 되었다.

이리하여, 그는 심오하고 풍부하게 층을 이룬 건축 – 그것을 통해, 각각의 장소가 정돈된 우주의 일부분으로서 좀 더 완전히 드러나게 되는 – 을 마음에 그리면서, 장소와 시간 둘 다와의 관계에 영향을 끼쳤다.

2 대륙이 그들의 현재 위치에 항상 고정되어 있지 않았다는 믿음은 20세기 오래 전에 생각되었다; 이러한 개념은 1596년 만큼 빠른 시기에 독일 지도 제작자 Abraham Ortelius에 의해 그의 작품 "Thesaurus Geographicus" 에서 처음으로 제시되었다. Ortelius는 미국은 "지진과 홍수에 의해 유럽과 아프리카로부터 떨어져 나온 것"이라고 말하며 계속해서 다음과 같이 말했다: "만일 누군가가 세계지도를 가져와 주의 깊게 3개 대륙의 해안선을 고찰해 보면, 단절의 흔적들이 자신들을 드러낸다." Ortelius의 개념은 19세기에 다시 출현했다. 그러나, 1912년이 되어서야, 움직이는 대륙에 대한 개념이 Alfred Lothar Wegener라는 이름의 32살의 독일 기상학자에 의해 출판된 두 개의 논설에 소개되어진 무르익은 과학적 이론(대륙이동설로 불리는)으로서 심각하게 고려되었다. 그는 대략 2억년 전에 초 대륙 팡게아가 갈라지기 시작했다고 주장했다. Johannesburg대학의 지질학 교수이자 Wegener 의 가장 든든한 후원자들 중의 한 사람인 Alexander Du Toit는 팡게아가 처음 북반구의 Laurasia 와 남반구의 Gondwanaland 라는 두 개의 큰 대륙 덩어리로 나누어 졌다고 제시했다. 그리고 나서, Laurasia와 Gondwanaland는 계속해서 분열하여 오늘날 존재하는 다양한 더 작은 대륙들이 되었다.

Wegener의 이론은 삼 백년 전에 Abraham Ortelius에 의해 처음으로 언급된, 남아메리카와 아프리카 대륙이 놀랄만하게 잘 들어맞는 것으로 보이는 것에 부분적으로 근거를 두고 있었다. Wegener 는 또한 특이한 지질학적 구조와 지금은 대서양에 의해 넓게 분리된 남아메리카와 아프리카의 잘 맞는 해안선에서 발견되는 식물과 동물화석의 발견에 흥미를 갖게 되었다. 그는 이러한 유기체들의 대부분이 거대한 대양을 가로질러 헤엄치거나 운반되는 것은 물리적으로 불가능하다고 판단했다. 그에게 있어서, 아프리카와 남아메리카의 근해 지방들을 따라 동일한 화석 종들이 존재하는 것은 그 두 개의 대륙이 한 때 합쳐져 있었다는 가장 강력한 증거였다.

Wegener의 생각에는, 팡게아의 분열 이후 대륙의 이동은 어울리는 화석의 발견뿐만 아니라, 몇몇 대륙에서의 극적인 기후 변화의 증거를 설명했다. 예를 들어, 남극 대륙에서 열대 식물 화석(석탄 매장물의 형태로)의 발견은 이 극한의 땅이 전에는 풀이 많고 습지의 초목이 자랄 수 있는 더 온화한 기후의, 적도에 더 가까이 위치했음이 틀림없다는 결론을 이끌었다. 지질과 기후의 다른 부조화들은 현재 극지방들에서 발견되는 특이한 화석 양치류들(Glossopteris)과 남 아프리카의 Vaal River 계곡과 같은 현재의 건조한 아프리카에서 빙하 매장물들이 발견되는 것을 포함했다

3 Jefferson Davis는 정치에 관심을 가지게 되었고, 1845년, 미 하원 의원이 되었다. 그는 하원에 오래 머물지 않았다. 1846년 6월, 그는 사임하여 멕시코 전쟁에서 대령이 되었고 Zachary Taylor 장관(후에 대통령이 된) 아래서 복무했다.

Davis는 1847년 미시시피 주지사에 의해 죽은 미국 상원의원의 임기를 채우도록 임명되었다. 다음해 그는 그 임기의 나머지 동안 근무하도록 미시시피 주 의회에 의해 선출되었고, 1850년 정식 임기 동안 근무하도록 선출되었다. 헌법의 엄격한 해석을 믿는 Davis는 논쟁에서 1850년의 절충안을 반대하는 쪽에 관련되었다. Davis는 남부 공민권의 지도자인 상원의원 John C. Calhoun의 헌신적인 지지자였다. Davis는 미시시피가 1850년의 절충안을 받아 들이지 말아야 한다고 믿었고, States' Rights Democrats Party의 후보자로서 미시시피 주지사에 출마하기 위해 상원에서 사임했다.

1857년, Davis는 미시시피 주에 의해 미국 상원에 재선출되었다. 상원에서, 그는 남부와 노예 제도의 권리를 옹호했다. 그는 의회가 그 지역에서 노예제도를 보호할 것을 요구했다.

Abraham Lincoln 이 1860년에 대통령으로 선출되었을 때, Davis는 상원에서 사임했다. 미시시피는 연방 탈퇴 법령을 통과시켰고, Davis는 남부 동맹군의 우두머리로 임명되기를 희망했다. 대신에, 그는 미국 남부 연합 주의 임시 대통령으로 지명되었다. 그는 1861년 2월 18일에 취임 선서를 했다. **Davis는 1년 후인 1862년 2월 22일에 취임했다.**

Davis는 남부 연합 주의 훌륭한 행정관이었으나, 결국에는, 서투른 입안자로 증명되었다. 그는 건강이 나빴으나, 헌신적으로 대통령으로서의 그의 임무를 해냈다.

남북전쟁 이후, Davis는 체포되어 Monroe 요새에 투옥되었다. 그는 반역죄로 기소되었고, 재판을 기다리기 위해 2년 동안 감옥에 있었다. Horace Greeley와 일단의 북부 사람들이 보석금을 내고 Davis를 감옥에서 빼냈다. 그는 결코 다시 재판 받지 않았다.

4   Donner 일행은 미국에 대서양에서 태평양까지 뻗는 "명백한 운명"을 가져올 이주자들의 물결 속에 존재했다. Sacramento 와 American Rivers (현재의 Sacramento)의 합류점에 요새를 가지고 있는 스위스인 John Sutter 와 Diablo 산 가까이에 대목장을 가졌던 John Marsh를 포함하는 캘리포니아 정착자들로부터의 보고서들은 매우 좋은 기후, 농업하기 용이함, 그리고 멕시코 정부의 유약함을 설명했다. 이러한 보고서들은 경제적으로 침체되어 있으며, 말라리아에 시달리는 미시시피 계곡으로부터의 이주를 조장했다.

1845년까지 출판된 여러 권의 책들은 캘리포니아로 가는 그 길에 대해 기술하고 있다. 그 책들에 나타나 있는 캘리포니아에서의 삶에 대한 찬사와 가는 길에 대한 정보는 횡단하기 위해 알 필요가 있는 모든 것을 제공하는 듯 보였다. 대략 2,700명의 사람들이 1846년에 그 길을 떠났다. 약 1,500명이 캘리포니아로 갔고, 나머지는 오레곤으로 갔다.

캘리포니아로 가는 길은 정부에 의해 만들어진 것이 아니라, 1840년대에 구성된 이주자 공동체의 회원들에 의해 만들어진 것이었다. 세 일행들의 노력으로 두 개의 주요 장애물들을 넘어 통행 가능한 마차 길이 만들어졌다: 유타의 Great Salt Lake 사막과 캘리포니아의 Sierra Nevada 산맥. 그 결과 한 번의 여름이나 가을에 2,000 마일의 여정이 되었는데, 황소나 말로 하루에 15마일 씩 걸리므로 이것은 약 다섯 달의 여행을 의미하는 것이었다.

캘리포니아로 가는 첫번째 마차 길은 Santa Fe를 통해 Los Angeles로 가는 오래된 스페인 길이었다. 오레곤으로 가는 첫번째 길은 Missouri 강 상류를 따라 오레곤으로 가는 Lewis 와 Clark 의 경로였다. 그러나, 1820년대에 여러 부족들의 저항은 모피 사냥꾼들이 남쪽 경로의 록키 산맥을 가로지르는 North Platte강을 따르는 길을 사용하도록 했다. 사냥꾼들은 그 곳에서부터 Snake 강에 있는 Hudson Bay 회사의 Fort Hall에 도달했다.

사냥꾼들은 the Great Salt Lake로부터 Nevada 사막을 거쳐 캘리포니아로 사냥감을 찾아다녔다. 1828년 봄, Jedediah Smith는 현재 Ebbetts 경로 근처의 Sierra 를 가로질러 캘리포니아로부터 돌아왔다.

Actual Test 1

1   이민 온 아이들을 "미국인화 한다" 는 결정에 의해 얼마간 자극 받은 공교육의 성장은 남북전쟁 이후에 새로운 미국의 출현을 빠르게 하는 데 이바지했다. 1870년대까지, 공교육에 대한 미국의 헌신은 거의 보편적이었다. 1870년에 공립학교에 7백만의 학생이 있었고, 1920년까지 그 숫자는 3배가 되어 있었다. 이러한 진전에도 불구하고, 교육계 지도자들은 공립학교에서의 일련의 정치적 임명, 부패 그리고 무능함에 대항해서 싸워야만 했다.

중등학교의 확산은 공립학교 입학 증가의 주 원인이었다. 전쟁 전 미국에서는, 사립 교육 기관들이 대학에 들어가려는 사람들을 준비시켰다. 남북전쟁 초기에, 나라 전역에 단지 백 여 개의 공립 고등학교가 있었으나, 그 숫자는 빠르게 증가하여 1880년에는 대략 800개, 그 세기의 전환기에는 6,000개에 이르렀다.

이 시대의 미국 대학들은 규율, 도덕성, 수학과 고전에 비중을 둔 교육 과정, 그리고, 주일 학교에서는 민족학, 수사학과 함께 신학을 가르치려고 했다. 역사, 현대 언어와 문학, 그리고 몇몇 과학 수업은 허용되었지만 실험은 보통 수업 중 교수의 시범으로 제한되었다. 대학 강사들은 일시적인 피난처를 찾으려는 젊은 사람이나 안전한 안식처를 찾는 지친 설교자들인 경우가 많았다. 1871년에 한 작가는 전형적인 교수는 "특징이 없는, 무엇이든지 다 할 수 있는, 측량술과 라틴어 수사법을 가르치는데 똑같이 준비가 된, 그리고 그의 급료가 학교 담장을 회칠 하기위해 삭감되지 않는다면 감사할 사람"이라고 칭했다.

그럼에도 불구하고, 고등 학문에 대한 수요는 1870년 5만2천명에서 1890년에 15만 7천명으로 그리고 1920년에는 60만 명으로 학생 수의 증가를 가져왔다. 같은 기간동안, 교육기관의 수는 563개에서 대략 1000개로 증가했다. 이렇게 증가하는 학생의 다양한 요구를 수용하기 위해서, 대학은 정확히 규정된 과목들에서 선택 과목제도로 바뀌었다. 그 새로운 접근은 학생들이 그들의 강점을 선호하고 대학들은 그들의 영역을 넓힐 수 있도록 했다. 그러나 Henry Cabot Lodge가 불평했던 것처럼, 그 접근은 또한 학생들로 하여금 "별 관련 없는 과목들을 단지 그 과목들이 쉽다는 이유로 또는 그것들을 가르치는 사람들에 의해 부과되는 짐이 가볍다는 이유로 눈치 빠르게 선택함으로써 배우는 것 하나도 없이 탈출하게 "만들었다."

2 건조와 반 건조 지역에서 발견되는 토양은 종종 무기성 광물질 소금이 높은 농도로 함유되어있다. 이러한 지역들에서 하부 토양 층으로 흘러가는 물의 양은 극미한데, 그 이유는 (그나마) 적은 강우량이 재빨리 증발하기 때문이다. 반대로, 습한 기후는 토양에서 소금을 걸러내 수로와 지하수로 보내기에 충분한 강우량을 가지고 있다. 농지로 물을 끌어들이는 것은 종종 더 소금기가 많아지는 결과를 가져온다. 또한, 물을 끌어들인 토양이 물에 잠기게 될 때, 소금은 지하수로부터 위쪽으로 표토까지 올라와 결정화된 지각으로 퇴적된다.

대부분의 식물은 소금기 많은 땅으로부터 그들이 필요로 하는 모든 물을 얻을 수 없는데 그 이유는 그러한 토양은 물 균형 문제를 가져오기 때문이다. 정상적인 상태에서, 식물세포의 수분이 많은 세포질에 용해된 물질은 토양의 그것보다도 더 낮은 물의 농도를 제공한다. 결과적으로, 물은 삼투성에 의해 토양에서 식물의 뿌리로 이동한다. 그러나, 토양의 수분이 다량의 용해된 소금을 함유할 때, 그것의 수분 농도는 식물세포의 수분농도보다 낮을 지 모르고 결과적으로, 물은 식물의 뿌리에서 빠져 나가 소금기 있는 토양으로 이동한다. 당연히 대부분의 식물들은 이런 조건 하에서 살아남을 수 없다. 염분을 함유한 토양에서 번성하는 식물 종들은 그것들이 많은 양의 소금을 견딜 수 있도록 하는 특별한 적응 방식들을 가지고 있다. 대부분의 농작물들은 유전적으로 높은 염분을 견디도록 선택되지 않았다면 염분이 있는 땅에서 생산적이지 못하다.

원칙적으로, 염분이 있는 토양에서 여분의 염분을 제거하기 위한 방법은 염분을 용해 시키기에 내기 위해 충분한 물을 공급하는 것이다. 이것이 간단하게 들리지만, 이것은 매우 어렵고, 많은 경우 불가능하다. 하나는, 염분이 있는 땅은 보통 물 공급이 부족한 건조와 반 건조 지역에 나타난다. 또한, 많은 토양이 배수가 잘 되는 특성을 가지고 있지 않으므로, 단순히 많은 물을 공급하는 것은 침수를 가져올 뿐이다. 간과해서는 안될 또 다른 요소는 만약 염분이 토양 밖으로 흘러나온다 할지라도, 어디로든 가야만 한다는 것이다. 여분의 염분은 보통 지하수나 강, 하천으로 운반되어 수질 오염물질이 된다.

3 째즈 연주자들은 그들이 선택한 스타일의 관습의 범위 안에서 즉흥연주를 한다. 전형적으로 즉흥연주는 대중적인 노래나 원곡의 반복되는 화음 진행에 의해 이루어진다. 악기 연주자들은 흑인 성악 스타일 – 글리산도(註: 음계를 빠르게 오르내리는 것)와 슬리이딩(註: 음이 점점 높아지거나 점점 낮아지는 것), 다양한 뉘앙스의 음조(블루스의 음계에서 미세하게 반음을 내린 음조인 블루노트를

포함하는) 그리고 으르렁거리는 소리나 울부짖는 소리와 같은 음조 효과 등이 사용되는 - 을 모방한다.

개인의 소리나 음조의 특색(리듬과 형식의 특유한 감각과 개인의 연주 스타일)을 개발하기 위한 노력으로, 연주자는 연속적인 싱커페이션(기대되지 않는 곳에서의 악센트)과 스윙 - 멜로디가 정해진 박자에 맞춰서, 다음엔 그 박자에 약간 엇갈려서, 번갈아 들릴 때 생기는 당김과 반동력의 느낌 - 에 의해 특징 지워지는 리듬을 만든다. 쓰여진 악보는, 있다면, 단지 지침서 - 즉흥연주가 이루어지는 틀을 제공하는 - 로만 사용된다. 전형적인 기악 편성은 피아노, 스트링 베이스, 드럼, 선택 사항인 기타로 구성되는 리듬 부분으로 시작하고, 그것에 여러 가지의 관악기들이 덧붙여지기도 한다. 대형 밴드에서, 관악기는 섹스폰, 트럼본, 트럼펫의 세 부류로 나뉜다.

비록 몇몇 스타일에서 예외가 있지만, 대부분의 재즈는 무한한 수의 멜로디가 모든 노래의 화음 진행에 적합할 수 있다는 원칙에 기초하고 있다. 음악가는 각 독창자가 노래를 할 때 화음 진행 - 계속적으로 반복되는 - 에 맞는 멜로디를 즉흥적으로 연주한다, 원하는 만큼 많은 후렴들을. 많은 서로 다른 형식을 가진 악보들이 즉흥 재즈연주를 위해 사용되지만, 특히 두 가지 형식이 재즈에 사용되는 노래들에서 자주 발견된다. 하나는 대중적 노래 후렴들의 AABA형식인데, 그것은 전형적으로 박자상 32소절을 구성하고, 그것은 다음과 같이 8소절의 4개 부분으로 나뉜다: 섹션 A; 섹션 A의 반복; 섹션 B (자주 새로운 조에서 시작하는 "경과부"나 "방출부"); 섹션 A의 반복. 두 번째 형태는 미국 흑인의 민속 음악에 깊이 뿌리내린 12소절의 블루스 형태이다. **32소절 AABA 형태와 달리, 블루스 노래는 상당히 통일된 화음 진행을 가지고 있다.**

4 고고학적 증거는 콘도르가 서부의 원주민들에 의해 수천년간 숭배되어왔고 이들의 전설과 의식에서 중요한 역할을 해왔음을 알려준다. 콘도르는 신성하고 초자연적인 신들 뿐만 아니라 초자연적인 세계와의 의사소통을 제공할 수 있다고 여겨졌다.

좀 더 최근에는, 캘리포니아 콘도르가 그들을 멸종에서 구하기 위한 열렬하고 때로는 논의의 여지가 있는 운동의 대상이 되었다. 콘도르의 급격한 감소에 맞서, 과학자들은 야생에 있는 알을 수집하고, 궁극적으로 캘리포니아 하늘의 올바른 위치에 콘도르를 복귀시킬 목적으로 그것들을 잡아놓고 기르기 위해 자유롭게 날아다니는 새들을 잡기 시작했다.

콘도르는 북미에서 아마도 결코 그 수가 많지 않았다. 이 종들은 한 때 British Columbia부터 Baja California에 이르는 태평양 해안 전역에 걸쳐 분포했었다. 텍사스, 플로리다, 뉴욕과 같이 동부의 먼 곳에서 화석들이 발견되어 왔다. 그러나 더욱 최근에, 그들은 Transverse 산맥과 Sierra Nevada산맥 남부, 해안에 위치한 산맥들의 일부분을 포함하는 캘리포니아의 편자 모양의 지역에 한정되었다.

비록 1890년대 이래로 이 종이 감소한다고 생각되어왔지만, 수년간 아무도 얼마나 많은 캘리포니아 콘도르가 존재하는지 정확히 알지 못했다. 한 추정에 따르면, 1940년대 초에 약 백 마리 정도의 수가 있다고 했다. 또 다른 추정은 1960년대 초에 50에서 60마리 정도가 있었다고 알려주었다. 1970년대 후반까지, 추정치는 25에서 30마리로 감소했다.

수 년간의 연구에도 불구하고, 과학자들은 이 새의 감소 이유를 정확히 집어낼 수 없었다. 몇몇 요인들은 콘도르와 그들의 알을 불법적으로 수집하는 것, 가축의 천적을 박멸하려는 농장주들이 놓아둔 물질을 먹고 중독되는 것, 콘도르가 먹이로 하는 동물의 시체에 깊게 박힌 총알들로부터 나온 납 조각들을 섭취해서 중독되는 것 그리고 전선과 같은 구조물에 충돌하는 것을 포함한다. 덧붙여, 도로, 도시 주택지역 그리고 현대 문명의 주말 산림 피서지는 콘도르가 먹이를 찾기 위해 필요로 하는 탁 트인 시골의 많은 부분을 대체해버리고 있다. 콘도르들의 낮은 출산율과 번식할 수 있을 정도의 성장을 하는 데 소요되는 수 년은 당연히 전체 콘도르들이 이러한 위협들에 훨씬 더 취약하도록 만든다.

1   역사가들은 "혁명" 이라는 단어를 폭력적인 봉기, 현저히 혁신적이고 영향력 있는 것, 심오하고 중요한 변화를 일으키는 과정의 여러 다른 의미로 사용한다. 혁명을 논할 때, 깨닫지 못한 채로 한 의미에서 다른 의미로 바꾸기는 쉽다. 이것은 특히 산업혁명 같은 것을 논할 때 피하려고 하는 것이다. 산업혁명은 세계에서, 특히 서구에서, 큰 변화를 가져 온 긴 과정이라고 주로 여겨지지만, 몇몇 작가들은 혁신을 강조하고 석탄 채굴과 사용, 증기 기관의 원리와 운영을 논하는데 많은 시간을 보내는 것을 선호한다. 그러나, 이것들 중 어느것도 특별히 새로운 것은 아니었다.

1092년에 Liege(현재의 벨기에)에 있는 Saint James 수도원의 한 수도사는 많은 "검은 암석"이 부근의 흙 아래서 발견되었고 이것은 "빈자들에게 온기를 주고 장인들에게 불을 주는" 대단한 이점들을 가지고 있다고 기록했다. 19세기에, 중요한 철강공장이 그 석탄 매장물을 사용하여 Liege 에 설립되었으나, 그 때까지도 개발되지는 않았다. 중세 사람들은 그들의 "검은 암석"이 유독한 증기 (우리가 "오염"이라 부를)를 내뿜는 것을 알고 사용을 금지하는 법을 통과시켰다. 그 당시 또한, 헬레니즘 시대로 거슬러 올라가 알렉산드리아 박물관에서 일하던 영리한 친구들 중 하나인, Hiero가 흥미로운 장치를 만들었다. 그는 꽉 끼는 뚜껑과 양쪽에 하나씩 반대방향을 가리키는 두개의 주둥이를 가진 구 모양의 차 주전자를 만들었다. 그는 그 안에 물을 넣고 조그만 불 위에 실을 이용해서 그것을 걸었다.

물이 끓기 시작하면서, 증기가 용기 안에서 쌓였고 주둥이를 통해 빠져나가기 시작했다. 증기가 반대방향으로 튀어 나왔고 금속 구는 더욱 빠르게 회전하기 시작했다. Hiero 는 이 장치를 공기로(爐)라고 불렀고 그의 친구들은 그것이 매우 독창적이라 생각했다. 하지만, 마야문명 사람들이 바퀴를 단지 당기는 장난감에만 사용한 것처럼, 그것도 교묘한 장난감에 지나지 않았다. 공기로는 많은 결함이 있었지만, 만약, Hiero와 그의 동료들이 그렇게 할 중요한 이유가 있었다면 그들은 틀림없이 그것을 더 나아가 효율적인 증기터빈으로 발전시켰을 것이다. 그러나, 그렇게 할 이유가 없었기에 공기로의 원리는 대부분 잊혀졌다.

2   대략 50억년 전까지, 태양 성운은 약 75%의 수소, 23%의 헬륨, 2%의 무거운 원소(가스, 먼지, 얼음)들을 포함하는 다른 물질로 이루어진 회전하는 원반 모양의 덩어리였다. 팔을 안으로 모으며 회전하는 스케이터처럼, 성운은 응축하면서 더 빨리 회전했다. 그 중심에 모인 물질들은 최초의 태양이 되었다. 외부에 있던 물질들의 대부분은 결국에는 별의 주위를 돌고 스스로의 빛에 의해 빛나지 못하는 작은 천체인 혹성이 되었다.

새로운 혹성들은 어린 태양 (원시 태양)을 둘러싼 먼지와 부스러기의 원반에서 융합(작은 입자들이 모여 큰 덩어리가 되는 것)이라 알려진 과정을 통해 형성되었다. 중력이 더 강한 더 큰 덩어리들이 응축하는 물질의 대부분을 잡아 당겼다. 원시 태양의 주변이 가장 온도가 높았는데, 가장 먼저 고체화한 것은 끓는 점이 높은 물질 (주로 금속과 특정한 광물질)이었다. 태양에서 가장 가까운 혹성인 수성은 철이 높은 온도에서 고체이므로 주로 철로 되어있다. 다소 먼 바깥의 더 차가운 지역들에서, 마그네슘, 규소, 물, 산소가 응축했다. 메탄과 암모니아는 혹한의 바깥 지역에서 축적되었다. 지구가 물, 규소-산소 화합물, 금속으로 이루어진 것은 그 융합하고 있는 구름 같은 것 내부의 중간에 위치한 결과이다. 바깥쪽 태양계의 혹성들 (목성, 토성, 천왕성, 해왕성)은 대부분 메탄과 암모니아 얼음으로 구성 되어있는데, 이는 이 가스들이 단지 매우 낮은 온도에서만 응결할 수 있기 때문이다.

융합 기간은 아마도 5천 만년에서 7천 만년까지 지속되었다. 내부 온도가 수소 원자들을 헬륨으로 융합하기에 충분하게 높아졌을 때 원시 태양은 별이 되었다. 이런 핵 반응의 격렬함은 방사능 - 내부의 행성들을 빠르게 지나치고, 여분의 입자들이 있는 지역을 깨끗이 하며, 빠른 융합의 시기를 끝내도록 한 - 을 내보냈다. 우리가 지금 거대한 외행성들에서 보는 것과 같은 가스들은 한 때는 내행성을 둘러싸고 있었을 지 모르지만, 이런 태양 에너지와 입자들의 급격한 움직임은 가스들을 벗겨 내 버렸다.

3   미국의 직접적인 개입이 상대적으로 짧았고(1917-1918), 그 사상자들이 유럽연합국과 적국의 사상자들보다 훨씬 적었던 사실에도 불구하고, 많은 역사가들은 두 세계대전 사이의 기간을 미국이 외상으로 인해 "성인이 된" 기간으로 묘사한다. John Dos Passos는 미국의 전후 환멸감을 그의 소설 "Three Soldiers" (1921)에서 표현했고, 문명은 "거짓의 거대한 건축이었고 전쟁은 그것의 파괴가 아니라, 가장 충분하고 궁극적인 표현이었다" 라고 기록했다. 충격을 받고 영구적으로 변한 미국인들은 본국에 돌아왔으나 그들의 순수성을 결코 되찾을 수 없었다. **시골에서 온 군인들도 쉽게 그들의 (정신적인) 고향으로 돌아갈 수 없었다.**

세계를 경험한 후, 많은 사람들이 이제는 현대적이고 도시적인 삶을 갈망했다. 파종기, 수확기, (짚)단 묶는 기계 등의 새로운 농기계들이 획기적으로 농사 일에 대한 요구를 감소시켰으나, 생산성이 증가했음에도 불구하고, 농민들은 가난했다. 도시 노동자들의 임금처럼, 농산물가격도 사업 이해관계에 의해 크게 영향을 받는, 제어되지 않는 시장의 힘에 좌우지 되었다: 농부들과 효과적인 노동조합에 대한 정부보조금은 아직 설립되지 않았었다. "미국민의 중요한 일은 사업이다" 라고 Calvin Coolidge 대통령은 1925년 선언했고, 대부분 이에 동의했다.

전후 "Big Boom" 때, 사업은 번성했고 성공한 사람들은 그들의 무모한 꿈을 넘어서는 성공을 이루었다. 처음으로 많은 미국인들은 고등교육을 위해 등록했는데 1920년대에 대학등록자수는 두 배가 되었다. 중산층이 번창했고, 이 시대에 미국인들은 세계에서 가장 높은 국민 평균소득을 누리기 시작했고, 많은 사람들이 최고 지위의 상징인 자동차를 구입했다. 전형적인 도시의 미국인 집은 전기불로 빛났고, 집과 바깥세계를 연결시키는 라디오와 전화, 사진기, 타자기 또는 재봉틀를 가진 것을 자랑했다. Sinclair Lewis의 소설 "Babbitt" (1922)의 사업가 주인공처럼, 보통의 미국인들은 기계들이 현대적이고 대부분 미국인들이 발명하고 만든 것이기에 이것들을 호의적으로 생각했다.

4   1950년대 초반까지, 수면에 대해 거의 알려진 것이 없었다. **그러다가 하나의 획기적인 발견이 생리학자 Nathaniel Kleitman - 수면에 대해 연구하느라 자신의 전 생애를 보낸 유일한 사람 -의 실험실에서 일어났다.** Kleitman은 그의 대학원생중의 한명인 Eugene Aserinsky에게 수면의 시작을 특징짓는 느리게 굴러가는 안구 움직임이 밤새 계속되는 지를 알아내는 지루한 과제를 주었다. 두 사람 모두 놀랍게도, Aserinsky는 안구 운동이 정말 일어나는데, 느린 것이 아니라 빠르다는 것을 발견했다. 뇌의 전기적 활동을 측정하는 뇌파전위 기록 장치를 사용하여, Kleitman의 학생들 중 또 다른 한명인 William Dement와 함께 이 연구자들은 수면자의 빠른 안구 움직임을 뇌파의 형태변화와 상호 관련시킬 수 있었다. 성인 지원자들이 실험실에서 밤에 자는 동안 과학자들은 그들을 관찰하고 그들의 뇌활동, 근육긴장, 호흡, 그 밖의 생리적인 반응들의 변화를 측정했다. 이 연구 결과, 오늘날 우리는 수면이 휴식의 연속상태가 아니라는 것을 안다. 성인에게서, 빠른 안구 운동(REM)은 평균 매 90분마다 반복되는 초일(超日)주기로 적은 안구운동, 즉, non-REM(NREM)과 교대로 나타난다. REM주기는 몇 분에서 길게는 한 시간, 평균적으로는 약 20분간 지속된다. REM이 시작될 때 마다, 수면자의 뇌에서 나오는 전기적인 활동의 형태는 바뀌어 깨어 있을 때의 것과 비슷하게 된다. Non-REM 상태는 그 자체가 더 짧고 뚜렷한 단계들로 나뉘고, 각각은 특별한 뇌파 형태와 관련이 있다.

당신이 처음 침대로 올라가서, 눈을 감고, 쉴 때, 당신의 뇌는 알파 파를 분출한다. 뇌파전위 기록장치의 기록에는, 알파 파가 규칙적인 리듬, 높은 진폭, 초당 8-12주기의 낮은 주파수를 가진다. 알파 파 활동은 휴식을 취하거나 특별히 어떤 일에 집중하지 않는 것과 연관되어 있다. 점차적으로, 이 파들은 점점 더 느려지고, 사람들은 고개를 끄덕이는 상태로 표류하여 각 단계가 전 단계보다 더 깊은 4단계를 거치게 된다. REM과 non-REM은 밤새 계속해서 교대로 나타나는데, REM주기는 시간이 흐르면서 더 길어지고 더 가까워지는 경향이 있다. 초기 REM주기는 단지 몇 분간만 지속하는 반면에, 후기 REM은 20-30분 정도 때로는 한 시간까지도 지속되는데, 그것이 자명종이 울릴 때 사람들이 꿈을 꾸고 있는 것 같은 느낌이 드는 이유이다.

5   crustose, foliose 그리고 fruticose라는 세 가지 서로 다른 성장 형태들 중의 하나를 전형적으로 가지는 약 20,000종의 이끼들이 있다.

이끼가 한 개의 유기체처럼 보이지만, 실제는 광합성 유기체와 진균류사이의 공생적 연합이다. 광합성을 하는 쪽은 보통 녹색 조류나 시아노 박테리아이고, 진균류는 대개 자낭균이다. 열대지방의 몇몇 이끼들에서, 균성 상대는 담자균이다. 이끼들에서 발견되는 조류나 시아노 박테리아는 생태계의 독립생활을 하는 종에서도 또한 발견되지만, 이끼의 균성 부분은 일반적으로 이끼의 부분으로서만 발견된다.

실험실에서 이끼의 진균류와 광합성 유기체는 분리되어 적절한 배양 환경에서 따로 따로 성장할 수 있다. 조류나 시아노 박테리아는 분리되었을 때 더 빨리 자라는 반면, 진균류는 천천히 자라고, 많은 복합 탄수화물을 제공하는 배양환경을 필요로 한다. 일반적으로, 진균류는 광합성 유기체와 분리되면 자실체(子實體)들을 생산하지 않지만, 이끼의 부분으로서 진균류는 자실체들을 생산하는데, 그것은 둘 중 하나만을 독립적으로 유지할 수 없는 조건의 배양환경에 함께 놓여지는 때이다.

과거에는 이끼가 상호주의, 즉 두 종류에 모두 똑같이 이익이 되는 공생관계의 명확한 표본으로 간주되었다. 광합성 유기체는 그 자신과 진균류를 위해 탄수화물 분자를 생산하는 광합성을 수행하고, 진균류는 그 광합성 파트너를 탈수로부터 보호할 뿐만 아니라 그것을 위해 물과 광물질을 흡수한다. **그러나, 어떤 생물학자들은 이끼의 공생관계는 상호부조론의 진정한 한 예가 아니라, 진균류에 의한 광합성 유기체의 통제된 기생생활의 예라고 생각한다.** 현미경 검사를 통해 몇몇 조류 세포들이 균사들에 의해 침투되고 파괴된다는 것이 드러난다.

Actual Test 3

1   남북전쟁이후, 도시산업은 급속하게 발전한 반면에 농업은 쇠퇴하기 시작했다. 농부들은 그들이 뒤처지고 있다는 것을 알았다. 그들은 이익에 대한 정부의 무관심과 적대 행위에 대해 의심했다. 미국의 농부들은 그들이 세계의 많은 곳에서 농업을 강타한 국제적 위기에 말려 들었다는 것을 이해하지 못했다.

수출 주요 농산물(예를 들어 밀과 면화)을 생산하는 농부들의 위기는 농업 생산물의 세계 시장을 창조한 통신과 수송 혁명에서 기인했다. 선박들이 처음 1869년 수에즈 운하를 통해 출항했고, 그 해 처음 기관차가 북아메리카 대륙을 횡단했다. 게다가, 광활한 넓이의 새로운 땅이 미시시피 강을 가로질러 서쪽뿐만 아니라 남아메리카 호주 그리고 캐나다에서 경작지가 되었고, 동시에 기계화된 경작의 새로운 기술이 생산성을 크게 증가시켰다. 1831년에 기계 수확기의 발명은 곡물 생산을 6배로 증가시켰다.

농부들은 그들의 경쟁자에 대한 보호 또는 세계적 생산고에 대한 통제 없이 세계 시장에서 경쟁하도록 강요되었다. 이리하여, 농산품의 가격은 생산성이 오르면서 떨어졌다. 1867년에, 미국 농부들은 1,700만 에이커의 땅에서 밀 2억 1,100만 부셸을 생산했고, 그들은 1부셸 당 평균 $2.01를 받았다. 1868년에, 미국 농부들은 1,900만 에이커의 땅에서 밀 2억 4,600만 부셸을 생산했고, 그들은 1부셸 당 평균 $1.46를 받았다. 1869년에, 미국 농부들은 2,100만 에이커의 땅에서 밀 2억 9,000만 부셸을 생산했고, 그들은 1부셸 당 평균 $.91를 받았다. 1870년부터 1873년까지 면화는 파운드 당 평균하여 약 15.1 센트 였고, 1894년부터 1898년 까지 그것은 파운드 당 평균 5.8 센트로 떨어졌다. 1889년에 옥수수는 캔사스에서 부셸 당 10센트로 팔리고 있었고, 농부들은 연료로 사용하기 위해 그것을 태웠다. 조지아 농부들은 생산하는데 파운드 당 약 7 센트의 비용이 드는 면화에 대해 파운드 당 5 센트를 받고 있었다.

2   1840년대 중반에 이르러, 미국은 두개의 바다를 둔 나라가 되어 있었다. 멕시코와의 Guadaloupe Hidalgo 조약과 영국과 오레곤 문제를 조기 해결한 결과, 미국은 캘리포니아, 오레곤 그리고 그 대륙 내부의 많은 부분에 대한 지배권을 가지게 되었다. 그 광대한 영역을 연결할 필요성을 인식하면서, 1853년 의회는 Jefferson Davis, 그 당시 국방장관에게 대륙간 철도에 대한 가능성 조사를 수행할 것을 명령했다. 가장 좋은 경로에 관한 수 년간의 논쟁 후에, 링컨 대통령은 1862년 7월 1일 태평양 철도 조약에 서명했고, 미국 역사상 가장 큰 모험 중의 하나가 시작되었다.

The Union Pacific과 the Central Pacific, 두 개의 철도 회사는 대륙의 양 끝을 연결할 철도와 전신선을 건설하도록 정식인가를 받았다. The Union Pacific은 대평원을 가로질러 (네브라스카 오마하 근처의) 100번째 자오선으로부터 서쪽으로 건설하게 되었고, the Central Pacific은 시에라 네바다 산맥을 거쳐 새크라멘토로부터 동쪽으로 건설하게 되었다.

토지 보조금과 더불어, 정부는 얼마나 많은 철도가 놓여지는가에 따라 각 철도회사에 재원을 약속함으로써, 두 회사 사이의 열렬한 경쟁을 유발했다. 유목 원주민, 모피 상인 그리고 탐험가들의 영역이었던 조용한 땅들이 측량 기사들, 등급을 매기는 사람들, 버팀 다리 건설자들, 터널 발파공들 그리고 못 박는 이들의 야단법석에 물려갔다. 남북 전쟁의 퇴역 군인들과 이민자들을 포함하여 수천명의 노동자들이 수목이 없는 사막을 가로지르고 높이 솟은 화강암 산을 통과하여 철도를 놓는 몹시 힘든 작업을 하기 위해 소집되었다. The Central Pacific과 the Union Pacific의 철도들이 서로 접근함에 따라, 그 두 철도 회사들은 만나는 지점에 대해 합의에 도달할 수 없었다. 해결책으로 그들은 320킬로미터 길이의 평행한 노반을 측량하고 등급을 매겼다. 결국, 그들은 유타 주의 Promontory를 만나는 지점으로 선택했고, 1869년 5월 10일에 전건(電鍵)은 그 선로의 완성을 알리는 소식을 전했다.

다음 20년 동안, 철도 회사들은 철도망에 176,000킬로미터를 더하고 결국에는 일곱 개의 대륙간 철도 선로를 건설하면서 최고의 성장을 경험했다. 1차 세계 대전 직전까지, 철도 회사들은 400,000 킬로미터가 넘는 철도 선로를 가지며, 미국에서 그들의 절정기에 도달했다.

3   태평양 연어종들의 사실상 절대적으로 확실한 귀소 본능은 믿기 어려울 정도다. 두 살 된 연어로 하류에 이주한 후, sockeye연어는 거의 4년 동안 태평양에 걸쳐 수백 마일을 배회하고, 무게가 2킬로그램에서 5킬로그램까지 자라면, 원래 시내의 상류에 알을 낳기 위해 태어난 시내까지 거의 실수 없이 돌아온다. 헤메는 일이 가끔 있긴 하지만, 이것은 유전자 흐름을 증가시키고, 새로운 시냇물에 살도록 하는 중요한 방법이다.

여러 실험들에서 귀소하는 연어가 그들의 원래 시내의 독특한 냄새를 따라 상류로 안내된다는 것을 보여준다. 연어가 최종적으로 그들의 부모가 산란한 자리(그들 자신이 부화되었던 곳)에 도달하면, 그들은 알을 낳고 죽는다. 그 다음해 봄, 새로 부화된 연어 새끼들은 하류 이동 전과 이주를 하는 동안 두 살 된 연어로 변한다. 이 때에 그들은 시내의 특유한 냄새에 강한 인상을 받는데, 이것은 분명히 원래 시내의 유역에 특징적인 초목과 흙에 의해 퍼진 혼합물들의 하나의 모자이크이다. 그들은 또한 강 아래로 이동하는 동안 그들이 지나치는 다른 시내들의 냄새들을 각인하는 것처럼 보이고, 되돌아가는 어른 연어로서 상류로 이주하는 동안 반대 순서로 이러한 냄새들을 지도로 사용하는 것처럼 보인다.

어떻게 연어는 길 없는 개방된 대양의 수 마일로부터 연안의 강 입구까지 그들의 길을 찾을까? 연어는 해안으로부터 수백 마일을 이동하는데, 너무나 멀어서 그들 원래 시내의 냄새를 탐지할 수 없다. 실험은 새들처럼 몇몇 이동하는 물고기들이 태양의 위치에 방위를 맞춤으로써 항해할 수 있다는 것을 시사한다. 그러나, 이주성의 연어는 흐린 날이나 밤에도 항해할 수 있는데, 이것은 태양을 이용한 항해가, 만약 사용된다 해도, 연어의 유일한 항해 단서가 될 수 없다는 것을 나타낸다. 또 새들처럼 물고기들 또한 지구의 자장을 감지할 수 있고 자장에 방위를 맞춤으로써 항해할 수 있는 듯하다. 마지막으로, 어류 생물학자들은 연어가 정확한 항해 능력을 전혀 필요로 하지 않을 지 모르고, 그 대신에 그들의 강이 위치한 일반적인 연안 지역에 도달하기 위해 대양 해류, 기온의 증감, 그리고 먹이의 이용 가능성을 사용할 지 모른다는 것을 인정한다. 이러한 점에서 보면, 그들은 그들이 출생한 시내에 도달할 때까지 각 시내의 합류점에서 정확히 방향을 바꾸면서 그들의 각인된 냄새 지도에 의해 항해할 것이다.

4 오늘날 대기가 따뜻해지고 있다는 사실을 의심하는 과학자는 거의 없다. 대부분은 또한 온난화의 속도가 빨라지고 있고 이러한 기온 변화의 결과들이 더욱 더 혼란을 일으킬 수 있다는 사실에 동의한다. 심지어 고등학생도 몇몇 투영된 결과들을 술술 이야기할 수 있다: 대양은 따뜻해질 것이고 빙하들이 녹아, 해수면이 올라가고 소금물이 많은 낮은 해안가의 부락을 침수시킬 것이다. 동시에, 농업에 적절한 지역들은 바뀔 것이다. 날씨 패턴 또한 더 변덕스러워지고 폭풍우가 더 심해질 것이다. 그러나 덜 친숙한 결과들이 똑같이 해로울 수 있다. 그 중에서도, 컴퓨터 모형은 지구 온난화와 그것이 야기하는 다른 기후 변화들이 많은 심각한 의학적 병의 발병률과 분포를 넓힐 것이라고 예측한다. 불안하게도, 이러한 예상들은 실현될 것 같다.
대기의 가열작용은 여러 경로를 통해 건강에 영향을 미칠 수 있다. 가장 직접적으로는, 그것은 더 많은 더욱 강하고 뜨거운 열파를 발생시킬 수 있는데, 그것은 만일 저녁시간이 냉각 교체를 가져오는데 실패한다면 특히 믿을 수 없이 되어버릴 것이다. 불행하게도, 밤의 냉각현상 부족이 있을 수 있다. 대기는 불균형적으로 가열되고, 밤과 겨울 그리고 약 50도 보다 더 높은 위도에서 가장 큰 상승을 보이고 있다. 몇몇의 장소에서, 열파와 관련된 사망자 수는 2020년까지 2배가 될 것으로 예상된다. 게다가 길어진 열은 스모그의 발생과 알레르기를 일으키는 물질들의 분산을 높일 것이다. 이 두 가지 효과는 호흡기 증상과 관련되어 있다.
지구 온난화는 또한 다소 덜 직접적이지만, 날씨 패턴을 수정함으로써 -특히 홍수와 가뭄의 빈도와 강도를 높이고, 날씨에서 급격한 변화를 야기시킴으로써- 인간의 복지를 심각하게 위협할 수 있다. 대기가 지난 세기에 걸쳐 따뜻해지면서, 건조한 지역의 가뭄이 더 오래 지속되었고, 강수량의 대규모 폭발이 더욱 흔한 일이 되었다. 물에 빠지거나 굶주림에 의해 죽음을 가져오는 것 이외에, 이러한 재앙은 다양한 방법으로 전염병의 출현, 부활 그리고 확산을 촉진한다.
이러한 예상은 전염병이 병에 다시 넣기가 매우 어려울 수 있는 마귀이기 때문에 큰 고민거리이다. 그것이 사나운 홍수나 장기간의 가뭄보다 일거에 더 적은 사람들을 죽일지도 모르지만, 일단 그것이 공동체에 뿌리를 내리면, 그것은 자주 박멸을 좌절시키고 다른 지역들을 침입할 수 있다.

Actual Test 4

1 음파탐지기 - 음파 항해와 음역 - 는 고주파 음의 짧은 파동이 물을 통해 발사되고, 되돌아 오는 것(핑하는 소리)이다. 수상선과 잠수함에 탄 선원들은 바다에 있는 물체들을 찾기 위해 수중 음파 탐지기를 사용한다. 1930년대 중위 Pryor의 작업 이래로 많은 진보가 이루어졌다. 현대적인 방식에서, 전류가 광석들을 통과하는데, 그것은 인간의 청력의 한계를 넘어서 조정된 강력한 소리 파동을 생산함으로써 반응한다. 발신기로부터 나오는 몇몇 소리는 사용되는 소리의 파장보다 더 큰 모든 물체에서 되 튀어, 마이크와 같은 감지기로 되돌아온다. 그 다음으로 신호 처리 장치들은 메아리를 증폭시키고, 그 소리의 진동수를 인간의 청력 범위 내로 줄인다. 노련한 수중 음파 탐지기 기사는 돌아온 핑 하는 소리의 특징들을 분석함으로써, 접촉한 물체의 방향, 그것의 크기와 진로 그리고 심지어는 그것의 구성(고래나 잠수함 또는 물고기 떼)에 대해 무언가를 알려줄 수 있다.
측면 감시 수중 음파 탐지기는 일종의 고성능 수중 음파 탐지기이다. 고음 진동수로 돌려진 많게는 60개의 라디오 송수신기와 함께 작용하면서, 배 아래의 잔잔한 물에서 견인된 측면 감시 기계 장치들은 거의 사진 같은 분석을 때때로 할 수 있다. 측면 감시 장치들은 지질 조사, 고고학 연구, 그리고 물에 빠진 배와 비행기들의 위치를 알아내는 데 사용된다.
음향 측심기도 또한 수중 음파 탐지기를 이용한다. 음향 측심기는 바다 밑바닥쪽으로 하나의 음파를 보내고, 변환기로부터 해저로 갔다가 돌아오는 소리의 왕복여행의 시간을 측정하고, 시간 지연으로부터 깊이를 추정하고 나서, 스크린과 스트립 차트(긴 띠 모양의 용지를 사용하는 장기간 기록도[기록 장치])위에 그 깊이를 표시한다. 이 방법은 대략 5,000미터의 깊은 곳들까지 사용될 수 있으나, 소리의 감소와 물의 상태에 대한 불확실성은 일반적으로 더 깊은 물에서 이 방법을 덜 정확하게 만든다.

더 깊은 수심 측량을 위해 또는 수면 아래의 침전물 층들을 "간파하기" 위해서, 지질학자들은 매우 활기찬 저주파 음파를 발생시키기 위한 강력한 전기 불꽃, 폭발물, 또는 압축된 공기를 사용하는 지진의 반향 윤곽도를 사용한다. 또한, 소리 파동들의 왕복여행 시간은 중요하다. 저주파 음향은 많은 세부사항을 해결할 수 없지만, 그 메아리는 보통 수면 아래 침전물 층들의 이미지를 제공할 수 있다. 저주파 음향은 또한 적게 흡수하며 효과적으로 이동하는 이점을 가지고 있다.

2 유일한 날아다니는 포유 동물 집단인 박쥐들은 야행성이므로, 대부분의 새들에 의해 점령되지 않은 적소를 차지한다. 그들의 성공은 다음 두 가지 덕분이다: 비행과 반향 정위(定位) 박쥐 등이 발사한 초음파의 반향으로 물체의 존재를 측정하는 능력에 의해 항행하는 능력. 이러한 적응 구조들이 모여 박쥐들이 칠흑 같은 암흑 속을 날면서 장애물을 피하고, 정확하게 곤충들의 위치를 알아내어 잡고, 그들이 낮에 자는 동굴(포유 동물들과 새들 둘 다에 의해 대부분 무시되는 서식지)속 깊이 길을 찾아가는 것을 가능하게 한다.

비행할 때, 박쥐는 입이나 코에서 좁은 유도된 줄기로 5에서 10 밀리세컨드 정도 지속되는 짧은 파동을 낸다. 각각의 파동은 진동수가 변화된다; 즉, 처음에 10만 헤르츠(1초당 1회)까지 올라가며 가장 높고, 마지막에는 약 3만 헤르츠로 급속히 하락한다. 이러한 진동수의 음향은 사람의 귀에는 초음파인데, 사람의 귀는 약 2만 헤르츠의 상위 한계를 가진다. 박쥐가 먹이를 찾고 있을 때, 초당 약 10개의 파동을 낸다. 만일 먹이가 탐지되면, 그 비율은 빠르게 증가하여 접근과 포획의 마지막 단계에서는 초당 200개의 파동을 낸다. 그 파동들은 일정한 간격이 유지되어, 각각의 메아리는 다음 파동이 방출되기 전에 접수되는데, 이것은 혼잡을 막는 적응 구조이다. 발신되고 수신되는 데 걸리는 시간이 박쥐가 물체에 접근하면서 줄어들기 때문에, 박쥐는 그 물체에 대해 더 많은 정보를 얻기 위해 진동수를 증가시킬 수 있다. 파동의 길이도 또한 박쥐가 물체에 가까워지면서 줄어든다. 박쥐의 몇몇 먹이들이, 예를 들어 특정한 야행성 나방들, 접근하는 박쥐들을 탐지하고 피하기 위해 사용되는 초음파 탐지기를 발달시켜 왔다는 사실은 흥미롭다.

박쥐의 외이는 트럼펫처럼 크고, 종 마다 다양한 모양을 하고 있다. 박쥐의 내이에 대해서는 덜 알려져 있지만, 그것은 분명히 발산된 초음파 소리를 받을 수 있다. 생물학자들은 박쥐의 비행이 매우 정확해서 박쥐가 주행성 동물의 시각적 이미지의 선명도에 근접하는 메아리 스캐닝으로부터 그것의 주변환경에 대해 머리속으로 이미지를 만들어간다는 사실을 믿는다.

3 불은 많은 생태계들의 본질적인 요소이다. 수 천년에 걸쳐, 이러한 생태계의 식물과 동물들은 주기적인 화재에 익숙해져 왔고, 실제로 몇몇은 불타는 것에 의존하게 되었다. 예를 들어, 특정 키 작은 떡갈나무 덤불 종들은 꽤 단단한 그들의 씨 위에 코팅이 입혀져 있다; 불에 타는 것은 씨에 상처를 내어 그것이 싹트도록 한다. Lodgepole 솔방울들은 송진으로 갇혀진 채 잡혀 있다. 불은 송진을 녹이고, 솔방울이 열려서 씨를 풀어놓도록 한다. 궁극적으로 그들을 죽일 진균류는 자주 1년 생 긴 잎 소나무 묘목들을 공격한다. 묘목의 두 번째 해 동안, 그것은 매우 길고 풀 같은 바늘 모양의 잎들의 덩어리를 생기게 하지만, 높이는 자라지 않는다. 불이 진균류를 죽일 것이지만, 풀이 우거진 덤불들은 묘목의 싹들을 보호하고, 그것이 1년에 몇 피트씩 자라기 시작하도록 한다. 불에 의존하는 생태계로부터 필요한 불의 요소를 억제하는 것은 물과 산소 또는 질소를 제거하는 것이 그렇듯이 확실히 그들의 생태학적 변화를 방해하는 것이다.

자연적인 상황에서 불은 일반적으로 덤불이나 풀과 관목을 통하여 빠르게 탄다. 주기적인 화재가 정기적으로 집을 깨끗이 하고, 연료가 쌓이는 것을 막기 때문에 연료 적재량이 적다. **그래서 그 불들은 강한 열이나 강도를 가지고 타지는 않는다.** 안정된 식물들과 흙은 보통 불리하게 영향을 받지 않고, 불에 의존하는 그러한 종들은 그들의 자연적 싸이클을 계속 유지한다. 반면에, 불의 빈번한 발생에 적응된 생태계에서 불을 억제하는 것은 높은 연료 밀도를 가지게 하는 것이다. 죽은 풀,

덤불, 나무, 작은 가지들, 나무 껍질들, 잎과 바늘모양의 잎들이 축적되어왔고, 이것들은 만일 주변 자연이 자연적 주기로 타도록 허락된다면 그러하지 않을 경우에서 보다 더 큰 들불을 부양하는 더 많은 연료를 공급하게 된다.

불은 번개나 사람들에 의해 발생한다. 사람들은 인류 역사에 걸쳐 불을 솜씨있게 다루어 왔다. 미국 원주민은 여러 가지 이유로 일부러 불을 놓았는데, 그 중에는 다음과 같은 것들이 있다: 원예를 위해 토지를 개간하는 것, 다양한 사냥감 종들을 유인할 수 있도록 식물계의 구성을 변화시키는 것, 그리고 접근성을 향상시키는 것. 초기 정착자들은 또한 농업에 쓸 땅을 마련하고, 지난해의 모든 농작물의 그루터기를 제거하기 위해 불을 놓았다. 오늘날, 토지 관리자들은 천연 자원들을 관리하기 위한 도구로 불을 사용한다.

4 1765년부터 1775년까지의 전쟁 전 10년 동안 영국의 전제 정치에 대항하는 선전을 위한 시각 매체들이 급증했다. 인쇄 업자들은 신문, 잡지에, 그리고 가게, (선)술집, 커피점에 붙여놓은 포스터에 정치적 시사 만화들을 출판했다. 인쇄업자이자 달력 출판업자인 Benjamin Franklin은 식민지에 대한 영국 의회의 독단적인 과세에 대영제국을 팔다리가 잘린 여성으로 표현함으로써 대응했다. 배경에는 그녀의 배들이 버려져 있고, 브리타니아 (Great Britain을 여성으로 의인화(擬人化)한 이름)는 그녀가 한 때 지배했던 지구에 무기력하게 기대고 있다. 창이 자멸적으로 그녀의 가슴을 향해 있다. (동부 13주의) 영국 식민지들을 의미하는 절단된 팔과 다리들이 땅 위에 흩어져 있다. 영국의 자기 파괴적인 제국 정책을 비난했을지라도, Franklin의 그림은 영국 의회가 세금과 무역 관세를 부과하는 것을 처음에 비난한 사람들 대부분이 정치적인 독립을 꿈꾸지는 않았다는 것을 보여주고 있다. 1765년 Franklin에게 있어서, 그 식민지들은 모국의 건강한 정치 조직에 전적으로 의존하는 단지 개별적인 팔다리들일 뿐이었다.

그러나, 무역 관세와 런던 상인들이 누리는 독점권에 반대하는 항의들이 격렬해지면서, 정치적인 출판물들은 모국에 의존하는 식민지적 모델을 풍자했다. 1773년 12월 16일, Mohawk 인디언으로 가장한 일단의 보스턴 사람들은 몰래 the East India Company의 배들에 타서, 식민지 무역에 대한 영국의 독점적인 지배를 상징하는 관세가 많이 붙는 차를 보스턴 항에 던졌다. 보스턴 차 사건에 뒤이어, 참가자 중의 한 명인 Paul Revere는 미국을 강간당한 인도의 공주로 의인화했다. 영국 정부 관료들은 그녀의 옷을 올려다 보고 그녀의 목구멍에 억지로 차를 밀어넣는다. 미국의 어머니, 브리타니아는 그녀의 딸이 성적으로 학대 당하는 동안 어찌하지 못한 채 방관한다. 독립 후, 인쇄 업자, 화가 그리고 조각가들은 미국의 화신을 서구 문명과 자유와 지혜라는 이상적인 목표들을 상징하는 그리스나 로마의 여신으로 바꾸었다. 보통 배의 이물에 장식한 조상들을 조각하는 미국의 나무 조각가들은 이제 자유와 지혜의 화신들로 법원 청사와 다른 공공 건물들을 장식하도록 요구되었다. **하얀 소나무 재목과 도료로, 그들은 고전적인 조각의 자연 그대로의 대리석을 흉내내었다.**

카톨릭 프랑스에게 캐나다를 포기하도록 강요한 7년간의 전쟁 후, 미국인들은 동부의 해안 지대 넘어 멀리 영토 확장을 꿈꾸면서, 문명화의 진행이 태양과 더불어 서쪽으로 이동하고 있다고 선언했다. 잡지와 신문들은 George Berkeley의 "Verses on the Prospect of Planting Arts and Learning in America" – 미국의 "처녀지" (천년간의 "황금 시대"를 위한 비옥한)와 쇠퇴하는 유럽을 대조 시키고 있는 – 를 인용하였다.

5 유성영화의 시대는 Warner Brothers의 "The Jazz Singer"의 엄청난 성공과 더불어 1927년 후반에 시작되었다. 첫번째 완전 유성 필름 "Lights of New York"이 1928년에 뒤이어 나타났다. 비록 음성과 화면을 일치시키는 실험이 영화 그 자체(예를 들어, Dickson은 1894년 Edison을 위해 그 두 가지를 서투르지만 일치하게 만들었다)만큼 오래 되었을지라도, 유성 영화의 가능성은 Warner Brothers가 1926년 Western Electric으로부터 디스크식 발성 영화기를 구입하고 나서야 널리 알려졌다. 최초의 디스크식 발성 영화기 시스템은 영화 그 자체에 사운드 트랙을 녹음(oscilloscope 원리에 기초하는)하는 보다 정확한 방법을 사용하기 보다는 오히려 사진과 개별적 축음기 디스크를 일

치시켰다. Warner Brothers는 최초로 디스크식 발성 영화기를 사용하여 고전적이고 대중적인 연기자들 모두를 주연 시키는 짧은 뮤지컬 영화를 만들어 그렇지 않으면 무성 영화가 되었을 영화에 뮤지컬 사운드 트랙을 녹음하였다. "The Jazz Singer"의 경우, Warner Brothers는 그 무성 영화에 화면과 일치하는 네 개의 음악 (반복 진행)들을 덧붙였다. Al Jolson이 노래하고 나서 몇 줄의 대화를 했을 때, 청중은 감전된 것처럼 충격을 받았다. 무성영화는 1년 내에 쓸모없게 되었다.

화면과 일치하는 음향으로의 전환은 영화산업에 심각한 문제들을 일으켰다. 음향 녹음은 어려웠고, 카메라들은 유리로 된 영사실 내부로 부터 촬영해야만 했고, 영화 촬영소들은 특별한 방음 무대들을 지어야만 했고, 극장들은 비싼 새로운 장비를 필요로 했고, 대화를 이해하는 작가들이 고용되어야만 했고, 자신들의 목소리가 그것을 전달할 수 있는 배우들을 찾아내야만 했다. 초기의 유성 영화들의 상당수는 천박하고 정적인 것으로 시각적 장면들이 끊임 없는 대화, 음향 효과, 노래가사에 단지 하나의 부속물로서 봉사하는 이었다. 진지한 영화 평론가들은 활동사진의 소멸을 슬퍼했는데, 그것은 더 이상 움직임이나 사진 둘 중의 하나를 포함하는 것으로 보이지 않았다.

가장 효과적인 초기 유성 영화들은 사진과 사운드 트랙의 결합을 가지고 가장 대담하게 연출한 것들이었다. Walt Disney는 그의 만화 영화들에서 활동적인 움직임과 음악적 리듬을 세심하게 배합하면서, 독창적인 소리들과 놀라운 장면들을 결합시켰다. Ernst Lubitsch 또한 음향을 가지고 매우 교묘하게 연출해서, 경탄할 만큼 재미있고 노출된 방법으로 사운드 트랙의 정보와 시각적으로 묘사된 연기를 대조시켰다. 1930년까지 미국 영화 산업은 장면과 음향을 조화롭게 사용하는 것에 관련된 기술적, 예술적인 문제들 둘 다를 극복했고, 유럽 산업이 재빨리 뒤를 따르게 되었다.

Actual Test 5

1 사람이 많이 살지 않는 거친 황야의 초기 정착민인 북미 인디언들은 서반구 신세계의 지도를 제작하고 설계한 유럽인들보다 앞서 나갔다. 그들은 환경에 이름을 붙이고 지도를 제작함으로써 자연과의 의미 있는 관계망을 만들어 냈다. 그들의 지도는 상거래와 의사소통의 지역 망을 구축했다. 미국 원주민 지도는 서로 다른 장소를 동물, 채소, 광물 자원뿐만 아니라 특정한 영적 힘과 신으로 연결하는, 즉, 경험적인 용어로 환경을 묘사했던 구두 전통의 일부분이었기 때문에 현재 거의 남아있지 않다. 필요할 때, 지도는 흙이나 모래 위에 기억한 것이 그려졌고 좀 더 영구적인 것으로는 동물의 가죽, 나무 껍질 그리고 바위와 같은 다른 자연 물질들 위에 그려졌다.

Idaho주 Givens Hot Springs근처의 Snake강에 있는 한 장소에서 콜럼버스 이전의 Shoshone 인디언 부족은 커다란 현무암 표석을 그림문자로 뒤덮었다. 지도 바위로 알려진 이 깊게 새긴 표시가 있는 바위 예술의 한 예로 암석조각은 분명히 Snake와 Salmon강을 중심으로 하는 Shoshone 부족의 영역을 보여준다. 다른 암석조각이 있는 영역 내에 그리고 4,000년 전부터 비롯된 인디언 거주지의 건축상의 유적 근처에 위치하여, 지도 바위는 인간의 형상과 버팔로, 사슴, 영양, 뿔 큰 사슴, 산양과 같은 동물을 그림으로 보여준다. 이러한 상들은 바위가 그 지역의 인간과 동물의 영역사이의 영적인 조화를 표시하면서 성공적인 사냥을 보장하는 실용적이고 관습적인 중요성을 포함했음을 시사한다.

자연을 정복하려 하거나 그 위에 자신들을 위치시키기 보다는 미국 원주민들은 대지와 물과 하늘의 자연적인 작용 안에서 그들의 위치를 발견하려고 애썼다. 그들은 땅을 개인 소유자의 독점적인 사용을 위해 팔리고 거래될 수 있는 하나의 상품으로 생각하지 않았다. 땅은 상호 동의에 의해 그것의 자원과 사용이 다른 부족과 공유된다 할지라도, 한 부족의 구성원들에 의해 공공으로 소유되었다. 어떤 인디언 집단도 전적으로 정착하지는 않았다. 음식 공급원에 따라, 부족들은 일반적으로 하나 이상의 집과 마을을 차지했고 계절의 변화에 따라 여름과 겨울 거주지 사이를 이동했다.

2 인간에 의한 것이 아닌 모든 의사소통 체계 중에서 가장 정교하고 복잡한 것 중의 하나는 벌들의 상징적인 언어이다. 꿀벌들은 주로 두 가지 형태의 춤을 춤으로써 의사소통 할 수 있다. 의사 소통에 있어서 가장 풍부한 형태는 흔드는 춤이다. 벌들은 마량 징발대원이 자양분이 많은 곳으로부터 다리 위의 털에 의해 형성된 바구니 같은 공간에 화분 낱알들을 꾸리거나 위 속에 벌꿀을 가지고 돌아왔을 때 이러한 춤을 가장 많이 춘다. 흔드는 춤은 대략 벌통안 벌집위의 수직면에 만들어진 팔자모양의 양식이다. 춤의 한 주기는 세가지 요소로 구성된다.: (1) 벌 길이의 대략 세배가량의 지름을 가진 원, (2) 맥박치는 저주파의 소리를 내고 좌우로 복부를 흔들면서 직선으로 날기, (3) 또 다른 원, 처음과 반대방향으로 돌기. 이 춤은 교대로 시계방향, 반 시계방향으로 빙빙 돌면서 여러 번 반복된다.

흔들면서 직선으로 나는 것은 춤의 중요한 정보적인 요소이다. 흔드는 춤은 거의 항상 태양의 명확한 위치에 따라 행해진다. 마량 징발대원이 일직선으로 태양을 향한 위치에 있는 먹이를 찾아냈다면, 벌집의 수직면 위로 위를 향해 일직선으로 날것이다. 먹을 것이 태양의 오른쪽 60도 각도에 위치해 있다면, 수직선의 오른쪽 60도 각도로 날것이다. 그 흔드는 춤은 음식이 태양과 관련하여 위치해 있듯이 수직선과 관련하여 똑같은 각도를 지시한다.

음식이 있는 곳까지의 거리는 벌 춤에 또한 암호화 되어있다. 음식이 벌통에 가까우면, 마량 징발대원은 둥근 춤으로 불리는 더 단순한 춤을 춘다. 마량 징발대원은 단순히 시계방향으로 한바퀴의 원을 돌고, 그리고 돌아서, 여러 번 반복되는 행위인 시계반대방향으로의 원을 끝낸다. 다른 일꾼들은 정찰병주위에 모이고 정찰병이 방문한 꽃들로부터 얻은 꿀과 화분 낱알들의 냄새뿐만 아니라 춤에 의해 자극을 받는다. 그러면 신병들은 날아가서 모든 방향으로 찾지만 멀리 뒤쳐지지는 않는다. 둥근 춤은 음식이 벌통 근처에서 발견될 거라는 메시지를 전한다.

3 미국 서부에서의 삶은 목장주들이 땅을 개간하도록 도운 단순한 도구, 철조망에 대한 일련의 특허에 의해 재형성되었다. 철사로 울타리를 두르는 것의 발달과 관련된 아홉 개의 특허권이 미국 특허청에 의해 1868년 11월 Michael Kelly로 시작하여 1874년에 11월 Joseph Glidden으로 끝나는 발명자들에게 주어졌다. 철조망은 목장주와 농부의 일을 단순화했을 뿐만 아니라, 그 지역 전역에 걸쳐 정치적, 사회적, 경제적 관행에 상당한 영향을 끼쳤다. 선호되는 울타리를 두르는 방법으로서 매우 효과적인 이러한 도구의 빠른 출현은 총, 육연발 권총, 전보, 풍차 그리고 기관차만큼 극적으로 그 지역의 삶에 영향을 끼쳤다.

철조망은 서부의 환경에 이상적인 것으로 증명되었기 때문에 널리 채택되었다. 광대하고 한정되지 않은 초원과 평야는 목장경영, 농업, 더 나아가 궁극적으로는 광범위한 개척지로 전락했다. 철조망의 사용이 증가함에 따라, 넓고 트인 공간들은 좁고 닫힌 그리고 넉넉하지 않은 공간이 되어 버렸고, 자유롭게 떠돌아다니는 목동이 배회하는 시대도 얼마남지 않게 되었다. 오늘날 목동의 시는 철조망이 공간을 장소로 변동시키고, 사유지에 새로운 의미를 부여하는 통제의 공인된 상징이 되기 이전에 존재했던, 삶의 향수를 불러 일으키는 것으로 남아있다.

철조망의 발명이전에 효과적인 울타리의 부족은 농업의 범위와 목장 일, 그와 더불어, 한 지역에 정착할 수 있는 사람들의 숫자를 제한했다. 나무 울타리는 비쌌으며, 나무가 거의 자라지 않는 초원이나 평야에서는 구하기도 어려웠다. 재목이 그 지역에서 매우 부족했기 때문에 농부들은 잔디로 집을 짓도록 강요되었다. **또한, 보통 뉴 잉글랜드에서 발견되는 돌담을 만드는데 필요한 돌 역시 평원에서는 드문 것이었다.** 나무와 돌로 된 울타리 재료의 초기 대체물이었던 관목과 생울타리들은 급속히 팽창하는 서부에서 널리 사용되기에는 기르는데 너무 오랜 시간이 걸렸다. 철조망은 더 싸고, 이러한 다른 대체 수단들 중 어느것 보다도 사용하기에 쉽고 더 빨랐다.

4 우리들 대부분이 상상하듯이, 미국 남서부의 사막들은 매우 덥고 건조한 지역이다. 좀 더 과학적으로, 건조한 지역이라고도 불리는 사막은 특정적으로 일년에 10인치도 못 미치는 강수량을 갖는다. 몇몇 사막에서는 증발량이 강우량보다 더 크다. 반 건조 지역들은 평균적으로 10에서 20인치의 한 해 강수량을 기록한다. 전형적으로, 사막의 수증기는 짧은 간격으로 발생하고 해마다 예측이 불가

능하다. 지구 땅 덩어리의 대략 삼분의 일이 건조에서 반건조이다 (사막 또는 반 사막).

증발은 또한 건조상태에 기여하는 중요한 요소이다. 몇몇 사막에서는, 증발하는 물의 양이 강우량을 초과한다. 상승하는 공기는 차가워지고 구름과 강우를 생성하면서 습기를 덜 함유하게 되고, 하강하는 공기는 따뜻해지면서 습기를 포함한다. 구름, 물, 초목이 적은 지역들은 태양방사선의 대부분을 흡수하고 그 결과, 흙 표면 근처의 공기를 뜨겁게 데운다. 더 습한 지역들은 구름, 물, 초목에서 열을 비껴가게 하면서 더 차갑게 유지시킨다. 탁 트인 시골에서의 높은 바람은 또한 증발의 원인이 되기도 한다.

대륙의 표류와 산맥들의 융기의 결과로 사막의 위치는 지질학적 시대에 걸쳐 변화해 왔다. 현대의 사막 지역들은 전형적으로 적도의 북위와 남위 15도와 30도 사이의 북회귀선 남회귀선에 양다리를 걸치고 무풍대에 집중되어있다. 중앙 아프리카의 Kalahari사막과 같은 곳들은 지질학적으로 오래된 것이다. 북 아메리카의 Sonoran사막은 지난 1만년 내에 북방 경계선에 도달한 반면에, 북 아프리카의 Sahara 사막은 6천5백만년의 나이를 가지고 있다.

열과 건조함과 같은 혹독한 극단에 자리를 잡고 있기 때문에, 사막은 지구상 가장 취약한 생태계 중에 하나이다. 북 아메리카의 네 개의 주요 사막 중 세 개가 동쪽으로는 Rocky 산맥과 서쪽으로는 Sierra Nevadas사이에 위치해 있는 Basin and Range 지방으로 불리는 지질학적 지역에 포함되어 있다. 개개의 사막의 특색이 그 곳에서 발견되는 (진화의 역사와 기후 양쪽에 의해 결정되는) 초목계의 유형에 기초를 두는 반면에, 이러한 세 개의 사막의 지질학적 구조는 다소 비슷하다.